The fifth edition of Gregg Typing

Volume One: General Course

JOHN L. ROWE, Ed.D.
Chairman, Business Education
College of Education
University of North Dakota

ALAN C. LLOYD, Ph.D.
Director, Typing Instructional
Services, Gregg Division
McGraw-Hill Book Company

FRED E. WINGER, Ed.D.
Professor, Office Administration
and Business Education
Oregon State University

GREGG DIVISION / McGraw-Hill Book Company

New York St. Louis Dallas San Francisco Düsseldorf Johannesburg Kuala Lumpur
London Mexico Montreal New Delhi Panama Rio de Janeiro Singapore Sydney Toronto

Library of Congress Cataloging in Publication Data
Rowe, John L., date.
Typing 300.
Previous editions published under title: Gregg typing.
CONTENTS: v. 1. General course.—v. 2. Vocational course.
1. Typewriting. I. Lloyd, Alan C., joint author.
II. Winger, Fred E., joint author. III. Title.
Z49.R8774 652.3 72-184506
ISBN 0-07-054090-X (v. 1)
ISBN 0-07-054094-2 (v. 2)

2 3 4 5 6 7 8 9 0 DODO 1 0 9 8 7 6 5 4 3

Contents

a·i·m PAGE

PART ONE
20 wam
2 minutes
4 errors

1 The machine 2
2 Home keys 4
3 Home keys 6
4 E key, U key 8
5 .... Review 9
6 G key, Right Shift 10
7 .... Review 11
8 R key, Period 11
9 .... Review 12
10 H key, Left Shift 13
11 I key 14
12 .... Review 15
13 O key, T key 16
14 Comma, C key 17
15 ....Scoring, Review 18
16 M key, Colon 20
17 W key, Y key 21
18 .... Review 22
19 V key, N key 23
20 X key, P key 24
21 .... Review 26
22 B key, Diagonal 27
23 ....SI score, Review 28
24 Z key, Hyphen 29
25 .... Review 30
26 Q key, ? key 31
27 .... Review 32
28 .... Review 33
29 .... Test preview 34
30 Part One Test 35

PART TWO
25 wam
2 minutes
4 errors

31 .... Skill drills 37
32 .... Skill drills 38
33 .... Skill drills 38
34 Tab stops, horizontal centering 39
35 Block centering 40
36 .... Skill drills 41
37 .... Skill drills 42
38 Vertical centering 43
39 All cap display 44
40 .... Skill drills 45
41 .... Skill drills 45
42 Spread centering 46
43 Centering practice 47
44 Paragraph spacing 48
45 Listening for bell 49
46 Word division 50
47 Centering practice 51
48 .... Skill drills 52
49 .... Test preview 53
50 Part Two Test 54

PART THREE
30 wam
3 minutes
5 errors

51 1 key, 2 key 56
52 3 key, 4 key 57
53 .... Review 58
54 7 key, 8 key 59
55 9 key, 0 key 60
56 .... Review 61
57 5 key, 6 key 62
58 ½ key, ¼ key 63
59 .... Review 64
60 .... Speed drive 65
61 Centering review 65
62 .... Speed drive 66
63 Underscore key, apostrophe key 67
64 Enumeration 68
65 .... Speed drive 69
66 Parentheses keys 69
67 Enumeration 70
68 .... Speed drive 71
69 Quotation key, use 72
70 Bibliography 73
71 Enumeration 74
72 Margin release, outline 74
73 Enumeration, poems 76
74 .... Test preview 77
75 Part Three Test 78

PART FOUR
30 wam
4 minutes
5 errors

76 .... Speed drive 80
77 Intro. to letters 81
78 Blocked letter 82
79 Blocked letters 85
80 Blocked letters 86
81 .... Speed drive 87
82 Personal letters 88
83 Personal letter 90
84 Personal letter 91
85 Blocked letter 92
86 .... Speed drive 92
87 Intro. to tables 93
88 Open tables 95
89 Open tables 96
90 Open table 97
91 .... Speed drive 97
92 Open tables, narrow column heads 98
93 Open tables 99
94 Open tables, wide column headings 100
95 Open table 101
96 .... Speed drive 102
97 Letter and table 103
98 Letter and table 104
99 .... Test preview 105
100 Part Four Test 106

PART FIVE
30 wam
5 minutes
5 errors

101 .... Speed drive 109
102 $ key, asterisk 110
103 % key, capital of period, comma 110
104 Envelopes 111
105 Letter, envelope 112
106 .... Speed drive 113
107 # key, ampersand 114
108 ¢ key, @ key 114
109 Postal cards 115
110 Postal cards 116
111 .... Speed drive 117
112 Symbols that must be constructed 119
113 !, +, and = keys 120
114 Form postal cards 121
115 Form postal cards 122
116 .... Speed drive 122
117 Memo, plain 124
118 Memo, printed 125
119 Invoice, plain 126
120 Invoice, printed 127
121 .... Speed drive 129
122 Blocked letter 130
123 Short invoices 130
124 .... Test preview 131
125 Part Five Test 132

PART SIX
35 wam
5 minutes
5 errors

126 .... Speed drive 135
127 Corrections 136
128 New letter parts, blocked letter 137
129 Blocked letter 138
130 Blocked letters 139
131 .... Speed drive 140
132 Revision marks 141
133 Two-page report 142
134 Report page 1 144
135 Report page 2 145
136 .... Speed drive 146
137 Long one-page blocked letters 148
139 Long two-page blocked letters 150
141 .... Speed drive 152
142 Report page 1 153
143 Report page 2 154
144 Report page 3 154
145 Report cover, contents, etc. 155
146 .... Speed drive 156
147 .... Test preview 157
148 .... Preview cont. 158
149 Part Six Test 159
150 Test cont. 160

PART SEVEN
36 wam
5 minutes
4 errors

151 .... Accuracy drive 162
152 Review of tables 163
153 Review of tables 164
154 Review of tables 165
155 .... Accuracy drive 165
156 Review of reports 167
157 Review of reports 168
158 Review of reports 169
159 .... Accuracy drive 169
160 Review of letters 170
161 Review of letters 172
162 Review of letters 172
163 .... Accuracy drive 173
164 .... Numbers drive 173
165 Review of memos 174
166 Review of printed forms, invoices 175
167 .... Test preview 176
168 .... Preview cont. 177
169 Part Seven Test 178
170 Test cont. 179

PART EIGHT
37 wam
5 minutes
4 errors

171 .... Accuracy drive 181
172 Ruled tables 182
173 Ruled tables 183
174 Ruled tables 184
175 .... Accuracy drive 184
176 Article page 1 185
177 Article page 2 186
178 Article retyped 186
179 .... Accuracy drive 187
180 Ruled tables 188
181 Ruled tables 189
182 Ruled tables 189
183 .... Accuracy drive 190
184 News release 191
185 News release 192
186 News release 192
187 .... Test preview 193
188 .... Preview cont. 194
189 Part Eight Test on mag. articles 194
190 and ruled tables 195

PART NINE
38 wam
5 minutes
4 errors

191 .... Accuracy drive 197
192 Blocked letters 198
193 Blocked letter 200
194 Blocked letters 200
195 .... Numbers drive 201
196 Index cards 202
197 Labels 203
198 Form postal cards 203
199 .... Accuracy drive 204
200 Blocked letter 205
201 Blocked letter 207
202 Blocked letters 207
203 .... Accuracy drive 207
204 Invoices 208
205 Credit memos 209
206 Statements 209
207 .... Test preview
208 on fill-in postal cards ... 210
and letters 211
209 Part Nine Test 211
210 Test cont. 212

PART TEN
39 wam
5 minutes
3 errors

211 .... Skill drive 214
212 .... Skill drive 215
213 Punctuation, stationery, letter 216
214 Monarch letter 218
215 Official letter 219
216 Two-page baronial 220
217 .... Skill drive 221
218 Report page 1 222
219 Report page 2 224
220 Book ms. page 225
221 Book ms. page 226
222 .... Skill drive 227
223 Letter styles 228
224 Letter styles 229
225 Semiblocked letter 230
226 Semiblocked letter 230
227 .... Test preview 231
228 .... Preview cont. 232
229 Part Ten Test 233
230 Test cont. 234

PART ELEVEN
40 wam
5 minutes
3 errors

231 .... Skill drive 236
232 Leadered menu 237
233 Leadered contents 238
234 Leadered schedule 238
235 Leadered program 238
236 .... Skill drive 239
237 Reconciliation 240
238 Balance sheet 241
239 Reconciliation 241
240 Income statement 242
241 .... Skill drive 242
242 Bill of sale 243
243 Bill of sale 244
244 Bill of sale form 245
245 Resolution, minutes of meeting 246
246 .... Skill drive 247
247 .... Test preview 248
248 .... Preview cont. 249
249 Part Eleven Test 249
250 Test cont. 250

PART TWELVE
40 wam
5 minutes
3 errors

251 Telegrams 252
252 "Copy" letter 253
253 Magazine article 254
254 Blocked letter 254
255 Open tables 255
256 Ruled tables 255
257 Dictated tables 257
258 Dictated tables 257
259 Membership bills 258
260 5 x 3 Index cards 258
261 Mailing labels 258
262 Newsletter 259
263 Term paper page 1 260
264 Term paper page 2 261
265 Term paper page 3 261
266 Term paper page 4 262
267 Objective test from Workbook 263
268 5-Minute TW 263
Blocked letter 264
269 Magazine article 264
Ruled table 265
270 Leadered program 265
Telegram 265

SUPPLEMENT I
Timed Writings

271 TW selection 1 266
272 TW selection 2 266
273 TW selection 3 267
274 TW selection 4 267
275 TW selection 5 268
276 TW selection 6 268
277 TW selection 7 269
278 TW selection 8 269
279 TW selection 9 270
280 TW selection 10 270
281 TW selection 11 271
282 TW selection 12 271
283 TW selection 13 272
284 TW selection 14 273
285 TW selection 15 274

SUPPLEMENT II
Motion Drills

286 Manual under 25 275
287 Manual 25 to 35 275
288 Manual 25 to 35 276
289 Manual 35 to 45 276
290 Manual 35 to 45 277
291 Manual 45 to 55 277
292 Manual 45 to 55 278
293 Electric under 25 278
294 Electric 25 to 35 279
295 Electric 25 to 35 279
296 Electric 35 to 45 280
297 Electric 35 to 45 280
298 Electric 45 to 55 281
299 Electric 45 to 55 281
300 Technique drills 282

index

DRILLS

Adjacent reaches, 46, 276, 277, 281
Aligning, 121, 136
Alphabetic paragraphs, 37–39, 41, 42, 45, 46, 48, 49, 52–55, 56–59, 62–64, 68, 70, 72, 95, 96, 98, 100–104, 109, 111, 115, 117, 120, 122, 128, 173, 182, 185, 188, 191, 204, 208, 215, 222, 227, 237, 243
Alphabetic sentences, groups of, 214, 215, 221, 227, 236, 240, 248; individual, all warmups beginning on page 50
Alphabetic word lines, warmups, 32–35, 37, 38, 40–48
Alternate-hand words, 32, 33, 37, 38, 275, 276, 278, 281
Bell, 49, 52–54, 57, 66, 67
Capitalizing, 282
Centering, horizontal, 40, 41, 52–54
Centering, spread, 46, 47
Concentration, 251
Double-letter words, 38, 43, 45, 48, 50, 275–278, 280, 281
Double-reach words, 45
Downhill runs, 42, 111
Down-motion words, 28, 275–279
Erasing, 136
Easy paragraphs for speed building, see very easy [VE] timed writing selections below
Easy sentences, groups of, 23, 120, 201, 214, 215, 221, 227, 236, 240, 248, 251; see also first line of all warmups
Experts' rhythm drill, warmups, 21, 23, 26 ff.
Eyes on copy, 282
Finger by finger, 6
In-motion words, 30, 276, 279, 280
Jump-row words, 276–278, 281
Key-jam prevention, 282
Left-hand runs, 275–277, 279, 280
Names, 39, 40, 41
Numbers, cumulative count, warmups, 136, 140, 141, 144, 146, 148, 149, 151, 152, 156, 157, 202, 204, 207, 208, 217, 228
Numbers, keys, 56–62, 174
Numbers, pair patterns [10 28 39 47 56], warmups, 63–72, 80, 87, 93, 95–101, 103, 105, 109–111, 113–117, 120–127, 129–132, 162, 163, 165, 169, 173, 176, 181, 237, 242, 243, 251
Numbers, paragraphs, 56–64, 110, 111, 114, 115, 233
Numbers, reviews, 58, 61, 64, 174
Numbers, sentences, 174, 201
Numbers "we 23," 63, 182, 184, 187, 188, 190, 193, 201
One-hand words, 39, 42
Out-motion words, 275, 276, 278, 279
Phrases, 16
Proximates, 275, 276, 278
Quotation mark sequences, 72–73
Right-hand runs, 278–281
Shift locking, 44, 46, 47
Space bar, 5, 282
Trill strokes, 37, 46
Up-motion words, 26, 277, 280
Vowels, 32, 33
Word division, 50–52

A

Abbreviations: a.m., p.m., 59, 60; bcc, 205; cc, 198; et al., 145; ibid., 145, 169; in re, 205; L.S., 245; op. cit., 145; re, 205; SI, 34; sic, 253; spacing after, 18, 21; state names, 164
Account, statement of, 209
Accuracy, 147; checklists for, 12, 19, 22, 69, 87, 173, 181, 184; see also selected drills in first column
Addresses: envelopes, 112; indexed on cards, 202, 203; labels, 203; postal cards, 116, 203, 212; punctuation styles, 216; return, envelope, 112; return, letter, 88; titles in, 137; use of st, d, th, etc., 225
Ages, expressing, 225
a·i·m explained, vi, 1
Alignment: dollar signs, 183; numbers in columns, 175; periods in enumeration, 68; pivoting, 178; reinsertion, 121; revision sign for, 141
All capitals, 44, 111; attention line, 198, company signature, 137, 262; legal display, 243–245; magazine style touch, 185, 186; marking, 141; shift lock, used for, 44; subject line, 205
Alphabet, see Keys introduced
Announcements, displayed, 47, 52, 66
Apostrophe, 67
Articles, magazine, 185–186
Artistic lettering, 258, 259
Asterisk in footnotes, 256
Attention Line, 198–199
Author, name of: in bibliography, 71, 73; in by-line, 76; in footnote, 145; in running head, 154, 186, 221

B

Backrolling, 159
Backspacing, 40; centering a line, 40; centering a table, 94; pivoting, 178; underscoring, 67
Balance sheet, 241
Bank reconciliation, 240
Baronial size [5½ x 8½"], 216, 217
BCC notations, 205, 206
Bell, adding 5 spaces for, 3; listening for, 49, 57
Bibliography, 71, 73, 155
Bill of Sale, 244, 245
Book manuscript, 222, 225, 226
Bound manuscript, 142, 222
Brackets, 119
Business forms, see Forms, types of
Business reports, 222–224
By-line, 76, 145, 223

C

Capitals, rules for, 226
Carbon copies, 156; assembling packs, 156; "bcc," "cc" notations, 149, 152, 205; erasing, 136; inserting thick packs, 194
Cards, 116, 121, 122, 202, 203, 212, 258
Care of typewriter, 78, 234
Carriage returning, 5
Centering, above columns, 100, 101; between points, 243; block, 41; by backrolling, 159; by backspacing, 40; by margin setting, 3; horizontal, 40; spread, 46; vertical, 43, 159, 195
Characters, constructing, 119; keyboard, see capital keys introduced
Checklists: accuracy, 12, 15, 19, 22, 24, 25, 69, 87, 146, 156, 173, 181, 184, 197; position, 16 [feet], 17, 24, 215 [elbows],

I

Inches, horizontal, 81; vertical, 43
Income summary, 242
Incoming letter, copying, 252, 253
Indenting, 48, 59, 68, 243
Index cards, 203, 258
Inferior figures, 119
Interoffice memo, 124–126, 174
Invoice, 127, 128, 174, 208, 258; on plain paper, 127
Italics, underscoring for, 147, 234

K

Key jams, 12, 97
Key stroking, 5, 15–17, 20, 24, 25, 97
Keys introduced:

A... 6	T...17	#...114
B...27	U... 8	$...110
C...18	V...24	%...111
D... 6	W...21	&...114
E... 8	X...25	(... 70
F... 6	Y...22	)... 70
G...10	Z...29	*...110
H...13	1...56	¢...115
I...15	2...56	@...115
J... 6	3...57	;... 6
K... 6	4...57	:... 21
L... 6	5...62	/... 27
M...20	6...62	?... 31
N...24	7...59	+...120
O...17	8...59	=...120
P...25	9...60	!...120
Q...31	0...60	–... 67
R...12	½...63	"... 72
S... 6	¼...63	'... 67

Others: comma, 18 [capped, 111]; hyphen, 29; lock, 44; period, 12 [capped, 111], shift keys, 10, 14; constructed characters, 119

L

Label, 203, 258
Leaders: hyphen, 243, 245; period, 236–238, 241, 242, 249, 253; spaced periods, 242
Legal-display papers, 243–246; agenda, 249; bill of sale, 244, 245; margins of, 243; minutes, 246; resolution, 246, 248, 250; seal [L.S.], 245; signature line, 245
Letters, composing, 91
Letters, parts of, 81; address, 81, 269; address below body, 232; attention line, 198, 199; "bcc" notation, 205, 206; body, 81; "cc" notation, 149, 152, 198, 199; closing lines, 81, 262; complimentary closing, 205, 262; "copy" notation, 253; date line, 81, 137, 142; display in body, 137, 141; "enclosure" notation, 81, 104; enumeration in body, 59, 60, 151, 152, 199; letterhead, 81, 151, 199 (typewritten, 253); page-2 heading, 150, 152, 220; postscript, 137, 138, 158, 206; punctuation styles, 216; quotation in body, 137, 138, 152, 160, 171; reference initials, 81, 83–85, 152, 199, 252; return address, 88; salutation, 81, 198; signature of company, 137, 171, 229, 261, 262; signature of individual, 81, 158, 171, 252, 261, 262; signature of a woman, 152, 219, 260–261; signer's identification, 81, 137, 171, 229; subject line, 205, 206; table in body, 137, 138, 253; title of addressee, 137; title of signer, 81, 137, 158, 171, 261, 262
Letters, placement, 81, 137, 148, 150, 170; adjustments for, 82; allowance for extra display lines, 170, 198; stationery sizes,

Production word count, 73
Programs, 238, 249
Proofreading, 19, 24, 25, 146, 197, 224
Punctuation styles, 83, 94, 171, 216

Q

Quotations: in correspondence, 137, 138, 152, 160, 171; in reports, 145, 146, 167, 168; punctuation sequences of, 72, 73

R

Reconciliation, bank, 240
Remedial, see column 1; 275–281, 282
Reports, parts of: bibliography, 71, 73, 155; by-line, 142, 154, 223; contents, 155, 238; cover, 155; enumeration, 68, 71, 225; footnotes, 145, 146, 167, 168; headings, summarized, 153–155; listings, 225; page-2 heading, 141, 144; paragraph headings, 142, 153; quotations, 145, 167, 168; reference numbers, 145, 168; rules governing, 141–144, 222–224; running heads, 222, 225, 226; side headings, 142, 154; subheadings, 145, 153; tables, 262; title, 154
Reports, placement, 141, 143, 222; in formal reports, 141; margins, 141–144, 167; when bound at left, 142, 222; when unbound, 142, 222
Reports, types and styles of: agenda, 238, 249; bibliography, 73, 155; bill of sale, 244, 245; book manuscript, 222, 225, 226; business report, 223, 224; contents page, 155, 238; correspondence manual, 260, 262; cover page, 155; enumeration, 68, 71, 225; formal, 142–144, 153–155; magazine article, 185–186; menu, 237, 238; minutes of meeting, 246; news release, 191–193; outlines, 75, 154; poems, 76; programs, 238, 249; resolution, 246, 248, 250; school reports ["term papers"], 141–146, 153–155, 167–169; script, 73; table of contents, 155; title page, 155
Resolution, 246, 248, 250
Return address, envelope, 112; letter, 89
Revision (rough draft) marks, 141
Roman numerals, 75
Rules for: bibliography, 71; capitalizing, 226; dividing words, 50; expressing numbers, 225; legal papers, 243; letters, 81, 137, 149; manuscripts, 142–144, 153–155; paragraphing, 25, 48; punctuation spacing, 18; quotations, 72; word division, 50
Ruling: financial statements, 240; horizontal lines, 182, 240, 245; legal papers, 243, 245; tables, 182; vertical, 243

S

Salutations, selecting, 198
Scoring employment tests, 224
Script, 73
Seal [L.S.], 245
Shift lock, 44
SI score, 28
Space bar, 5
Spacesaver arrangement, 222–224
Spacing, 4; after abbreviations, 18, 21; after punctuation, 18, 21; before and after ruled lines, 182; between columns, 93, 94, 240, 241; between paragraphs, 25, 48; when spread-centering, 46
Special characters, 199
Speed: checklists, 14, 15, 69, 71, 109, 117, 152, 156; computation, 19, 223; drills, see column 1 and 275–281
Spreading: centered lines, 46; corrections

TESTS

Part	Preptest	Test
One	34	35
Two	53	54
Three	77	78
Four	105	106
Five	131	132
Six	157	159
Seven	176	178
Eight	193	194
Nine	210	211
Ten	231	233
Eleven	248	249
Twelve	...	263

TIMED WRITINGS

Words	SI	Form	Page
100	VE	Typed	34
100	VE	Typed	35
120	E	Print	54
120	VE	Typed	65
140	VE	Print	67
140	VE	Print	69
150	VE	Print	71
150	FE	Print	77
150	FE	Print	78
200	VE	Print	80
155	VE	Print	87
200	VE	Print	93
200	VE	Print	98
140	VE	Print	103
120	FE	Print	103
120	FE	Print	105
120	FE	Print	106
200	FE	Print	107
200	VE	Typed	109
200	VE	Print	113
400	VE	Typed	118
400	VE	Typed	123
372	VE	Print	129
200	FE	Print	131
200	FE	Print	133
300	E	Typed	135
300	VE	Typed	140
335	E	Print	147
225	VE	Print	156
265	FE	Print	157
265	FE	Print	159
204	VE	Typed	162
432	E	Typed	166
192	N	Print	170
204	FE	Print	173
310	N	Print	176
285	N	Print	178
370	FE	Print	181
370	N	Print	186
370	N	Print	190
380	E	Print	197
380	N	Print	204
190	N	Print	210
320	N	Print	211
195	FE	Typed	214
195	N	Typed	215
250	N	Print	221
250	N	Print	227
276	FE	Print	236
400	FE	Print	239
400	N	Print	247
326	N	Print	250
336	N	Print	263
144	N	Typed	266
144	N	Typed	266
204	N	Typed	267
408	N	Typed	267
252	N	Print	268
506	N	Print	268
294	N	Print	269
490	N	Print	269
294	N	Print	270
504	N	Print	270
294	N	Print	271
490	N	Print	271
560	N	Print	272
560	N	Print	273
547	N	Print	274

proofreading, 19, 24, 25, 146, 197, 224; routines 6, 7, 11, 23, 113, 201; speed, 14, 15, 69, 71, 109, 117, 152, 156; stroking, 15–17, 20, 24, 25, 97; technique, 14, 23, 24, 97, 190
Chemical symbols, 119
Cleanup routine, 11
Clearing machine, 94
Closed punctuation, 216, 218
Complimentary closing, selection of, 205, 207
Composing letters, 91; tables, 255, 257
Contents, table of, 155, 238
Copying: exact, 77, 253; incoming letter, 253; italic printing, 147, 234; previous financial statements, 240
Corrections: erasing, 136; inserting, 121, 136; marks for, 141; spreading, 136; squeezing, 136
Correspondence manual, 260–262
Cover for manuscript, 155
Credit Memorandum, 209
Crowding (squeezing), 136

D

Dash, 31
Decimal omitted, 208, 209
Desk arrangment, 2
Difficulty of copy [SI], 28
Division of words, 49–54
Drills, see column 1

E

Elbow position, 17, 24, 215
Electric typewriters: apostrophe, 67; asterisk, 110; at [@], 115; backspacing, 40; carriage return, 5; cent [¢], 115; margin setting, 3, 4; quotation mark, 72; underscore, 67
Elite spacing, 12 to inch, 81
Ellipsis [. . .], 119
Employment tests, 223, 224
Enumeration, 59, 68; in letters, 59, 60, 151, 199; in reports, 68, 71, 225
Envelopes, 112
Erasing, 136; permitted, 137
Errors, 19, 192; penalized, 224
Exclamation mark, 67
Eye control, 14, 190, 282

F

Feet and inches, 119
Filing cards, 202, 258
Financial statements, 240–242, 249, 253
Finger position, 5, 6
Folding, of letters, 112
Foot position, 16
Footnotes, in reports, 145, 146, 167, 168; in tables, 256
Forms, parts of: column 128, 243; guide lines, 128; guide words, 124, 128, 174; heading, 124; leaders, [hyphens], 243; margins, 124, 128, 174; totals line, 127, 128, 174; typed on plain paper, 124, 127, 243
Forms, placement, 124–126, 174, 175, 243
Forms, types of: bill of sale, 245; credit memo, 209; interoffice memo, 124–126, 174; invoice, 127, 128, 174, 208, 258; label, 203; news release, 191, 192; postal card, fill-in, 121, 203, 212; statement of account, 209; telegram, 252
Fractions, 58

G

Graph lines, 119

H

Halfspacing, 136
Hand position checklists, 22, 49, 71, 122, 165, 207, 242
Home keys, 5, 6
Horizontal center, 3, 243
Horizontal centering, 40, 46, 243
Horizontal ruling, 182, 240, 245
Horizontal spacing, 81

Letters, stationery: baronial [$5\frac{1}{2}$ x $8\frac{1}{2}$"], 216, 217; envelopes, 112; folding, 112; monarch [$7\frac{1}{4}$ x $10\frac{1}{2}$"], 216, 218; official [8 x $10\frac{1}{2}$"], 216, 219; standard [$8\frac{1}{2}$ x 11"], 216
Letters, types and styles of, 227; blocked, 81, 83, 84, 88, 171, 217–219; formal, 232; full (extreme) blocked, 229; indented, 229; personal, 88, 89; semiblocked, 229, 253; with address below body, 232; with attention line, 199, 229; with "bcc" notation, 205, 206; with "cc" notation, 149, 152, 198, 199, 229; with closed punctuation, 216, 218; with "copy" notation, 253; with double-spacing, 232; with "enclosure" notation, 81, 104; with enumeration, 59, 60, 151, 152, 199; with page-2 heading, 150, 152, 220; with postscript, 137, 138, 158, 206; with quotation, 137, 138, 152, 160, 171; with subject line, 205, 206; with table, 137, 138, 253
Lines to inch, 43

M

Machines, 2–4; care of, 78, 234
Magazine article, 185–186, 194, 195, 254, 264,
Mailing lists, 202, 258
Margin bell, 3, 49
Margin release, 75
Margins: calculation of, 3; for legal papers, 243; for letters, 81, 216; for magazine articles, 185; for memos, 124, 125; for manuscripts [formal], 141–144, 167; for postal cards, 116; for practice papers, 3; for reports, 222; setting of, 3–4
Married woman, signature of, 152, 219, 260, 261
Mathematical symbols, 119
Memorandum: credit, 206; interoffice, printed form, 126; interoffice, wholly typed, 124
Menu, 237, 238
Minutes and seconds, 119
Minutes of meetings, 246

N

Net speed, 224
News letter, 259
News release, 191–193
Notice, postal card, 116, 212
Numbers: drills, see column 1; alignment in columns, 175; dividing, 51; fractions, 58; roman, 75; rules for expressing, 225; street names, 225, 226

O

O'clock, numbers with, 225
Open punctuation, 216, 217
Outlines, 75, 154

P

Page numbers, 221; in legal papers, 243, 245; in letters, 150, 220; in reports, 141, 222, 224; in magazine articles, 186
Paper, 247; carbon, 156; center of, 3, 243; inserting, 3; reinserting, 121; stationery sizes, 216–219; straightening, 3
Paper guide, adjusting, 3
Paragraphs: headings of, 154; indentions of, 48; spacing between, 25, 48
Percent, 111, 256
Performance goals:

Part 1......	1	Part 7	161
Part 2......	36	Part 8	180
Part 3......	55	Part 9	196
Part 4......	79	Part 10......	213
Part 5......	108	Part 11......	235
Part 6......	134	Part 12......	251

Personal letter, 88–90
Pica spacing, 10 to inch, 81
Pivoting, 178, 236
Poems, 76
Postal cards, 116, 121, 122, 203, 212
Postscripts, 137, 138, 158, 206
Posture illustrated, 4; checklist, 13, 15, 80, 92, 142, 162, 165, 187; discussed, 147

Sprints, 24, see also Easy sentences in column 1
Squeezing: corrections, 136; letters, 82
State abbreviations, 2-letter, 164
Statement of account, 209
Stationery, 216
Street names, numbers, 225
Stroking checklists, 15–17, 20, 24, 25, 97
Subject line, 205, 206
Superior figures, 119
Syllabic intensity, 28

T

Tables, parts of, 93, 256; column heads, blocked, 99, 163; column heads centered, 100, 101, 164
Tables, placement: backspace centering, 94; in letters, 137, 138; in manuscripts, 262; key line, 94; spacing between columns, 94, 95, 101, 162, 256; spacing between money columns, 162, 240–242; spacing, vertical, 94, 102, 246; spacing with ruled lines, 182; when using leaders, 241, 242, 253
Tables, types and styles of: dictated, 255, 257; financial statements, 240, 242; leader tables, 241, 242, 249, 253; open tables, 94, 256; ruled tables, 182–184, 256; with extra spacing, 102, 183; with footnotes, 256, 260; with leaders, 241, 242, 249, 253; with totals, 183
Tabulation, see Tables
Technique, see drills in column 1; 14, 23, 24, 97, 190
Telegrams, 252
Tests, centering names, 54
Tests, display, 265
Tests, enumeration, 78
Tests, forms, 133, 179, 212, 265
Tests, legal-style, 250
Tests, letters, 107, 133, 160, 178, 212, 233, 264
Tests, manuscripts, 195, 264
Tests, reports, 159, 178, 234
Tests, tables, 107, 178, 195, 249, 265
Tests, timings on straight copy, 35, 54, 77, 107, 133, 159, 178, 195, 211, 233, 250, 263
Time, expressing, 57, 225
Timed writings, see column 1 list and table of contents, ii
Title page, 50, 51
Titles, of books and magazines: in bibliographies, 73, 155; in context, 172; in footnotes, 145, 146, 167, 168
Titles, of individuals: in addresses, 137; in context, 226; in signatures, 261
Transposition error, 19, 141
Two-page letters, 150, 151, 220
Typewriters, care of, 78, 234; parts of, 2–4
Typist's initials (URS), 81, 83–85, 152, 199, 252

U

Unarranged tables, 255–257
Underscoring: basics, 67; book titles, 71; footnotes, 145, 146, 167, 168; italics, 147, 234; open vs solid, 67; signature line, legal, 246; tables, 182

Variable spacer, 121
Vertical centering, 43, 159
Vertical ruling, legal paper, 243

W

"We 23" drills, 63, 182, 184, 187, 188, 190, 193, 201
Word division, 41–54; rules, 50
Words a minute: allowance for machine operation [production word count], 25, 73; computing, 19, 223; in production jobs, 73
Work station, 4

Z

ZIP Code, 93, 131
Zero, military, 119

preface

Before you start using TYPING 300, you should know three things about it: (1) It is more than a book—it is a whole "system" of books and learning aids that fit together. (2) As the newest in the unbroken sequence of typing programs dating all the way back to 1902, TYPING 300 includes the best features developed in prior editions. (3) TYPING 300 introduces many new learning aids, some of which will prove to be landmark innovations.

The Typing 300 Program

This is a two-year program of materials for developing and using typing skill. Materials included are:

☐ **Two textbooks,** one for each year. Volume One is the General [basic] Course. Volume Two is the Vocational Office [advanced] Course.

☐ **Four workbooks,** each entitled Learning Guides and Working Papers, one for each semester.

☐ **Keyboard** instructional tapes/cassettes.

☐ **Procedures** tapes/cassettes, for repeat use with patterned-alike lessons.

☐ **Speed** and accuracy improvement drive tapes, for use with the supplement of timings and drills.

☐ **Four kits of special transparencies,** one kit for each semester in the TYPING 300 program.

☐ **Teacher's service manual,** including keys, methods discussions, and leaflets for research reports.

Continued Gregg Features

TYPING 300 includes many features that were pioneered in prior Gregg typing books and are included because they have passed the test of time and use:

☐ Production word count on all job material.

☐ Copy control of the length and difficulty of all material used for skill building and production.

☐ Backspace-centering method of tabulation.

☐ Inclusion of tests in the textbook.

☐ Sight-saver-size print in the early lessons, when learners are reading letter by letter at arm's length.

☐ Machine settings given in every lesson heading.

☐ Separate drills for electric machines.

☐ Use of visual placement guides.

☐ Programmed-instruction "Learning Guides."

☐ Double-blocking of timed-writing selections, so lines will end even to assist quick proofreading.

Typing 300 Innovations

Changes in today's educational scene have set the stage for most of the innovations in Typing 300:

☐ **20-Minute Modules.** A great many schools are switching to computer scheduling, extended periods, flexible schedules, independent-progress laboratory plans, open classrooms, and so on. A working module is needed that is flexible enough for both the new and the old kinds of schedules. Accordingly, the activities in TYPING 300 are designed in 20-minute segments. Each is an Applied Instructional Module, or a·i·m, for short. Each volume of TYPING 300 has 300 such modules [hence the title of the program]. One a·i·m is a computer-schedule unit. Two modules fit a standard class period of 40–45 minutes. Three fit an extended period of 60–70 minutes. For a learner progressing by himself, one a·i·m is precisely the right amount of work for one sitting.

☐ **Performance Goals.** Specific goals are stated at the outset of each Part in the book and in the heading of every a·i·m; there is never doubt about them.

☐ **Visual Goals.** And when the a·i·m concerns production work, the heading also includes a miniature replica of the work that is to be done. The replica not only gives clues but also serves as a visual goal.

☐ **Goal Targets.** The exact point in the copy where the learner achieves his goal is signaled by a marker that resembles a target, like this: ⚲

☐ **Quantitative Timings.** In many timed writings and production jobs, the learner is given exactly enough material to equal the goal—another way of establishing performance goals, a way that reduces frustration for the learner.

☐ **Less Reading, More Typing.** The 20-minute module cannot afford much time for reading, so each a·i·m concentrates on more typing and less reading; what reading there is falls in the "very easy" category.

☐ **Special Supplement.** Thanks to recent research, it is possible to prescribe the proper drills for a learner stalled at any given point of progress. TYPING 300 has a supplement weighted with such prescription drills, to which the learner is directed frequently and systematically in many of the skill drives. Main result: higher achievement in accuracy.

Acknowledgment

And, speaking of research, the authors wish to acknowledge and to express appreciation for the research of scores of graduate students and the experience reports of hundreds of teachers who explored with us and stabilized for us the innovations in TYPING 300.

—John L. Rowe, Alan C. Lloyd, Fred E. Winger

Overview

In Part One you will master the essentials of operating a typewriter. You will learn to adjust the machine, manage the paper, control keys by touch, and perform all the basic motions.

This will be easy for you because everything to be learned has been divided into short (20 minute) experiences of reading and typing, and arranged in the way that will help you most.

a·i·m Each 20-minute experience is an Applied Instructional Module, or a·i·m for short. There are 30 a·i·m experiences in Part One. Each a·i·m (after the first introductory ones) opens with a warmup review. Each then includes either (a) something new to be learned, like a new key, or (b) exercises to help your speed and accuracy.

⚲ ⚲ ⚲ Each a·i·m includes in its heading a list of goals that you will, or should, attain in that a·i·m. Among the exercises is one or more goal symbols, like ⚲, at the points where you have attained a goal. You will always know what your goal is, and the symbol will tell you when you've reached it.

Performance Goals

When you finish Part One, you should be able to demonstrate the following abilities when you take the test in a·i·m 30, page 35:

1. Touch Typing While keeping your eyes on the material you are copying, you will operate letter and punctuation keys with correct fingering and return and indent the carriage by touch and proper controls.

2. Adjustments You will correctly set the paper guide, margin stops, tab stops, and linespacing. You will use the carriage releases and tab-stop clear, set, and action keys.

3. Checking You will proofread work, mark mistakes, count errors, and compute speed.

4. Technicalities You will score at least 80 percent on an objective test covering the technical information in Part One (names of machine parts, spacing after punctuation, etc.).

5. Skill You will type 40 words or more in 2 minutes within 4 errors as you copy alphabetic paragraph material line for line.

Routines and Procedures

Schedule An average learner will finish an a·i·m readily in 20 minutes if he moves quickly from one exercise to the next and makes exactly the number of copies directed. If your practice period is 40 to 50 minutes, you will complete two a·i·m experiences in the period. If you have time to spare (if you have 25 or more minutes for each a·i·m, for example), you should do extra practice on what is in the two a·i·m sets—you should not start another a·i·m that you cannot finish.

Copies The minimum number of copies to be made of each exercise is always indicated in the margin. It is the number an average learner will complete; if you can do more copies, do so.

Timesaving Machine adjustments are consistent throughout Part One: 40-space line and single-spacing. The extra-large typewriter type will help you read and type letter by letter.

Ready . . . Start!

As you turn the page to a·i·m 1, do so with confidence: more than 5 million beginners like you learn to type each year. You will find the course easy, interesting, and rewarding.

 300

FOR ALL TYPISTS WHO NEED TECHNIQUE IMPROVEMENT

DIRECTIONS

1. Using your last 5-minute timed writing paper, analyze the work for each of the flaws listed in the left margin. Select the three flaws that proved to be the most troublesome.

2. For each of the three selected flaws, type the matching drill once for every 10 words a minute you typed in that timed writing. For example, if you typed in the 30's, type the pair of drills 3 times each. Then type all the drills once or twice for general improvement.

FLAWS		CORRECTIVE DRILLS		
1. Capitals appear above the line.	1A	L Li Liz D Da Dan J Jo Joe S Sa Sam H Ho How R Re Red L Lois		12
	1B	T Th The K Ke Ken S Su Sue M Ma May F Fl Flo P Pa Pam D Dora		24
2. Some letters are very, very light.	2A	These small firms found their steel costs could mount daily.		12
	2B	They will lend them some more cash that they will soon need.		24
3. Some letters are very, very dark.	3A	They might help quite a lot if you would ask for their help.		12
	3B	We owe it to you to try to write or type all of your poetry.		24
4. Words omitted or words inserted.	4A	now. for need we that size the just is box this that think I	Start	12
	4B	.senioM seD dna ytiC awoI tisiv ot nalp ennA dna ,liaG ,naeJ	Start	24
5. Extra spaces have been inserted.	5A	Well, the skill, or art, of typing is, or should be, useful.		12
	5B	Miss Day paused . . . smiled wanly . . . and fell. I raced.		24
6. Some spaces were left out.	6A	v f x ; b k n d s g , h o y / q z j u l r . a e t p w c i m!		12
	6B	Frank knew why you used data about the early years so often.		24
7. You had some key jams or pile-ups.	7A	Sue and the new boy got the red car she and her dad had won.		12
	7B	Bob and the man did not get all the pay for the one day off.		24
8. You remember that you stalled when typing long words.	8A	To tolerate or organize an analysis of offerings is so easy.		12
	8B	An elementary way to emphasize any new concept is essential.		24
9. You remember that you looked up or lost your place.	9A	D--r M-ss P-rk-r: W- -r- pl--s-d t- -ckn-wl-dg- --r r-c--pt	Insert Vowels	12
	9B	-f y--r l-tt-r -f S-pt-mb-r 11, -b--t y--r -v-rd-- p-ym-nts.		24
10. You are slowed when indenting (tab every 10).	10A	the and for but did own		12
	10B	they wish form when them then		24
11. You lean palms on the machine.	11A	oxen many view snow zero snip brew nope veer join taxi pint		12
	11B	upon text only curb limp crib numb rove pony exit coin next		24

GOALS ◦ *To learn the names, location, and use of principal operating parts.* ◦ *To learn how to adjust the machine at the start of each session.*

DIRECTIONS *Read the information. Then, with your teacher's help, make the necessary adjustments.*

DESK ARRANGEMENT

MAIN PARTS

Carriage top, moving part that carries paper

Carriage release lever at each end of carriage to release it for easy repositioning by hand

Carriage return lever or key used for returning carriage

Carriage scale counts and numbers spaces, like a ruler

Cylinder large roller in middle of the carriage

Margin set key, lever, or button to adjust the setting of margin stops

Off-On switch to control power to motor

Paper guide a blade against which paper is placed when inserted

Paper bail holds paper in place

Paper rest paper rests against it

Paper release lever to loosen paper

Print point the place where typebars strike paper

Print-point indicator the marker pointing to the space at which the machine is ready to print

Spacing regulator lever that controls the space between lines of typing ◦

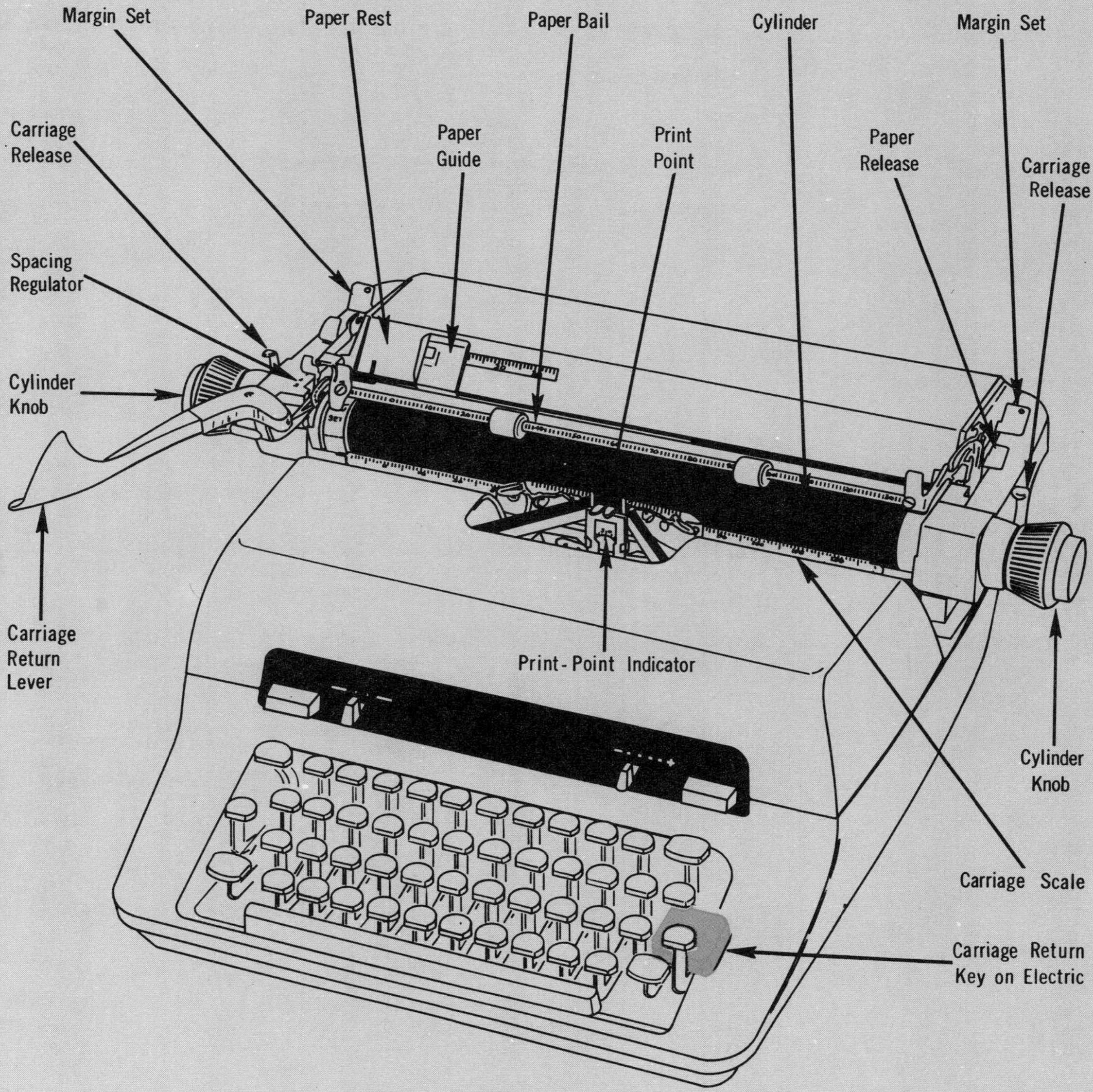

Margin Set
Paper Rest
Paper Bail
Cylinder
Margin Set
Carriage Release
Paper Guide
Print Point
Paper Release
Carriage Release
Spacing Regulator
Cylinder Knob
Carriage Return Lever
Print-Point Indicator
Cylinder Knob
Carriage Scale
Carriage Return Key on Electric

a·i·m 298

FOR ELECTRIC TYPISTS WHO ARE TYPING 45 TO 55 WAM • 5 COPIES

ACCURACY

Alternates
Adjacents
Double letters

1 ask woe here true weeks their power usual glass works newer 12
2 chassis bushels period thrown wheels where roads error well 12
3 Ross works with power tools for three of six class periods. 12
4 Bertrand took eight weeks to prepare a report for the firm. 12

|1 |2 |3 |4 |5 |6 |7 |8 |9 |10 |11 |12

SPEED

Right-hand runs
Adjacents
Jump reaches

5 china train equip choir doing never mines coin hope buy him 12
6 milling reverse dinner happen filler being climb doing foil 12
7 Thomas is going to train there as soon as we finish moving. 12
8 Vernon will never be willing to join your union until July. 12

|1 |2 |3 |4 |5 |6 |7 |8 |9 |10 |11 |12

ACCURACY

9 The powerful threshers that puffed their wood soot are 12
10 through. Many areas do reenact the era with thresher bees. 24

SPEED

11 Copper mining in open mines has become common in a few 36
12 areas. Ore trucks cling to inner areas for clearer vision. 48

a·i·m 299

FOR ELECTRIC TYPISTS WHO ARE TYPING 45 TO 55 WAM • 5 COPIES

ACCURACY

Alternates
Adjacents
Double letters

1 buy err cure view class spend owner issue truth flash teeth 12
2 channel socials pepper height bottle firms flash occur port 12
3 Russell paid the owner of the resort to keep the new skiff. 12
4 Sherry has to report there a few weeks before they open up. 12

|1 |2 |3 |4 |5 |6 |7 |8 |9 |10 |11 |12

SPEED

Right-hand runs
Adjacents
Jump reaches

5 thing verse inner print limit trims shops join very owe inn 12
6 winning between import lining senior mixer miner while foil 12
7 Bonnie was willing to join a beginning choir in her region. 12
8 Ronnie has nine reports on new import and export contracts. 12

|1 |2 |3 |4 |5 |6 |7 |8 |9 |10 |11 |12

ACCURACY

9 There are many wells where coins are tossed for better 12
10 luck. There are good reports of sending them to charities. 24

SPEED

11 Chinese coins were initially minted with center holes. 36
12 Reverses would portray mints where coins were being minted. 48

CARRIAGE RELEASE

To free the carriage so that you can move it freely, left or right, (1) brace your left hand against the left cylinder knob as (2) you press the adjacent carriage release lever. Practice control of the carriage: move it to 40 (release the lever when the carriage is at 40 on the scale) . . . move it to 70 . . . move it to 30.

PAPER GUIDE

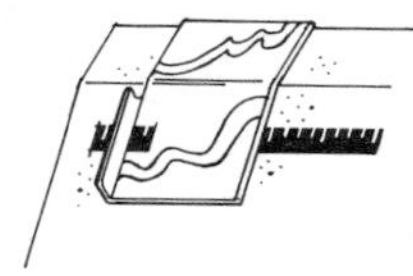

The paper guide should be set so that the paper, when inserted, will center at 50 on the scales. Take these seven steps to determine where it should be (do these steps just once, and afterward you will know where the paper guide belongs):

1. Pull the paper bail forward or up.

2. Move the paper guide as far to the left as it can go.

3. Set the carriage or carrier (if you are using a Selectric machine) at 50.

4. Mark the center of the top of a sheet of paper by creasing it.

5. Insert the creased sheet: grasp it in the left hand, set it behind the cylinder, and draw it into the machine by turning the knob by the right-hand fingers.

6. After depressing the paper release to loosen the paper, slide the paper left or right until the center crease is at the printing point—the point where the printing occurs. Then release the paper release.

7. Slide the paper guide to the right until its upright blade edge is snugly against the side of the sheet of paper.

Note on the guide scale exactly where you have set the paper guide. Now you will be able to confirm or correct the position of the paper guide very easily and quickly. Do so each time you come to the typewriter.

PAPER HANDLING

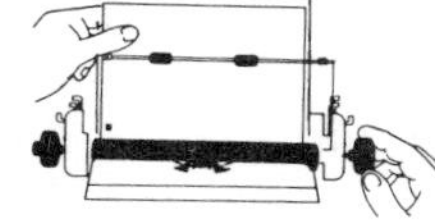

Practice paper handling several times:

1. Confirm setting of paper guide.

2. Pull paper bail forward or up.

3. With your left hand, place the paper behind the cylinder against the paper guide, then use your right hand to turn the right cylinder knob to draw in the paper. Advance the paper until about a third of it is in sight.

4. Confirm that the paper is straight by pressing back the visible part; the top and bottom should line up at the paper guide. If they do not, loosen the paper (by depressing the paper release) and straighten it.

5. Place the paper bail back against the paper. Adjust the small rollers on the bail so they are spread evenly across the paper.

6. Turning the right-hand cylinder knob, back down the paper until only a quarter inch or so shows above the bail. Now the paper is in the position it should be for the warmup review at the start of each session.

7. To remove the paper, draw the bail forward or up. Then depress the paper release (right hand) as you silently draw out the paper (left hand) and then restore the paper release to its normal position.

MARGIN PLANNING

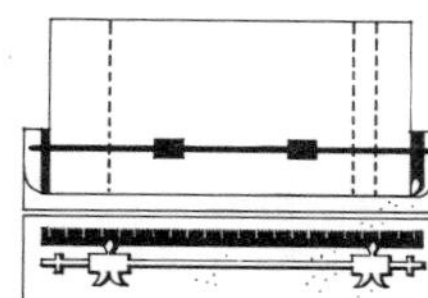

Margins at the sides of a typed page are controlled by "margin stops" that limit the line of writing. The length of the writing line is always indicated. "Line 40," for example, means you are to set the margin stops for a line of 40 spaces. Plan the left and right settings separately:

For the left margin, subtract half the desired line from the center. For a 40-space line, 50 (center) minus 20 (half of 40) = 30, the scale point at which the left margin stop is to be set.

For the right margin, add half the desired line and 5 extra spaces (an allowance for line-ending adjustments) to the center. For a 40-space line, for example, 50 (center) plus 20 (half of 40) plus 5 = 75, the point at which the right margin stop is to be set.

The settings you will use most often:

Line	Left Margin	Right Margin
40	50 − 20 = 30	50 + 20 + 5 = 75
50	50 − 25 = 25	50 + 25 + 5 = 80
60	50 − 30 = 20	50 + 30 + 5 = 85

SETTING MARGIN STOPS

Spring-Set Machines Royals, Smith-Coronas, and some Allens have a margin-set key at each end of the carriage. **For the left margin,** (1) press the left margin-set key,

SPEED

11 Boy Scouts have carried rations in the canvas knapsack 36

12 for years. These packs are seen very often on our streets. 48

|1 |2 |3 |4 |5 |6 |7 |8 |9 |10 |11 |12

a·i·m 296

FOR ELECTRIC TYPISTS WHO ARE TYPING 35 TO 45 WAM • 4 COPIES

ACCURACY

Double letters
Right-hand runs
In motions

1 adds pour yarn boom plum stop pipe good puff past mile flue 12

2 copy toys poor come spur week mate done rely tour coop atom 12

3 Donna will stop at our room on her last tour of our county. 12

4 Aaron is going to ration that milk supply on a weekly plan. 12

|1 |2 |3 |4 |5 |6 |7 |8 |9 |10 |11 |12

SPEED

Double letters
Left-hand runs
Up reaches

5 been yard uses less west tees safe part sell owes ties drew 12

6 feel wash mass rest away wild crew this puff nest life sees 12

7 Edward has thirteen acres of good trees at that hilly area. 12

8 Everett was feeling good after he was awarded that new car. 12

|1 |2 |3 |4 |5 |6 |7 |8 |9 |10 |11 |12

ACCURACY

9 Roller skills are coming on at a fast pace. People do 12

10 know races are put on, but seemingly enjoy all rough stuff. 24

SPEED

11 Steelhead eggs are hatched for mass release into water 36

12 reserves. Research stresses what took place after release. 48

a·i·m 297

FOR ELECTRIC TYPISTS WHO ARE TYPING 35 TO 45 WAM • 4 COPIES

ACCURACY

Double letters
Right-hand runs
In motions

1 pop coy soil well marks fluid stout merry party going spill 12

2 are off soon tour weeks topic stout rooms stone poppy about 12

3 Allyn put poppy seeds on our ground south of that building. 12

4 Mary would like to donate her copper spoons to a poor club. 12

|1 |2 |3 |4 |5 |6 |7 |8 |9 |10 |11 |12

SPEED

Double letters
Left-hand runs
Up reaches

5 asset pages yards still herds wares tiles nest hard sew odd 12

6 offer award sewer teeth safes press boost part last few too 12

7 Ward was willing to boost his offer for that large dresser. 12

8 Jeff still likes to get away to watch that large press run. 12

|1 |2 |3 |4 |5 |6 |7 |8 |9 |10 |11 |12

ACCURACY

9 A mass piling of car hulks all along our roads arouses 12

10 one. Machines that roll steel chunks from cars are coming. 24

SPEED

11 The good airlines want good food served to passengers. 36

12 Great stress is invested in seeing that few patrons suffer. 48

SPRING SET

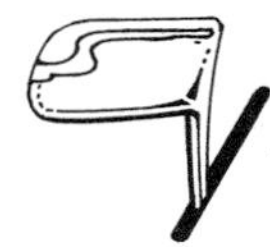

HAND SET

HOOK ON

LINESPACING

(2) move the carriage to the desired scale point, and (3) release the set key. **For the right margin,** (1) press the right margin-set key, (2) move the carriage to the desired scale point, and (3) release the set key.

Hand-Set Machines The margin stops of Underwoods, IBM Selectrics, Olympias, Remingtons, some Allens, and most portables are adjusted by hand without use of a set key. Set each margin stop separately: (1) press down the top of the margin stop, (2) slide the stop right or left to the desired scale point, and (3) release the stop.

Hook-On Machines Electric Underwoods, typebar IBMs, and some Remingtons have hook-on margin stops. **For the left margin,** (1) move the carriage to the left margin, (2) hook onto the left margin stop by holding down the margin-set key on the keyboard, (3) move the carriage to the desired scale point, and (4) release the set key. **For the right margin,** (1) move the carriage to the right margin, (2) hook onto the right margin stop by holding down the set key on the keyboard, (3) move the carriage to the desired point, and (4) release the set key.

Right now, set a "Line 40" (30 and 75).

The blank space between the lines of typing is controlled by the spacing regulator. Set it at "1" for single-spacing, which provides no

At "1"	At "2"	At "3"
single	double	triple
single	------	------
single	double	------
single	------	triple

blank space between typed lines, and "2" for double-spacing, which provides 1 blank line between lines of typing; and at "3" for triple-spacing, which provides 2 blank lines between typed lines. Many machines also have $1\frac{1}{2}$-spacing and $2\frac{1}{2}$-spacing, which are not used very often.

Right now, adjust the linespacer of your machine for "Spacing 1" (single-spacing).

a·i·m 2

GOALS *To sit in correct typing position. To place hands in correct "home position." To type the home keys and space bar by touch (without looking at them).*

DIRECTIONS *Spacing 1. Line 40. Tape K 1.*

POSITION

Sit like the typist in the picture:

Head erect, facing the book, which should be at the right of the machine, tilted to reduce shine on the paper.

Back straight and body leaning forward slightly; **shoulders** level.

Body a handspan from the machine, centered opposite the J key.

Feet apart, firmly braced on the floor, one foot ahead of the other.

Fingers curled tightly, as though you were pulling a heavy bar.

ACCURACY

SPEED

Every person in the timber belt finds their views very 12
fine. The sight of pure snow on every tree top opens eyes. 24
The sweet cherry ranks up near the peak on good taste. 36
A cup full of clean cherries can cap off a first-rate meal. 48

|1 |2 |3 |4 |5 |6 |7 |8 |9 |10 |11 |12

a·i·m 294

FOR ELECTRIC TYPISTS WHO ARE TYPING 25 TO 35 WAM • 3 COPIES

ACCURACY

Down reaches
Right hand runs
Out motions

bank coin ripe twin inks more bump knot mind cups poor type 12
poor gain link note nine scan unit coin camp lips rink snow 12
Danny knows he cannot hope to reach the mining camp by two. 12
Winn can gain more pointers by going to a full summer camp. 12

|1 |2 |3 |4 |5 |6 |7 |8 |9 |10 |11 |12

SPEED

Left hand runs
In motions
Down reaches

baby care load rare yarn vast hear toys cast fast four tree 12
dark last wear cabs farm past jack mast back pure wear puff 12
Bart had a very bad race at our early track meet last week. 12
Barbara cares a great deal about the fact that we are last. 12

|1 |2 |3 |4 |5 |6 |7 |8 |9 |10 |11 |12

ACCURACY

SPEED

Baseball can really move its fans to support a winning 12
group. Fans will shout, hoot poor calls, and trample cups. 24
Each area should draft axioms to stop the vast mass of 36
garbage. Garbage wastes can stack up at a very quick rate. 48

a·i·m 295

FOR ELECTRIC TYPISTS WHO ARE TYPING 25 TO 35 WAM • 3 COPIES

ACCURACY

Down reaches
Right hand runs
Out motions

bay now pop lax two coin wipe mind knee mood bump snow damp 12
mop cap not gay tip know ramp poor moot knit more noun join 12
Nora knows Ivan cannot join the baseball fans on two trips. 12
Timmy hopes to bank the minimum amount of money next month. 12

|1 |2 |3 |4 |5 |6 |7 |8 |9 |10 |11 |12

SPEED

Left hand runs
In motions
Down reaches

area back stay dead cast stop yarn sack coy par rag are bad 12
east flue heat care part vary mast pack wee van add pie bar 12
Grace made four copies of each part after the last meeting. 12
Max barely made it back after an early tour at our capital. 12

|1 |2 |3 |4 |5 |6 |7 |8 |9 |10 |11 |12

ACCURACY

Banks now supply all kinds of means for banking money. 12
A number of people now enjoy doing banking jobs from a car. 24

HOME KEY POSITION

Left Hand Place your fingertips on **A S D** and **F,** with your left thumb (it is not used) close to your forefinger.

Right Hand Place your fingertips on **J K L** and **;** keys, with your right thumb extended over the center of the space bar.

Curl the fingers tightly, so that only their tips lightly touch the keys. Your fingers are named for the home keys on which they rest: "A-finger, S-finger, D-finger," etc., ending with "Sem-finger" for the little finger on the **;** key.

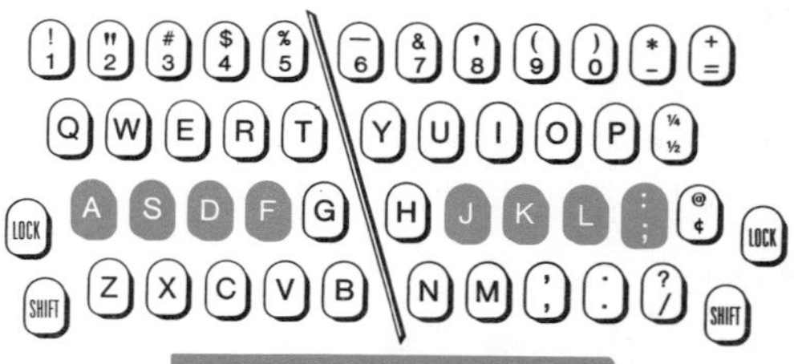

This is a "keyboard chart." The eight color keys are the "home keys."

SPACE BAR

With all fingers motionless on or above the home keys **A S D F** and **J K L ;** and with both hands as low as you can hold them without having your palms or wrists touch the front of the machine, sharply tap the space bar with your right thumb. Make the thumb *bounce* off the space bar. Practice spacing:

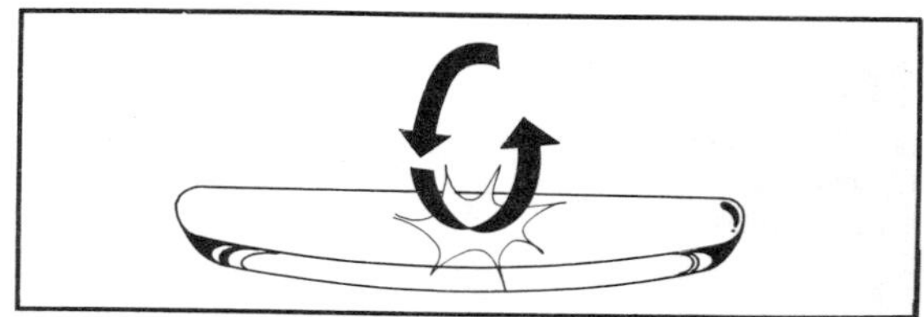

Strike the center of the space bar.

Space once [TAP THE SPACE BAR ONCE] . . . **twice** [TAP THE SPACE BAR TWICE] . . . **once** . . . **once** . . . **twice** . . . **once** . . . **twice** . . . **once** . . . **twice** . . . **twice** . . . **once** . . . **once** . . . **Repeat**

CARRIAGE RETURN

Manual Machine Place forefinger and next two fingers against the return lever; flip the lever with a toss of the wrist, returning the carriage to the margin; and return the hand to home-key position. Practice the drill below:

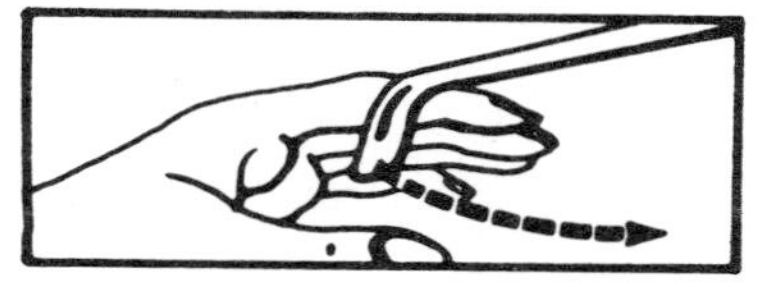

Electric Machine Extend the Sem-finger to the adjacent carriage-return key; lightly press the return key, causing the carriage to return automatically; and return the hand to home-key position. Practice the drill below:

Space once . . . twice . . . once . . . twice . . . Ready to return [MOVE HAND TO RETURN LEVER OR FINGER TO RETURN KEY]—**Carriage!** [RETURN IT] . . . **Home!** [FINGERS ON HOME KEYS] . . . **Repeat**

STROKING PRACTICE

Strike the F and J and space strokes shown in the drill lines below. Experiment to see how hard you must tap the keys to get them to print evenly. Type each line once.

Left forefinger, right thumb	`fff fff ff ff f f ff ff f f`	and return.
Right forefinger, right thumb	`jjj jjj jj jj j j jj jj j j`	and return.
Both forefingers, right thumb	`fff jjj ff jj f j ff jj f j`	and return.

SPEED (Cont.)

7 Linda will soon be willing to supply things for your pupil. 12

Right-hand runs
Proximates

8 Kim likes to draw pictures to exhibit in all our new homes. 12

|1 |2 |3 |4 |5 |6 |7 |8 |9 |10 |11 |12

ACCURACY

9 Extra efforts are used to get ahead in all areas. The 12
10 status seeker will see that greater rewards call up stress. 24

SPEED

11 A bill which calls for using braille in printing money 36
12 will really help all blind people in feeling money amounts. 48

a·i·m 292

FOR MANUAL TYPISTS WHO ARE TYPING 45 TO 55 WAM • 5 COPIES

ACCURACY

Double letters
Up reaches
Left-hand runs

1 wall tiles award stuff waists parrot estate appears statues 12
2 ages teeth drawn seems lights rotten states guesses watches 12
3 Gerald hopes to award those coffee makers at weekly drives. 12
4 Gerry heard that all those last guests were sorry to leave. 12

|1 |2 |3 |4 |5 |6 |7 |8 |9 |10 |11 |12

SPEED

Double letters
Right-hand runs
Proximates

5 winning linings typing tennis simply fines could blind cook 12
6 raining willing timing smiles piling clips miles ships hill 12
7 Lorrine would like to win that tennis award in your school. 12
8 Jim hopes to pull out a winning number in the next drawing. 12

|1 |2 |3 |4 |5 |6 |7 |8 |9 |10 |11 |12

ACCURACY

9 There are boaters who seem to taunt good sense at sea. 12
10 These boaters will cross bars against gales and bad swells. 24

SPEED

11 The striking of proof coins imposes select handling in 36
12 minting. All these proof coins will command higher prices. 48

a·i·m 293

FOR ELECTRIC TYPISTS WHO ARE TYPING UNDER 25 WAM • 2 COPIES

ACCURACY

Alternates
Jump reaches
Adjacents

1 aid fin wet big mid try cow not say dog rim pop end ten new 12
2 pork very worn sort trim turn more inch main give mire move 12
3 Dorene might rent them the boxer dog for their ninth mixer. 12
4 We were there in time to report on every level being timed. 12

|1 |2 |3 |4 |5 |6 |7 |8 |9 |10 |11 |12

SPEED

Down reaches
Double letters
Out motions

5 bay all day can fan ill lax gay off van hoe too job rip odd 12
6 trip bank type cuff show date rail hogs cans hood tubs knee 12
7 Todd will call the bank to clear up their shortage of cash. 12
8 Dana hopes to choose all those proofs to show to each camp. 12

LEFT HAND

Forefinger . . . . . F
Second finger . D
Third finger . . . S
Fourth finger . . A

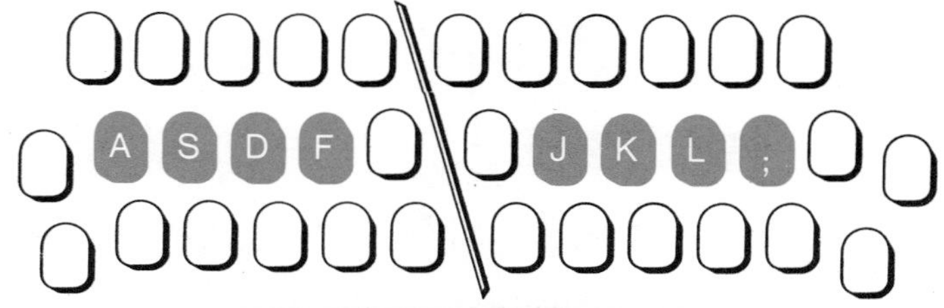

RIGHT HAND

J ...... Forefinger
K ... Second finger
L ...... Third finger
; ... Fourth finger

Space Bar ... Right thumb

F AND J Use forefingers and right thumb.	1	fff fff jjj jjj fff jjj ff jj ff jj f j	Return
	2	fff fff jjj jjj fff jjj ff jj ff jj f j	Return
	3	fff fff jjj jjj fff jjj ff jj ff jj f j	Return twice
D AND K Use second fingers.	4	ddd ddd kkk kkk ddd kkk dd kk dd kk d k	
	5	ddd ddd kkk kkk ddd kkk dd kk dd kk d k	
	6	ddd ddd kkk kkk ddd kkk dd kk dd kk d k	
S AND L Use third fingers.	7	sss sss lll lll sss lll ss ll ss ll s l	
	8	sss sss lll lll sss lll ss ll ss ll s l	
	9	sss sss lll lll sss lll ss ll ss ll s l	
A AND ; Use fourth fingers.	10	aaa aaa ;;; ;;; aaa ;;; aa ;; aa ;; a ;	
	11	aaa aaa ;;; ;;; aaa ;;; aa ;; aa ;; a ;	
	12	aaa aaa ;;; ;;; aaa ;;; aa ;; aa ;; a ; ⚲	

PREPARE a·i·m WB 1–4

GOALS ⚲ *To reinforce control of home keys.* ⚲ *To type words on home keys.* ⚲ *To type 60 strokes (12 words) or more in 1 minute on home key words.*

DIRECTIONS *Spacing 1. Line 40. Tape K 2.*

START-UP ROUTINE

1. Read the "Goals" carefully.
2. Read the "Directions" and adjust your machine accordingly.
3. Scan nearest keyboard chart.
4. Begin the Warmup Review.

WARMUP REVIEW

L = left hand
R = right hand

	L1	R1	L2	R2	L3	R3	L4	R4	L1	R1	
1	fff	jjj	ddd	kkk	sss	lll	aaa	;;;	fff	jjj	Return
2	fff	jjj	ddd	kkk	sss	lll	aaa	;;;	fff	jjj	Return
3	fff	jjj	ddd	kkk	sss	lll	aaa	;;;	fff	jjj	Return twice

SPEED

Double letters
Up reaches
Down reaches

5 ball arts haul vans fees flax file goes tall gray hose jobs 12

6 axle blow deed hail scab edge sell tubs away loss this word 12

7 Jill will appeal to those local banks to award school kits. 12

8 Barry waited for his good friend to mail those local gifts. 12

|1 |2 |3 |4 |5 |6 |7 |8 |9 |10 |11 |12

ACCURACY

9 There have been very few persons who have never become 12

10 very excited over flying kites in one period in their past. 24

SPEED

11 Those who like to travel can easily fill a schedule by 36

12 looking at small places off regular roads and local trails. 48

a·i·m 290

FOR MANUAL TYPISTS WHO ARE TYPING 35 TO 45 WAM • 4 COPIES

ACCURACY

Jump reaches
Adjacents
Left-hand runs

1 mob buy pop gas add cove dash reel song size rims into next 12

2 win err try sad wet crop even free inch text trim mine crew 12

3 Rex saw seven new mowers on review in their recent meeting. 12

4 Everett is being trained as an expert in import and export. 12

|1 |2 |3 |4 |5 |6 |7 |8 |9 |10 |11 |12

SPEED

Double letters
Up reaches
Down reaches

5 tank call shoe rail mess used plea oral see way can sea sky 12

6 jobs wife cuff sets nets lose kits loss odd tax raw old van 12

7 Will thinks his rates have been too low to allow valid pay. 12

8 Howard called the school to schedule a buffet for his club. 12

|1 |2 |3 |4 |5 |6 |7 |8 |9 |10 |11 |12

ACCURACY

9 There have been recent reports in respect to moving to 12

10 a new mixture of certain shades on our present paper money. 24

SPEED

11 Those who like to discuss varied issues or causes will 36

12 like to defray a few hours in a village and gab with folks. 48

a·i·m 291

FOR MANUAL TYPISTS WHO ARE TYPING 45 TO 55 WAM • 5 COPIES

ACCURACY

Double letters
Up reaches
Left-hand runs

1 see too away fees worse staff fuses guest petty mails gears 12

2 egg ate data gets vests shall gates heard issue pleas array 12

3 Howard seems eager to start searching for those lost balls. 12

4 Aileen feels that the best results were attained last week. 12

|1 |2 |3 |4 |5 |6 |7 |8 |9 |10 |11 |12

SPEED

Double letters

5 teeth would thing smile mines limit award hook pile ill beg 12

6 rooms while still pupil lines hinge alive ship will bin cry 12

WHEN YOU PRACTICE

1. Note how many copies of a line you are to make—one, two, or (as here) three.
2. If uncertain where a key is, look at the nearest keyboard chart, not at your fingers.
3. After completing a set of lines, return the carriage an extra time.

WORD BUILDING

3 copies (as shown)

4 aaa lll lll all all aaa ddd ddd add add Return
5 aaa lll lll all all aaa ddd ddd add add Return
6 aaa lll lll all all aaa ddd ddd add add Return twice

7 ddd aaa ddd dad dad lll aaa ddd lad lad
8 ddd aaa ddd dad dad lll aaa ddd lad lad
9 ddd aaa ddd dad dad lll aaa ddd lad lad

10 aaa sss ;;; as; as; jjj aaa lll jal jal
11 aaa sss ;;; as; as; jjj aaa lll jal jal
12 aaa sss ;;; as; as; jjj aaa lll jal jal

13 fff aaa ddd fad fad aaa sss kkk ask ask
14 fff aaa ddd fad fad aaa sss kkk ask ask
15 fff aaa ddd fad fad aaa sss kkk ask ask

WORD PYRAMIDS

3 copies (as shown)

16 a as ask asks asks; f fa fal fall falls
17 a as ask asks asks; f fa fal fall falls
18 a as ask asks asks; f fa fal fall falls

19 a al ala alas alas; f fl fla flas flask
20 a al ala alas alas; f fl fla flas flask
21 a al ala alas alas; f fl fla flas flask

1-MINUTE GOAL

Copy 22–23 in 1 minute. 2 tries

22 sad sad lad lad ask ask fad fad dad dad
23 fall fall asks asks [60 strokes]

SPEED

In motions
Double letters
Adjacents

5 sour dash reel some adds clad buys muff pick will song fire 12

6 road adds were flag week iron made push sure toys pass spur 12

7 Asher has had one week to add three women to our new staff. 12

8 Aaron put her rough copy of that report on top of our list. 12

|1 |2 |3 |4 |5 |6 |7 |8 |9 |10 |11 |12

ACCURACY

9 The total of basic mailings that fail to arrive at the 12

10 right dwelling might be because of faulty use of full data. 24

SPEED

11 There were three very good toys on that store counter. 36

12 One freak toy had three large wheels that were really flat. 48

a·i·m 288

FOR MANUAL TYPISTS WHO ARE TYPING 25 TO 35 WAM • 3 COPIES

ACCURACY

Proximates
Alternates
Out motions

1 bin via who wit ail goes vote slip high rail inch self jots 12

2 six two dry toe fin peak eyes rain fuse fail type take wife 12

3 Norm believes Craig should be boxing again within six days. 12

4 Darlene believes she should help them display those horses. 12

|1 |2 |3 |4 |5 |6 |7 |8 |9 |10 |11 |12

SPEED

In motions
Double letters
Adjacents

5 wire tops spur dome open fall slat view say add son off coy 12

6 stag done mass bomb sane only pure puff sad wee lad ask out 12

7 Aarron has had all women come to our home after sour dough. 12

8 Terry was about to report all her new bonds on our reports. 12

|1 |2 |3 |4 |5 |6 |7 |8 |9 |10 |11 |12

ACCURACY

9 Benign citizens believe they should cleanup or sustain 12

10 those beaches to give full benefits for those who see them. 24

SPEED

11 Most foodstuffs that are prepared on outdoor fires are 36

12 very good. There are very few persons about to oppose one. 48

a·i·m 289

FOR MANUAL TYPISTS WHO ARE TYPING 35 TO 45 WAM • 4 COPIES

ACCURACY

Jump reaches
Adjacents
Left-hand runs

1 wind adds tree over very fire beet even come bind crop here 12

2 buys mass into time week note owes mine ever been were nine 12

3 Everett has to report on the new concrete street next week. 12

4 Robert never expects to invent any number of better levers. 12

|1 |2 |3 |4 |5 |6 |7 |8 |9 |10 |11 |12

aim 4

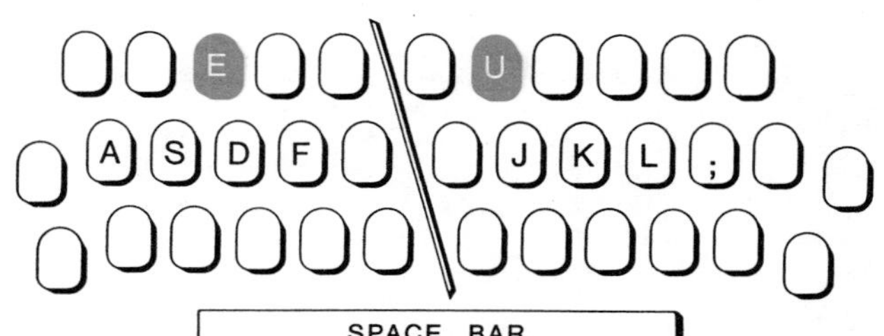

GOALS *To control E and U keys. To type 60 strokes or more in 1 minute on 10 keys.*

DIRECTIONS *Spacing 1.* Line 40. *Tape K 3.*

WARMUP REVIEW

2 copies

1 fff jjj ddd jjj sss kkk aaa ;;; fff jjj

2 sss aaa ddd sad sad aaa sss kkk ask ask

E KEY

D-finger
3 copies

3 ddd ded eee ddd ded eee ddd ded eee ded

4 ded see see ded fee fee ded lee lee ded

5 ded led led ded fed fed ded fee fee ded

U KEY

J-finger
3 copies

6 jjj juj uuu jjj juj uuu jjj juj uuu juj

7 juj dud dud juj due due juj sue sue juj

8 juj us; us; juj use use juj uke uke juj

WORD BUILDING

2 copies

9 d du dus dusk dusk; j je jel jell jells

10 f fu ful full full; l le lea leak leaks

1-MINUTE GOAL

2 tries

When you do drills like the ones above, you have two objectives: to master whatever is new (like the E and U keys) and to combine the new things with what you already know.

The 1-Minute Goal is a checkup to tell you whether you achieve your objectives.

The material to be typed below (the full line 11 + the partial line 12) is exactly the amount you should be able to type in 1 minute if you *have mastered* the new keys and blended them with other keys you know. You are to make two tries (a third is acceptable, if you have time for it). If you finish the material in 1 minute on the very first try, see on the second attempt whether you can do it again with fewer mistakes. If you don't make it the first time, you probably will succeed the second time because you will have practiced the material.

If you do not make the goal in two tries, figure out why not. Need extra practice on the new-key drills? Need to push harder? After you decide, act accordingly on the next 1-Minute Goal assignment.

11 jell jell seek seek add; add; full full

12 jell seek add; full [60 strokes]

These are remedial drills. Do ONLY the ones designed for your need. Note this table:

Tapes	Speed	Manuals	Electrics	Copies
SAID 1	→ 25	a·i·m 286	a·i·m 293	2
SAID 2	25 → 35	a·i·m 287, 288	a·i·m 294, 295	3
SAID 3	35 → 45	a·i·m 289, 290	a·i·m 296, 297	4
SAID 4	45 → 55	a·i·m 291, 292	a·i·m 298, 299	5
SAID 5	All	a·i·m 300	a·i·m 300	3

Use a 60-space line and single-spacing.

Speed Do drills given for the speed span in which your last 5-minute TW falls. Also do the technique drills in a·i·m 300.

Manuals/Electrics Do only the drills for the machine on which you are practicing.

Copies Copy each drill line and paragraph the number of times indicated for your speed span. **Note:** If you made 6 or more errors on your last 5-minute writing, repeat drill lines in whole groups, as though they were paragraphs; repeat single drill lines only when your error score on a 5-minute writing is 5 or fewer errors.

Follow-up After doing the drills, turn to any of the timed-writing selections in a·i·m group 271–285 and take a 5-minute writing on it, to measure your progress and define your next goal.

Limit You may use the appropriate a·i·m set as many times as you wish, but never work on the drills more than 30 minutes in one day.

a·i·m 286

FOR MANUAL TYPISTS WHO ARE TYPING UNDER 25 WAM • 2 COPIES

ACCURACY

Left-hand runs
Double letters
Out motions

1 bay too art cup see few gay odd gas lip ill raw who err set 12
2 week tray seat pass seen real mass legs here easy case away 12
3 Darr was here last week to show off all those small horses. 12
4 Wess was not ready to take care of each of those tax cases. 12
|1 |2 |3 |4 |5 |6 |7 |8 |9 |10 |11 |12

SPEED

Double letters
Alternates
Down reaches

5 all got bay odd ham can off key ink too day lax oak van pan 12
6 lack hand boot auto bake cuff dish cans knee firm able door 12
7 Ross may have to carry all the fuel and bait for that trip. 12
8 Diane may have to pay for all the food for their fall camp. 12
|1 |2 |3 |4 |5 |6 |7 |8 |9 |10 |11 |12

ACCURACY

9 Skeet shooters shoot fast after a target is fired off. 12
10 Those who shoot well are very steady and show great skills. 24

SPEED

11 When do they plan to go back to the city? We can call 36
12 the bank and borrow cash for them to keep that room a week. 48

a·i·m 287

FOR MANUAL TYPISTS WHO ARE TYPING 25 TO 35 WAM • 3 COPIES

ACCURACY

Proximates
Alternates
Out motions

1 belt also bugs fail hose crow ants find inch auto chip lawn 12
2 lies does gain flip bent days hail damp jots cuts buck move 12
3 Gail and Linda think they might both fail to gain a rating. 12
4 Does Wanda live in their house by the bay to raise a quota? 12
|1 |2 |3 |4 |5 |6 |7 |8 |9 |10 |11 |12

a·i·m 5

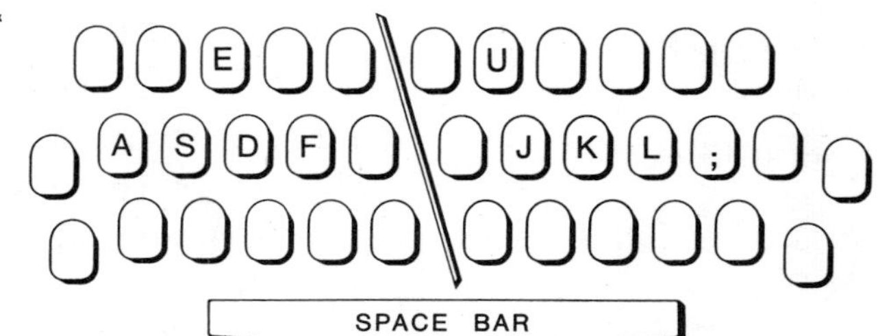

GOALS *To boost speed and accuracy, type 2 copies of the Improvement Practice. To type 65 strokes or more in 1 minute.*

DIRECTIONS *Spacing 1. Line 40.*

WARMUP REVIEW

2 copies

1 aaa sss ddd eee fff jjj uuu kkk lll ;;;

2 sss uuu eee sue sue ddd uuu ddd dud dud

PRETEST

1 copy (as shown)

3 all sad due elf fed jel use kee lea ;;;

4 all sad due elf fed jel [65 strokes]

Type two copies of each of the lines below. Note that the first word in each line corresponds to a word in the Pretest. For each word in the Pretest in which you make an error, type a remedial [additional] copy of the drill line that begins with that word.

IMPROVEMENT PRACTICE

2 copies of each line + remedials

5 all add add ask ask fall fall lake lake

6 sad see see sue sue sell sell sled sled

7 due dee dee dad dad dull dull dell dell

8 elf ell ell eel eel feed feed feel feel

9 fed fad fad fee fee full full fade fade

10 jell jell jade jade jude jude jess jess

11 uses uses dusk dusk dual dual fuel fuel

12 keel keel asks asks leak leak seek seek

13 lead lead leaf leaf less less fell fell

14 ; ;; see; fee; fee; all; all; add; add;

POST-TEST

Type the Pretest in 1 minute. 2 tries

a·i·m 285
Spacing 2
Line 70 Tab 5
Level: 1.41N

More and more people are learning to fly their very own airplane 14
every day. It used to be, many years ago, that only very rich people 28
were able to afford to learn how to fly and purchase their own plane. 42
This is not the case today, however. It is really not that expensive 56
to learn how to fly, and smaller airplanes do not cost very much more 70
than that expensive automobile; in fact, perhaps even less than some. 84

It was not until after World War II that so many suddenly became 98
interested in learning to fly. Many of the men who became trained to 112
be pilots during that war started flying schools and became active in 126
recruiting people to learn to fly. About that same time, many plants 140
which had been used to manufacture planes for the war converted 153
their equipment and began to produce small, light airplanes at a 166
reasonable price; however, they are still quite expensive for many, 179
many people. 182

Not everyone is capable of flying; however, most of us are. You 196
must, of course, be in sound physical shape. However, the most vital 210
factors are wanting to learn to fly and then not being afraid to fly 224
a plane by yourself. A few persons who have completed their training 238
never really do become good pilots simply because, although they 251
have mastered the subject matter, they become frightened while in 265
the air, by themselves. Just remember, flying an airplane is actually 279
no more difficult or dangerous than driving an automobile. The fact 293
is, many people would consider motoring down the busy freeway 305
during rush hour traffic more dangerous than flying that airplane; 318
in fact, much more. 323

If you think you would like to learn to fly, you should find out 337
as soon as possible. Locate the pilot schools in your area and visit 351
each of them. After talking to the people in charge, return home and 365
think about it for several days. If any questions come to your mind, 379
be sure to go back and find the answers. If you then decide that you 393
really want to learn to fly, then by all means sign up in that school 407
of your choice. Get involved and really buckle down to your studies. 421

After you complete the training you may not want to buy a plane. 435
Very often, several people will go together and lease an airplane and 449
maintain it as the group venture. A complete schedule is made out as 463
to who is to use it and when they are to use it. Every person shares 477
in the expense of the upkeep in such items as engine tune-ups, tires, 491
and other maintenance. However, each pilot is responsible for paying 505
for the fuel consumed on his own trip. What a pride of ownership, to 519
walk out on that airstrip and know that part of that airplane or even 533
all of it belongs to you. It has freed you from the confines of all. 547

|1 |2 |3 |4 |5 |6 |7 |8 |9 |10 |11 |12 |13 |14

 6

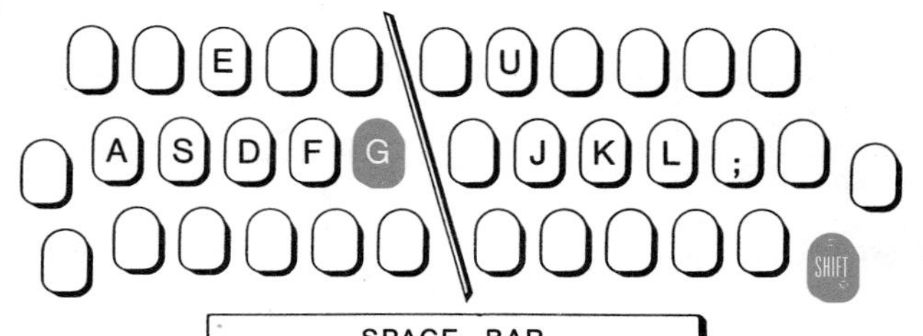

GOALS *To control G and Right Shift. To type 65 strokes or more in 1 minute on 11 keys (including capitals, too).*

DIRECTIONS *Spacing 1. Line 40. Tape K 4.*

WARMUP REVIEW

2 copies

1 `aaa ;;; sss lll ddd kkk fff jjj ded juj`

2 `uuu sss eee use use ddd uuu eee due due`

G KEY

F-finger
3 copies

3 `fff fgf ggg fff fgf ggg fff fgf ggg fgf`

4 `fgf lag lag fgf jag jag fgf sag sag fgf`

5 `fgf dug dug fgf lug lug fgf jug jug fgf`

RIGHT SHIFT KEY

Sem-finger
3 copies

Use the Right Shift key to capitalize letters typed by the left hand. Use a 3-step sequence of motions like this:

1. "CAP!" Keeping J-finger in home position, extend Sem-finger to press and hold down firmly the Right Shift key.

2. "Strike!" [or the name of the letter to be capitalized]. While the Shift is still depressed, strike with the left hand the letter to be capitalized.

3. "Home!" Release the Shift key and return all fingers to their home position.

For a capital A, for example, you would think "Cap!" as you press the Shift, "A!" as you strike the letter, and "Home!" as all fingers snap back to home position.

6 `;;; A;; A;; ;;; S;; S;; ;;; D;; D;; ;;;`

7 `;;; Ask Ask ;;; Alf Alf ;;; Ada Ada ;;;`

8 `;;; See See ;;; Sal Sal ;;; Del Del ;;;`

WORD BUILDING

2 copies

9 `F Fl Fla Flag Flags j ju jug jugs jugs;`

10 `D Da Dal Dale Dale; a as ask aske asked`

1-MINUTE GOAL

2 tries

11 `Saul Saul jade jade fake fake egg; egg;`

12 `Saul jade fake egg; asks` [65 strokes]

a·i·m 284
Spacing 2
Line 70 Tab 5
Level: 1.41N

People the world over know of West Point and Annapolis, for 13
much of our nation's and the modern world's history has been punctu- 26
ated by the valorous deeds of men whose training began on the march- 40
ing fields and in the stern classrooms of these institutions. Now there's 55
a new school, a school for skymen, perched within the shadow of the 68
Rockies in a valley just an hour's drive from Denver; and though it is 83
young, the new school augurs well to emulate the qualities of the 96
other two. 98

This new school is the new Air Force Academy, where two thou- 111
sand young men take a four-year course in the engineering and liberal 125
arts that are necessary for careers as Air Force officers. The cadets get 140
little flight training (which explains why the crags and peaks of the 154
Rockies are no hazard to the young men); they learn to fly light air- 168
planes and to navigate them, but the pilot training in the big planes 182
comes later (to those who qualify) in special flying schools operated 196
by the Air Force. The cadets take a program that is similar to those 210
of many colleges, but this program is buttressed also by great stress 224
on physical fitness, on military science, and on both the mathematics 238
and the physics that are important in the ballistics of space flight. 252

Visitors to the Academy find much to admire. The buildings have 266
a design that is oddly right, blunt and solid like the mountains that 280
stand behind them and yet sleek with long clean lines and chrome in a 294
fashion that suggests the steel needles of missiles of the space age. 308

Some of the traditions of the other two academies have appeared, 322
as you would expect, in the life of the new school. Standard "plebe" 336
customs, like dining at attention, walking at attention in the living 350
areas, and so on, are observed. Athletics have sprung into full life 364
with the falcon as the Academy's equivalent of the Army mule and 377
Navy goat. Within four years of the time that Congress passed the 390
bill to set up the school, the Falcons were being cheered in the Cotton 404
Bowl. 406

You would learn much if you could make a visit to the Academy, 420
a half dozen miles on the Denver side of Colorado Springs. How men 434
can carve out a mountainside to build a beautiful and useful plain, 449
where once was only wilderness, and how they can cloak the raw earth 463
with a green cover of trees and grass and can grace it with fine build- 477
ings—this is one thing you might learn by a visit. How a nation, re- 491
solved to find and train the best minds and bodies of its youth and 505
dedicate them to its armor, takes steps to do so—this is another il- 518
lustration to be observed. And how these men so selected and so 531
observed, these men most likely to be independent by nature, disci- 542
pline themselves to the rigorous life they have chosen—this, too, is 556
worth going to see. 560

|1 |2 |3 |4 |5 |6 |7 |8 |9 |10 |11 |12 |13 |14

7

GOALS ⚲ *To boost speed and accuracy, type 2 copies of the Improvement Practice.* ⚲ *To type 70 strokes or more in 1 minute.*

DIRECTIONS *Spacing 1. Line 40.*

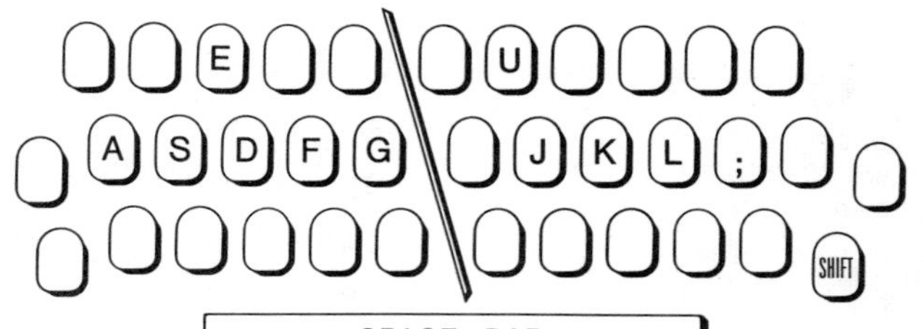

WARMUP REVIEW

2 copies

1 aaa ;;; sss lll ddd kkk fff jjj aaa ;;;

2 ded juj fgf juj ded fgf juj ded juj fgf

PRETEST

1 copy (as shown)

3 alas slug duke fade Gus; jell kegs legs

4 alas slug duke fade Gus; jell [70 strokes] ⚲

IMPROVEMENT PRACTICE

Each line twice plus once more if first word in line was typed wrong in the Pretest.

5 alas alas ages ages gala gala Ada; Ada;

6 slug slug sage sage seek seek sulk sulk

7 duke duke deal deal dull dull Dad; Dad;

8 fade fade feel feel fake fake full full

9 Gus; Gus; eggs eggs sags sags flag flag

10 jell jell jags jags jugs jugs jade jade

11 kegs kegs kale kale desk desk dusk dusk

12 legs legs lake lake gull gull luke luke⚲

POST-TEST

Type the Pretest in 1 minute. 2 tries

8

GOALS ⚲ *To control R and Period.* ⚲ *To type 70 strokes or more in 1 minute on 13 keys.*

DIRECTIONS *Spacing 1. Line 40. Tape K 5.*

CLEAN-UP ROUTINE

- 1. Paper—out.
- 2. Bail—against cylinder.
- 3. Carriage—centered (only approximately).
- 4. Covers—on (at end of last period).

WARMUP REVIEW

2 copies

1 aaa sss ded fff fgf jjj juj kkk lll ;;;

2 use use dug dug due due lug lug lea lea

a·i·m 283

Spacing 2
Line 70 Tab 5
Level: 1.41N

The visitor to New York City always has a list of sights he must 14
see before he heads back home. He must see the Empire State Building 28
and Radio City, for example; he just doesn't believe it's possible to 42
stack that much masonry that high. He must see the Statue of Liberty 56
because all the youngsters in his neighborhood will ask him about it. 70
He would like to see a fashionable stage play. He would enjoy having 84
dinner at Sardi's. He would like to see Yankee Stadium; or (if he is 98
a she) she would like to "do the shops on Fifth Avenue," which is her 112
way of saying that she hopes to see a three-thousand-dollar mink in a 126
window at Bonwit Teller and a ten-thousand-dollar ring in the display 140
panel at Tiffany's just so she can tell The Girls about what she saw. 154

There is, however, a phenomenon so important to visitors that it 168
will even outpull the Statue and the Empire, and that is Times Square 182
after dark. Even potentates and dictators schedule sightseeing tours 196
about the city timed to catch Times Square at night. It has to be at 210
night. In the daytime the Square is simply one more lively crossroad 224
where several thoroughfares come together and whose signals blink too 238
quickly for you to get across the street without panic. After dinner 252
it's different. It's entirely different! It is a panoply of lights, of sound, 268
of action, of noise, of color, of music and laughter, of so many things 282
all whirled together that they make a kaleidoscope of all the bright- 295
nesses there are. Fifteen minutes in Times Square at night gives a 309
visitor more things to remember, more vivid things to hold in memory, 323
than will an entire day in any other place you could mention. 336

It's the "spectaculars" that fascinate you, those giant displays 350
of lights and motion which catch your eyes and strain your credulity. 364
Where else does a billboard, forty feet high, blow smoke rings twenty 378
feet across? Where else will you find, three stories up, a waterfall 392
that is fifty feet high and a city block long, festooned in a rainbow 406
of changing hues from flickering spotlights? Where else do you watch 420
the headline news of the day run around buildings in ribbons of light 434
bulbs? Where else do fifty-foot sheets of Kleenex (in lights) spring 448
from a box the size of a house? Where else does coffee cascade sixty 462
feet from a coffee pot as big as a railroad water tank into a cup the 476
size of a backyard swimming pool? Where else do cartoons flicker all 490
evening on a screen of bulbs so enormous it is visible two miles off? 504

Up and down the side streets on both sides of the Square you see 518
the names, often in blazing letters six feet high, of the great stars in the 533
theaters; in the middle of the Square may be a destroyer or an 546
enormous tank or even a cottage. Oh, to see Times Square after dark! 560

|1 |2 |3 |4 |5 |6 |7 |8 |9 |10 |11 |12 |13 |14

If your keys get tangled, stop typing. Using both hands, GENTLY untangle the typebars. Let them fall back into the basket. Never pull or tug them.

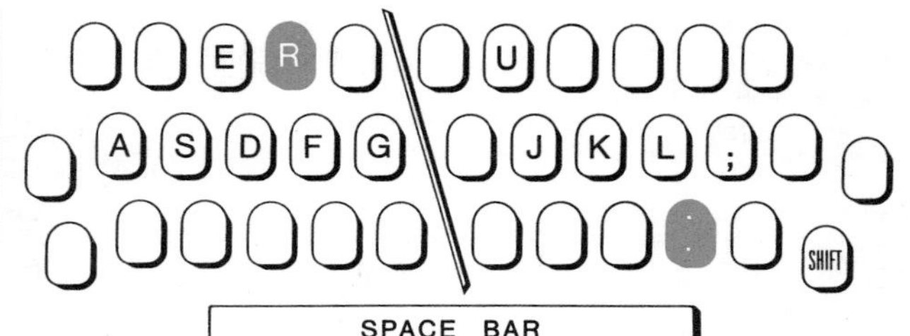

R KEY

F-finger
3 copies

3 fff frf rrr fff frf rrr fff frf rrr fff

4 frf fur fur frf far far frf jar jar frf

5 frf err err frf ere ere frf are are frf

. KEY

L-finger
3 copies

6 lll l.l ... lll l.l ... lll l.l ... l.l

7 l.l dr. dr. l.l sr. sr. l.l fr. fr. l.l

8 l.l Dr. Dr. l.l Sr. Sr. l.l Fr. Fr. l.l

WORD BUILDING

2 copies

9 u ur urg urge urges f fl fla flak flake

10 j ju jud judg judge G Ga Gal Gale Gale.

1-MINUTE GOAL

2 tries

11 Dad fed us. See a red fur. See a jug.

12 Sara Reed fed Dr. Gee a salad. [70 strokes]

 **9**

GOALS *To boost speed and accuracy, type 2 copies of the Improvement Practice. To type 75 strokes or more in 1 minute.*

DIRECTIONS *Spacing 1. Line 40.*

SPELL TO YOURSELF

1. To help accuracy, and
2. to reduce looking up, and
3. to make more even printing,

spell to yourself each letter and space you type. Do this without speaking aloud.

WARMUP REVIEW

2 copies

1 aaa ;;; sss l.l ded kkk frf juj fgf jjj

2 red red rug rug Dr. Dr. see see lee lee

a·i·m 281
Spacing 2
Line 70 Tab 5
Level: 1.40N

They say that opportunity never knocks twice. This is not true. 14
Maybe you just do not hear it knocking. Many people fail to take the 28
advantages offered in life. Even worse, they are so busy looking for 42
the "golden" opportunity, that they never see the simple obvious ones 56
that are given to them every day. All they can see are those unusual 70
doors leading to a pot of gold at the end of a rainbow, but never can 84
find that rainbow. The doors of opportunity never seem to unlock for 98
them no matter how hard they look. You must proceed slowly, and 111
look into life, and live it to find opportunities for advancement in life. 126

To succeed, you must be willing to work hard and even to give up 140
a few pleasures to get ahead. However, you must not make the 153
mistake of trying to get ahead by being oblivious to other people 166
around you. Other people's ideas and interests are important to you 180
as well as to them. If you have to obstruct others to push ahead, then 194
you are not finding the real opportunity, only making it. There are 208
tiny, subtle opportunities to prove that you are aware of humanity. 222
You can steal a few moments out of your busy life to be kind, to be 235
generous, or to be a real friend, to those who are in need of friendship. 250
This could put a zest in your life. You will find that if you do take 265
advantage of those tiny opportunities, your own life will be enhanced 279
more than you can imagine. You must work hard and plan carefully 292
to get ahead. 294

|1 |2 |3 |4 |5 |6 |7 |8 |9 |10 |11 |12 |13 |14

a·i·m 282
Spacing 2
Line 70 Tab 5
Level: 1.38N

Almost everyone does something in life that he enjoys doing. If 14 259
that something is not connected to his daily work day, it is called a 28 273
hobby. A hobby can be almost anything, from carving stone to 40 286
growing flowers to sky-diving. But the one essential ingredient 53 299
involved, in a hobby, is that you must enjoy doing it with zest and 67 312
zeal. A hobby is not difficult to get started; all you need is to schedule 81 326
a little time from each day in which to work on, and to enjoy, your 94 340
hobby. If you just can't seem to get started on anything new or 108 353
exciting, pay a visit to your local craft shop. There you will find 121 367
myriads of ideas from which to get a start. You should visit local 135 380
fairs and exhibits to learn new ideas. Possibly you have a hidden and 149 394
buried talent for a new and unique hobby that has not yet been 162 407
discovered and explored. 167 412

You might enjoy nature as your hobby. You can watch birds, hunt 181 426
for unusual plant life, or you might even try becoming a hunter of an 195 440
old fossil or rocks. A hobby such as this would not be expensive and 209 454
difficult. All you need is time and ambition, and a zest for finding 223 468
and doing the unknown. Perhaps, you can find a friend who would like 237 482
to join you in your pursuit of a hobby. 245 490

|1 |2 |3 |4 |5 |6 |7 |8 |9 |10 |11 |12 |13 |14

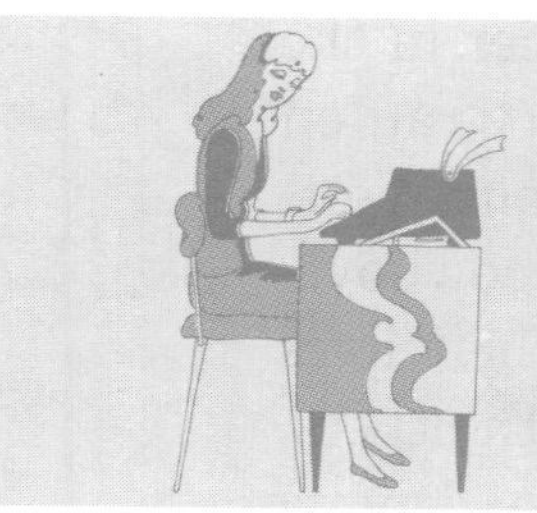

CHECK YOUR POSTURE

- **Feet** ... apart, on floor.
- **Back** ... erect, leans forward.
- **Hands** ... close, curled, low.
- **Eyes** ... focused on book.

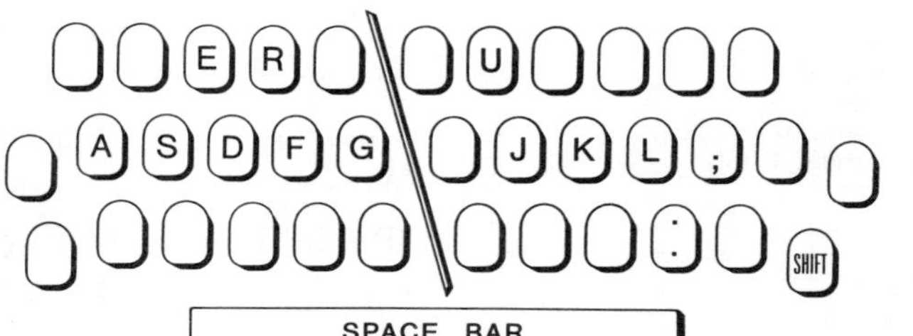

PRETEST

1 copy (as shown)

3 adds sure dark full gear jars keel led.

4 adds sure dark full gear jars keel [75 strokes]

IMPROVEMENT PRACTICE

Each line twice plus once more if first word in line was typed wrong in the Pretest.

5 adds adds area area are; are; ark; ark;

6 sure sure seed seed sees sees fees fees

7 dark dark dare dare dale dale dads dads

8 full full fuss fuss furl furl flag flag

9 gear gear gaff gaff glee glee glad glad

10 jars jars jugs jugs jell jell jade jade

POST-TEST

Type the Pretest in 1 minute. 2 tries

11 keel keel lake lake sake sake rake rake

12 led. led. less less sell sell dell dell

a·i·m 10

GOALS *To control H and Left Shift. To type 75 strokes or more in 1 minute on 14 keys.*

DIRECTIONS *Spacing 1. Line 40. Tape K 6.*

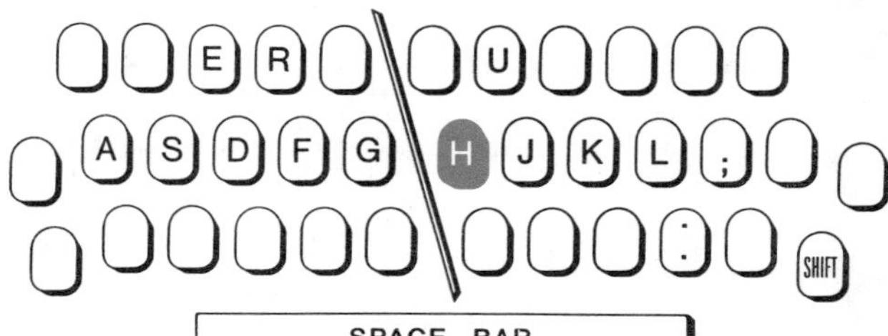

WARMUP REVIEW

2 copies

1 aaa ;;; sss lll ddd kkk fff jjj A;; A;;

2 fff frf jjj juj fff fgf lll l.l ddd ded

H KEY

J-finger 3 copies

3 jjj jhj hhh jjj jhj hhh jjj jhj hhh jhj

4 jhj had had jhj hag hag jhj has has jhj

5 jhj he; he; jhj she she jhj her her jhj

a·i·m 279
Spacing 2
Line 70 Tab 5
Level: 1.40N

Many pioneers and explorers bravely opened a new frontier in the 14
western part of our country. The trail was long; the blue sky ran on 28
forever. There were brave people who went on the long road out West. 42
Among those brave explorers was a unique group called cowboys. 55
Their lives were filled with zestful adventure. Sometimes their lives 69
were lonely, although at times they found companionship with others. 83
They spent long, hard days riding around the herds of cattle, driving 97
them to distant points. Through the day they would ride through all 111
kinds of weather, inclement and fair. They would sweat on the dusty 125
plains and freeze on a hilltop or mountain. They went through the 138
dangerous plains for miles, and rode through the beautiful, scenic 152
mountains of America. When they came upon a stream, there was the 165
clear icy water gurgling through the arid soil. At night, the unusual 179
songbird would sing very softly in the dusk; the shadows lengthened 193
around the butte of the hill. The life of a cowboy was adventurous, 207
unusual, and full of many rewards. The quietness of the evenings, the 221
warmth and close companionship of fellow cowboys, the soft lowing 234
of cattle, the daily campfire, the stars in the sky, or the end of the 248
trail were all full rewards for the cowboy. The cowboy was truly the 262
explorer, who first traveled on that long road west and made the way 276
for others to travel on the same route later on with safety. They were 290
true trailblazers. 294

|1 |2 |3 |4 |5 |6 |7 |8 |9 |10 |11 |12 |13 |14

a·i·m 280
Spacing 2
Line 70 Tab 5
Level: 1.38N

A jet plane is a marvelous, intricate machine. This craft truly 14 266
imitates a bird, a graceful creature of the sky. The plane navigates 28 280
easily and quickly, making a tiny ripple of air as it flies. It will 42 294
glide through those fleecy billowy clouds without disrupting even one 56 308
single cloud. The wings hold it delicately high like a giant, though 70 322
graceful bird. The tail glides along, as if it were floating through 84 336
the air with no visible way of support. It is a giant graceful bird. 98 350

Yes, the jet plane is a far cry from the plane of the past. The 112 364
plane of yesterday rumbled, roared, and jogged along. It was quite a 126 378
clumsy, almost crippled, bird trying to experience the joy of flying. 140 392
It was a poor imitation of those graceful birds that soared overhead, 154 406
and did not reach out and kiss the clouds easily. It lurched through 168 420
the air like the proverbial ugly duckling. This airplane of today is 182 434
truly a work of art. It can carry cargoes of people, luggage, autos, 196 448
animals, and mail to far off lands. It can soar through the air with 210 462
great zest and zeal, yet it smoothly glides through the sky. But the 224 476
most wonderful thing of all about the jet plane is that it brings the 238 490
world closer together. Within hours anyone can be jetted anywhere. 252 504

|1 |2 |3 |4 |5 |6 |7 |8 |9 |10 |11 |12 |13 |14

KEEPING EYES ON COPY IS EASIER IF YOU—

- 1. Understand how the line is arranged.
- 2. Review the chart for key positions.
- 3. Maintain an even pace.
- 4. Resist the temptation to look up.

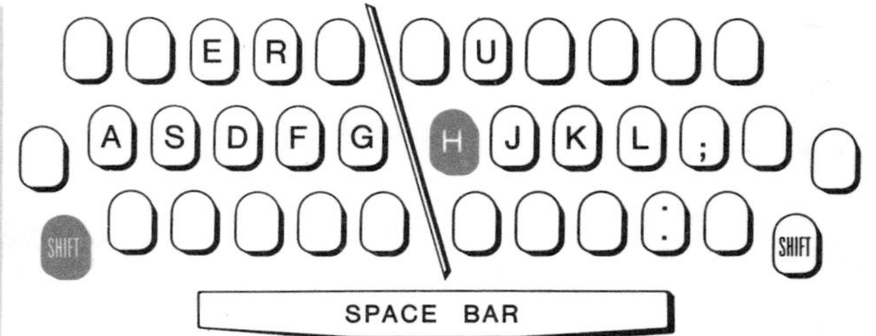

LEFT  KEY

A-finger
3 copies

Use the Left Shift key to capitalize letters typed by the right hand. Signals:

1. "Cap!" Keeping F-finger in home position, extend your A-finger to press and hold down firmly the Left Shift key.

2. "Strike!" While the Shift is still depressed, strike with the right hand the letter that is to be capitalized.

3. "Home!" Release the Shift and return all fingers to home position.

6 aaa Jaa Jaa aaa Kaa Kaa aaa Laa Laa aaa

7 aaa Jed Jed aaa Lea Lea aaa Hal Hal aaa

8 aaa Her Her aaa Has Has aaa Had Had aaa

WORD BUILDING

2 copies

9 J Ja Jak Jake Jake; L La Lar Larg Large

10 h hu hus hush hush; f fr fre free freed

1-MINUTE GOAL

2 tries

11 He sees us. He sees Hale. Gus feeds a

12 red deer. Dr. Hall sued Jake Lee. [75 strokes]

a·i·m 11

GOALS *To control I key. To type 80 strokes or more in 1 minute on 15 keys.*

DIRECTIONS *Spacing 1. Line 40. Tape K 7.*

TO TYPE FASTER

- 1. Try for smoothness, not speed.
- 2. Read copy before typing it.
- 3. Type with fingers curled.
- 4. Match strokes with someone who types at about your speed.

WARMUP REVIEW

2 copies

1 aaa ;;; sss lll ded kkk frf juj fgf l.l

2 Lee Lee Sue Sue Hal Hal Red Red Les Les

a·i·m 277

Spacing 2
Line 70 Tab 5
Level: 1.40N

What is so rare as a day in June? Although this is a queer, old 14
saying, it is a true saying. When you think of it, what really is it 28
about the day in June that brings all sorts of pictures to your mind? 42
Is it the brilliant warm sunshine that beams and glows softly around; 56
or is it the odor of fragrant flowers in full blossom? Perhaps it is the 71
lazy buzzing of an insect, while you are sitting quietly thinking 84
about all the joyous adventures in life. The June rain falls softly; 98
it gives off a sparkling clean odor of new beginnings and refreshes 112
the dusty earth. The trees are greener and the flowers are gorgeous. 126
All of nature puts on a new garment of cleanliness and zest for life. 140

June is also that time for initiating many new jobs and hobbies. 155
You can begin planting a vegetable garden or mow a lawn. You will be 169
transported to adventure by reading a book under that shady old 181
tree. You can gaze toward a huge, brilliant cosmic sky above and 195
make cloud pictures. You can imagine various types of adventures 208
and stories by gazing at the fleecy, fluffy, moving clouds. This is an 222
old and true relaxation. Although others may say you are being lazy, 236
you are not, really; you are truthfully creating. You might be able to 251
accomplish these things on that quiet day in June. Of course, you can 265
do almost anything on any rare day of any month. All that is re- 278
quired is time, and some imagination to make that day truly a 289
memorable one yourself. 294

|1 |2 |3 |4 |5 |6 |7 |8 |9 |10 |11 |12 |13 |14

a·i·m 278

Spacing 2
Line 70 Tab 5
Level: 1.38N

Goals require industrious and diligent labor. You may initially 14 265
determine your exact goal or goals. Too many go through life without 28 279
ever realizing what their exact goals for that day, that year, or the 42 293
future will be. They stumble blindly, trying to go everywhere, never 56 307
knowing where they are traveling. To determine your own goal in life 70 321
you must first decide which direction you would like to push. Do not 84 335
travel in the direction immediately, but meditate about the different 98 349
routes toward the goal and what you should find at the end. Think of 112 363
the final result, of all those possible goals that you may personally 126 376
want to attain. Use your energies to determine what you really want. 140 389

When you have decided on your goal, whether it be a short-termed 154 403
goal or a long-range goal, decide how best to reach it. Most of your 168 417
goals are reached through long, hard, and dedicated work. Do not let 182 431
yourself believe even for one moment that your goal will come to you. 196 445
You must go toward your goal. You must strive with all of your might 210 459
and wits to reach to your goal. Do not allow any distractions of the 224 463
everyday world to pull your sights away from your goal. You must not 238 477
lose sight of your goal all the time you are working toward it. 251 490

|1 |2 |3 |4 |5 |6 |7 |8 |9 |10 |11 |12 |13 |14

YOUR BODY SHOULD BE

- A handspan of space from the typewriter.
- Centered opposite the J key.
- Erect, with spine straight.
- Leaning forward—slightly—from the waist.

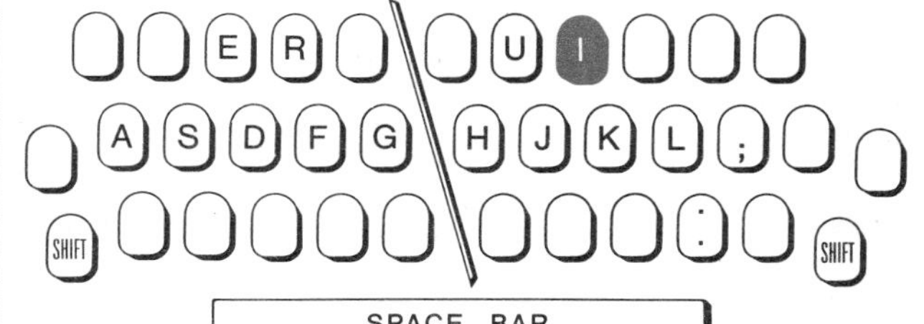

I KEY
K-finger
3 copies

kkk kik iii kkk kik iii kkk kik iii kik
kik air air kik fir fir kik sir sir kik
kik kid kid kik did did kik rid rid kik ⚲

WORD FAMILIES
3 copies

ire; ire; hire hire fire fire sire sire
ill; ill; fill fill dill dill sill sill
air; air; fair fair hair hair lair lair

WORD BUILDING
2 copies

H Ha Hal Half Half; g gi gir girl girls
J Ja Jad Jade Jade; d du dus dusk dusk.

1-MINUTE GOAL
2 tries

Jill is here; Jeff said she is. He has
a red rug. I guess she likes red rugs. ⚲ [80 strokes]

 **12**

GOALS ⚲ *To boost speed and accuracy, type 2 copies of the Improvement Practice.* ⚲ *To type 80 strokes or more in 1 minute.*

DIRECTIONS *Spacing 1. Line 40.*

TYPE WITH STEADY STROKES

- When you make capitals.
- When you tap the space bar.
- Whether words are long or short.
- Whether words are easy or hard.

WARMUP REVIEW
2 copies

aaa ;;; sss l.l ded kik frf juj fgf jhj
add add fee fee err err all all see see

PRETEST
1 copy
(as shown)

Jake Rash Jell Fire Hers Fish Lugs Dare
Jake Rash Jell Fire Hers Fish Lugs Dare [80 strokes] ⚲

a·i·m 275

Spacing 2
Line 60 Tab 5
Level: 1.38N

A late summer shower is a joyous experience. After it has been hot 15
and the humidity has been extremely high there is nothing more 27
beautiful than summer rain. Usually before rain, you can see a sky 41
warning; you might see thunderheads ominously forming on the 53
serene horizon. Then quickly, you will see them begin to turn darker. 67
Perhaps they will turn into ominous, angry, or very, very threatening 81
clouds. The excitement begins to build within you. You look to see the 96
flashes of lightning up in the summer sky. You may be able to hear 110
the distant clap of thunder. You may begin to feel those few drops of 124
rain, and the air becomes refreshing and clean. You may realize 137
suddenly that the rain is upon you. 144

Almost instantly the rainy deluge surrounds you. Rain may gush 159
down in torrents, or it may fall gently and slowly toward the soil. 172
Very soon the grass will be a rich, dark, fresher shade of green. 185
Flowers quickly begin to spring up their sad, drooping heads as if 199
quite glad for a refreshing drink. Then, as suddenly as the storm 212
came up, it is over. The air is fresh and pure, the puddles begin 225
slowly seeping into the soil, and you feel quite refreshed. It has been 240
a good rain. You know you will look forward to the next one. 252

|1 |2 |3 |4 |5 |6 |7 |8 |9 |10 |11 |12 |13 |14

a·i·m 276

Spacing 2
Line 60 Tab 5
Level: 1.38N

If you and your friends have never spent time camping, close to 14 267
nature, you are in for a great thrill. Camping is an experience which 28 281
you never forget. It seems to fill you full of vim, vigor, and zest. The 43 296
great outdoors gives you a feeling of being alive and close to nature. 58 311
Many persons are discovering this great feeling each summer as they 71 324
pack up their gear and enthusiasm and take off for the wonderful 84 337
experience of being able to spend amounts of time outdoors. 96 350

A novice at camping must first learn a few broad basic safety rules. 111 365
These items are designed to protect you from the dangers. There are 125 378
several good handbooks available in dealing with this subject. You 139 392
should never try to camp in the wilderness unless you know those 152 405
safety rules. Always, you should be aware of the rules of courtesy 165 418
while camping. Nothing will ruin good camping for others than to be 179 432
around anyone who is rude and not considerate of others' feelings. 193 446
As far as what to take with you, you will find the supplies and needs 207 460
vary from one camper to another. Perhaps you can refer to a camping 221 474
handbook, or maybe ask the other campers what they find that they 234 497
need while camping. You will find that you will enjoy camping and 247 501
will want to go back again. 253 506

|1 |2 |3 |4 |5 |6 |7 |8 |9 |10 |11 |12 |13 |14

YOUR FEET SHOULD BE—

- Both in front of the chair.
- Firmly placed on the floor, square, flat.
- Set apart, 6 or 7 inches between ankles.
- One foot a little ahead of the other.

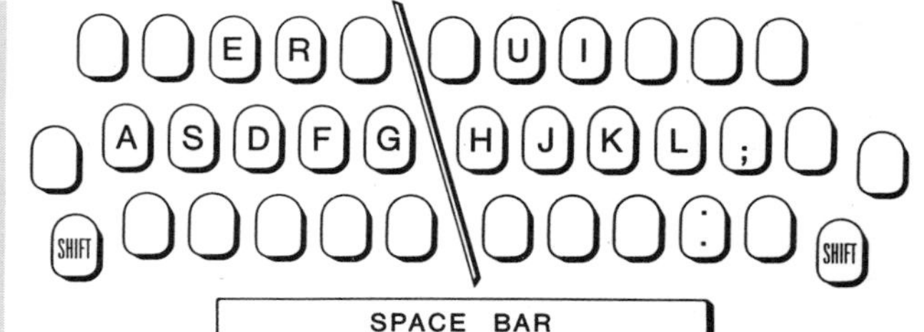

IMPROVEMENT PRACTICE

Each line twice, plus once more if first word in line was typed wrong in the Pretest.

5 Jake Jake lake lake sake sake fake fake
6 Rash Rash sash sash hash hash lash lash
7 Jell Jell fell fell sell sell dell dell
8 Fire Fire dire dire hire hire sire sire

9 Hers Hers herd herd hard hard lard lard
10 Fish Fish dish dish dash dash gash gash
11 Lugs Lugs jugs jugs hugs hugs rugs rugs
12 Dare Dare hare hare fare fare far; far;

Phrases:

13 if he; if he; if she; if she; if she is

POST-TEST

Type the Pretest in 1 minute. 2 tries

14 he is; he is; she is; she is; if he is;
15 a rug a rug a fill a fill a lake a lake

a·i·m 13

GOALS *To control O and T keys. To type 80 strokes or more in 1 minute on 17 keys.*

DIRECTIONS *Spacing 1. Line 40. Tape K 8.*

ON THE UP REACHES—

- Just move the finger; keep the arm as motionless as you can.
- Keep the finger curled; don't let it straighten or stiffen.
- Keep A or F and J or ; "at home."

WARMUP REVIEW

2 copies

1 aaa sss ded frf fgf jhj juj kik l.l ;;;
2 ask ask fed fed rig rig jug jug his his

a·i·m 273

Spacing 2
Line 60 Tab 5
Level: 1.39N

Have you ever thought about sounds? There are lots of many interesting kinds of sounds to meditate about. For an example, when walking you can hear feet scraping, scuffing, clomping, and stomping. If listening to wet water, you can hear it gurgle, ripple, bubble, or rumble. Individuals can scrunch, crunch, yip, zoom, and squawk. Papers can rustle, crackle, flop, or pop. Even your voice can portray certain moods like crying, giggling, whining, laughing, or sobbing.

Shut your eyes for a few minutes and try listening for different sounds. Try to find out from where they might be coming. Try to classify each sound that you hear and match it with images in your mind. Most of us seem to go through life without hearing the many, many delightful sounds which are all around us. We hear without hearing; we see without seeing; and we really live without living. Most of us have not heard the very sad sound of a loon crying across a lake or the soothing sound of whippoorwills in the evening dusk.

|1 |2 |3 |4 |5 |6 |7 |8 |9 |10 |11 |12

a·i·m 274

Spacing 2
Line 60 Tab 5
Level: 1.39N

Did you ever stop to cogitate about the vast amount of knowledge you can obtain by browsing through the ads in the newspaper? It does not matter which newspaper you may read or look at, for the huge amount of printed advertising will surprise you. You will notice many types of helpful items.

The classified section of the newspaper is many things to many different people. For example, you might either be a buyer or seller of items. As a seller it may be your own wares, or you could be selling goods for someone else. Any wares could be listed in the paper. However, as the buyer, you might be trying quite hard to buy a certain object that you have wanted for a long time, or you may just be looking for general items. You can find, if you want, where trucks are fixed, what kinds of schooling are offered, how to find a job, where to find a lost puppy or bicycle, what types of houses are available, and many, many more kinds of valuable information. Try scanning those ads today; you will learn.

WATCH YOUR ELBOWS

- Let them hang limply, just as they are when you let your arms drop down all the way.
- Don't let them swing in and out as you type.
- Hold your shoulders naturally—don't let them sag and don't raise them unusually high.

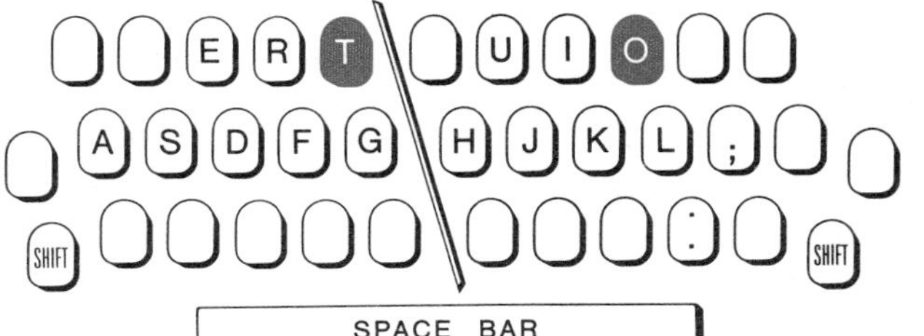

O KEY
L-finger
3 copies

3 lll lol ooo lll lol ooo lll lol ooo lol
4 lol log log lol jog jog lol dog dog lol
5 lol off off lol odd odd lol old old lol

T KEY
F-finger
3 copies

6 fff ftf ttt fff ftf ttt fff ftf ttt ftf
7 ftf aft aft ftf its its ftf hat hat ftf
8 ftf too too ftf toe toe ftf the the ftf

WORD BUILDING
2 copies

9 o ot oth othe other t tr tru trus trust
10 t to tot tota total j jo jol jolt jolts
11 d di dis disk disk; g go gol golf golf.

1-MINUTE GOAL
2 tries

12 Joe had a fall. He hurt his foot. His
13 dad asked Dr. Good to look at the foot. [80 strokes]

GOALS *To control Comma and C keys. To type 80 strokes or more in 1 minute on 19 keys.*

DIRECTIONS *Spacing 1. Line 40. Tape K 9.*

ON THE DOWN REACHES—

- Curl the finger under.
- Keep your hand in home position.
- Try to move only the striking finger.
- Don't let hand or arm move down.

WARMUP REVIEW
2 copies

1 aaa ;;; sss lll ddd kkk fff jjj aaa ;;;
2 lol ded l.l frf kik ftf juj fgf jhj frf

SUPPLEMENT 1 EXTRA TIMED WRITINGS

The following 15 timed-writing selections are for use, as your teacher may elect—

A. In regular timed-writing tests.

B. In connection with the remedial drills, as explained on page 275.

C. In this special skill-building plan:

Step 1. Type your goal at the top of the paper; it should be not less than the goal in your last text a·i·m that included a skill goal.

Step 2. Read the material and practice any word that you think might be difficult.

Step 3. Take a 5-minute writing, pausing for a few seconds' rest after each minute.

Step 4. Type 3 times each line of your typing that contains an error or in which you recall that you had any difficulty.

Step 5. Starting where the timed writing ended, type an additional line's worth of material; type it at least 3 times. If this does not reach your goal, type 3 times all the remaining material right up to your speed goal.

Step 6. Now take an uninterrupted 5-minute writing, trying to complete all the material you have practiced in Steps 3–5.

a·i·m 271

Spacing 2
Line 60 Tab 5
Level: SI 1.39N

Keeping in top physical condition is definitely one of 12
the most important things in life that you will accomplish. 24
There are several ways to maintain top physical fitness and 36
all methods are also devised to help you go through life by 48
being active. You may want to do a quick, zesty, exercise. 60
If you do, you should do the same kinds every day. You can 72
exercise to rhythms to make them quite suitable. You might 84
like to go out for sports such as skating, dancing, hiking, 96
swimming, biking or some other activities. Along with good 108
exercise and activity, you might need to be aware of proper 120
nutrition and follow the diet carefully to be sure that you 132
are getting the required types of food to keep you healthy. 144

|1 |2 |3 |4 |5 |6 |7 |8 |9 |10 |11 |12

a·i·m 272

Spacing 2
Line 60 Tab 5
Level: 1.38N

Millions of Americans have become addicted to a method 12
of living that may seem unusual to some. That is the habit 24
of keeping a domestic pet. Household pets could range from 36
a loving dog or cat to a pet turtle or a zany hamster. The 48
type of pet really does not matter. The important thing is 60
that you get a good pet of which you are fond and will take 72
good care of it. The pet should be adaptable to everyone's 84
household routine and not be a distraction. Perhaps, it is 96
easier for you to keep turtles than to accommodate a puppy. 108
Make your choice carefully and thoughtfully. When you have 120
made a decision as to the type of pet, remember a pet needs 132
lots of love and care to mature and grow into a loving pet. 144

SPACING AFTER PUNCTUATION MARKS

- Space twice after the end of any sentence.
- Space once after a comma.
- Space once after a period that follows an abbreviation.
- Space once after a semicolon.

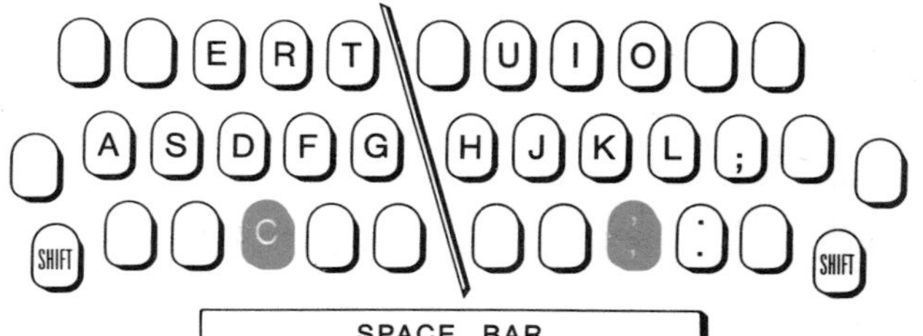

, KEY

K-finger
3 copies

3 kkk k,k ,,, kkk k,k ,,, kkk k,k ,,, k,k

4 k,k as, as, k,k is, is, k,k us, us, k,k

5 k,k to, to, k,k do, do, k,k so, so, k,k

C KEY

D-finger
3 copies

6 ddd dcd ccc ddd dcd ccc ddd dcd ccc dcd

7 dcd cad cad dcd cod cod dcd cud cud dcd

8 dcd ice ice dcd ace ace dcd act act dcd

WORD BUILDING

2 copies

9 o oc occ occu occur l la lac lack lack,

10 t tr tru truc truck s si sid side side;

11 f fi fig figh fight j ju jus just just.

1-MINUTE GOAL

2 tries

12 The chocolate cake looks good, Joe said

13 to Chris as she cut it. He likes food. [80 strokes]

PREPARE a·i·m WB 7–10

 **15**

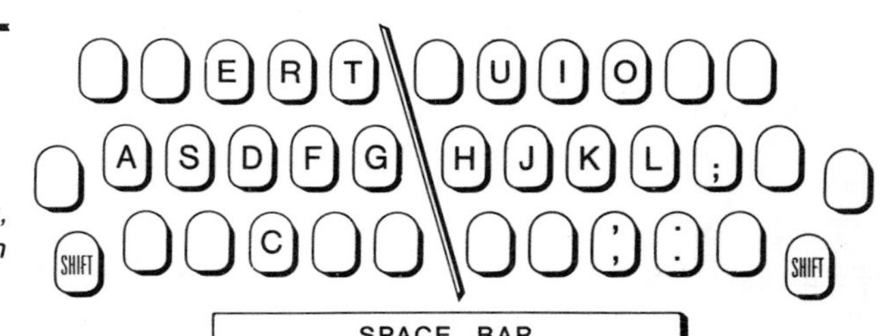

GOALS *To learn to count words and errors. To boost speed and accuracy, type 2 copies of the Improvement Practice. To type 32 words or more in 2 minutes within 4 errors.*

DIRECTIONS *Spacing 1. Line 40.*

WARMUP REVIEW

2 copies

1 a ; aa ;; ss ll dd kk ff jj gg hh ff jj

2 this this rock rock huge huge coat coat

TEST 12-E

RULED TABLE
Spacing 2
Workbook 281
Rearrange highest "next year" first

QUARTERLY BUDGET FOR ADVERTISING 19

July Through September, 19— 31

45

Media	Last Year	This Year	Next Year	
				56 / 68
Catalog	$ 7,000	$10,000	$12,500	108
Direct Mail	18,000	17,000	18,250	78
Magazines	2,000	3,500	2,500	138
Newspapers	14,000	15,000	16,500	99
Radio Spots	10,500	11,000	11,500	118
Television	18,500	7,500	5,300	128
Trade Journals	10,000	11,000	14,500	89
				152
Totals	$80,000	$75,000	$81,050	161

174

TEST 12-F

PROGRAM WITH LEADERS
Line 60
Workbook 283

```
                 C O M M E N C E M E N T

                   [Your] High School

PROCESSIONAL ..................... Dr. Ronald O'Toole, Marshal
                                 Principal of [Your] High School

NATIONAL ANTHEM ...................... The Star Spangled Banner

INVOCATION ................. The Reverend Graham N. Williams

INTRODUCTION OF SPEAKERS ......... Dr. Phillip S. Hutchinson
                                   Superintendent of Schools

    The Heritage ....... Holly Ann Biltomore, Salutatorian
    The Challenge ..........               Valedictorian
    The Opportunity .......... The Honorable Percy Mohler
                                  Member of The Congress

PRESENTATION OF DIPLOMAS ............ Dr. Martin J. Ebertson
                                          Board of Education

BENEDICTION ................. The Reverend Harold W. Jenkins

RECESSIONAL ................. John N. Vaughn, Marshal
                              President, Graduating Class

                       June 29, 19--
                  High School Auditorium
```

TEST 12-G

TELEGRAM
Workbook 284

Charge to Sender / *To* The Hon. Percy Mohler / Member of Congress / Washington, DC 20515 / *Telephone* 883-7573 / Proud you will participate in commencement. Can we provide transportation or make reservations for you? / Ronald O'Toole / Green Bay High School / *Sender's telephone* 266-8008 / *Sender's address* 3800 Racine Avenue / Green Bay, WI 54301.

WHAT ABOUT ERRORS?

- "To err is human" is just as true about typewriting as anything else people do.
- Errors tell you what to practice next. Don't worry about errors—instead, use them.
- Check errors only on Pretests and Post-tests.

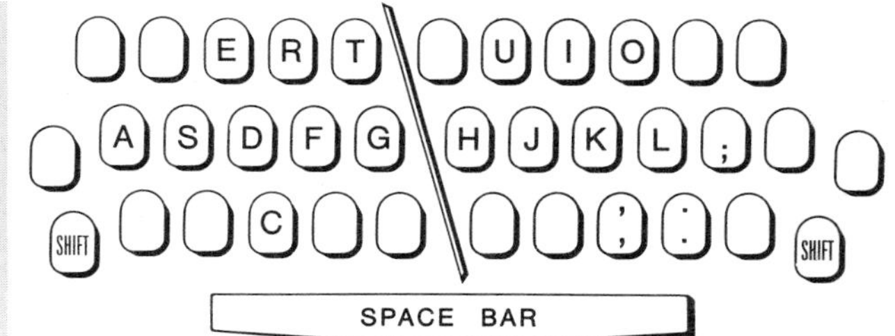

COUNTING ERRORS

```
Carl had a fakl; he hurt his right leg,            (1) (2)
Dr. Jack  told us togo o t to see Carl.            (3) (3) (4)
Carl had a fall; he hurt his rgohr leg.            (5) (6)
     Dr. Jack told to go out to to see Carl.       (7) (8) (9)
|1     |2     |3     |4     |5     |6     |7     |8
```

1. Draw a loop around any word in which there is an error.
2. Count a word as an error if the punctuation after it is typed incorrectly.
3. Count a word as an error if the spacing after it is incorrect.
4. Count a word as an error if it contains a letter so light you can't read it.
5. Count a word as an error if it contains an incomplete capital letter.
6. Count only 1 error against 1 word, no matter how many errors it may contain.
7. Count each failure to follow directions in spacing, indenting, and so forth.
8. Count each word that is omitted as an error.
9. Count each word that is repeated incorrectly as an error.

FIGURING SPEED

1. Find how many "average" words you type in the time allowed. Every 5 strokes count as 1 "average" word. A 40-stroke line is 8 words long; two such lines count as 16 words. For an incomplete line, use the scale: the number above (or below) which you stop is your word count for that incomplete line. **Example** If you type lines 3 and 4 below and start over, getting as far as "fall;" in line 3, you've typed $16 + 4 = 20$ words. "Fall;" counts as 4 because it has a character in the fourth word group—a fraction counts as a whole word.
2. Divide the word total by the number of minutes you typed. **Example** 37 words in 2 minutes would be $37 \div 2 = 18\frac{1}{2} = 19$ wam (words a minute). Count a fraction as a whole.

PRETEST

2 copies or type for 2 minutes, then figure score.

```
3   Carl had a fall; he hurt his right leg.      8
4   Dr. Jack told us to go out to see Carl.     16
    |1   |2   |3   |4   |5   |6   |7   |8
```

IMPROVEMENT PRACTICE

```
5   Cora core code coal coat cost colt Cora      8
6   Ella tell sell jell dell fell cell Ella     16
7   Ruth ruse rude rule role rose rise Ruth     24
8   Tess tell teal teak tear tare tore Tess     32
```

TEST 12-C

BLOCKED LETTER WITH SUBJECT
Punctuation standard
Tab center
Workbook 278

Date | Mr. Wayne L. Neale | Features Editor | The Secretary's Journal 20
| 1029 Muskogee Street | Tulsa, Oklahoma 74104 | Salutation | 34
SUBJECT: Another Manuscript! 41
I am delighted to learn that you are printing the article I sent 54
to you last week. I have inquired, as you asked, to see whether my 68
company would mind your using my professional title with the article; 82
it will be agreeable. My superiors are delighted to have the title 96
used this way. 100
I was so pleased to learn that you like my article that I had to 113
do another one right away, and here it is! It deals with the reference 127
values of the office files, something that new employees ought to 140
know but too often do not. I am sending with it a table that might 154
be used as an illustration. 161
Naturally, I hope that I shall hear that you want to print this 174
one, too; but if you don't, simply send it back to me in a week or 187
two. So far as I know, there has been nothing like it published. 201
Complimentary closing | Gwen Thiels, Director | Office Services | 219
Initials | Enclosure notation? | cc Mr. Kennedy 225

|1 |2 |3 |4 |5 |6 |7 |8 |9 |10 |11 |12 |13 |14 SI 1.41N

TEST 12-D

TWO-PAGE MAGAZINE ARTICLE
Line exactly 40
Style as on page 185–186
Tabs 5, center
Workbook 279

STUDY THE FILES! | By Gwen Thiels | Director of Office Services | 25
Hall-Odee, Inc. | (30 Lines of 40 Spaces) 56
DO YOU WISH to amaze your employer by the amount of work you 69
can produce right away in exactly the form he likes best? Then learn 83
how to "read" his office files. 90
Perhaps your employer gives you some letters to type first. 103
Instead of asking about their arrangement, lay them on your desk 116
and walk quickly to the file cabinet. Remove one of the thickest file 130
folders and examine its contents, noting the pattern of his letters. 144
Then, hustle back to your machine and type the letters in "his style" 158
without a question. 162
Next, he gives you a quarterly sales report and asks you to type 176
it. You ask no questions. Again you refer to the file cabinet, you find 191
the last similar report, you put it in your typewriter, you copy its 205
margin stops and tab stops, (PAGE 2 BEGINS NEAR HERE) and you clip 227
off the report not only in record time but also in correct style. 243
SEE WHAT I MEAN? The file cabinet has copies, properly arranged, 256
of almost all the work you might be asked to type. It is a fine office 270
tutor. The typist who will get ahead on the job is the one who asks 284
his questions of that tutor instead of bothering the employer with 297
questions whose answers are in the file cabinet. (END) SI 1.41N 313

AS YOU STRIKE EACH KEY—

- Make it print as dark as the other keys.
- Snatch your finger off the key as though it were red hot—don't let the finger get burned.
- Move instantly to the next letter; don't rest.
- Make the typebar BOUNCE off the paper.

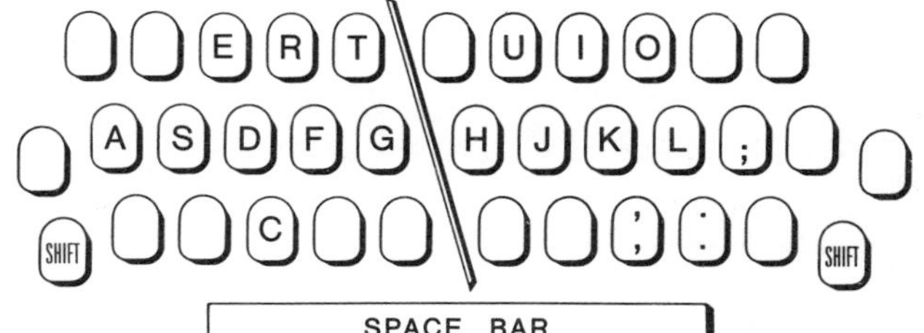

|1 |2 |3 |4 |5 |6 |7 |8

IMPROVEMENT PRACTICE continued

9 Ulla uses used user fuse fuss cuss Ulla 8

10 Ilka silk silt gilt hilt lilt list Ilka 16

11 Olga ours hour dour tour four sour Olga 24

12 Lola cola cold gold fold told sold Lola 32

Phrases:

POST-TEST

Type Pretest twice in 2 minutes. 2 tries

13 to do, to do so; to go, to go to; to us 8

14 it is, it is so; if he, if he is; he is 16

15 go to us; to go to her; is to go to her 24

|1 |2 |3 |4 |5 |6 |7 |8

 **16**

GOALS *To control the M and Colon keys. To type 32 words or more in 2 minutes within 4 errors on 20 keys.*

DIRECTIONS *Spacing 1. Line 40. Tape K 10.*

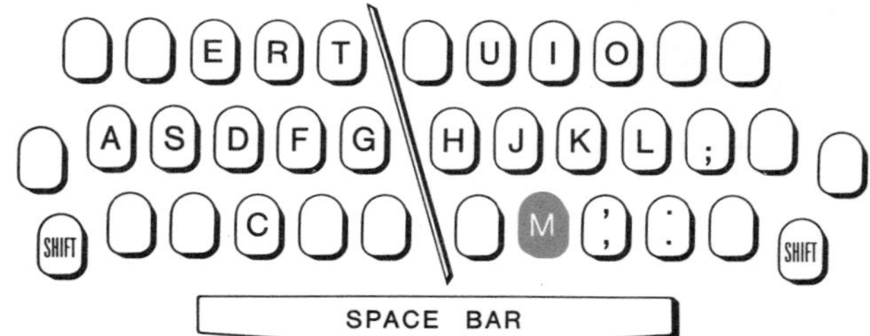

WARMUP REVIEW

2 copies

1 ; a ;; aa ll ss kk dd jj ff hh gg jj ff 8

2 high high true true dock dock grid grid 16

|1 |2 |3 |4 |5 |6 |7 |8

M KEY

J-finger
3 copies

3 jjj jmj mmm jjj jmj mmm jjj jmj mmm jmj 8

4 jmj jam jam jmj ham ham jmj him him jmj 16

5 jmj mar mar jmj mat mat jmj mad mad jmj 24

a·i·m 267–270

Project 5 is a comprehensive inventory. Each assignment is to be typed on the official Workbook page (or other paper your instructor may provide) for that assignment. The test will require four or more a·i·m sessions and encompasses everything that an employment test might include. Your instructor may permit you to omit parts of this inventory. The general schedule is given in the box at the right.

a·i·m	Test	Content	Text	Work
267	12-A	Objective Test	. . .	275–276
268	12-B	5′ Timed Writing	263	277
	12-C	Blocked Letter	264	278
269	12-D	Magazine Article	264	279
	12-E	Ruled Table	265	281
270	12-F	Leadered Program	265	283
	12-G	Telegram	165	284

TEST 12-A

Take a general information test. It may be the one on Workbook pages 275–276 or a similar test that your teacher may give you or may dictate to you.

TEST 12-B

5-MINUTE TW
Line 70
Spacing 2
Tab 5
Workbook 277

Of all the magic moments when calm is everywhere and man can 13
let his soul stretch and relax, any sailor will tell you that the best is 28
the moment just before dawn when you are a hundred miles at sea. 41
For an instant earth seems motionless. You're surrounded by the 54
darkness and silence of night's black veil all around, except for a hand- 68
ful of stars peacefully gazing down at you without winking. Then the 82
breeze begins to stir, flapping the signal halyards and making the ship 97
heel over slightly. You experience an eerie feeling of quiet expectation. 112
Then the sun springs over the horizon. It doesn't appear little 126
by little; it arrives in a flash of magnificent splendor; it explodes in 140
brilliance. One moment you are standing in darkness, and the next 154
instant you stand in full daylight, just as though someone had pushed 168
a button. The light was out, and then it appeared. But the light is 182
very soft, an artistic blending of yellow with white and pastel pink. 196
It's a pleasant scene to remember when the day's activities grow 210
frantic, when pressure increases and frustration jangles your temper, 224
when the demands of life press too insistently. Let go and relax for 238
a moment as you turn your mind to the calmness of the sea, the velvet 252
breeze on your arm, the gentle lapping of water. Sense the quietness 266
of the night. Listen for the foam of the water as it curls back from the 281
bow; listen for the soft hum of the signal lines. Then, remember (and 295
smile at yourself for the fears and tensions) that morning comes only 309
after the very darkest part of night; and the drearier the night around 324
you, the earlier will day's dawning arrive to give you relief. 336

|1 |2 |3 |4 |5 |6 |7 |8 |9 |10 |11 |12 |13 |14 SI 1.41N

SPACING AFTER PUNCTUATION MARKS

Space TWO times—

- After a colon, as in line 12 below.
- After the end of a sentence.

Space ONE time—

- After a comma, a semicolon, and a period that follows an abbreviation.

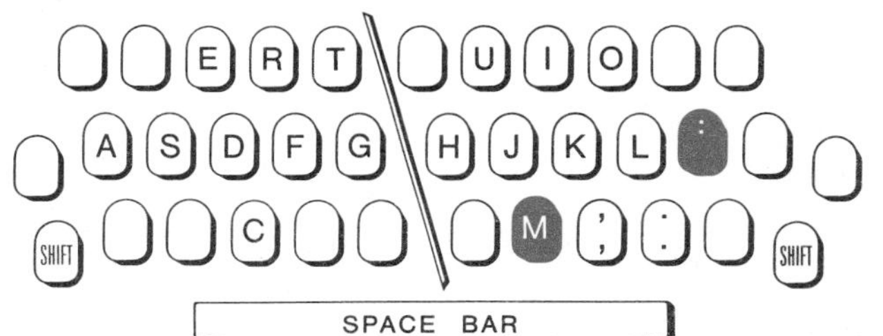

: KEY

Sem-finger
Capital of ;
3 copies

Space twice after a colon.

6 ; ; ; ; : ; : : : ; ; ; ; : ; : : : ; ; ; ; : ; : : : ; : ; 8

7 Dear Al: Dear Jo: Dear Lu: Dear Sir: 16

8 Mr. Em: Dr. Doe: Miss Ree: Mrs. Mor: 24

WORD BUILDING

2 copies

9 D De Dea Dear Dear: c ch chu chum chum; 8

10 e ei eig eigh eight m mo mol mola molar 16

11 M Ma Maj Majo Major F Fr Fra Frak Frake 24

2-MINUTE GOAL

2 copies in 2 minutes. 2 tries

12 Dear Jack: Let us make sure that there 8

13 is some ice cream for Gus to sell them. 16

|1 |2 |3 |4 |5 |6 |7 |8

a·i·m 17

GOALS To control W and Y keys. To type 32 words or more in 2 minutes within 4 errors on 22 keys.

DIRECTIONS *Spacing 1. Line 40. Tape K 11.*

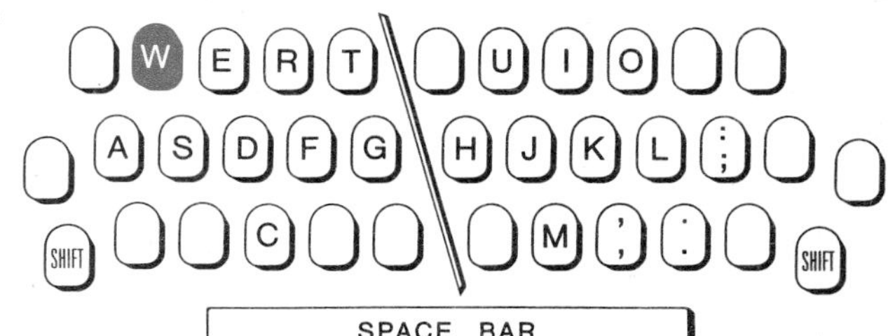

WARMUP REVIEW

2 copies

1 a ; s l d k f j g h a ; s l d k f j g h 8

2 drag lock sham jets fame item film cute 16

|1 |2 |3 |4 |5 |6 |7 |8

W KEY

S-finger
3 copies

3 sss sws www sss sws www sss sws www sws 8

4 sws sow sow sws sew sew sws saw saw sws 16

5 sws low low sws mow mow sws wow wow sws 24

JOB 266·1

REPORT
PAGE 4

Run horizontal rules to page width; pivot from right to find starting point of second column.

In each case, leave just 2 blank lines in each signature space.

Leave 3 blank lines between a table or a display and following text of the report.

REPRESENTATIVE FORMS OF SIGNATURE ARRANGEMENTS 36

		48
Cordially yours,	Yours very sincerely,	59
		61
General Manager	Personnel Department	71
		84
Yours very sincerely,	Respectfully submitted,	95
		97
Head, Credit Bureau	Tom Everett, Secretary	106
		119
Very truly yours,	Yours sincerely,	128
		129
THE TURNER CORPORATION	WILSON CONSTRUCTION COMPANY	141
		143
Elaine J. Perkins	Richard F. Hughes	154
President	Vice President, Sales	163
		177
Yours truly,	Very cordially yours,	188
INTERNATIONAL ARBOR COMPANY	S T Y L E , I N C .	211
		213
Mrs. Ellen Park	Miss Reuters Huntington	229
Chairman of the Board	Advertising Department	247
		261

↓4

264

arrangement of women's signatures, the use or absence of a 274
company name, and the display of the title of the signer. 284

When differences in spacing and indenting are added to 294
the other variants, the possibilities seem without limit. 303

The display above, reproduced from a textbook,[9] shows 317
how much signatures can be like, yet unlike, each other. 327

331

9. Rowe, op. cit., page 262. 338

Formal Manuscript with a Special Display

CHECK YOUR HANDS

- Palms are low but do not touch the machine.
- Hands are flat, level, across their backs.
- Right thumb $\frac{1}{4}$ inch above the space-bar CENTER.
- Hands so close you could lock the thumbs.
- All fingers are curled; you type on the tips.

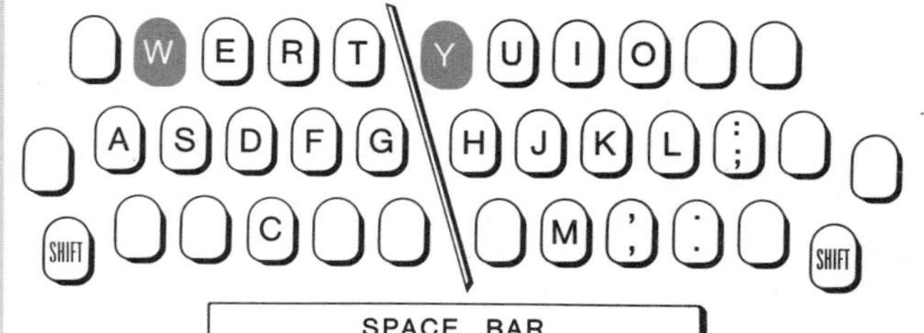

Y KEY

J-finger
3 copies

6 jjj jyj yyy jjj jyj yyy jjj jyj yyy jyj 8
7 jyj sly sly jyj shy shy jyj sky sky jyj 16
8 jyj yes yes jyj yet yet jyj you you jyj ⚲ 24

WORD BUILDING

2 copies

9 www hhh yyy why why sss kkk yyy sky sky 8
10 www eee ,,, we, we, www hhh ooo who who 16
11 www aaa yyy way way mmm aaa yyy may may 24

2-MINUTE GOAL

1 copy in 2 minutes. 2 tries

12 Dear Wes: I hear that your team is all 8
13 ready for the game with West City. Jim 16
14 Dear Jim: You are right; we are set to 24
15 fly to West City sometime Tuesday. Wes ⚲ 32

|1 |2 |3 |4 |5 |6 |7 |8

18

GOALS ⚲ *To boost speed and accuracy, type 2 copies of the Improvement Practice.* ⚲ *To type 34 words or more in 2 minutes within 4 errors.*

DIRECTIONS *Spacing 1. Line 40.*

ABOUT ACCURACY

- Strive for it; no one ever typed accurately by accident.
- First fundamental: good posture.
- Second fundamental: typing very evenly.

WARMUP REVIEW

2 copies

1 a ; s l d k f j g h f j d k s l a ; s l 8
2 you tie jet cow has wad yes elk arm fog 16

|1 |2 |3 |4 |5 |6 |7 |8

JOB 264·1

REPORT PAGE 2

5] If she is a Miss, she does not have to take any special pains because, 22
as Gavin and Sabin state, "it is assumed that a woman is Miss unless Mrs. 37
is clearly indicated."3 (footnote: Ibid., p. 207.) One exception: if 51
the first name could be either man or woman, the writer should indicate 65
which personal title is appropriate: 73

Miss Kenny Hall 77
Miss Don Carr 81
Mr. Roe Lynn 84

If she is a Mrs., she is expected to say so. She might give indication 106
in the letterhead of the firm, if her name is printed on it, or in the sig- 121
nature lines of the letter. The indication of Miss, Mrs., or Mr., if in- 141
cluded, may be made by typing the title before the typed name or penning 155
the title in parentheses before the written signature, like these: 169

Mary Smith	(Mrs.) Mary Smith	(Miss) Dana Hall	186
Mrs. Mary Smith	Mary Smith	Dana Hall	198

2. COMPANY SIGNATURES 203

One textbook says that the Company name, if used, should be typed "in all 217
caps a double space below the [complimentary] closing,"4 (footnote: John L. Rowe 234
et al., Typing 300, Volume 1, "General Course," McGraw-Hill Book Company, New 254
York, 1972, p. 137) and Gavin and Sabin agree with that arrangement.5 (footnote: 271
Gavin and Sabin, op. cit., p. 206). 279

In some companies, the typists are permitted to use the company name when- 294
ever the letter needs to be lengthened (if the tone of the letter does not make 310
the use of the firm name unsuitable),6 (footnote: Interview with Miss Jean Court, 328
United Weston Company.) but in general the company name is "if the employer wants 345
it or if the letter is a contract."7 (footnote: Rowe, Loc. cit.) Also: 360

JOB 265·1

REPORT PAGE 3

A company signature may be used to empha size 372
the fact that a letter represents the views of the 384
company as a whole (and not merely the individual 396
who has written it) 8 (footnote: Gavin and Sabin, loc. cit.) 411

3. THE SIGNER'S TITLE 420

The choice of using one's name, or title, or department, or combination of 436
these is the writer's choice. The sequence is not a choice, however: name, 451
t itle, departmnnt is the one correct sequence for the elements typed. When 470
there is more than 1 line to the identification of the signer, effort is 485
made to have them about equal: 491

John E. Horton, Head of the 497
Accounting Department 504

Richard A. Featheringham 510
Head, of the Credit Bureau 517

D. Summary. The preceding remarks show indicate that there really is wide 538
variation possible in the closing lines, thanks to differences in all the 552

SHORT TIMED WRITINGS

- They are good for increasing speed.
- Use easy sentences (as in lines 6–13 below).
- On $\frac{1}{2}$-minute writings, speed is the number of words × 2.
- On 12-second writings, each stroke is 1 word a minute—43 strokes would be 43 words a minute.

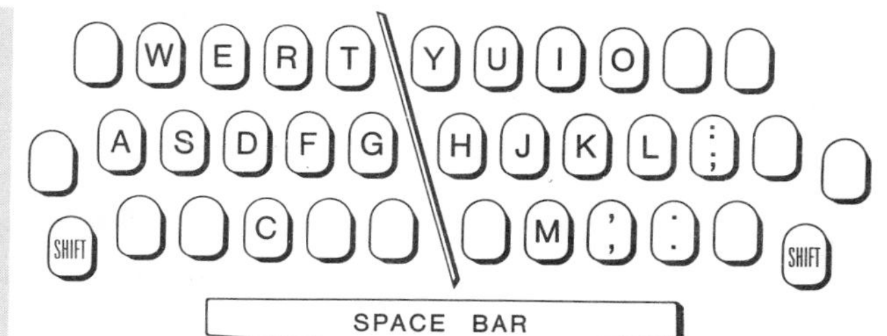

PRETEST

2 copies or type for 2 minutes, then figure score

3 I would like to ask you what Major Crag 8
4 would say if I asked Jack for some more 16
5 work. 17

|1 |2 |3 |4 |5 |6 |7 |8

IMPROVEMENT PRACTICE

2 copies of each line

6 Grace had to miss school all this week. 8
7 The two aides had to lock the old door. 16
8 Two or three girls told me to meet you. 24
9 We will go to the old store if we must. 32
10 She will try to get the day off for us. 8
11 We must go if we wish to get to school. 16
12 I wish I had a tree we could take away. 24
13 He had to go to the office for the day. 32

|1 |2 |3 |4 |5 |6 |7 |8

POST-TEST

Type Pretest twice in 2 minutes. 2 tries

a·i·m 19

GOALS *To control V and N keys. To type 34 words or more in 2 minutes within 4 errors on 24 keys.*

DIRECTIONS *Spacing 1. Line 40. WB 11–12. Tape K 12.*

YOU'RE EFFICIENT IF—

- You can insert paper, straighten it, bail it in 7 seconds.
- You can remove paper, insert a new sheet, etc., in 9 seconds.
- You can reset margins in 5 seconds.

WARMUP REVIEW

2 copies

1 a;sldkfjgh a;sldkfjgh a;sldkfjgh a;sldk 8
2 silk mail gulf jury come hold with much 16

|1 |2 |3 |4 |5 |6 |7 |8

PREPARE a·i·m WB 273–274

project 4

a·i·m 263–266

GOALS *To review the technicalities of a formal manuscript. To execute a four-page formal manuscript. To review technical niceties in letter writing: women's signatures, company names, display closings, etc.*

Your employer is a college student, Otis Fitzgerald, who is paying you to type a report that he has drafted for his Business Communications course.

The paper is to go in a binder [wide left margin!] and be given full formal treatment—better review pages 141–146 and 167–169 to brush up on footnotes, margins, spacing, and the like. Use a visual guide if you wish. Make one carbon copy.

Mr. Fitzgerald has pieced and taped his draft together; if you note discrepancies, correct them.

JOB 263·1

REPORT
PAGE 1

*

LET TER SIGNATURES 10

(A report for Business Comm. 211) 37

By Otis Fitzgerald ↓3 52

A. Purpose — center → 64

5 It has been stated[1] (footnote: Blanche T. Minotty, "Dress-Up Close," 79
Today's Secretary, July, 1971, pp. 84-88) that the signature arrangement of a 101
business letter lends it self to variety more than any other section of the let- 117
ter does. What are some of the arrangements that are most commonly used? The 131
purpose of this report is to look into and report the answer. 150

B. Sources — to that intriguing question. 160

The research behind this report included interviewing two office workers, 176
scanning several issues of Today's Secretary magazine, studying ② typewriting 198
texts, and looking in a reference manual for answers to specific questions on 214
the topic. The reference manual[2] (footnote: Ruth E. Gavin and William A. Sabin, 228
Reference Manual for Stenographers and Typists, 4th ed., McGraw-Hill Book Com- 261
pany, New York, 1970, pp. 206-209) proved to be extremely helpful. 275

C. Findings 285

5 The findings are grouped in ③ areas: the treatment of women's signatures, 302
the treatment of company names, and the treatment of the business title of the signer. 320

1. WOMEN'S SIGNATURES 324

When writing a business letter to a lady, any writer's first question is 340
"Should I address her as Miss or Mrs.?" 347

*Word count is for the material as arranged here, with footnotes run in.

fff fvfvvv fff fvf vvvfff

IF your work has omitted spaces, as above, then—

- Check that your palms do not touch the machine.
- Think "space" for each space-bar stroke.
- Type calmly, evenly—not hastily or hurriedly.
- Check that thumb stays $\frac{1}{4}$ inch above space bar.

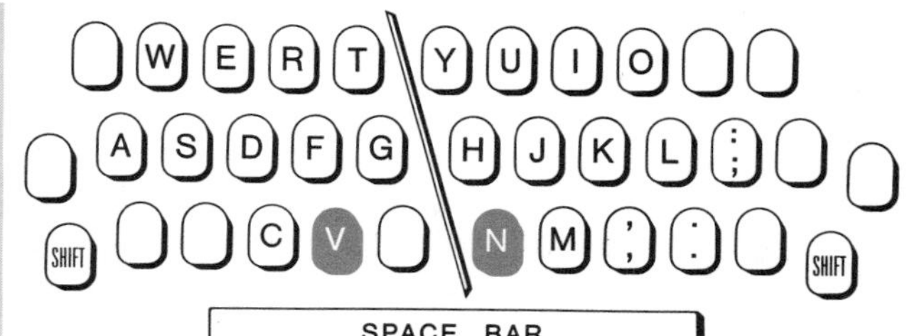

V KEY
F-finger
3 copies

3 fff fvf vvv fff fvf vvv fff fvf vvv fvf 8
4 fvf vie vie fvf vim vim fvf via via fvf 16
5 fvf vet vet fvf vat vat fvf eve eve fvf 24

N KEY
J-finger
3 copies

6 jjj jnj nnn jjj jnj nnn jjj jnj nnn jnj 8
7 jnj nun nun jnj run run jnj sun sun jnj 16
8 jnj not not jnj now now jnj nor nor jnj 24

WORD CHAINS
2 copies

9 not not nor nor now snow snow know know 8
10 vim vim vie vie vin vine vine vane vane 16
11 ivy ivy ive ive ave have have save save 24

2-MINUTE GOAL
2 copies in 2 minutes. 2 tries

12 Dear Jay: It is very good news to your 8
13 friends to know that you will soon come 16
14 home. 17

|1 |2 |3 |4 |5 |6 |7 |8

 20

GOALS To control X and P keys. To type 34 words or more in 2 minutes within 4 errors on 26 keys.

DIRECTIONS *Spacing 1. Line 40. Tape K 13.*

WATCH YOUR ELBOWS

- Don't let them swing out when you reach for the X and P.
- Keep shoulders level to make it easier to relax elbows.
- Do stroking with FINGERS only.

WARMUP REVIEW
2 copies

1 a;sldkfjgh ghfjdksla; a;sldkfjgh ghfjdk 8
2 dry vim cut fog jaw let ask ham way any 16

|1 |2 |3 |4 |5 |6 |7 |8

```
mmmm  mmm  mmm  mmm  mmmm  m m      mmmm  mmm  mmm  mmm  mmmm  mmmm
m  m  m m   m   m m  m  m  m m      m  m  m    m    m m  m  m  m  m
mmmm  m m   m   mmm  mmmm  mmm      mmmm  mm   m    m m  mmmm  m  m
m m   m m   m   m m  m m    m       m m   m    m    m m  m m   m  m
m  m  mmm   m   m m  m  m   m       m  m  mmm  mmm  mmm  m  m  mmmm
```

Volume 21, No. 12 Islip, Long Island May 10, 19--

SPEAKER FOR NEXT WEDNESDAY

A famous croporation lawyer will be our speaker at the luncheon meeting next wednesday. He is Carson Garett, brother-in-law to Steve Casino, with whom he will be visiting at a family get-together at Steve's home. He is the lawyer who brought about that big Anderson-Lee Merger a year ago. Mr. Garret is going to tell us what House Bill 317 will mean to owners of business grossing under $600,000 a year, if it passes. ~~Reservation in?~~

RECYCLING DRIVE IS FALTERING

Nobody wants to bother. That's the opinion of Ellwood Featherstone, chairman of our paper-recycling project. "With all the newspaper publicity and even one TV bit to help, we got off to a great start," says Roy. "But as soon as the fanfair stopped, so did the paper." He is calling a committee meeting (attention Joe, Bob, and Harrison) for Thrusday night at his house, 8 p.m.

MILD DRIVE IS DOING VERY WELL

A nickle here and anickle there adds up to success in the milk drive, according to the counter-top collection committee. Last week the committee collected a bonanza of more than $30 (well, $30.72, to be exact) in coins at checkout and cash-register counters. Tim O'Leary also reports that Ken Ewell has joined the committee, filling the vacancy created ~~with~~ Tom ~~Klein~~ moved to Kansas City last month.

NEW PROGRAM COMMITTEE

Alex Swantz has appointed a new committee to ~~build~~ the program ~~of~~ speakers and events for the luncheons. The new committee, effective June 1, will be Lincoln Garr, chairman; and Ted Young, Jim Cordite, and Sam Kling. Alex also asks for a round of applause for Cather Poe and his committee for the programs of the past nine weeks. Lincoln wants a meeting of his committee right ~~after~~ the luncheon next week.

OFFICE VISITS ~~WEEK~~ COMING

Our future employees will be visiting us in the near future: Thursday, May 18, to be exact. This is the annual visit to our offices by ~~the local~~ high school seniors who are office trainees and to our stores by those who are merchandising trainees. Each student visits one place in the morning, a different one in the afternoon. Schedules will be mailed to you sometime next week.

Manuscript Page for a "Newsletter"

a as ak asks aks

If your work has omitted letters, as above, then—

- Check that you are not typing too rapidly.
- Strike the keys hard enough for them to print.
- Keep your eyes on the copy!
- Say each letter to yourself for even rhythm.

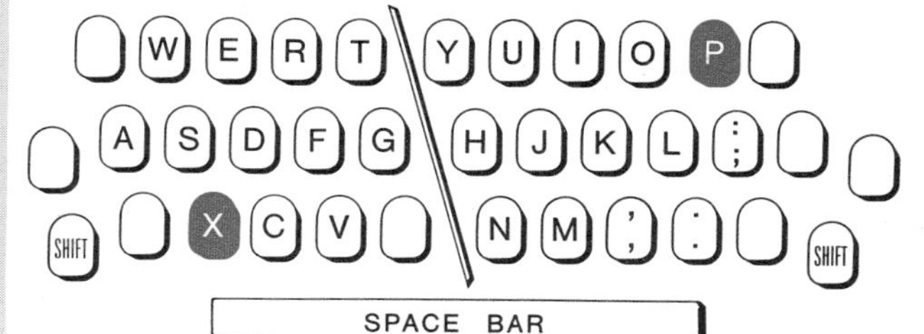

X KEY

S-finger
3 copies

3 sss sxs xxx sss sxs xxx sss sxs xxx sxs 8
4 sxs six six sxs nix nix sxs fix fix sxs 16
5 sxs wax wax sxs tax tax sxs lax lax sxs 24

P KEY

Sem-finger
3 copies

6 ;;; ;p; ppp ;;; ;p; ppp ;;; ;p; ppp ;p; 8
7 ;p; lap lap ;p; nap nap ;p; map map ;p; 16
8 ;p; pin pin ;p; pen pen ;p; pan pan ;p; 24

WORD CHAINS

2 copies

9 put put pat pat pad paid paid pair pair 8
10 lox lox lax lax tax taxi taxi text text 16
11 pen pen pan pan pin spin spin span span 24

2-MINUTE GOAL

1 copy in 2 minutes. 2 tries

When single-spacing is used as here, leave a blank line after the salutation and between paragraphs—simply return the carriage one extra time. In scoring timed writings, the extra blank line counts as 1 word. This allowance is included in the word count.

12 Dear Tex: 2
3
13 The next time we fly to Texas I hope we 11
14 can visit the Astrodome. I would enjoy 19
15 a chance to see it. 23
24
16 Perhaps we could ask George to go to it 32
17 with us. 34

|1 |2 |3 |4 |5 |6 |7 |8

project 3

a·i·m 259–262

GOALS *To review the quick production of mailing labels and dues bills. To learn how to create display lettering. To produce a newsletter-style bulletin.*

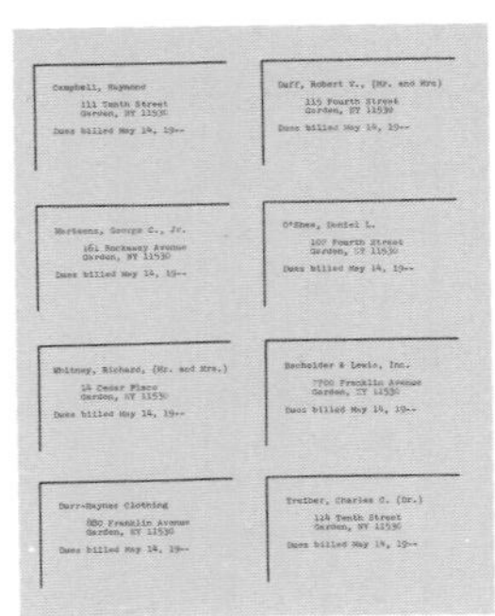

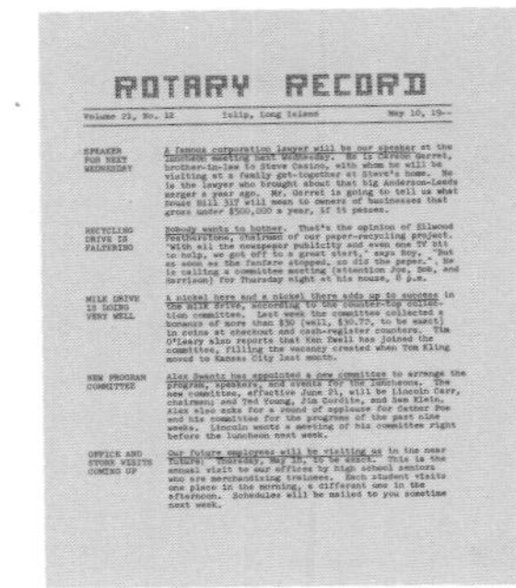

ROTARY RECORD

Your employer is Patricia Dugan, manager of Eagle Printers and Mailers, Inc., of 1800 Nassau Boulevard, Mineola, NY 11528. The firm specializes in work with organizations like PTAs, property associations, Kiwanis and Rotary Clubs, and the like.

JOB 259·1

DUES INVOICES — Workbook 267–270 Spacing 2; Tab for fill-in amount

"We have a contract with the Property Association of the community of Garden to send a membership bill like this—

PROPERTY ASSOCIATION, INC.

BOX 15 GARDEN, N. Y. 11530

Mr. Fred C. Doyle, Jr.
7 Carteret Place
Garden, NY 11530

PLEASE RETURN THIS STUB WITH YOUR CHECK

Membership Dues for the Property
Association, Inc., for One year
Beginning June 1 . . . . 5.00

—to each newcomer to that community. We type the address in the boxed space (which lets us use a window envelope) and the amount due at the right. The dues are $5.00 for individuals, $10 for firms. Here are the names and addresses, all of them having the same post office, of course, Garden, NY 11530. Please prepare the bills for these eight addressees—"

Mr. Raymond Campbell, 111 Tenth Street
Mr. and Mrs. Robert V. Duff, 115 Fourth Street
George C. Marteens, Jr., 161 Rockaway Avenue
Daniel L. O'Shea, 102 Fourth Street
Mr. and Mrs. Richard Whitney, 14 Cedar Place
Bachelder & Lewis, Inc., 2700 Franklin Avenue
Durr-Haynes Clothing, 880 Franklin Avenue
Dr. Charles C. Treiber, 114 Tenth Street

JOB 260·1

INDEX CARDS — Use 5 x 3 cards or slips of paper; Reference page 202

"—and, for each addressee, an index card like this one, with today's date of billing added on."

Doyle, Fred C., Jr.

7 Carteret Place
Garden, NY 11530

Dues billed May 14, 19--

JOB 261·1

MAIL LABEL — Workbook 271 or page divided into eighths; Reference page 203

"Please prepare, also, mailing labels for us to use when we ship each of the eight addressees a copy of the Garden 'community calendar book.' "

JOB 262·1

NEWSLETTER — Paper plain Line 70 Tab 16; Reference page 222

"One of our contracts," says Miss Dugan, "is for editing, duplicating, and mailing a weekly newsletter for the Rotarians in Islip. Here [page 259] is the draft that we received from the secretary of the group, with my corrections and changes. Please retype it, ready for duplicating. To make the display lettering, copy the lettering on the worksheet: type what shows as lines 1, 3, and 5, then adjust the variable spacing and insert the strokes of the other two rows.

```
mmm mmm mmm
     m m  m m
mmm mmm mmm
           m m
m m  m m  m m
```

21

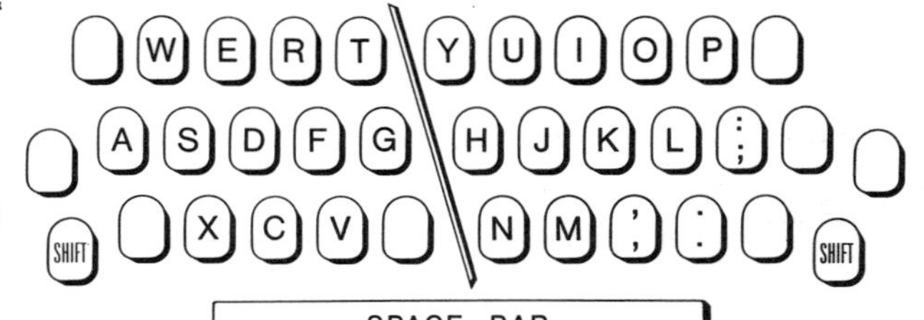

GOALS To boost speed and accuracy, type 2 copies of lines 3–10. To type 36 words or more in 2 minutes within 4 errors.

DIRECTIONS *Spacing 1. Line 40.*

WARMUP REVIEW

2 copies

1 a;sldkfjghfjdksla; : a;sldkfjghfjdksla; 8

2 six vat mop can jug sly her kid few pad 16

|1 |2 |3 |4 |5 |6 |7 |8

UP REACH PRACTICE

2 copies

3 Your paper will arrive within the hour. 8

4 frf from frf free frf fret frf frey frf 16

5 juj just juj jugs juj judo juj junk juj 24

6 ded deal ded dent ded deep ded desk ded 32

7 kik kick kik king kik kite kik kilt kik 40

8 sws swim sws swam sws swan sws swap sws 48

9 lol load lol lock lol lots lol loaf lol 56

10 Your paper will arrive within the hour. 64

1·1·2·2 TW 2-MINUTE GOAL

1 copy in 2 minutes. 2 tries

A 2-minute goal is often easier to reach if you practice the first minute's worth, then the second minute's worth, then put the two together: the "1·1·2·2" plan. When you see such figures as a heading, they mean—

"1" Type for 1 minute, then rest.
"1" Starting where the first minute left off, type for an additional minute.
"2" Type for 2 minutes without stopping.
"2" Try the 2 minutes a second time.

11 Dear Jack: 2

3

12 I think that two dollars is rather high 11
13 for a ticket to a class play. 17

18

14 Dear Max: 20

21

15 Two dollars is not so much when half of 29
16 it is given over to the Red Cross. 36

|1 |2 |3 |4 |5 |6 |7 |8

JOB 256·2

(Continued)

3. Our Milwaukee branch, aiming for $126 thousand, edged up to 70
$130 thousand, for 103 percent of budget. 74
4. In Oklahoma City, the budget was for $205 thousand, but 79
actuals were $194 thousand, just 95 percent of what we expected. 84
5. In Seattle, our branch was budgeted for $150 thousand but 88
dropped off to $127 thousand in actual sales, just 85 percent of goal. 93
But that branch was closed for two weeks because of the fire in 127
August—make a footnote explanation about that, please. 129
The totals should be $831 thousand budgeted, but only $803 106
thousand actually sold, for an overall performance of 97 percent. ⊙ 118

JOB 257·1

OPEN TABLE
Date it for next week.

*
Here is the schedule for *Noon-Hour Duty* for the *Week of January 27,* 24
in three columns, headed (1) *Day* (2) *Telephones* (3) *Reception.* 42
On Monday, Carmen Seveille covers phones and Roberta Miller 51
takes the reception desk. On Tuesday, Anne Parker covers the tele- 56
phones and Joan Hamilton takes the reception desk. On Wednesday, 61
Susan Fields covers the telephones and Dorothy Asperri takes the 68
reception desk. On Thursday, Alice Fisher covers the telephones and 73
Evelyn Farmer covers the reception desk. On Friday, Patricia Evans 82
covers the telephones and Ruth Montgomery covers the reception 86
desk. As standby, Jean Ingot covers the phones; Margaret Thompson 98
is to be standby on the reception desk. ⊙ 99

JOB 258·1

RULED TABLE

*
Mr. Oberndenfer says: "I have prepared for Mr. Richmond, our 6
vice president, a table on *the largest arenas in America,* including 23
capacity in thousands. Three columns: *Arena* and *Location* and 39
Capacity. Ready?" 45
The Municipal Stadium, in Philadelphia, holds 105 thousand. 55
The Coliseum, in Los Angeles, holds 101 thousand. The Rose Bowl, in 64
Pasadena, holds 100 thousand. Michigan Stadium, in Ann Arbor, 75
holds 100 thousand. 77
Stanford Stadium, in Stanford, holds 90 thousand. Soldier Field, 89
in Chicago, holds 85,000. The Memorial Stadium, in Berkeley, holds 100
82 thousand. The Indianapolis Speedway holds 82 thousand, too. 111
Tulane Stadium, in New Orleans, holds 81 thousand. The Uni- 120
versity Stadium, in Columbus, holds 80 thousand. The Orange Bowl, 130
in Miami, and Spartan Stadium, in East Lansing, both hold 76 143
thousand. ⊙ 145

JOB 258·2

OPEN TABLE

Mr. Oberndenfer looks at your *Arenas* table and says: "You know, I think this might look better in open style. With the 12 arenas grouped in threes. Please retype this for me." ⊙

***Word count** is for arranged table, not for copy as shown.

 22

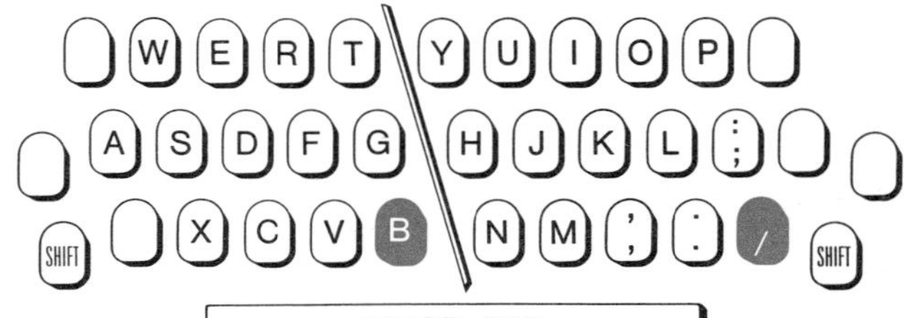

GOALS *To control the B and Diagonal keys. To type 36 words or more in 2 minutes within 4 errors on 28 keys.*

DIRECTIONS *Spacing 1. Line 40. Tape K 14.*

WARMUP REVIEW

2 copies

1 ;p; aaa lol sws kik ded juj frf jyj ftf 8
2 jhj fgf jnj fvf jmj dcd k,k sxs l.l ;:; 16
|1 |2 |3 |4 |5 |6 |7 |8

B KEY

F-finger
3 copies

3 fff fbf bbb fff fbf bbb fff fbf bbb fbf 8
4 fbf fob fob fbf job job fbf rob rob fbf 16
5 fbf bud bud fbf but but fbf bug bug fbf 24

/ (DIAGONAL) KEY

Sem-finger
3 copies

6 ;;; ;/; /// ;;; ;/; /// ;;; ;/; /// ;/; 8
7 ;/; his/her ;/; him/her ;/; we/they ;/; 16
8 Two kinds of current: the a/c and d/c. 24
9 There is no charge. Mark the bill n/c. 32

WORD CHAINS

2 copies

10 Ben Ben Bob Bob bow bowl bowl bows bows 8
11 Ben/Bea will bring his/her report soon. 16
12 rob rob rub rub rib crib crib ribs ribs 24

1·1·2·2 TW 2-MINUTE GOAL

1 copy in 2 minutes. 2 tries

13 Dear Bob: 2
3
14 I think we can count on Alex and/or Jake 11
15 to take us over to the game. 17
18
16 Dear Vic: 20
21
17 I think you are wrong. Both of the guys 29
18 have told me that they are tied up. 36
|1 |2 |3 |4 |5 |6 |7 |8

Arrange a sequence in some definite pattern. Here, items are in alphabetic sequence.

Display the column headings by underscoring them and centering them over their columns.

Align words at the left.

Place an asterisk (it does not count in column width) in front of an item in a column of words, but after an item in a column of numbers.

ANNOUNCEMENT OF CHANGE OF PRICES

Effective July 1, 19--

Item	Warehouse Number	Old Price	New Price
Chair	EC18	$34.40	$37.80
Chair	GC37	22.50	24.75
Chair	SC11	28.80	31.68
*Desk	ED12	75.50	83.05
Desk	SD93	42.75	47.02
Files	FF19	35.25	38.77
Files	FF23	38.50	42.35

* To be discontinued September 1

Put 6 spaces between columns unless there is some special reason for more or fewer.

Count a $ sign in width of column, but ignore OR count it (whichever seems more convenient) when centering the heading and column. Here $ is ignored.

Align numbers at the right. Align decimals.

Separate a footnote by a 1-inch line. Center OR block a 1-line footnote.

JOB 255-1: "Open Style" Table, Illustrating Many Arrangement Guides

Arrange a sequence in a definite pattern. Here, items are by percentages.

A miscellaneous item is always put last.

Repeat % sign after each percent number; the % sign is not typed just once, then discontinued (as a $ sign is). It is wise to use the % sign, even though the column heading says "percent," if other columns have numbers that are not percent figures.

Block any summary word like "Totals" or "Averages."

Table 12

WHERE OUR EMPLOYEES WENT FOR VACATIONS
AND WHAT THEY SPENT EACH DAY AWAY

(Summer, 19--)

Place	Percent Employees	Daily Expense
Metropolitan city	38%	$14.00
Seaside resort	32%	19.00
Mountain resort	23%	11.50
Motor trip	20%	13.75
Lake resort	9%	12.50
Miscellaneous	18%*	11.75
AVERAGES	23%	$13.80

* That is, 18 percent of employees collectively had other kinds of vacations.

Tables in a series are numbered and displayed as shown here.

Display the column heads by centering each above its column. Align all headings at bottom.

Align the $ sign at top of column with $ sign at the bottom of column.

To get 1 blank line above and below a ruled line, single-space before typing the line and double-space after typing it.

Arrange as shown here any footnote with more than one line.

JOB 256-1: "Ruled Style" Table, Illustrating More Arrangement Guides

 23

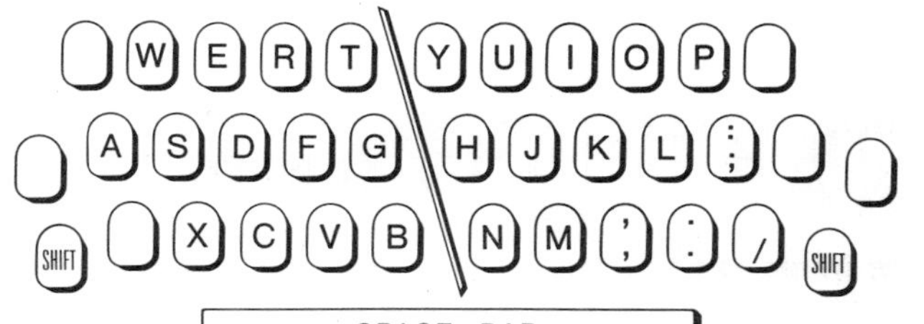

GOALS *To boost speed and accuracy, type 2 copies of lines 3-10. To understand and use the Difficulty Index. To type 38 words or more in 2 minutes within 4 errors.*

DIRECTIONS *Spacing 1. Line 40.*

WARMUP REVIEW

2 copies

1 a;sldkfjghfjdksla; : a;sldkfjghfjdksla; 8
2 jam nod cub fir yes hug kit wax lap eve 16

|1 |2 |3 |4 |5 |6 |7 |8

DOWN REACH PRACTICE

2 copies

3 Vic and Jim saved six men in this cave. 8
4 fvf five fvf save fvf pave fvf nave fvf 16
5 jnj June jnj Joan jnj Jane jnj Jean jnj 24
6 dcd dice dcd dock dcd iced dcd deck ded 32
7 jmj jams jmj jump jmj drum jmj slum jmj 40
8 sxs axes sxs next sxs text sxs axis sxs 48
9 k,k ink, k,k elk, k,k ark, k,k irk, k,k 56
10 Vic and Jim saved six men in this cave. 64

SI	Difficulty	Code
1.00+	Very Easy	VE
1.15+	Easy	E
1.25+	Fairly Easy	FE
1.35+	Normal	N
1.45+	Fairly Hard	FH
1.55+	Hard	H
1.65+	Very Hard	VH

Difficulty Index Many factors affect the difficulty of copy. One that summarizes the others in a general way is the average number of syllables per word—the Syllabic Intensity (SI). The "difficulty index" is given under the word-count column. For example, the 1.16E below means "The material averages 1.16 syllables per word, which is easy."

Very easy material (SI score of 1.00 to 1.15) is fine for building speed, which is why so many very easy selections appear in the early Parts of this book. Anytime you wish to boost speed, turn back to one of these VE or E selections—it is to help you then that the difficulty index is given now, even though everything you type right now may seem difficult.

1·1·2·2 TW 2-MINUTE GOAL

1 copy in 2 minutes. 2 tries

11 Dear Max: 2

3

12 Dad says we may have the car on Friday. 11
13 We will leave here at two. Janice will 19
14 provide the food. I am looking forward 27
15 to our visit to the beach. I hope that 35
16 we have sun. 38

|1 |2 |3 |4 |5 |6 |7 |8 SI 1.16E

PREPARE a·i·m WB 261–262

project 2

a·i·m 255–258

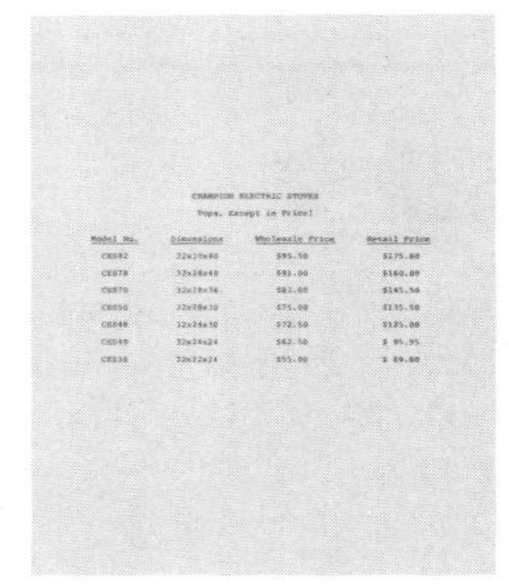

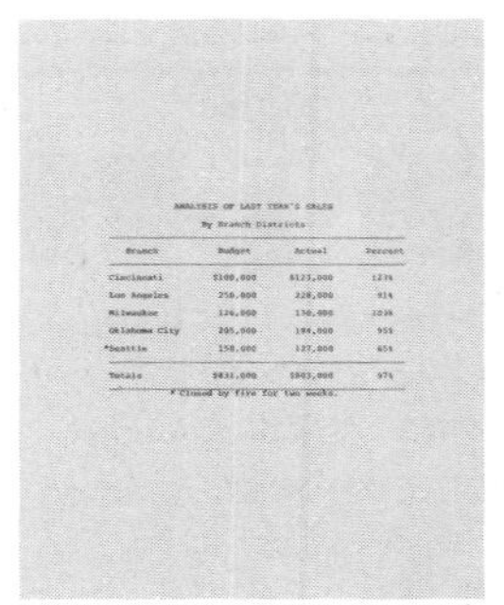

GOALS *To review essentials of open and ruled tables. To type tables from dictation. To create original tables. To do assignments by direction. To experience work-flow.*

Your employer is Fred Obernderfer, assistant manager and statistician at the headquarters office of Pappas Heath & Marbut, Inc. Address: 288 Dixon Avenue, Lincoln, NE 68508. He often dictates tables (you make a pencil draft as he talks, then type the table he has dictated) or asks you to compose them for him.

JOB 255·1

OPEN TABLE
Reference pages 163–165

Giving you the table at the top of page 256, Mr. Obernderfer says, "Please retype this for me, making one change: all the *New Price* items should be rounded off to the nearest dollar. The *$37.80* of the first line should be *$38.00,* for example. The *$42.35* of the bottom line should be *$42.00.* We'll need an original and one carbon copy."

*

JOB 255·2

OPEN TABLE
Reference pages 163–165

Let's draft a circular about *Champion Electric Stoves.* They are 18
Tops, Except in Price! I'll read the information for columns headed 29
(1) *Model No.* (2) *Dimensions* (3) *Wholesale Price* (4) *Retail Price.* 49
Model CES82 is 32x30x40 inches, $95.50 wholesale, $175 retail. 57
Model CES78 is 32x28x40 inches, $91.00 wholesale, $160 retail. 65
Model CES70 is 32x28x36 inches, $83 wholesale, $145.50 retail. 73
Model CES50 is 32x28x30 inches, $75 wholesale, $135.50 retail 81
Model CES48 is 32x24x30 inches, $72.50 wholesale, $125 retail. 89
Model CES40 is 32x24x24 inches, $62.50 wholesale, $95.95 retail. 97
Model CES38 is 32x22x24 inches, $55 wholesale, $89 retail. 115

JOB 256·1

RULED TABLE
Reference pages 182–184

Giving you the table at the foot of page 256, Mr. Obernderfer says, "Please retype this table for me. It is arranged now by percentage. I need to have it arranged by highest expense—that is, the *Seaside resort* line, at $19.00, should be first; the *Metropolitan city,* at $14.00, should be second; and so on. An original and one carbon, please."

*

JOB 256·2

RULED TABLE
Reference pages 182–184

***Word count** is for arranged table, not for copy as shown. More dictated tables are on Workbook 263–264

Your employer says: Well, I've drafted my *analysis of last year's* 14
sales. Let's type it, shall we? I'll give you the figures in nearest thou- 17
sands, reading across four columns headed (1) *Branch* (2) *Budget* 42
(3) *Actual* (4) *Percent.* Ready? 47
1. Our Cincinnati branch, budgeted for $100 thousand in sales, 52
actually did better: $123 thousand, a 123 percent performance. 56
2. Our Los Angeles branch was budgeted for $250 thousand, 61
slipped down to $228 thousand, a 91 percent performance. [Turn to page 257.] 65

aim 24

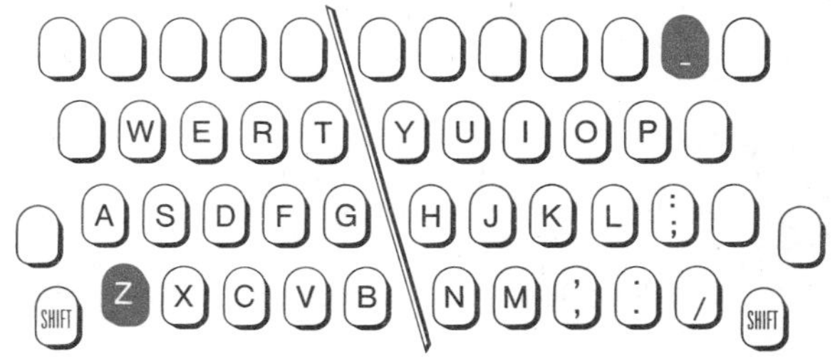

GOALS *To control the Z and Hyphen keys. To type 38 words or more in 2 minutes within 4 errors on 30 keys.*

DIRECTIONS *Spacing 1. Line 40. Tape K 15.*

WARMUP REVIEW

2 copies

1 a;sldkfjghfjdksla; : a;sldkfjghfjdksla; 8

2 ark bad cud fig job lax map set why van 16

|1 |2 |3 |4 |5 |6 |7 |8

Z KEY

A-finger
3 copies

3 aaa aza zzz aaa aza zzz aaa aza zzz aza 8

4 aza zip zip aza zig zig aza zag zag aza 16

5 aza zoo zoo aza zed zed aza zee zee aza 24

- (HYPHEN) KEY

Sem-finger
3 copies

6 ;;; ;p; ;p-p ;--; ;;; ;p; ;p-; ;--; ;-; 8

7 ;p- ;-; blue-gray ;p- ;-; one-third ;-; 16

8 ;p- ;-; one-fifth ;p- ;-; part-time ;-; 24

WORD CHAINS

2 copies

9 d di diz dizz dizzy l la laz lazy lazy; 8

10 a am ama amaz amaze j ja jaz jazz jazz. 16

11 half half fare fare half-fare half-fare 24

12 over over size size over-size over-size 32

1·1·2·2 TW 2-MINUTE GOAL

1 copy in 2 minutes. 2 tries

13 Dear Kip: 2

3

14 I have a lot of old jazz records that I 11
15 wish to sell. I was told that you col- 19
16 lect Dixieland. I am wondering whether 27
17 you wish to buy my Count Basie records. 35
18 Let me know. 38

|1 |2 |3 |4 |5 |6 |7 |8 SI 1.21FE

JOB 253·1

MAGAZINE ARTICLE

Line 45 Spacing 2
Carbon copy 1
Reference pages 185–186

"Please type this manuscript for the *Stationers' Journal*," says Mr. Dennis, handing you the timed-writing selection on page 247. "Type it in magazine style and entitle it *I Trust My Stationer*."

Checking the magazine, you find that it uses a 45-space line. It also uses not only the name of a contributor but also his business title and his company's name. The magazine uses brief sideheadings of two or three words (each sideheading and the extra blank space above it count as 2 lines). You decide to insert this sideheading before paragraph 3—

PAPER, FOR EXAMPLE

—and this sideheading before paragraph 5—

CARBON PAPER, TOO

You will indent paragraphs just 3 spaces and, of course, will use double-spacing throughout.

JOB 254·1

2-PAGE
BLOCKED LETTER

Page baronial (5½ x 8½)
Letterhead Workbook 259
Reference pages 216–220

This letter, please, to Mr. Ennis. I am 32
pleased to send you, at last, what you asked 41
me for: an article that would serve you as 50
the basis for an editorial on the need today 59
for stationers to have a high standard of 68
ethical conduct in advising their customers. 77
I know you will excuse my pretense of 85
so much ignorance about the qualities to be 93
found in paper. I thought I could serve our 102
common purpose better by pretending that 111
I, like most office executives, depend com- 119
pletely on my stationer—which, come to 127
think of it, is actually the case! 135
Thus, it seems to me, you could write 143
an editorial that says stationers owe it to 152
themselves and to the industry, as well as to 162
the public, to become experts in knowledge 170
of their wares. Working on the basis of paper 179
[getting near the bottom of the page?] and 180
carbon paper, you should not find it too dif- 188
ficult to add other [bottom of page yet?] 212
products, such as ink pens versus ball pens, 221
big staplers versus small ones, and the whole 230
world of printed letterheads and envelopes. 240
If the manuscript is not exactly what 248
you wish, let me know. / Cordially yours, / 261
Paul B. Dennis / Vice President / *and so on.* 273

|1 |2 |3 |4 |5 |6 |7 |8 SI 1.45N

JOB 254·2

2-PAGE
BLOCKED LETTER

Paper baronial (5½ x 8½)
Letterhead Workbook 259
Reference pages 216–220

This letter, please, to Mrs. Walters, the 11
Spokane lady to whom we sent the telegram. 35
Much as I appreciate the courtesy and the 43
honor you extended to me when you asked 51
me to take part in the survey you plan to 59
make of the Spokane business-training pro- 68
gram, I must, as I said in my wire, decline 76
this opportunity. 81
I truly regret this decision, but in the 89
past few months I have taken on some new 98
duties not only in my office but also in a 106
professional group in which I have long been 115
active. As you can see, my work load is such 124
that I could not do real justice to you if I 133
were also to try to participate in your 141
survey. 144
Might I suggest the name of another 151
man, one who is quite eligible and is perhaps 161
free to take my place on your committee? 170
I should like to suggest Dr. E. F. Price, 178
who is in charge of the business program at 187
Clayton College, in St. Louis. Doctor Price 196
has just finished work on a project in Knox- 225
ville and, so far as I know, is not busy right 235
now. As a former high school teacher, he 243
would bring fine perspective to your survey. 253
Again, let me tell you that I am truly 261
sorry that I am not able to join you. Cor- 272
dially yours, *and so on, bcc Doctor Price.* 293

|1 |2 |3 |4 |5 |6 |7 |8 SI 1.37N

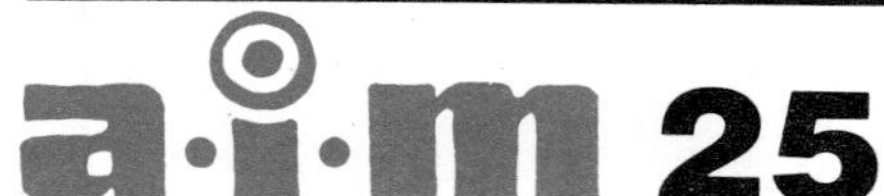

25

GOALS To boost speed and accuracy, type 2 copies of lines 3-10. To type 40 words or more in 2 minutes within 4 errors.

DIRECTIONS *Spacing 1. Line 40.*

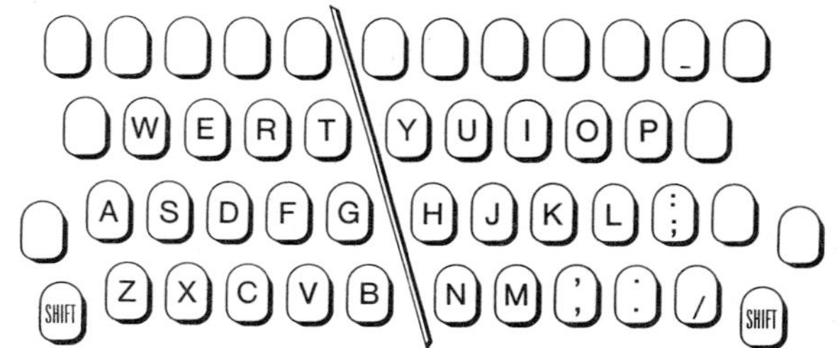

WARMUP REVIEW

2 copies

1 a;sldkfjghfjdksla; : a;sldkfjghfjdksla; 8

2 fed jug hay elk nob mix sac war vat zap 16

|1 |2 |3 |4 |5 |6 |7 |8

INWARD REACH PRACTICE

2 copies

3 The jury thinks a fight is never right. 8

4 ftf gift ftf lift ftf rift ftf sift ftf 16

5 jyj jays jyj joys jyj jury jyj jays jyj 24

6 fgf frog fgf flog fgf flag fgf fang fgf 32

7 jhj josh jhj rush jhj gush jhj push jhj 40

8 ftg twig ftg tags ftg tugs ftg togs ftg 48

9 jyh holy jyh shay jyh ahoy jyh they jyh 56

10 The jury thinks a fight is never right. 64

1·1·2·2 TW 2-MINUTE GOAL

1 copy in 2 minutes. 2 tries

11 Dear Mr. Zimmer: 4

5

12 Dixon and I want to thank you very much 13
13 for letting us do the job. We will ar- 21
14 rive there in good time. All our elec- 29
15 tric tools are a/c. I hope that a/c is 37
16 what you have. 40

|1 |2 |3 |4 |5 |6 |7 |8 SI 1.17E

JOB 252·1

EXACT COPY: INCOMING SEMIBLOCKED LETTER
Line 60 Spacing 1
Tabs 5, 10, 30, 41, 49

Typing shown here in color is what typist adds as he copies original.

COPY shows letter is not an original

(SIC) shows that error was in the original letter.

Indent table 5 spaces from each margin.

Copyist shows who signed the letter.

Copyist adds his initials.

Shown in pica 1/4 reduced

Line 6 AMERICAN STATIONERS LEAGUE 16
17
Line 8 99 Boulder Avenue 30
31
Line 10 Denver, Colorado 80205 49
50
51
52
53
Line 15 May 17, 19-- 60
61
62
C O P Y 67
68
Mr. Paul B. Dennis 71
H. P. Lebrad, Inc. 75
221 Mercer Avenue 79
Newark, New Jersey 07103 84
85
Dear Mr. Dennis: 89
90

I am pleased to tell you that, at the meeting last 102
night, the ASL Board gave its full approval to the plans that 114
you and your chairmen have proposed for our meetings in New 126
York City next fall. At the same time, the Board past (sic) 139
on your budget just as you sent it to us: 147
148

Income 157
158

From League account	$2,500		170
From rental of display space	2,500		180
Total income		$5,000	195

196

Expenses 207
208

Hotel space and service	$2,000		218
Fees and expenses of speakers	2,000		227
Expenses of the League staff	500		237
Reserve	500		249
Total expenses		$5,000	264

265

This, then, is to serve as the "go ahead!" sign to 277
you and your district chairmen. When you want the staff here 290
to help you out, just let us know your needs. 299
300

With best wishes, 307
308
P. J. Dwight (signed) 315
316
Staff Director 322
323

PJD/ssm/urs 325
cc Minutes 326
SI 1.45N

Typist's Exact Copy of an Incoming Semiblocked Letter with Deep Paragraph Indentions and a Leadered Table in the Body

a·i·m 26

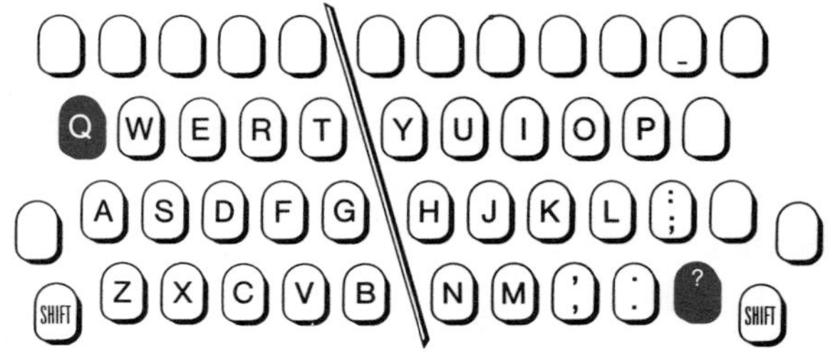

GOALS *To control Q and Question Mark Keys. To type 40 words or more in 2 minutes within 4 errors on 31 keys.*

DIRECTIONS *Spacing 1. Line 40. Tape K 16.*

WARMUP REVIEW

2 copies

1 a;sldkfjghfjdksla; : a;sldkfjghfjdksla; 8

2 boy cap fox hug jam lad irk sew vat zen 16

|1 |2 |3 |4 |5 |6 |7 |8

Q KEY

A-finger
3 copies

3 aaa aqa aqqa aqqa aaa aqa aqqa aqqa aqa 8

4 aqa aqa quit quit aqa aqa quip quip aqa 16

5 aqa aqa quiz quiz aqa aqa quay quay aqa 24

? KEY

Sem-finger
3 copies

6 ;;; ;/; ;/?; ;??; ;;; ;/; ;/?; ;??; ;?; 8

7 ;/; ;?; who? who? ;/; ;?; how? how? ;?; 16

8 ;/; ;?; why? why? ;/; ;?; you? you? ;?; 24

STYLE NOTE

USES OF THE HYPHEN

1. Dash The dash consists of two consecutive hyphens, with no spaces:

> Mr. Smith--I think you know him--came over to see John.

2. Word Division The hyphen is to indicate that a word is divided:

> They had far too much home-
> work to do on Friday night.

3. Compounds The hyphen is used, without spaces, to tie words together in compound expressions, as:

> She admired the first-class sketch her son-in-law made.

1·1·2·2 TW 2-MINUTE GOAL

1 copy in 2 minutes. 2 tries

9 Dear Jack and Rex: 4

5

10 Did you do very well on the quiz? Vera 13

11 said she thought--well, hoped--that she 21

12 did well. She said she spent a tremen- 29

13 dous study-review hour with you. Thank 37

14 you for that. 40

|1 |2 |3 |4 |5 |6 |7 |8 SI 1.21E

project 1

a·i·m 251–254

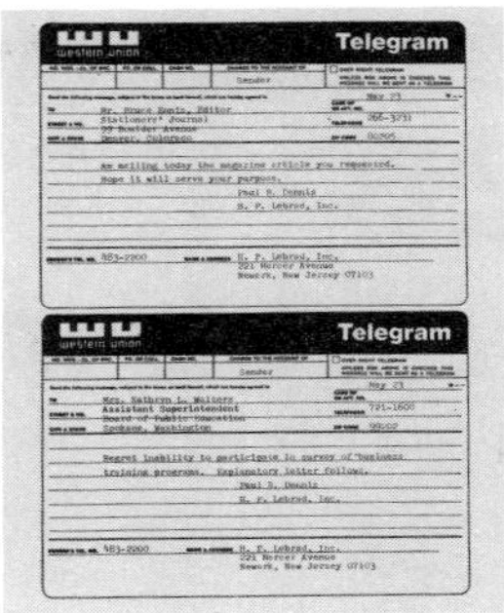

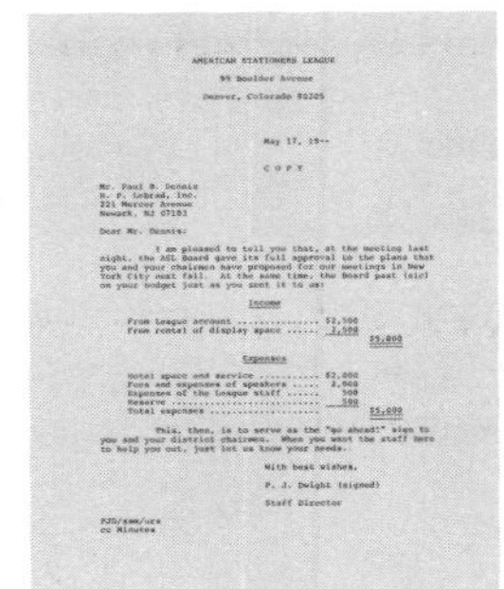

GOALS *To learn to fill in telegram blanks. To learn how to make and identify an exact copy of a letter. To obtain and use in production the data used in prior jobs. To experience work-flow.*

Your employer is Paul B. Dennis, vice president of H. P. Lebrad, Inc., located at 221 Mercer Avenue, Newark, New Jersey 07103. His telephone is Area 201 Local 483-2200. For his letters, Mr. Dennis prefers blocked letter style, standard punctuation, and baronial stationery. He wishes both his name and title shown under his signature on letters. Mr. Dennis says to you—

JOB 251·1–2
TWO TELEGRAMS

Service full rate
Forms Workbook 257
Reference illustration below

Please send this full-rate telegram to Mr. Bruce Ennis, Editor / Stationers' Journal / 99 Boulder Avenue / Denver, Colorado 80205 / *Telephone* 266-3231 / Am mailing today the magazine article you requested. Hope it will serve your purpose. / Paul B. Dennis / H. P. Lebrad, Inc.

Send this full-rate telegram to Mrs. Kathryn L. Walters / Assistant Superintendent / Board of Public Education / Spokane, Washington 99202 / *Telephone* 721-1600 / Regret inability to participate in survey of business training programs. Explanatory letter follows. / Paul B. Dennis *and so on as usual.*

JOB 252·1
EXACT-COPY LETTER

Carbon copies 1
Paper plain
Reference page 253

"I need two copies of this letter," says Mr. Dennis, giving you the original of the letter on page 253. You find that the office photocopying machine is out of order. You will have to type the duplicate copies. You do so, making the technical additions shown in color.

western union — Telegram

NO. WDS.–CL. OF SVC. | PD. OR COLL. | CASH NO. | CHARGE TO THE ACCOUNT OF: Sender | OVER NIGHT TELEGRAM — UNLESS BOX ABOVE IS CHECKED THIS MESSAGE WILL BE SENT AS A TELEGRAM

Send the following message, subject to the terms on back hereof, which are hereby agreed to — May 16 197-

TO: Mr. P. J. Dwight — CARE OF OR APT. NO.
STREET & NO.: American Stationers League — TELEPHONE: 266-3237
CITY & STATE: 99 Boulder Ave., Denver, CO — ZIP CODE: 80205

How soon will the Board meet and decide on budget for
New York City conference?
Paul B. Dennis
H. P. Lebrad, Inc.

SENDER'S TEL. NO.: 483-2200 — NAME & ADDRESS: H. P. Lebrad, Inc.
221 Mercer Avenue — Newark, NJ 07103

western union — Telegram

NO. WDS.–CL. OF SVC. | PD. OR COLL. | CASH NO. | CHARGE TO THE ACCOUNT OF: Sender | OVER NIGHT TELEGRAM — UNLESS BOX ABOVE IS CHECKED THIS MESSAGE WILL BE SENT AS A TELEGRAM

Send the following message, subject to the terms on back hereof, which are hereby agreed to — May 16 197-

TO: Mr. P. J. Dwight — CARE OF OR APT. NO.
STREET & NO.: American Stationers League
99 Boulder Ave. — TELEPHONE: 266-3237
CITY & STATE: Denver, CO — ZIP CODE: 80205

How soon will the Board meet and decide on budget for
New York City conference?
Paul B. Dennis
H. P. Lebrad, Inc.

SENDER'S TEL. NO.: 483-2200 — NAME & ADDRESS: H. P. Lebrad, Inc.
221 Mercer Avenue
Newark, NJ 07103

Printing is 1½-spaced, to accommodate handwriting. Typing telegrams is easy with 1½-spacing (left). If machine doesn't have 1½-spacing, use single-spacing (right) and merely approximate the alignment with guides. Western Union is more anxious for complete data than in typing alignment. Set margin at V of "Service" and tabs at R of "Charge" and T of "Night."

27

GOALS To boost speed and accuracy, type 3 copies of lines 3–12. To type 40 words or more in 2 minutes within 4 errors.

DIRECTIONS *Spacing 1. Line 40.*

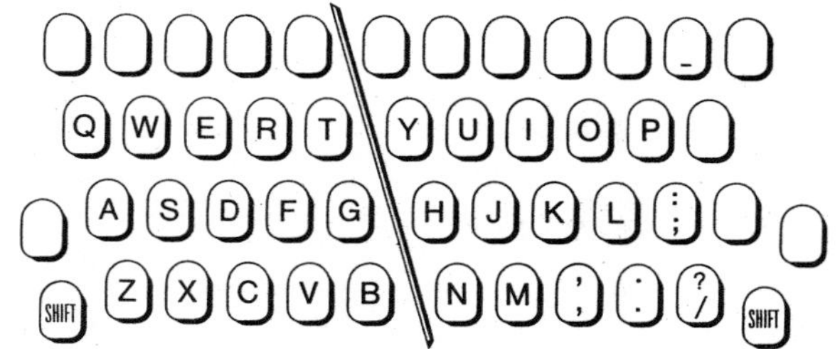

WARMUP REVIEW

2 copies

1 aim bow fit hug icy jig kit lid mad net 8
2 orb pit quo sir taz use vie why yet zoo 16

|1 |2 |3 |4 |5 |6 |7 |8

ACCURACY DRILL

3 copies

3 aa apt aa all aa aid aa area aa away aa 8
4 ee end ee eye ee eke ee edge ee else ee 16
5 ii its ii ice ii ire ii into ii idea ii 24
6 oo old oo our oo out oo odor oo oleo oo 32
7 uu use uu ups uu urn uu upon uu undo uu 40

SPEED BOOSTER

3 copies

8 land lame laud lard lab lad lag law lap 8
9 sofa soap sock soak son sod sox sob sow 16
10 maid malt mane make mar mad map man may 24
11 done dorm down dock don dog dob dot doe 32
12 name nays nape naps nag nab nan nay nap 40

1·1·2·2 TW 2-MINUTE GOAL

1 copy in 2 minutes. 2 tries

13 Dear Vic: 2
3
14 The new coach will be here on the sixth 11
15 of June. I fear that my size will keep 19
16 me off the squad, for he likes the team 27
17 to be big fellows. Well, hope we win a 35
18 lot of games this year. 40

|1 |2 |3 |4 |5 |6 |7 |8 SI 1.02VE

Overview

Part Twelve consists of four office-style projects and a final test. It is intended for all who have achieved at least the minimum skill goal for this course: 200 words within 5 minutes [40 words a minute] within 3 errors.

Discuss these alternatives with your teacher:

1. If you have not achieved the minimum skill goal, reaching it is more important than typing the assignments in Part Twelve. So, turn to page 266, read the directions for building skill on the materials in the two Supplements, and start a skill drive. Return here when you have achieved the minimum skill goal.

2. If you have achieved the goal but feel you need more skill, review Part Twelve with your instructor and decide which assignments can be left out. Use the time of such assignments for skill practice in the Supplements; start by reading the directions on page 266. With your teacher, work out a schedule of skill sessions vs. production assignments in Part Twelve.

3. If you have achieved the skill goal and feel that further skill drill would be less rewarding than the interesting assignments in Part Twelve, start the projects. They are for you. You will enjoy the realistic style of the directions.

Performance Goals

When you finish the 20 a·i·m sessions in Part Twelve and take the test on pages 263–265, you should be able to demonstrate these abilities:

1. Technicalities You will score 90 or more percent correct on an objective test covering the technical information in the Part.

2. Production Working from unarranged material, you will produce letters, tables, forms, and manuscripts of average difficulty and complexity in correct form without coaching.

3. Skill You will type at least 200 words in 5 minutes (230–235 is more likely) within 3 errors on normal paragraphs whose line endings you will have to determine by listening for the bell.

Routines and Procedures

Whichever of the three options you elect, each day turn here first and do a warmup on the lines below, then turn to your project work for the Part Twelve assignments or to the Supplements, beginning on page 266, for your skill-development work.

WARMUP		**Each day type one sentence from each pair. Type it three times.**	
Speed	1A	They paid for the pen and the box, so I paid for the chair.	12
	1B	Both the men may go to town if he pays them for their work.	24
Accuracy	2A	Because he was very lazy, Jack paid for six games and quit.	12
	2B	Zoe enjoys Pam's diving board, which is quick but flexible.	24
Numbers	3A	Send us 10 of No. 28, and 39 of No. 47, and 56 of No. 1028.	12
	3B	They were assigned rooms 10, 28, and 39. We got 47 and 56.	24
Concentration	4A	jo anne invited sue ellen to visit kay at easter in denver.	12
(insert caps)	4B	there are mr. and mrs. roper p. hale, of chicago, illinois.	24

a·i·m 28

GOALS *To boost speed and accuracy, type 3 copies of lines 3–12. To type 40 words or more in 2 minutes within 4 errors.*

DIRECTIONS *Spacing 1. Line 40.*

WARMUP REVIEW

2 copies

1 lid nut man ice kid jag fur box hem gap 8

2 sir tux per tip qui why vie zip yet use 16

|1 |2 |3 |4 |5 |6 |7 |8

ACCURACY BOOSTER

3 copies

3 aa sea aa lea aa tea aa papa aa data aa 8

4 ee eve ee elk ee dew ee ease ee haze ee 16

5 ii rip ii fin ii ink ii five ii tidy ii 24

6 oo two oo out oo low oo solo oo polo oo 32

7 uu but uu cub uu due uu bulk uu true uu 40

SPEED BOOSTER

3 copies

8 their they them then than that this the 8

9 lends lent leap less lean lead lest let 16

10 ducks dusk dune duty dumb duns duke due 24

11 hairy hale hang halt hair hand hams hay 32

12 coals corn cork comb come cost cold cob 40

1·1·2·2 TW 2-MINUTE GOAL

1 copy in 2 minutes. 2 tries

13 Dear Vick: 2

3

14 Did I tell you that Robert has been as- 11
15 signed to a jet squadron? His plane is 19
16 equipped with six giant pods. It is so 27
17 fast and goes so high that the sound is 35
18 more a fizz than a roar. 40

|1 |2 |3 |4 |5 |6 |7 |8

SI 1.10VE

TEST 11-C

RESOLUTION IN LEGAL STYLE
Line 60
Spacing 2
Start line 14
Tabs 10, center

R E S O L U T I O N / WHEREAS the number of students who attend 23
Roosevelt High School is nearly two times the number for which it 36
was built in 1955; and 41
WHEREAS the average class size is far higher than the size that is 55
recommended by the State Department of Public Instruction; and 68
WHEREAS ground has been broken for the building of apartment 81
dwellings that will house two hundred families and will add to the 94
enrollment at the said Roosevelt High School: Therefore be it 107
RESOLVED, that the officers, and the directors, and the members of 121
the Community Council do approve and do urge others to approve a 135
one million dollar school bond issue for the addition of a wing to the 149
said Roosevelt High School; and in proof of that approval do direct 162
our Secretary to sign and to deliver a copy of this resolution to the 176
School Board. 179

____________________________ 187
Secretary 192
Today's Date 196

|1 |2 |3 |4 |5 |6 |7 |8 |9 |10 |11 |12 |13 |14 SI 1.47FD

TEST 11-D

5-MINUTE TW
Line 70
Spacing 2
Tab 5

The error into which the majority of us fall is in thinking that 14
we can grasp a new lease on life whenever we decide to do so. We may 28
coast along, telling ourselves that whenever our big opportunity pops 42
up, an opportunity worth a real effort, that is when we will stretch. 56
We couldn't be more mistaken. Once we get the habit of coasting, the 70
habit gets us. We continue to coast. There is only one direction we 84
can coast: downhill. To be a climber, you have to use your muscles. 98
This might seem theoretical, but it means dollars in your pocket 112
when you begin working. As a beginner, you'll be given the easy jobs 126
and most will be tolerant of all your mistakes; no one really expects 140
very much of you. Now what happens? On one hand you might relax 153
and start taking it easy, with the result that you stop growing and 166
begin to coast. On the other hand you might take advantage of the 180
easiness of your assignment and, by pushing avidly, not only master 193
the duties but also amaze the world with the rate at which you 206
make progress and the speed of your promotion. Taking it easy is 219
likely to cost a lot. 224
You see, getting ahead in business is not easy, a very fortunate 238
thing for you; if it were easy, the ladder would be full of those who 252
got there ahead of you. Sometimes the ladder of advancement trembles 266
and quakes, and you with it. Sometimes the rungs seem far apart—too 280
far apart. But only when the stretching is longest, and the climbing 294
is toughest, can your strength and determination and drive enable you 308
to accomplish the rung that others couldn't reach. You have probably 322
heard it said that success is a habit; it is—the habit of hard work. 336

|1 |2 |3 |4 |5 |6 |7 |8 |9 |10 |11 |12 |13 |14 SI 1.41N

a·i·m 29

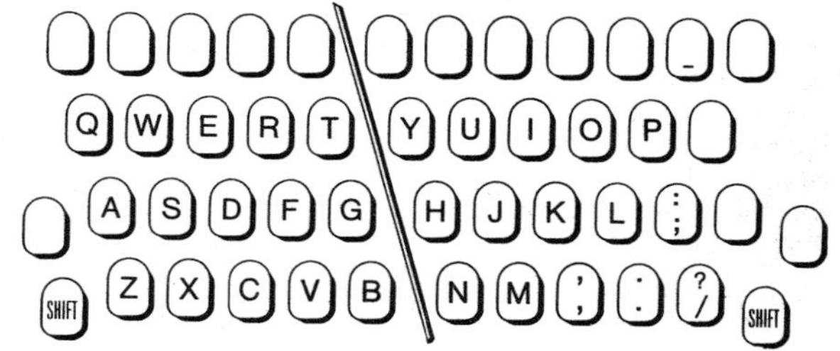

GOALS *To boost speed and accuracy, type 40 words in 2 minutes within 4 errors. To preview a·i·m 30 Test.*

DIRECTIONS *Spacing 1. Line 40.*

WARMUP REVIEW

2 copies

1 a;sldkfjghfjdksla; : a;sldkfjghfjdksla; 8

2 back fled high jinx many quiz rots wavy 16

|1 |2 |3 |4 |5 |6 |7 |8

TEST PREPPING

1. Review the objective-information test on Workbook pages 13–14. Do not mark the test, but look up any details you do not already know.

2. Take a 2-minute writing on the following material, as though it were the test you will take in a·i·m 30 to show how much you have learned in Part One.

3. Build reserve speed and accuracy power for the a·i·m 30 test by using the material below for a 1·1·2·2 timed-writing series.

3 Dear Al: 2

3

4 I wish that you had been with us to see 11
5 the new jet planes smack the sky in the 19
6 air show. It was great. 24

25

7 The six big jets took off with a scream 33
8 of engines to soar up and zoom over our 41
9 heads like a squadron of comets. For a 49
10 while we could see the white trail, but 57
11 soon it faded away. 61

62

12 Rod and Jane did not want to leave, for 70
13 they thought the group might circle the 78
14 field and then come back to give us an- 86
15 other of those skyrocket displays. You 94
16 would have loved the affair. 100

|1 |2 |3 |4 |5 |6 |7 |8

SI 1.12VE

TEST PREP 4

TABULAR DISPLAY WITH LEADERS
Line 60
Tabs 30, 61
Spacing 2
Center

Remember to underscore words shown in italic (slanted) print.

Pappas, Heath & Marbut		12
SPECIAL MEETING OF STOCKHOLDERS		33
June 8, 19—		44
Welcome..................................	Raymond H. Pappas	64
Old Business		79
Minutes of the Last Meeting....................	Charles C. Laird	102
Report of the Treasurer..........................	Scott Marbut, Jr.	116
Report of the Chairman of the Board...............	Paul J. Heath	134
New Business		146
Should We Merge with Chase & Sons?............	John Lawrence	164
Other Stock Plans...............................	Alice Pappas Heath	184
Major Stock Rights Plan..........................	Scott Marbut, Sr.	203
Other New Business that May Be Brought		211
to the Floor..	Stockholders	229
Adjournment		240

SI 1.41N

a·i·m 249-250

GOALS To type 200 or more words in 5 minutes within 3 errors on average listen-for-bell copy. To produce a financial statement with solid leaders. To produce a resolution in legal style. To score 90% or higher on an objective test on technical information in Part 11.

DIRECTIONS *Warmup page 243. WB 255–256.*

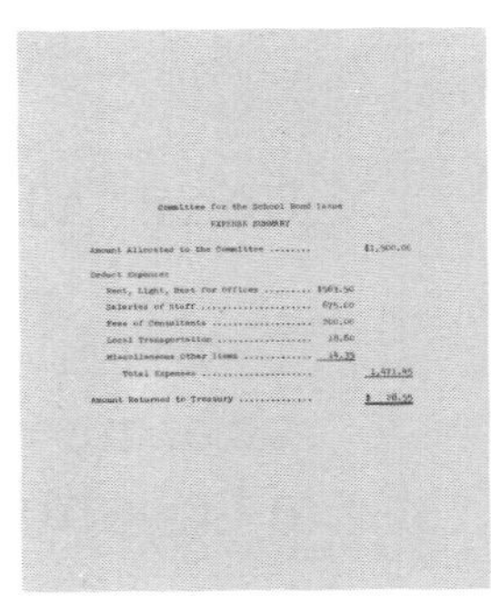

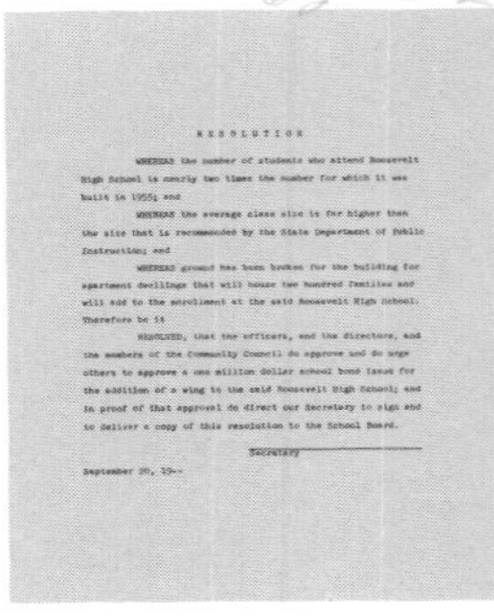

TEST 11-A

Take a general information test. It may be the one on Workbook 255–256 or a similar test that your teacher may give you or may dictate to you.

TEST 11-B

EXPENSE REPORT WITH LEADERS
Line 60
Spacing 2
Center on a full page
Tabs 2, center, and columns

Committee for the School Bond Issue		21
EXPENSE REPORT		31
		43
Amount Allocated to the Committee		57
Deduct Expenses		60
Rent, Light, Heat for Offices		71
Salaries of Staff		81
Fees of Consultants		91
Local Transportation		102
Miscellaneous other items		115
Total Expenses to Be Deducted		127
Amount Returned to Treasury		146

a·i·m 30 TEST

GOALS *To score 80 percent or more correct on an objective test on technical information presented and practiced in Part One. To type 40 words or more in 2 minutes within 4 errors on alphabetic copy, by touch.*

DIRECTIONS *Spacing 1. Line 40. WB 13–14.*

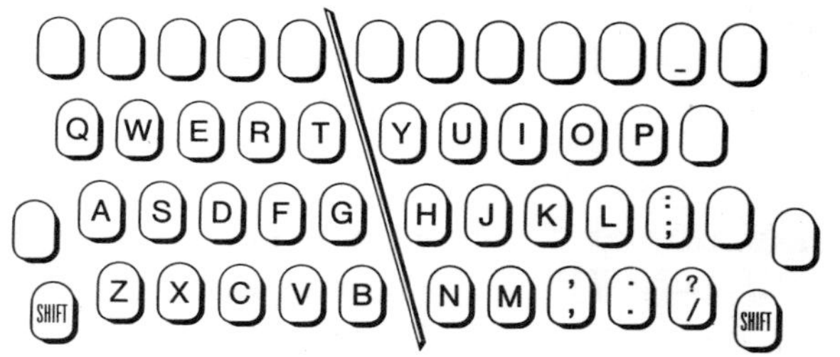

WARMUP REVIEW

2 copies

a;sldkfjghfjdksla; : a;sldkfjghfjdksla; 8
deaf hazy joke lame monk plug quit very 16

|1 |2 |3 |4 |5 |6 |7 |8

TEST 1-A

Take a general information test. It may be the one on Workbook pages 13–14 or any similar one that your teacher may give or dictate to you.

TEST 1-B

Type as much of the following "letter" as you can in 2 minutes. Control your pace carefully so that you maintain a speed of at least 20 words a minute without making more than 4 errors. Your teacher will inspect you for correct operating techniques as you type. Your teacher may authorize a second attempt on this test.

Dear Lou: 2

3

Yes, I wish that I had been with you at 11
the air show. I would have enjoyed the 19
jets and their act. I am sorry to have 27
missed the show, but I had to be at the 35
store all day. 38

39

The six planes flew over the store with 47
a sizzle that made the lima beans quake 55
in their jars. I raced out for a look, 63
but the jets were over the horizon with 71
nothing in the sky but the vapor trail. 79

80

Next time, please let me know the plans 88
in advance so that I can arrange to get 96
off and go with you. 100

|1 |2 |3 |4 |5 |6 |7 |8 SI 1.11VE

SPEED SENTENCES

For 1′ TW

33 Eight of the men may go right to the big field with Tod and Henry. 13.3
34 They may wish to blame Sue or me for the fight to end the problem. 13.3
35 Helen may wish to pay both of the men if and when they go to work. 13.3

|1 |2 |3 |4 |5 |6 |7 |8 |9 |10 |11 |12 |13

ACCURACY SENTENCES

For 1′ TW

36 Having typed exercises very lazily, we both acquired jerky habits. 13.3
37 Mrs. Moxley served Jack, the quaint wag, a pizza and black coffee. 13.3
38 Very quickly, Jean froze both the mixtures in the deep brown jugs. 13.3

a·i·m 247-248

GOALS To type 200 or more words in 5 minutes within 3 errors on average listen-for-bell copy. To preview the test in a·i·m 249–250. To execute a resolution and a program involving pivoting and use of leaders.

DIRECTIONS *Spacing 1. Line 60. Line 70 for Warmup lines 35 and 38 above. WB 255–256.*

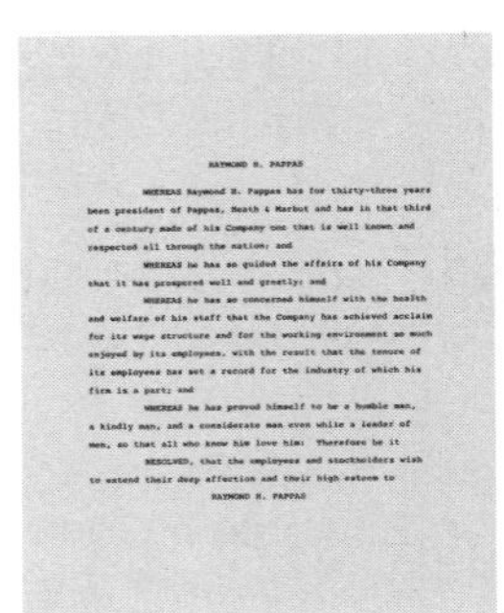

RAYMOND H. PAPPAS

WHEREAS Raymond H. Pappas has for thirty-three years been president of Pappas, Heath & Marbut and has in that third of a century made of his Company one that is well known and respected all through the nation; and

WHEREAS he has so guided the affairs of his Company that it has prospered well and greatly; and

WHEREAS he has so concerned himself with the health and welfare of his staff that the Company has achieved acclaim for its wage structure and for the working environment so much enjoyed by its employees, with the result that the tenure of its employees has set a record for the industry of which his firm is a part; and

WHEREAS he has proved himself to be a humble man, a kindly man, and a considerate man even while a leader of men, so that all who know him love him: Therefore be it

RESOLVED, that the employees and stockholders wish to extend their deep affection and their high esteem to

RAYMOND H. PAPPAS

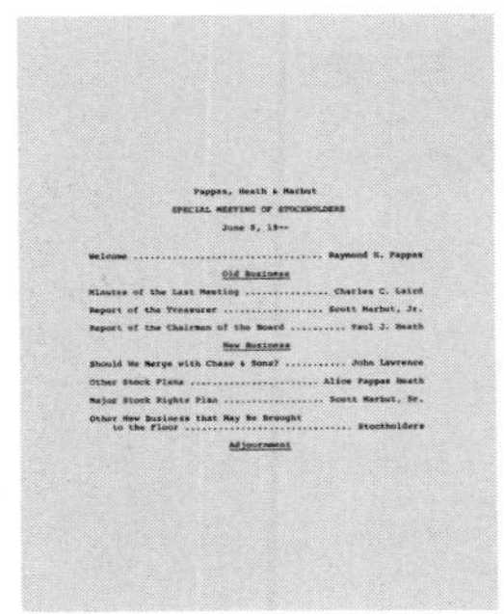

Pappas, Heath & Marbut

SPECIAL MEETING OF STOCKHOLDERS

June 5, 19--

Welcome .... Raymond H. Pappas

Old Business

Minutes of the Last Meeting .... Charles C. Laird

Report of the Treasurer .... Scott Marbut, Jr.

Report of the Chairman of the Board .... Paul J. Heath

New Business

Should We Merge with Chase & Sons? .... John Lawrence

Other Stock Plans .... Alice Pappas Heath

Major Stock Rights Plan .... Scott Marbut, Sr.

Other New Business that May Be Brought to the Floor .... Stockholders

Adjournment

TEST PREP 1

Review the objective information test on Workbook 255–256. Do not mark the pages, but look up any details of which you are not sure; be ready to score well.

TEST PREP 2

5-MINUTE TW

Using lines 18–32 on page 247, take a 5-minute writing to show that you can type at goal rate or better: 200 or more words in 5 minutes within 3 errors.

TEST PREP 3

RESOLUTION IN LEGAL STYLE
Line 60
Spacing 2
Paragraph indentions 10
Tabs 10, center
Start line 14

1 RESOLUTION / WHEREAS Raymond H. Pappas has for 21
2 thirty-three years been president of Pappas, Heath & Marbut and 34
3 has in that third of a century made of his Company one that is 47
4 well-known and respected all through the nation; and 57
5 WHEREAS he has so guided the affairs of his Company that it 70
6 has prospered well and greatly; and 78
7 WHEREAS he has so concerned himself with the health and 90
8 welfare of his staff that the Company has achieved acclaim for its 103
9 wage structure and for the working environment so much enjoyed 118
10 by its employees, with the result that the tenure of its employees 131
11 has set a record for the industry of which his firm is a part; and 145
12 WHEREAS he has proved himself to be a humble man, a kindly 157
13 man, and a considerate man even while a leader of men, so that all 171
14 who know him love him: Therefore be it 179
15 RESOLVED, that the employees and stockholders wish to ex- 191
16 tend their deep affection and their high esteem to / RAYMOND H. 212
17 PAPPAS 216

|1 |2 |3 |4 |5 |6 |7 |8 |9 |10 |11 |12 |13 SI 1.41N

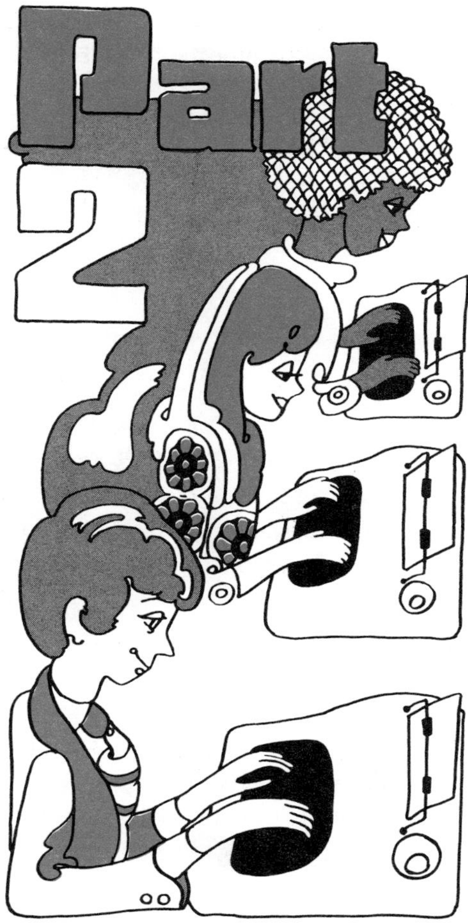

Overview

In Part Two you will concentrate on three main kinds of activities: (1) You will strengthen your typing speed and accuracy. (2) You will practice many elements of display typing, including horizontal centering, vertical centering, spread centering, block centering, and use of all capitals. (3) You will learn how to end typing lines from the sound of the margin bell, without looking up from the copy; you will be able to divide words correctly when necessary.

There are 20 a·i·m experiences in Part Two. As before, each a·i·m provides about 20 minutes of reading and typing practice. In general, there are two or three a·i·m sets on skill building, then two or three on display typing.

The skill gains are spelled out in the goals listed in the heading of each a·i·m for skill building. These goals will press you to reach for 1 additional word in 2-minute writings in each skill a·i·m, which is merely ½ word a minute. This will be well within your grow power.

Performance Goals

When you finish Part Two, you should be able to demonstrate the following abilities when you take the test in a·i·m 50, page 54:

1. Touch Typing You will control all letter and punctuation keys by touch. You will use the main operating parts, like the carriage return and tabulator, correctly and by touch. You will return the carriage, indent, even double-indent with the tabulator, all by touch.

2. Technicalities You will score at least 80 percent on an objective test that reviews both Part One and Part Two. The test includes items on word division, names of machine parts, score keeping, spacing after punctuation, etc.

3. Production You will be able to display typed material by centering it vertically on the paper, with individual or groups of lines centered horizontally. You will be able to spread words and to type them in all capitals.

4. Skill You will type at least 50 words in 2 minutes within 4 errors as you copy alphabetic paragraph material whose line endings are not shown—that is, you must listen for the margin warning bell and decide on line endings.

Routines and Procedures

Pretest|Post-test The skill-building routine that you will use most frequently is one that has three steps in it. First you will take a preliminary test ("Pretest") to see whether you need to accent speed more than accuracy or accuracy more than speed. Then you will do accuracy and speed drills, accenting one kind a little more than the other kind. Finally, as the third step, you will take another test (the "Post-test") to measure your gains.

Skill Drills The drills you do in the middle step involve lines of words with motions in them that you need to practice. The directions usually tell you to make two copies, but make more copies if your time schedule permits.

Post-test The Post-test involves more than merely writing for 2 minutes. It involves a sequence of timings: 1·1·2·2. You write for a minute, rest, continue for another minute; then you try to cover both minutes' worth of practice material in 2 minutes without pause; and finally you make a second effort for 2 minutes. This is the big one in which you will make (or even surpass!) your skill goal for that a·i·m.

a·i·m 246

GOAL ⚲ *To type 200 or more words within 5 minutes and 3 errors on listen-for-bell copy of normal difficulty.*

DIRECTIONS *Spacing 2 for Pretest, Post-test; 1 for others. Line 70. Tab 5.*

HOW TO MAKE ERRORS

- Get angry with yourself.
- Get angry with your machine.
- Get angry with your neighbor.
- Get angry with the requirements.
- Get upset. Lose your self-control.

WARMUP PREVIEW

2 copies

responsibility specialist illustrate century effects juggle 12
acquaintance wastebasket information flexible chemical toss 12

SKILL DRIVE

See page 214.

② is minimal 2-minute goal.

The subject of paper is so broad that, if somebody said I had to 14
accept responsibility for buying it for an office, I would take steps to 29
strike up an acquaintance with a specialist on paper, a stationer. 42
I am no expert on the topic, but I do know that paper is made in 56
many sizes and in many grades; and just knowing this is enough to 69
tip me off that there must be a lot to know about it.② 80
Take the life of paper, for example. If you are buying paper to use 95
in a circular that is destined to end in a wastebasket, would you buy 109
the same quality of paper that you need for the financial records you 123
are required to keep on file for a decade? I think not. "Record paper," 138
as that kind is called, has to stay flexible and white—tough enough to 152
last a century. Now, a stationer can tell you how to order the proper 166
paper for the right purpose, and so you realize why I said I would get 180
to know one of those gentlemen: if I am to be the office expert on 194
paper, he may become my coach. ⚲ 200

|1 |2 |3 |4 |5 |6 |7 |8 |9 |10 |11 |12 |13 |14 SI 1.35N

ALTERNATE SKILL DRIVE

or a·i·m 247 5-minute TW

There really is a lot of technical information involved. Let me il- 14 | 214
lustrate. Paper comes from rag fiber and wood fiber and chemicals. 28 | 228
The folks who manufacture it juggle the ratio of these three elements 42 | 242
to get special effects. The more wood they use, the shorter the life but 57 | 257
the lower the price of the stuff. The more rag they toss in, the longer 71 | 271
will be the life and the higher the price.② 80 | 280
Carbon paper is just as complex as paper; typists may think that 94 | 294
all carbons are alike, but they are not. You can purchase thin kinds 107 | 307
that don't last long but let you make many copies at one time, or you 122 | 322
can purchase thick carbon, soft carbon, tough carbon, colored carbon, 136 | 336
carbon of different sizes and shapes, carbon of just about every kind 150 | 350
of quality which you can define and for which you are willing to pay. 164 | 364
Only a person who knows all the brands and all the qualities and 178 | 378
all the uses can guide a purchaser in getting the right carbon or the 192 | 392
right stationery; know anyone like that? ⚲ 200 | 400

|1 |2 |3 |4 |5 |6 |7 |8 |9 |10 |11 |12 |13 |14 SI 1.40N

a·i·m 31

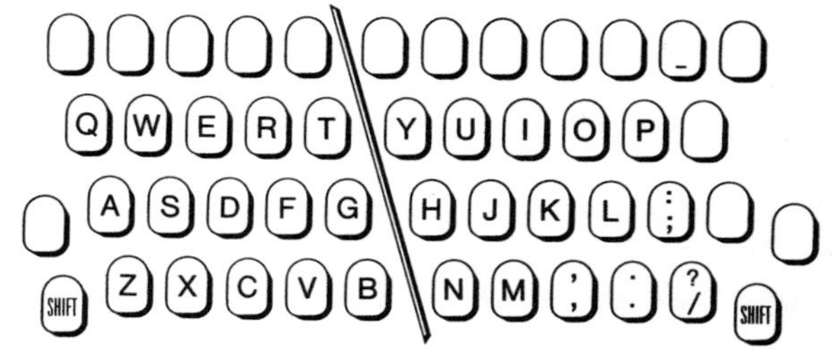

GOALS ⚲ *To type 41 words or more in 2 minutes within 4 errors.* ⚲ *To boost accuracy and speed, practice typing lines 8–15.* ⚲ *To use new drill routine.*

DIRECTIONS *Spacing 1. Line 50.*

WARMUP PREVIEW

2 copies

1 lock jade oxen cafe type brim silk whig quiz five 10

2 mesquite sizzling through rabbit steer patch exam 10

|1 |2 |3 |4 |5 |6 |7 |8 |9 |10

PRETEST

1 copy or 2-minute TW

3 Dear Vic: 2

3

4 I really did hit that exam like a steer chasing a 13
5 jolly jack rabbit through a mesquite patch. This 23
6 man was sizzling, I tell you. For once I had the 33
7 angle: in other words, I passed it. ⚲ 41

|1 |2 |3 |4 |5 |6 |7 |8 |9 |10 SI 1.26E

IMPROVEMENT PRACTICE

If you make more than 4 errors on the pretest, stress *accuracy* in this practice time. If you made 4 or fewer errors, however, stress *speed* in this practice period.

Accuracy Stress Make 3 copies of the accuracy drills, then 1 copy of the speed drills.

Speed Stress Make 1 copy of the accuracy drills, then 3 copies of the speed drills. ⚲

ACCURACY

3|1 copies

8 ere mom ewe non dad lily data none rare pipe solo 10

9 tot gag pop eve pup baby yoyo even nine here lull 10

10 bag yon sax fat joy bath your herd mint owes mine 10

11 Dad gave the judge seven or nine very rare pipes. 10

SPEED

3|1 copies

12 angle endow they lend wish pane and for the it is 10

13 right bugle work form duty with rib vow men or it 10

14 gland their when than risk then pan rid owl do so 10

15 They do their work right when they do their duty. ⚲ 10

POST-TEST 1·1·2·2 TW

on Pretest

When you complete the speed and accuracy drills, do a 1·1·2·2 series on the pretest material. Your final 2-minute writing should be the one that fulfills your goal of writing much better on the post-test than you achieve in an honest effort on the original pretest.

THOMAS WALTER HOLCOMB

WHEREAS Thomas Walter Holcomb will retire from the
presidency of The Business Club of Wayne High School, upon

Resolution, with Legal-Style Display

JOB 245·1 Spacing 2 Line 60 Tab 10
Start on line 12 Display as shown

RESOLUTION

THOMAS WALTER HOLCOMB ↓3 13
WHEREAS Thomas Walter Holcomb will 24
retire from the presidency of The Business 32
Club of Wayne High School, upon his grad- 40
uation at the end of this school year, having 50
served as President of the Club for the past 59
eight months; and 62
WHEREAS he has devoted all his skill and 74
much of his time to the development, ex- 82
pansion, and services of the Club, to the end 93
that under his leadership the Club has 101
grown both in its contribution to and in its 110
prestige in Wayne High School; and 117
WHEREAS he has proved himself a gener- 129
ous and most thoughtful leader, a warm 136
and kindly associate, and a person much 144
endowed with the ability to inspire others, 153
to the end that his fellow Members in the 162
Club will always and ever respect his name 170
and record: Therefore be it 176
RESOLVED, that the Officers, Members, 188
and Initiates of The Business Club of 195
Wayne High School do on this eighth day 203
of May, nineteen hundred and *[year, spelled* 212
out], truly compliment and commend for 218
his devotion to them and to the Club and 226
for his leadership in their and in its behalf, 236
THOMAS WALTER HOLCOMB 251

The Business Club
MINUTES OF THE MONTHLY MEETING
April 21, 19--

ATTENDANCE

The regular meeting of The Business Club of Washington
Senior High School was held in Room 212, Jay Anne Carson,
presiding. The meeting began at 2:45 and ended at 3:30 p.m.
All officers, all members except Graham Dorsky, and the
faculty sponsor were present.

OLD BUSINESS

Minutes, in Business-Report (Binder) Style

JOB 245·2 Spacing 1 Line 60 (binding)
Tabs 5, center Start line 7

MINUTES

Personnel Committee 12
MINUTES OF THE SPECIAL MEETING 34
Today's Date 50

53
ATTENDANCE
A special meeting of the Personnel 61
Committee was held in the office of Mr. 69
Quinn, who presided at the meeting. The 77
session began at two o'clock and adjourned 86
at four. All members were there except Ruth 95
Ann Schmidt, who was represented by 102
Helen Sampson. 107

OLD BUSINESS 111
The secretary read the minutes of the 119
last monthly conference, which were ap- 127
proved with one small change that was duly 136
noted. 138
Mr. Stern reported on the survey of 146
ages of company employees; a copy of the 155
survey is attached to and becomes part of 163
these minutes. 168

NEW BUSINESS 172
Mr. Quinn then introduced the need for 181
planning a campaign to let job applicants 189
know of the openings that now exist in our 198
office. Steps for action were planned: Miss 207
Verne will write to all the local training 215
schools, Miss Burns will place ads in the 224
papers, and Mr. Kern will send a note to all 233
members of the staff to ask them to look for 242
job seekers who would fit into our jobs. 251
Respectfully submitted, ↓4 261

Beth Dawson, Secretary 268

a·i·m 32

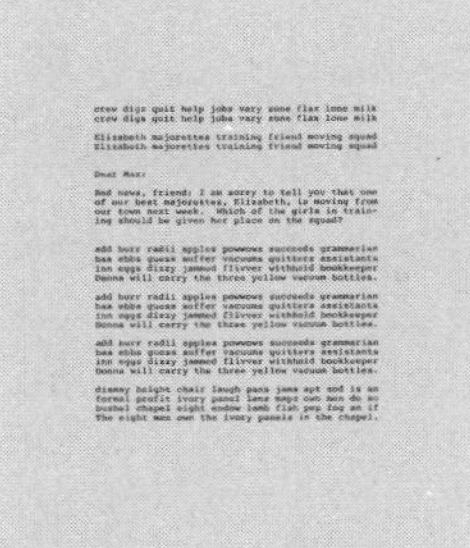

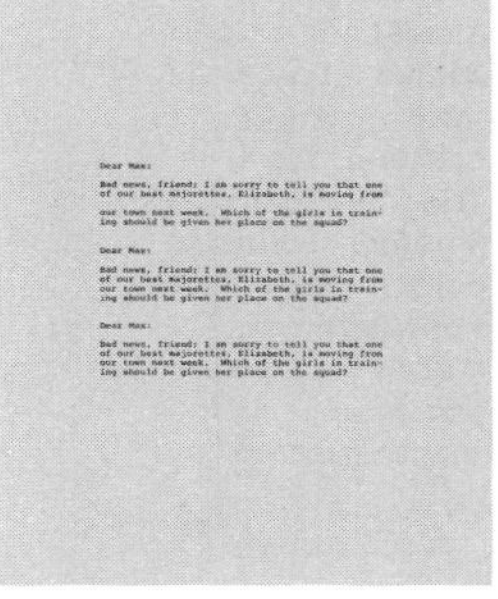

GOALS ⚲ *To type 42 words or more in 2 minutes within 4 errors.* ⚲ *To boost accuracy and speed, practice typing lines 8–15.*

DIRECTIONS *Spacing 1. Line 50.*

WARMUP PREVIEW
2 copies

```
1   crew digs quit help jobs vary zone flax lone milk     10
2   Elizabeth majorettes training friend moving squad     10
    |1   |2   |3   |4   |5   |6   |7   |8   |9   |10
```

PRETEST
1 copy or
2-minute TW

```
3   Dear Max:                                              2
                                                           3
4   Bad news, friend; I am sorry to tell you that one     13
5   of our best majorettes, Elizabeth, is moving from     23
6   our town next week.  Which of the girls in train-     33
7   ing should be given her place on the squad?         ⚲ 42
    |1   |2   |3   |4   |5   |6   |7   |8   |9   |10   SI 1.20E
```

ACCURACY
3|1 copies

```
8   add burr radii apples powwows succeeds grammarian     10
9   baa ebbs guess suffer vacuums quitters assistants     10
10  inn eggs dizzy jammed flivver withhold bookkeeper     10
11  Donna will carry the three yellow vacuum bottles.     10
```

SPEED
3|1 copies

POST-TEST
1·1·2·2 TW
on Pretest

```
12  dismay height chair laugh pans jams apt sod is an     10
13  formal profit ivory panel lens maps own men do so     10
14  bushel chapel eight endow lamb fish pep fog an if     10
15  The eight men own the ivory panels in the chapel.⚲    10
```

a·i·m 33

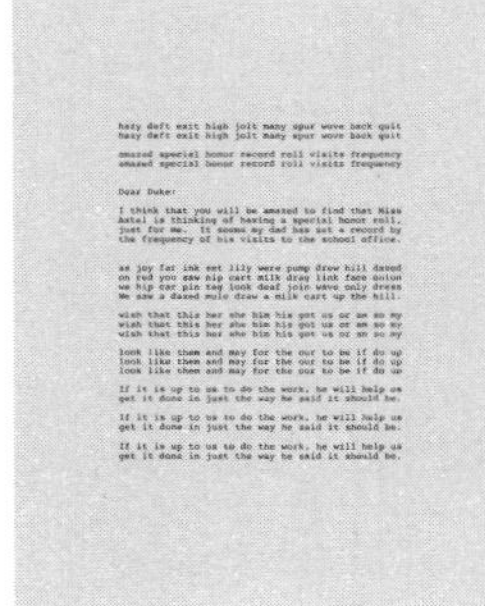

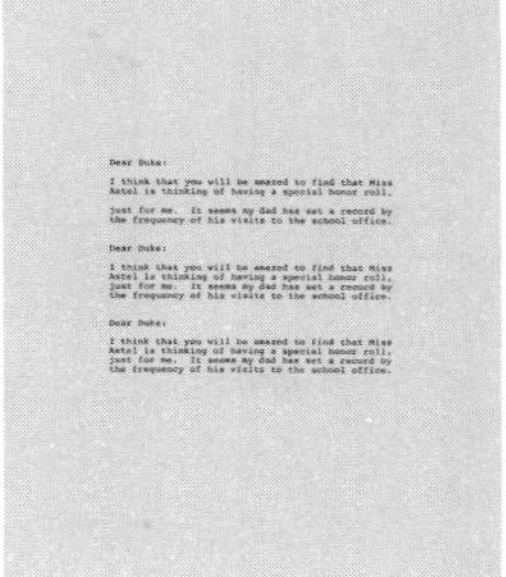

GOALS ⚲ *To type 43 words or more in 2 minutes within 4 errors.* ⚲ *To boost accuracy and speed, practice typing lines 8–14.*

DIRECTIONS *Spacing 1. Line 50.*

WARMUP PREVIEW
2 copies

```
1   hazy deft exit high jolt many spur wove back quit     10
2   amazed special honor record roll visits frequency     10
    |1   |2   |3   |4   |5   |6   |7   |8   |9   |10
```

Signature line begins at center, and witness line runs from margin to center of the area. The witness-to-signing section is called an "acknowledgment." If done by a notary public, it is called a "notarization."

Final page number is typed a triple space under witness line, not at foot of page.

BILL OF SALE [Continued]

Line 10 → IN WITNESS WHEREOF, I have hereunto set my hand and 288

seal the sixth day of May in the year one thousand nine hundred 300

and [year, spelled out]. ↓2 304

↓ Start at center (L.S.) 312

↓2

Sealed and Delivered 316

in the Presence of 320

(L.S.) means "place of the seal." It is typed without a space.

______________________________ 327

↓3

Page 2 of 2 335

Page 2 of a Fully Typed Legal Document: Bill of Sale

JOB 244·1

BILL OF SALE (FORM) Use form on Workbook page 251 or type as a document, like 242·1.

JOB 244·2

BILL OF SALE (FORM) Retype Job 242·1 on Workbook 253, or retype this form like the 243·1 document.

Shown in pica, ¼ reduced

BILL OF SALE

Know all Men by these Presents,

That I, Roy Andrew Harkley, of 297 Eureka Drive, Las Vegas, Clark County, State of Nevada, ---------------------------------- of the first part, for and in consideration of the sum of One Thousand Dollars ($1,000) -------------- -- lawful money of the United States, to me ----- in hand paid, at or before the ensealing and delivery of these presents by Howard Potter & Sons, of 44 Bryce Avenue, Madison, Dane County, State of Wisconsin, -- of the second part, the receipt whereof is hereby acknowledged, have bargained and sold, and by these presents do sell, grant and convey unto the said party -- of the second part, its -- executors, administrators and assigns my working model of a machine to simplify the binding of bristles in the construction of paint brushes. -------------- -- -- -- --

To have and to hold the same unto the said party -- of the second part, its - executors, administrators and assigns forever. And do I for me and my ---- heirs, executors and administrators, covenant and agree, to and with the said party -- of the second part, to warrant and defend the sale of the aforesaid machine ---------------------- hereby sold unto the said party - of the second part, its - executors, administrators and assigns, against all and every person and persons whomsoever.

In Witness Whereof, I - have hereunto set my hand - and seal - the sixth ----- --------- day of March ----- in the year one thousand nine hundred and [year, spelled out]

Sealed and Delivered in the presence of

________________________ ______________________________[L.S.]

Printed Legal Form: Bill of Sale

PRETEST

1 copy or
2-minute TW

3 Dear Duke: 2

3

4 I think that you will be amazed to find that Miss 13
5 Axtel is thinking of having a special honor roll, 23
6 just for me. It seems my dad has set a record by 33
7 the frequency of his visits to the school office. 43

|1 |2 |3 |4 |5 |6 |7 |8 |9 |10 SI 1.26FE

ACCURACY

3|1 copies

8 as joy far ink set lily were pump drew hill dazed 10
9 on red you saw nip cart milk drag link face onion 10
10 we hip car pin tag look deaf join wave only dress 10
11 We saw a dazed mule draw a milk cart up the hill. 10

SPEED

3|1 copies

12 wish that this her she him his got us or am so my 10
13 look like them and may for the our to be if do up 10
14 If it is up to us to do the work, he will help us 10
15 get it done in just the way he said it should be. 20

|1 |2 |3 |4 |5 |6 |7 |8 |9 |10

POST-TEST
1·1·2·2 TW

on Pretest

PREPARE a·i·m WB 15–16

GOALS *To set and clear tab stops. To use the backspace key in centering. To center horizontally each name in a list of names.*

DIRECTIONS *Spacing 1 for drills, 2 for Jobs. Line 50.*

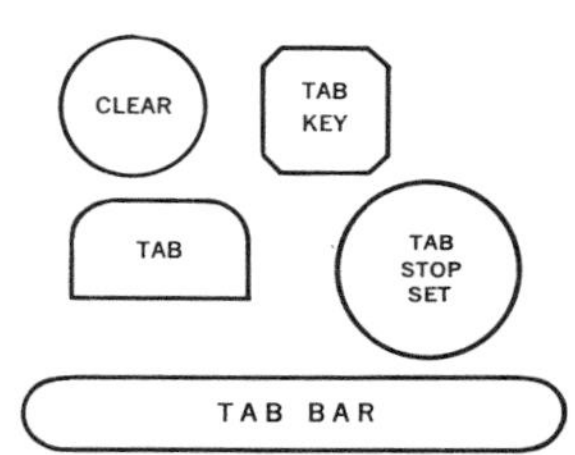

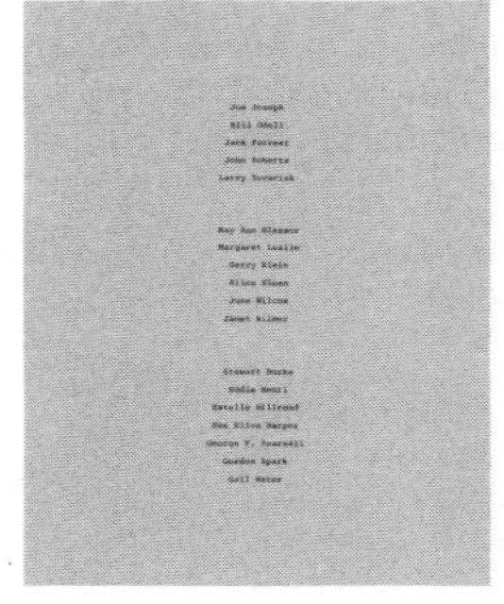

WARMUP PREVIEW

3 copies

1 back dual from high jest lock lazy quip wave next 10
2 Margaret Estelle George Larry Eddie John Bill Joe 10
3 to do so, if it is, in or on, to or of, at or as, 10

|1 |2 |3 |4 |5 |6 |7 |8 |9 |10

TAB STOPS

To make the carriage jump to a selected point and stop there, set a Tab Stop at that point and use the Tabulator for the jumping. Steps:

1. To eliminate any stop that may be in the way, press the All Clear key if your machine has one, or move the carriage to the right margin and then hold down the Tab Clear key as you return the carriage.

2. To set the stop at the point where you want the carriage to stop, move the carriage

JOB 242·1

2-PAGE BILL OF SALE
Paper 8½ by 11, with margin rules
Tabs 10 and center
Spacing 2 Top 2″

JOB 243·1

1-PAGE BILL OF SALE
Paper 8½ by 11, with margin rules
Directions Center entire Bill of Sale on one page, using single-spacing for paragraphs. You can count the Job 242·1 lines.

Shown in pica on 8½ x 11 paper, reduced one-fourth to fit page.

B I L L O F S A L E ↓3 ← Line 13 14

KNOW ALL MEN BY THESE PRESENTS 21

10 → THAT I, Owen Taylor Ardell, of 4811 Montcalm Avenue, 33
Richmond, Henrico County, State of Virginia, of the first part, 45
for and in consideration of the sum of One Hundred Twenty-Five 58
Dollars ($125) lawful money of the United States, to me in hand 70
paid, at or before the ensealing and delivery of these presents 83
by John Lee Guest, of 229 Lanier Drive, Savannah, Chattam County, 96
State of Georgia, of the second part, the receipt whereof is 109
hereby acknowledged, have bargained and sold, and by these pres- 121
ents do sell, grant and convey into the said party of the second 134
part, his executors, administrators and assigns my Ajex Motor 147
Scooter, 1973 model, serial number A-642-57. ↓3 or 4 156

157

TO HAVE AND TO HOLD the same unto the said party of 168
the second part, his executors, administrators and assigns for- 181
ever. And I do for me and my heirs, executors and administra- 193
tors, covenant and agree, to and with the said party of the 205
second part, to warrant and defend the sale of the aforesaid 217
machine hereby sold unto the said party of the second part, his 230
executors, administrators and assigns, against all and every 242
person and persons whomsoever. ↓3 249

Page 1 of 2 [Continued next page.] 256

there and press the Tab Set key.

3. To test the setting, draw the carriage back to the left margin, then press the Tabulator key or bar; hold it down firmly until the carriage stops moving. It should stop at the point where you set the stop.

Practice Set a tab stop at 50, then type your first name three times there, like:

50
Ray
Ray
Ray

TO CENTER HORIZONTALLY

1. Set the carriage at the center (50).

2. Find the backspace key (upper left or right corner of the keyboard). Control it with the nearest finger.

3. Say the strokes (including spaces) to yourself in pairs, depressing the backspace key once after you say each pair. If you have an odd letter left over after calling off all pairs, do *not* backspace for it.

4. Type the material. It should appear in the middle of the paper.

Practice Using double-spacing, center each name in these lists. Leave 5 blank lines above each list. **Check** Letter O should line up in Problem 1, Letter L in Problem 2, and Letter R in Problem 3. If the letters do not line up that way, repeat the list correctly.

CENTERING

Change to Spacing 2

JOB 34·1

Joe Joseph
Bill Odell
Jack Forrest
John Roberts
Larry Tovarisk

JOB 34·2

May Ann Blessor
Margaret Leslie
Gerry Klein
Alice Sloan
June Wilcox
Janet Wilmer

JOB 34·3

Stewart Burke
Eddie Henri
Estelle Hillroad
Sue Ellen Harper
George F. Pearsall
Gordon Spark
Gail Water

 35

GOAL *To block-center a list of names, using backspace key, margin set, and tab set correctly.*

DIRECTIONS *Spacing 1 for drills, 2 for Jobs. Line 50.*

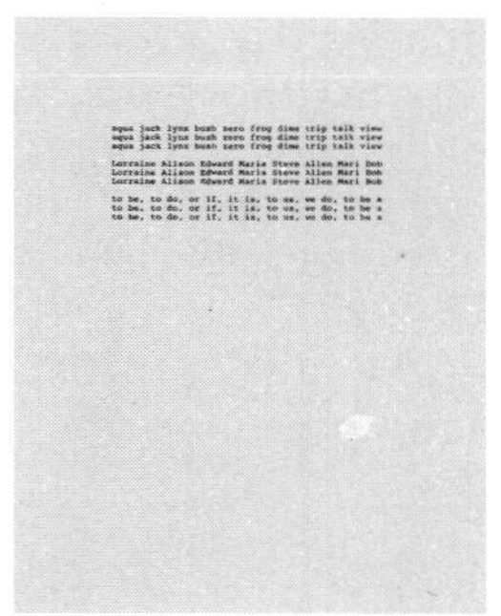

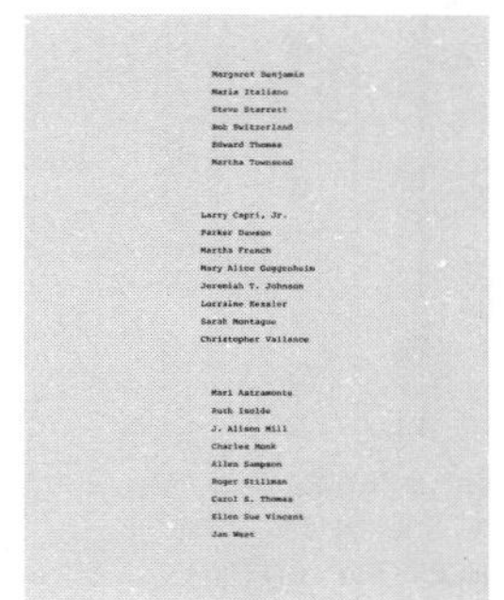

WARMUP PREVIEW

3 copies

```
1  aqua jack lynx bush zero frog dime trip talk view      10
2  Lorraine Alison Edward Maria Steve Allen Mari Bob      10
3  to be, to do, or if, it is, to us, we do, to be a      10
   |1   |2   |3   |4   |5   |6   |7   |8   |9   |10
```

PREPARE a·i·m WB 249–250

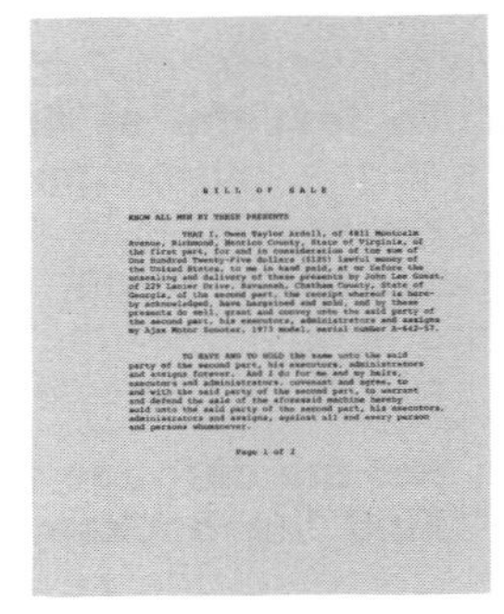

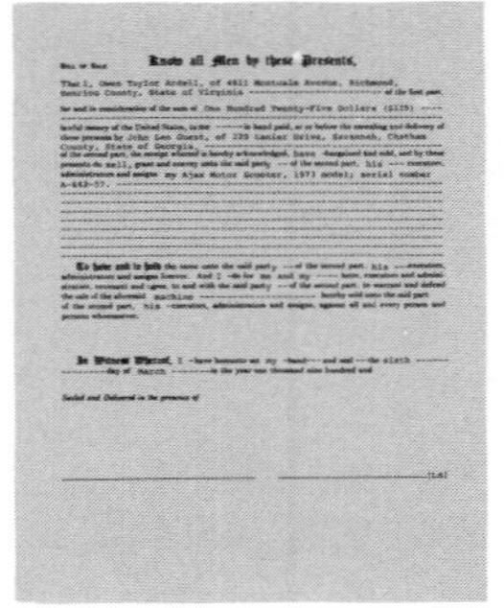

a·i·m 242–245

GOALS ⚲ *To execute legal documents that are wholly typed.* ⚲ *To execute legal documents that are filled-in forms.* ⚲ *To type 200 or more words within 5 minutes and 3 errors on ordinary listen-for-bell copy.*

DIRECTIONS *Spacing 1 for drills, 2 for TW. Line 60 drills, 70 TW with Tab 10. WB 251–254.*

WARMUP REVIEW

2 copies in each a·i·m

```
If he is to do the ad for us, he can do it in a day or two.      12
My speaker, James C. Viking, analyzed a few banquet hoaxes.      12
They were assigned rooms 10, 28, and 39.  We got 47 and 56.      12
|1  |2  |3  |4  |5  |6  |7  |8  |9  |10  |11  |12
```

5-MINUTE TW GOAL WRITING

2 copies within 5 minutes
Daily until 200/3 goal is reached

	1	2
Sometimes one will need to find the exact horizontal center between	16	115
two points or two lines. For example, the margins on a legal document	30	129
are unequal: the left one is one and a half inches wide and the right	44	143
one is just a half inch. Where is the center? To find it, insert the	57	156
paper, observe at what scale points the margin lines fall, then average	72	171
(add and divide by two) the two figures. If the margins are at 20 and	86	185
95, for example, midway between them will be half their total, or 58.	100	200 ⚲
|1 |2 |3 |4 |5 |6 |7 |8 |9 |10 |11 |12 |13 |14		SI 1.35N

LEGAL PAPERS

Read, remember

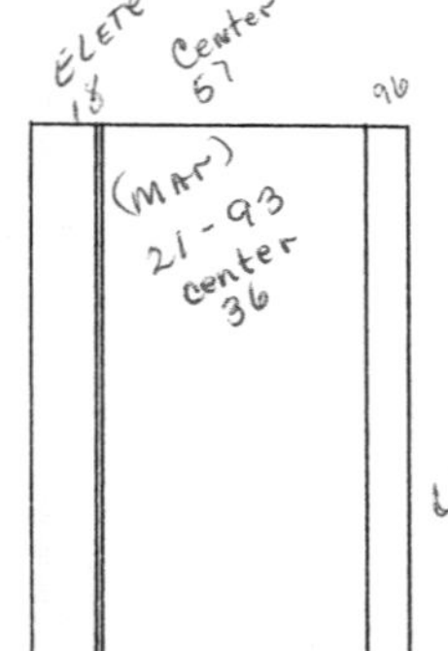

Regular $8\frac{1}{2}$ by 11 paper can be used for legal documents, but offices use $8\frac{1}{2}$ by 13 or 14. A double rule is printed or drawn $1\frac{1}{2}$ inches from the left edge, a single rule $\frac{1}{2}$ inch from the right.

FULLY TYPED DOCUMENTS

The legality of a paper doesn't depend on its typed arrangement, but most legal typists follow these guides:

1. Double-spacing.

2. Ten-space paragraph indention.

3. Margins set 2 or 3 spaces inside the vertical rules, for a 6-inch writing line.

4. Top margin 2 inches on first page, $1\frac{1}{2}$ inches on others, to permit top binding.

5. Page numbers 1 inch from foot of the page, centered between the ruled lines a triple space below the body. Phrasing is "Page 1 of 6," "Page 2 of 6," etc. Omit page number from a 1-page document.

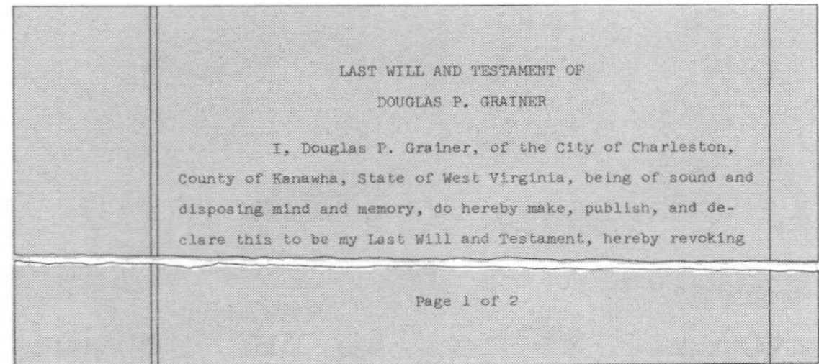

LAST WILL AND TESTAMENT OF
DOUGLAS P. GRAINER

I, Douglas P. Grainer, of the City of Charleston, County of Kanawha, State of West Virginia, being of sound and disposing mind and memory, do hereby make, publish, and declare this to be my Last Will and Testament, hereby revoking

Page 1 of 2

Legal documents are embellished manuscripts.

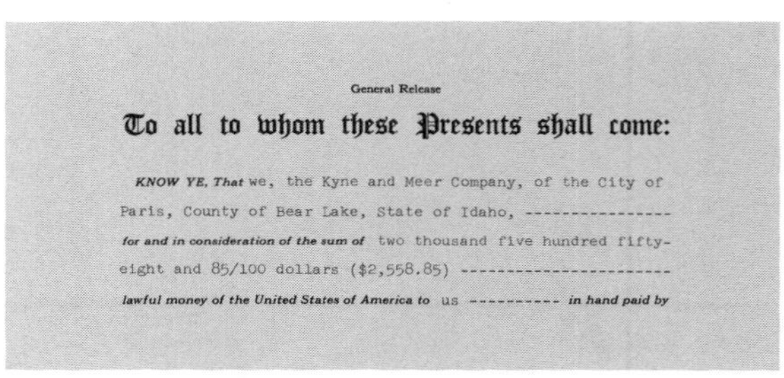

General Release

To all to whom these Presents shall come:

KNOW YE, That we, the Kyne and Meer Company, of the City of Paris, County of Bear Lake, State of Idaho, ---------------- *for and in consideration of the sum of* two thousand five hundred fifty-eight and 85/100 dollars ($2,558.85) ---------------------- *lawful money of the United States of America to* us ---------- *in hand paid by*

Legal forms are easy but require care.

LEGAL FILL-IN FORMS

6. Insertions aligned at bottom of adjacent printed or duplicated words.

7. Blank areas filled in with rows of hyphens. Consistently do or do not leave a blank space before and after hyphen rows.

8. Word insertions separated from preceding printed word by 1 space.

9. Word completions typed as close to the incomplete root word as possible.

10. Margins align with those of form.

Note that erasing is not permitted on any key factor, like dates, addresses, amounts of money, names, and the like.

BLOCK CENTERING

Spacing 2
Tab center

When you have a group of lines to be centered, it is often quicker and easier to center them as a block than as individual lines. Steps:

1. Select the longest line.
2. Backspace to center that longest line.
3. Set left margin at point you reach.
4. Type the block of lines, starting each line at the left margin stop.

Practice Using double-spacing, center each block of names, like the first one is shown. Leave 5 blank lines above each group. **Check** Problem 35·1 aligns at the T, 35·2 at the R, and 35·3 at the S. If the letters in a list do not line up that way, repeat that list.

JOB 35·1

Margaret Benjamin
Maria Italiano
Steve Starrett
Bob Switzerland
Edward Thomas
Martha Townsend

JOB 35·2

Larry Capri, Jr.
Parker Dawson
Martha French
Mary Alice Guggenheim
Jeremiah T. Johnson
Lorraine Kessler
Sarah Montague
Christopher Vallance

JOB 35·3

Mari Astramonte
Ruth Isolde
J. Alison Mill
Charles Monk
Allen Sampson
Roger Stillman
Carol S. Thomas
Ellen Sue Vincent
Jan West

a·i·m 36

GOALS *To type 44 words or more in 2 minutes within 4 errors. To boost accuracy and speed, practice typing lines 9–14.*

DIRECTIONS *Spacing 1. Line 50. Tab center.*

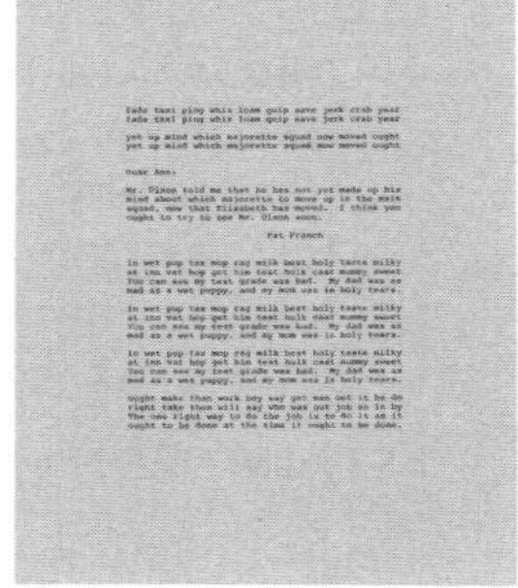

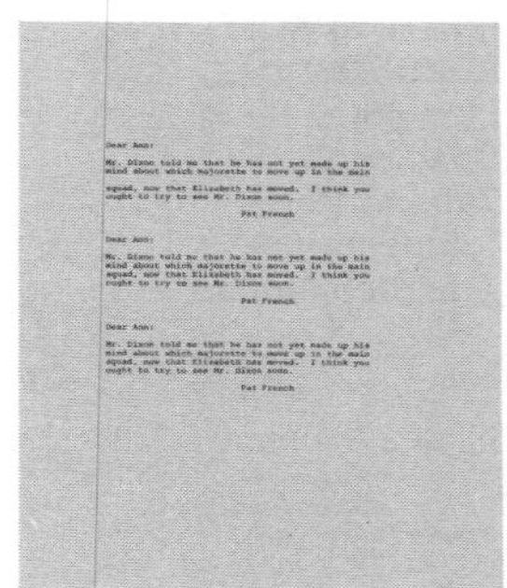

WARMUP PREVIEW

2 copies

1 fade taxi ping whiz loam quip save jerk crab year 10
2 yet up mind which majorette squad now moved ought 10

|1 |2 |3 |4 |5 |6 |7 |8 |9 |10

PRETEST

1 copy or
2-minute TW

At the end of the letter, use the tab to position the closing line. Using the tab is counted always as one word extra in the cumulative word count.

3 Dear Ann: 2
3
4 Mr. Dixon told me that he has not yet made up his 13
5 mind about which majorette to move up in the main 23
6 squad, now that Elizabeth has moved. I think you 33
ought to try to see Mr. Dixon soon. 40
7 41
8 TAB → Pat French 44

|1 |2 |3 |4 |5 |6 |7 |8 |9 |10 SI 1.21E

SPACED LEADERS

"Spaced" leaders (alternate periods and spaces) are slower to type than solid leaders but look better when a table has some very short items in Column 1.

When you determine where the last period in the first line of leaders will fall, note whether it falls in an odd-number or even-number space on the scale; use this fact when you start each subsequent leader line. You will often need to space twice at the start of a leader line to keep all the periods aligned.

a·i·m 240

JOB 240·1

INCOME SUMMARY (WITH SPACED LEADERS)
Line 60
Spacing 1
Tabs 3, 6, and for columns

JOB 240·2

INCOME SUMMARY (WITH SPACED LEADERS)
Line 65
Spacing 2
Tabs 5, 10 (for indentions), and columns

The Business Club Lettershop

INCOME STATEMENT SUMMARY

For School Year Ended May 10, 19-- ↓3

SALES OF GOODS AND SERVICES		$1,375.00
DEDUCT COST OF GOODS SOLD:		
Supplies inventory, school opening . .	$104.75	
Supplies purchased during year	309.35	
Total available for sale	$414.10	
Supplies inventory, school closing . .	213.60	
Cost of supplies sold		200.50
GROSS PROFIT ON SUPPLIES SOLD		$1,174.50 ↓3
DEDUCT EXPENSES:		
Incentive payments to staff	$150.00	
Laboratory space charge by school . .	100.00	
Replacement of damaged typewriters . .	275.45	
Delivery expenses	85.35	
Repair service	25.00	
Total expenses		635.80
NET INCOME FOR SCHOOL YEAR		$ 538.70

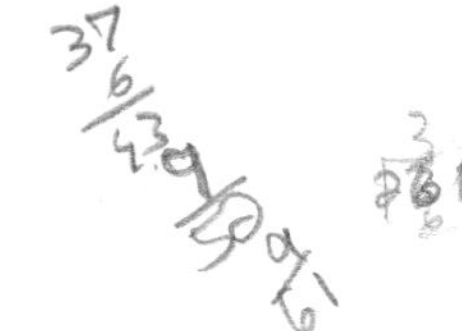

GOAL *To bolster skill (200 or more words in 5 minutes within 3 errors) on fairly easy listen-for-bell copy.*

DIRECTIONS *Spacing 2 for Pretest, Post-test; 1 for others. Line 60 drills, line 70 TW with tab 10. After Warmup below, use timed-writing materials on pages 239 and 240.*

CHECK YOUR HAND POSITION

- Wrists low but not touching machine.
- Wrists so close together you could (but don't!) lock your thumbs as you type.
- Small fingers hugging home anchors.
- Hands flat across the backs.

WARMUP REVIEW

2 copies

1 When did they find that they must have more cash with them? 12
2 The banquet speaker, James Carvings, analyzed a few hoaxes. 12
3 He has 10 or 28. She has 39 or 47. I have 10 or maybe 56. 12
4 Turn to page 239 and use lines 18–32 for a skill drive.

ACCURACY
3|1 copies

9 in wet pup tax mop rag milk best holy taste milky 10
10 at inn vat hop get him test hulk cast mummy sweet 10
11 You can see my test grade was bad. My dad was as 10
12 mad as a wet puppy, and my mom was in holy tears. 20
|1 |2 |3 |4 |5 |6 |7 |8 |9 |10

SPEED
3|1 copies

13 ought make than work boy say get man out it he do 10
14 right take then will say who was out job an in by 10

POST-TEST
1·1·2·2 TW
on Pretest

15 The one right way to do the job is to do it as it 10
16 ought to be done at the time it ought to be done. 20
|1 |2 |3 |4 |5 |6 |7 |8 |9 |10

37

GOALS ◦ *To type 45 words or more in 2 minutes within 4 errors.* ◦ *To boost accuracy and speed, practice typing lines 10–17.*

DIRECTIONS *Spacing 1. Line 50. Tab center.*

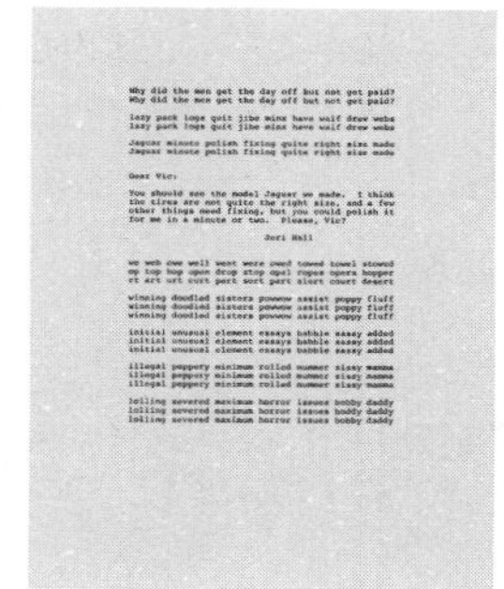
Why did the men get the day off but not get paid?
Why did the men get the day off but not get paid?

lazy pack logs quit jibe minx have waif drew webs
lazy pack logs quit jibe minx have waif drew webs

Jaguar minute polish fixing quite right size made
Jaguar minute polish fixing quite right size made

Dear Vic:

You should see the model Jaguar we made. I think
the tires are not quite the right size, and a few
other things need fixing, but you could polish it
for me in a minute or two. Please, Vic?

Jeri Hall

we web owe well went were owed towed towel stowed
op top hop open drop stop opal ropes opera hopper
rt art wrt curt port sort part alert court desert

winning doodled sisters powwow assist poppy fluff
winning doodled sisters powwow assist poppy fluff
winning doodled sisters powwow assist poppy fluff

initial unusual element essays bubble sassy added
initial unusual element essays bubble sassy added
initial unusual element essays bubble sassy added

illegal peppery minimum rolled summer sissy mamma
illegal peppery minimum rolled summer sissy mamma
illegal peppery minimum rolled summer sissy mamma

lolling severed maximum horror issues bobby daddy
lolling severed maximum horror issues bobby daddy
lolling severed maximum horror issues bobby daddy

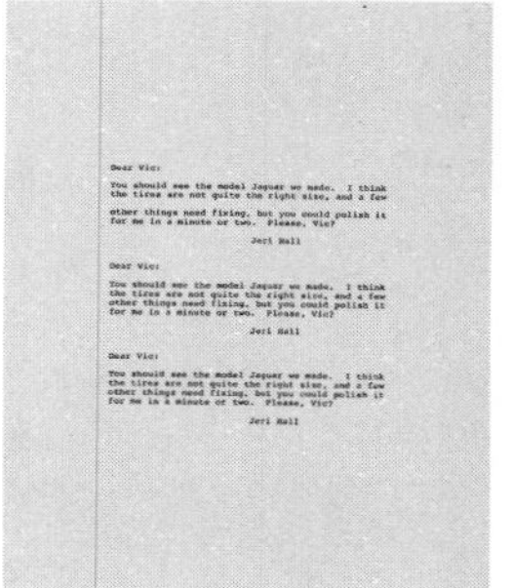
Dear Vic:

You should see the model Jaguar we made. I think
the tires are not quite the right size, and a few

other things need fixing, but you could polish it
for me in a minute or two. Please, Vic?

Jeri Hall

Dear Vic:

You should see the model Jaguar we made. I think
the tires are not quite the right size, and a few
other things need fixing, but you could polish it
for me in a minute or two. Please, Vic?

Jeri Hall

Dear Vic:

You should see the model Jaguar we made. I think
the tires are not quite the right size, and a few
other things need fixing, but you could polish it
for me in a minute or two. Please, Vic?

Jeri Hall

WARMUP PREVIEW
2 copies

1 Why did the men get the day off but not get paid? 10
2 lazy pack logs quit jibe minx have waif drew webs 10
3 Jaguar minute polish fixing quite right size made 10
|1 |2 |3 |4 |5 |6 |7 |8 |9 |10

PRETEST

4 Dear Vic: 2
3
5 You should see the model Jaguar we made. I think 13
6 the tires are not quite the right size, and a few 23
7 other things need fixing, but you could polish it 33
8 for me in a minute or two. Please, Vic? 41
42
9 TAB → Jeri Hall ◦45
|1 |2 |3 |4 |5 |6 |7 |8 |9 |10 SI 1.16E

a·i·m 238

WARMUP REVIEW

2 copies in each a·i·m

A proprietorship inventory withdrawn refunded accounts senior 12

B liabilities membership receivable lettershop payable profit 12

C Why did Professor Black give you a quiz on the major texts? 12

D Repeat the page 239 5-minute TW if you have not made the 200/3 goal.

MORE ABOUT FINANCIAL STATEMENTS

1. If you must spread or condense a financial statement, to match other statements or the margins of other pages, adjust the space after Column 1. The statement below, for example, has been spread to fill a line of 65 spaces.

2. Use leaders to guide the eye over the wide space following Column 1.

3. To locate the start of the money columns and the spot for the last leader in the first row, pivot from the end of the designated line of writing.

4. Use whatever "style touches" your employer prefers or have been used previously: spacing? any all cap lines? totals blocked? subheadings underscored? etc.

JOB 238·1

BALANCE SHEET (WITH LEADERS)
Line 65
Spacing 2

JOB 238·2

BALANCE SHEET (WITH LEADERS)
Line 70
Spacing 1

a·i·m 239

JOB 239·1

RECONCILIATION (WITH LEADERS)
Line 60
Spacing 1

JOB 239·2

RECONCILIATION (WITH LEADERS)
Line 55
Spacing 2

The Business Club 10

SUMMARY BALANCE SHEET 24

For the School Year Ended June 19, 19__ ↓3 49

			51
A S S E T S			58
Supplies inventory	$213.60		73
Cash in bank, lettershop account	36.40		84
Cash in bank, membership account	20.50		96
Accounts receivable, lettershop	32.55		107
Accounts receivable, membership	8.40		123
TOTAL ASSETS		$311.45 ↓3	143
			145
L I A B I L I T I E S			158
Accounts payable, club emblems and cards	$ 18.75		173
Accounts payable, school fund (party)	25.00		184
Dues to be refunded to withdrawn members	2.00		199
TOTAL LIABILITIES		$ 45.75 ↓3	212
			214
O W N E R S ' E Q U I T Y			231
Capital (membership treasury, September)	$ 75.00		246
Capital (lettershop treasury, September)	50.00		257
Capital (gift of senior club members)	10.00		268
Profit from year's club activities	130.70		283
TOTAL OWNERS' EQUITY		265.70	299
TOTAL LIABILITIES AND OWNERS' EQUITY		$311.45	320

Summary Balance Sheet, Double-Spaced, with Totals Lines Blocked in All Capitals

ACCURACY
3|1 copies

10 we web owe well went were owed towed towel stowed 10
11 op top hop open drop stop opal ropes opera hopper 10
12 rt art urt curt pert sort part alert court desert 10
13 hu hug hut hung hurt huff hull chuck shuts chunks 10

SPEED
3|1 copies

POST-TEST
1·1·2·2 TW
on Pretest

14 winning doodled sisters powwow assist poppy fluff 10
15 initial unusual element essays babble sassy added 10
16 illegal peppery minimum rolled mummer sissy mamma 10
17 lolling severed maximum horror issues bobby daddy 10

PREPARE a·i·m WB 17–18

a·i·m 38

GOALS *To center a group of lines vertically and horizontally on a half page.*

DIRECTIONS *Spacing 1. Line 50. Tab center.*

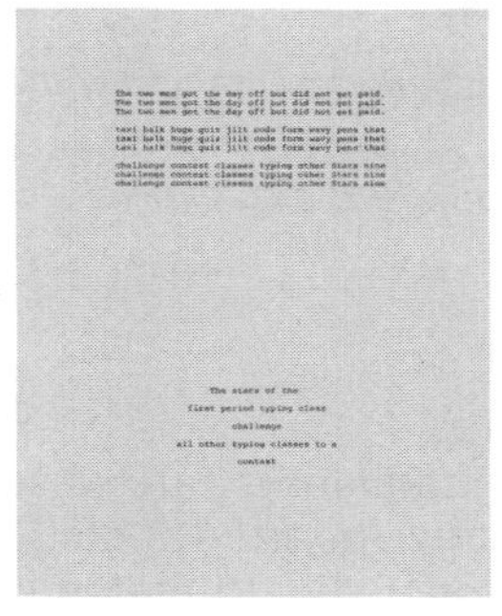

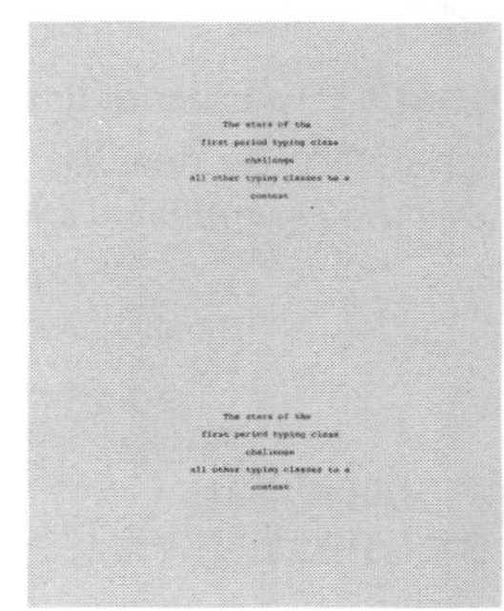

WARMUP PREVIEW
3 copies

1 The two men got the day off but did not get paid. 10
2 taxi balk huge quiz jilt code form wavy pens that 10
3 challenge contest classes typing other Stars nine 10

|1 |2 |3 |4 |5 |6 |7 |8 |9 |10

VERTICAL SPACING

Most typewriters space 6 lines to an inch. Standard typing paper is 11 inches long, so you can get 11 × 6 = 66 lines on a full page or 33 lines on a half page. (Some special and imported typewriters space 5¼ lines to an inch; giving 57 lines, full page and 28 lines, half page.

1	single	double	triple
2	single	------	------
3	single	double	------
4	single	------	triple
5	single	double	------
6	single	------	------
7	single	double	triple

VERTICAL CENTERING

For material to look centered, the top margin must be a line or two narrower than the bottom margin. To center a group of lines and provide this desirable difference:

1. Count the lines (including blank ones) that the material will occupy when typed.

2. Subtract that number from the number of lines you can type on your paper.

3. Divide the difference by 2 (count a fraction as a whole number) to find the number of the line, counting from the top, on which you should begin typing.

Example To center 5 double-spaced lines on a half sheet, you need 9 lines (5 typed, 4 blank); 33 − 9 = 24, and 24 ÷ 2 = 12, the line from the top on which to begin typing.

Practice Center the following display on a half sheet of paper, top to bottom, and when

SPEED SENTENCES

33 The girl got eighty snaps of an authentic whale by the big island. 13.3
34 The six forms the auditor got for the firm may do for the problem. 13.3
35 The man did their work; then they sign for it and make the profit. 13.3
|1 |2 |3 |4 |5 |6 |7 |8 |9 |10 |11 |12 |13

ACCURACY SENTENCES

36 Jinx gave back the prize money she won for her quaint little doll. 13.3
37 The very tough quiz on black pigments taxed a few juniors' brains. 13.3
38 Merek will exhibit a few unique zinc and ivory jewels this spring. 13.3

PREPARE a·i·m WB 245–246

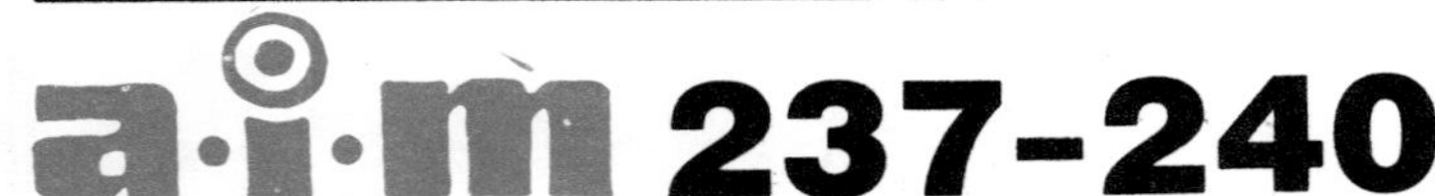

a·i·m 237–240

GOALS *To execute financial statements with and without leaders.*

DIRECTIONS *Spacing 1. Line 70. Warmup on lines 33 and 36 above, then start the assignments shown below. WB 247–248.*

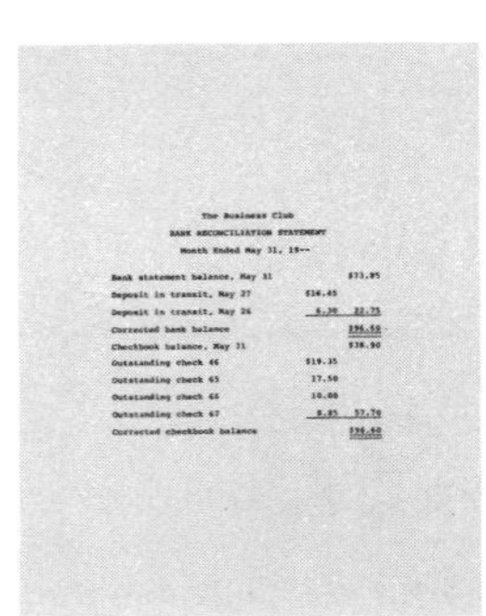

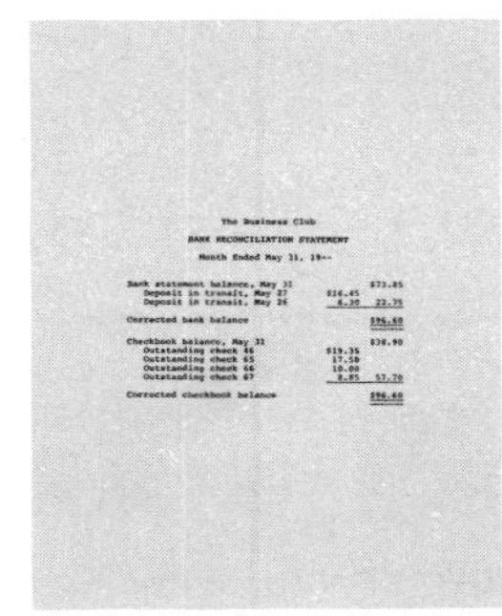

FINANCIAL STATEMENTS

Read, remember

1. Statements are issued on a schedule (monthly, quarterly, etc.). The form of a new statement should match that of the old.

The Business Club

BANK RECONCILIATION STATEMENT

Month Ended May 31, 19--

Bank statement balance, May 31		$73.85
Deposit in transit, May 27	$16.45	
Deposit in transit, May 26	6.30	22.75
Corrected bank balance		$96.60
Checkbook balance, May 31		$38.90
Outstanding check 46	$19.35	
Outstanding check 65	17.50	
Outstanding check 66	12.00	
Outstanding check 67	8.85	57.70
Corrected checkbook balance		$96.60

Bank statement balance, May 31 123456 $16.45 12 $73.85

2. Double-space the heading and follow it by 2 blank lines. Type the name of the statement in all capitals.

3. Leave 6 or more spaces after the first column but only 2 spaces between adjacent money columns.

4. You may type any statement as a table (as here), with a key line guiding the horizontal placement of the columns.

5. Single-space or double-space the table, depending on the employer's preference and the length of the statement.

6. In the body, capitalize consistently, like (a) only the first word of each line or (b) the first and all principal words in each line.

7. Type an underscore line to show addition or subtraction. Type a double line to show totals. For the second line, advance the paper 1/3 line, using the variable spacer in the left cylinder knob.

JOB 237·1 Center this Bank Reconciliation Statement on a full sheet.

JOB 237·2 Type another copy in double-spaced, blocked (no indentions) arrangement. If you have the Workbook, insert the "April file copy" on page 247 or 248 and use it as your guide.

finished, fold the paper, top to bottom, and crease it at the center. The crease should be close to the point indicated by the arrow. Make 3 copies of the assignment.

JOB 38·1

Spacing 2
Tab center
3 copies

```
          The stars of the
      first period typing class
CENTER →       challenge
CHECK
    all other typing classes to a
               contest
```

39

GOALS *To learn use of the Shift Lock and to practice typing in all capitals.*

DIRECTIONS *Spacing 1. Line 50. Tab center.*

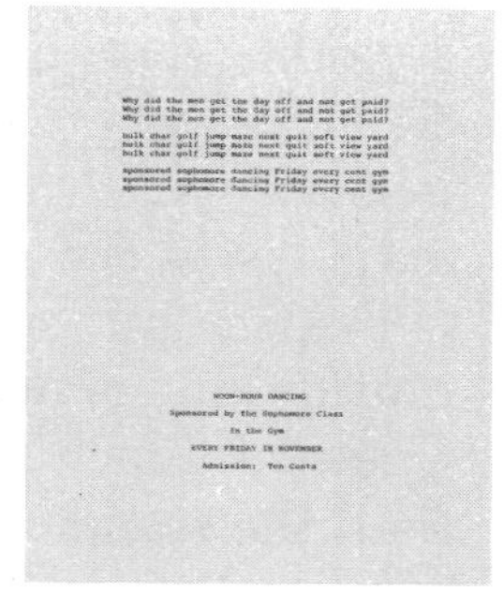

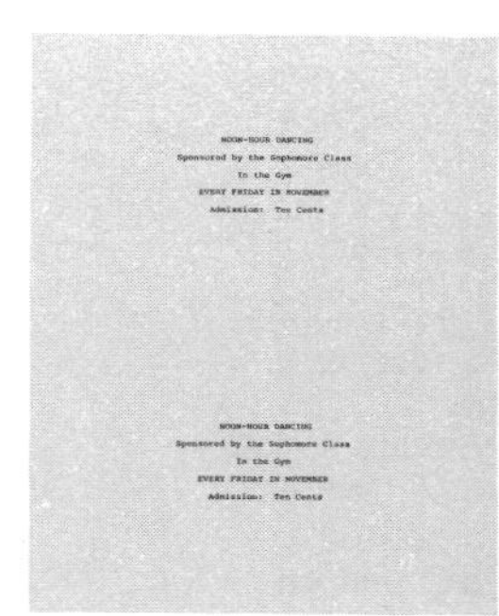

WARMUP PREVIEW

3 copies

```
1   Why did the men get the day off and not get paid?   10
2   bulk char golf jump maze next quit soft view yard   10
3   sponsored sophomore dancing Friday every cent gym   10
    |1   |2   |3   |4   |5   |6   |7   |8   |9   |10
```

TYPING ALL CAPS

1. Press the shift lock. It is above one or both of the shift keys.

2. Type the words to be in all capitals.

3. Release the lock by touching the opposite shift key. (**Caution** Release the lock before typing a stroke that, like a hyphen, cannot be typed as a capital.)

Practice Center the following display on a half sheet of paper, top to bottom, and when finished, fold the paper, top to bottom and crease it at the center. The crease should be close to the point indicated by the arrow. Make 3 copies of the assignment.

JOB 39·1

Spacing 2
Tab center
3 copies

```
          NOON-HOUR DANCING
   Sponsored by the Sophomore Class
→             In the Gym
        EVERY FRIDAY IN NOVEMBER
         Admission:  Ten Cents
```

a·i·m 236

GOAL *To type 200 or more words within 5 minutes and 3 errors on fairly easy listen-for-bell copy.*

DIRECTIONS *Spacing 2 for Pretest, Post-test, 1 for others. Line 70. Tab 10.*

KEEP EYES ON THE COPY—

- When you return the carriage (carrier).
- When you reach for a figure key.
- When you indent for a paragraph.
- When you type intricate material.

WARMUP PREVIEW

2 copies

```
antiquated paragraph executor assigns legal truth after all  12
manuscript tradition majority touches fancy flair typed day  12
```

SKILL DRIVE

See page 214. Note 10-space paragraph indentions

Pretest up to the (2)
Practice 1′ TW on sentences on page 240.
Post-test on lines 3–17.

Most of us have great respect for the law, for we feel that it 14
is complex and full of fine points that might trip us in some way. As 28
a result, there is a tradition, or what amounts to one, that legal 41
typing is very hard. Nothing could be further from the truth. Legal 55
jobs are quite easy to type, much easier, come to think of it, than a 69
majority of the jobs that are typed each day in the office.(2) 80
After all, such documents are nothing more or less than the 93
routine kind of manuscript with some fancy touches to impress people. 107
One such touch is the flair of indenting paragraphs ten spaces rather 121
than the standard five spaces. One more such flair is the antiquated 135
wording that is used time and again, such as "executors and heirs and 149
assigns forever." A wise typist just smiles, knowing that such terms 163
become easy to type when they are typed often enough. After a while, 177
the typist learns how to zip off such turns of words in nothing flat; 191
and there are few numbers for him to type. 200

|1 |2 |3 |4 |5 |6 |7 |8 |9 |10 |11 |12 |13 |14 SI 1.30FE

a·i·m 241 SKILL DRIVE

Pretest up to the (2)
Practice 1′ TW on sentences on page 240.
Post-test on lines 18–32.

An extra legal touch in most states is using vertical lines to show 15 | 215
you where to set the margin stops. The lines are in color in most 27 | 227
cases, giving a bright but stern and official look to the papers on 40 | 240
which they appear. What is typed on the paper is supposed to stay 55 | 255
between the ruled lines without touching either of them; so the smart 69 | 269
typist sets the stops two or three spaces inside them.(2) 80 | 280
But the splendor of this lavish treatment of manuscripts is 93 | 293
dimming. One can find most of these papers in printed form at a dime 107 | 307
a dozen in any stationery shop, and one just inserts a few words here 121 | 321
and there on the form. Gone are the rows of shouting capitals. Gone 135 | 335
are the deep bows at the starts of the paragraphs. Gone are the firm 149 | 349
but colorful rules that fenced in the majestic words. And to replace 163 | 363
them, what have we? We have a printed form, a form full of holes and 177 | 377
gaps in which we insert a word, a name, a date, an amount, and 191 | 391
enough hyphens to fill any extra room left over in that gap. 200 | 400

|1 |2 |3 |4 |5 |6 |7 |8 |9 |10 |11 |12 |13 |14 SI 1.30FE

a·i·m 40

GOALS ⚲ *To type 46 words or more in 2 minutes within 4 errors.* ⚲ *To boost accuracy and speed, practice typing lines 10–17.*

DIRECTIONS *Spacing 1. Line 50. Tab center.*

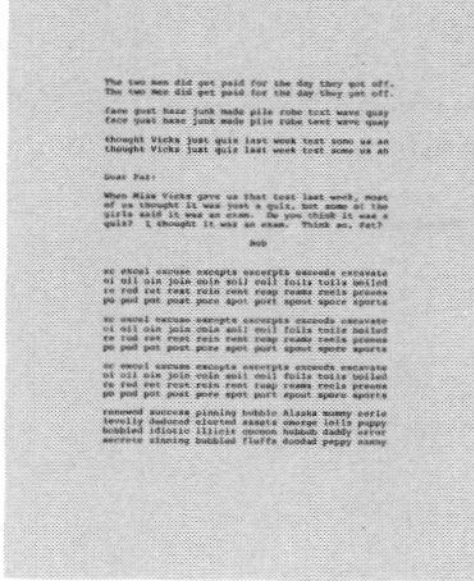

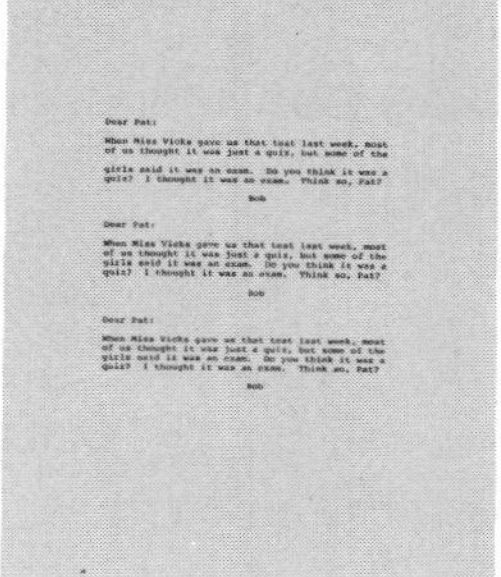

WARMUP PREVIEW
2 copies

1 The two men did get paid for the day they got off. 10
2 face gust haze junk made pile robe text wave quay 10
3 thought Vicks just quiz last week test some us an 10

|1 |2 |3 |4 |5 |6 |7 |8 |9 |10

PRETEST

4 Dear Pat: 2

3

5 When Miss Vicks gave us that test last week, most 13
6 of us thought it was just a quiz, but some of the 23
7 girls said it was an exam. Do you think it was a 33
8 quiz? I thought it was an exam. Think so, Pat? 43

44

9 Bob ⚲46

|1 |2 |3 |4 |5 |6 |7 |8 |9 |10 SI 1.04VE

ACCURACY
3|1 copies

POST-TEST
1·1·2·2 TW

10 xc excel excuse excepts excerpts exceeds excavate 10
11 oi oil oin join coin soil coil foils toils boiled 20
12 re red ret rest rein rent reap reams reels preens 30
13 po pod pot post pore spot port spout spore sports 40

SPEED
3|1 copies on Pretest

14 renewed success pinning bubble Alaska mummy eerie 10
15 levelly deduced elected assets emerge lolls puppy 20
16 bobbled idiotic illicit cocoon hubbub daddy error 30
17 secrete sinning bubbled fluffs doodad peppy nanny 40

a·i·m 41

GOALS ⚲ *To type 47 words or more in 2 minutes within 4 errors.* ⚲ *To boost accuracy and speed, practice typing lines 11–18.*

DIRECTIONS *Spacing 1. Line 50. Tab center.*

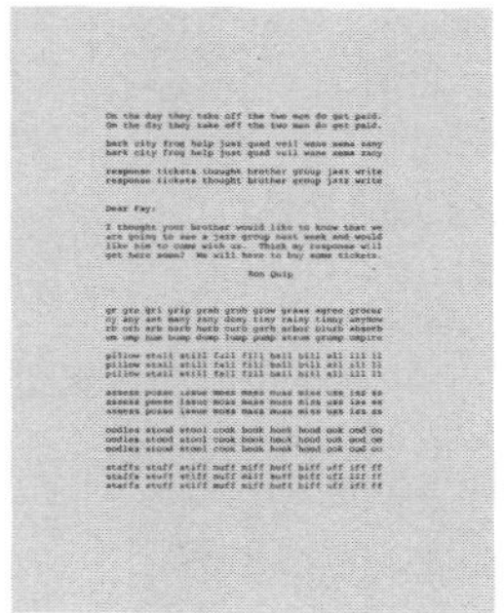

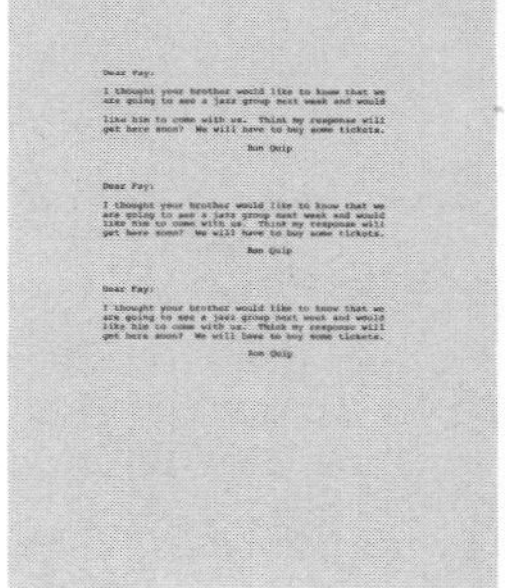

WARMUP PREVIEW
2 copies

1 On the day they take off the two men do get paid. 10
2 bark city frog help just quad veil wane xema zany 10
3 response tickets thought brother group jazz write 10

|1 |2 |3 |4 |5 |6 |7 |8 |9 |10

JOB 233·1

CONTENTS PAGE

Arrange as a 2-column table with leaders. Tabs 5, column 2
Spacing 2 uniformly

TABLE OF CONTENTS ↓3 10

12

1. The Arrangement of Letters 1 21
2. The Arrangement of Manuscripts 9 30
3. The Arrangement of Legal 35
   Documents 15 44
4. The Arrangement of Tabulations 23 52
5. The Arrangement of Financial 59
   Statements 32 67
6. The Arrangement of Printed and 74
   Duplicated Business Forms 39 83
7. The Arrangement of Legal Forms 51 91
8. The Arrangement of Postal Cards 57 100
9. The Arrangement of Index Cards 61 109
   Special Supplement 66 117
   Appendices I–IX 71 126
   Index to the Publication .... 80⊚ 134

8. The Arrangement of Postal Cards 123456 57

JOB 234·1

SCHEDULE

Arrange as a 2-column table with leaders. Tabs 5, center, column 2
Spacing 1, with display blanks

CALENDAR OF ACTIVITIES ↓2 13

Friday Morning ↓3 24

1. Convocation of Delegates 9:00 35

2. Presentation of Reports-- 40
   A. By Secretary-General 9:15 49
   B. By Treasurer-General 9:25 57
   C. By National Organizer 9:35 66

3. Sectional Meetings of Groups 73
   of Regional Delegates 9:45 82
   Group A (East) in Parlor A 88
   Group B (South) in Room 21 95
   Group C (West) in Parlor B 101
   Group D (North) in Room 9 107

4. Reports of Chairmen of the 114
   Groups of Delegates 11:00 123

5. Summary by the President 11:45 133

6. Adjournment for Luncheon .... 12:15⊚ 142

3. SeGroup B (South) in Room 21 123456 11:00

JOB 235·1

DISPLAY MENU

Arrange as a 2-column table with leaders. Tabs 5, center, column 2
Spacing 1 with display blanks

COMPANY LUNCHROOM 10

Menu for April 26 ↓3 24

26

Plate Lunches 41

Chicken Salad, French Dressing, 48
Hot Rolls, Potato Waffles .... .75 57
Hot Roast Beef, Mashed Potatoes, 64
Peas, Coleslaw, Hot Rolls .... .95 ↓3 72

74

Sandwiches 86

Vegetable Salad, Large Roll .... .35 96
Grilled American Cheese, with 102
Tomato Slices .... .40 111
Frankfurter Garni on Roll .... .45 ↓3 119

121

Special Desserts 139

Chocolate Layer Cake .... .15 149
Apple, Peach, or Cherry Pie .... .20 158
Butterscotch-Vanilla Peach Sundae .... .25⊚ 166

JOB 235·2

PROGRAM

Shown on 42-space line; spread to fill 50 spaces. Tabs center, column 2 (from which to backspace column 2 items)

MUSIC WITH THE WENDALLS 14

Marilyn Wendall, Soprano 30
Frank Wendall, Baritone ↓3 45

47

P R O G R A M ↓3 56

58

Student Prince (Selections) .... Romberg 73

The Red Mill (Selections) 88

Desert Song (Selections) .... Romberg ↓3 101

103

Intermission 112

114

Scottish Airs .... Old Ballads 128

Sweethearts (Selections) .... Herbert 144

Famous Lullaby .... Hahn ↓3 162

164

Eight O'Clock, April 26 179
High School Auditorium 194
Sponsored by the Senior Class⊚ 210

PRETEST

4 Dear Fay: 2
3
5 I thought your brother would like to know that we 13
6 are going to see a jazz group next week and would 23
7 like him to come with us. Think my response will 33
8 get here soon? We will have to buy some tickets. 43
44
9 Ron Quip 47

|1 |2 |3 |4 |5 |6 |7 |8 |9 |10 SI 1.09VE

ACCURACY
3|1 copies

11 gr gre gri grip grab grub grow grass agree grocer 10
12 ny any ant many zany deny tiny rainy tinny anyhow 20
13 rb orb arb barb herb curb garb arbor blurb absorb 30
14 um ump hum bump dump lump pump strum grump umpire 40

SPEED
3|1 copies

POST-TEST
1·1·2·2 TW
on Pretest

15 pillow stall still fall fill ball bill all ill ll 10
16 assess posse issue moss mass muss miss uss iss ss 20
17 oodles stood stool cook cook hook hood ook ood oo 30
18 staffs stuff stiff muff miff buff biff uff iff ff 40

a·i·m 42

GOALS ⚲ *To "spread" words.* ⚲ *To center lines with spread words in them.* ⚲ *To produce centered announcements on half sheets.*

DIRECTIONS *Spacing 1 for drills, 2 for Jobs. Line 50. Tab center.*

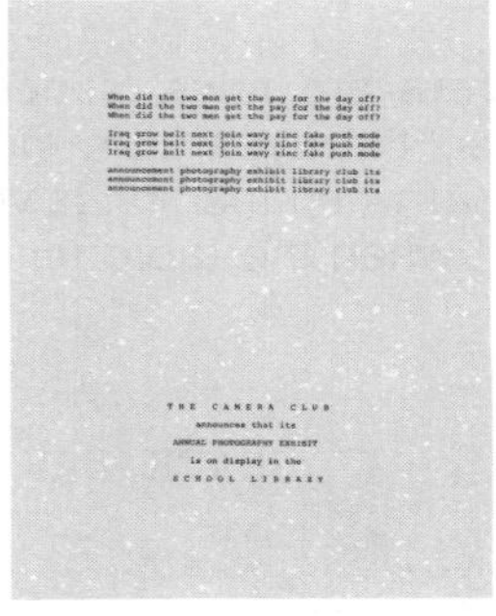

When did the two men get the pay for the day off?
When did the two men get the pay for the day off?
When did the two men get the pay for the day off?

Iraq grow belt next join wavy zinc fake push mode
Iraq grow belt next join wavy zinc fake push mode
Iraq grow belt next join wavy zinc fake push mode

announcement photography exhibit library club its
announcement photography exhibit library club its
announcement photography exhibit library club its

T H E   C A M E R A   C L U B
announces that its
ANNUAL PHOTOGRAPHY EXHIBIT
is on display in the
S C H O O L   L I B R A R Y

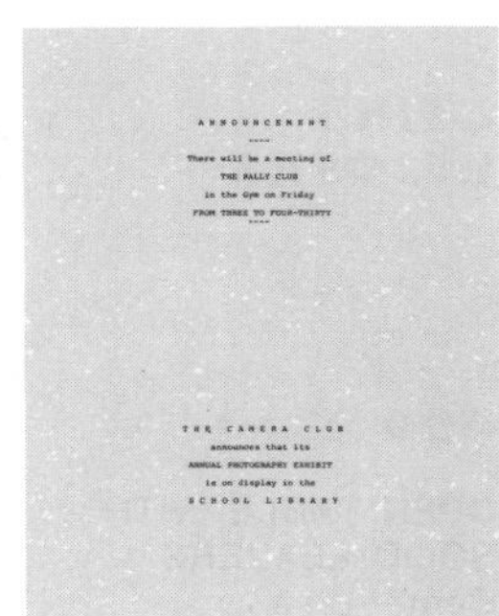

A N N O U N C E M E N T

There will be a meeting of
THE RALLY CLUB
in the Gym on Friday
FROM THREE TO FOUR-THIRTY

T H E   C A M E R A   C L U B
announces that its
ANNUAL PHOTOGRAPHY EXHIBIT
is on display in the
S C H O O L   L I B R A R Y

WARMUP PREVIEW
3 copies

1 When did the two men get the pay for the day off? 10
2 Iraq grow belt next join wavy zinc fake push mode 10
3 announcement photography exhibit library club its 10

|1 |2 |3 |4 |5 |6 |7 |8 |9 |10

SPREAD CENTERING

1. To make a word longer or to display a line more prominently, you may "spread" it by inserting 1 blank space after each letter and 3 blank spaces between words, like:

. . . .
T H E   M E N U

2. To center a spread line, you may use the standard backspacing method: call the letters and spaces in pairs, backspacing from the center once for each complete pair. You would backspace 7 times for this line:

T H E   M E N U

Practice Using double-spacing, center each of these displays on a half sheet, then repeat whichever one you wish.

a·i·m 232-235

GOALS *To use leaders correctly. To type menus, contents, schedules, programs, and other tabular displays that involve using leaders. To type 200 words within 5 minutes and 3 errors.*

DIRECTIONS *Spacing 1. Line 60.*

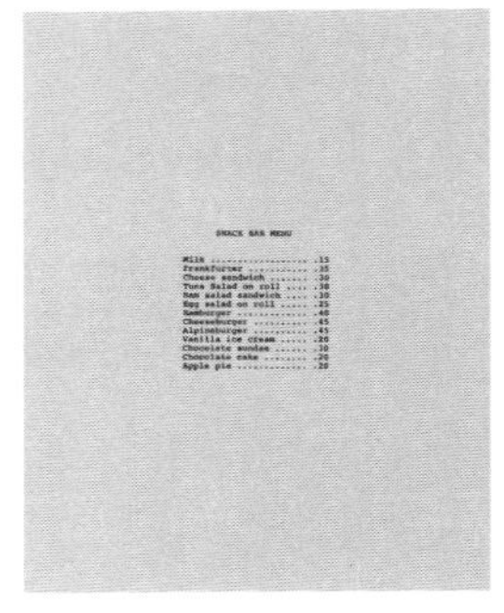

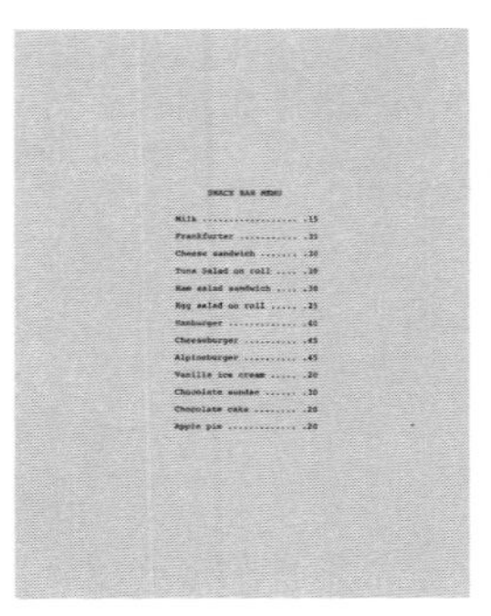

WARMUP REVIEW

2 copies in each a·i·m

Ask the new man who had the red car why you did not get it.	12
Gabe quickly won five more prizes and junked the xylophone.	12
We checked on pages 10, 28, and 39 but did not on 47 or 56.	12

|1 |2 |3 |4 |5 |6 |7 |8 |9 |10 |11 |12

5-MINUTE TW GOAL WRITING

3 copies within 5 minutes in each a·i·m

		1	2	3
Leaders can be solid or spaced. Lines of leaders most		12	79	146
frequently are solid, one period after another, for this is		24	91	158
the quick way to execute them. Spaced leaders have a space		36	103	170
after each period. The leaders in one line must align with		48	115	182
those above and below. This isn't hard to do, but one must		60	127	194
realize that it slows the job.	SI 1.40N	66	133	200

USING LEADERS

Leaders are rows of periods used in tables to lead the eyes from the first column to the next (a) when the first is very irregular in width or (b) when the table must be spread to fill a preassigned line length. A row of leaders consists of at least 3 periods and is always preceded and followed by at least 1 blank space.

Typing a table with leaders involves 5 steps. Apply them, now, to the typing of Job 232·1 at the left.

Step 1. Figure the top margin, to center the table. Insert paper to the proper line and center the title in all capitals.

Step 2. Ignoring leaders for a moment, backspace-center to set the left margin stop and whatever column tabs are needed.

Step 3. Still ignoring the leaders, type the first line in all columns. In the sample problem, you type "Milk" in Column 1 and ".25" in Column 2.

Step 4. Draw the carriage (carrier) back to the first column and carefully insert the row of periods. Remember to leave a blank space before and after the row.

Step 5. Now continue the table, typing the item in Column 1, then looking up as you type leaders, then typing the item in Column 2—line after line. Careful! Looking up for the leaders is slow—and risky!

JOB 232·1

OPEN TABLE WITH SOLID LEADERS
Center on a full page with spacing 1

JOB 232·2

OPEN TABLE WITH SOLID LEADERS
Center on a full page with spacing 2

```
           SNACK BAR MENU ↓3
Milk ................... .25
Frankfurter ............ .50
Cheese sandwich ........ .50
Tuna salad on roll ..... .65
Ham salad sandwich ..... .60
Egg salad on roll ...... .55
Hamburger .............. .75
Cheeseburger ........... .80
Alpineburger ........... .80
Vanilla ice cream ...... .25
Chocolate sundae ....... .50
Chocolate cake ......... .30
Apple pie .............. .30

Tuna salad on roll      .65
                  123456
```

Table with Solid Leaders

PROBLEMS

Center on a half page.
Spacing 2
Tab center

JOB 42·1

A N N O U N C E M E N T

There will be a meeting of

THE RALLY CLUB

→ in the Gym on Friday

FROM THREE TO FOUR-THIRTY◎

JOB 42·2

T H E   C A M E R A   C L U B

announces that its

ANNUAL PHOTOGRAPHY EXHIBIT

→ is on display in the

S C H O O L   L I B R A R Y◎

a·i·m 43

GOALS ◎ *To center displays on full sheets.* ◎ *To use inventive spacing in display.* ◎ *To create and center an original announcement or other display.*

DIRECTIONS *Spacing 1 for drills, 2 for Jobs. Line 50. Tab center.*

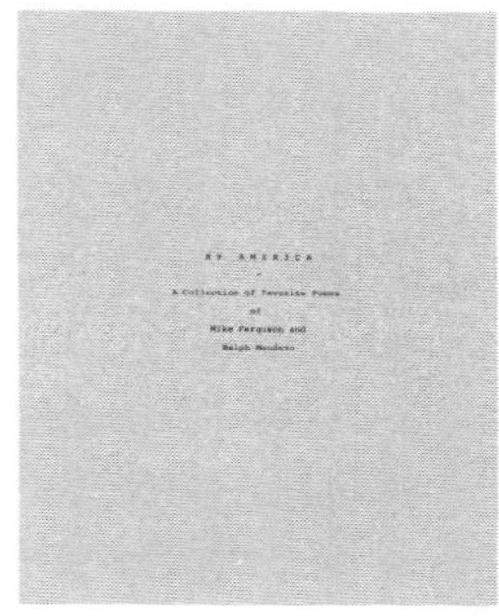

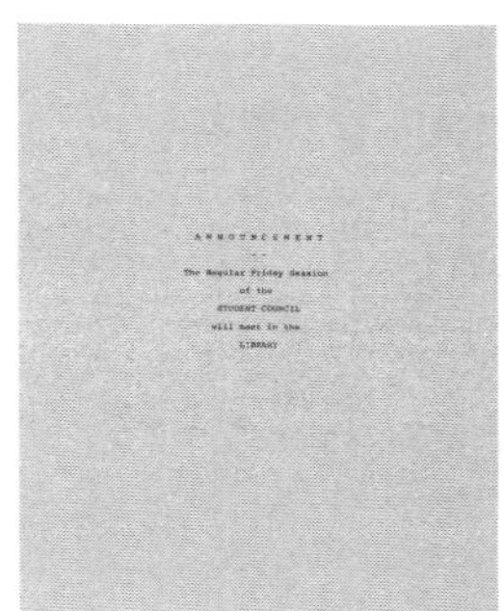

WARMUP PREVIEW

3 copies

1 How soon did the men get the pay for the day off? 10
2 club jeer maze dirk quit hugs oxen pave ways fuss 10
3 collection favorite regular session council poems 10
|1 |2 |3 |4 |5 |6 |7 |8 |9 |10

PROBLEM SOLVING

Spacing 2
Tab center

Practice Center each of these displays on a full sheet, then compose an additional display of your own and center it on a half sheet. If you wish to allow extra space between any lines, do so—but remember to allow for these spaces when you plan the vertical centering.

JOB 43·1

MY AMERICA

—

A Collection of Favorite Poems

→ *of*

Mike Ferguson and

Ralph Mendez ◎

JOB 43·2

ANNOUNCEMENT

— —

The Regular Friday Session

→ *of the*

STUDENT COUNCIL

will meet in the

LIBRARY ◎

a·i·m 231

GOAL *To type 200 or more words within 5 minutes and within 3 errors on fairly easy listen-for-bell copy.*

DIRECTIONS *Pretest, Post-test: spacing 2, line 50, tab 5. Others: spacing 1, line 70.*

REMEMBER THE SCHEDULE:

Warmup on preview words	1′
Pretest (2-minute TW) and score	3′
Drill (six 1-minute TW)	9′
Post-test (5-minute TW) and score	7′
Total time used in session	20′

WARMUP PREVIEW

2 copies

1 determine becoming tidbits hazard lunch take menu help many 12
2 five-inch standard leaders bridge lines will vary with most 12

|1 |2 |3 |4 |5 |6 |7 |8 |9 |10 |11 |12

SKILL DRIVE

See page 214.

The ② represents your 2-minute goal for the pretest.

Pretest up to the ②
Practice 1′ TW on lines 25–27 or 28–30
Post-test on lines 3–24

3 Leaders, as lines of periods are called, are quite a help in many a 15
4 special typing task. Take a menu as an example. At the left is a 28
5 column of food words, and the column will vary in its width as much 41
6 as do the foods in the column; some items are just tidbits, while 55
7 others are whole dinners. At the right you have a column of prices, 68
8 as thin and flat as your wallet will be after your lunch.② 80
9 How can we secure these columns together, so that the eye can zip 94
10 from one to the other? This is where leaders go to work; they bridge 108
11 the gap. 110
12 The first thing you do is determine the line of writing to use. You 125
13 may experiment with lines of various sizes, but most likely you will 139
14 end up with a five-inch line, which is becoming standard for this sort 153
15 of work. After you type an item in Column One, you leave one space 167
16 and then type the leaders. You have to be sure you stop the row of 181
17 periods in time, though, so that you will leave a blank space before 194
18 the amount item in Column Two. 200
19 One way to avoid this hazard is to pivot the last period: you back- 216
20 space from the right margin to the exact spot where the last leader 229
21 should be typed. If Column Two is jagged, as in a program, you have 243
22 to pivot each line; but if Column Two is uniform in size, as in menus, 257
23 you must pivot only the first line because you can make all the other 271
24 lines end even with it. 276

|1 |2 |3 |4 |5 |6 |7 |8 |9 |10 |11 |12 |13 |14 SI 1.25FE

SPEED SENTENCES

25 If the men do their work by six, they may go to the island social. 13.3
26 The profit of eighty bushels of corn may pay for the enamel chair. 13.3
27 He and I go to work for the Lake Island firm by the eighth of May. 13.3

|1 |2 |3 |4 |5 |6 |7 |8 |9 |10 |11 |12 |13

ACCURACY SENTENCES

28 Jack's man excitedly found an old quarter in the woven zipper bag. 13.3
29 Max worked quietly, alphabetizing the census cards for vital jobs. 13.3
30 The wizard quickly made his dogs jump over a pyramid of new boxes. 13.3

 44

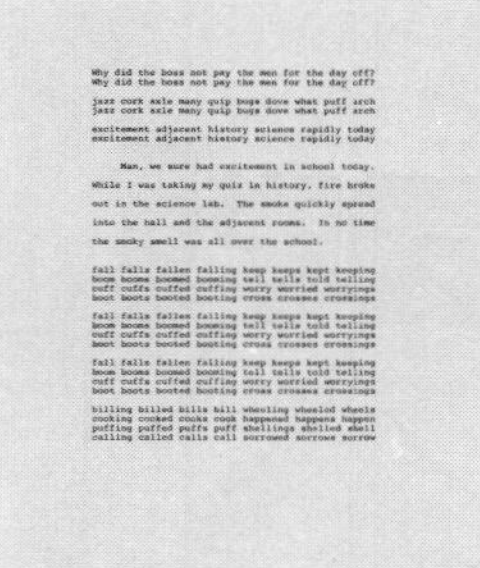

GOALS *To type 48 words or more in 2 minutes within 4 errors. To boost accuracy and speed, practice typing lines 9–16. To learn to tab-indent paragraphs. To use double-spacing in timed writings.*

DIRECTIONS *Spacing 1 for drills, 2 for TW. Line 50. Tab 5.*

WARMUP PREVIEW

2 copies

1 Why did the boss not pay the men for the day off? 10
2 jazz cork axle many quip bugs dove what puff arch 10
3 excitement adjacent history science rapidly today 10
|1 |2 |3 |4 |5 |6 |7 |8 |9 |10

PARAGRAPH STYLES

1. Leave 1 blank line between paragraphs that are single- or double-spaced.

2. The start of a single-spaced paragraph may be indented or blocked (not indented), depending on the task to be done.

3. The start of a double-spaced paragraph should always be indented (as shown below).

4. The standard indention of a paragraph is 5 spaces. It counts as 1 word in timed writtings. The word count assumes you will indent paragraphs when you should indent them.

5. To indent the start of a paragraph, set a tab stop and thereafter use the tabulator. The signal "Tab 5" in the Directions reminds you to prepare to do so.

6. When a timing begins with an indention, as below, have the carriage at the margin. Do not indent until you hear the "Go!" signal. Indenting is part of the timed writing.

PRETEST

4 TAB Man, we sure had excitement in school today. 10
5 While I was taking my quiz in history, fire broke 20
6 out in the science lab. The smoke quickly spread 30
7 into the hall and the adjacent rooms. In no time 40
8 the smoky smell was all over the school. 48
|1 |2 |3 |4 |5 |6 |7 |8 |9 |10 SI 1.26E

ACCURACY

3|1 copies

9 fall falls fallen falling keep keeps kept keeping 10
10 boom booms boomed booming tell tells told telling 20
11 cuff cuffs cuffed cuffing worry worried worryings 30
12 boot boots booted booting cross crosses crossings 40

SPEED

3|1 copies

13 billing billed bills bill wheeling wheeled wheels 10
14 cooking cooked cooks cook happened happens happen 20
15 puffing puffed puffs puff shellings shelled shell 30
16 calling called calls call sorrowed sorrows sorrow 40

POST-TEST 1·1·2·2 TW

on Pretest

Overview

In Part Eleven you will hold tight on your accuracy control while pushing your speed up one more word a minute for 5 minutes. You will also learn to use leaders in tabular display and in financial statements and to type basic kinds of legal manuscripts.

Skill Your goal will be to type with no more than 3 errors while working at 40 wam for 5 minutes. Four a·i·m sessions will be focused on helping you meet this objective.

Leaders Leaders are rows of periods or (in legal documents) hyphens that lead the eye from one place to another. Leaders are used in menus, program listings, tables of contents, and other kinds of tabular display. They are also used in balance sheets, income summaries, and other accounting statements. You will type many Jobs involving the use of leaders.

Legal Legal documents, like wills and bills of sale, may be elaborate manuscripts (with streams of all caps, deep paragraph indentions, and so on) or fill-in forms. You will type some of these in Part Eleven. You will also type similar documents (like resolutions) that are not legal documents, strictly speaking, but are arranged like them for sheer impressiveness.

Performance Goals

When you complete the 20 a·i·m sessions in Part Eleven and take the test on pages 249–250, you should be able to demonstrate as follows:

1. Technicalities You will score 90 or more percent correct on an objective test covering the technical information introduced in Part Eleven (plus a review of previous instruction, too).

2. Production Working from a rough draft, you will execute a financial statement (an expense summary) with leaders; and working from complete but unarranged material, you will type in correct legal style a formal resolution.

3. Skill You will type at least 200 words in 5 minutes (225 or 230 is more likely!) within 3 errors on narrative paragraph material whose line endings you will have to determine for yourself.

Routines and Procedures

You will continue the skill-drive routine that you began in Part Ten: the 2-minute pretest, then 1-minute writings on either speed sentences or accuracy sentences—depending on the number of errors in your pretest—and then a 5-minute TW to confirm the gains you have made in skill.

You should take at least one 5-minute TW daily while working in Part Eleven if you are not able to achieve the 200/3 goal (200 words within 3 errors) for 5 minutes, using paragraphs provided for the purpose.

You will spend more time on production jobs in Part Eleven: the program is arranged for you to follow each skill a·i·m with a cluster of four production a·i·m assignments on some one kind of production work.

PREPARE a·i·m WB 21–22

 45

GOALS *To type 49 words or more in 2 minutes within 4 errors. To boost speed and accuracy, practice typing lines 10–18. To learn how to make line-ending decisions.*

DIRECTIONS *Spacing 1 for drills, 2 for TW. Line 50. Tabs 5 (spaces in from left margin), center.*

HAND POSITION

- Wrists low but not touching the typewriter.
- Wrists close but not touching.
- Fingers curled, almost clenched.
- Hands flat across the backs.

WARMUP PREVIEW

2 copies

```
1   The fog may help the two men who came on the jet.      10
2   A quick tally shows that taxi drivers whiz along.      10
3   surprise exciting Jenkins getting grade best ever      10
    |1   |2   |3   |4   |5   |6   |7   |8   |9   |10
```

MARGIN BELL

A bell rings when the carriage is a few spaces from the right margin stop. For example, if you want lines to end near 75 and so have set the margin stop at 80, the bell rings when the carriage gets to 72 or 73. [**Check your machine** How many strokes must you type after the bell rings before you reach the desired line-ending point?]

When the bell rings, end the line as near the desired ending point as you conveniently can, preferably without word divisions. Here are some typical line-ending decisions:

BELL ↓ DESIRED ENDING ↓ ↓ LOCK	RETURN CARRIAGE AFTER TYPING
I realize their.	realize
Now, we must be.	we
possibility you.	possibility
a philosophical.	philo-

PRETEST

This short note is shown to you on a 60-space line. You are to type it on a 50-space line and decide how to end each line. If you do so correctly, all full lines will end even.

Try to type the whole note (including the tab at the start of the first paragraph and the two tabs to the signature) without looking at the machine, your fingers, or the paper.

Spacing 2. Tabs 5, center.

```
4   Dear Vic:                                                        2
5        This has been a dozen days in one.  The main exciting      14
6   thing in it has been my getting the best grade in the science   26
7   quiz, which was as much of a surprise to me as it was to Mr.    38
8   Jenkins.  Did you ever do that?                                 45
9                             Bob Polk                              49
    |1   |2   |3   |4   |5   |6   |7   |8   |9   |10   |11   |12   SI 1.16E
```

TEST 10-D

PAGE 1 OF A BUSINESS REPORT

Spacing 1
Start line 13
Refer page 223.
Note: Be sure to underscore all material shown here in italic (slanting) printing.

THE HIGH COST OF TYPEWRITER REPAIRS 22

Chester Dailey, Manager 29
Office Services Department 36
Fourth Floor, Room 411 44

Today's Date 59

EXTENSION 1212 63

As every typist in the company knows, you dial 1212 when 75
you need first aid for your typewriter. *It is a number that is used* 100
too often. Our typists average twice as many service calls as do 117
typists in other companies our size. 125

Some of the calls would seem funny if they were not so 151
ridiculous. Nine typists pressed the ratchet release and then 163
called us to report that the cylinder didn't click anymore. Four 177
electric typists forgot to check that the electric cord was firmly 190
in the wall socket. Seven girls tried to put Underwood ribbons on 203
Royals. 206

These calls were in February. We asked our repairmen to 219
list their March calls. *Here are the results:* 238

FACTS AND FIGURES 243

One call in every five means ribbon trouble. It is not clear 273
why typists have trouble putting on new ribbons, but they do. 286
They twist ribbons, put spools backwards in their sockets, use 299
the wrong kind of ribbon, etc. 306

One call in every three means machine abuse. Typebars are 336
bent by carelessness in untangling key jams. The margin stops 349
are broken by heavy carriage returns. Banging thumbs break 361
space bars. 364

Two calls in every five mean improper care. Keys stick 393
when grit and eraser crumbs fill in the slots. The carriage or 406
carrier sticks when too much oiling has gummed the rails. 419

Only one call in twenty is the machine's fault. Parts break 451
and springs and screws loosen and fall out, but only one call in 464
twenty is due to such a reason. 470

|1 |2 |3 |4 |5 |6 |7 |8 |9 |10 |11 |12 |13 SI 1.40N

IMPROVEMENT PRACTICE

2 copies

As you type each line, insert a hyphen into each word as shown in the first line of each group. Try to do this without looking up from the copy.

```
10   shrug-ging trot-ting swim-ming ship-ping win-ning     10
11   strapping shopping stunning stepping padding          10
12   scrubbing slugging chopping spinning putting          10

13   stress-ing spill-ing swell-ing chill-ing yell-ing     10
14   squalling shelling quelling dressing fussing          10
15   appalling smelling pressing spelling willing          10
```

POST-TEST 1·1·2·2 TW

on Pretest, page 49

```
16   shud-der sput-ter let-ter mid-dle sup-per rub-ber     10
17   stubble clipper winner sorrow ladder dinner           10
18   shipper clutter nibble bitter runner borrow           10
```

PREPARE a·i·m WB 23–24

 46

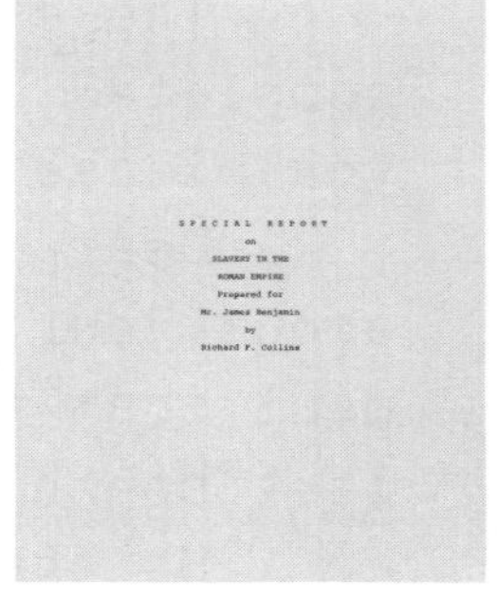

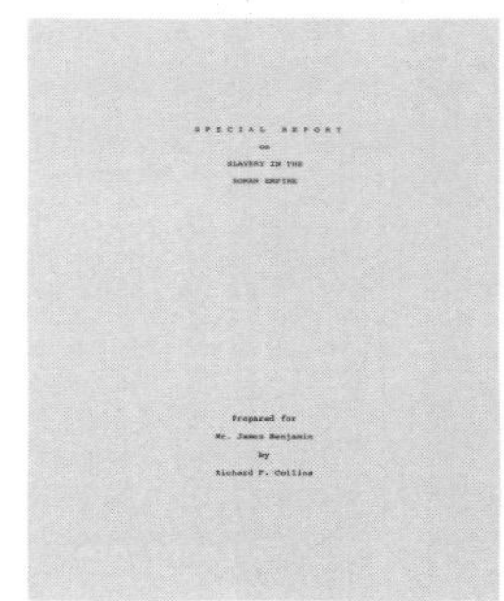

GOALS ◎ *To center displays on both half and full sheets.* ◎ *To study the rules of word division.*

DIRECTIONS *Spacing 1. Line 50. Tab center.*

WARMUP PREVIEW

3 copies

```
1    How can the fog help the men who came on the jet?     10
2    The camera showed quick taxi drivers whizzing by.     10
3    Benjamin Richard slavery special Empire Roman Mr.     10
     |1   |2   |3   |4   |5   |6   |7   |8   |9   |10
```

WORD BUILDING

2 copies, type with hyphens as in line 4.

```
4    excite-ment state-ment ship-ment ele-ment ce-ment     10
5    management merriment filament comment lament          10
6    instrument amusement document ferment foment          10
```

DIVISION RULES

ABSOLUTE RULES

1. Do not divide a word pronounced as one syllable (shipped), any contraction (can't, shouldn't), or any abbreviation (U.S.N.R. or UNICEF).

2. Divide only between whole syllables. If uncertain where a syllable ends, check in a dictionary. Some words are tricky; for example, it's "prod- uct," not "pro- duct."

3. Leave on the upper line a syllable of at least 2 letters; and carry to the next line a syllable of (a) at least 3 letters or (b) 2 letters and a punctuation mark. Thus, "an- swer" and "teach- ers" but not "a- ground" or "heart- y."

PREFERENTIAL RULES

Any division fulfilling rules 1–3 is acceptable. When space allows alternative choices, rules 4–8 can be used as guides.

a·i·m 229-230

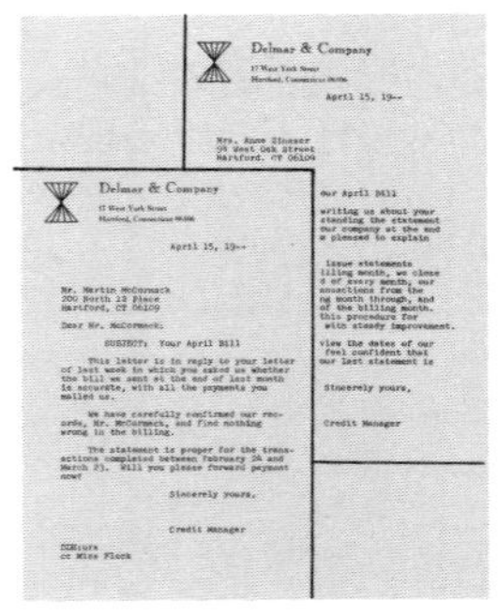

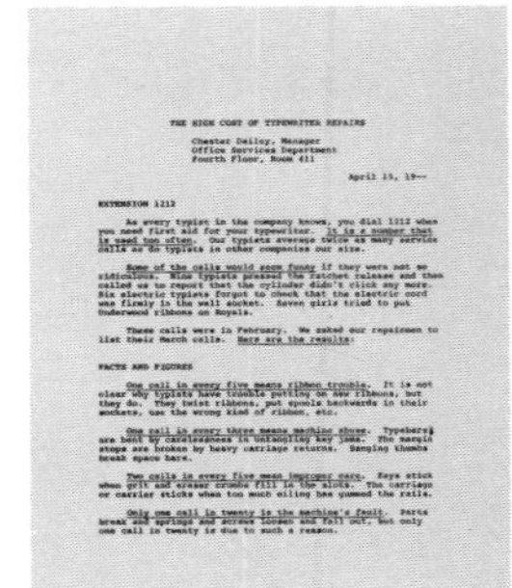

GOALS *To type 195 or more words in 5 minutes within 3 errors on facsimile copy of average difficulty. To produce semiblocked letters, with a subject line and a cc notation, on baronial stationery. To execute a page of business report in "newsletter style" from a revised draft. To score 90% or higher on an objective test on technical information in Part Ten.*

DIRECTIONS *Warmup page 231. WB 241–244.*

TEST 10-A

Take a general information test. It may be the one on Workbook 241–242 or a similar test that your teacher may give you or may dictate to you.

TEST 10-B

5-MINUTE TW
Line 50
Tab 5
Spacing 2

```
     Dear Mr. McCormack:  This letter is in reply     10
to your letter of last week in which you asked us     20
whether the bill we sent at the end of last month     30
is accurate, with all the payments you mailed us.     40
     We have carefully confirmed our records, Mr.     50
McCormack, and find nothing wrong in the billing.     60
     The statement is proper for the transactions     70
completed between February 24 and March 23.  Will     80
you please forward payment now?  Sincerely yours,     90
     Dear Mrs. Zinsser:  Thank you for writing us    100
about your difficulty in understanding the state-    110
ment that we mailed to your company at the end of    120
last month.  I am pleased to explain the routine.    130
     So that we may issue statements promptly for    140
each billing month, we close our books on the 23d    150
of every month; our statement covers transactions    160
from the 24th of the preceding month through, and    170
including, the 23d of the billing month.  We have    180
been using this procedure for about seven months,    190
with steady improvement.                             195
     If you will review the dates of our invoices    205
to you, we feel confident that you will find that    215
our last statement is in order.  Sincerely yours,    225
|1   |2   |3   |4   |5   |6   |7   |8   |9   |10    SI 1.40N
```

TEST 10-C

SEMIBLOCKED LETTERS
Workbook 243

Both Letters Insert centered line, **SUBJECT: Your April Bill,** and a **"cc"** note for **Miss Fleck.** Letter is from **Credit Manager (DDH).** Today's date.

Letter 1 (1–9) Mr. Martin McCormack, 200 North 12 Place, Hartford, CT 06109.

Letter 2 (10–23) Mrs. Anne Zinsser, 94 West Oak Street, Hartford, CT 06109

4. Divide compounds at their point of compound (if a hyphen is there, do not add another hyphen). "Father- in-law" is better than "Fa- ther-in-law." "Under- stand" is better than "Un- derstand."

5. If two accented vowels occur together, divide between them. "Radi- ation" is better than "Radia- tion."

6. If a one-letter syllable occurs in the middle of a root word, divide after it. "Sepa- rate" is better than "Sep- arate."

7. Avoid breaking compound prefixes and suffixes. "Intro- duce" is better than "In- troduce," and "Possibil- ities" is better than "Possibili- ties."

8. Avoid separating elements that must be read as units, such as dates (May 3), amounts ($10 million or $10,000,000), titles and names (Mr. Hall), reference numbers (page 54, Unit 6), and so on.

CENTERING

46·1 Center this 8-line display on a full sheet. Use whatever display procedures and spacing you wish, but be sure to center the display vertically.

46·2 At the left edge of a sheet of paper, lightly crease or mark the middle of the paper. Then center lines 7–10 in the top half (top 33 lines) and 11–14 in the bottom half (bottom 33 lines).

Suggestion Substitute your name for that of Richard F. Collins.

7 SPECIAL REPORT
8 on
9 SLAVERY IN THE
10 ROMAN EMPIRE
11 Prepared for
12 Mr. James Benjamin
13 by
14 Richard F. Collins

 47

GOALS *To center a grouped display. To block-center a grouped display. To modify an announcement.*

DIRECTIONS *Spacing 1 for drills, 2 for displays. Line 50. Tab center.*

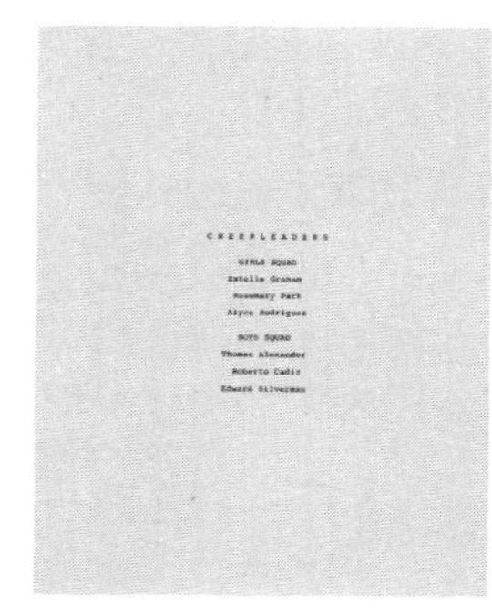

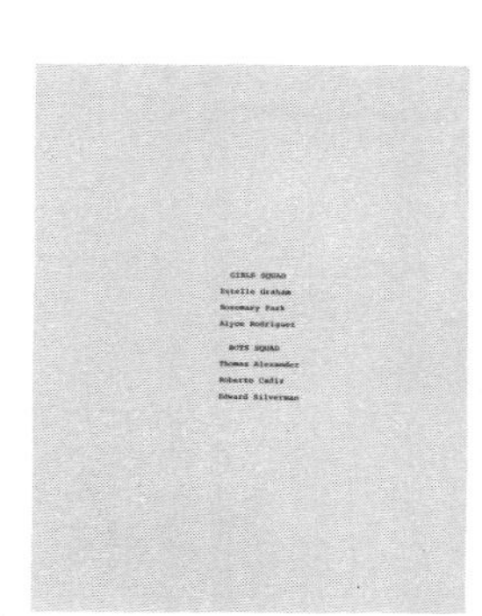

WARMUP PREVIEW

2 copies

```
1  The fog did not help the men who came on the jet.       10
2  We saw taxi drivers quickly whizzing by the Home.       10
3  Rosemary Estelle Roberto Edward Thomas Alyce Park       10
   |1   |2   |3   |4   |5   |6   |7   |8   |9   |10
```

WORD BUILDING

3 copies

Type with hyphens, as in line 4.

```
4  demoli-tion commo-tion trac-tion suc-tion ac-tion       10
5  aspiration reduction position mention notion            10
6  resolution promotion fraction section lotion            10
7  exhalation partition sanction portion potion            10
```

TEST PREP 4

PAGE ONE OF A
BUSINESS REPORT
Line 6 inches
Spacing 1
Tabs 5, center
Review page 223

line 13

SPECIAL LETTER PROBLEMS 18

19

Block Center

Kay Anne Weller, Counselor 36
Office Placement, Inc. 41
Des Moines, Iowa 50311 47

48

April 29, 19-- 51

52

BULLETIN TO CLIENTS 56

SS

You are not likely to be frowned at for what you do to normal 71

employment

letters. After all, your test proved that you could manage them. 86
It is the special letters, ~~with problems in them~~ that will spotlight 113
your performance on the job. the problem ones, 130

132

BEING
~~WHEN TO BE~~ FORMAL 134

expect to
For example, your boss will ~~require~~ ~~that~~ you know when you 148
should give a letter the formal look (you transfer the inside ad- 172
dress to the foot of the letter, remember? 181
Answers: ~~Make it formal~~ when the letter is to your boss's bosses 193
. . . or to someone who is much older than he is . . . to a public 207
figure or churchman ~~official~~ . . . in a note of condolence or ~~sympathy or~~ of congratula- 220
tions to someone woh is on ~~his~~ the staff. 228

230

VERY, VERY SHORT 233

And what do you do when a letter is very short? You know the 258
kind: ~~your employer dictates:~~ "Dear Sir: Thanks for telling me all 267
about your insurance plans. I don't want any. Yours truly." 280
Possibilities: ~~you can investigate:~~ Use banonial ~~(5½ by 8½)~~ 288
paper; most ~~modern~~ offices have some--this is what ~~that size paper~~ it 297
is for . . . ~~you might~~ double-space the whole letter from address 308
to enclosure note (but if you do this you must indent the para- 318
graphs). 322
And don't for get the most use ful of all the "tricks of the 340
trade," the blanace line. That's the line ~~that~~ you ~~compose and~~ 353
type low on the page when you find your work looks too high on the 369
page ~~and you want to do something about it~~. 382
Run in If a letter is so short that it is ~~much~~ too high, ~~when you type~~ 392
~~it,~~ drop the reference ~~initials or enclosure or other final~~ lines 397
as far down ~~the page~~ as you want them to be. ~~to balance the page.~~ 404

331

339

... or allow two blank lines each place you would normally leave one blank line.

SI 1.36N

CENTERING

Spacing 2

47·1 Center a double-spaced copy of this display on a full sheet, with each line centered horizontally. Allow one extra blank line between lines 8–9 and between lines 12–13.

47·2 Center another double-spaced copy of this display, this time *block centering* the listings in the manner you did in problem 35·1, page 41.

47·3 Repeat either 47·1 or 47·2, adding your name in the appropriate squad. Insert your name in the proper place for the alphabetic sequence.

8 C H E E R L E A D E R S ↓3

9 GIRLS SQUAD

10 Estelle Graham

11 Rosemary Park

12 Alyce Rodriquez ↓3

13 BOYS SQUAD

14 Thomas Alexander

15 Roberto Cadiz

16 Edward Silverman

a·i·m 48

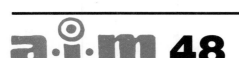

GOALS *To type 50 words or more in 2 minutes within 4 errors. To improve typing skill in word division by typing lines 9–16.*

DIRECTIONS *Spacing 1 for drills, 2 for TW. Line 50. Tab 5.*

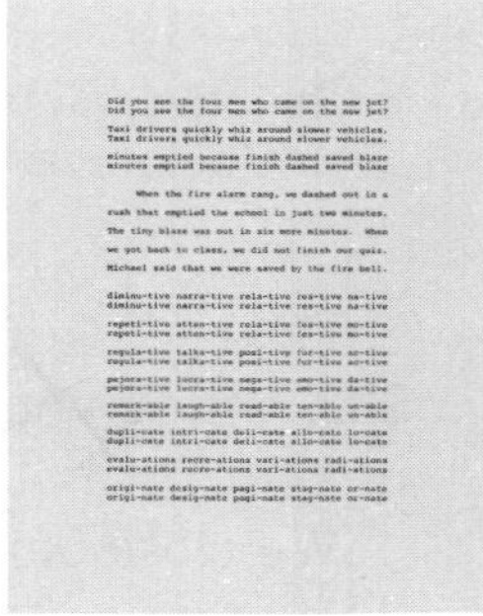

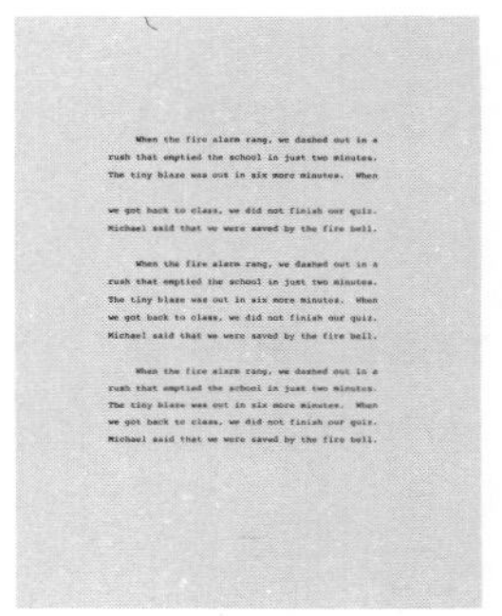

WARMUP REVIEW

2 copies

```
1  Did you see the four men who came on the new jet?    10
2  Taxi drivers quickly whiz around slower vehicles.    10
3  minutes emptied because finish dashed saved blaze    10
   |1   |2   |3   |4   |5   |6   |7   |8   |9   |10
```

PRETEST

1 copy or a 2-minute TW. Use 50-space line, listen for the bell.

```
4      When the fire alarm rang, we dashed out in a rush that    12
5  emptied the school in just two minutes.  The tiny blaze was    24
6  out in six more minutes.  When we got back to class, we did    36
7  not finish our quiz.  Michael said that we were saved by the    48
8  fire bell.                                                      50
   |1   |2   |3   |4   |5   |6   |7   |8   |9   |10   |11   |12   SI 1.14VE
```

IMPROVEMENT PRACTICE

2 copies

```
9   diminu-tive narra-tive rela-tive res-tive na-tive    10
10  repeti-tive atten-tive rela-tive fes-tive mo-tive    10
11  regula-tive talka-tive posi-tive fur-tive ac-tive    10
12  pejora-tive lucra-tive nega-tive emo-tive da-tive    10

13  remark-able laugh-able read-able ten-able un-able    10
14  dupli-cate intri-cate deli-cate allo-cate lo-cate    10
15  evalu-ations recre-ations vari-ations radi-ations    10
16  origi-nate desig-nate pagi-nate stag-nate or-nate    10
```

POST-TEST 1·1·2·2 TW

on Pretest

a·i·m 227–228

GOALS ⚲ *To type 195 or more words in 5 minutes within 3 errors on average listen-for-the-bell copy.* ⚲ *To preview the test in a·i·m 229–230.* ⚲ *To produce a newsletter-style business report and a semiblocked letter on baronial-size stationery.*

DIRECTIONS *Spacing 1 for jobs, 2 for TW. Tabs 5, center. WB 239–242.*

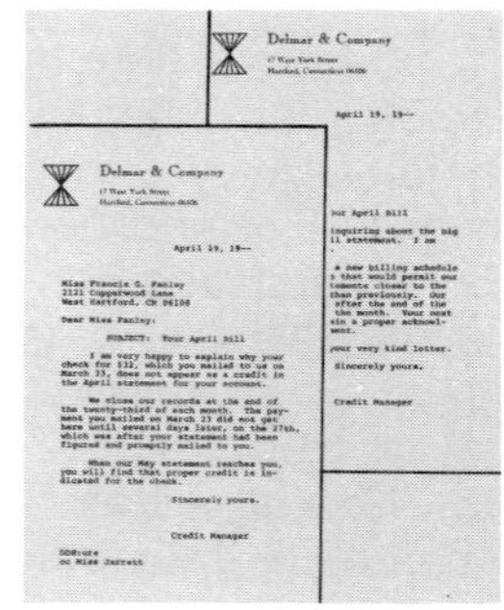

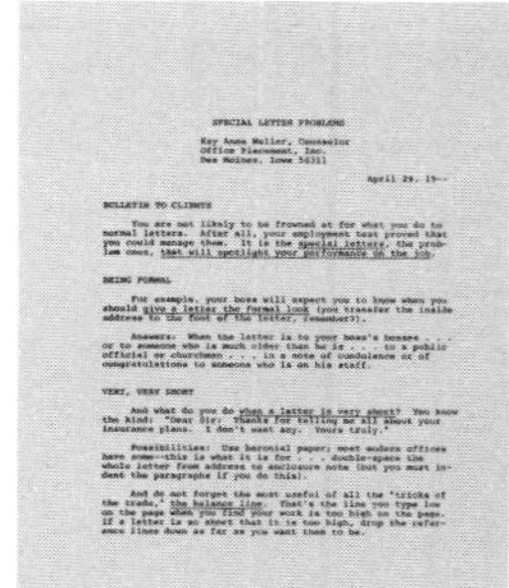

WARMUP REVIEW

2 copies

Did you not get any pay at all for the one day you had off? 12
Mack gave four equal prizes to Bud, Huey, Jinx, and Wendel. 12
Did he win 1 or 2 or 3 or 4 or 5 or 6 or 7 or 8 or 9 times? 12
|1 |2 |3 |4 |5 |6 |7 |8 |9 |10 |11 |12

TEST PREP 1

Review the objective information test on Workbook 241–242. Do not mark the pages, but look up any details of which you are uncertain; be ready to score high.

TEST PREP 2

5-MINUTE TW
Spacing 2

Dear Miss Fanley: I am very happy to explain why your check for 14
$32, which you mailed to us on March 23, does not appear as a credit 28
in the April statement for your account. 36
We close our records at the end of the twenty-third of each month. 51
The payment you mailed on March 23 did not get here until several 64
days later, on the 27th, which was after your statement had been 77
figured and promptly mailed to you. 84
When our May statement reaches you, you will find that proper 98
credit is indicated for the check. Sincerely yours, 108

Dear Mr. Luzor: Thank you for inquiring about the big "error" 122
in your April statement. I am happy to clarify it. 132
We adjusted to a new billing schedule a few weeks ago, one that 146
would permit our issuing monthly statements closer to the first of 160
the month than previously. Our records are figured after the end of 174
the twenty-third day of the month. Your next statement will contain 187
a proper acknowledgment of your payment. ⚲ 195
Thank you for your very kind letter. Sincerely yours, 207
|1 |2 |3 |4 |5 |6 |7 |8 |9 |10 |11 |12 |13 |14 SI 1.40N

TEST PREP 3

SEMIBLOCKED LETTERS
Spacing 1

The two letters above (lines 4–12, 13–20) are from the **Credit Manager** of Delmar & Company (his initials are **DDH**) to two of his customers. Each letter needs to have a subject line, **SUBJECT: Your April Bill,** centered at the appropriate point.

Type the two letters in semiblocked style. Use Baronial stationery (Workbook 239 or plain paper, $5\frac{1}{2}$ by $8\frac{1}{2}$ inches). Add one "cc" note: **cc Miss Jarrett**

Letter 1 should be addressed to **Miss Frances G. Fanley, 2121 Copperwood Lane, West Hartford, CT 06108.**

Letter 2 should be addressed to **Mr. Igor T. Luzor, Apartment 19-J, Fairmont Apartments, Hartford, CT 06107.** ⚲

a·i·m 49

GOALS ⚲ *To type 50 or more words in 2 minutes within 4 errors while listening for the bell.* ⚲ *To center a display on a full page.* ⚲ *To preview a·i·m 50 Test.*

DIRECTIONS *Spacing 2. Line 50. Tabs 5, center. Use any prior material for warmup. WB 25–26.*

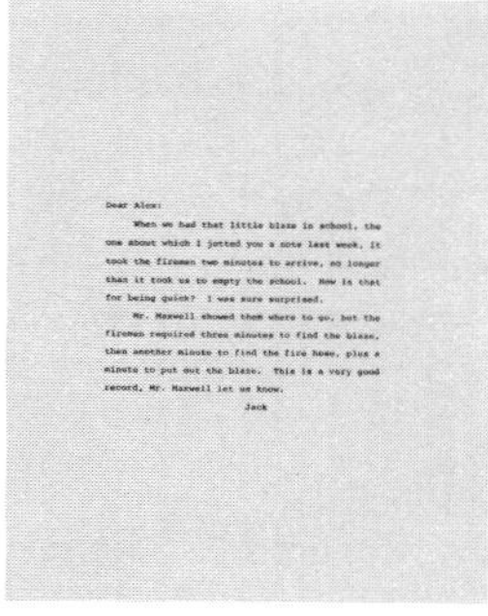

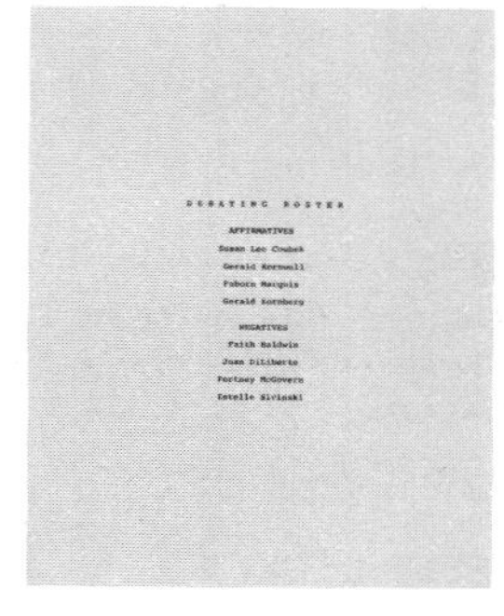

TEST PREP 1

Review the objective-information test on Workbook pages 25–26. Do not mark the test, but look up any details of which you are not positive. Be ready to score well.

TEST PREP 2

2-Minute TW Attempt 1

```
Dear Alex:                                                      2
     When we had that little blaze in school, the one about    14
which I jotted you a note last week, it took the firemen two   26
minutes to arrive, no longer than it took us to empty the      38
school.  How is that for being quick?  I was sure surprised.  ⚲50
                                                        SI 1.25E
|1   |2   |3   |4   |5   |6   |7   |8   |9   |10   |11   |12
```

2-Minute TW Attempt 2

Start name at center. Tab twice to it.

```
     Mr. Maxwell showed them where to go, but the firemen re-  12
quired three minutes to find the blaze, then another minute    24
to find the fire hose, plus a minute to put out the blaze.     36
This is a very good record, Mr. Maxwell let us know.           47
                              Jack                            ⚲50
|1   |2   |3   |4   |5   |6   |7   |8   |9   |10   |11   |12
```

TEST PREP 3

Center on full page.

D E B A T I N G   R O S T E R ↓3 — 18

20

AFFIRMATIVES — 28

Susan Lee Coubek — 39

Gerald Kornwall — 49

Faborn Marquis — 59

Gerald Kornberg ↓3 — 69

71

NEGATIVES — 77

Faith Baldwin — 86

Juan DiLiberte — 96

Fortney McGovern — 107

Estelle Sinvinski ⚲ — ⚲118

TEST PREP 4

If you have time, do a 1·1·2·2 TW on lines 1 to 5 above.

WARMUP PREVIEW

2 copies in each a·i·m

A date meet nine four from five this hour then keep will know 12
B inconvenient imaginative engagement briefcase o'clock April 12
C Liza packed six new bags, quit her job, and moved far away. 12
D Repeat the page 228 5-minute TW if you have not made the 195/3 goal.

JOB 225·1

SEMIBLOCKED LETTER

Punctuation open
Stationery Monarch (Workbook 233)
Body 65 words + ?? Extras

Date/Mr. Chad. V. Weiss/Weiss & Clem, 12
Inc./Law and Finance Building/Detroit, 22
Michigan 48201/*Salutation?* / 30
SUBJECT: Could We Save an Hour? 39
Could we change our April 27 date, Mr. 47
Weiss, to meet from nine until four o'clock 56
instead of from ten o'clock until five? 65
I would not ask this change had you not 74
originally suggested the earlier hour. 83
If the change is inconvenient, then let's 93
keep our present engagement; but if you can 102
change our appointment without difficulty, 110
please do so. Will you let me know? 119
Closing? / Kelly Bevin, President / 134
Initials? / cc Mr. Druid / cc Miss Vance 141

|1 |2 |3 |4 |5 |6 |7 |8 SI 1.41N

JOB 226·1

SEMIBLOCKED LETTER

Punctuation open
Stationery Monarch (Workbook 235)
Body 122 words + ?? Extras

Date / Mrs. M. W. Snow / 122 Planter 14
Street / Williamston, NC 27892 / *Salu-* 23
tation? 25
SUBJECT: A Brand New Idea 31
It has been much too long since you 39
have come in to brainstorm with us. Do you 48
think you could come in some day next week 57
and look at a new product with us? We are 65
not happy about it and really need your 74
help. 76
We are trying to design a briefcase just 85
for women, but we keep running into one 93
snag; whatever we design still looks like a 102
briefcase instead of something chic, femi- 110
nine, and so attractive that women will 118
want it. 121
Let me know when you might come in 129
so that I can have samples of our best 137
efforts ready for you to tear apart and re- 145
build in that imaginative way of yours. 153
Remember, we are counting on your help! 163
Closing? / Kelly Bevin, President / 178
Initials? / cc Miss Vance 182

|1 |2 |3 |4 |5 |6 |7 |8 SI 1.39N

JOB 226·2

SEMIBLOCKED LETTER

Punctuation open
Stationery Monarch (Workbook 237)
Body 110 + ?? Extras

Date / Mr. Edward K. Eyster / Phillips 14
Leather Goods / 2795 Manitowoc Street / 21
Madison, WI 35705 / *Salutation?* 29
SUBJECT: Your Overdue Account 36
I am relieved to learn from your re- 45
cent letter that you still wish delivery 53
of the 2,500 pieces of hand luggage that 61
you ordered six weeks ago. The luggage 69
is loaded in three vans that are in a garage 78
two or three miles from your store. 86
As our frequent letters have reminded 95
you many times, your account is now four 104
months overdue. We do not feel that we 111
should deliver $25,000 worth of luggage 119
to you unless you pay for it in advance. 128
As soon as you give a certified check 137
to our man, Robert Davie, who will call 145
at your office daily, the luggage will be 154
brought to your store. 159
Closing? / Kelly Bevin, President / 175
Initials? / cc Mr. Davie 179

|1 |2 |3 |4 |5 |6 |7 |8 SI 1.40N

a·i·m 50 TEST

GOALS To type 50 words or more in 2 minutes within 4 errors. To center a display on a full page. To score 80 percent or more correct on an objective test on technical information presented in Part Two.

DIRECTIONS *Spacing 2. Line 50. Tabs 5, center. WB 25–26. Use any prior material for warmup.*

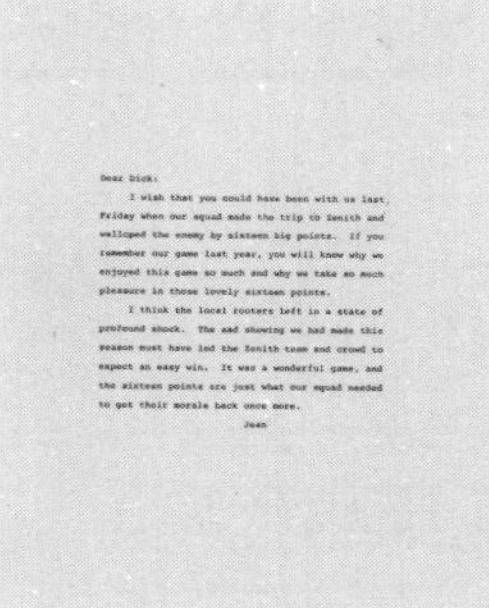

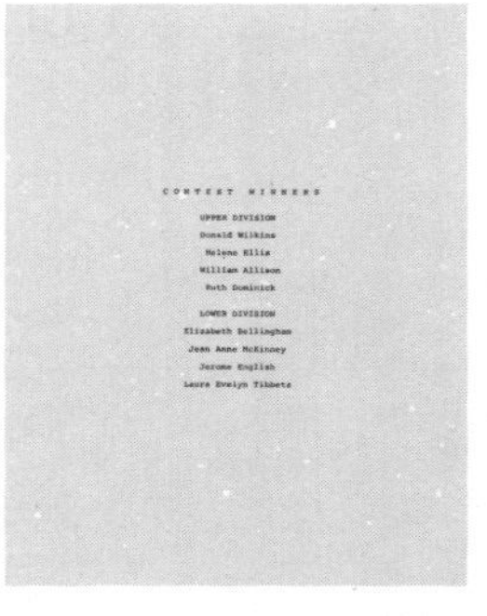

TEST 2-A Take a general information test. It may be the one on Workbook pages 25–26 or a similar one that your teacher may give or dictate to you.

TEST 2-B

Attempt 1
2 Minutes
Use plain paper.

1 Dear Dick: 2
2 I wish that you could have been with us last Friday when 14
3 our squad made the trip to Zenith and walloped the enemy by 26
4 sixteen big points. If you remember our game last year, you 38
5 will know why we enjoyed this game so much and why we take so 50
6 much pleasure in those lovely sixteen points. 60

|1 |2 |3 |4 |5 |6 |7 |8 |9 |10 |11 |12 SI 1.21E

ATTEMPT 2

7 I think the local rooters left in a state of profound 12 | 72
8 shock. The sad showing we had made this season must have led 24 | 84
9 the Zenith team and crowd to expect an easy win. It was a 36 | 96
10 wonderful game, and the sixteen points are just what our 47 | 107
11 squad needed to get their morale back once more. 57 | 117
Jean 60 | 120

|1 |2 |3 |4 |5 |6 |7 |8 |9 |10 |11 |12

TEST 2-C

Center on a full sheet of paper.

12 CONTEST WINNERS ↓3 18
20
13 UPPER DIVISION 29
14 Donald Wilkins 39
15 Helene Ellis 47
16 William Allison 57
17 → Ruth Dominick ↓3 66
68
18 LOWER DIVISION 78
19 Elizabeth Bellingham 91
20 Jean Anne McKinney 103
21 Jerome English 113
22 Laura Evelyn Tibbets 126

FULL BLOCKED STYLE

EVERY LINE BEGINS AT THE LEFT MARGIN STOP

April 17, 19--

Purchasing Department
Continental Box Company
1801 Topeka Boulevard
Shawnee Mission, KS 66201

Attention of Mr. C. R. Stone

Gentlemen:

Thank you very much for the order that you sent to us last week. We were pleased to receive it.

Your order did not include any payment. Since your account is now more than 75 days overdue, we cannot send the merchandise unless you settle your account or accompany your order with full payment.

We hope, therefore, that you will send us your check very quickly so that we may proceed to fill and send your order to you. We have full inventory and can ship your order within 24 hours after your payment reaches us.

Yours very truly,

ALL-STAR ELECTRIC COMPANY

Credit Manager

HIS/urs

cc Sales Manager
cc Miss Foster

1. FULL BLOCKED STYLE . . . all lines begin at left margin . . . about 5 percent of letters are in this easy style . . . also shown here: standard punctuation, attention line, company signature, cc notations.

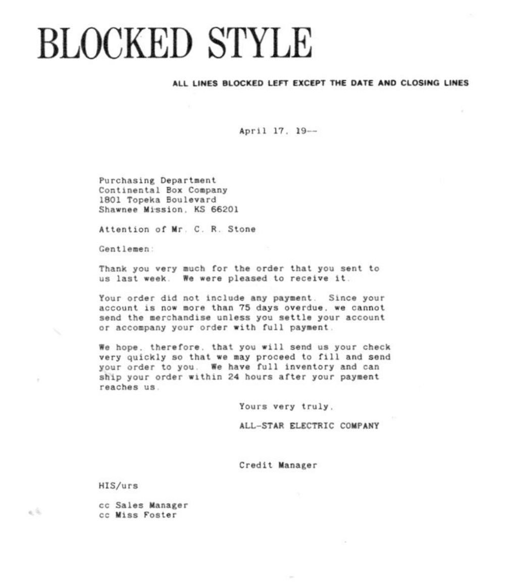

BLOCKED STYLE

ALL LINES BLOCKED LEFT EXCEPT THE DATE AND CLOSING LINES

April 17, 19--

Purchasing Department
Continental Box Company
1801 Topeka Boulevard
Shawnee Mission, KS 66201

Attention of Mr. C. R. Stone

Gentlemen:

Thank you very much for the order that you sent to us last week. We were pleased to receive it.

Your order did not include any payment. Since your account is now more than 75 days overdue, we cannot send the merchandise unless you settle your account or accompany your order with full payment.

We hope, therefore, that you will send us your check very quickly so that we may proceed to fill and send your order to you. We have full inventory and can ship your order within 24 hours after your payment reaches us.

Yours very truly,

ALL-STAR ELECTRIC COMPANY

Credit Manager

HIS/urs

cc Sales Manager
cc Miss Foster

2. BLOCKED STYLE . . . like Full Blocked except that date and closing are indented to the center . . . this is most popular style; about 45 percent of business letters are typed in this arrangement.

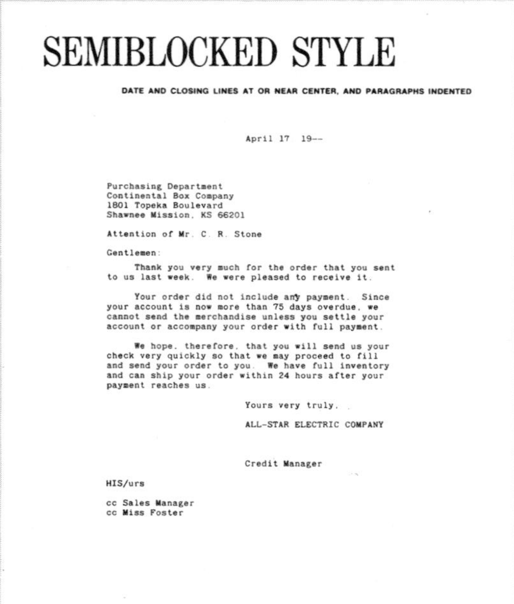

SEMIBLOCKED STYLE

DATE AND CLOSING LINES AT OR NEAR CENTER, AND PARAGRAPHS INDENTED

April 17 19--

Purchasing Department
Continental Box Company
1801 Topeka Boulevard
Shawnee Mission, KS 66201

Attention of Mr. C. R. Stone

Gentlemen:

Thank you very much for the order that you sent to us last week. We were pleased to receive it.

Your order did not include any payment. Since your account is now more than 75 days overdue, we cannot send the merchandise unless you settle your account or accompany your order with full payment.

We hope, therefore, that you will send us your check very quickly so that we may proceed to fill and send your order to you. We have full inventory and can ship your order within 24 hours after your payment reaches us.

Yours very truly,

ALL-STAR ELECTRIC COMPANY

Credit Manager

HIS/urs

cc Sales Manager
cc Miss Foster

3. SEMIBLOCKED STYLE . . . like Blocked except that paragraphs are indented—usually 5 spaces but could be 10 or any other consistent number . . . about 40 percent of business letters are typed like this.

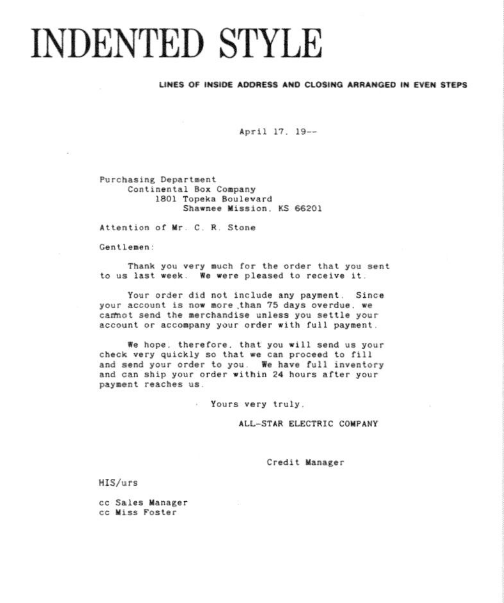

INDENTED STYLE

LINES OF INSIDE ADDRESS AND CLOSING ARRANGED IN EVEN STEPS

April 17, 19--

Purchasing Department
Continental Box Company
1801 Topeka Boulevard
Shawnee Mission, KS 66201

Attention of Mr. C. R. Stone

Gentlemen:

Thank you very much for the order that you sent to us last week. We were pleased to receive it.

Your order did not include any payment. Since your account is now more than 75 days overdue, we cannot send the merchandise unless you settle your account or accompany your order with full payment.

We hope, therefore, that you will send us your check very quickly so that we can proceed to fill and send your order to you. We have full inventory and can ship your order within 24 hours after your payment reaches us.

Yours very truly,

ALL-STAR ELECTRIC COMPANY

Credit Manager

HIS/urs

cc Sales Manager
cc Miss Foster

4. INDENTED STYLE . . . like Semiblocked except that the lines of the inside address and closing are stepped in 5-space indentions . . . rarely used in America, this style is popular in many other countries.

The Four Basic "Styles" for Business Letters

Overview

In Part Three you will review everything you have learned so far and will focus on three principal kinds of practice:

(1) You will increase your speed from 25 words a minute for 2 minutes to 30 words a minute for 3 minutes.

(2) You will master the number keys and the punctuation keys you have not yet had—apostrophe, quotation mark, underscore, parentheses.

(3) You will begin production work by producing enumerations and assignments that are arranged somewhat like enumerations.

There are 25 a·i·m experiences in Part Three. As before, each affords about 20 minutes of study and practice. And, also as before, the last a·i·m in Part Three (a·i·m 75) is a test on the Part, and the a·i·m before it is a practice run on the Part Three test.

Performance Goals

When you finish Part Three, you should be able to demonstrate the following abilities when you take the test in a·i·m 75, page 78:

1. Touch Typing In addition to the letters and punctuation keys you already know, you will control by touch the number keys, fraction keys, and the punctuation marks not previously learned. Also, you will develop greater touch power in returning and indenting the carriage.

2. Technicalities You will score at least 80 percent on an objective test that reviews Parts One and Two and includes a great deal of new information from Part Three: how to arrange an outline, type a poem, arrange a script, and execute other "enumeration" kinds of assignments.

3. Production Not only will you understand the technical principles in arranging enumerations, but also you will have the experience of typing them. Most of the assignments are accompanied by counts so that you can use them for timed practice, too, and thereby become as competent in typing them in arranged form as you are in copying ordinary paragraph material.

4. Skill You will type at least 90 words in 3 minutes within 5 errors as you copy alphabetic paragraph material whose line endings are not shown—that is, you must listen for the bell and decide how and where to end each line of typing.

Routines and Procedures

1·1·1·3·3 TW The basic skill-improvement serial 3-minute writing is a derivative of the 1·1·2·2 concept of Part Two. In the 1·1·1·3·3 routine, you (1) take three consecutive 1-minute writings with a brief rest after each, then (2) a 3-minute timing to see whether you can cover all the practiced material in an unbroken 3-minute stretch, and then (3) one more 3-minute writing to surpass the speed and/or accuracy score of the first 3-minute effort. You will use this routine 20 or more times in Part Three.

Speed Drive In four a·i·m sessions (60, 62, 65, and 68) you will spend the whole session driving for speed. Using extremely easy material, you will work in three stages: first, a complete set of 1·1·1·3·3 timings; second, concentrated practice on more lines of the copy; and third, one more 3-minute timing to see how much more you can type than you did in the 1·1·1·3·3 sequence.

Technical Rules You will be helped to master two different kinds of guidelines, such as: (1) basic ones, like the rules for underscoring (do you or do you not underscore spaces, too?) and using quotation marks (does the quotation mark follow or precede the final punctuation mark?); and (2) general ones, like the precise arrangement of a typewritten outline or bibliography.

And when you complete a·i·m 75, you will be ready to type personal and business letters!

a·i·m 223–226

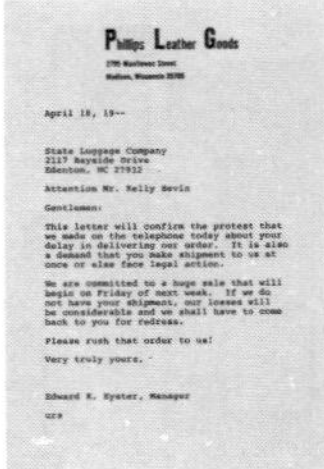
Phillips Leather Goods

April 18, 19--

State Luggage Company
2117 Bayside Drive
Edenton, NC 27932

Attention Mr. Kelly Bevin

Gentlemen:

This letter will confirm the protest that we made on the telephone today about your delay in delivering our order. It is also a demand that you make shipment to us at once or else face legal action.

We are committed to a huge sale that will begin on Friday of next week. If we do not have your shipment, our losses will be considerable and we shall have to come back to you for redress.

Please rush that order to us!

Very truly yours,

Edward K. Eyster, Manager

urs

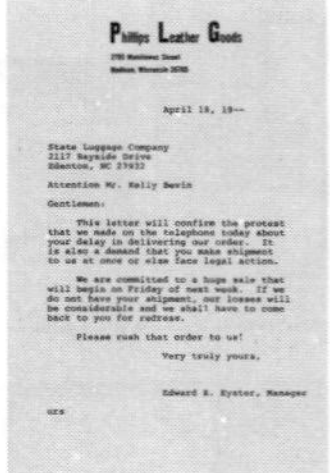

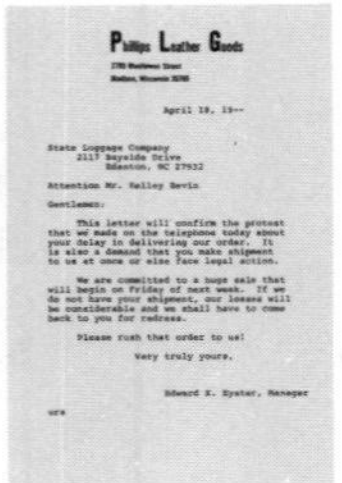

GOALS ⚲ *To distinguish the four basic letter styles.* ⚲ *To produce a short letter in each style.* ⚲ *To type 195 or more words of normal copy within 5 minutes and 3 errors.*

DIRECTIONS *Spacing 1. Line 60. Tab 5. WB 229–237.*

WARMUP REVIEW

2 copies in each a·i·m

Did the boy get his cup and the map off the lid of the box? 12
Liza quit her new job, packed six bags, and moved far away. 12
Ask us for 1 or 2 or 3 or 4 or 5 or 6 or 7 or 8 or 9 or 10. 12

|1 |2 |3 |4 |5 |6 |7 |8 |9 |10 |11 |12

5-MINUTE TW

GOAL WRITING
2 copies within 5 minutes and 3 errors

Spacing 1

	1	2
The "style" of a letter is its basic pattern for using	12	110
indentions. A letter with no indentions at all is known as	24	122
Full Blocked. If we indent the date and the closing lines,	36	134
the style is known as Blocked. If we also indent the start	48	146
of each paragraph, the style is Semiblocked. If we indent,	60	158
in a series of equal steps, the lines of the inside address	72	170
and the lines of the closing, the style is called Indented.	84	182
There are also variations of these four letter styles.	97	195 ⚲

|1 |2 |3 |4 |5 |6 |7 |8 |9 |10 |11 |12 SI 1.39N

FOUR BASIC LETTER STYLES

See page 229.

Refer to page 216 for placement plan.

The four basic "styles" of letters are (1) Full Blocked, (2) Blocked, (3) Semiblocked, and (4) Indented. All use the same placement plan, punctuation pattern, and stationery. They differ only in their patterns of indention.

Practice After studying the illustrations on page 229, type the short letter below once in each style. Use baronial stationery. (Workbook 229–231 or plain paper 5½ by 8½ inches) with a 4-inch line.

Job 223·1 Full Blocked copy
Job 223·2 Blocked copy
Job 224·1 Semiblocked copy
Job 224·2 Indented copy

Body 82 words + attention 20

Today's date/State Luggage Company/2117 Bayside Drive/ 16
Edenton, NC 27932/Attention Mr. Kelly Bevin/Gentlemen: 31
This letter will confirm the protest that we made on the telephone 46
today about your delay in delivering our order. It is also a demand 60
that you make shipment to us at once or else face legal action. 73
We are committed to a huge sale that will begin on Friday of next 97
week. If we do not have your shipment, our losses will be considerable 101
and we shall have to come back to you for redress. 112
Please rush that order to us! 119
Very truly yours,/Edward K. Eyster, Manager/urs ⚲ 131

|1 |2 |3 |4 |5 |6 |7 |8 |9 |10 |11 |12 |13 |14 SI 1.43N

 51

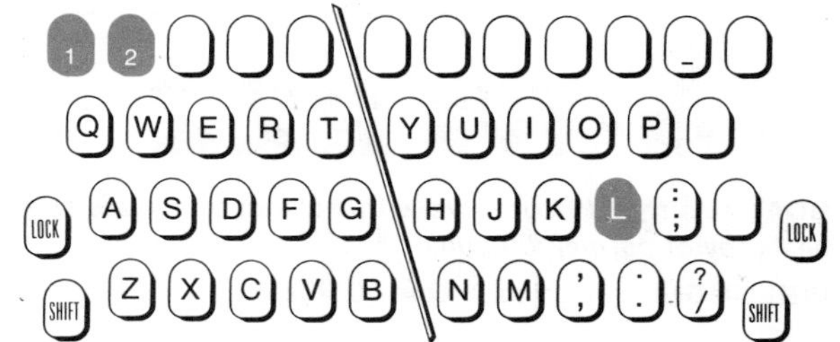

GOALS *To control 1 and 2 keys. To type 75 or more words in 3 minutes within 5 errors on paragraph copy that includes the 1 and 2 keys.*

DIRECTIONS *Spacing 1. Line 50. Tabs 5, center. Tape K 17.*

WARMUP PREVIEW

2 copies

1 The six new men may get the cab you saw turn off. 10
2 Pat just said that this quiz took very hard work. 10
3 quarterback scoreboard because relief losing toss 10

|1 |2 |3 |4 |5 |6 |7 |8 |9 |10

 **KEY**

Use A-finger (or L-finger on small l)
2 copies

4 aqla aqla alla alla alal alal all 111 and 111,111 10
5 11 arts 11 axes 11 aims 11 alms 11 aces 1.11 1:11 10
6 We need 11 pairs of size 11 shoes for the 11 men. 10

2 **KEY**

Use S-finger
2 copies

7 sw2s sw2s s22s s22s s2s2 s2s2 all 222 and 112,122 10
8 22 sons 22 sums 22 seas 22 sips 22 suns 2.22 2:22 10
9 The 12 men and the 22 boys played 122 full games. 10

1·1·1·3·3 TW

Spacing 1

The 1·1·1·3·3 signal shows how to practice timed writings in this Part: three consecutive 1-minute efforts, then two 3-minute writings. It is normal at this point to be able to finish this selection within 3 minutes and within 5 errors. If time permits, use Workbook pages 27 and 28 for pacing practice.

10 Dear Jim: 2
3
11 TAB Well, we took Quinette High by a score of 22 13
12 to 12, thanks to a toss of 22 yards by Zipper and 23
13 a couple of 11-yard runs by Dick Dixon. The very 33
14 fine work of our quarterback was a joy to behold. 43
44
15 The lights on the scoreboard, 22 to 12, were 54
16 a joy to behold, too. It was also a relief to me 64
17 because I had worried about losing. 71
72
18 TAB TAB Jack 75

|1 |2 |3 |4 |5 |6 |7 |8 |9 |10 SI 1.22E

a·i·m 222

GOAL *To type 195 or more words within 5 minutes and 3 errors on listen-for-bell copy of normal difficulty.*

DIRECTIONS *Spacing 2. Line 60. Tab 5.*

TYPE WITH STEADY, EVEN STROKES—

- When you shift for capital characters.
- When you strike the space bar.
- When you shift from short to long words.
- When you type both hard and easy strokes.

WARMUP

2 copies

1 "full blocked" distinction indention courtesy bizarre style 12
2 "semiblocked" punctuation "blocked" orthodox antique fuzzy, 12

|1 |2 |3 |4 |5 |6 |7 |8 |9 |10 |11 |12

SKILL DRIVE

See page 214.

Pretest on lines 3–8
Practice 1′ TW on lines 22–24 or 25–27
Post-test on lines 3–17

3 The design of the letterhead and the size of paper are two sources 14
4 that make a letter distinctive when it might be quite orthodox in other 29
5 ways. Pattern of punctuation might be a third source, although the 42
6 standard pattern is used so widely that a writer might be considered 56
7 bizarre if he used one of the others. There is one other source worth 70
8 noting: the indention style he uses. 78
9 The extent to which business letters do or do not have their parts 92
10 indented is a major quirk of distinction. Some writers claim that an 106
11 indention is a waste of time and is a sign of fuzzy, antique thinking. 121
12 Some others say that that which appears antique smacks of honesty 134
13 and courtesy to the reader, and the more such smacks the better. 147
14 Besides, they point out, the tab key cuts down the "waste of time." 161
15 Most businessmen walk a middle path, preferring the "blocked" 173
16 or "semiblocked" styles, which involve just simple indentions. 186
17 Just the same, some men do prefer the "full blocked." 197
18 This maze of ways to make letters different from other letters might 212
19 alarm the young typists, new on the job, were it not for the office 225
20 files. Five minutes used in checking the files can show the novice the 240
21 letter form, styles, etc., that will be expected or required. 252

|1 |2 |3 |4 |5 |6 |7 |8 |9 |10 |11 |12 |13 |14 SI 1.40N

SPEED SENTENCES

Line 65

22 Bob and Glen got the girls the right forms and the six big jobs. 13
23 He is to go to work for the big audit firm by the eighth of May. 13
24 The man is to go to town and then make six panels for the girls. 13

|1 |2 |3 |4 |5 |6 |7 |8 |9 |10 |11 |12 |13

ACCURACY SENTENCES

Line 65

25 Because he was very lazy, Jack paid for six games and then quit. 13
26 On his way here, the quick fox jumped back over a brown gazelle. 13
27 Dave quickly froze the two brown mixtures in the four deep jugs. 13

a·i·m 52

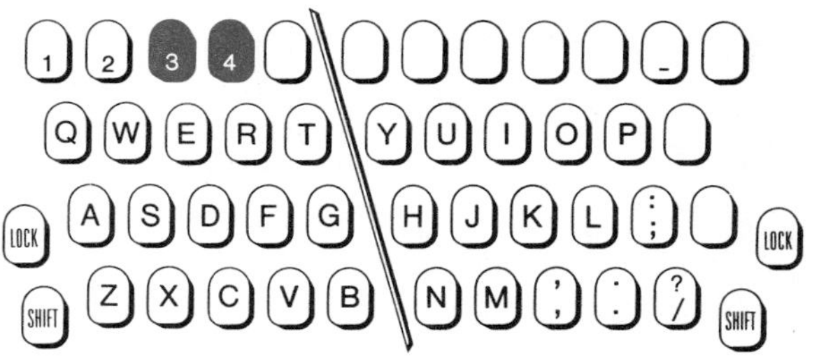

GOALS *To control 3 and 4 keys. To type 76 words or more in 3 minutes within 5 errors on material involving 4 number keys and requiring listening for the bell.*

DIRECTIONS *Spacing 1. Line 50. Tabs 5, center. Tape K 18.*

WARMUP REVIEW

2 copies

1 The six new men did not get the cab that you saw. 10
2 Pat said that your quiz took just a little study. 10
3 The 12 men and the 12 boys played 212 full games. 10

|1 |2 |3 |4 |5 |6 |7 |8 |9 |10

3 KEY

Use D-finger
2 copies

4 de3d de3d d33d d33d d3d3 d3d3 all 333 and 123,123 10
5 33 dads 33 dips 33 dues 33 dots 33 dogs 3.13 3:13 10
6 Did the 3 men catch 31 or 33 fish in the 13 days? 10

4 KEY

Use F-finger
2 copies

7 fr4f fr4f f44f f44f f4f4 f4f4 all 444 and 123,441 10
8 44 furs 44 fins 44 fish 44 fell 44 flew 4.14 4:14 10
9 The 44 boys lost only 14 of their 144 golf games. 10

1·1·1·3·3 TW

Use 50-space line and listen for bell. Spacing 1

The material here is shown on a longer line than the 50-space line you are to use. You will therefore have to be guided by the margin-warning bell on your machine.

Check that the right-hand margin stop is set where it should be for your 50-space line [review page 3], so the bell rings properly.

Respond to the bell signal by deciding where to end the line. Do this mentally without looking up and—hopefully—without even pausing.

You will often find timed-writing selections in this form to give you practice in a skill that is really urgent: ending lines expertly and correctly dividing words if necessary.

10 Dear Jack: 2
11 How in the world did little Quinette score 2 touch- 13
12 downs, or was it 4 field goals, on all those giants on your 25
13 team? Were Dick and Zipper really playing? How could they 37
14 score only 3 touchdowns? Why, Quinette is so tiny that I 49
15 doubt it even has a second team. I thought your guys would 61
16 build a wide margin, like 23 or 24 extra points. 71
17 Jim Vanderslice 76

|1 |2 |3 |4 |5 |6 |7 |8 |9 |10 |11 |12

SI 1.23E

a·i·m 221
WARMUP PREVIEW

2 copies A–C

A many week name kind used rule even some most what when word 12

B capitalized possessive capitalize preceded definite capital 12

C Jane seized the wax buffer and removed a big patch quickly. 12

D Repeat page 222 TW if you have not yet made the 195/3 goal.

JOB 221·1

BOOK MANUSCRIPT Continued Tabs 5 and 10

1" Margin ↓ — 1" Margin

ENGLISH FOR BUSINESSMEN 143 7

9

there is a word between the building number and street number: 20
<u>11 North 11 Street</u>, <u>330 West 42 Street</u>. The trend is not defi- 47
nite; be guide(d) by what is on the in coming letterhead. ↓3 59

61

<u>18. Most Common Uses of Capitals</u> 81

Some rules about the use of capitals are ~~used~~ applied so often 93
that we do not even thing(s) of ~~their being~~ them as rules. Every busi- 104
nessman knows, ~~we trust,~~ surely to use a capital letter: 114

1. To begin proper names 122
2. To begin sentences 127
3. To begin direct quotations 136
4. To Begin lines in out lines and poems 146

The first rule is used the most, ~~often,~~ of course, for there 159
are so many kings(d) of names. Use a capital for names of: 169

1. People: John Bates, Joan K. Hall 180
2. Firms: Smith Bros., Brown Box Co. 190
3. Trade Names: Old Dutch Cleanser 198
4. Places: West Coast, Maine, Butte 108
5. Days of the week, months, holidays 208

Any word substituted for a name begins with a capital, too: 231
<u>the Bay State</u>, <u>Honest Abe</u>, <u>on the West Coa~~sh~~st</u>. 252

Titles are sometimes a problem. A word used as a family 264
title is ~~capped~~ capitalized if it is not preceded by a possessive pronoun: 278
<u>Father told Mother . . . my father told my mother</u>. 309

A business or public title is capitalized when it precedes 322
a name but not when it follows a name: <u>There is Judge Lake</u> 343
<u>with Ralph Parke, the mayor</u>. But note that the title of a very high offi- 367
cial is always capitalized: <u>He got the ~~story~~ news from John Jay</u>, 391
<u>who was then Secretary of State</u>. 411

Revised Page of a Book Manuscript with Displayed Listings

SI 1.40N

GOALS To review control of 1–4 keys. To construct fractions. To type 77 words or more in 3 minutes within 5 errors on material including four number keys.

DIRECTIONS *Spacing 1. Line 50. Tabs 5, center.*

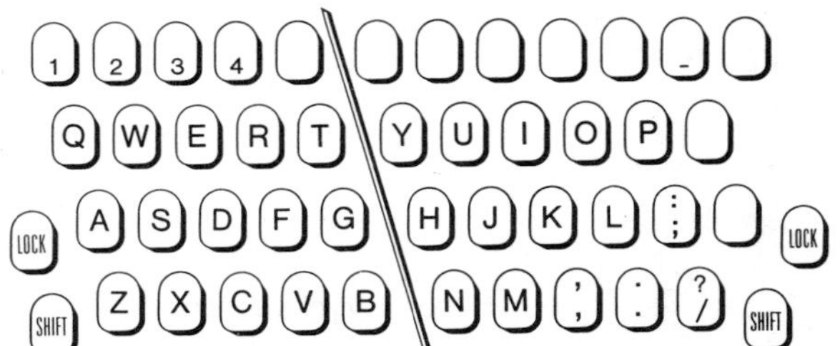

WARMUP REVIEW
2 copies

1 The new man did get the one old cab you had seen. 10
2 Jaqueline felt the big exam took too much review. 10
3 The 12 men and 34 boys played 11,324 quoit games. 10

1 2 3 4 5 6 7 8 9 10

REVIEW
2 copies

4 aqla 1 aunt 1 arch 1 alley 1 aunt 1 arch 1 alley. 10
5 sw3s 2 sons 2 sips 2 sighs 2 sons 2 sips 2 sighs. 10
6 de3d 3 dogs 3 days 3 dried 3 dogs 3 days 3 dried. 10
7 fr4f 4 fell 4 furs 4 foxes 4 fell 4 furs 4 foxes. 10

FRACTIONS
2 copies

Use the diagonal to build a fraction. Mixed fractions require a blank space between the whole number and the fraction. If one fraction in a sentence has to be constructed, build all the fractions that occur in that same sentence.

8 He worked between 1/4 and 1/3 of an hour for Tom. 10
9 I worked 1 1/3 hours, but Joe worked 2 1/2 hours. 10

1·1·1·3·3 TW
Spacing 1

10 Dear Mr. Zaner: 3
4
11 I am happy to answer your question about the 14
12 hours I have put on the painting job you gave me. 24
25
13 I worked 4 hours each on the last 3 Saturday 35
14 mornings, for 12 hours. I also worked 2 1/3 more 45
15 hours on each of 3 Fridays plus 2 more on each of 55
16 2 Tuesdays, for 11 more hours. I think the total 65
17 comes to exactly 23 hours. Right? 72
73
18 Andy Kerr 77

1 2 3 4 5 6 7 8 9 10 SI 1.23E

a·i·m 220
WARMUP PREVIEW
2 copies A–C

A when they inch feet paid many used quit out are ten six old 12
B approximate indefinite bargains together exact boxes ago or 12
C Jane seized a big wax buffer and quickly removed the patch. 12
D Repeat page 222 5-minute TW if you have not made the 195/3 goal.

1½" MARGIN 19 — 90 — 1" MARGIN

ENGLISH FOR BUSINESSMEN Line 7 → 142 7

2 blank lines here 9

17. The Expression of Numbers 26

When should numbers be typed as figures and when 37
should they be spelled out? The general guide is to spell ~~them~~ numbers 50
out when they are small or approximate and to use figures when 63
the numbers are exact or when there are ~~many~~ several of them appearing 76
close together. Here are the rules to ~~be~~ remembered: 86

1. Spell out ten and lower numbers: 95
four jets, six boys . . . 18 riders, 14 boxes. 107

JOB 220·1
BOOK MANUSCRIPT
Tabs 5 and 9
Spacing 1 or 2 as shown

2. Spell out round numbers, except in advertising: 119
five hundred voters . . . 1,000 bargains! 130

3. Spell out indefinite amounts of money: 141
hundreds of dollars . . . contributed $25. 151

4. Spell out numbers that begin sentences: 162
Fourteen quit. Thirty-eight voted. ~~for him.~~ 172

5. Spell out numbers used as adjectives: 182
twelfth game, Forty-second Regiment 191

6. Spell out informal and o'clock times: 202
at ten, about six o'clock . . . 8:45 a.m. 212

7. Spell out years and ages when approximate: 224
ten years ago, two years old . . . 9 years 234
and 1 month ago, 11 years and 1 week old. 245

8. Use figures in dimensions and measurements: 256
3 quarts, 14 by 25 feet, 6 feet 1 inch. ~~tall~~ 266

9. Use figures with ~~any~~ all symbols: 275
order #188, an 8% discount, paid $16. 285

10. Use figures for many numbers and for numbers 297
in series: found 8 bags, 4 boxes, 2 crates. 307

For numbers used as street names, spell out ten and lower 321
numbers: <u>on Sixth Avenue, at 111 Fifth Street</u>. Use figures 347
for higher numbers: <u>21st Street, at 111 91st Road</u>. There is 371
a marked trend toward omitting the endings <u>st</u>, <u>d</u>, <u>th</u>, and so on, when 388

SI 1.41N

Revised Page of a Book Manuscript with a Displayed Enumeration

a·i·m 54

GOALS *To control 7 and 8 keys. To type 78 words or more in 3 minutes within 5 errors on material involving 6 number keys.*

DIRECTIONS *Spacing 1. Line 50. Tabs 4, center. Tape K 19.*

WARMUP REVIEW

2 copies

1 Why did the six new men not take the cab you had? 10

2 The lazy girl quit work when they gave this exam. 10

3 There were 21 men and 34 boys in the third group. 10

|1 |2 |3 |4 |5 |6 |7 |8 |9 |10

7 KEY

Use J-finger
2 copies

4 ju7j ju7j j77j j77j j7j7 j7j7 you 777 for 123,477 10

5 77 jugs 77 jars 77 jigs 77 jets 77 jogs 7/17 7:17 10

6 On June 7, the 7 men left Camp 7 on the 7:17 bus. 10

8 KEY

Use K-finger
2 copies

7 ki8k ki8k k88k k88k k8k8 k8k8 irk 888 for 123,478 10

8 88 kits 88 keys 88 kids 88 inks 88 inns 8/18 8:18 10

9 Train No. 188 departs at 11:18 a.m. or 12:18 p.m. 10

1·1·1·3·3 TW

If paragraphs are numbered, as here, space twice after the period. Use tab to indent lines 14 and 16. Spacing 1

10 Dear Jim: 2

3

11 It may be November 7 or 8 before I have the exact 13
12 counts worked out, but here is the present score: 23

24

13 1. I think that 43 or 44 juniors will attend the 34
14 banquet. 37

38

15 2. I am sure that there will be 71 or 72 seniors 48
16 attending. 51

52

17 The size of the group, about 114, will require us 62
18 to find a larger room than we used last Saturday. 72

73

19 Carole Giuliano 78

|1 |2 |3 |4 |5 |6 |7 |8 |9 |10 SI 1.26FE

a·i·m 219 **WARMUP PREVIEW**

2 copies A–C

A copy bell pays know test make read line four find work test 12
B proofreading practicing interview yourself subtract warning 12
C Quickly Jane seized the big wax buffer and removed a patch. 12
D Repeat page 222 5-minute TW if you have not made the 195/3 goal.

JOB 219·1

BUSINESS REPORT (Continued)

TYPING TESTS / 2 3

5

You copy simple essay material from a leaflet for the 10 19
minutes. You listen for the warning bell; you do not copy line 39
for line as the material is printed. You use a 70-space line 65
and double-spacing. 77

Scoring involves four steps. First, you proof read the work 95
and encircle the errors. Second, you find the total number of 108
words typed. Third, from that total you subtract 10 for each er- 120
ror. Fourth, you divide what is left by 10 (the number of minutes 134
to get your "net" words a minute. This is your score. 154

For example, in 10 minutes you type 575 words and you make 5 167
errors. You subtract 50 from 575, to get 525; and you divide the 180
525 by 10, (minutes), to get 52.5 net words a minute as your score. 192
In effect, you lose 1 wam for each error. Accuracy pays. 216

218

PREPARING FOR THE TEST 222

Don't make the mistake of practicing 10-minute writings one 260
after another. If you do, you will get tired and simply drill 276
yourself in typing with poor posture, poor stroking, etc. In- 286
stead, take one 10-minute writing a day preceding this practice 303
by short writings in which you get the feel of a pace that you 316
can manage to sustain for 10 minutes. 321

Don't make the mistake of pushing for speed. If you do, you 353
invite errors; at fifty strokes each, they cost you too much. 364
Do practice changing the paper quickly. With practice, you 393
can get it down to 2 or 3 seconds. 400

Do sharpen your proofreading. A paper with even just one 423
unmarked error is likely to stamp you as unreliable and to end in 436
the wastebasket along with all your application papers. 448
If you can type at a net rate of 50.0 or more for 10 minutes 469
let us know. We will test you to confirm your score and arrange 482
for your placement interview and official test by the employer. 498

Joyce L. Neitz 504

April 12, 19-- 509

SI 1.39N

Revised Last Page of a Manuscript Typed in Business-Report Form

55

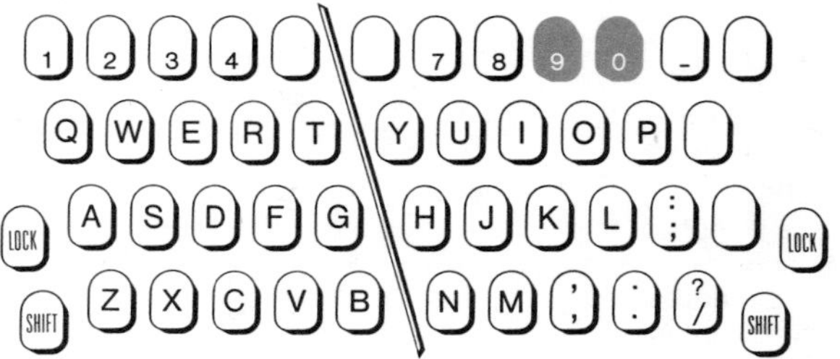

GOALS *To control 9 and 0 keys. To type 79 words or more in 3 minutes within 5 errors on material involving 8 number keys.*

DIRECTIONS *Spacing 1. Line 50. Tabs 4, center. Tape K 20.*

WARMUP REVIEW

2 copies

1 The six new men did not see the cab that you had. 10
2 The lazy girl quit her job when she saw the exam. 10
3 Is the campaign dated 1/23 to 2/7 or 1/24 to 2/8? 10

|1 |2 |3 |4 |5 |6 |7 |8 |9 |10

 KEY

Use L-finger
2 copies

4 lo91 lo91 1991 1991 1919 1919 all 999 for 234,789 10
5 99 lots 99 lids 99 laws 99 logs 99 less 9/19 9:19 10
6 In 1919, there were 199 men in each of 19 lodges. 10

0 KEY

Use sem-finger
2 copies

7 ;p0; ;p0; ;00; ;00; ;0;0 ;0;0 dip 000 for 347,890 10
8 10 pegs 10 pins 10 play 10 paid 10 push 1/10 1:10 10
9 Meet them at 10:00 a.m. or 1:00 p.m. for a snack. 10

1·1·1·3·3 TW

Tab-indent lines 14 and 16. Tab two times to the final line. Spacing 1

10 Dear Jake: 2
3
11 Thank you for your note of 10/8. I need the fol- 13
12 lowing banquet details not later than 10/17: 22
23
13 1. Your guess as to the final number of tickets, 33
14 since this affects the size of the room. 42
43
15 2. Your guess as to when we might give the exact 53
16 count to the hotel; we must give it by 10/19. 63
64
17 Jake, I am very, very grateful for all your help. 74
75
18 Jim Barr 79

|1 |2 |3 |4 |5 |6 |7 |8 |9 |10 SI 1.24E

a·i·m 218

JOB 218·1

PAGE ONE OF A BUSINESS REPORT
Line 6 inches
Spacing 1
Tabs 5 and at a point to block-center the three subtitle lines.

TAKING TEN-MINUTE TYPEWRITING TESTS 21

22

Joyce L. Neitz, Counselor 39
Office Placement, Inc. 46
Des Moines, Iowa [3 spaces] 50311 53

54

April 12, 19-- 69

70

BULLETIN TO CLIENTS 74

75

A large [East Coast] firm, extending its operations to the west, is open- 90
ing a district office in Des Moines next month. <u>Needed: about</u> 108
<u>325 office workers within three months</u>. 132

133

To attract ~~superior~~ [top-drawer] talent, the firm ~~plans to~~ [will] pay 5 to 10 145
per cent above present rates in this city. So: <u>There will be</u> 162
<u>stiff competition for these ~~attractive~~ positions</u>. 185

[2 blank] 186

187

CAUTION 189

[1 blank] 190

Applicants for typing positions in most ~~of our~~ Des Moines 201
firms are given <u>a qualifying test</u>. Usual base: ~~60~~ [50] words a min- 221
ute, 5 minutes, 3 or fewer errors, better of 2 efforts. 232

233

But the new ~~office~~ [firm], to get a better staff in ~~exchange~~ [return] for 245
better pay, plans to use <u>a competititive test</u>, not a qualifying 265
test. The test will be for 10 minutes. Speed will be charged 277
50 strokes (10 words) for each error. <u>Those who make the top</u> 299
<u>scores will get ~~the~~ first consideration for the jobs</u>. 328

329

If you hope to land [10] one of these ~~superior~~ [better] jobs, <u>learn how</u> 345
<u>to take and to score</u> a ~~ten~~-minute typewriting test. 363

364

365

TAKING THE TEST 368

369

You start 9 or 10 lines from the top [of the paper]. You stop typing [about] an 385
inch or so from the bottom of the sheet, change paper quickly, 397
and continue on another sheet. 404

405

(To speed up paper change: Make a double crease about an 417
inch and a half from the bottom of the paper; your typing will 430
sound ~~a lot~~ different when you reach the creases. Do not use 441
the paper bail. Use two sheets of paper; when you remove the 454
two, ~~shove~~ [move] them straight back across the top of the cylinder and 466
reinsert both, bringing the clean ~~paper~~ [sheet] up in ~~the~~ front. ¶ 477

SI 1.39N

Revised Page One of a Business Report with Highlighting Underscores

a·i·m 56

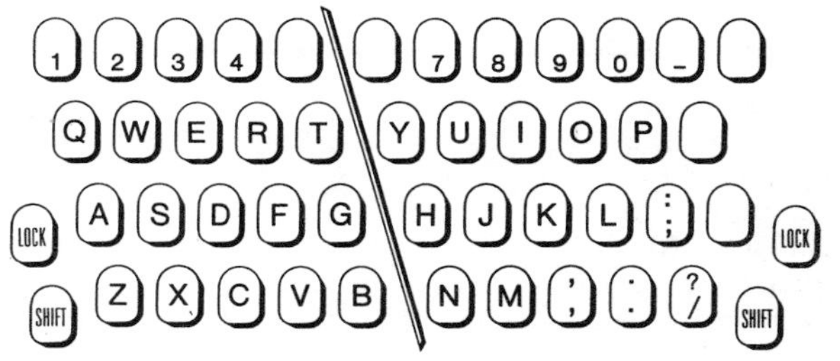

GOALS ⚲ *To improve number controls by reviewing 1–4 and 7–0 keys.* ⚲ *To type 80 words or more in 3 minutes within 5 errors on alphabet number-weighted material.*

DIRECTIONS *Spacing 1 for drills, 2 for TW. Line 50. Tab 5.*

WARMUP REVIEW
2 copies

The six new men did not want the cab you had had. 10
Some lazy guy said the quiz was too hard for him. 10
He did problems 10 and 28 while we did 39 and 47. 10
|1 |2 |3 |4 |5 |6 |7 |8 |9 |10

IMPROVEMENT PRACTICE
2 copies

aqla 1 auto 1 army 1 apple 1 auto 1 army 1 apple. 10
sw2s 2 sirs 2 sods 2 spots 2 sirs 2 sods 2 spots. 10
de3d 3 dots 3 deer 3 disks 3 dots 3 deer 3 disks. 10
fr4f 4 firs 4 fish 4 falls 4 firs 4 fish 4 falls. 10

ju7j 7 jays 7 joys 7 jibes 7 jays 7 joys 7 jibes. 10
ki8k 8 kits 8 kids 8 kings 8 kits 8 kids 8 kings. 10
lo9l 9 lots 9 less 9 limes 9 lots 9 less 9 limes. 10
;p0; 10 put 10 ;py 10 push 10 put 10 pay 10 push. ⚲ 10

1·1·1·3·3 TW
Spacing 2

The changes in rules seemed to bring about a 10
quick rise in the scores we made. In 1970, teams 20
seemed to average only 38 to 40 points a game. A 30
year later, in 1971, most Arizona squads averaged 40
71 or 72 points a game. New Mexico tried out the 50
new rules, too, with the same result: the scores 60
went up from 41 or 42 per game to about 71 or 72. 70
The teams did not get better; just the rules did. ⚲ 80
|1 |2 |3 |4 |5 |6 |7 |8 |9 |10 SI 1.20E

a·i·m 218–221

GOALS ◉ *To prepare a manuscript in business-report arrangement.* ◉ *To prepare a manuscript in book-manuscript arrangement.* ◉ *To type 195 or more words of fairly difficult material within 5 minutes and within 3 errors.*

DIRECTIONS *Spacing 1 for drills, 2 for TW. Line 60. Tab 5.*

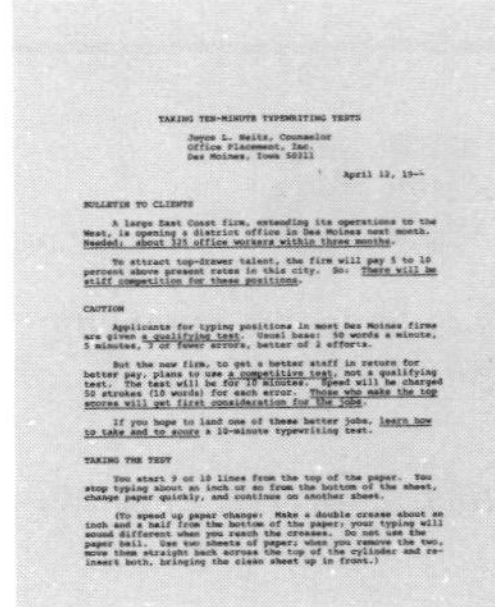
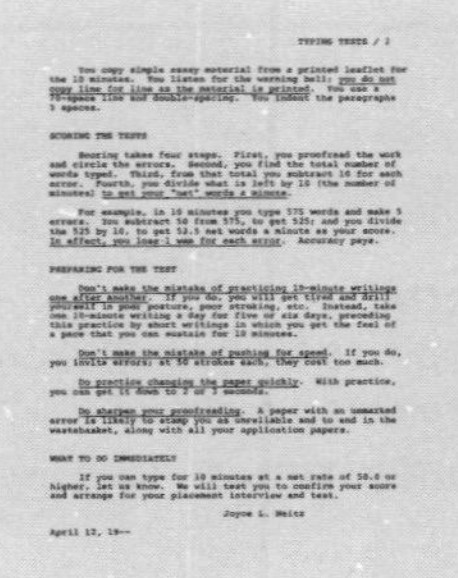

Two Pages of a Business Report

BUSINESS REPORT

See pages 223 and 224.

A business report is typed (as shown above) like other manuscripts in that:

1. Line is 6″, centered.

2. Top margin is 2″ on page 1 and 1″ on the following pages.

3. Bottom margin is 1″ to 1½″.

4. Two blank lines should precede subheads and the text on each page.

Business reports are usually, but not necessarily, unique in these regards:

1. Spacing is single, to save supplies, postage, time, filing space (most business reports get wide distribution).

2. A running head (short form of the report title) is typed in front of each page number after the first page.

BOOK MANUSCRIPT

See pages 225 and 226.

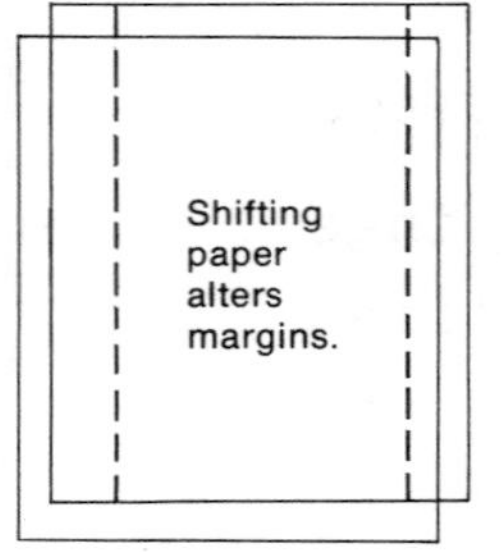
Shifting paper alters margins.

A book manuscript is like any formal manuscript (double-spaced text, 6″ line, etc.), but note two modifications:

1. A running head (short form of the chapter title) is typed in all caps at the left margin parallel to page number.

2. Binding space should be left in the left margin so pages can be accumulated in a 3-ring or clamp binder. Shift the paper guide and paper a quarter inch to the left to provide the binding space.

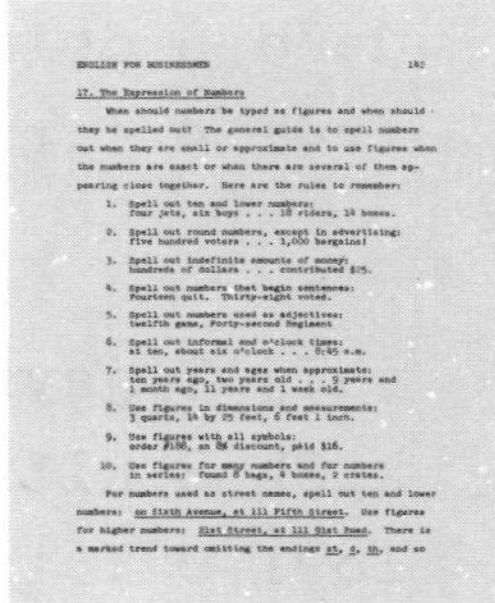
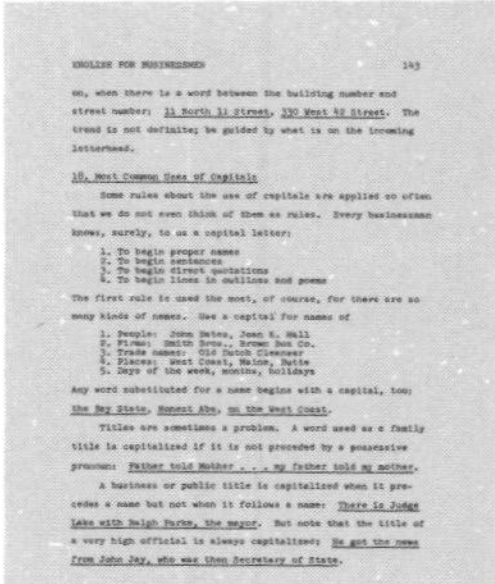

Two Pages of a Book Manuscript

WARMUP PREVIEW

2 copies

```
accumulation oversized emerging "bound" binder placed clamp    12
department experiment quarterly journal margin likely pages    12
Jane quickly seized the wax buffer and removed a big patch.    12
|1   |2   |3   |4   |5   |6   |7   |8   |9   |10   |11   |12
```

5-MINUTE TW

GOAL WRITING 3 copies within 5 minutes and 3 errors

Spacing 2

```
     What is a "bound" manuscript?  It is most likely to be    12
an accumulation of writing in a three-ring or clamp binder.    24
Placed in such a binder would be pages of an emerging book,    36
or journal notes on an experiment, or the quarterly reports    48
of a department.  To fit into the binder, the pages need an    60
oversized left margin.◉                                        65
|1   |2   |3   |4   |5   |6   |7   |8   |9   |10   |11   |12   SI 1.51FD
```

a·i·m 57

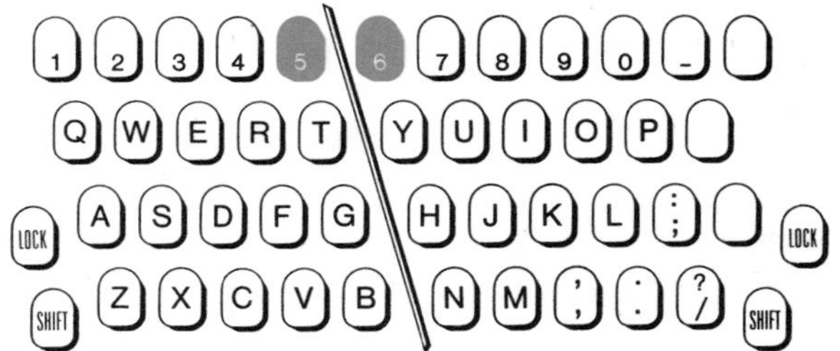

GOALS ⚲ *To control 5 and 6 keys.* ⚲ *To type 81 words or more in 3 minutes within 5 errors on review material.*

DIRECTIONS *Spacing 1. Line 50. Tab center. Tape K 21.*

WARMUP REVIEW

2 copies

1 The six did not ask the girl for the cab you saw. 10
2 Jippy said your size shoe was quite hard to find. 10
3 He ordered 10 of No. 28, but he got 39 of No. 47. 10

|1 |2 |3 |4 |5 |6 |7 |8 |9 |10

5 KEY

Use F-finger, keep A-finger on the A key.
2 copies

4 f55f f55f f5f5 f5f5 5 falls 5 fires 5 folks 5 red 10
5 55 fell 55 find 55 fewer 55 fix 55 fuss 5/55 5:55 10
6 The answer to No. 155 is either 55 1/2 or 55 2/5. ⚲ 10

6 KEY

Use J-finger, keep Sem-finger on home key.
2 copies

7 jy6j jy6j j66j j6j6 6 jays 6 jumps 6 jugs 6 jades 10
8 66 join 66 jump 66 more 66 must 66 have 1/66 1:66 10
9 We shall need 36 pencils or 6 pens for the 6 men. ⚲ 10

1·1·1·3·3 TW

Spacing 1

10 Dear Mr. Cory: 3
4
11 It is only 40 to 50 miles from your place over to 14
12 Jasper Park. Highway No. 77 is a good one, so it 24
13 should not take you more than 60 or 70 minutes to 34
14 whiz over in a car. There is a quaint yellow bus 44
15 that makes the trip five or six times a day, too, 54
16 taking about 2 hours for the trip. 61
62
17 I hope that you will make plans to join the Class 72
18 of 1966 at its reunion. 77
78
19 Ann Shaw ⚲ 81

|1 |2 |3 |4 |5 |6 |7 |8 |9 |10 SI 1.15E

 217

GOAL To type 195 or more words within 5 minutes and 3 errors on listen-for-bell copy of normal difficulty.

DIRECTIONS *Spacing 2. Line 60. Tab 5.*

AS YOU STRIKE EACH KEY—

- Make it print as dark as the others.
- Snap your finger off the key top.
- Move to the next stroke instantly.
- Make the typebar bounce off the paper.

WARMUP REVIEW

2 copies

1 information continuing separated diagonal version lone page 12
2 "running head" identify parallel magazine heading same line 12

|1 |2 |3 |4 |5 |6 |7 |8 |9 |10 |11 |12

SKILL DRIVE

See page 214.

Pretest on lines 3–8
Practice 1′ TW lines 22–24 or 25–27
Post-test on lines 3–17

3 Whenever there is more than one page to something that is typed, 14
4 there is always the chance that a lone page might become separated 27
5 from the others. Each page should include in its heading enough 40
6 information to identify it. There is no problem with letters, since the 55
7 standard heading for all continuing pages serves very well. But what 69
8 about headings on the pages of manuscripts? 78
9 That question is answered by the "running head" on the manu- 91
10 script page, typed on exactly the same line as the page number. For 105
11 a magazine piece, the running head may be just the name of the 117
12 author, typed in front of the number of the page and separated from 131
13 it by a diagonal or a dash. A page in a business report will have a 145
14 short version of the title of the report in the position of the author's 159
15 name. A page for a book will have a short version of the chapter name 173
16 at the left margin, parallel to the number. In all cases, the running 188
17 head gives the clue to where the page belongs. 197
18 In other words, any typed piece of paper that is found on the floor 212
19 of an office must be identifiable at a glance, and if it is not, some 226
20 scheme of running headings should be established for the use of all 239
21 the typists in the firm. No mystery papers should be permitted. 252

|1 |2 |3 |4 |5 |6 |7 |8 |9 |10 |11 |12 |13 |14 SI 1.40N

SPEED SENTENCES

Line 65

22 Lena paid for the six pens, but I paid the man for the big fish. 13
23 Jane got both forms for us and may do the audit for the socials. 13
24 She is busy with the work but is to go to town to get the panel. 13

|1 |2 |3 |4 |5 |6 |7 |8 |9 |10 |11 |12 |13

ACCURACY SENTENCES

Line 65

25 As Elizabeth requested, Jack will pay for fixing my silver vase. 13
26 Jeff quietly moved the dozen steel boxes by using a power truck. 13
27 Jinx gave back the cash prize money she won for her quaint doll. 13

a·i·m 58

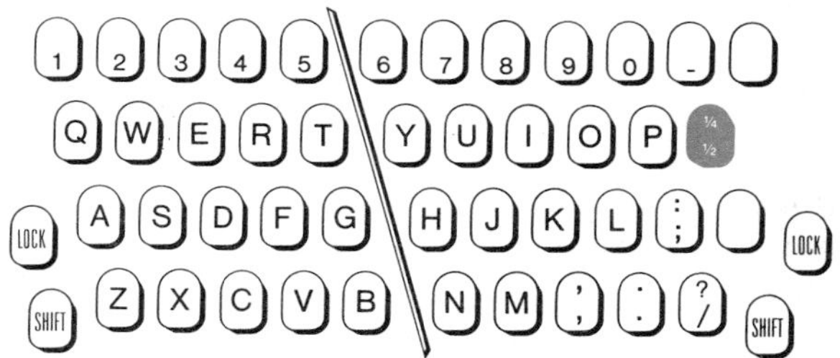

GOALS *To control the ½/¼ key. To type 82 words or more in 3 minutes within 5 errors on review materials.*

DIRECTIONS *Spacing 1 for drills, 2 for TW. Line 50. Tab center. Tape K 22.*

WARMUP REVIEW

2 copies

The six men got bus No. 22A, not the cab you had. 10
Jerry Quill could not find one shoe in your size. 10
The sum of 10 and 28 and 39 and 47 and 56 is 180. 10

|1 |2 |3 |4 |5 |6 |7 |8 |9 |10

½ KEY

Use Sem-finger, keep J on home key. 2 copies

;½½; ;½½; ;½;½ ;½;½ ½ pay; ½ mile; ½ hour; ½ week 10
Yes, 4 is ½ of 8, 4½ is ½ of 9, and 7 is ½ of 14. 10
He worked 10½ hours in May and 11½ hours in June. 10

¼ KEY

This is cap of ½ key. 2 copies

;½¼; ;½¼; ;¼;¼ ;¼;¼ ¼ pay; ¼ mile; ¼ hour; ¼ week 10
Yes, 2 is ¼ of 8, 2¼ is ¼ of 9, and 7 is ¼ of 28. 10
We gave ½ to him and ¼ to her; I got the other ¼. 10

1·1·1·3·3 TW

Dear Mr. Quinette: 4

We are pleased with the design of the school 14
emblems you have shown us. We wish to order some 24
of them. 26

Please ship us 10 dozen of the 37-inch green 36
pennants and 4 dozen of the wide 25-inch red felt 46
ones. Send us also ½ gross of the 10-inch decals 56
and ¼ gross of the 8- or 9-inch hexagons. Let us 66
have ¼ gross of the narrow 6-inch jade bookmarks. 76

Yours very truly, 82

|1 |2 |3 |4 |5 |6 |7 |8 |9 |10 SI 1.26FE

a·i·m 216 WARMUP PREVIEW

2 copies A–C

A know that will able meet both them soon come with make hope 12
B participate experiment permission delighted advisable extra 12
C Jack quietly seized the big ball of wax and moved up front. 12
D Five-minute TW on page 215 if you have not yet made the 195/3 goal.

JOB 216·1

TWO-PAGE BLOCKED LETTER

Punctuation open
Stationery Baronial Workbook 225
Plain half-sheet for second page

Date / Dr. Wayne T. Glover / School of 14
Engineering/Detroit College of Technology 22
/ Detroit, Michigan 48226 / *Salutation?* 33
I am delighted to know that you will be 42
able to participate in the experiment and 51
that Dean Toll has given permission for 59
Miss Jaboski and Mr. Harris to assist you. 67
I am eager to meet both of them. 75
I agree that it would be advisable for us 85
to have a planning session as soon as possible 94
so that we may come to grips with the de- 102
tails of the study. I shall be in Detroit for 111
another engagement on April 27 and will 119
make plans to remain an extra day, the 28th, 128
for a conference with you and your two new 137
assistants. 141
We might be able to get a start the eve- 149
ning before. I hope to finish my day's work 158
by late afternoon. 163
Could the three of you have dinner with 172
me at the Manger on the 27th? 179

```
1
2
3
4
5
6
7    Dr. Wayne T. Glover
8    Page 2
9    April 19, 19--
               ↓3
```

Example of a page 2 heading 203

By the time we get together, could you 212
and your assistants have some kind of tenta- 220
tive schedule ready for the study? It would 229
be helpful for our conference if you could, 238
for example, estimate the number of hours 247
the computer would be used, both for its 255
programming and for its running of the data. 265
Let me say once more how pleased I am 274
to know that our firm is to have your help in 283
the study. I have a firm feeling that what 292
we are investigating will turn out to be so 300
significant that your work and findings will 309
be quoted by others for years to come. 318
Complimentary closing? Punctuation? / 326
Michael R. Phillips / Director of Research 337
/ urs 338

|1 |2 |3 |4 |5 |6 |7 |8 SI 1.39N

OPTIONAL JOB 216·2

BLOCKED LETTER

Punctuation open
Stationery Baronial Workbook 225
Body 70 words + Attention Line 20

Date / Hotel Manger / 1857 Dodge Street / 14
Detroit, Michigan 48231 / Attention of the 24
Reservations Manager / *Salutation?* 32
Please reserve for Mr. Michael R. Phillips 40
a large single room, with bath or shower, 48
for April 26, 27, and 28. He would like to 57
have one of your large rooms in the new 65
wing. 69
Mr. Phillips will arrive late in the evening 78
on April 26. We enclose a $10 deposit to 87
hold the room for his late arrival. 96
Please let us have a prompt confirmation 104
of this request. 110
Complimentary closing? Punctuation? 116
Assume that you are signing the letter / 121
Secretary to Mr. Phillips / *Initials? Other* 129
reference? 131

|1 |2 |3 |4 |5 |6 |7 |8 SI 1.43N

a·i·m 59

GOALS ⚲ *To review all the number keys.* ⚲ *To type 83 words or more in 3 minutes within 5 errors.*

DIRECTIONS *Spacing 1. Line 50. Tab center.*

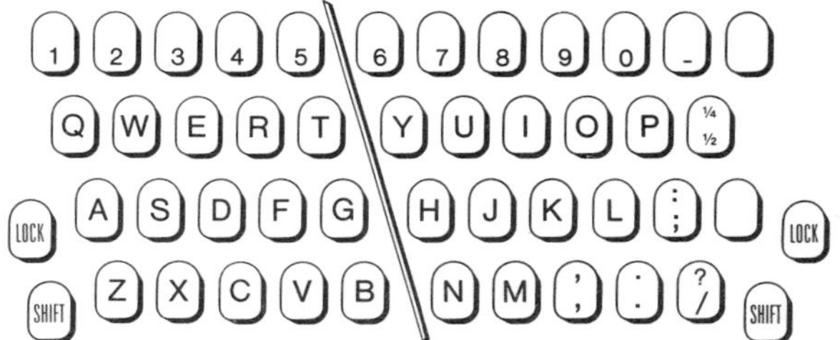

WARMUP REVIEW

2 copies

1 Why did the six men take the bus and not the cab? 10

2 Jill Mazurak was quite excited over a poor fight. 10

3 How much are $10\frac{1}{2}$ and $28\frac{1}{2}$ and $39\frac{1}{2}$ and $47\frac{1}{2}$ and $56\frac{1}{2}$? 10

|1 |2 |3 |4 |5 |6 |7 |8 |9 |10

PRETEST

1 copy or 3-minute TW

4 Dear Mr. Quinette: 4

5

5 We hope that you have not yet shipped the emblems 15
6 that we ordered, for we want to change the order. 25

26

7 Please ship us just 5 dozen of the 37-inch length 36
8 pennants but 9 dozen of the wide 25-inch red felt 46
9 ones. We still want $\frac{1}{2}$ gross of the 10-inch decal 56
10 emblems and $\frac{1}{4}$ gross of the 8-inch hexagons. Send 66
11 also 4 gross of the narrow 6-inch jade bookmarks. 76

77

12 Very sincerely yours, ⚲83

|1 |2 |3 |4 |5 |6 |7 |8 |9 |10 SI 1.25E

ACCURACY

3/1 copies

13 we 23 24 25 we 23 24 25 we 23 24 25 we 23, 24, 25 10

14 ow 92 93 94 ow 92 93 94 ow 92 93 94 ow 92, 93, 94 10

15 it 85 86 87 it 85 86 87 it 85 86 87 it 85, 86, 87 10

16 to 59 60 61 to 59 60 61 to 59 60 61 to 59, 60, 61 ⚲ 10

|1 |2 |3 |4 |5 |6 |7 |8 |9 |10

SPEED

3/1 copies

17 The total of 10, 28, 39, 47, and 56 is about 180. 10

18 Now, please total 10 and 28 and 39 and 47 and 56. 10

POST-TEST 1·1·1·3·3 TW

on Pretest

19 The sum of 10, 28, 39, 47, and 56 is exactly 180. 10

20 Do problems 10, 28, and 39; and review 47 and 56. ⚲ 10

a·i·m 215 WARMUP PREVIEW

2 copies A–C

A committee session attend cannot accept sorry shall tell see 12
B appropriations sincerely, pleasant graduate chapter program 12
C Jack seized the big ball of wax quietly and moved up front. 12
D Five-minute TW on page 215 if you have not yet made the 195/3 goal.

JOB 215·1

BLOCKED LETTER
Shown in pica (1/6th reduced)
Stationery Official
Workbook 223
Body 140 words
Line 5 inches
Tabs 5, center

Official is 8″ by 10½″.

HOUSE OF REPRESENTATIVES

FEDERAL APPROPRIATIONS COMMITTEE

Administration Building
Washington, DC 20515

Line 14 April 18, 19-- 3

7

Line 19 Dean Ralph E. Peterson 11
Colorado State University 17
300 North Pond Drive 21
Denver, CO 80202 24

25

Dear Dean Peterson: 29

30

I regret very, very much that I shall not be able to 41
take part in your FBLA workshop. The dates of your 51
program are ones when the Appropriations Committee 62
holds hearings, and I must attend each session. 71

72

I am <u>so</u> sorry that I cannot be there for your fine 83
program. It would have been pleasant for me to see 94
you and to have talked with your FBLA students and 104
sponsors. In fact, it would have served as a double 115
reunion for me, since I am both a graduate of CSU 125
and a former president of an FBLA chapter. 133

134

Please give my regrets to the Members of the Board 145
and tell them that, if I am invited for another FBLA 155
program on a date when I am free to attend, I shall 166
be pleased to be present and to take part. 174

175

Very sincerely yours, 181

184

Mrs. Andrew F. Tazewell 190
Legal Counsel 193

194

URS 195

SI 1.35N

Blocked Letter (1/6th Reduced) with Standard Punctuation, on Official Stationery

a·i·m 60

GOAL To build a speed reserve (100 words or more in 3 minutes within 5 errors) on very easy material.

DIRECTIONS *Spacing 1 for drills, 2 for TW. Line 50. Tab 5.*

STEPS FOR A SPEED DRIVE

1. Do a 1·1·1·3·3 on easy material.
2. Type a line of each word you typed incorrectly.
3. Type 6 more words, 3 times each.
4. Do one more 3′ TW; try to include the new words.

WARMUP REVIEW

2 copies

Jim has two pals who can fix the old car you use. 10
He quickly extinguished the most dangerous blaze. 10
He selected Nos. 10, 28, 39, 47 and 56 to review. 10

|1 |2 |3 |4 |5 |6 |7 |8 |9 |10

SPEED DRIVE

Remember the four steps in a speed drive (see box).

The two men went with me down the long road, 10
and in no time at all we had reached the lake and 20
found the path up to the spring. We had made the 30
hike in less than two hours; the day was good for 40
it, mild and cool, and the three of us felt well. 50
Jan and I sat down on a stone ledge near the 60
spring and gave our legs a rest, but Dick felt an 70
urge to scout for game and so told us not to talk 80
while he went on the prowl. We could hear him as 90
he shoved his way through the trees and brush; if 100
we could hear him, of course the game could, too, 110
which made us smile a bit, but we did keep still. 120

SI 1.00VE

a·i·m 61

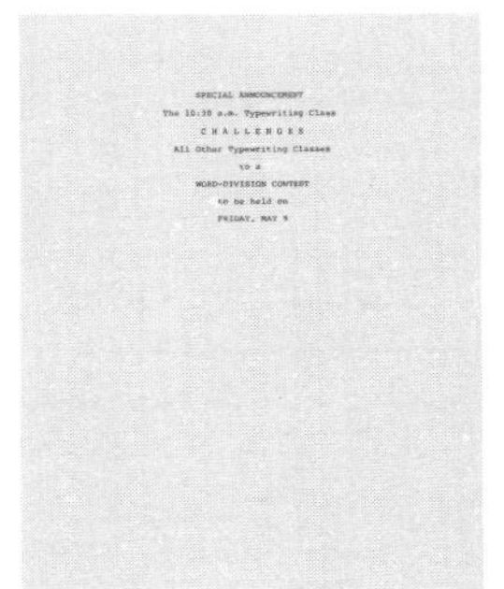

SPECIAL ANNOUNCEMENT
The 10:30 a.m. Typewriting Class
C H A L L E N G E S
All Other Typewriting Classes
to a
WORD-DIVISION CONTEST
to be held on
FRIDAY, MAY 9

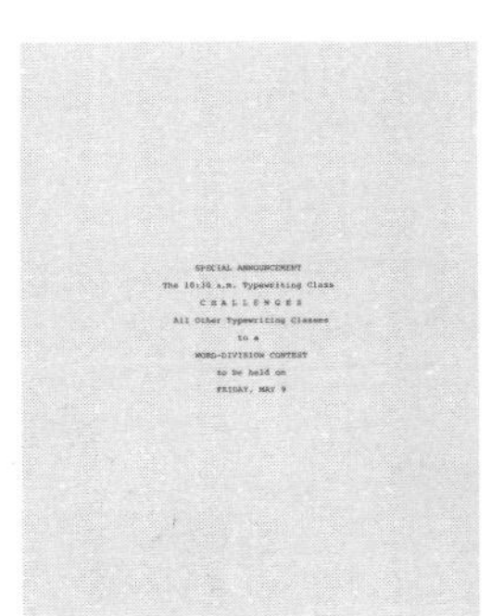

SPECIAL ANNOUNCEMENT
The 10:30 a.m. Typewriting Class
C H A L L E N G E S
All Other Typewriting Classes
to a
WORD-DIVISION CONTEST
to be held on
FRIDAY, MAY 9

GOALS To review the ending of lines. To review display centering.

DIRECTIONS *Spacing 1 for drills, 2 for Jobs. Line 50. Tab center.*

WARMUP PREVIEW

2 copies

Who are the men who can fix the old car Jim uses? 10
Did Ed extinguish a dangerous blaze very quickly? 10
I took 10 and 28, but June picked 39, 47, and 56. 10

|1 |2 |3 |4 |5 |6 |7 |8 |9 |10

a·i·m 214
WARMUP PREVIEW

2 copies A–C

A FBLA talk meet your this hour when take you but him and the 12
B Department conclusion invitation workshop conflict again it 12
C Jack seized the big ball of wax and quietly moved up front. 12
D Five-minute TW on page 215 if you have not yet made the 195/3 goal.

JOB 214·1

BLOCKED LETTER
Shown in pica (1/6th reduced)
Stationery Monarch (Workbook 221)
Body 174 words
Line 5 inches
Tabs 5, center

Woodbine Paper Company
Concord, New Hampshire 03301
Los Angeles ✱ *New York* ✱ *Concord*

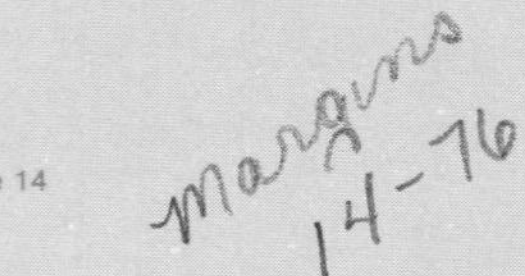

Line 14 April 18, 19--. 3

7

Line 19 Dr. Ralph E. Peterson, 12
Dean of Instruction, 16
Colorado State University, 22
Denver, Colorado 80202. 27

28

My dear Ralph: 31

32

It is kind of you to invite me to speak at the FBLA 42
workshop dinner. I am pleased to accept your invi- 52
tation. My talk will be called "Business Training, 63
an Investment in a Career." The talk will be light 73
in tone but add up to a thoughtful conclusion. 83

84

Thanks, too, Ralph, for the offer to meet my plane 94
and to make my hotel reservation. I shall arrive 104
on United Flight 219 at 3:45 on April 30. I know 114
this hour will conflict with some meetings of the 124
workshop, so I shall take a cab to the Hilton if I 134
find that you cannot meet my plane. 141

142

A special question: Could I arrange for a minute 152
or two with Dr. John Banks, of your Art Department? 163
He was one of my instructors when I went to Penn, 173
many years ago. It would be a pleasure to see him 183
again and to congratulate him on his advancement. 193

194

I am looking forward to visiting with you, Ralph, 204
and to taking part in the program of the workshop. 215

216

Very sincerely yours, 221

224

Robert S. Clemente, 229
Vice President, Research. 236

237

urs. 238

Blocked Letter (1/6th Reduced) with Closed Punctuation, on Monarch Stationery SI 1.39N

Monarch is 7¼" by 10½".

BELL RE-SPONDING

1 copy
Spacing 2

Type the paragraph below on a 50-space line, using the margin bell (check margin stop position) as your guide to line endings. Done correctly, all the lines will end at the same point.

4 Bob, how did you do it? I was worried about you, knowing that you 13
5 were quite tied up with the play rehearsals while the rest of us were 26
6 studying for examinations. Then you made honors grades. What 40
7 magical trick did you perform to do that, friend? 50

|1 |2 |3 |4 |5 |6 |7 |8 |9 |10 |11 |12 |13 |14 SI 1.21E

CENTERING

Spacing 2

61·1 Center the following announcement on a half sheet of paper. Beware the pitfall in Line 13: the hyphen is not a capital. Substitute your class starting time for the 10:30 a.m. in line 9 and next Friday's date in line 15.

61·2 Center the display on a full page.

Both Use the center tab stop to reposition the carriage for each new line.

8 SPECIAL ANNOUNCEMENT
9 The 10:30 a.m. Typewriting Class
10 CHALLENGES spread
11 All Other Typing Classes
12 to a (center check)
13 WORD-DIVISION CONTEST
14 to be held on
15 FRIDAY, MAY 9

a·i·m 62

GOALS To practice listening for the bell. To build a speed reserve (100 words or more in 3 minutes within 5 errors) on material that is very easy but requires listening for the bell.

DIRECTIONS *Spacing 1. Line 50. Tab 5.*

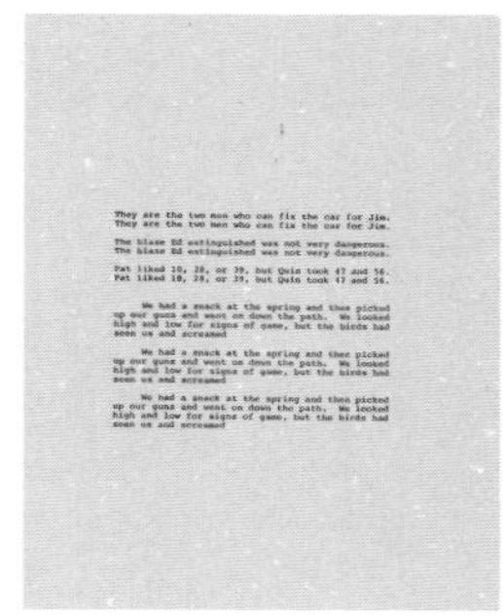

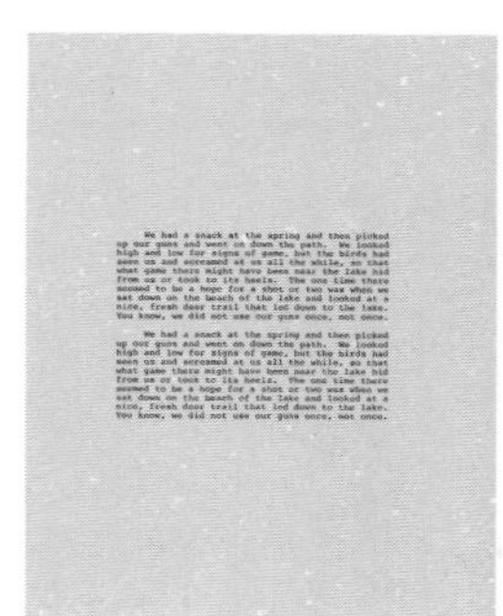

WARMUP REVIEW

2 copies

1 They are the two men who can fix the car for Jim. 10
2 The blaze Ed extinguished was not very dangerous. 10
3 Pat liked 10, 28, or 39, but Quin took 47 and 56. 10

|1 |2 |3 |4 |5 |6 |7 |8 |9 |10

a·i·m 213 WARMUP REVIEW

2 copies A–C

A They must have good jobs with very good pay, they told her. 12
B James Lennox, the banquet speaker, analyzed a few carvings. 12
C Blend 2 or 4 or 6 or 8 or 10 or 12 or 14 or 16 or 18 or 20. 12
D Five-minute goal-writing on page 215 if you have not already made the goal.

JOB 213·1

BLOCKED LETTER
Shown in elite
Stationery (Workbook 219)
Body 106 words
Line 4 inches
Tab center

F·B·L·A NATIONAL HEADQUARTERS
1251 16th Street N.W. Washington, DC 20036

Line 12

April 7, 19-- 4
5
6
7

(Baronial) Line 16

Dean Ralph E. Peterson 12
Colorado State University 17
Denver, Colorado 80202 22
23
Dear Dean Peterson 27
28
Thank you for the letter giving all the details 37
of our FBLA workshop. Thank you, too, for your 47
offer to meet my plane on April 30. 54
55
I shall get in at 9:28 a.m. on United Flight 18. 65
I do know that this hour may conflict with your 75
other morning meetings; so if you are not at the 84
airport, I shall take a taxi to the hotel and 94
plan to be at your office by eleven o'clock. 103
104
I have shipped to you a carton of books and one 113
large box of workshop guides. Would you arrange 123
for them to be held for my use at the workshop? 133
134
Cordially yours 138
139
(Mrs.) Ruth Rawlins 140
141
Program Aide 145
146
RR/urs 147

|1 |2 |3 |4 |5 |6 |7 |8 |9 |10 SI 1.35N

Blocked Letter, with Open Punctuation, on Baronial Stationery

"Baronial size" is 5½ by 8½ inches (half page turned sideways).

SPEED DRIVE

Spacing 2
See page 65 for speed drive procedure.

4 We had a snack at the spring and then picked up our guns and went 14
5 on down the path. We looked high and low for signs of game, but the 28
6 birds had seen us and screamed at us all the while, so that what game 42
7 there might have been near the lake hid from us or took to its heels. 56
8 The one time there seemed to be a hope for a shot or two was when we 68
9 sat down on the beach of the lake and looked at a nice, fresh deer 83
10 trail that led down to the lake. You know, we did not use our guns once, 98
11 not once. 100

1 2 3 4 5 6 7 8 9 10 11 12 13 14 SI 1.00VE

a·i·m 63

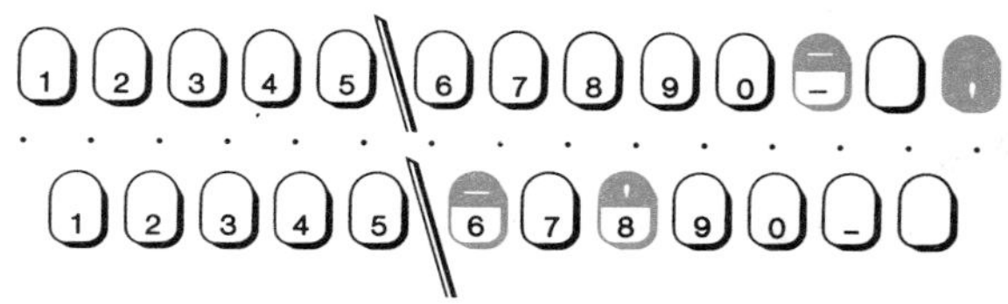

GOALS *To control the underscore key. To control the apostrophe. To type 84 words or more in 3 minutes within 5 errors.*

DIRECTIONS *Spacing 1. Line 50. Tape K 23.*

WARMUP PREVIEW

2 copies

```
1  Why did the new man not take the job you had had?   10
2  Quickly pack the box with five dozen modern jugs.   10
3  The stores are 10, 28, 39, 47, and 56 miles away.   10
   1    2    3    4    5    6    7    8    9    10
```

UNDERSCORE KEY

J-finger or Sem-finger

Check If your underscore is on 6 key, use J-finger; type line 4M, omit 4E. If underscore is on hyphen key, use Sem-finger; omit line 4M, type line 4E. Two style points to remember:

To group words (line 5), underscore both the words and the spaces between them, solidly.

To stress words individually (line 6), underscore the words but not the spaces between them.

```
4M  j6j j_j j6j j_j He did say he would not ask Paul.   12
4E  ;-; ;_; ;-; ;_; He did say he would not ask Paul.   12
5   I have not read that new book, Paying the Winner.   18
6   Remember, Al is not to help you on this new test.   16
```

APOSTROPHE KEY

K-finger or Sem-finger.
2 copies

Check If your apostrophe is on 8 key, use K-finger; type line 7M, omit 7E. If apostrophe is beside the semicolon key, omit line 7M and type 7E. To make the exclamation (line 8), type a period, backspace once, then type an apostrophe above the period.

```
7M  k8k k'k k8k k'k It's John's job to get Dad's car.   10
7E  ;'; ''' ;'; ''' It's John's job to get Dad's car.   10
8   We can't find Joanne's cap.  Help us look for it!   10
9   A dog's bark isn't as bad as his growl, I'm told.   10
```

a·i·m 213–216

GOALS *To distinguish display-line punctuation patterns. To distinguish stationery sizes. To produce blocked letters in different punctuation patterns on different stationery sizes. To type 195 or more words of normal copy within 5 minutes and within 3 errors.*

DIRECTIONS *Spacing 1. Line 60. Tabs 5, center. WB 219–225.*

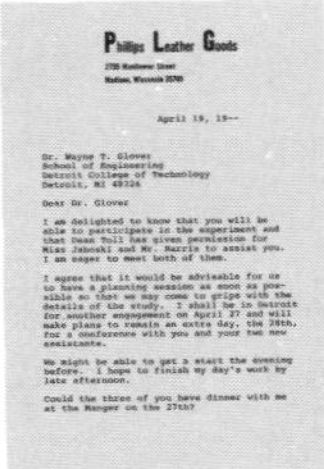

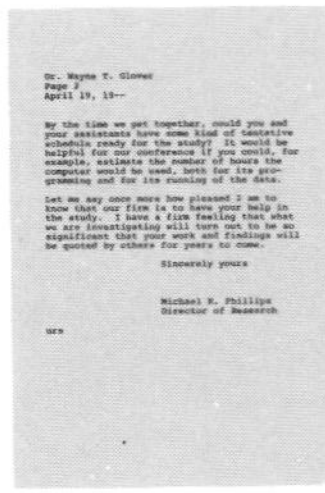

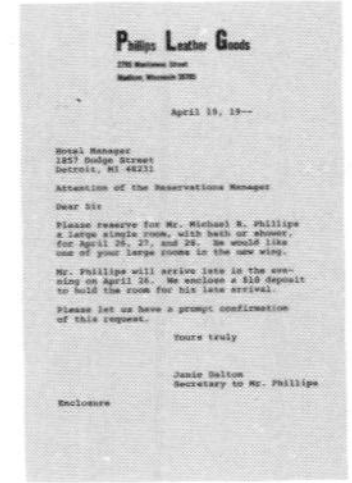

PUNCTUATION PATTERNS

Punctuation patterns do not concern letter bodies, but only the display lines above and below the bodies. In all cases, periods follow abbreviations.

Always use the Standard pattern except when specifically directed to use some other.

```
                    May 3, 1975

Mr. Stephen Kerr
Assistant Manager
The Bergen Press
313 North Brock Blvd.
San Jose, CA 95113

Dear Mr. Kerr:
.................................
            Yours sincerely,

            SWISHER COMPANY



            Sales Manager

HIS/urs
Enclosure
```

Standard Pattern, page 219

```
                    May 3, 1975

Mr. Stephen Kerr
Assistant Manager
The Bergen Press
313 North Brock Blvd.
San Jose, CA 95113

Dear Mr. Kerr
.................................
            Yours sincerely

            SWISHER COMPANY



            Sales Manager

HIS/urs
Enclosure
```

Open Pattern, page 217

```
                    May 3, 1975.

Mr. Stephen Kerr,
Assistant Manager,
The Bergen Press,
313 North Brock Blvd.,
San Jose, CA 95113.

Dear Mr. Kerr:
.................................
            Yours sincerely,

            SWISHER COMPANY,



            Sales Manager.

HIS/urs,
Enclosure.
```

Closed Pattern, page 218

Standard: colon after salutation, comma after complimentary closing. A period after an abbreviation and a comma after city are required regardless of pattern.

Open: No punctuation at line ends, not even colon or comma.

Closed: Every line ends in comma or period as shown in illustration.

STATIONERY SIZES

Always use Standard paper for the Jobs except when directed to use another size.

When you do use other sizes, you may refer to this page to check paper dimensions and your placement plan.

Most business letters are typed on the "standard" ($8\frac{1}{2}$ by 11) paper. Most government and military correspondence is typed on "official" (8 by $10\frac{1}{2}$) paper. Typists use similar placement plans for both. Increasing numbers of executives, however, prefer the "monarch" ($7\frac{1}{4}$ by $10\frac{1}{2}$) or "baronial" ($5\frac{1}{2}$ by $8\frac{1}{2}$) size. These smaller pages are distinctive, but their limits force typists to alter the letter-placement plan and to use two pages for many letters that would fit on one larger size page.

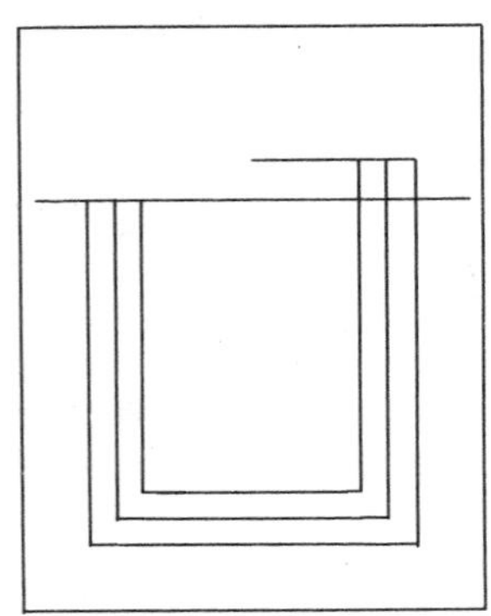

Standard $8\frac{1}{2}$ by 11″
Date on Line 15
Address on Line 20
Lines 6, 5, and 4″

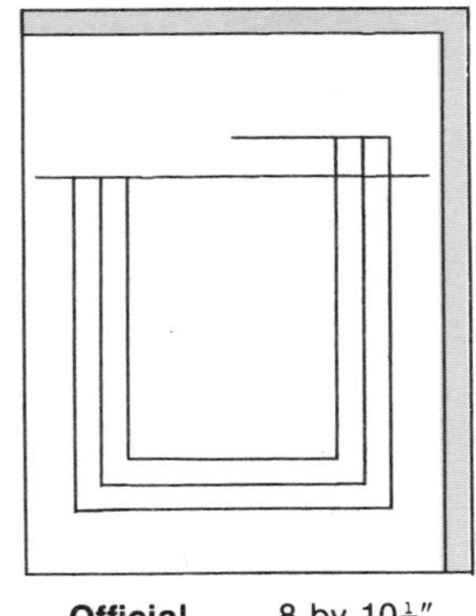

Official 8 by $10\frac{1}{2}$″
Date on Line 14
Address on Line 19
Lines 6, 5, and 4″

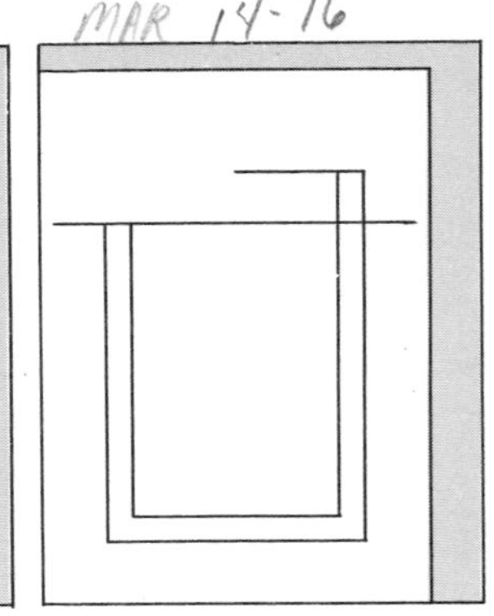

Monarch $7\frac{1}{4}$ by $10\frac{1}{2}$″
Date on Line 14
Address on Line 19
Lines 5 and 4″

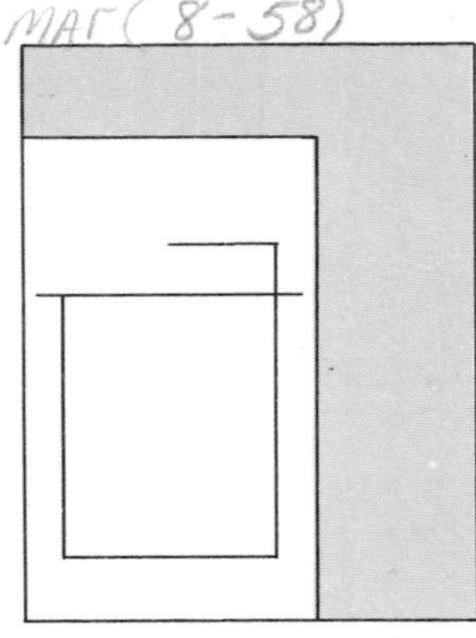

Baronial $5\frac{1}{2}$ by $8\frac{1}{2}$″
Date on Line 12
Address on Line 16
Lines Only 4″

1·1·1·3·3 TW

Note: Underscored words are tripled in the count. Spacing 1

Dear Jill: 2
3
The scout march sure was a wet one! It rained so 13
hard that we stopped in a cave and made a fire to 23
get dry and warm. Did that fire feel extra good! 33
34
Dave turned out to be our clown. You <u>always</u> have 47
one, you know. As we stood around, putting twigs 57
on the fire, he pushed in a wet one. It sizzled, 67
it squeaked, it smoked. We all yelled at him and 77
jumped back, but he was laughing. 84

|1 |2 |3 |4 |5 |6 |7 |8 |9 |10 SI 1.10VE

a·i·m 64

GOALS To type 85 or more words of production copy in 3 minutes within 5 errors. To produce a centered enumeration on a full sheet of paper.

DIRECTIONS *Spacing 1. Line 50. Tab 4.*

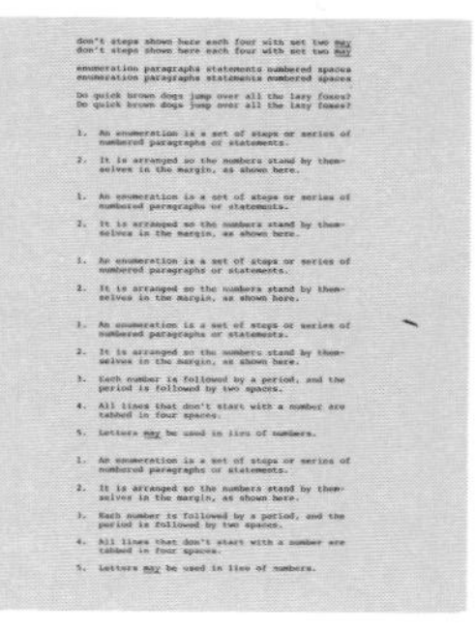

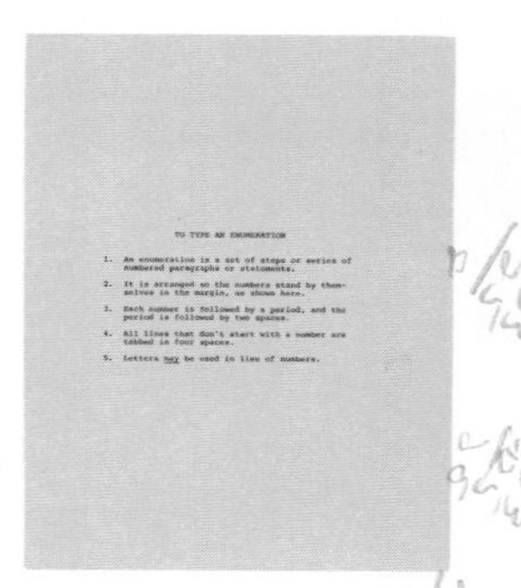

WARMUP PREVIEW

2 copies of A B C

Here is the first of many 4-line Warmup Previews. Type line A B C twice, do Line D once. Note that the words in lines A and B are from the production exercise that follows.

A don't steps shown here each four with set two <u>may</u> 11
B enumeration paragraphs statements numbered spaces 10
C Do quick brown dogs jump over all the lazy foxes? 10
D To practice tab-indenting run-over lines, type the first word in each line.

1·1·1·3·3 TW

Omit heading. Spacing 1

TO TYPE AN ENUMERATION ↓3

1. An enumeration is a set of steps or series of 10
numbered paragraphs or statements. 18
19
2. It is arranged so the numbers stand by them- 29
selves in the margin, as shown here. 37
38
3. Each number is followed by a period, and the 48
period is followed by two spaces. 56
57
4. All lines that don't start with a number are 67
tabbed in four spaces. 73
74
5. Letters <u>may</u> be used in lieu of numbers. 85

|1 |2 |3 |4 |5 |6 |7 |8 |9 |10 SI 1.35N

JOB 64·1 ENUMERATION

Center on a full sheet.

a·i·m 212

GOAL *To type 195 or more words within 5 minutes and within 3 errors on facsimile copy of normal difficulty.*

DIRECTIONS *Spacing 2. Line 60. Tab 5.*

WHEN YOU ARE TYPING—

- Your hands are low and close together.
- Your palms never touch the machine.
- Your elbows are close to your side.
- Your hands are flat across the backs.

WARMUP PREVIEW

2 copies

like some want into just good inch half size also with make 12
"executive" "official" "monarch" printing trimming squeezed 12
|1 |2 |3 |4 |5 |6 |7 |8 |9 |10 |11 |12

SKILL DRIVE

See page 214.

Pretest on lines 3–9
Practice 1′ TW lines 20–22 or 23–25
Post-test on lines 3–19

An example of how men like to be similar but different 12
is to be found in their stationery. One man wants color in 24
the printing. One man wants the paper to be colored. Some 36
want big letters in the printing; some want the printing to 48
be in tiny letters squeezed into one corner. Another wants 60
a picture used. Each man wants a normal letterhead that is 72
just a little distinctive. 78

Anything standard is a target for change by the writer 90
who wants to make his letters different. Paper is one good 102
example. Standard typing paper, eight and a half inches by 114
eleven, has been trimmed down to many other sizes. Govern- 126
ment bureaus use paper that is eight by ten and a half. It 138
is called "official" size. On this size, cut three-fourths 150
of an inch off the width, making a page seven and a quarter 162
by ten and a half inches; this is a size that is so popular 174
with executives that it is known as "executive" size. By a 186
quirk of humor, this is also known as "monarch" size. 195

SI 1.40N

SPEED SENTENCES

Line 65

Helen paid the city firm for the field she got down by the lake. 13
If they handle the panel right, the girls may make a big profit. 13
The eight men may run downtown and then to the field in the bus. 13
|1 |2 |3 |4 |5 |6 |7 |8 |9 |10 |11 |12 |13

ACCURACY SENTENCES

Line 65

Vic quickly mixed some grape juice with the frozen strawberries. 13
Tex may give quite a few prizes back but not that model jukebox. 13
Jack quietly moved up front and kicked the sizzling ball of wax. 13

a·i·m 65

GOALS ⚲ *To practice listening for margin bell.* ⚲ *To build a speed reserve (100 or more words in 3 minutes within 5 errors) on very easy material.*

DIRECTIONS *Spacing 1. Line 50. Tab 5.*

TYPING SPEED COMES FROM—

- Not losing time.
- Not jamming keys.
- Not breaking rhythm.
- Not losing the place.
- Smooth, steady typing.

WARMUP REVIEW

2 copies

The two new men <u>can't</u> fix up the old car for Jim. 12
Was the blaze that I extinguished very dangerous? 10
Queenie picked 10, 28, 39, 47, and 56 for Sunday. 10

|1 |2 |3 |4 |5 |6 |7 |8 |9 |10

SPEED DRIVE

Review page 65.
Spacing 1

When the two of us got back from our hike to the lake, we found 14
that there had been a big fire in one of the homes down the street 27
from where we live. No one had been hurt in the blaze, but the 40
flames had left just a shell of what had been one of the best old 53
homes in that whole part of town. 60

Doc and I went down for a look and were told that no one was in 73
the house when the fire began, which was why it had a big head 86
start by the time the fire trucks got there. While we stood there, ⚲ 100
some man came out of the wet ruins with a strange look on his 111
face and a black oil can in his hand. 120

For the next week or two, all we did was try to guess who the 132
man was and why he had that can. 140

|1 |2 |3 |4 |5 |6 |7 |8 |9 |10 |11 |12 |13 |14 SI 1.00VE

a·i·m 66

GOALS ⚲ *To control the parentheses keys.* ⚲ *To type 86 words or more in 3 minutes within 5 errors on alphabetic copy.*

DIRECTIONS *Spacing 1. Line 50. Tab 5. Tape K 24.*

TYPING ACCURACY COMES FROM—

- Giving equal time and attention to each key.
- Saying every letter to yourself (but don't move your lips).
- Smooth, steady typing.

WARMUP REVIEW

2 copies

I'm told the man who has the job now gets no pay! 10
Quietly pack the crate with five dozen gum boxes. 10
Study pages 10 through 28, 39, and 47 through 56. 10

|1 |2 |3 |4 |5 |6 |7 |8 |9 |10

a·i·m 211

GOAL *To type 195 or more words within 5 minutes and within 3 errors.*

DIRECTIONS *Spacing 2. Line 60. Tab 5. WB 215.*

NEW ROUTINE TIMETABLE

Warmup on preview words	1′
Pretest (2-minute TW) and scoring	3′
Drill (six 1-minute TW)	9′
Post-test (5-minute TW) and scoring	7′
Total time used in the a·i·m	20′

NEW SKILL ROUTINE

1. Warmup Each line twice.

2. Pretest Type first paragraph within 2 minutes with 0 or 1 error; or make one copy of it with 0 or 1 error.

3. Drill If you make more than 1 error on the Pretest, use the accuracy sentences; otherwise use the speed sentences. Type each sentence six times or, better, take two 1-minute TW on it—three copies in 1 minute = your goal of 39 wam.

4. Post-test Type both paragraphs within 5 minutes and within 3 errors.

WARMUP

2 copies

were them much they tiny ways from this goes back most wish 12
distinguishes different recognize neckties uniformly unique 12

|1 |2 |3 |4 |5 |6 |7 |8 |9 |10 |11 |12

PRETEST

Paragraph 1 within 2 minutes and 1 error

POST-TEST

Both paragraphs within 5 minutes and 3 errors

If you were to collect business letters and study them 12
in detail, you would be pleased to find how much alike they 24
are in general. But you would also be amazed by the number 36
of tiny ways in which they differ from one another. Why is 48
this so? Well, it goes back to the nature of men. Most of 60
the breed wish to be judged a little different from others, 72
a little unique in some way. 78

They do not wish to be a lot different, only a little. 90
They are like football players—want to dress uniformly but 102
to have their own numbers. They want their neckties in the 114
shape and size that is right, but in a unique design. They 126
want their letters to be standard in general but to have an 138
extra something that distinguishes them from other letters. 150
They want the letter to have all the usual parts, let there 162
be no mistake about that; the letter must conform to letter 174
patterns, so everyone will recognize that it is a fine one. 186
But just the same, each man seeks an extra something. 195

SI 1.33FE

SPEED SENTENCES

Line 65

Yes, the boy may ask you how you use the tab key and why you do. 13
Why not ask the boy how the tab can aid him do all the new work? 13
The two men may ask the boy how and why he set the one tab stop. 13

|1 |2 |3 |4 |5 |6 |7 |8 |9 |10 |11 |12 |13

ACCURACY SENTENCES

Line 65

Jeff quickly amazed the audience by giving them six new reports. 13
Jacqueline was very glad her family took five or six big prizes. 13
Judy gave a quick jump back as the zebra and lynx wildly fought. 13

PARENTHESES KEYS

Use L- and Sem- fingers.

4 191 l(l 191 l(l ;0; ;); ;0; ;); (1) (9) (10) (11) 10
5 The captain (John, that is) caught the long pass. 10
6 Bob is (1) tall, (2) dark, and (3) very handsome. 10
7 They need (a) six brunettes and (b) four blondes. 10

1·1·1·3·3 TW

Spacing 1

8 Dear Jake: 2

3

9 I sure wish you could see our new car! It's 13
10 beautiful and it rides like a cloud. The roof is 23
11 green and the body is a kind of tan; the paint is 33
12 glazed so that it seems newly shined. 41

42

13 It's a compact Olds (but it seats six). The 52
14 car has power steering and power disk brakes. It 62
15 takes corners like a race car. It is just <u>great</u>, 74
16 and my folks are quite happy about it. 82

83

17 Lew 86

|1 |2 |3 |4 |5 |6 |7 |8 |9 |10 SI 1.20E

67

GOALS To type an enumeration correctly. To type 87 words or more in 3 minutes within 5 errors, while arranging the body of an enumeration correctly.

DIRECTIONS *Spacing 1. Line 50. Tabs 4, center.*

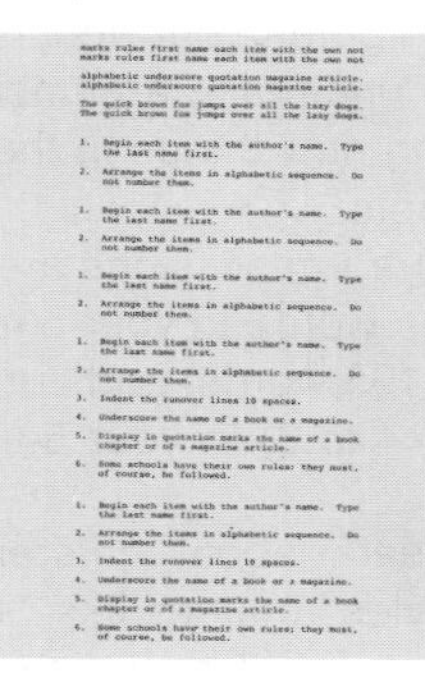

marks rules first name each item with the own not
marks rules first name each item with the own not

alphabetic underscore quotation magazine article.
alphabetic underscore quotation magazine article.

The quick brown fox jumps over all the lazy dogs.
The quick brown fox jumps over all the lazy dogs.

1. Begin each item with the author's name. Type the last name first.
2. Arrange the items in alphabetic sequence. Do not number them.

1. Begin each item with the author's name. Type the last name first.
2. Arrange the items in alphabetic sequence. Do not number them.

1. Begin each item with the author's name. Type the last name first.
2. Arrange the items in alphabetic sequence. Do not number them.

1. Begin each item with the author's name. Type the last name first.
2. Arrange the items in alphabetic sequence. Do not number them.
3. Indent the runover lines 10 spaces.
4. Underscore the name of a book or a magazine.
5. Display in quotation marks the name of a book chapter or of a magazine article.
6. Some schools have their own rules; they must, of course, be followed.

1. Begin each item with the author's name. Type the last name first.
2. Arrange the items in alphabetic sequence. Do not number them.
3. Indent the runover lines 10 spaces.
4. Underscore the name of a book or a magazine.
5. Display in quotation marks the name of a book chapter or of a magazine article.
6. Some schools have their own rules; they must, of course, be followed.

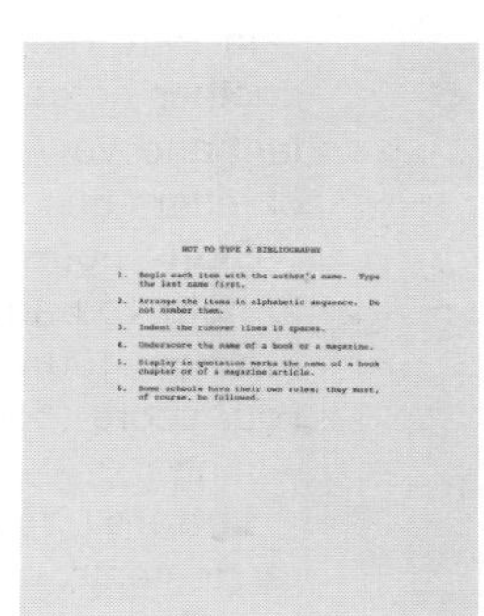

HOW TO TYPE A BIBLIOGRAPHY

1. Begin each item with the author's name. Type the last name first.
2. Arrange the items in alphabetic sequence. Do not number them.
3. Indent the runover lines 10 spaces.
4. Underscore the name of a book or a magazine.
5. Display in quotation marks the name of a book chapter or of a magazine article.
6. Some schools have their own rules; they must, of course, be followed.

WARMUP PREVIEW

2 copies

A marks rules first name each item with the own not 10
B alphabetic underscore quotation magazine article. 10
C The quick brown fox jumps over all the lazy dogs. 10
D To practice tab-indenting run-over lines, type the first word in each line.

|1 |2 |3 |4 |5 |6 |7 |8 |9 |10

Overview

In Part Ten you will tighten your accuracy controls another notch and will undertake a number of important and very interesting new things in the production of letters and manuscripts.

Skill Four of the 20 a·i·m sessions are skill drives to help you add 5 more words to your 5-minute count (up from 190 words to 195 words) and cut 1 error from your score (down from 4 to 3) in your 5-minute timed writings.

Letters You will learn about different letter arrangements, called "styles" (names like "full blocked" and "indented," and so on, will become familiar). You will learn also about stationery sizes (expressions like "monarch size" and "baronial size" will become familiar). You will learn, too, about the three punctuation patterns called "open," "standard," and "closed."

Manuscripts You will learn the difference between business reports and formal manuscripts; and you will also learn how to arrange the pages of a manuscript for a book (in case you or some future employer decide to write one).

Performance Goals

When you finish the 20 a·i·m sessions in Part Ten and take the test on pages 233–234, you should be able to demonstrate these abilities:

1. Technicalities You will score 90 or more percent correct on an objective test covering the technical information introduced and practiced in Part Ten (plus some review of prior Parts).

2. Production Working from unarranged material, you will execute letters in semiblocked style on baronial stationery, with subject lines and "cc" notations. You will also type the first page of a business report in correct arrangement, working from a revised draft with many alterations.

3. Skill You will type at least 195 words in 5 minutes (225 words is more likely!) within 3 errors on production matter of normal difficulty.

Routines and Procedures

The skill-drive routine has been altered from what it was in Part Nine. You will now (1) take a 2-minute pretest, (2) follow that by a series of 1-minute timed writings on either speed sentences or accuracy sentences—depending on the number of errors in your pretest—and (3) take a 5-minute writing to cement your gains in skill.

You will take at least one 5-minute writing each day that you work on Part Ten if you are not able to reach the "195/3" goal (195 words within 3 errors in 5 minutes), using portions of production Jobs or special paragraphs given for this purpose.

On many occasions you will follow the standard three-step production-practice routine (warmup, 5-minute writing on production material, then Job production) that you have used in most Parts.

1·1·1·3·3 TW

Omit heading. See example of bibliography on page 73. Spacing 1

```
                HOW TO TYPE A BIBLIOGRAPHY ↓3

1.  Begin each item with the author's name.  Type        10
    the last name first.                                  15
                                                          16
2.  Arrange the items in alphabetic sequence.  Do        26
    not number them.                                      31
                                                          32
3.  Indent the run-over lines 10 spaces.                  40
                                                          41
4.  Underscore the name of a book or a magazine.          51
                                                          52
5.  Display in quotation marks the name of a book        62
    chapter or of a magazine article.                     70
                                                          71
6.  Some schools have their own rules; they must,        81
    of course, be followed.                               87
|1   |2   |3   |4   |5   |6   |7   |8   |9   |10      SI 1.40N
```

center check →

JOB 67·1

ENUMERATION Center on a full sheet.

a·i·m 68

GOALS *To practice listening for the bell. To build a speed reserve (100 or more words in 3 minutes within 5 errors) on very easy material.*

DIRECTIONS *Spacing 1. Line 50. Tab 5.*

TO INCREASE SPEED

- Curl fingers as mucn as you can; keep them curled while you type.
- Keep wrists low—almost but not quite touching the front of the machine.
- Claw the keys—that is, hit the key top on the run, like a tiger's blow.

WARMUP REVIEW

2 copies

```
Why can't the two new men fix up the car for Jim?        10
Do quick brown dogs jump over all the lazy foxes?        10
Problems 10, 28, and 39 are easy; 47 and 56, hard.       10
|1   |2   |3   |4   |5   |6   |7   |8   |9   |10
```

SPEED DRIVE

See page 65. Spacing 1

If there is one thing that all of us like to watch, it is the way that (15) folks get on one of the huge new jets. These planes are so big that (29) they have to have three or four doors in the side, and twin doors (42) at that, so that all who are set for a sky ride can mount the plane (56) two by two, like the twos who got on the Ark, and do so in a big (69) rush. (70)

It is quite a sight to see, but we do not go just to watch the folks (86) go in the door. We think as we watch them. We think of where they (100) are off to, of the far parts of our land or of the world. We think (115) of why they must leave and why they must fly to get where they (126) wish to go. We look at the face of each, to see if we can tell its tale; (141) and we dream our own tales from what we think we see. (150)

|1 |2 |3 |4 |5 |6 |7 |8 |9 |10 |11 |12 |13 |14 SI 1.00VE

TEST 9-C

BLOCKED LETTER
Body 148 words
+ subject line
+ cc line
+ bcc line
1 carbon copy
WB 209

In this letter (a) center *Subject: Interviews with Tra*... 48
caps at the proper point, (b) insert a "cc" notation for *Dover Schoo*... 229
Board at the proper point, and (c) indicate on the carbon copy a 230
"bcc" notation for Mr. S. R. Sturgis. 250

Today's date / Mr. Blair N. Poe / Supervising Principal / Harrison 18
High School / Dover, DE 19901 / *Salutation?* / 28

We want to thank you, Mr. Poe, for sending so quickly the informa- 62
tion for which we asked about the number of students who will 74
graduate from your programs in office training and in industrial arts 88
next June. We hope that we shall be able to recruit some of these 102
young men and women for our firm. 109

Might we ask your help, also, in arranging for interviews with 122
these trainees? If you approve, we could send a man to give, right 136
in your typing room, our test for office employment. We could send 150
someone, also, to give a shop test. The next day, then, we could 163
send a team of several persons to interview those who made good 176
scores on the tests. 180

Would you be kind enough, Mr. Poe, to tell us whether and when 194
this plan, or some such plan, could be arranged? We should be 206
grateful. 208

Complimentary closing? / John A. Byrd, Personnel / *Anything else?* 226

|1 |2 |3 |4 |5 |6 |7 |8 |9 |10 |11 |12 |13 |14 SI 1.41N

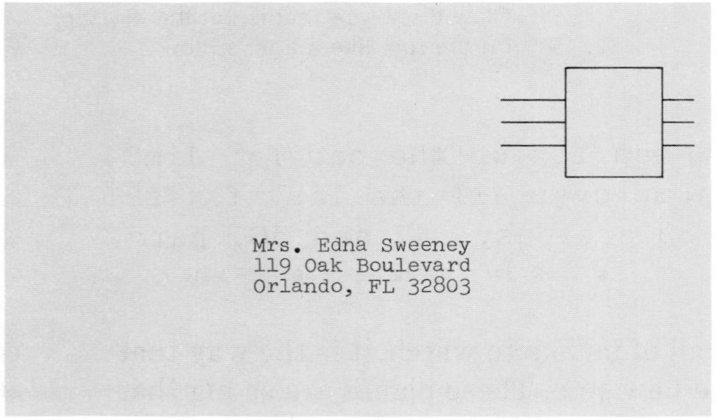

Mrs. Edna Sweeney
119 Oak Boulevard
Orlando, FL 32803

Address Side of Form Postal Card

THE P.T.A. OF BABSON TECH
Babson Technical High School Baton Rouge 70803

April 3, 19--

Dear Mrs. Sweeney:

The next meeting of the Babson PTA Executive Board:

8:30 Friday Evening
April 14, 19--
In the School Library

We shall count on your attendance.

Janet Womack, Secretary

URS

Form Postal Card, with Message Inserted

TEST 9-D

FILL-IN CARDS
WB 211

Using the "duplicated" form postal cards on Workbook 211, send notifications of the next meeting. It will be held at 8:30 on Friday of next week in the school library. [If you do not have the workbook forms, use simulated cards (slips of paper $5\frac{1}{2}$ by $3\frac{1}{4}$ inches) on which you type the complete message, not just the inserts.]

Send the cards to Mr. Gerald Fortune (378 Princess Street), Miss Miriam G. Baker (402 East 21 Road), and Dr. Merwin K. Ormond (833 West 67 Avenue), all located in your city and your ZIP zone.

|1 |2 |3 |4 |5 |6 |7 |8 |9 |10 |11 |12 |13 |14

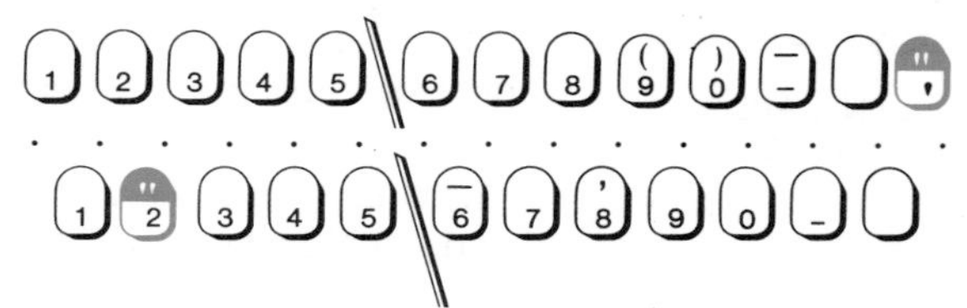

GOALS To control the quotation mark key. To learn the rules governing the sequence of punctuation at the end of a quotation. To type 88 words or more in 3 minutes within 5 errors from copy that requires listening for the margin bell.

DIRECTIONS *Spacing 1. Line 50. Tabs 5, center. Tape K 25.*

WARMUP REVIEW

2 copies

1 Joe (the man who got the job) didn't get <u>any</u> pay! 11
2 Quietly pick up the box with five dozen gum jars. 10
3 Helen lost these checks: 10, 28, 39, 47, and 56. 10

|1 |2 |3 |4 |5 |6 |7 |8 |9 |10

END OF A QUOTATION

As you look at lines 4–6, note that the quotation mark at the end of the quotation is sometimes before and sometimes after the final punctuation mark. These are the guidelines:

The final quotation mark always follows a comma (A) and a period (B), but always precedes a semicolon (C) and a colon (D).

A quotation mark follows a question mark (E) or exclamation mark (F) unless the quoted words do not ask a question (G) or make an exclamation (H), in which cases the quotation mark comes first.

QUOTATION KEY

Cap of 2, use s-finger. Cap of apostrophe, use Sem-finger. 2 copies

4M s2s s"s s2s s"s "Well,"Ⓐ he said. "Hello, again."Ⓑ 10
4E ;'; ;"; ;'; ;"; "Well,"Ⓐ he said. "Hello, again."Ⓑ 10
5 Joe "hurried";Ⓒ so did I. He "mewed":Ⓓ "Who, me?"Ⓔ 10
6 I called, "Help!"Ⓕ Did he "beg"?Ⓖ How he "cried"!Ⓗ 10

1·1·1·3·3 TW

Words shown in italics, like *"The Record,"* must be underscored. Spacing 1

7 Dear Customer: 3

4

8 I'm quite sorry that your copy of *The Record* was not delivered 22
9 here by Tony last night, as you expected. You see, Tony had an 35
10 accident while he was going for the papers. A large car "jumped" 48
11 a light on 12th street and struck him and his bike. 58

59

12 Tony will be hospitalized, we think, for two or three weeks. He 73
13 is at the Downtown Clinic, if you wish to write. 83

84

14 Yours truly, 88

|1 |2 |3 |4 |5 |6 |7 |8 |9 |10 |11 |12 |13 |14

TEST PREP 4

FILL-IN CARDS
Workbook 206

Using the postal cards on Workbook 206, acknowledge the requests of these persons for copies of "Credit Around the World":

1. Mrs. Thursa H. Sotak / 1733 Westchester Avenue / New Haven, CT 06511

2. Dr. A. James Lemaster / Apartment 411-A / 260 West Columbus Avenue / New York, NY 10017

3. Mr. Stewart K. Bessemer / 2317 Skyline Drive / Omaha, NE 68104 ⚲

a·i·m 209–210

GOALS ⚲ *To type 190 or more words in 5 minutes within 4 errors on normal listen-for-bell copy.* ⚲ *To produce a letter with an attention line and both "cc" and "bcc" references.* ⚲ *To produce fill-in postal cards.* ⚲ *To score 85% or higher on an objective test on Part Nine.*

DIRECTIONS *Warmup from the review on page 208. WB 207–211.*

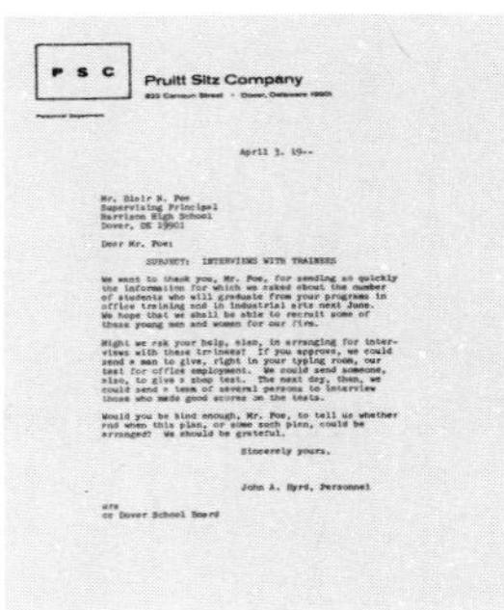

P S C Pruitt Sitz Company

April 3, 19--

Mr. Blair N. Poe
Supervising Principal
Harrison High School
Dover, DE 19901

Dear Mr. Poe:

SUBJECT: INTERVIEWS WITH TRAINEES

We want to thank you, Mr. Poe, for sending so quickly the information for which we asked about the number of students who will graduate from your programs in office training and in industrial arts next June. We hope that we shall be able to recruit some of these young men and women for our firm.

Might we ask your help, also, in arranging for interviews with these trainees? If you approve, we could send a man to give, right in your typing room, our test for office employment. We could send someone, also, to give a shop test. The next day, then, we could send a team of several persons to interview those who made good scores on the tests.

Would you be kind enough, Mr. Poe, to tell us whether and when this plan, or some such plan, could be arranged? We should be grateful.

Sincerely yours,

John A. Byrd, Personnel

urs
cc Dover School Board

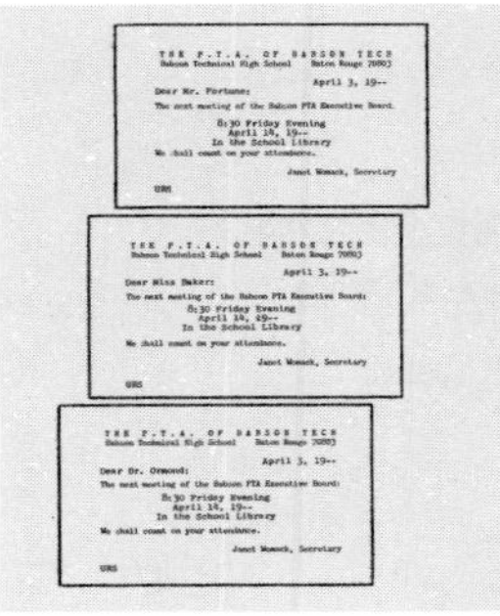

THE P.T.A. OF BABSON TECH
Babson Technical High School Baton Rouge 70803
April 3, 19--
Dear Mr. Fortune:
The next meeting of the Babson PTA Executive Board:
8:30 Friday Evening
April 14, 19--
In the School Library
We shall count on your attendance.
Janet Womack, Secretary
URS

THE P.T.A. OF BABSON TECH
Babson Technical High School Baton Rouge 70803
April 3, 19--
Dear Miss Baker:
The next meeting of the Babson PTA Executive Board:
8:30 Friday Evening
April 14, 19--
In the School Library
We shall count on your attendance.
Janet Womack, Secretary
URS

THE P.T.A. OF BABSON TECH
Babson Technical High School Baton Rouge 70803
April 3, 19--
Dear Dr. Ormond:
The next meeting of the Babson PTA Executive Board:
8:30 Friday Evening
April 14, 19--
In the School Library
We shall count on your attendance.
Janet Womack, Secretary
URS

TEST 9-A

Take a general information test. It may be the one on Workbook 207–208 or a similar test that your teacher may give you or may dictate to you.

TEST 9-B

5-MINUTE TW
Line 60
Spacing 2
Tab 5

Someone once said that the whole city of Boston should be set 13
aside as a kind of national shrine to liberty and to the roots of our 27
history. Most of the citizens of the city would probably object to 41
this. After all, they would point out, Boston is no relic of the past 55
but instead is a modern city that is pacing other cities in many ways. 70
But there's much that can be said for the shrine idea, so much that 83
the businessmen of the city are now backing a unique and exciting 96
display of colonial history: Boston's "Freedom Trail." 108
The Trail is a route that takes a visitor past a dozen or more 121
landmarks, ranging from the quaint house where Paul Revere lived 134
to the Old North Church, from the piers of the Boston Tea Party to 148
Bunker Hill. It takes an hour to cover the Trail by auto. A rapid 161
walker can do it in an hour and a half, although it is hard to believe 176
that anyone would be able to resist the temptation to stop and ponder. ⚲ 190
Along this Trail are guideposts and historical plaques to steer the 205
visitor and explain what he sees. How are the signs kept in good con- 218
dition? Here is the perfect example, if there ever was one, of Yankee 233
ingenuity. At each change of direction there is a vending machine 246
from which you buy, if you wish, and many do, a stamp that is a 259
memento of that point in the Trail. There are eight machines, and 272
together they dispense enough stamps to pay the upkeep of the Trail. 286
The next time you travel through the New England area, you must 300
be sure to stop in Boston and visit these exciting landmarks. It will 314
be an experience you will never forget. 322

|1 |2 |3 |4 |5 |6 |7 |8 |9 |10 |11 |12 |13 |14 SI 1.39N

a·i·m 70

GOALS *To apply the end-of-quotation punctuation rules. To practice using the quotation marks. To type a bibliography correctly.*

DIRECTIONS *Spacing 1. Line 50. Tab 10.*

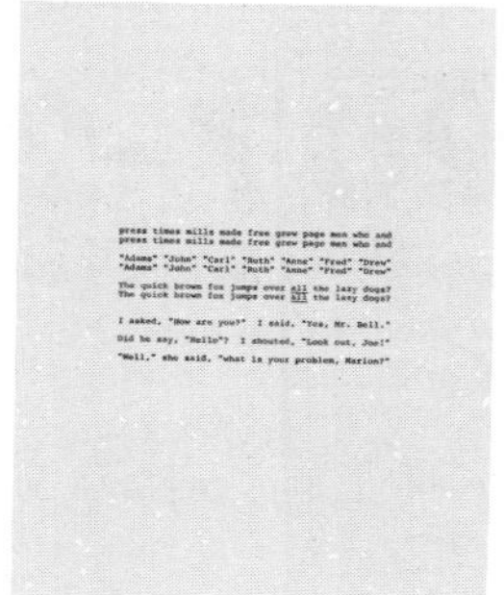

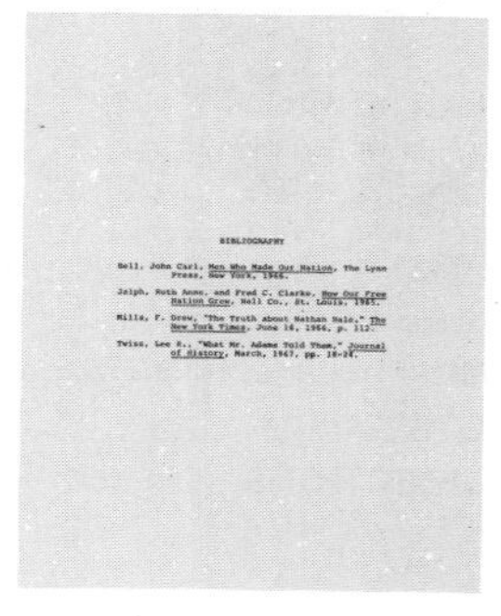

WARMUP PREVIEW

2 copies

1 press times mills made free grew page men who and 10
2 "Adams" "John" "Carl" "Ruth" "Anne" "Fred" "Drew" 10
3 The quick brown fox jumps over <u>all</u> the lazy dogs? 11

|1 |2 |3 |4 |5 |6 |7 |8 |9 |10

QUOTATION PRACTICE

Complete each line after reviewing rules, page 72.

4 I asked, "How are you___ I said, "Yes, Mr. Bell___ 10
5 Did he say, "Hello___ I shouted, "Look out, Joe___ 10
6 "Well___ she said, "what is your problem, Marion___ 10

JOB 70·1

BIBLIOGRAPHY Center on full page. Review page 71.

7 BIBLIOGRAPHY ↓3 7
9
8 Bell, John Carl, <u>Men Who Made Our Nation</u>, The Lynn 28
9 Press, New York, 1966. 34
35
10 Jalph, Ruth Anne, and Fred C. Clarke, <u>How Our Free</u> 50
11 <u>Nation Grew</u>, Hall Co., St. Louis, 1965. 63
64
12 Mills, F. Drew, "The Truth about Nathan Hale," <u>The</u> 76
13 <u>New York Times</u>, June 16, 1966, p. 112. 89
90
14 Twiss, Lee R., "What Mr. Adams Told Them," <u>Journal</u> 103
15 <u>of History</u>, March, 1967, pp. 18–24. 115

|1 |2 |3 |4 |5 |6 |7 |8 |9 |10 SI 1.28FE

PRODUCTION WORD COUNT

In addition to giving credit for each key stroke, the word counts of the Jobs include credit for these machine operations:

Centering Each stroke in a centered word or line counts as 3 strokes.

Underscoring Any stroke that is underscored counts as 3 strokes.

Tabulating An indention or other tabulator hop counts 5 strokes (1 word).

Blank lines involving an extra carriage (carrier) return count 1 word each.

Hand operations, like turning the cylinder or setting a tab stop, count as 10 strokes (2 words) each.

a·i·m 207-208

GOALS *To type 190 or more words in 5 minutes within 4 errors on average listen-for-the-bell copy. To preview the test in a·i·m 209–210. To produce a letter with special display lines and missing parts. To produce three form postal cards.*

DIRECTIONS *Line 60. Tab 5. Warmup page 208. WB 205–206.*

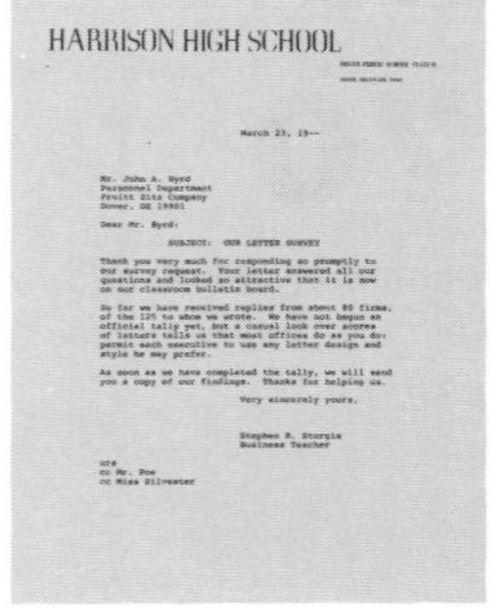

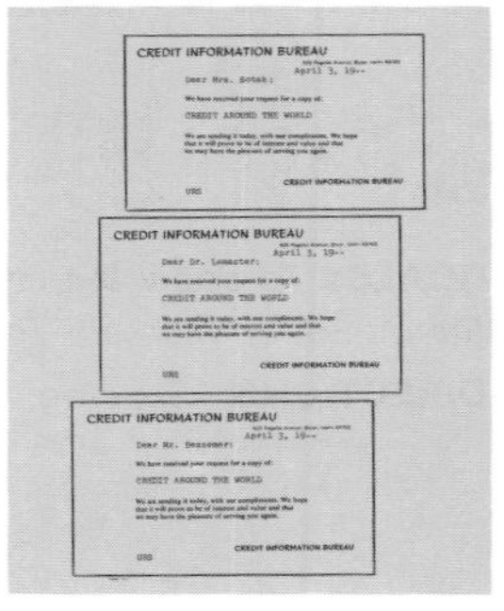

TEST PREP 1

Review the objective information test on Workbook pages 207–208. Do not mark the pages, but look up any details about which you are uncertain; be ready to score high.

TEST PREP 2

5-MINUTE TW
Spacing 2

One of the most prized animals in all the world is the camel, called 15
the "ship of the desert" because it can carry heavy loads for long 28
journeys across the desert wastes with very little food or water. Its 42
long hair can be woven into tough cloth for tents and blankets or 55
exquisite, soft cloth for clothing. Its owner values it equally for the 68
milk and meat and leather it gives him. The camel is valued highly. 84
Now, you would expect that an animal so prized must be much 97
loved, but that's not the case with the camel. Nobody loves a camel. 111
Nobody even likes one. The camel is simply too exasperating. It is 125
mean. It bites and kicks and even spits at its master; it tries to bite 139
any rider. The camel will not work without bellowing in anger, and 153
it frequently tries to shake off its load. Like goats, it chews anything 168
it can reach. And it is so stupid that the only trick that it learns to 182
do is kneel at its master's command. 190

|1 |2 |3 |4 |5 |6 |7 |8 |9 |10 |11 |12 |13 |14 SI 1.39N

TEST PREP 3

BLOCKED LETTER
Body 107 words
+ subject 20
+ two cc 10s
Workbook 205

In this letter, center *Subject: Our Letter Survey* in all caps at the 48
proper point and add "cc" notations for Mr. Poe and Miss Silvester. 191
Today's date / Mr. John A. Byrd / Personnel Department / Pruitt 17
Sitz Company / 822 Carroun Street / Dover, DE 19901 / *Salutation?* 31
Thank you very much for responding so promptly to our survey 61
request. Your letter answered all our questions and looked so attrac- 75
tive that it is now on our classroom bulletin board. 86
So far we have received replies from about 80 firms, of the 125 to 100
whom we wrote. We have not begun an official tally yet, but a casual 114
look over scores of letters tells us that most offices do as you do: 128
permit each executive to use any letter design and style he may prefer. 142
As soon as we have completed the tally, we will send you a copy of 157
our findings. Thanks for helping us. / *Complimentary closing?* 169
Stephen R. Sturgis / Business Teacher / urs / *Anything else?* 185

|1 |2 |3 |4 |5 |6 |7 |8 |9 |10 |11 |12 |13 |14 SI 1.43N

GOALS ⚲ *To type an enume* … *typing.* ⚲ *To type 89 words in 3 minutes within 5 errors.*

DIRECTIONS *Spacing 1. L…*

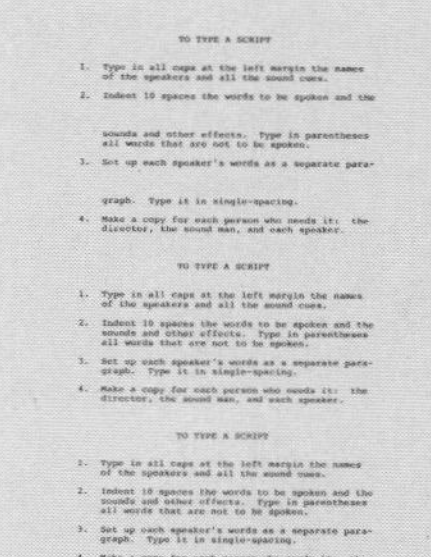

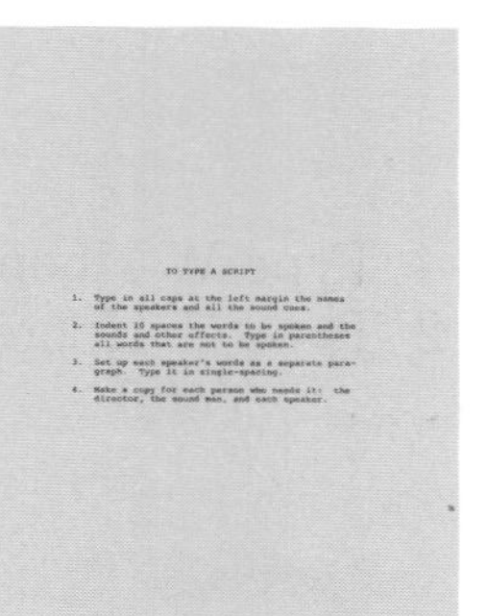

WARMUP PREVIEW

2 copies

A `names sound words caps cues each make set all the` 10
B `single-spacing parentheses paragraph separate and` 10
C `Did my quick brown dog jump over both lazy foxes?` 10
D Practice tabulating (Tab 4) the indented lines—by touch! 10

|1 |2 |3 |4 |5 |6 |7 |8 |9 |10

1·1·1·3·3 TW

Spacing 1
Omit heading.

JOB 71·1

ENUMERATION
Center on a full page.

1 TO TYPE A SCRIPT ↓3

2 1. Type in all caps at the left margin the names 10
3 of the speakers and all the sound cues. 19
20
4 2. Indent 10 spaces the words to be spoken and the 30
5 sounds and other effects. Type in parentheses 40
6 all words that are not to be spoken. 50
51
7 3. Set up each speaker's words as a separate para- 61
8 graph. Type it in single-spacing. 69
70
9 4. Make a copy for each person who needs it: the 80
10 director, the sound man, and the speaker. ⚲ ⚲89

|1 |2 |3 |4 |5 |6 |7 |8 |9 |10 SI 1.31FE

a·i·m 72

GOALS ⚲ *To use the margin-release key correctly.* ⚲ *To center an enumeration.* ⚲ *To learn the procedure for typing an outline.* ⚲ *To type 90 words or more in 3 minutes within 5 errors.*

DIRECTIONS *Spacing 1. Line 50. Tabs 4, center.*

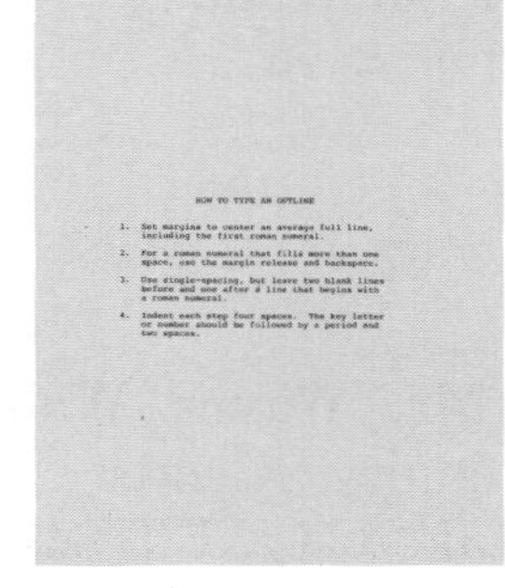

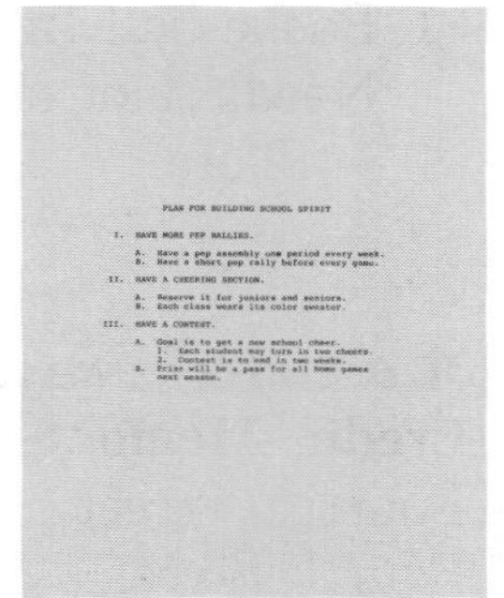

WARMUP PREVIEW

2 copies

A `line, roman blank each step line that set one two` 10
B `backspace including numeral average period margin` 10
C `Lazy brown dogs do not jump over the quick foxes.` 10
D Practice touch-tabulating the indented lines: type first word in each line.

|1 |2 |3 |4 |5 |6 |7 |8 |9 |10

4 Type W Hoops @ 5 00	20 00
2 Type K Hoops @ 5 25	10 50
Total	122 30

WSG WHOLESALE SPORTING GOODS COMPANY
Pend Oreille Drive
Spokane, Washington 99209

Credit Memorandum
No. 843

TO Finch and Gale Bros., Inc.
520 First Street
Fort Pierce, FL 33450

DATE April 3, 19--

Your Account has been Credited as follows

QUANTITY	DESCRIPTION	UNIT PRICE	AMOUNT
12	Regulation Type F Basketballs, damaged in transit	4 90	58 80
1	Basketball Inflation Pump and Needle, not ordered	3 75	3 75
	Total		62 55

A Standard Credit Memorandum Form

A credit memorandum tells a customer that an adjustment in his favor has been made in his account.

JOB 205·1 WB 201

Credit Memo 842 / Finch and Gale Bros., Inc. / 520 First Street / Fort Pierce, FL 33450 / Account credited for:

12 Regulation Type F Basketballs, damaged in transit @ 4 90	58 80
1 Basketball Inflation Pump and Needle, not ordered @ 3 75	3 75
Total	62 55

JOB 205·2 WB 201

Credit Memo 843 / Mr. Wayne Williams / Fourth Street Community Center / 1800 Fourth Street / Salt Lake City, UT 84101 for:

7 Regulation Type L Basketballs, returned as credit on order of Invoice No. 25992 @ 2 75	19 25
2 Type W Hoops, damaged in transit @ 5 00	10 00
Total	29 25

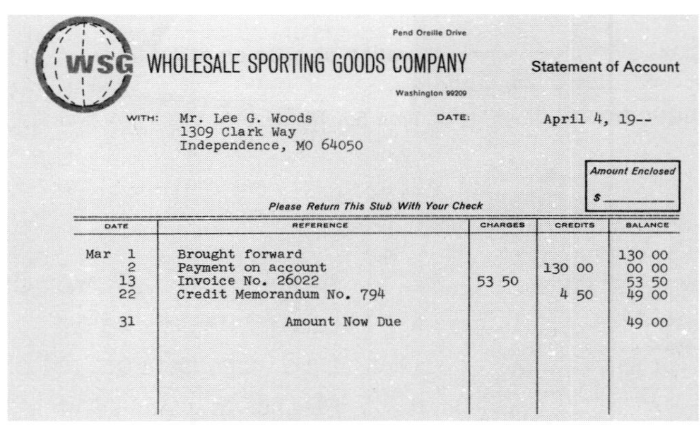

WSG WHOLESALE SPORTING GOODS COMPANY
Pend Oreille Drive
Washington 99209

Statement of Account

WITH: Mr. Lee G. Woods
1309 Clark Way
Independence, MO 64050

DATE: April 4, 19--

Amount Enclosed $ ______

Please Return This Stub With Your Check

DATE	REFERENCE	CHARGES	CREDITS	BALANCE
Mar 1	Brought forward			130 00
2	Payment on account		130 00	00 00
13	Invoice No. 26022	53 50		53 50
22	Credit Memorandum No. 794		4 50	49 00
31	Amount Now Due			49 00

A Standard Statement of Account Form

A statement is a summary of transactions with a customer during a month (or other stated period).

JOB 206·1 WB 203

Statement of account with Mr. Lee G. Woods / 1309 Clark Way / Independence, MO 64050.

		Balance
Mar 1	Brought Forward	130 00
Mar 2	Payment on Account, Credit 130 00	00 00
Mar 13	Invoice No. 26022 Charges 53 50	53 50
Mar 22	Credit Memorandum 794 Credit 4 50 Balance	49 00
Mar 31	Amount Now Due	49 00

JOB 206·2 WB 203

Statement of account with Mrs. Theodore J. Quill / 1524 Jane Street West / North Platte, NE 69101.

		Balance
Mar 1	Brought Forward	125 45
Mar 11	Payment on Account Credit 125 45	00 00
Mar 29	Invoice No. 27103 Charges 97 60	97 60
Mar 30	Credit Memorandum 867 Credit 18 30 Balance	79 30
Mar 31	Amount Now Due	79 30

MARGIN RELEASE KEY

The margin release (top left or right corner of the keyboard, possibly marked "Mar Rel" or "MR") releases the margin stop so you can type in a margin area. You do this to get another stroke or two at the end of a line. Occasionally you use the release so you can align roman numerals in the left margin. **Practice** Type **I** at the left margin, then use the margin release so you can backspace into the margin to align the other roman numerals.

```
   I.
 III.  (Backspace 2 times)
   V.
VIII.  (Backspace 3 times)
   X.
```

1·1·1·3·3 TW

Omit heading. Spacing 1 Note that "roman" is spelled with a small r.

JOB 72·1

ENUMERATION Center on a full page.

HOW TO TYPE AN OUTLINE ↓3

1. Set margins to center an average full line, 10
   including the first roman numeral. 18

19

2. For a roman numeral that fills more than one 29
   space, use the margin release and backspace. 39

40

3. Use single-spacing, but leave two blank lines 50
   before and one after a line that begins with 60
   a roman numeral. 65

66

4. Indent each step four spaces. The key letter 76
   or number should be followed by a period and 86
   two spaces. 90

|1 |2 |3 |4 |5 |6 |7 |8 |9 |10 SI 1.45N

OPTIONAL JOB 72·2

OUTLINE Center on a full page.

PLAN FOR BUILDING SCHOOL SPIRIT 19

21

I. HAVE MORE PEP RALLIES. 26

27

A. Have a pep assembly one period every week. 38
B. Have a short pep rally before every game. 48

50

II. HAVE A CHEERING SECTION. 58

59

A. Reserve it for juniors and seniors. 68
B. Each class wears its color sweater. 78

80

III. HAVE A CONTEST. 86

87

A. Goal is to get a new school cheer. 95
   1. Each student may turn in two cheers. 107
   2. Contest is to end in two weeks. 116
B. Prize will be a pass for all home games 124
   next season. 128

SI 1.27FE

a·i·m 204–206

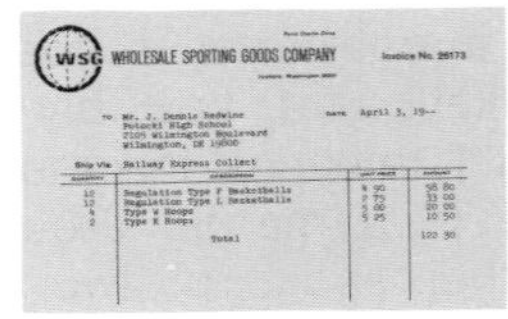

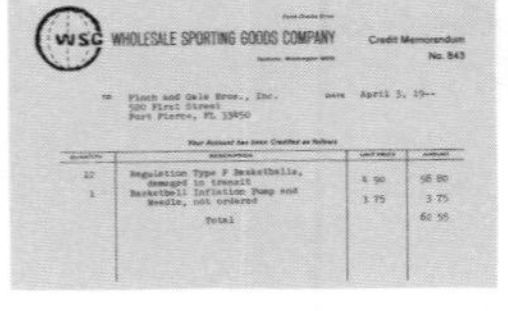

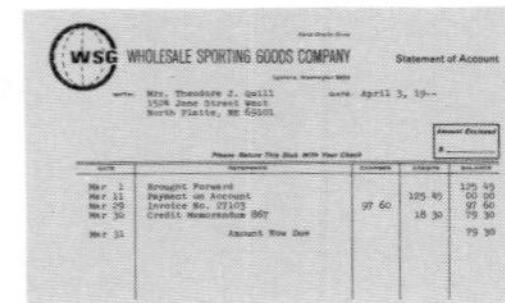

GOALS *To review the typing of invoices. To learn how to type credit memos. To learn how to type monthly statements. To type 190 or more words of repetitive copy in 5 minutes within 4 errors.*

DIRECTIONS *Spacing 1 for drills, 2 for TW. Line 60. Tab 5. WB 199–203.*

WARMUP REVIEW

2 copies

```
They will note this thin line when they look over this job.     12
The banquet speaker analyzed a few major carvings by Lenox.     12
Ship 1 or 2 or 3 or 4 or 5 or 6 or 7 or 8 or 9 or 10 or 11.     12
|1   |2   |3   |4   |5   |6   |7   |8   |9   |10   |11   |12
```

5-MINUTE TW GOAL WRITING

2 copies in 5 minutes

Repeat in a·i·m 205 a·i·m 206

```
                                                                 1 |  2
     The majority of typists approach forms typing somewhat     12 | 107
gingerly, because they know it is hard and hazardous.  Note     24 | 119
that it's what you type on forms that is hard and hazardous     36 | 131
and not any form itself.  The material is full of pitfalls,     48 | 143
like numbers and capitals and tab jumps and addresses, none     60 | 155
of which is easy.  Moreover, there is no way to spot errors     72 | 167
as you can with sentences, and so you have to exert special     84 | 169
care.  To be skillful with forms is quite a challenge.          95 | 190
```

SI 1.42N

JOB 204·1

INVOICE
WB 199
Review pages 127, 128

Invoice No. 26171 / Finch and Gale Bros., Inc. / 520 First Street / Fort Pierce, FL 33450 / shipped Railway Express Collect for:

24	Regulation Type F Basketballs @ 4 90	117 60
12	Regulation Type L Basketballs @ 2 75	33 00
4	Laminated Backboards, with Mounting Rods @ 15 50	62 00
6	Type K Hoops @ 5 25	31 50
	Total	244 10

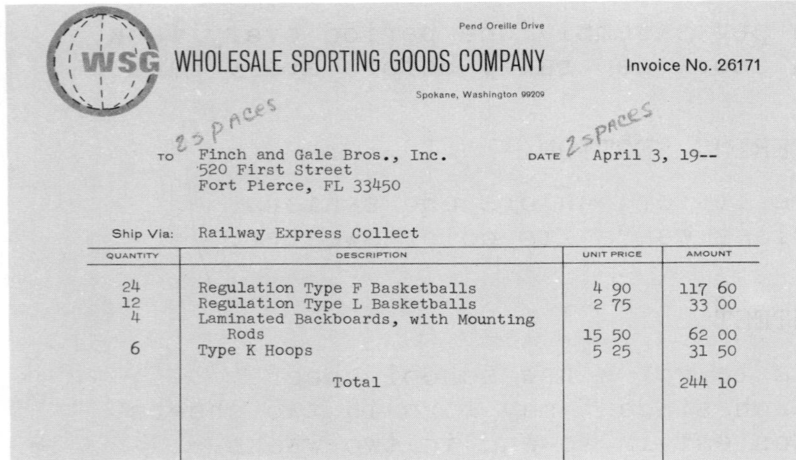

Pend Oreille Drive

WSG WHOLESALE SPORTING GOODS COMPANY — Invoice No. 26171

Spokane, Washington 99209

TO Finch and Gale Bros., Inc.
520 First Street
Fort Pierce, FL 33450

DATE April 3, 19--

Ship Via: Railway Express Collect

QUANTITY	DESCRIPTION	UNIT PRICE	AMOUNT
24	Regulation Type F Basketballs	4 90	117 60
12	Regulation Type L Basketballs	2 75	33 00
4	Laminated Backboards, with Mounting Rods	15 50	62 00
6	Type K Hoops	5 25	31 50
	Total		244 10

A Standard Invoice Form, with Space Instead of Decimals

JOB 204·2

WB 199

Invoice No. 26172 / Mr. J. Dennis Redwine / Potocki High School / 2105 Wilmington Boulevard / Wilmington, DE 19800 / Railway Express Collect for:

12	Regulation Type F Basketballs @ 4 90	58 80
12	Regulation Type L Basketballs @ 2 75	33 00

[TURN PAGE]

a·i·m 73

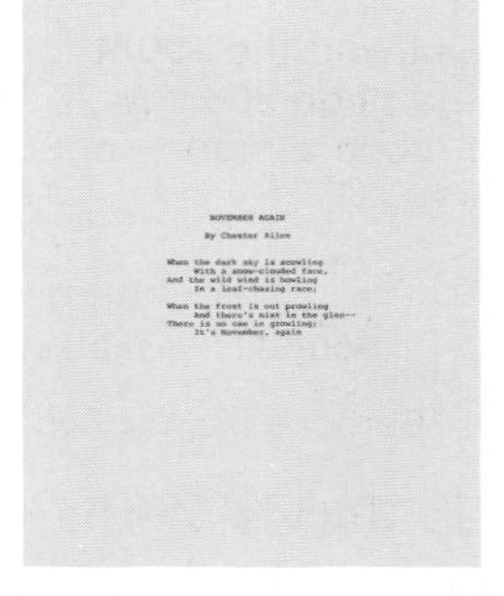

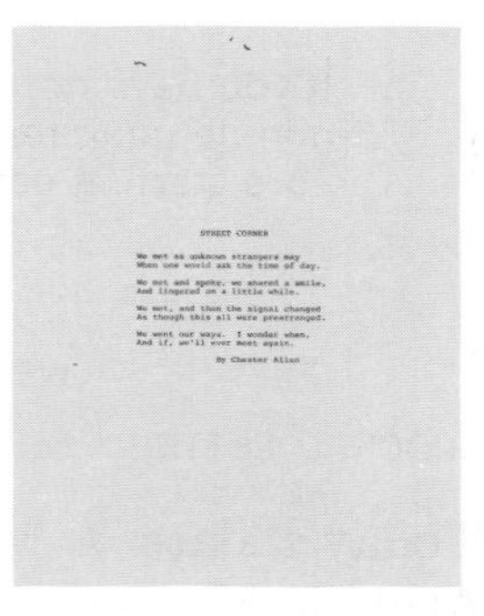

GOALS *To type verses with correct display. To type 90 words or more in 3 minutes within 5 errors.*

DIRECTIONS *Spacing 1. Line 50. Tabs 4, center.*

WARMUP PREVIEW

2 copies

A verse <u>extra</u> blank size want some poem you use all 12
B displayed subtitle author's rhyming special might 10
C All quick brown dogs do jump over the lazy foxes. 10
D Practice touch-centering the three titles shown in this a·i·m.

|1 |2 |3 |4 |5 |6 |7 |8 |9 |10

1·1·1·3·3 TW

Omit title.

TO TYPE A POEM OR VERSE ↓3

1. Center it on the paper. You might use an odd size paper if you want some special effect. 10 20
2. Center the title of the poem in all caps. 30
3. Type the author's name as a subtitle or as a line displayed under the last verse. 41 50
4. Begin each line with a capital letter. 60
5. Leave one <u>extra</u> blank line between the verses. 73
6. Show the rhyming scheme by indenting lines or using extra blank lines. 84 90

SI 1.34FE

OPTIONAL JOB 73·1

ENUMERATION Center on a full page.

POEMS

JOB 73·2

NOVEMBER AGAIN ↓2 9

By Chester Allen ↓3 19

21

When the dark sky is scowling 27
    With a snow-clouded face, 34
And the wild wind is howling 39
    In a leaf-chasing race; 45

46

When the frost is out prowling 52
    And there's mist in the glen-- 59
There is no use in growling: 66
    It's November, again! 71

JOB 73·3

STREET CORNER ↓3 8

We met as unknown strangers may 16
When one would ask the time of day. 24

25

We met and spoke, we shared a smile, 31
And lingered on a little while. 38

39

We met, and then the signal changed 46
As though this all were prearranged. 54

55

We went our ways. I wonder when, 61
And if, we'll ever meet again. 68

69

By Chester Allen 73

If you have not yet achieved the 190/4 5-minute goal, repeat the page 206 TW before starting each of these assignments.

JOB 201·1 WB 193 Body 117 + subject 20 +
BLOCKED LETTER cc 10 Carbons file, cc, bcc

Today's date / Mr. T. Jarvis Zorbach / 12
Athletic Manager / Harrison High School / 28
Dover, DE 19901 / *Salutation?* 36
Subject: Football Schedule 42
I do not know when I have been so 50
pleased by one letter as I was when I re- 58
ceived your offer of a game this fall. Because 68
you fielded your first team just a few years 77
back, you most likely remember clearly the 85
problems involved in getting a squad 93
started. 95
We accept your invitation for Friday, 103
October 18. I know our field will not be 112
in operating condition this fall; we shall 120
be grateful for the chance to play under 128
the lights on the fine Harrison field. 136
Complimentary closing? / Denton Jason / 150
Athletic Director / urs / cc Mr. Flynn 159
PS: I look forward to meeting you at 168
one of the conferences of the league this 176
spring. I know that you can help me solve 185
many more of my problems. 190
bcc Mr. Hale 210

|1 |2 |3 |4 |5 |6 |7 |8 SI 1.42N

JOB 202·1 WB 195 Body 94 + subject 20 + bcc
BLOCKED LETTER + co. signature Carbons ?

Today's date / Miss Nina Wamsley, Dean / 13
Petrie School of Business / 1600 Liberty 21
Avenue / Philadelphia, PA 19104 / *Saluta-* 32
tion? / Subject: Harrison Career Day 38
This year Harrison High School will hold 48
its annual Career Day on Tuesday, April 3. 56
Enclosed is a copy of the program from last 65
year; we plan to use the same type this 73
spring, too. 76
As you know and as the program shows, 85
last year you sent a member of your staff 93
to attend the sessions and to speak. We 101
should like to invite you to send a speaker 111
again this year. If you can do so, please 119
fill out the enclosed form and return it to 127
me by the end of the month. 133
Complimentary closing? / HARRISON 142
HIGH SCHOOL / Guidance Counselor / 152
ILS/urs / 2 Enclosures / bcc Mr. Ford 178

|1 |2 |3 |4 |5 |6 |7 |8 SI 1.40N

JOB 202·2 WB 197 Repeat 202·1, for
BLOCKED LETTER new addressee Carbons

Today's date / Miss Jean Spear, Director / 13
Copeland School for Nurses / 200 Avery 20
Street / Baltimore, MD 21217 / *Saluta-* 27
tion? / Subject: Harrison Career Day 37

a·i·m 203

GOAL *To bolster skill (190 or more words in 5 minutes within 4 errors) on normal listen-for-bell copy on material on page 204.*

DIRECTIONS *Spacing 1 for drills, 2 for TW. Line 60. Tab 5.*

WATCH THE WRISTS!

- Keep them low (don't touch machine).
- Keep them close (thumbs could lock).
- Keep them level with one another.
- Keep them quiet (fingers do the work).

WARMUP REVIEW

2 copies

1 Why did she not buy the lid for the new pan she got for us? 12
2 Jake Westman found exactly five quarters in the zipper bag. 12
3 For 1 for 2 for 3 for 4 for 5 for 6 for 7 for 8 for 9 for 0 12
4 Turn to page 204 and use lines 19–33 for an accuracy drive.

 74

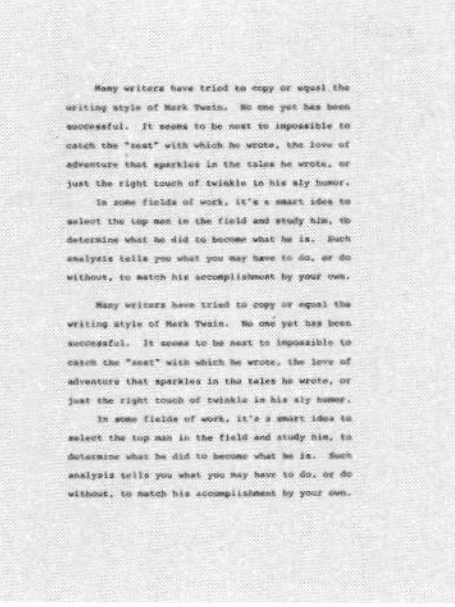

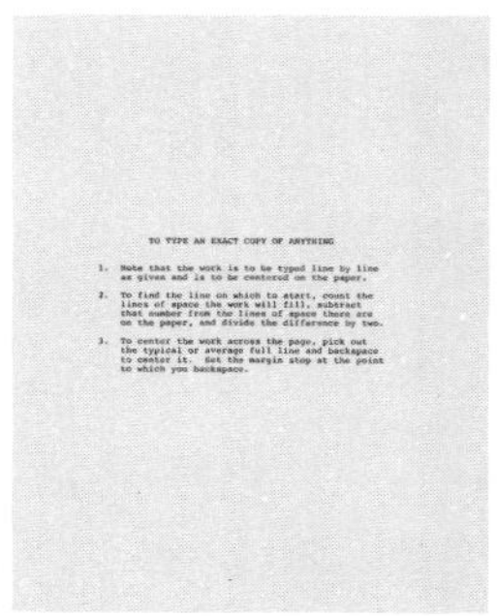

GOALS ⚲ *To type 90 words or more in 3 minutes within 5 errors on alphabetic paragraphs, with listening to the margin bell required.* ⚲ *To center an enumeration correctly on a full sheet.* ⚲ *To preview a·i·m 75 Test.*

DIRECTIONS *Spacing 2 for TW, 1 for enumeration. Line 50. Tabs 5 for TW, 4 and center for enumeration. WB 31, 32.*

TEST PREP 1

Review the objective-information test on Workbook pages 31–32. Do not mark the test, but look up any details of which you are not positive. Be ready to score well.

TEST PREP 2

3-Minute TW
2 attempts

Many writers have tried to copy or equal the writing style 13
of Mark Twain. No one yet has been successful. It seems to be 26
next to impossible to catch the "zest" with which he wrote, the 38
love of adventure that sparkles in the tales he wrote, or just the 52
right touch of twinkle in his sly humor. 60
In some fields of work, it's a smart idea to select the top man 74
in the field and study him, to determine what he did to become 87
what he is. ⚲Such analysis tells you what you may have to do, or 100
do without, to match his accomplishment by your own. 110
But this plan does not work when you turn to writing for a 123
career. Oh, a study of the working methods of good authors is 136
helpful, but only in a technical way; it doesn't tell you what to write. 150

|1 |2 |3 |4 |5 |6 |7 |8 |9 |10 |11 |12 |13 SI 1.29FE

TEST PREP 3
ENUMERATION

Center on a full page. Use the correct enumeration form—do not use the style shown here.

TO TYPE AN EXACT COPY OF ANYTHING ↓? 13

1. Note that the work is to be typed line by 25
line as given and is to be centered on the paper. 35
36
2. To find the line on which to start, count 46
the lines of space the work will fill, subtract 56
that number from the lines of space there are on 65
the paper, and divide the difference by two. 75
76
3. To center the work across the page, pick 86
out the typical or average full line and backspace 96
to center it. Set the margin stop at the point to 106
which you backspace. ⚲ 110

|1 |2 |3 |4 |5 |6 |7 |8 |9 |10 SI 1.22E

bcc Mr. Caspar 225
bcc Miss Kearney 228

JOB 200·1

BLOCKED LETTER
Shown in pica
Body 139 words
+ Subject + PS
Workbook 191

March 22, 19-- 4

8

Mr. Stephen R. Sturgis 13
Business Teacher 16
Harrison High School 20
Dover, DE 19901 23

Dear Mr. Sturgis: 27

SUBJECT: Our Current Letter Practices 36

I am pleased to cooperate with you and your class. 48
I made a quick survey among our office personnel, 58
and so I can now answer the questions you raised. 68

I found that our executives differ widely in their 79
use of the attention and subject lines. One writer 90
in the Advertising Department is the only man who 100
uses the attention line often, and writers in Legal 110
and in Collections are the only ones who often use 120
the subject line. The older men prefer these lines 131
centered; the young men like them blocked. 140

As you might guess from what I have said, we have 151
not adopted any one letter style. As in most com- 160
panies, each writer uses the style that he prefers. 171
My survey shows that two-thirds of us use blocked 181
form, as shown by this letter; the others vary. 190

Hope this fills the bill! 195

198

John A. Byrd, Personnel 204
urs 205

PS: And I am the only one who likes a postscript! 216

SI 1.39N

Carbon Copy of Blocked Letter with Subject Line, Postscript, and "bcc" Notation

a·i·m 75 TEST

GOALS *To type 90 or more words in 3 minutes within 5 errors on alphabetic paragraphs involving listening for the margin bell. To arrange and center an enumeration on a full page. To score 80% or more on an objective test on Part Three technical information.*

DIRECTIONS *Spacing 2 for TW, 1 for enumeration. Line 50. Tabs 5 for TW, you decide for enumeration. WB 31–32.*

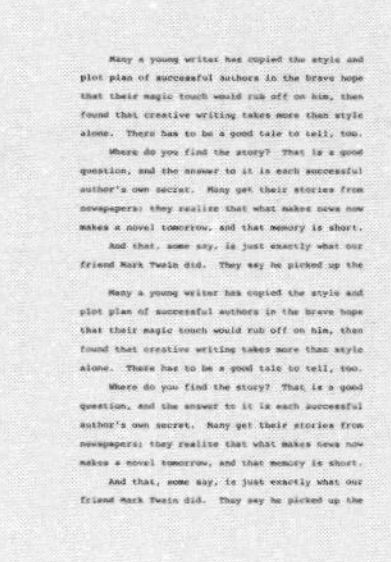

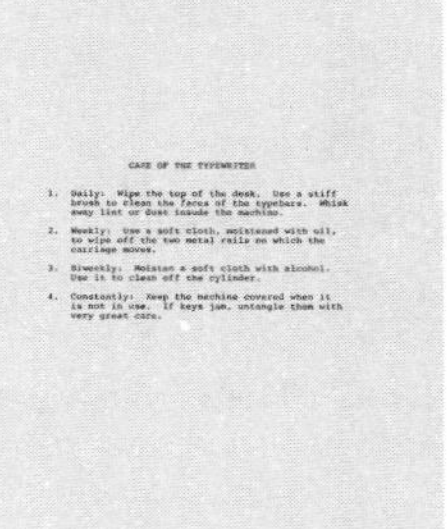

TEST 3-A

Take a general information test. It may be the one on Workbook pages 31–32 or a similar test that your teacher may give you or may dictate to you.

TEST 3-B

3-Minute TW
2 attempts

Many a young writer has copied the style and plot plan of 13
successful authors in the brave hope that their magic touch 25
would rub off on him, then found that creative writing takes 37
more than style alone. There has to be a good tale to tell, too. 50
Where do you find the story? That is a good question, and 63
the answer to it is each successful author's own secret. Many get 76
their stories from newspapers; they realize that what makes 88
news now makes a novel tomorrow, and that memory is short. 101
And that, some say, is just exactly what our friend Mark 113
Twain did. They say he picked up the stories that people read 125
and talked about and put them together like so many sausage 138
links. If so, certainly he was a cook who could dish up a meal! 150

|1 |2 |3 |4 |5 |6 |7 |8 |9 |10 |11 |12 |13 SI 1.29FE

TEST 3-C

Center on a full page. Use correct form for enumeration (not the style shown here).

CARE OF THE TYPEWRITER 13

1. Daily: Wipe the top of the desk. Use a 25
stiff brush to clean the faces of the typebars. 35
Whisk away lint or dust inside the machine. 45

2. Weekly: Use a soft cloth, moistened with 55
oil, to wipe off the two metal rails on which the 66
carriage moves. 71

3. Biweekly: Moisten a soft cloth with al- 81
cohol. Use it to clean off the cylinder. 90

4. Constantly: Keep the machine covered 100
when it is not in use. If keys jam, untangle 110
them with very great care. 116

|1 |2 |3 |4 |5 |6 |7 |8 |9 |10 SI 1.30FE

a·i·m 200–202

GOALS *To learn correct form for a subject line in a letter. To learn how to choose a complimentary closing. To use "bcc" notations correctly. To type 190 or more words of production copy in 5 minutes within 4 errors.*

DIRECTIONS *Spacing 1. Line 60. Tab center. WB 191–197.*

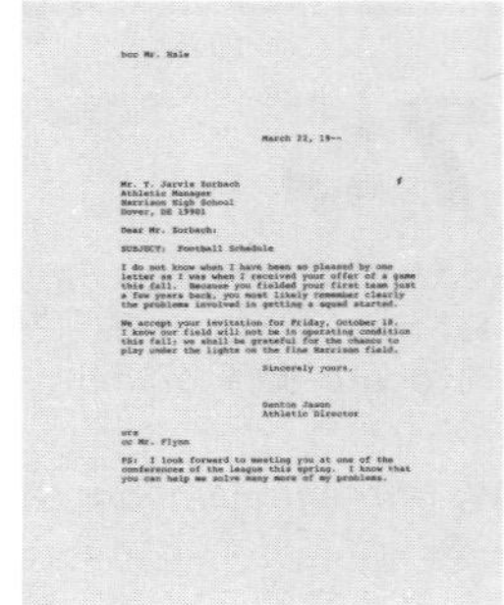

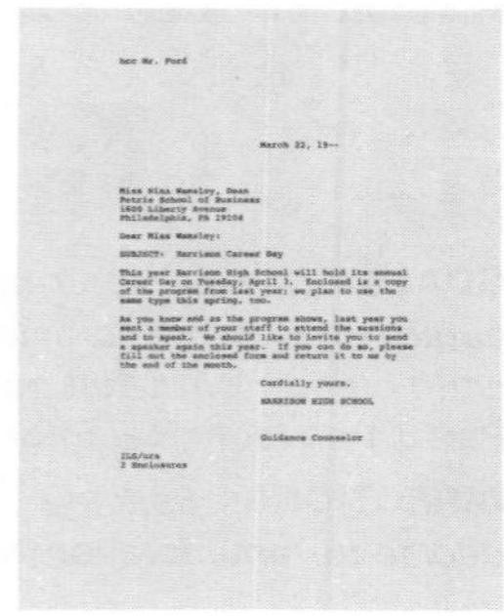

SUBJECT LINE

See example on page 206.

Many writers use a subject line to indicate what a letter concerns. The line may be used to arouse interest in a proposal. It may be used simply to save a reader's time by telling him what previous letter, file number, case, invoice number, or other reference he should have at hand as he reads the letter.

Guide 1 A subject line, if used, is typed between the salutation and body.

Guide 2 A subject line is usually introduced by the word "Subject" (or, in a legal office, by the Latin terms "in re" or "re") in all caps followed by a colon.

Guide 3 The words after "subject" (or after "in re" or "re") may be displayed with underscores and/or all caps.

Guide 4 The subject line may be centered or blocked at the left margin.

Examples:

```
 SUBJECT:  Invoice 663-12
SUBJECT:  CHANCE TO GET RICH!
 IN RE:  Carlton vs. Smith
 RE:  The State vs. Wilcox
```

COMPLIMENTARY CLOSINGS

Guide 1 Use "Yours truly," with or without "very," when (a) the salutation is "Gentlemen" or "Dear Sir" or (b) when the tone of the letter is cool or formal.

Guide 2 Use "Sincerely yours" or "Cordially yours," with or without "very," if the name of a person is used in the salutation of a letter whose tone is personal, casual, or friendly.

Guide 3 Use "Respectfully yours," with or without "very," when a letter is to a person to whom great respect is due, such as a public official, a much older person, a churchman, and the like.

Guide 4 If in doubt, it is always safe to use one of the "truly" closings.

Guide 5 Use an informal close ("See you soon!") only if it is dictated.

BCC NOTATIONS

See example on page 206.

If a writer does not wish his correspondent to know of the distribution of some copies, these copies and the file (bottom) copy are given a "bcc" [blind carbon copy] notation. After finishing the letter and removing the carbon pack, the typist peels off the original copy and all carbon copies on which the "bcc" is not to appear. Then he reinserts the remainder of the carbon pack and types the "bcc" notation in the blank space at the top (the space filled by the letterhead on the original copy), starting at the left margin on line 6.

Examples:

```
bcc Credit ✓        BCC Miss Carr
bcc Mr. Colt        BCC Akron Office ✓
```

WARMUP PREVIEW

2 copies A–C

```
A   The hat you got for the old man was the one you had for me.    12
B   Collections Advertising question whatever survey shown bill    12
C   Jack's man found exactly a quarter zipped in the woven bag.    12
```

D Take a 5-minute goal writing (190/4) on Job 200·1, date through body.

Overview

In Part Four you will review much of what you have learned to this point, and move ahead on three aspects of growth and new learning:

1. You will extend the base of your skill. In the Part you have just finished, your goal was to type *at least* 30 words a minute for 3 minutes within 5 errors. In Part Four you will sustain that level of skill, or higher, for another whole minute without making any more errors. To help you build a speed reserve that will make it easier to reach the goal, you will also have several a·i·m speed drives on smooth paragraphs of easy copy.

2. You will type letters. In Part Four you will learn the blocked letter arrangement and will type short business letters (as well as some short *personal*, or family, business letters) in that arrangement.

3. You will type data in tables. You will learn to arrange material in open-style form and will become familiar with columns, column headings, titles, subtitles, and so on. Near the end of this Part, the tables will serve as enclosures to the letters you type.

There are 25 a·i·m experiences in Part Four, each providing about 20 minutes of study and/or guided practice. As in the preceding Parts, the last a·i·m is a test on the Part and the a·i·m before it is a practice run on the Part Four test.

Performance Goals

When you finish Part Four, you should be able to demonstrate the following skills and abilities when you do the test in a·i·m 100, page 106:

1. Touch Typing You will operate all keys by touch. You will use the tabulator unhesitatingly as you tab-indent the date and the closing lines in a letter and as you tabulate from one column to another in the typing of a table.

2. Technicalities You will score 80 or more percent on an objective test that reviews the preceding Parts and includes much information from Part Four—names of letter parts, steps in producing letters and tables, and so on.

3. Production You will use at least 60 percent of your basic (straight copy) typing skill in the production of a business letter and at least 50 percent in the production of data tables.

4. Skill You will type *at least* 120 words in 4 minutes within 5 errors as you copy alphabetic paragraph material that is not arranged line for line (the 120 is minimal; 140 is more nearly the average expectation).

Routines and Procedures

Speed Drives There are five speed drives in Part Four—a·i·m sessions 76, 81, 86, 91, 96—in which the whole session is devoted to increasing power. Using extremely easy material, you work in four steps: (1) take a 4-minute timing to get the feel of the copy, (2) take two 2-minute timings for intensive practice, (3) practice an additional line's worth of copy, then (4) take a final 4-minute writing in which you increase your rate to a new record high—all within good control. The 4·2·2·4 routine replaces the 1·1·1·3·3 plan you used so successfully in Part Three.

Production Writings To help you build typing power and to learn to apply it to production work, many of the a·i·m sessions require you to take a timed writing on the body of a letter or other production task. Note that you are not likely to achieve higher scores on such timings than you do on the simple paragraph writings, but the scores on the production timed writings are much more important—they are the *real* typing.

Technical Rules In Part Four you will establish the base of all the letters and tables that lie ahead. Letters and tables can be arranged in many different ways, but all the ways are based on what you do as you type the kinds of letters and tables that are given in Part Four.

Now turn the page and start the timings assigned in a·i·m 76. The material is so easy you will set a record, and as you do so you'll pause to think how far you have come in this course!

a·i·m 199

GOAL *To bolster skill (190 or more words in 5 minutes within 4 errors) on as fairly easy or normal copy.*

DIRECTIONS *Spacing 1 for drills, 2 for TW. Line 60. Tab 5.*

WATCH THE SHOULDERS!

- Keep them level with one another.
- Keep them up but not all the way up.
- Keep them loose, so elbows dangle.
- Wobble them for a moment, to relax.

WARMUP REVIEW

2 copies

She did not see the big lid for the new pan she had for us. 12
My folks proved his expert eloquence was just a big hazard. 12
The 1 the 2 the 3 the 4 the 5 the 6 the 7 the 8 the 9 the 0 12
1 2 3 4 5 6 7 8 9 10 11 12

ACCURACY DRIVE

See page 162

Spacing 2

One of the most thriving kinds of business in this day and age is 14
the business of designing business forms. True, almost all stationers 28
have standard forms on their shelves; but it is true, too, that many 40
big firms bring in an expert who will analyze all the forms they use 56
and then design new forms that are easier to use and that save time 70
for all who execute them. You would not suppose that a company 83
selling jars of medicine would use the same invoices as a firm that 97
sells tin hats. A requisition form for steel beams will be different 111
from one for rugs. 114
Good forms are organized on sound principles. Experts will concur 128
that forms are supposed to use standard spacing without squeezing or 142
adjusting the paper. Each form should have guide words or signals so 156
that you will know what must be typed in each part. Each form should 170
be like a letter—that is, you type things in the same sequence you 184
would say them in a letter. 190
1 2 3 4 5 6 7 8 9 10 11 12 13 14 SI 1.30FE

ACCURACY DRIVE

For a·i·m 203

Once you have used a half dozen or more business forms often 13 204
enough to understand them well, you should be able to adjust your- 26 217
self rather quickly to the use of other business forms. This is fortunate, 41 232
for many thousands of forms have been designed and printed. No one 55 245
could ever practice them all in a lifetime of typing; no one could even 69 260
keep up with them, for new ones are generated faster than a pro- 82 272
fessional typist could fill them in. So it's a good thing that forms 96 286
are built on principles; once you grasp the principles, you can use 110 299
just about any form. 114 304
The main similarity of all good forms is that they are typed and 128 319
read in the same sequence as a letter. They have a letterhead. They 142 333
are addressed to someone. They deliver a message in itemized detail. 156 347
They are signed at the foot. Just visualize a check, for example, or 170 361
a receipt, invoice, bid, or any other form you've seen: they're simply 185 375
letters in a fill-in style. 190 380
1 2 3 4 5 6 7 8 9 10 11 12 13 14 SI 1.40N

a·i·m 76

GOALS ⚲ *To practice listening for the bell.* ⚲ *To build a speed reserve (135 or more words in 4 minutes within 5 errors) on very easy material.*

DIRECTIONS *Spacing 1 for drills, 2 for TW. Line 50. Tab 5.*

CORRECT POSITION

- **Feet** apart, braced on the floor
- **Back** erect, leaning forward
- **Hands** low, fingers curled
- **Eyes** unwaveringly on the copy

WARMUP PREVIEW

3 copies

```
The man who lost the big box did not fix its lid.    10
strength naught churns storms tough whole ship is    10
Racer No. 10 won over numbers 28, 39, 47, and 56.    10
Joe quietly took the zippers from the woven bags.    10
|1   |2   |3   |4   |5   |6   |7   |8   |9   |10
```

SPEED DRIVE 4·2·2·4 TW

If you respond correctly to the bell, lines will end even.

If you can reach the 135-word goal in 4 minutes within 5 errors on the first attempt, you may (if you wish and if your teacher approves) omit the rest of a·i·m 76 and advance to a·i·m 77. But if you do not make the goal on the first try, or if you wish to press for a higher goal, then:

1. Take two 2-minute timings, starting the second where the first one ended.
2. Type three copies of one more line beyond where the second timing ended.
3. Take a 4-minute timing in which you try to cover within 5 errors all the material you typed in steps 1 and 2.

The ships that go down the sea lanes have to be tough and are tough. 15
The storms they may have to face can be worse than the worst ones on 29
land, for the land has hills and woods and all kinds of things to slow 43
the wind and soak up the rain, but there are none of these at sea. The 58
gale runs on with naught to stop it. The waves it churns will heave up 72
and lift whole ships as though they were but chips. Not all storms are 86
so bad, but a ship is built so it will last through the worst storms. 100

But if the ships are tough, so are the crews that sail them. The 115
sea has no place for the man who is weak or soft; such a man will make 129
but one trip—his first and last. ⚲ 135

It takes strength for a man to fight the sea and sun and wind and 150
rain and heat and cold. The man who can stand watch through the night 164
and yet work hours in the day, who can prowl the decks or climb the 178
mast in a gale, who can guide the wheel as well in a storm as in a 191
calm, this man is what makes a ship what it is. 200

|1 |2 |3 |4 |5 |6 |7 |8 |9 |10 |11 |12 |13 |14 SI 1.00VE

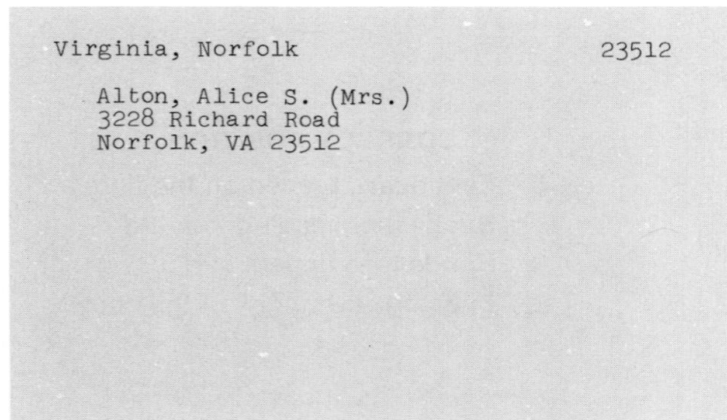

Virginia, Norfolk 23512

Alton, Alice S. (Mrs.)
3228 Richard Road
Norfolk, VA 23512

5 x 3 Card for Geographic Address File

JOB 196·2 Index Cards Using 5 x 3 cards or slips of paper, (a) prepare a geographic file of the names and addresses on page 202 and (b) arrange them alphabetically in geographic sequence.

Guide 1 On line 2, starting 3 or 4 spaces from the edge, type state and city; type the ZIP so it ends 3 or 4 spaces from right-hand edge. After 1 blank line, indent the other lines 3 or 4 spaces (tab); single-space them.

Guide 2 Arrange the indented portions the same way you do an alphabetic file.

THE HARTMANN COMPANY
28 MUSKOGEE BOULEVARD OKLAHOMA CITY, OKLAHOMA 73106

Mrs. Alice S. Alton
3228 Richard Road
Norfolk, VA 23512

Typical Business Mailing Label

JOB 197·1 Labels Using Workbook 185 or a sheet of paper creased in eighths, address a mailing label to each of these educators (full names and address are on page 202):

1	5
2	6
3	7
4	

1 Alton
2 Krawchuk
3 Malone
4 Patton
5 Pepper
6 Plimpton
7 Yates

Use the labels in the sequence illustrated; shift the margin stop for the second "strip." Start addresses 1 inch from left edge. Single-space them. Center each vertically, by estimate, on its label.

LAKE ALUMNI ASSOCIATION
Lake High School -- Austin, Texas 78700

April 2, 19--

Dear Miss Dailey:

We should like to acknowledge receipt of your contribution of $10 to the Veteran Memorial Fund of Lake High School. The Association, the school, and the committee in charge of the project all wish to express their gratitude.

Marsha Abbott, Chairman

stu

Duplicated Fill-In Postal Card

JOB 198·1 Form Cards Using the postal cards on Workbook 187, acknowledge the contributions of these three alumni:

1 Daily, $10
2 Landers, $10
3 Ortland, $5

Insert the date, salutation, amount of contribution, and typist's (your) initials. Center the contribution in the space provided for it.

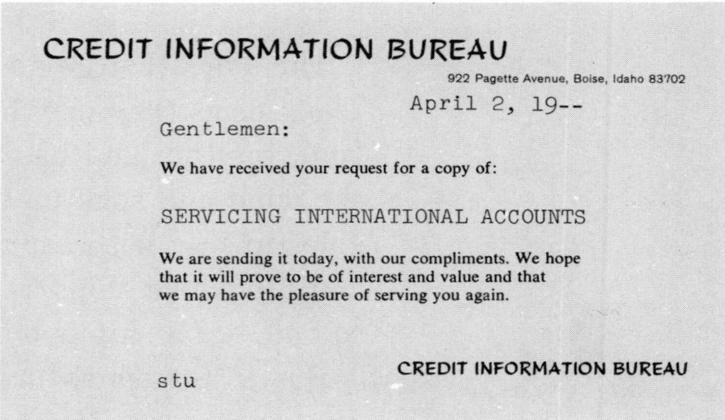

CREDIT INFORMATION BUREAU
922 Pagette Avenue, Boise, Idaho 83702

April 2, 19--

Gentlemen:

We have received your request for a copy of:

SERVICING INTERNATIONAL ACCOUNTS

We are sending it today, with our compliments. We hope that it will prove to be of interest and value and that we may have the pleasure of serving you again.

stu CREDIT INFORMATION BUREAU

Printed Fill-In Postal Card

JOB 198·2 Form Cards Using the postal cards on Workbook 189, acknowledge the requests of Bamberger-Hart, Dr. Pepper, and Mr. Woods for a copy of "Servicing International Accounts."

The insertions include today's date, a suitable salutation, the full title of the desired publication, and the typist's (your) initials.

a·i·m 77

GOALS ⚲ *To learn the names of the letter parts.* ⚲ *To learn how to arrange a letter in "blocked style."* ⚲ *To learn the placement of a short business letter on stationery.* ⚲ *To distinguish pica and elite printing.*

DIRECTIONS *Spacing 1. Line 4 inches (40 pica spaces, or 50 elite spaces). Tab center. WB 37–39.*

PICA vs. ELITE

Type periods on your machine and see which of these it matches.

```
Elite...........   (12 to an inch)
Pica..........     (10 to an inch)
```

LETTER PARTS

Read and remember.

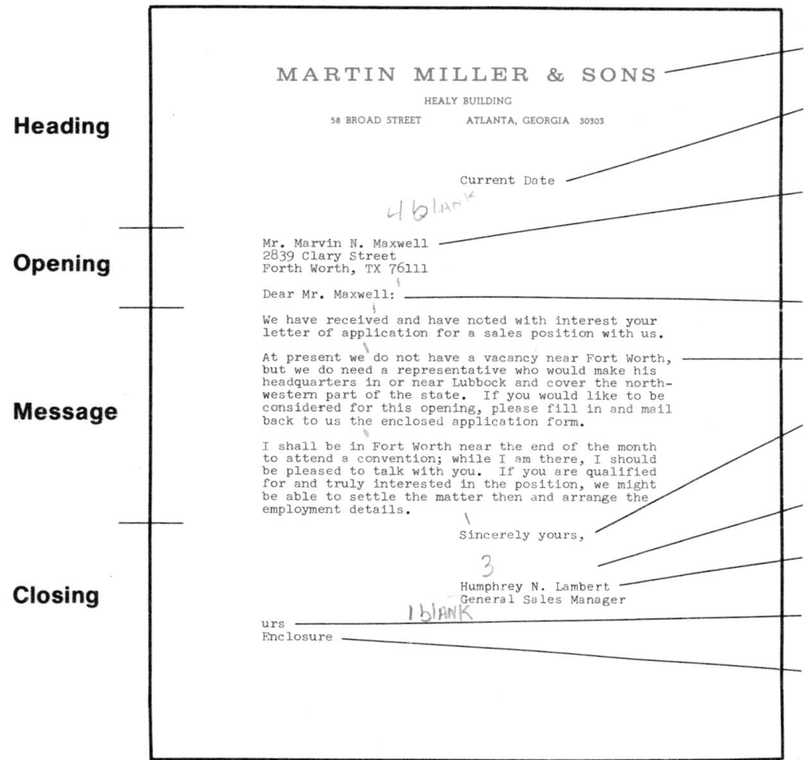

MARTIN MILLER & SONS
HEALY BUILDING
58 BROAD STREET ATLANTA, GEORGIA 30303

Current Date

Mr. Marvin N. Maxwell
2839 Clary Street
Forth Worth, TX 76111

Dear Mr. Maxwell:

We have received and have noted with interest your letter of application for a sales position with us.

At present we do not have a vacancy near Fort Worth, but we do need a representative who would make his headquarters in or near Lubbock and cover the northwestern part of the state. If you would like to be considered for this opening, please fill in and mail back to us the enclosed application form.

I shall be in Fort Worth near the end of the month to attend a convention; while I am there, I should be pleased to talk with you. If you are qualified for and truly interested in the position, we might be able to settle the matter then and arrange the employment details.

Sincerely yours,

Humphrey N. Lambert
General Sales Manager

urs
Enclosure

BLOCKED LETTER STYLE

Letterhead your company's printed name and address

Date Line date (month, day, year) the letter is typed; starts at center of line 15.

Inside Address party and address to which you are writing; starts at margin, line 20.

Salutation opening greeting, like "Dear Mr. Maxwell"

Body text of letter, typed in single-spaced paragraphs

Complimentary Closing parting phrase, like "Sincerely yours"; starts at center.

Signature Space usually 3 to 5 blank lines.

Writer's Identification signer's name, or title, or both

Reference Symbols initials of dictator and/or typist (you)

Enclosure Notation reminder if letter has an enclosure

MARGINS

Read and remember.

All letters have the same top margin (the date is on line 15), but side and bottom margins depend on the number of words (estimated in letter body). Line length to use:

For this many words in the letter body:	*Use this line length*		
	Inches	*Pica*	*Elite*
under 100	4	40	50
100–200	5	50	60
above 200	6	60	70

The beginning letters you type will have fewer than 100 words in the body, so you will type them on a 4-inch line (40-space line on pica machines, 50-space on elite).⚲

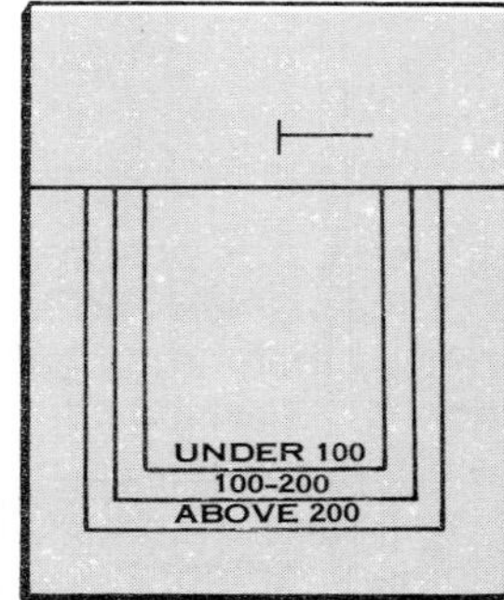

Short letters use shorter lines than do average or long letters.

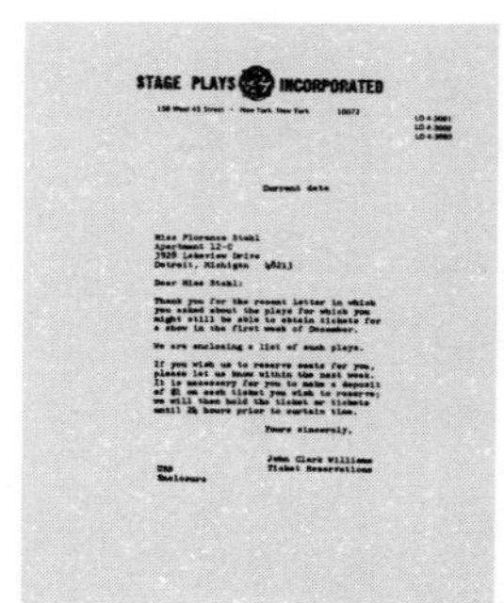

Use 4-inch line on short letter. With 50 center, pica is 30–75, elite is 25–80.⚲

a·i·m 196–198

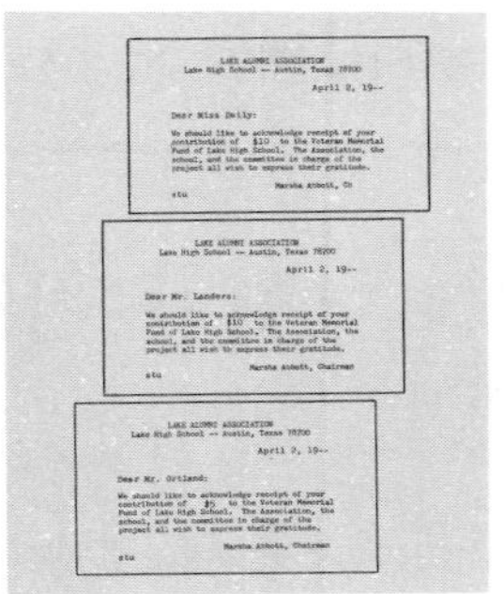

GOALS ◉ *To type on index cards.* ◉ *To address mailing labels.* ◉ *To type and address fill-in postal cards.* ◉ *To type at least 190 words of mailing list copy in 5 minutes within 4 errors.*

DIRECTIONS *Spacing 2. Line 70. Tabs 25, 50. WB 185–189.*

WARMUP REVIEW

2 copies

1 They will find some more work when they have done your job. 12
2 James Boxell, the banquet speaker, analyzed a few carvings. 12
3 One 1 two 2 three 3 four 4 five 5 six 6 seven 7 and eight 8 12
|1 |2 |3 |4 |5 |6 |7 |8 |9 |10 |11 |12

5-MINUTE TW

GOAL WRITING
Spacing 2
Use tabs 25, and 50
Repeat in a·i·m 197
a·i·m 198

4	Mrs. Alice S. Alton	3228 Richard Road	Norfolk, VA 23512	13
5	Bamberger-Hart Co.	896 Checker Circle	Cicero, IL 62822	25
6	Miss Suzanne Dailey	2007 Blake Street	Paynesville, OH 44077	39
7	Mr. Norman Krawchuk	10017 Heath Street	Covington, KY 41011	52
8	Mr. Lawrence Landers	2181 Little Lane	Austin, TX 78707	65
9	Miss Mary M. Malone	2403 Maxwell Road	Austin, TX 78711	77
10	Mr. Owen L. Ortland	513 Brindley Street	Pueblo, CO 81004	90
11	Mr. Phillip Patton	1411 Bartlett Avenue	Lincoln, NE 68502	104
12	Dr. Paul C. Pepper	2322 Faculty Annex	Chattanooga, TN 73402	117
13	Miss Ellen Plimpton	2124 Sorority Square	Middlebury, VT 05753	131
14	Mrs. T. J. Quill	1524 Jane Street West	North Platte, NE 69101	146
15	Mr. J. Dennis Twiff	8904 Wilmington Road	Wilmington, DE 19800	159
16	Mr. Lee G. Woods	1309 Clark Way	Independence, MO 64050	172
17	Dr. Wendell L. Yates	Barr University		180
		932 North Troy Road	Terre Haute, IN 47801 ◉	190

|1 |2 |3 |4 |5 |6 |7 |8 |9 |10 |11 |12 |13 |14

SI 1.44FD

JOB 196·1

INDEX CARDS

Using 5 x 3 cards or slips of paper, (a) prepare a file of the names and addresses above and (b) arrange them in alphabetic sequence.

Guide 1 Start on the second line, 3 or 4 spaces from the left edge. Leave 1 blank line, then tab-indent the other lines 3 or 4 spaces; use single-spacing.

Guide 2 When the first line is a person's name, invert it into filing sequence: last name first. Omit "Miss" and "Mr." Show all other titles in parentheses. ◉

Alton, Alice S. (Mrs.)

3228 Richard Road
Norfolk, VA 23512

5 x 3 Card for Alphabetic Address File

LETTER PROCEDURE

Produce a short letter experimentally.

To practice typing a business letter, copy the one on page 83 or 84. You may use the visual guide in your Workbook (page 37) or follow these standard steps:

Step 1. Machine. Set linespacer for single-spacing [business letters are almost always single-spaced]. The directions in the margin of the letter say it contains 89 words, so it is short and takes a 4-inch line of writing; set the margins for that line: 40 pica or 50 elite spaces. [The body count always determines the line length.]

Step 2. Stationery. Insert the *Kingman* letterhead, Workbook page 39. If you do not have a letterhead, insert plain paper and, to represent the depth of a printed letterhead, type a line of hyphens on line 9, margin to margin.

Step 3. Type date, starting it at center on line 15. Use today's month, day, and year.

Step 3

Step 4. Type letter, including the inside address, salutation, body, and complimentary closing. Stop to proofread and plan signature space.

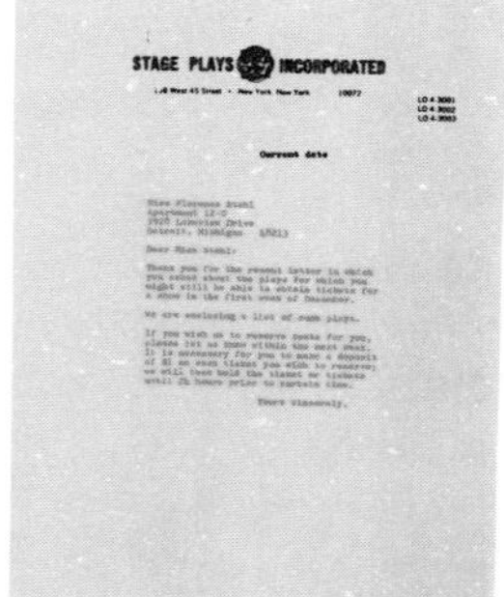

Step 4

Step 5. Finish it. It is normal to drop down 4 lines to the signer's identification and then 2 more lines to the initials. You may need to adjust this spacing, however, to get good letter balance:

5a. If body fills 14 or fewer lines (including blanks), drop 6 lines and finish.

5b. If body fills 15 or 16 lines, drop 5 lines and finish.

5c. If body fills 17 or more lines, drop down 4 lines to signer's identification and allow no blank lines above the reference initials.

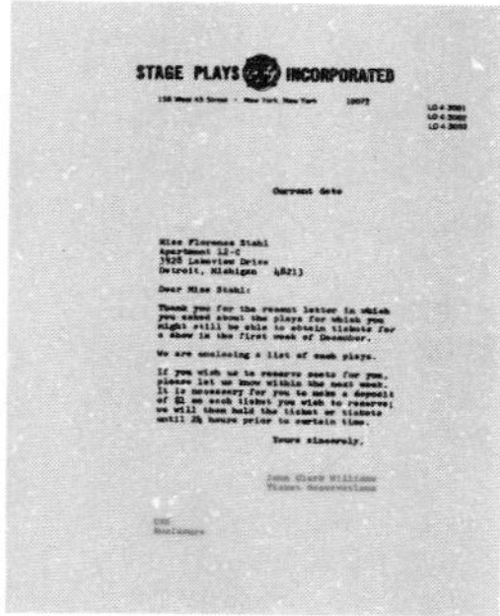

Step 5

a·i·m 78

GOALS *To type 105 words or more in 4 minutes within 5 errors on part of a letter [salutation through complimentary closing, page 83]. To copy a short letter, arranging it correctly. To type it within 7 minutes.*

DIRECTIONS *Spacing 1. Line 50 for TW. Tab center. WB 41.*

WHEN YOU TYPE A LETTER

- Position it with correct margins.
- Type all parts in correct arrangement.
- Try to type with no or few errors.
- Type efficiently; get it done quickly.

WARMUP PREVIEW

2 copies

A `last send here left date stop you sir and use let` 10

B `principal Thursday blocked explain except 109 tab` 10

C `Jo quietly picked six zippers from the woven bag.` 10

D Practice typing the date, inside address, and closing—by touch!

PRACTICE ROUTINE

Step 1. To build letter-typing power, take a 4-minute timing on the page 83 letter. To make your speed goal, type from salutation through the closing within 4 minutes and within 5 errors.

Step 2. Using the *Kingman* letterhead on Workbook page 41 or plain paper with a hyphen row on line 9, type another copy—a better one—of the page 83/84 letter. Try to finish it within 7 minutes.

 195

GOALS ⚲ *To build a speed reserve (at least 45 words in 1 minute with 1 or 0 errors) on easy sentences.* ⚲ *To review and strengthen number-key controls.*

DIRECTIONS *Spacing 1. Line 60.*

> **REPETITION REMINDER**
> When goal is speed, repeat each line by itself. When goal is accuracy, repeat each group of 3 lines as though the 3 lines were a paragraph for you to repeat.

WARMUP REVIEW
2 copies

```
1  The man got out the box for the new hat and the new gloves.   12
2  I quickly explained that many big jobs involve few hazards.   12
3  3,900 2,800 4,700 5,600 1,000 3,900 2,800 4,700 5,600 1,000   12
   |1   |2   |3   |4   |5   |6   |7   |8   |9   |10   |11   |12
```

NUMBER DRIVE
2 copies

```
4  we 23 wee 233 weep 2330 weepy 23306 pi 08 pie 083 pier 0834   12
5  pi 08 pit 085 pity 0856 piety 08356 yo 69 you 697 your 6974   12
6  tour 5974 pour 0974 pipe 0803 ripe 4803 wore 2943 tore 5943   12
   |1   |2   |3   |4   |5   |6   |7   |8   |9   |10   |11   |12
```

SKILL SPRINT
Each line: 1′ TW or 4 copies

```
7  All the men hope that they have a chance to win the trophy.   12
8  All they want to do is to sit in the shade of the big oaks.   12
9  The man and the boy did not see the old car you had for me.⚲  12
   |1   |2   |3   |4   |5   |6   |7   |8   |9   |10   |11   |12
```

NUMBER DRIVE
2 copies

```
10  The 39 boys and 28 men had 47 pies or 56 cakes for 10 days.   12
11  I sold 3,900 of No. 2,800 and 4,700 of No. 5,600 in 1 week.   12
12  Prisoner 3928 served 4,756 days; No. 1028 served out 3,947.   12
    |1   |2   |3   |4   |5   |6   |7   |8   |9   |10   |11   |12
```

SKILL SPRINT
Each line: 1′ TW or 4 copies

```
13  The job has to be done, so why not get at it and do it now?   12
14  The four boys said they will work when they walk over here.   12
15  The men did not cut the log the way you did the job for us.⚲  12
    |1   |2   |3   |4   |5   |6   |7   |8   |9   |10   |11   |12
```

NUMBER DRIVE
2 copies To improve concentration, double all numbers.

```
16  Please order 10 cakes, 20 pies, and 30 quarts of ice cream.   12
17  The golden ballroom is 100 by 110 feet and is 15 feet high.   12
18  The bus was going at 45 m.p.h. and skidded nearly 150 feet.   12
    |1   |2   |3   |4   |5   |6   |7   |8   |9   |10   |11   |12
```

SKILL SPRINT
Each line: 1′ TW or 4 copies

```
19  They hope your next journey with us will be a pleasant one.   12
20  They said that they felt that your coat must have been cut.   12
21  The boy hid the new hat and got out the old red one for me.⚲  12
    |1   |2   |3   |4   |5   |6   |7   |8   |9   |10   |11   |12
```

OPTIONAL 5′ TIMED WRITING If time permits, turn back to page 197 and take a 5-minute writing on the bottom part of the page—lines 18–32. Target on 190 words within 4 errors in 5 minutes.

The Kingman Studios
PROGRAM DEPARTMENT ■ GREYBAR BUILDING
NEW YORK CITY, NEW YORK 10017

JOB 78·1

BLOCKED LETTER
Line 4 inches
Tab center
Spacing 1
Start line 15
Body 89 words
Workbook 41

October 15, 19-- ↓5 **Use today's date and type the year in full.** 4

8

Mr. Frank C. Taylor 12
Taylor and Smythe, Inc. 17
109 Barnes Street 20
Houston, TX 77012 24

25

Standard punctuation has a colon after the salutation and comma after the closing phrase.

Dear Mr. Taylor: 4 29

5 30

When we talked at the letter clinic last Thursday, 15 40
I promised to send you a letter in blocked form. 25 50
Well, sir, here it is. 30 55

31 56

All lines begin at the left margin except for three 41 66
parts of the letter: the date line, the closing 51 76
phrase, and the name or title of the writer. Most 61 86
typists set a tab stop at the center to save time 71 96
when they type these three parts. 78 103

79 104

If there is anything else that you would like me to 89 114
explain about blocked letters, please let me know. 100 125

101 126

Yours sincerely, ↓6 105 130

135

Reference initials are (a) dictator's and yours, with a colon between, if his name isn't typed anywhere; or (b) only yours, if his name is typewritten.

Director of Training 140

141

RWC:URS 143

|1 |2 |3 |4 |5 |6 |7 |8 |9 |10

SI 1.27FE

Short Business Letter in Blocked Style (Elite). **See page 84 for Pica.**

JOB 193·1

BLOCKED LETTER — WB 177 — cc 10 — Body 122 + attention 20 + Carbons file and cc

Today's date / Athletic Department / 12
Potocki High School / Wilmington, DE 19
19800 / Attention Football Coach / *Salu-* 27
tation? 29
We have just learned that you are plan- 37
ning to build a football squad next fall and 46
to apply for a league membership the fol- 54
lowing season. That is good news to us. As 63
your nearest neighbor, we are pleased to 72
welcome you to competition. 77
Remembering how difficult it was for us 86
to schedule any games in our first season, 95
we should like to help you by offering a 103
game for this fall. We have two open dates— 112
October 18 and November 1. We should be 120
pleased to schedule either date. 127
These dates are for Friday nights. If 135
you would like to move one of them to the 144
following Saturday afternoon or evening, 152
we should be glad to change our schedule 160
to fit yours. 163
Yours very truly, /Athletic Manager / 177
TJZ / urs / cc Mr. Carlton 183

|1 |2 |3 |4 |5 |6 |7 |8 SI 1.42N

JOB 194·1

BLOCKED LETTER — WB 179 — cc 10 + co. sig. 20 — Body 148 + attention 20 + Carbons 2

Today's date / Placement Department / 12
Harrison High School / Dover, DE 19901 / 20
Attention of the Placement Director / 28
Salutation? / The Federal Government has 37
come to us to ask us to take on a number of 46
defense contracts. Civic leaders in this region 56
have urged us to accept these contracts, for 65
they know what an expansion of our plant 73
and payroll would mean to the area. 80
We cannot accept them, however, unless 89
we find there is a strong likelihood of adding 99
to the number of our plant and office 106
workers. So, we ask for your help: we 114
should like to know how many students 122
will graduate from your programs in indus- 130
trial arts and office training in June. Too, 139
we should like to know if we might be able 148
to talk with them. 152
We do not want to impose on you, but we 161
hope that you agree with us in feeling that 170
this matter is so important to you, the 178
school, and the community that it warrants 186
this request. / Yours very truly, / PRUITT 198
SITZ COMPANY ↓4 John A. Byrd, 208
Personnel / *Initials?* / cc Dover School 215
Board 216

|1 |2 |3 |4 |5 |6 |7 |8 SI 1.42N

JOB 194·2

BLOCKED LETTER — WB 181 — cc 10 — Body 156 + attention 20 + Carbons file and cc

Today's date / Vocational Department / 12
Dover County College / 2831 Bay Boule- 19
vard / Dover, DE 19905 / Attention 27
Miss Prue Ann Hildred / *Salutation?* 34
There is a likelihood that our company 43
will soon undertake some new defense con- 51
tracts. If we do, we will need a great many 60
more office workers. I am writing to you, 68
therefore, to inquire about the credentials 77
of your trainees who will finish in June. 86
It looks as though we may need three who 95
qualify as executive secretaries and four or 104
five others for private secretaries. Our pay 113
scale is top for Dover, as you probably 121
know, and we are proud of the comfort and 130
the quality of our offices. 135
If you have some good candidates whom I 144
could meet, with an eye to employing them 153
when they graduate in June, I would be 160
pleased to visit your offices at any time on 169
Friday of next week to interview them. My 178
phone number is 220-7878, and I would be 186
grateful if you would phone me and tell me 195
whether I might plan for some interviews. 203
Yours very truly, / John A. Byrd, Per- 213
sonnel / *Initials?* / cc Dean Steele 219

|1 |2 |3 |4 |5 |6 |7 |8 SI 1.43N

The Kingman Studios

PROGRAM DEPARTMENT ■ GREYBAR BUILDING
NEW YORK CITY, NEW YORK 10017

JOB 78·2

BLOCKED LETTER
Line 4 inches
Tab center
Spacing 1
Start line 15
Body 89 words
Workbook 41

Standard punctuation has a colon after the salutation and comma after the closing phrase.

Reference initials are (a) dictator's and yours, with a colon between, if his name isn't typed anywhere; or (b) only yours, if his name is typewritten.

October 15, 19-- ↓5 4

Use today's date and type the year in full.

8

Mr. Frank C. Taylor 12
Taylor and Smythe, Inc. 17
109 Barnes Street 20
Houston, TX 77012 24

25

Dear Mr. Taylor: 4 29

5 30

When we talked at the letter clinic last 13 38
Thursday, I promised to send you a letter 21 46
in blocked form. Well, sir, here it is. 30 55

31 56

All lines begin at the left margin except 39 64
for three parts of the letter: the date 47 72
line, the closing phrase, and the name or 56 81
title of the writer. Most typists set a 64 89
tab stop at the center to save time when 72 97
they type these three parts. 78 103

79 104

If there is anything else that you would 87 112
like me to explain, please let me know. 95 121

100 125

101 128

Yours sincerely, ↓5 105 130

135

Director of Training 140

141

RWC:URS 143

|1 |2 |3 |4 |5 |6 |7 |8

Short Business Letter in Blocked Style (Pica). See page 83 for Elite.

HARRISON HIGH SCHOOL

DOVER PUBLIC SCHOOL SYSTEM

DOVER, DELAWARE 19901

JOB 192·1

BLOCKED
LETTER
Body 114 words
+ 20 att. line
+ 10 cc note
Line 5 inches
Tabs 4, center
Workbook 175

March 20, 19-- 4
↓5
8

Pruitt Sitz Company 12
822 Carroun Street 16
Dover, Delaware 19901 20
21
Attention Training Director 27
28
Gentlemen: 30
31
The typing students in this high school are making a survey 43
to find what kinds of letter arrangements are popular among 55
the firms that employ our alumni. Since you are such a 66
firm, please tell us: 71
72
1. Has your company adopted some one letter style that is 84
used in all outgoing letters? 91
92
2. Do your writers usually use an attention line? Do they 104
have a preference in its arrangement? 113
114
3. Do your writers like to use a subject line? Do they have 126
a preference in its arrangement? 134
135
My students and I would be most grateful if we could receive 147
a letter that answers the above questions and illustrates the 160
most popular style of letter. 166
167
Yours very truly, 172
↓4
175

Stephen R. Sturgis 181
Business Teacher 187

urs 188
cc Mr. Poe 190

Blocked Business Letter with Attention Line, Enumeration, and Carbon-Copy Notation

a·i·m 79

GOALS *To type 107 or more words in 4 minutes within 5 errors on part of a letter (salutation through complimentary closing). To produce a business letter.*

DIRECTIONS *Spacing 1. Line 50. Tab center. WB 43, 45.*

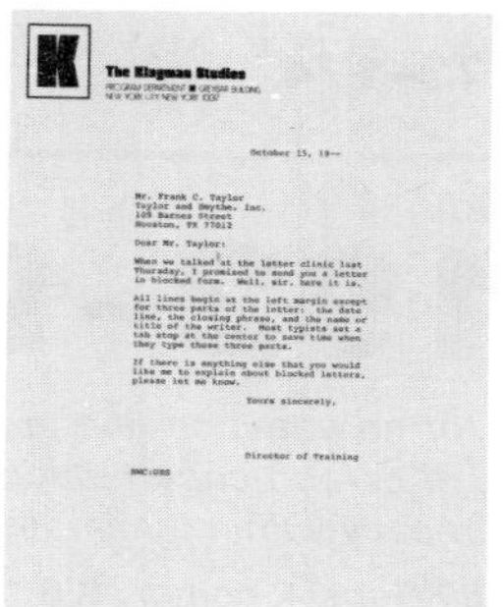

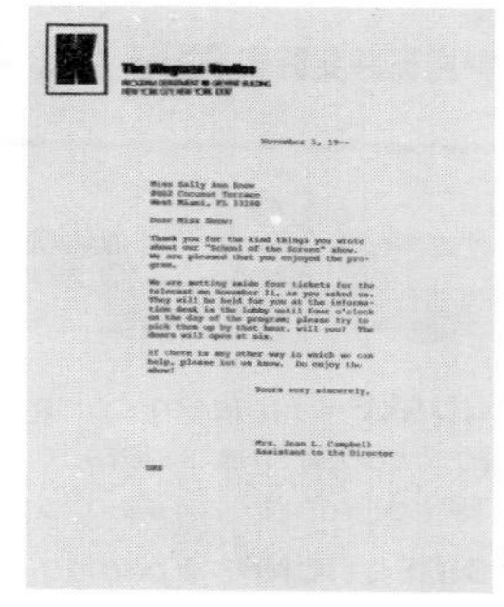

WARMUP PREVIEW

2 copies

A fine list that sent very them have gone over your 10
B suggestions conference excellent "School" Program 10
C Quietly Jo picked zippers for the six woven bags. 10
D Speed up carriage (carrier) returns: type first word in each line.

4-MINUTE TW

Lines 5 through 14
Spacing 1

JOB 79·1

BLOCKED LETTER
Line 4 inches
Tab center
Date line 15
Body 92 words
Workbook 43

The dictator's name is typed, so you do not need to include his initials in the reference initials.

Current date ↓ 5 | 4
Miss Jane E. Toulaine | 12
The Gabled Towers Hotel | 17
42 East 330 Avenue | 21
Boston, MA 02116 | 25

Dear Miss Toulaine: | 4 | 30

Thank you for the fine list of ideas that you sent to us in your recent | 19 | 45
letter. We are very grateful to you for sending them. | 31 | 56

The members of the "School of the Screen" have gone over your | 44 | 70
suggestions. We think so highly of four of them that we wonder | 57 | 82
whether you could meet with us in New York to discuss them. We | 70 | 95
should be pleased to pay your expenses, of course. | 80 | 106

We meet at ten o'clock on Monday mornings. Could you meet with | 94 | 119
us within the next two or three weeks? | 102 | 127

Sincerely yours, ↓ 6 | 107 | 133

George W. Strang | 142
Program Director | 146

URS | 148

|1 |2 |3 |4 |5 |6 |7 |8 |9 |10 |11 |12 |13 |14 · SI 1.32FE

OPTIONAL JOB 79·2

BLOCKED LETTER
Line 4 inches
Tab center
Date line 15
Body 91 words
Workbook 45

Dr. Thomas D. French, Dean | 13
School of Higher Education | 19
New Dorp State College | 23
New Dorp, NY 10028 | 27

Dear Dean French: | 32

The staff of "School of the Screen" read with great interest your | 46
recent talk on "You Can Teach Your Fingers to Spell." (Turn page) | 57

PREPARE a·i·m WB 173–174

a·i·m 192–194

GOALS *To learn correct form for an attention line in a letter. To learn how to choose the salutation. To use carbon-copy notations correctly. To type 190 or more words of production copy within 5 minutes and 4 errors.*

DIRECTIONS *Spacing 1. Line 60. Tabs 4, center. WB 175–181.*

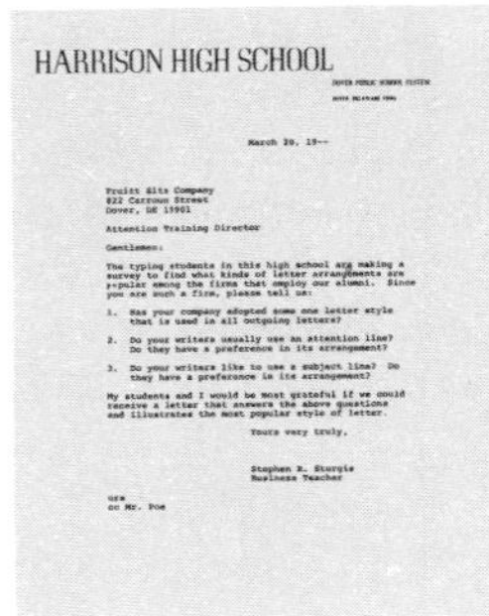

HARRISON HIGH SCHOOL

March 20, 19--

Pruitt Alts Company
822 Carroun Street
Dover, DE 19901

Attention Training Director

Gentlemen:

The typing students in this high school are making a survey to find what kinds of letter arrangements are popular among the firms that employ our alumni. Since you are such a firm, please tell us:

1. Has your company adopted some one letter style that is used in all outgoing letters?
2. Do your writers usually use an attention line? Do they have a preference in its arrangement?
3. Do your writers like to use a subject line? Do they have a preference in its arrangement?

My students and I would be most grateful if we could receive a letter that answers the above questions and illustrates the most popular style of letter.

Yours very truly,

Stephen R. Sturgis
Business Teacher

urs
cc Mr. Poe

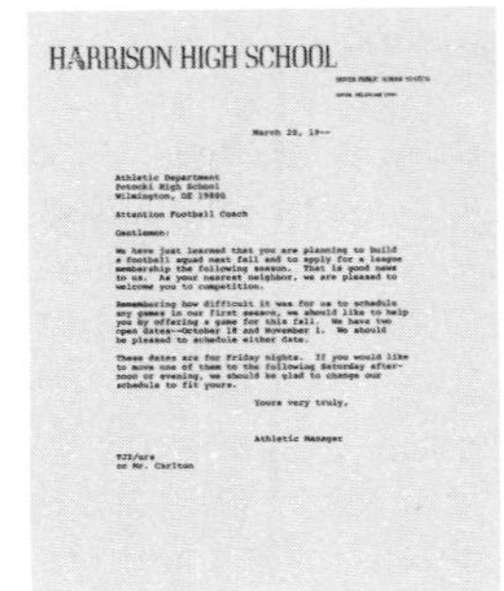

HARRISON HIGH SCHOOL

March 20, 19--

Athletic Department
Potocki High School
Wilmington, DE 19800

Attention Football Coach

Gentlemen:

We have just learned that you are planning to build a football squad next fall and to apply for a league membership the following season. That is good news to us. As your nearest neighbor, we are pleased to welcome you to competition.

Remembering how difficult it was for us to schedule any games in our first season, we should like to help you by offering a game for this fall. We have two open dates--October 18 and November 1. We should be pleased to schedule either date.

These dates are for Friday nights. If you would like to move one of them to the following Saturday afternoon or evening, we should be glad to change our schedule to fit yours.

Yours very truly,

Athletic Manager

TJI/urs
cc Mr. Carlton

ATTENTION LINE

Note example on page 199.

When estimating the body count, count an extra 20 if a letter has a subject line or an attention line.

Legal reasons sometimes make it important for a letter to be addressed to a company rather than to an individual or department in it. If the writer knows what person or department will handle the letter, he may expedite matters by indicating the person, by name or title, or department in an attention line typed between the inside address and the salutation.

Guide 1 An attention line is usually typed without display, at the left margin.

Guide 2 Some employers like attention lines to be displayed. You might use centering, underscoring, and/or all capping:

```
ATTENTION SALES MANAGER
ATTENTION: Sales Manager
Attention of Mr. Wayne Neale
Attention Sales Department
```

Guide 3 If the attention line is used, the salutation should be "Gentlemen."

Guide 4 The legal reasons for addressing a letter to a firm instead of a person do not apply to envelopes. It is normal simply to type the name, title, or department as the first line of the envelope address, even though an attention line may appear in the letter.

SALUTATIONS

Note problems on page 200.

Guide 1 If a letter is to a firm, use "Gentlemen" as the salutation.

Guide 2 If a letter is to a person whose name is known, use the name in the salutation, like "Dear Mr. Smith."

Guide 3 If a letter is to a person whose name is not known but whose title is known (like "Advertising Manager"), use "Dear Sir" as the salutation.

Guide 4 If the letter is to two persons, use both names in the salutation, like "Dear Mr. and Mrs. Smith" or "Dear Miss Smith and Miss Jones." If the letter is for several persons, use a collective term, like "Dear Committee Members."

Guide 5 Professional titles, like Doctor, Colonel, Professor, may be either abbreviated or spelled out, as you prefer.

CARBON COPY NOTATIONS

Note example on page 199. Each cc line adds 10 words to your estimated body word count.

Business letters are typed with at least one carbon copy, for filing. Most letters have several carbon copies so that everyone concerned may receive a copy.

CC [Carbon Copy] Notation If a writer wishes his correspondent to know to whom copies have been distributed, the typist gives this information in a "cc" notation under the other reference symbols:

```
DIC:TYP              DIC/typ
cc Miss Adams ✓      Enclosure
cc Home Office       cc Mr. Davis ✓
```

The cc note follows the initials and, if there is one, the enclosure notation.

On each copy the typist puts a check mark after the name of the person, office, or agency who is to receive that copy.

WARMUP PREVIEW

2 copies A-C

A `shared would write some with our ask you how to if is to us` 12

B `information typewriting position subject styles apply firm.` 12

C `Jack's man found exactly a quarter in the woven zipper bag.` 12

D Try to copy Letter 192·1 as a goal writing: within 5 minutes and 4 errors.

8 We believe that this subject would lend itself to excellent screening 72
9 as a part of the series that we are doing on new schools of thought. 86
10 We would like to explore this whole matter with you to find out 99
11 whether we could "teach fingers to spell" on our screens. 111

12 Would it be possible for you to come to New York City in a week 126
13 or two for a conference? 130

14 Sincerely yours, ↓ 5 or 6 135
140

The initials "URS" remind you to type your own initials.

15 George W. Strang 145
16 Program Director ↓ 2 149
17 URS 151

|1 |2 |3 |4 |5 |6 |7 |8 |9 |10 |11 |12 |13 |14 SI 1.33FE

80

GOALS *To type 108 or more words in 4 minutes within 5 errors on part of a letter (salutation through complimentary closing). To produce in correct blocked style two business letters from unarranged material.*

DIRECTIONS *Spacing 1. Line 50. Tab center. WB 47, 49.*

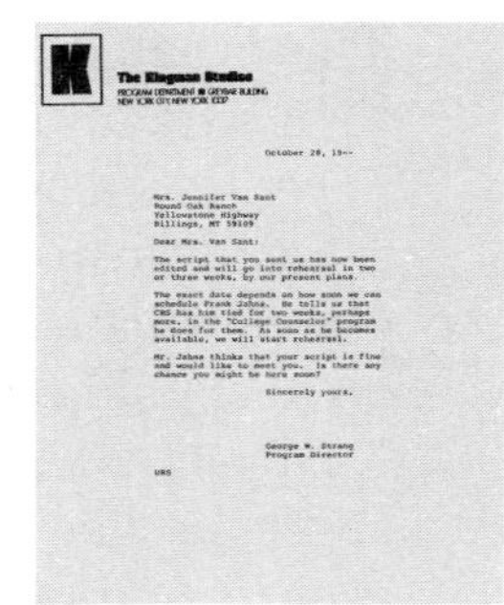

The Kingman Studios
PROGRAM DEPARTMENT ■ GREYBAR BUILDING
NEW YORK CITY, NEW YORK 10017

October 28, 19--

Mrs. Jennifer Van Sant
Round Oak Ranch
Yellowstone Highway
Billings, MT 59109

Dear Mrs. Van Sant:

The script that you sent us has now been edited and will go into rehearsal in two or three weeks, by our present plans.

The exact date depends on how soon we can schedule Frank Jahns. He tells us that CBS has him tied for two weeks, perhaps more, in the "College Counselor" program he does for them. As soon as he becomes available, we will start rehearsal.

Mr. Jahns thinks that your script is fine and would like to meet you. Is there any chance you might be here soon?

Sincerely yours,

George W. Strang
Program Director

URS

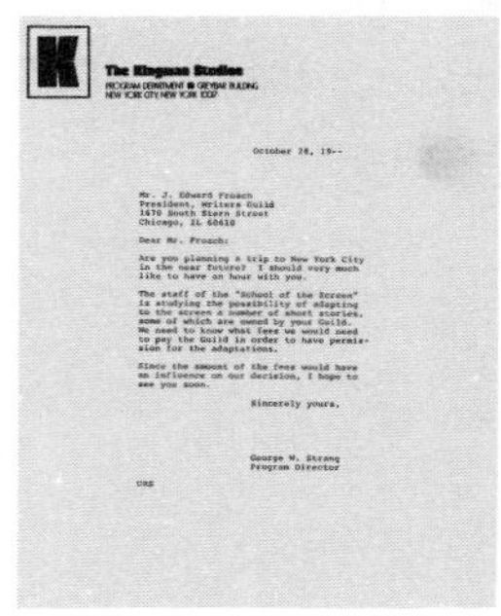

The Kingman Studios
PROGRAM DEPARTMENT ■ GREYBAR BUILDING
NEW YORK CITY, NEW YORK 10017

October 28, 19--

Mr. J. Edward Frosch
President, Writers Guild
1670 South Stern Street
Chicago, IL 60610

Dear Mr. Frosch:

Are you planning a trip to New York City in the near future? I should very much like to have an hour with you.

The staff of the "School of the Screen" is studying the possibility of adapting to the screen a number of short stories, some of which are owned by your Guild. We need to know what fees we would need to pay the Guild in order to have permission for the adaptations.

Since the amount of the fees would have an influence on our decision, I hope to see you soon.

Sincerely yours,

George W. Strang
Program Director

URS

WARMUP PREVIEW

2 copies

A exact weeks might date into here soon two has him 10
B available rehearsal counselor "college script CBS 10
C Jo quietly picked sixty sizes from the woven bag. 10
D Type by touch two copies of the inside addresses in these letters.

4-MINUTE TW

Lines 3 through 11
Spacing 1

JOB 80·1

BLOCKED LETTER
Line 4 inches
Tab center
Date line 15
Body 91 words
Workbook 47

1 *Today's date* ↓5 /Mrs. Jennifer Van Sant/Round Oak Ranch/Yellow- 17
2 stone Highway/Billings, MT 59109 ↓2 23
3 Dear Mrs. Van Sant: ↓2 4 29
4 The script that you sent us has now been edited and will go into 18 43
5 rehearsal in two or three weeks, by our present plans. 29 54
6 The exact date depends on how soon we can schedule Frank Jahns. 43 68
7 He tells us that CBS has him tied for two weeks, perhaps more, in the 57 82
8 "College Counselor" program he does for them. As soon as he becomes 71 96
9 available, we will start rehearsal. 79 103
10 Mr. Jahns thinks that your script is fine and would like to meet 93 117
11 you. Is there any chance you might be here soon? ↓2 /Sincerely yours, 108 133
12 George W. Strang/Program Director ↓2 /URS 147

|1 |2 |3 |4 |5 |6 |7 |8 |9 |10 |11 |12 |13 |14 SI 1.31FE

a·i·m 191

GOALS *To bolster skill (190 or more words in 5 minutes within 4 errors) on easy listen-for-bell copy.*

DIRECTIONS *Spacing 1 for drills, 2 for TW. Line 60. Tab 5.*

CHECK EVERY EXERCISE FOR—

- Flying caps (must be sitting off center).
- Spacing errors (table not right height).
- Top-row errors (not leaning forward).
- Irregular left margin (feet not braced).

WARMUP REVIEW

2 copies

```
James said he must work on his plans for the next big show.      12
Why did Max become eloquent over a zany gift like jodhpurs?      12
3,000 9,000 2,000 8,000 4,000 7,000 5,000 6,000 1,000 9,000      12
|1    |2    |3    |4    |5    |6    |7    |8    |9    |10   |11   |12
```

ACCURACY DRIVE

See page 162.

Spacing 2

If you have been out in a small boat, you have learned that the one 15
movement of the craft that is sure to give you a queasy sense is a roll. 29
This is caused when a swell or a wave comes up to the side of the boat, 44
then tilts and lifts that side with a surge, and then fades off, letting 58
it roll back with a lurch into the trough. Giant waves can capsize 72
a boat, turning it upside down. Judging where you might be in that 85
case is what makes you feel a bit anxious when your boat rolls. Even 99
on a big ship, the lurch as a ship rights itself is risky to all aboard. 114
All kinds of tales are told by those who were made ill by such rock 129
and roll. The standard joke, for example, has to do with a man so ill 143
that he fears he will die, and then he gets so much worse that he fears 157
he will not. Steamship lines and the Navy do not see it as a joke; 171
they have spent vast sums to find means to stabilize ships and thus 184
conquer the heaving seas. 190

|1 |2 |3 |4 |5 |6 |7 |8 |9 |10 |11 |12 |13 |14 SI 1.11VE

OPTIONAL OR ALTERNATIVE ACCURACY DRIVE

Well, if you feel a bit squeamish as you think of your next journey 15 | 205
at sea, you will be happy to know that the men who design ships 27 | 218
have learned a new trick that will get rid of most of the roll. They 41 | 232
found that putting two tiny fins on each ship, one on each side at 55 | 245
the exact point where the bow flattens into the sides of the hull, 68 | 259
will stabilize the ship. The fins are known as "gyrofins." They do 82 | 273
more than put an end to the rolling. They also diminish the pitching 96 | 287
of the ship as it plows directly through the wave crests in a roaring 110 | 300
and pounding storm. 114 | 304
The little fins are flexible. The officer of the deck can retract 129 | 319
them when the ship moves up to a dock. He also can adjust the angles 143 | 333
of the fins so as to equalize them to the flow of wind and wave. 156 | 347
Each fin is hinged; it will fold back if a submerged object is hit. 170 | 360
Should the ship develop a list, the fins can level the ship. The new 183 | 374
fins give new stability to a ship. 190 | 380

|1 |2 |3 |4 |5 |6 |7 |8 |9 |10 |11 |12 |13 |14 SI 1.22E

OPTIONAL JOB 80·2

BLOCKED LETTER
Line 4 inches
Tab center
Date Line 15
Body 94 words
Workbook 49

Today's date $\downarrow_5$ /Mr. J. Edward Frosch/President, Writers Guild/ 17
1670 South Stern Street/Chicago, IL 60610 $\downarrow_2$ /Dear Mr. Frosch: $\downarrow_2$ 30
Are you planning a trip to New York City in the near future? I 44
should very much like to have an hour with you. 54
The staff of the "School of the Screen" is studying the possibility 68
of adapting to the screen a number of short stories, some of which are 82
owned by your Guild. We need to know what fees we would need to pay 96
the Guild in order to have permission for the adaptations. 108
Since the amount of the fees would have an influence on our decision, 123
I hope to see you soon. $\downarrow_2$ /Sincerely yours, $\downarrow_5$ 134
George W. Strang/Program Director $\downarrow_2$ /URS 148

1 2 3 4 5 6 7 8 9 10 11 12 13 14 SI 1.36N

a·i·m 81

GOALS ◉ *To practice listening for the bell.* ◉ *To build speed reserve (135 or more words in 4 minutes within 5 errors) on very easy material.*

DIRECTIONS *Spacing 1 for drills, 2 for TW. Line 50. Tab 5 only.*

ERROR STOPPERS

- Read material before you type it.
- Practice words that you recall gave you trouble previously.
- Keep small fingers at "home."

WARMUP PREVIEW

3 copies

```
Why did the man who lost the box not fix the lid?    10
against whether instead leaners bought glance bit    10
Joe took quite a few zippers from that woven bag.    10
Anne lost checks 10, 28, and 39 but not 47 or 56.    10
1    2    3    4    5    6    7    8    9    10
```

SPEED DRIVE 4·2·2·4 TW

See page 80.

You can tell a great deal about a man if you know what kind of 14
books he does or does not read. 20
You watch him at a book stall. He takes one book from a shelf, 34
he turns a page or two, and he puts the book back. It is not what 47
he wants. If you could glance at the book, you would know what he 61
shuts out of his mind. 65
He might not put the book back. Instead, he may read a page 79
with a new look on his face. Now is the time to see what he does. 92
If he has found the kind of book he likes, he will look for a bit 106
of wall he can lean against as he scans the book. The next time 119
you are in a place where there is a choice of books, note how many 132
leaners there are.◉ 135
What does it mean if he looks for a chair in place of a wall? 150
Just that he has time to spare. 155

1 2 3 4 5 6 7 8 9 10 11 12 13 14 SI 1.04VE

Overview

Part Nine extends the accuracy drive that you began in Part Seven and introduces advanced training (compared to what you have previously typed) in letters and business forms.

Accuracy Four of the 20 a·i·m sessions in Part Nine are focused on skill drives. You use the same routine of 3-minute and 5-minute writings, with remedial practice between them. The skill goal for Part Nine is only 5 words higher (up to 190 words, now) than in Part Eight, but the material is harder and you will nearly always have to listen for the bell and make your own line-ending decisions.

Letters In Part Nine you will learn how to display attention lines, subject lines, "cc" notations, and "bcc" notations, as well as review the placement of titles, postscripts, and so on. You will also learn how to select (in case your employer wants you to do so) proper salutations and complimentary closings.

Forms You will get extensive experience with index cards and files, fill-in postal cards, invoices, credit memos, and statements of account.

Performance Goals

When you finish the 20 a·i·m sessions in Part Nine and take the test on pages 211 and 212, you should be able to demonstrate these abilities:

1. Technicalities You will score 85 or more percent correct on an objective test covering the technical information introduced and practiced in Part Nine, with some review of prior learnings.

2. Production Working from unarranged material into which you must make insertions of proper details, you will execute blocked letters with correct display of carbon notations, subject line, and other technical elements, including the making and annotating of carbons; and will execute three fill-in announcement form postal cards.

3. Skill You will type at least 190 words in 5 minutes (220–225 is more likely!) within 4 errors on paragraph material that requires your listening for the bell and making line-ending decisions.

Routines and Procedures

You will continue to use the same accuracy-drive routine: a 3-minute pretest, followed by remedial practice if needed and/or sustained 5-minute efforts. But there will also be a special skill drive in a·i·m 195, page 201, to help you speed up controls on the number keys (which you use extensively in business forms) without diminishing speed or accuracy on letter keys.

The production exercises will be direct and interesting, but there is one problem that you will wish to discuss with your instructor when you do the letter-typing assignments: should you make carbon copies? If you can obtain and use carbon paper, the answer is *yes*, for you can learn how to make "cc" and "bcc" notations more easily with the carbon copies that they concern.

82

GOALS *To type 109 or more words in 4 minutes within 5 errors on part of a letter (salutation through complimentary closing). To copy a short personal-business letter in correct blocked form.*

DIRECTIONS *Spacing 1. Line 50. Tab center.*

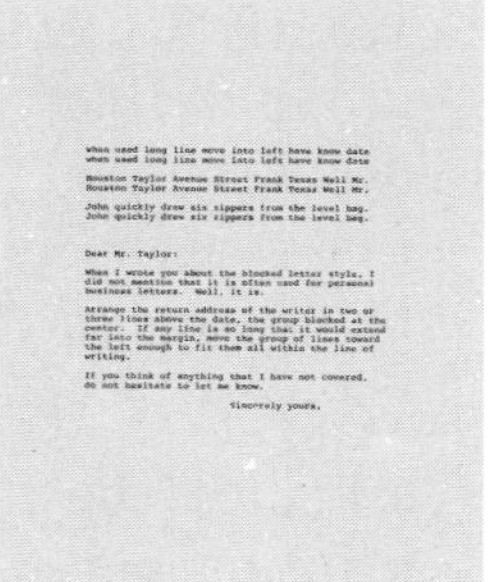

when used long line move into left have know date
when used long line move into left have know date

Houston Taylor Avenue Street Frank Texas Well Mr.
Houston Taylor Avenue Street Frank Texas Well Mr.

John quickly drew six zippers from the level bag.
John quickly drew six zippers from the level bag.

Dear Mr. Taylor:

When I wrote you about the blocked letter style, I did not mention that it is often used for personal business letters. Well, it is.

Arrange the return address of the writer in two or three lines above the date, the group blocked at the center. If any line is so long that it would extend far into the margin, move the group of lines toward the left enough to fit them all within the line of writing.

If you think of anything that I have not covered, do not hesitate to let me know.

Sincerely yours,

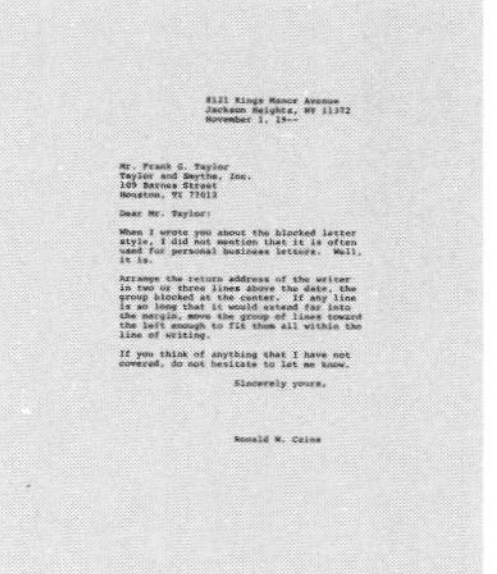

8121 Kings Manor Avenue
Jackson Heights, NY 11372
November 1, 19--

Mr. Frank C. Taylor
Taylor and Smythe, Inc.
109 Barnes Street
Houston, TX 77012

Dear Mr. Taylor:

When I wrote you about the blocked letter style, I did not mention that it is often used for personal business letters. Well, it is.

Arrange the return address of the writer in two or three lines above the date, the group blocked at the center. If any line is so long that it would extend far into the margin, move the group of lines toward the left enough to fit them all within the line of writing.

If you think of anything that I have not covered, do not hesitate to let me know.

Sincerely yours,

Ronald W. Cains

WARMUP PREVIEW

2 copies

A when used long line move into left have know date
B Houston Taylor Avenue Street Frank Texas Well Mr.
C John quickly drew six zippers from the level bag.
D Practice every word or number that is followed by punctuation.

|1 |2 |3 |4 |5 |6 |7 |8 |9 |10

4-MINUTE TW

Lines 8 through 20
Line 50
Spacing 1

JOB 82·1 (ELITE)

BLOCKED LETTER
Read page 89.
Line 4 inches
Tab center
Start line 13
Date line 15
Body 95 words

1	Line 13 8121 Kings Manor Avenue		5
2	Line 14 Jackson Heights, NY 11372		11
3	Line 15 November 1, 19-- ↓5		16
			20
4	Mr. Frank C. Taylor		24
5	Taylor and Smythe, Inc.		29
6	109 Barnes Street		32
7	Houston, TX 77012		36
			37
8	Dear Mr. Taylor:	4	41
		5	42
9	When I wrote you about the blocked letter style, I	15	52
10	did not mention that it is often used for personal	26	62
11	business letters. Well, it is.	32	69
		33	70
12	Arrange the return address of the writer in two or	43	80
13	three lines above the date, the group blocked at the	54	90
14	center. If any line is so long that it would extend	65	101
15	far into the margin, move the group of lines toward	75	111
16	the left enough to fit them all within the line of	85	122
17	writing.	87	124
		88	125
18	If you think of anything that I have not covered,	97	135
19	do not hesitate to let me know.	103	141
		104	142
20	Sincerely yours, ↓6	109	147
			151
21	Ronald W. Cains		155

|1 |2 |3 |4 |5 |6 |7 |8 |9 |10 SI 1.30FE

Short Personal-Business Letter in Blocked Style (Elite). Page 89 for Pica.

TEST 8-B

5-MINUTE TW
Spacing 2
Line 60
Tab 5
⚲ 185

HERE IS A TRICK of the trade every typist can use to center a 13
group of lines vertically on a paper. It is based on the same plan you 28
use when you center a line horizontally: you backspace once for each 41
two spaces the line will fill. Now learn how to "backroll," instead of 56
backspacing, to center. ↓4 61

WHEN YOU HAVE inserted and straightened the sheet of paper, 74
advance the sheet until the vertical center of the sheet is at the 87
printing point. Then, grasping a cylinder knob with one hand while 101
you point with the other one at the lines in the copy, turn the roller 115
back one click for each two lines in the material you wish to center. 129
You are "backrolling." ↓4 134

TEST 8-C

MAGAZINE ARTICLE
Type this as a magazine article on a 40-space line. Do only page 1. Entitle it "Centering by Backrolling." You are the author. Fills 44 lines.

ONE PROBLEM you have to solve in advance is discovering the 147
vertical midpoint of the paper, which is a trick in itself. 159
1. Fold a sheet of paper from top to bottom and crease it across 173
the center, so that you know where the center is. 183
2. Insert ⚲ the creased page; verify that it's straight. 196
3. Roll the paper forward until the top and the bottom edges 209
meet when you gently press down on the page of paper. 220
4. Now carefully advance the paper, counting the lines or clicks 234
as you advance it, until the creased line appears at the printing 247
point. Remember how many lines you counted as you advanced 259
the paper. It is your "correction" number. 268
So from now on you can work the centering trick of the trade. You 283
insert the paper. You advance it until the top meets the bottom. 296
You "correct" the paper the "correction" number of lines, to bring 309
it to its midpoint. You backroll the paper once for every two lines. 324
You are ready to type. ⚲ 328

|1 |2 |3 |4 |5 |6 |7 |8 |9 |10 |11 |12 |13 |14 SI 1.38N

TEST 8-D

RULED TABLE
Center on a full page.
Spacing 2

ENROLLMENTS IN THE CITY HIGH SCHOOLS 22

Spring Semester 33

High School	Boys	Girls	Totals	
				42
				51
				60
Adams	1,072	1,008	2,080	67
Carver	1,291	1,132	2,423	74
Kennedy	863	719	1,582	82
Roosevelt	1,038	887	1,925	89
Technical	1,466	1,229	2,695	97
Washington	987	1,102	2,089	105
				114
Totals	6,717	6,077	12,794	121
			⚲	130

PERSONAL-BUSINESS LETTERS

The blocked letter style can readily be used for *personal*-business letters. You simply type your return address above the date. All lines begin at the left margin except the heading and closing, which begin at or near the center.

1. Margin settings are the same as in other business letters. A short letter takes a 4-inch line (40 pica spaces, below; 50 elite spaces, page 88).

2. The return address starts at the center or, if there is a very long line in the return address, left of center. To find where to start the heading in that case, pick out the longest line in the return address and backspace from the left margin once for each letter and space in that line; start all heading lines at the point to which you backspace.

3. Begin the return address on line 13 so that the date will then fall on line 15.

4. Use no reference initials.

5. Use plain typewriting paper.

JOB 82·1. Make a copy of the letter to Frank Taylor. If your machine has pica type, copy the letter as it is shown below, but if your machine has elite type, copy the letter as it is shown on page 88.

JOB 82·1 (PICA)

BLOCKED LETTER
Line 4 inches
Tab center
Start line 13
Date line 15
Body 95 words

8121 Kings Manor Avenue
Jackson Heights, NY 11372
November 1, 19-- ↓5

Mr. Frank C. Taylor
Taylor and Smythe, Inc.
109 Barnes Street
Houston, TX 77012

Dear Mr. Taylor:

When I wrote you about the blocked letter style, I did not mention that it is often used for personal business letters. Well, it is.

Arrange the return address of the writer in two or three lines above the date, the group blocked at the center. If any line is so long that it would extend far into the margin, move the group of lines toward the left enough to fit them all within the line of writing.

If you think of anything that I have not covered, do not hesitate to let me know.

Sincerely yours, ↓5

Ronald W. Cains

SI 1.30FE

Short Personal-Business Letter in Blocked Style (Pica). Page 88 for Elite.

TEST PREP 2

5-MINUTE TW
Spacing 2
Line 60
Tab 5

WHEN YOU ARE MAKING just three or four carbon copies, it is easy to 14
insert the thin pack of papers into the typewriter. You simply press 28
the paper release; doing this opens up the paper grippers under the 41
cylinder so that the pack of paper slides right into position. This 55
is easy; this is obvious. 60
When you are making more than four carbon copies, however, the 74
paper pack will probably be too thick to slide in even though you 87
depress the paper release. What do you do? 96
There is a good way out of the quandary. All you need is any size 111
of card, sheet of paper, or envelope. With its help, you can insert 124
the thickest pack in three easy steps. ↓4 132

HERE ARE THE three steps. They are quicker to take than to read 148
about, once you have tried them out a couple of times. 158
First, insert the card or whatever you are using. Insert it part 173
way, about as far as two roller clicks permit. 182
Second, place the carbon pack between the cylinder and the end 196
of the guide card extending toward the paper table. 206
Third, turn the cylinder. The paper will go into your machine 221
very readily, for the card helps squeeze the carbon pack between the 234
big cylinder and the small paper grippers. 242

|1 |2 |3 |4 |5 |6 |7 |8 |9 |10 |11 |12 |13 |14 SI 1.37N

TEST PREP 3

MANUSCRIPT

Arrange the preceding timed writing selection as an article for a magazine that uses a 50-space line of writing. Use all cap paragraph display and this heading:

Line 13 INSERTING CARBON PACKS

Line 15 By (Your Name)

Line 17 (28 Lines of 50 Spaces)

TEST PREP 4

RULED TABLE

Turn to page 184. On a full sheet, center a copy of Optional Job 174·3 as a ruled table. Use double-spacing. Allow 6 spaces between the columns.

a·i·m 189–190

GOALS *To type 185 or more words in 5 minutes within 4 errors on average production copy requiring bell listening ◦ To produce page 1 of a magazine article. ◦ To produce a ruled table from rough-draft copy ◦ To score 85% or higher on an objective test on Part Eight.*

DIRECTIONS *Optional warmup from the review on page 193. Settings as indicated for each exercise. WB 171–172.*

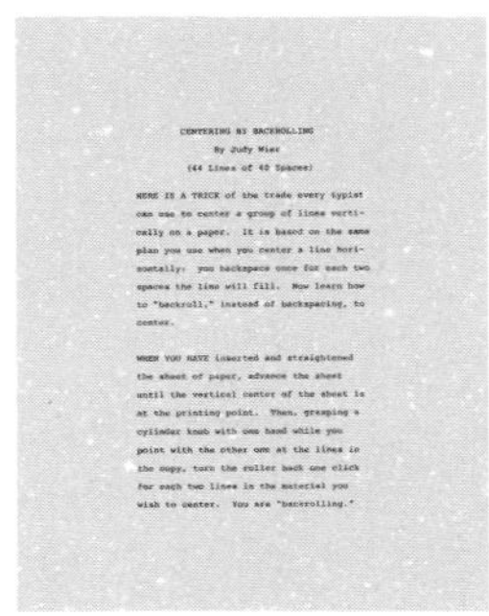

CENTERING BY BACKROLLING

By Judy Wier

(44 Lines of 40 Spaces)

HERE IS A TRICK of the trade every typist can use to center a group of lines vertically on a paper. It is based on the same plan you use when you center a line horizontally: you backspace once for each two spaces the line will fill. Now learn how to "backroll," instead of backspacing, to center.

WHEN YOU HAVE inserted and straightened the sheet of paper, advance the sheet until the vertical center of the sheet is at the printing point. Then, grasping a cylinder knob with one hand while you point with the other one at the lines in the copy, turn the roller back one click for each two lines in the material you wish to center. You are "backrolling."

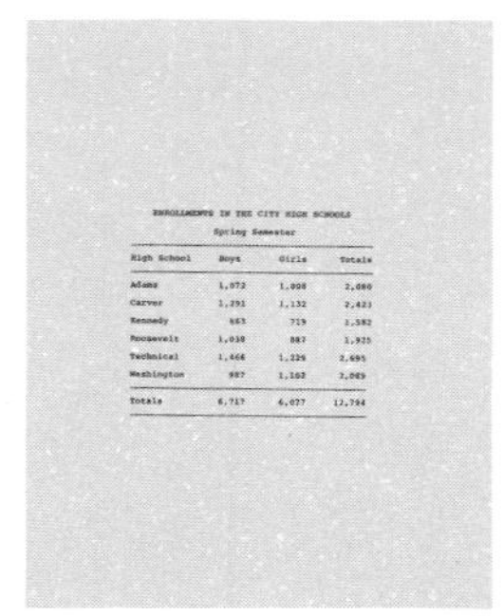

ENROLLMENTS IN THE CITY HIGH SCHOOLS

Spring Semester

High School	Boys	Girls	Totals
Adams	1,072	1,008	2,080
Carver	1,291	1,132	2,423
Kennedy	863	719	1,582
Roosevelt	1,038	887	1,925
Technical	1,466	1,229	2,695
Washington	987	1,102	2,089
Totals	6,717	6,077	12,794

TEST 8-A

Take a general information test. It may be the one on Workbook pages 171–172 or a similar test that your teacher may give you or may dictate to you.

 83

GOALS ⚲ *To type 110 words or more in 4 minutes within 5 errors on part of a letter (salutation through complimentary closing).* ⚲ *To type a short personal-business letter, arranging it in blocked style.*

DIRECTIONS *Spacing 1. Line 50. Tab center.*

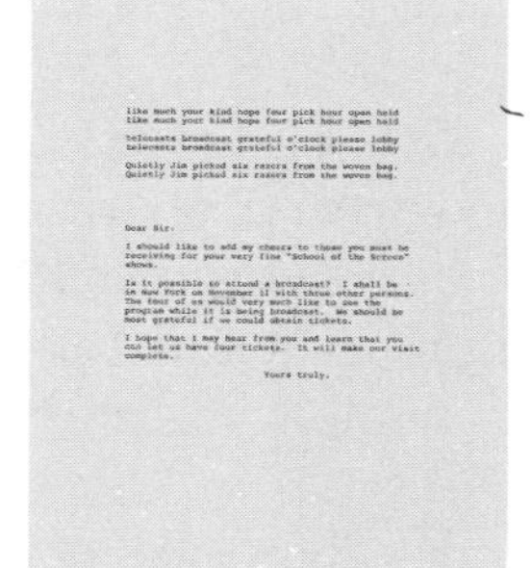

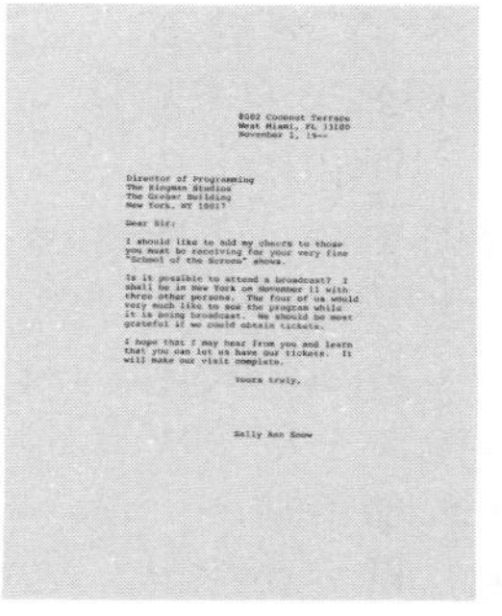

WARMUP PREVIEW

2 copies

A	like much your kind hope four pick hour open held	10
B	telecasts broadcast grateful o'clock please lobby	10
C	Quietly Jim picked six razors from the woven bag.	10
D	Practice the word before and after each punctuation mark.	

4-MINUTE TW

Lines 8 through 17
Lines 4 inches
Spacing 1

Before typing letter 83·1, review the information and model on page 89. If your machine is pica, remember to use a 40-space line and listen for the bell. If your machine is elite, use a 50-space line and listen for the bell.

JOB 83·1

BLOCKED LETTER
Line 4 inches
Tab center
Date line 15
Body 95 words

8002 Coconut Terrace		4
West Miami, FL 33100		9
Today's Date ↓5		14
		18
Director of Programming		23
The Kingman Studios		27
The Grebar Building		31
New York, NY 10017		35
		36
Dear Sir:	2	38
	3	39
I should like to add my cheers to those you must be receiving for	16	52
your very fine "School of the Screen" shows.	26	62
	27	63
Is it possible to attend a broadcast? I shall be in New York on	40	76
November 11 with three other persons. The four of us would very	58	99
much like to see the program while it is being broadcast. We should	72	108
be most grateful if we could obtain tickets.	81	117
	82	118
I hope that I may hear from you and learn that you can let us have	95	131
four tickets. It will make our visit complete.	105	141
	106	142
Yours truly, ↓6	⚲110	146
		150
Sally Ann Snow ⚲		154

|1 |2 |3 |4 |5 |6 |7 |8 |9 |10 |11 |12 |13 |14 SI 1.32FE

sadly said at a press conference at the local 44
college today. 47

Injured in the game with La Grange last 56
Friday, when he collided with a guard and 63
broke his left ankle, Hondo takes away the 71
Cougar hopes for a league title and the big 81
ticket to the Easter tournament in Madison 89
Square Garden, New York. 94

Hondo had scored more than 900 points 103
in the season and was high man in the Texas 112
League. Captain of the Cougars, he has been 121
the spark plug and hero of the Cougar fans. 130
Now the team must build its offense around 139
Blake Jourdan, Cougar guard, and Stew 146
Burr, relief center for the past year. 154

"We are not out of it," Gaines told the 163
press, "but we will have a rough time 171
without Red on the team." (END) 177

|1 |2 |3 |4 |5 |6 |7 |8 SI 1.47FD

OPTIONAL JOB 186·2 NEWS RELEASE
Use plain paper

News release from the Civil Service Commission, City of South Roselle, South Roselle, New Hampshire 03308. Release on March 15. From Guy S. Firestone. Title: "Civil Service Tests in April."

South Roselle, NH, Feb. 29—Office 8
workers who wish jobs when the new City 16
Hall of South Roselle opens in June will be 25
tested on April 1 and 15. Announcement of 33
the test schedule was made by H. J. Prentiss, 43
civil service commissioner. 48

"We will need 40 to 50 more office work- 57
ers in June, and we want to have them 65
ready," he said in an announcement sent 73
to all public and private schools in the 81
Concord area. 84

Commissioner Prentiss said that appli- 92
cants should report to the Commission 100
office in Garvey House on April 1 between 108
9:30 a.m. and 4:00 p.m. to file their papers 117
and take a test on general skills like spelling, 127
adding, and the like. 132

Those who pass this easy test will then 141
be told at what time on April 15 to report 150
to the senior high school for the tests 157
in typing and related skills. (END) 165

|1 |2 |3 |4 |5 |6 |7 |8 SI 1.43N

a·i·m 187–188

GOALS *To type 185 or more words in 5 minutes within 4 errors on normal listen-for-the-bell narrative copy. To preview the test in a·i·m 189–190. To produce a magazine article and a ruled table.*

DIRECTIONS *Warmup spacing 1, line 60. Other settings as directed for each exercise. WB 171–172.*

OPTIONAL WARMUP REVIEW

```
1  Why did you not ask the two old men who had dug the jar up?  12
2  Weekly magazines request help by and for junior executives.  12
3  we 23 25 27 or 94 96 98 it 85 87 89 up 70 72 74 ow 92 94 96  12
   |1   |2   |3   |4   |5   |6   |7   |8   |9   |10   |11   |12
```

TEST PREP 1 Review the objective information test on Workbook pages 171–172. Do not mark the pages, but look up any details about which you are uncertain; be ready to score high.

a·i·m 84

GOALS ⚲ *To type 111 words or more in 4 minutes within 5 errors on part of a letter (salutation through complimentary closing).* ⚲ *To type a short personal-business letter, arranging it in blocked style.*

DIRECTIONS *Spacing 1. Line 50. Tab center.*

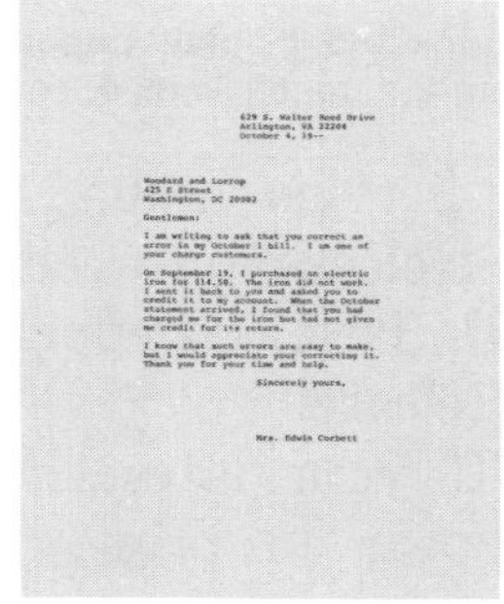

629 S. Walter Reed Drive
Arlington, VA 22204
October 4, 19--

Woodard and Lorrop
425 E Street
Washington, DC 20002

Gentlemen:

I am writing to ask that you correct an error in my October 1 bill. I am one of your charge customers.

On September 19, I purchased an electric iron for $14.50. The iron did not work. I sent it back to you and asked you to credit it to my account. When the October statement arrived, I found that you had charged me for the iron but had not given me credit for its return.

I know that such errors are easy to make, but I would appreciate your correcting it. Thank you for your time and help.

Sincerely yours,

Mrs. Edwin Corbett

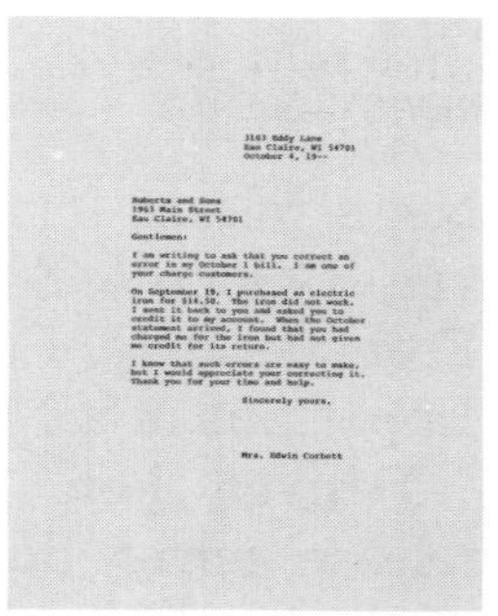

3163 Eddy Lane
Eau Claire, WI 54701
October 4, 19--

Roberts and Sons
1963 Main Street
Eau Claire, WI 54701

Gentlemen:

I am writing to ask that you correct an error in my October 1 bill. I am one of your charge customers.

On September 19, I purchased an electric iron for $14.50. The iron did not work. I sent it back to you and asked you to credit it to my account. When the October statement arrived, I found that you had charged me for the iron but had not given me credit for its return.

I know that such errors are easy to make, but I would appreciate your correcting it. Thank you for your time and help.

Sincerely yours,

Mrs. Edwin Corbett

WARMUP PREVIEW

2 copies

A October appreciate customers purchased would iron 10
B Washington, DC arrived writing credit you account 10
C The fog was so thick Ozzi could not see the road. 10
D Practice touch-tabbing and typing lines 1–3 and 16 and 17.

COMPOSING LETTERS

A convenient formula for writing a personal-business letter is to divide it into these parts:

1. **Introductory paragraph,** in which you explain why you are writing and, if the correspondent does not know you, who you are.
2. **Message paragraph** (or paragraphs), in which you explain the details of the matter.
3. **Sign-off paragraph,** in which you end the letter pleasantly, urging your correspondent to take the action about which you are writing him.

Note how this formula is applied in the letters in this Part, including the letter below.

Job 84·1 Copy this letter, using your own name and home address and the name and address of any department store.

4-MINUTE TW

Lines 7 through 16
Line 4 inches
Spacing 1

JOB 84·1

BLOCKED PERSONAL–BUSINESS LETTER
Line 4 inches
Tab center
Body 98 words

1 629 S. Walter Reed Drive 5
2 Arlington, Virginia 22204 11
3 Today's Date ↓5 16
4 Woodard and Lorrop 24
5 425 E Street 27
6 Washington, D C 20002 31
7 Gentlemen: 2 34
8 I am writing to ask that you correct an error in my October 1 bill. 17 49
9 I am one of your charge customers. 24 56
10 On September 19, I purchased an electric iron for $14.50. The iron 39 71
11 did not work. I sent it back to you and asked you to credit it to my 53 85
12 account. When the October statement arrived, I found that you had 66 98
13 charged me for the iron but had not given me credit for its return. 80 112
14 I know that such errors are easy to make, but I would appreciate your 95 127
15 correcting it. Thank you for your time and help. 105 137
16 Sincerely yours, ↓6 ⚲111 143
17 Mrs. Edwin Corbett ⚲ 152

|1 |2 |3 |4 |5 |6 |7 |8 |9 |10 |11 |12 |13 |14 SI 1.31FE

JOB 184·1
NEWS RELEASE

Workbook 165 (or plain paper)
Spacing 2. Line 6″. Tabs 5, center.

News release for Press Service Club, Den-
ver, Colorado 80202. Release on receipt.
From Paul N. Cantrell. Title: "Typing Is
Important in a News Release."

Denver, Feb. 25—If your latest news 8
release never does appear in print, you 16
might be able to blame your typist. 24

This is what Henry Lee, wire chief of the 33
Journal Press, told 200 members of the 45
Press Service Club meeting here at the 53
Denver Hilton for their eleventh national 62
convention. 64

"An editor gets a hundred or more news 73
releases a day," Lee told his audience. "He 82
is human. When he has an extra inch or 90
two to fill, he looks for the items that are 99
easiest to use without change. Make a re- 107
lease easy for him to use." 113

Lee offered five guides for improving a 122
news release: 125

1. Use a title line that tells the story at 135
a glance. 137

2. Tell who released the story, so the 146
editor knows to whom he can turn for con- 154
firmation or more details. 159

3. Start the story with a date line, even 169
if the story is local. It may hit the big 177
news circuits. 181

4. So that the editor will have room for 190
wielding his pen, double-space and make 198
margins at least an inch wide. 204

5. Be sure the typing is correct. An error 214
hints that the news release may not be 222
reliable enough to use. (END) 228

|1 |2 |3 |4 |5 |6 |7 |8 SI 1.38N

JOB 185·1
NEWS RELEASE

Workbook 167 (or plain paper)
Spacing 2. Line 6″. Tabs 5, center.

Prepare a news release for the Sky Mine
High School of Sky Mine, West Virginia
24306, for release at once. It is released by
Mark Jaderstrom, Acting Principal. Story
title: "Boys Take Most Typing Honors."

Sky Mine, W. Va., Feb. 27—This moun- 8
taintop town gained a new distinction today. 17
Not only is it the highest mining town in 26
the United States but it is also the place 34
where boys type faster than girls—in the 43
contests, that is. 47

Steve Cheney, 18, Sky Mine High School 55
senior, took the typing honors from the 63
girls today by writing at a speed of 74 71
words a minute for 10 minutes in the mid- 79
year contest sponsored by the high school. 88
He used an electric machine, as did the 97
other contestants. His 74 score set a 105
school record. 108

Runners-up in the contest were Al Har- 117
mon, 17, a junior, with 70 words a minute; 125
and Alex Dennis, 18, a senior, with 69 133
words a minute and a record of making no 141
errors at all. 145

In the 5-minute contest for students in 154
their first year of typing, first place went to 163
Vic Brill, 16, a tenth grader, with 51 words 172
a minute. In second place was the only 180
girl to place in the honors, Ruth Cheney, 189
16-year-old sophomore sister of the cham- 197
pion, with 50. Third place went to Stan 205
Hart, 16, with 48 words a minute. (END) 213

|1 |2 |3 |4 |5 |6 |7 |8 SI 1.36N

JOB 186·1
NEWS RELEASE

Workbook 169 (or plain paper)
Spacing 2. Line 6″. Tabs 5, center.

News release from the Athletic Department
of Costa Community College in San Marcos,
Texas 78666. Release immediately. From
Ben Carter, Athletic Director. Title:
"Hondo Out for the Season."

San Marcos, Tex., Feb. 28—Red Hondo, 9
star center of the CCC Cougars, will be 17
off the floor for the rest of this year's basket- 26
ball season. This is what Coach Tom Gaines 35

85

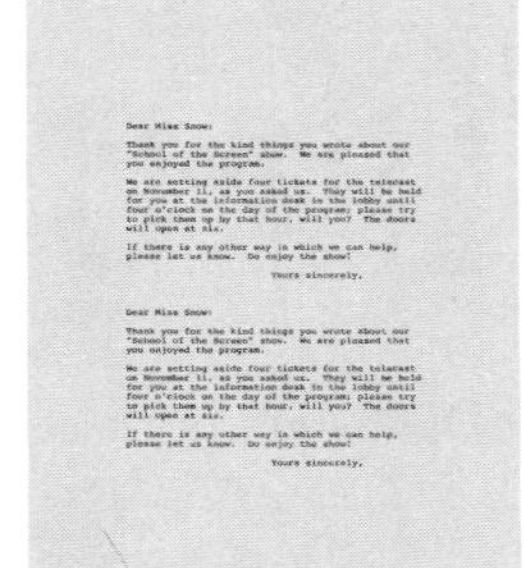

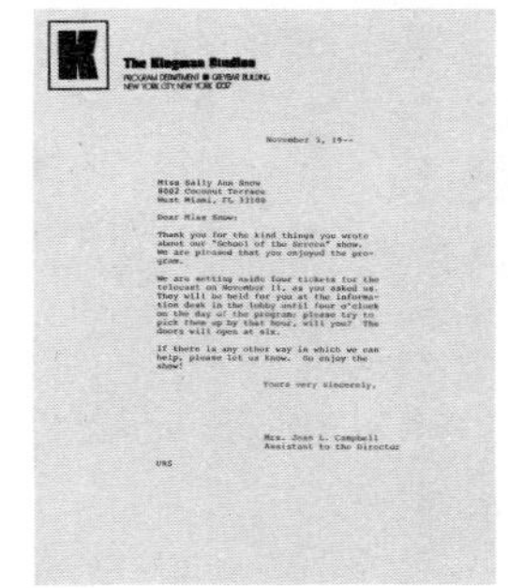

GOALS ⚲ *To type 112 words or more in 4 minutes within 5 errors on part of a letter (lines 3–11 below).* ⚲ *To type a short business letter from unarranged material, arranging it correctly in blocked form.*

DIRECTIONS *Spacing 1. Line 50. Tab center. WB 51.*

WARMUP PREVIEW

2 copies

```
A  thank write about four kind held pick are for the      10
B  information sincerely, November "Screen" telecast      10
C  Jim quietly picked up six zippers for the valise.      10
```

D Speed up carriage (carrier) returns: type first word shown in each line.

4-MINUTE TW

Lines 3 through 11
2 attempts
Line 4 inches
Spacing 1

JOB 85·1

BLOCKED LETTER
Line 4 inches
Tab center
Body 98 words
Workbook 51

1	*Today's date* ↓7 /Miss Sally Ann Snow/8002 Coconut Terrace/West		17
2	Miami, FL 33100 ↓?		20
3	Dear Miss Snow:/Thank you for the kind things you wrote about	14	36
4	our "School of the Screen" show. We are pleased that you have enjoyed	28	50
5	the program.	31	53
6	We are setting aside four tickets for the telecast on November 11,	45	67
7	as you asked us. They will be held for you at the information desk in	59	81
8	the lobby until four o'clock on the day of the program; please try to	73	95
9	pick them up by that hour, will you? The doors will open at six.	87	109
10	If there is any other way in which we can help you, please let us	101	123
11	know. Do enjoy the show!/Yours very sincerely, ↓?	⚲ 112	135
12	Mrs. Jean L. Campbell/Assistant to the Director/URS⚲		153

|1 |2 |3 |4 |5 |6 |7 |8 |9 |10 |11 |12 |13 |14

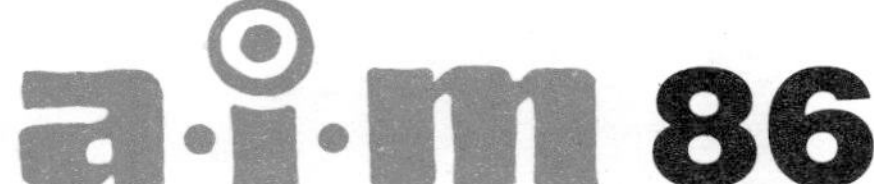

86

GOALS ⚲ *To practice listening for margin bell.* ⚲ *To build a speed reserve (140 words or more in 4 minutes within 5 errors) on very easy material.*

DIRECTIONS *Spacing 1 for drills, 2 for TW. Line 50. Tab 5 only.*

ALIGNING THE BODY

- Sit very tall, very erect.
- Lean forward slightly from waist.
- Center body opposite the J key.
- Have handspan of space between your body and the frame of the machine.

WARMUP PREVIEW

3 copies

```
1  The man who had the hat did not get the hat back.      10
2  country figures address number corner zone ZIP is      10
3  I quickly extinguished the other dangerous blaze.      10
4  Jim did problems 10, 28, and 39; I did 47 and 56.      10
```

a·i·m 184–186

GOALS ⚲ *To produce news releases on both plain paper and printed release sheets.* ⚲ *To type 185 or more words of normal repetitive copy within 5 minutes and 4 errors.*

DIRECTIONS *Spacing 1. Line 60. Tab 5. WB 165–169.*

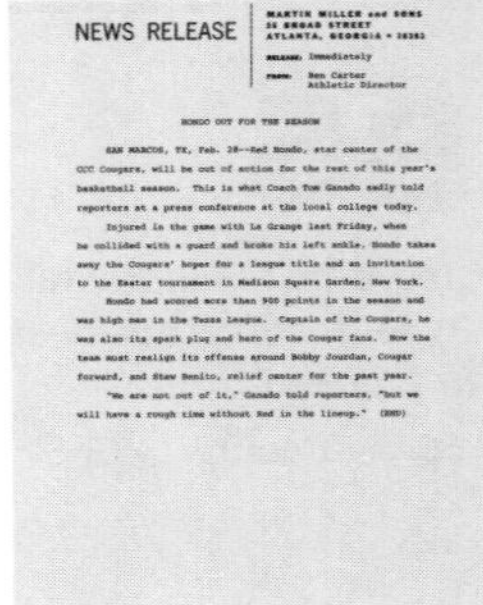

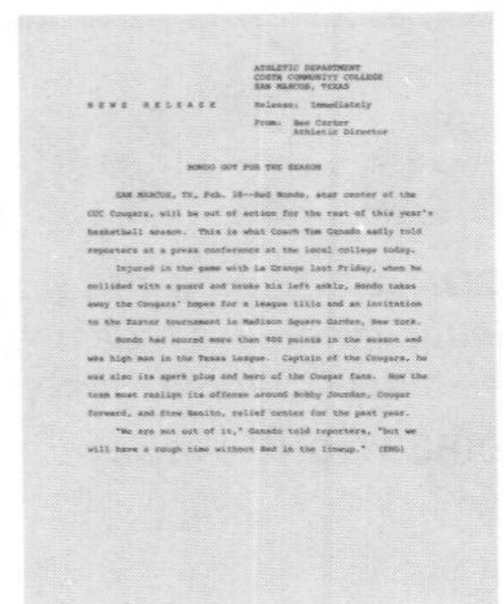

WARMUP REVIEW

2 copies

```
They will sell both lots when they feel they need more men.     12
Ziggy jumped up and quickly paid Bertha for five new taxis.     12
we 23 22 23 24 23 it 85 84 85 86 85 wo 29 28 29 30 29 28 27     12
|1   |2   |3   |4   |5   |6   |7   |8   |9   |10  |11  |12     1 | 2
```

5-MINUTE TW

GOAL WRITING
Spacing 1
2 copies in 5 minutes

```
     The majority of papers and magazines get far more news    12 | 105
releases and articles than they can publish.  Articles from    24 | 117
expert writers and news from a wire service are sure to get    36 | 129
a quick reading, but whatever looks as though it comes from    48 | 141
an amateur is certain to be ignored.  With so much material    60 | 153
he can use, the editor is not going to waste time rewriting    72 | 165
a story when he has others he can use.  If you want a story    84 | 177
used, write it the way he prefers it.                          92 | 185⚲
                                                                 SI 1.40N
```

NEWS RELEASES

For the Jobs on pages 192–193, use either the workbook forms or plain paper. Use a 6-inch line and tabs 5 and center in either arrangement.

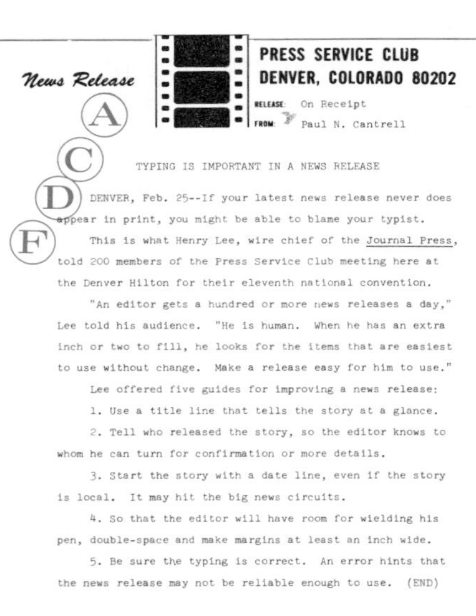

News Release (A)

PRESS SERVICE CLUB
DENVER, COLORADO 80202

RELEASE: On Receipt
FROM: Paul N. Cantrell

(C) TYPING IS IMPORTANT IN A NEWS RELEASE

(D) DENVER, Feb. 25--If your latest news release never does appear in print, you might be able to blame your typist.

(F) This is what Henry Lee, wire chief of the Journal Press, told 200 members of the Press Service Club meeting here at the Denver Hilton for their eleventh national convention.

"An editor gets a hundred or more news releases a day," Lee told his audience. "He is human. When he has an extra inch or two to fill, he looks for the items that are easiest to use without change. Make a release easy for him to use."

Lee offered five guides for improving a news release:

1. Use a title line that tells the story at a glance.

2. Tell who released the story, so the editor knows to whom he can turn for confirmation or more details.

3. Start the story with a date line, even if the story is local. It may hit the big news circuits.

4. So that the editor will have room for wielding his pen, double-space and make margins at least an inch wide.

5. Be sure the typing is correct. An error hints that the news release may not be reliable enough to use. (END)

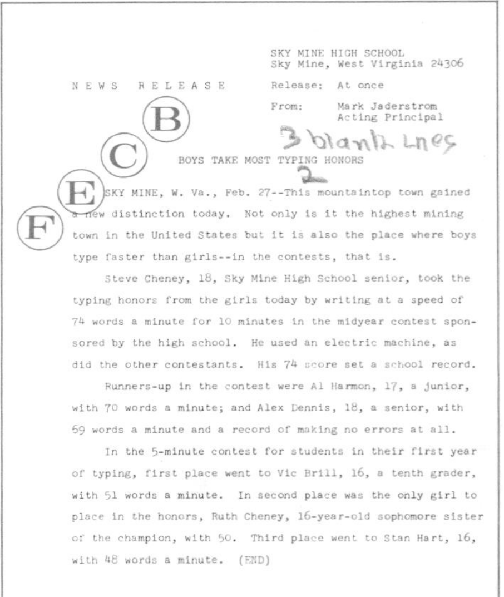

SKY MINE HIGH SCHOOL
Sky Mine, West Virginia 24306

N E W S   R E L E A S E (B)

Release: At once

From: Mark Jaderstrom
Acting Principal

(C) BOYS TAKE MOST TYPING HONORS

(E) SKY MINE, W. Va., Feb. 27--This mountaintop town gained a new distinction today. Not only is it the highest mining town in the United States but it is also the place where boys type faster than girls--in the contests, that is. (F)

Steve Cheney, 18, Sky Mine High School senior, took the typing honors from the girls today by writing at a speed of 74 words a minute for 10 minutes in the midyear contest sponsored by the high school. He used an electric machine, as did the other contestants. His 74 score set a school record.

Runners-up in the contest were Al Harmon, 17, a junior, with 70 words a minute; and Alex Dennis, 18, a senior, with 69 words a minute and a record of making no errors at all.

In the 5-minute contest for students in their first year of typing, first place went to Vic Brill, 16, a tenth grader, with 51 words a minute. In second place was the only girl to place in the honors, Ruth Cheney, 16-year-old sophomore sister of the champion, with 50. Third place went to Stan Hart, 16, with 48 words a minute. (END)

Heading may be typed (A) on a printed form or (B) on plain paper, with data aligned at the center tab stop.

Title (C) is all capped, centered and is preceded by 3 blank lines and followed by 2 blank lines of space.

Date line is (D) city name in all caps, abbreviated date, and a dash before first sentence. It includes state (E) only if city is small or shares a popular name.

Text (F) is double-spaced on a 6-inch line with 5-space paragraph indentions.

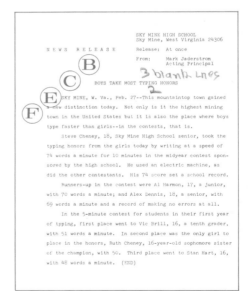

SPEED DRIVE 4·2·2·4 TW

See page 80.

The ZIP code is a number that you are to put in each address you 14
write. It goes at the end of the line in which you put the town and 28
state, one space after the name of the state. That is where the ZIP 42
has to be typed. No place else is right. 50
Come to think of it, though, the ZIP is more than just a number. It 65
is a plan, and the number is one small part of the plan. The plan is a 79
way to speed up the mail so that each piece you write will reach 94
where it has to go in a lot less time. 100
The plan has to use five figures. The first three steer the mail so 115
it goes to the right town in the right corner of our country. The last 129
two tell you in which zone of the town the street is. 140
If you had to sort out a lot of mail, as the men in the post office 155
do, you would find that it takes less time when you sort by number 169
than when you sort by name. That fact is the base on which the 181
whole ZIP code plan is built. To make it all work, of course, we 195
have to use the right number! 200

|1 |2 |3 |4 |5 |6 |7 |8 |9 |10 |11 |12 |13 |14 SI 1.05VE

PREPARE a·i·m WB 53–54

a·i·m 87

Tables

GOALS *To learn the names of the parts of a table. To learn "open" arrangement of a table. To produce a simple table in open arrangement.*

DIRECTIONS *Spacing 2. Line 50. No tabs.*

WARMUP REVIEW

3 copies

```
He may or may not be the man we want for the job.   10
The big man quickly fixed five jeopardized wires.   10
I retyped tables 10 and 28 but not 39, 47, or 56.   10
|1   |2   |3   |4   |5   |6   |7   |8   |9   |10
```

TABLE PARTS

Read and remember.

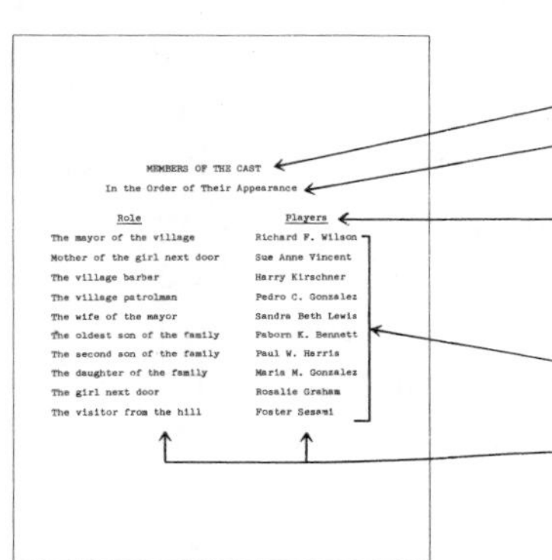

MEMBERS OF THE CAST

In the Order of Their Appearance

Role	Players
The mayor of the village	Richard F. Wilson
Mother of the girl next door	Sue Anne Vincent
The village barber	Harry Kirschner
The village patrolman	Pedro C. Gonzalez
The wife of the mayor	Sandra Beth Lewis
The oldest son of the family	Faborn K. Bennett
The second son of the family	Paul W. Harris
The daughter of the family	Maria M. Gonzalez
The girl next door	Rosalie Graham
The visitor from the hill	Foster Sesami

Title identifies table, is centered in all capitals.
Subtitle gives more information about table, is centered a double space below title, with principal words capitalized.
Column heads tell what is in columns, may be blocked at the start of each column or (more frequently) centered over it, is preceded by 2 blank spaces and followed by 1 blank space.
Body the columns, centered horizontally, normally with 6 spaces between columns.
Column listing, includes the column head, is considered to be as wide as the longest item in the column.

a·i·m 183

GOAL *To strengthen skill (185 words or more in 5 minutes within 4 errors on normal but listen-for-bell copy.*

DIRECTIONS *Spacing 1 for drills, 2 for TW. Line 60. Tab 5,*

FOR FASTER GAINS

- **Eyes:** don't let them look back.
- **Eyes:** don't let them get more than five strokes ahead of your fingers.
- **Eyes:** keep them on the copy.
- **Eyes:** keep them relaxed; no squint.

WARMUP REVIEW

2 copies

```
Dick will give them back the money they gave him last week.    12
Ziggy James quickly paid us for the five new Rambler taxis.    12
we 23 22 21 or 94 93 92 to 59 58 57 it 85 84 83 tu 57 56 55    12
|1  |2  |3  |4  |5  |6  |7  |8  |9  |10  |11  |12
```

ACCURACY DRIVE

See page 162.

Spacing 2

The aircraft to watch in the future is the helicopter, one of our most 15
amazing machines. This extraordinary thing goes straight up and 28
down, as well as sideways and forward, so it qualifies for so many jobs 42
that we may expect to find this marvel filling the skies in coming 56
decades. Right now the jet plane and the space missile take the head- 70
lines, and they do their tasks quite well. But the day of whirlybirds is 84
coming up fast. They do everything from spraying fields and forests to 98
lifting steel girders for the highest floors of skyscrapers. 111

The helicopter is not an impressive sight when you see it on the 125
ground. A jet plane, now, with its long fuselage and needle nose, with 140
its zooming tail and swept wings, has exquisite beauty built right into 154
it. Not even the deepest fan of the whirlybird will say it is pretty. To 169
be honest, it looks like a cross between a big, bent grasshopper and 182
a mosquito. 185

|1 |2 |3 |4 |5 |6 |7 |8 |9 |10 |11 |12 |13 |14 SI 1.40N

ACCURACY DRIVE

(For optional practice)

But whether a helicopter is pretty or not, it has made a performance 15 | 201
record that is unquestionably impressive. It has rescued hurt climbers 29 | 215
from mountain precipices. It has transferred sick men at sea from ship 44 | 230
to ship. In times of flood, the helicopter has taken doctors, clothing, 58 | 244
and food where no other vehicle could go. The lack of beauty hasn't 72 | 258
mattered to the hundreds of wounded it has rescued from the blaze 85 | 271
of battle, the crews whose planes have fallen at sea, the men it has 99 | 285
picked from steaming jungles, or many others it has saved. 111 | 296

For all the drama of these events, the real value that the whirly- 125 | 311
bird offers the world is its use in routine work. The taxi service that 140 | 326
the machine provides the President in his frequent trips to the 153 | 338
Washington airport is well known, as are also the taxi flights that 166 | 352
link the airfields around our cities and give us the traffic reports 179 | 364
which we hear on the radio. 185 | 370

|1 |2 |3 |4 |5 |6 |7 |8 |9 |10 |11 |12 |13 |14 SI 1.40N

STEPS IN TWO-COLUMN TABLE

1. **Clear the machine:** move margin stops to the end of the cylinder, clear out tab stops.
2. **Compute top margin:** find on what line to type the title, to center the table.
3. **Pick key line:** this is 6 blank spaces (between columns) plus the longest entry in each column: Astronauts, Edwin Jorgenson:

   `123456AstronautsEdwin Jorgenson`

4. **Set left margin:** from the center backspace to center the key line and set the left margin stop there:

   `123456AstronautsEdwin Jorgenson`

5. **Set Column 2 tab stop:** space over to Column 2 (tap the space bar enough to cross the first column and the 6 blank spaces) and set a tab stop at the start of Column 2:

   `Astronauts123456`

6. **Type the table:** insert paper to starting line and type the job, using the tabulator to hop to Column 2 on each line. Note:

Type →	tables →	line
by →	line →	just
the →	way →	you
are →	reading →	this ⚲

JOB 87·1

OPEN TABLE
Center on a full page.
Spacing 2

To triple-space after the title when spacing is set for 2, turn paper up 1 line by hand, then return carriage.

1		TEAM CAPTAINS ↓3	8
			10
2	Astronauts	Kenneth d'Alou	16
3	Bengals	Graham Jenkins	22
4	Eagles	Benjamin Kerr	27
5	CENTER → Leopards	David Renshaw	33
6	Mavericks	Fillippe Ryan	38
7	Panthers	Edwin Jorgenson	44
8	Royals	Caesar Corinni	49
9	Wings	John Hamilton ⚲	54

KEY Astronauts 123456 Edwin Jorgenson

OPTIONAL JOB 87·2

OPEN TABLE
Center on a full page.
Spacing 2
Use same steps as in 87·1.

1		NEW CHEER LEADERS ↓3	10
			12
2	Florenz Donaldson	Stephen T. Ford	20
3	Marguerite Djara	Nathan Krevalier	28
4	→ Esther Lea Fox	Josef Martinez	35
5	Eliza Gittins	Fenn L. Riley	41
6	Sue Anne Hunter	Fred Van Wilhelms	49
7	Donna Mari Williams	Victor Xavier	57

Donna Mari Williams 123456 Fred Van Wilhelms

a·i·m 181

WARMUP REVIEW
2 copies (A-C)

A Why did you use the old car when you went down to the city? 12
B Cincinnati Milwaukee Angeles Seattle Boston Tampa City, Los 12
C Jack lazily typed a requisition for moving the white boxes. 12
D Repeat the page 188 TW if you have not already reached the goal.

JOB 181·1

RULED TABLE
Center on a full page.
Make changes indicated.
Spacing 2

OPTIONAL JOB 181·2

OPEN TABLE
Retype 181·1 in open style.

ANALYSIS OF DECEMBER SALES 16

Based on Feb. 1 Figures 32

Branch	Budget	Actual	Percents	
				43
				56
				67
Boston, ~~MA~~	$ 9,000	$ 10,500	116.7%	78
Cincinnati, ~~OH~~	10,500	11,900	113.3%	89
Los Angeles, ~~CA~~	28,000	28,200	100.7%	99
Milwaukee, ~~WI~~	12,000	12,800	106.7%	109
Oklahoma City, ~~OK~~	21,000	21,700	103.3%	120
Seattle, ~~WA~~	]16,000]	17,500	109.4%	129
Tampa, ~~FL~~	9,500	9,400	98.9%	139
				152
Totals	$106,000	$112,000	105.7%	162
				173

a·i·m 182

WARMUP REVIEW
2 copies (A-C)

A The old car was not a good one for a trip down to the city. 12
B Jack was dazzled by a requisition for moving the top boxes. 12
C 111.7% 110.0% 109.0% 105.3% 103.4% 101.4% 92.0% plus 90.0%. 12
D Repeat the page 188 TW if you have not already reached the goal.

JOB 182·1

RULED TABLE
Center on a full page.
Spacing 2

OPTIONAL JOB 182·2

OPEN TABLE
Retype 182·1 in open style.

ANALYSIS OF JANUARY SALES 16

Based on February 28 Figures 32

BRANCH	BUDGET	ACTUAL	PERCENTS	56
Boston	$ 8,000	$ 8,270	103.4%	78
Cincinnati	9,000	10,050	111.7%	89
Los Angeles	25,000	23,000	92.0%	99
Milwaukee	15,000	15,800	105.3%	109
Oklahoma City	20,000	22,000	110.0%	120
Seattle	15,000	13,500	90.0%	129
Tampa	9,000	9,810	109.0%	139
Totals	$ 101,000	$ 102,430	101.4%	173

aim 88

GOALS To type 113 or more words in 4 minutes within 5 errors on an alphabetic paragraph. To produce in correct form a simple open table with three columns.

DIRECTIONS *Spacing 1. Line 50. Tab 5.*

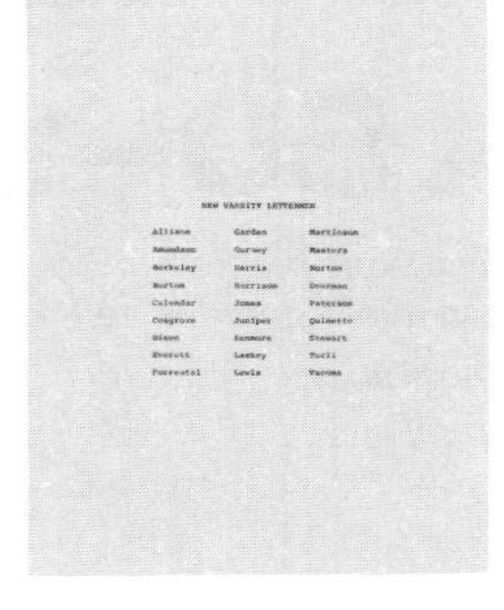

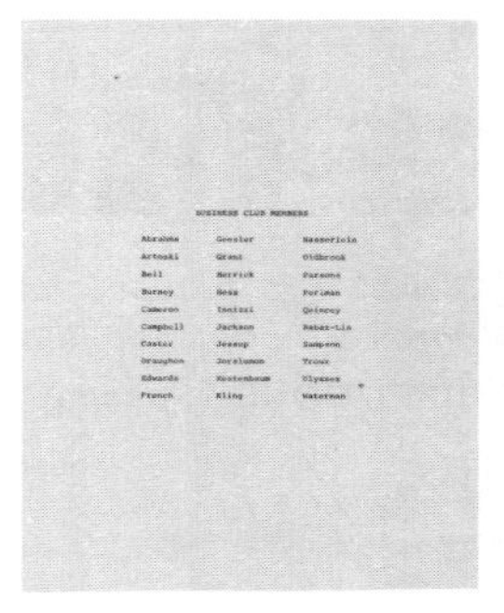

WARMUP PREVIEW

2 copies in 4 minutes Spacing 1

```
amaze seems other vast type form will but are put      10
required contents columns example numbers program      10
Five big men quickly fixed the jeopardized wires.      10
I lost Nos. 10 and 28, but Al has 39, 47, and 56.      10
|1    |2    |3    |4    |5    |6    |7    |8    |9    |10      1 | 2
```

4-MINUTE TW

(2 copies in 4 minutes)

```
     The word table seems to suggest vast columns      10 |  67
of numbers, but the kinds of other things that we      20 |  77
type in column form will amaze you.  They are put      30 |  87
in columns just for ease of reading.  A roster or      40 |  97
program or a table of contents, for example, will      50 | 107
be required to be in columns.                          56 | 113
```

SI 1.32FE

STEPS IN MULTICOLUMN TABLE

1. **Clear** the machine: margins, tabs.
2. **Compute** the top margin, to center.
3. **Pick key** line: this is 6 spaces for each between-column blank plus the longest entry in each of the columns.
4. **Set left** margin: from the center backspace to center the key line; set margin.
5. **Set columnar** tab stops: space across the paper to the start of each column, setting a tab stop at each starting point.
6. **Type** the table.

Practice. Job 88·1 and Optional Job 88·2 should be centered on full pages with double-spacing, 6 spaces between columns.

JOB 88·1

NEW VARSITY LETTERMEN ↓3 — 13

			15
Allison	Garden	Martinson	22
Amundson	Gurney	Masters	29
Berkeley	Harris	Norton	35
Burton	Harrison	Overman	42
→ Calendar	Jones	Paterson	49
Cosgrove	Juniper	Quinette	56
Dixon	Kenmore	Stewart	62
Everett	Laskey	Turli	69
Forrestal	Lewis	Vacoma	75

```
Forrestal      Harrison      Martinson
         123456        123456
```

OPTIONAL JOB 88·2

BUSINESS CLUB MEMBERS ↓3 — 13

			15
Abrahms	Geesler	Nasserlein	22
Artoski	Grant	Oldbrook	29
Bell	Herrick	Parsons	35
Burney	Hess	Perlman	41
→ Cameron	Innizzi	Quincey	48
Campbell	Jackson	Rabaz-Lin	55
Caster	Jessup	Sampson	62
Draughon	Joralemon	Troux	69
Edwards	Kestenbaum	Ulysses	76
French	Kling	Waterman	82

a·i·m 180–182

GOALS *To produce ruled tables from problem copy. To type 185 or more words of normal repetitive copy within 5 minutes and 4 errors.*

DIRECTIONS *Spacing 1. Line 60. Tab 5.*

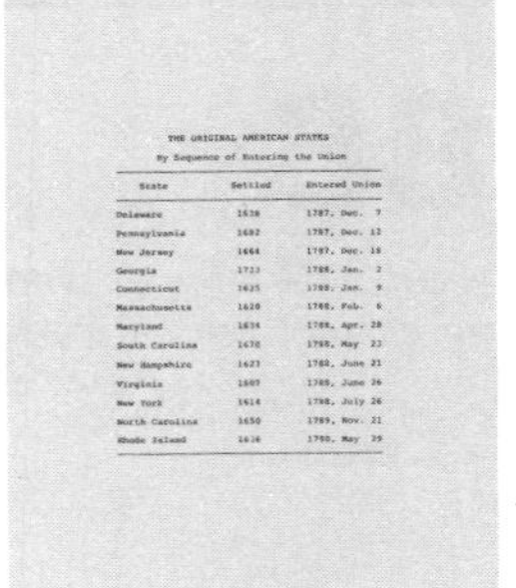

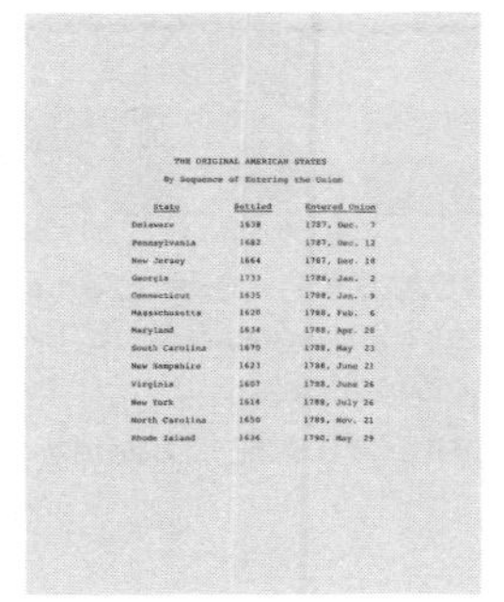

WARMUP REVIEW

2 copies

```
They will sell him some more lots when they need more cash.    12
Junior executives requested help for the biweekly magazine.    12
we 23 22 23 it 85 84 85 yo 69 68 69 or 94 93 94 wu 27 26 27    12
```

|1 |2 |3 |4 |5 |6 |7 |8 |9 |10 |11 |12

5-MINUTE TW

GOAL WRITING
Spacing 1
2 copies in 5 minutes

Text	1	2
There are many ways any table can be arranged, but the	12	105
majority of tables are typed in ruled or open style. These	24	117
styles are so nearly equal that one wonders for what reason	36	129
you might pick the one over the other. Well, it's size. A	48	141
table with many columns or narrow columns will be better in	60	153
ruled style. Tables with only two or three columns or with	72	165
very wide columns and tables with just a few lines are best	84	177
when displayed in the open arrangement.	92	185

SI 1.38N

JOB 180·1

RULED TABLE
Center on a full page.
Make changes indicated.
Spacing 2

THE ORIGINAL AMERICAN STATES 17

By Sequence of Entering the Union 39

State	Settled	Entered Union	
			49
			57
			68
Delaware	1638	1787, Dec. 7	75
Pennsylvania	1682	1787, Dec. 12	83
New Jersey	1664	1787, Dec. 18	91
Georgia	1733	1788, Jan. 2	98
Connecticut	1635	1788, Jan. 9	106
→ Massachusetts	1620	1788, Feb. 6	114
Maryland	1634	1788, Apr. 28	121
South Carolina	1670	1788, May 23	129
New Hampshire	1623	1788, June 21	137
Virginia	1607	1788, June 26	145
New York	1614	1788, July 26	152
North Carolina	1650	1789, Nov. 21	160
Rhode Island	1636	1790, May 29	168
			179

OPTIONAL JOB 180·2

OPEN TABLE
Retype 180·1 in open style.

a·i·m 89

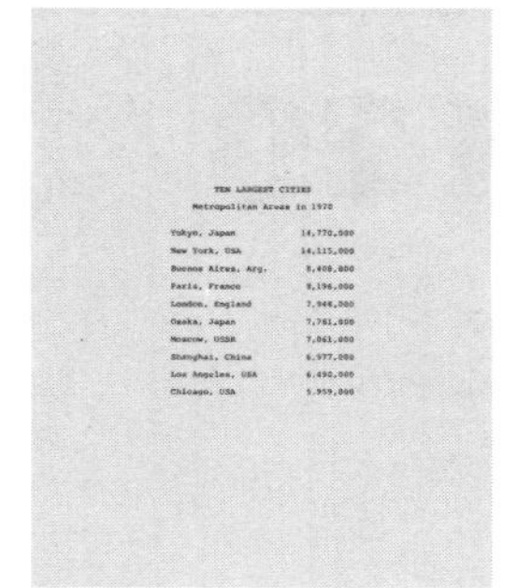

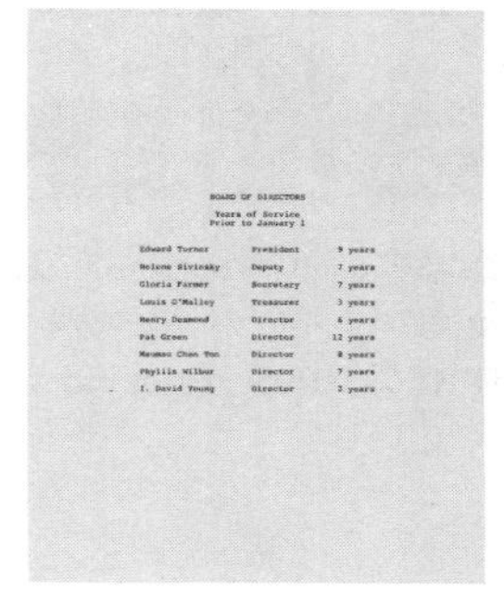

GOALS *To type 114 or more words in 4 minutes within 5 errors on an alphabetic paragraph. To produce in correct form an open table with a subtitle.*

DIRECTIONS *Spacing 1 for drills, 2 for TW. Line 50. Tab 5.*

WARMUP PREVIEW

2 copies

money names clear some data sure high you can low	10
alphabetize sequence figures amounts adjust versa	10
Five big men jeopardized the quickly fixed wires.	10
Look for 10 and 28 first, then for 39, 47, or 56.	10
1 2 3 4 5 6 7 8 9 10	

4-MINUTE TW

2 copies in 4 minutes

	1	2
If you must make a table from some data, you	10	67
must be sure to set it up in some clear way. You	20	77
would alphabetize names, for example, and arrange	30	87
amounts of money from high to low, or vice versa.	40	97
You cannot juggle figures, but you can adjust the	50	107
sequence in which you present them.	57	114

SI 1.33FE

SUBTITLES

If a table has a subtitle, center it. Capitalize the first and all major words. Allow 1 blank line before it and 2 after it. If it takes more than one line, single-space the group of subtitle lines.

Practice Job 89·1 and Optional Job 89·2 should be centered on full pages with double-spacing, with 6 spaces between the columns.

JOB 89·1

TEN LARGEST CITIES 11

Metropolitan Areas in 1970 29

Tokyo, Japan	14,770,000	37
New York, USA	14,115,000	43
Buenos Aires, Arg.	8,408,000	50
Paris, France	8,196,000	56
London, England	7,948,000	62
Osaka, Japan	7,781,000	68
Moscow, USSR	7,061,000	74
Shanghai, China	6,977,000	79
Los Angeles, USA	6,490,000	86
Chicago, USA	5,959,000	91

Buenos Aires, Arg. 14,770,000
123456

OPTIONAL JOB 89·2

BOARD OF DIRECTORS 11

Years of Service 23
Prior to January 1 38

Edward Turner	President	9 years	48
Helene Sivinsky	Deputy	7 years	56
Gloria Farmer	Secretary	7 years	65
Louis O'Malley	Treasurer	3 years	73
Henry Desmond	Director	6 years	82
Pat Green	Director	12 years	90
Maumau Chen Ton	Director	8 years	98
Phyllis Wilbur	Director	7 years	107
J. David Young	Director	2 years	115

a·i·m 179

GOAL ⚲*To strengthen skill (185 words or more in 5 minutes with 4 errors on fairly easy listen-for-bell copy).*

DIRECTIONS *Spacing 1 for drills, 2 for TW. Line 60. Tab 5.*

WHEN YOU SPEED UP

- **Fingers** stay curled at all times.
- **Wrists** stay low, almost touch machine.
- **Lips** are motionless; don't move them to spell or to exclaim.
- **Body** leans forward a bit from waist.

WARMUP REVIEW

2 copies

```
Dick will sell four lots when they find the cash they need.   12
The biweekly magazine for junior executives requested help.   12
we 23 24 23 24 25 ri 48 49 48 49 50 ty 56 57 56 57 58 57 58   12
|1    |2    |3    |4    |5    |6    |7    |8    |9    |10    |11    |12
```

ACCURACY DRIVE

See page 162.

Spacing 2

Being one of a group of commuters who ride together is a lot of fun 15
in a lot of ways. If one of the group hears a good story, he saves it 29
for the following morning; and then he tells it to the most apprecia- 42
tive audience there is. We listen raptly and roar with laughter, for 56
each man of us is aware that within an hour we will be telling the 70
same story to the men who work with us in our offices; we are studying 84
how to tell the story as much as listening to what is said. Since every 98
day someone has a story, we arrive at our desks with a smile. 111
My own favorite line is to discuss stocks with the men in my group 125
and then announce that I have purchased a share of stock—yes, one 139
share—in the company for which a member of our group works. This 152
makes me his employer. Naturally I inquire about why he takes so 165
many vacation days, how his sales are coming, and so on. I get a lot 179
of mileage out of this joke. ⚲ 185

|1 |2 |3 |4 |5 |6 |7 |8 |9 |10 |11 |12 |13 |14 SI 1.30FE

ACCURACY DRIVE

(For optional practice)

There are some serious moments, of course, when groups like ours 14 | 199
cooperate and work together. One of our guys was up for election in 28 | 212
the local village, and we announced that we would campaign for him 41 | 226
just so he couldn't say we didn't help him; we got him elected, too. 55 | 240
About twice a year, Old Man Winter knocks out our railroad; when 68 | 253
the weather begins to threaten, we make our own emergency trans- 81 | 265
portation plans so that nobody becomes stranded. When one of our 94 | 279
group was hospitalized, we flooded him with cards and got him 106 | 291
through a tough time. 111 | 296
In other words, nobody wants the air-conditioning unit to conk out 125 | 310
or the train to be canceled or slivers of glass from a shattered window 139 | 324
to glint on the seats, and any such sign of neglect is inexcusable. 153 | 338
Just the same, such perils and annoyances are not hard to bear when 167 | 352
you endure them as a member of a group that faces life with a helping 181 | 366
hand and laughter. ⚲ 185 | 370

|1 |2 |3 |4 |5 |6 |7 |8 |9 |10 |11 |12 |13 |14 SI 1.40N

a·i·m 90

GOALS *To type 115 or more words in 4 minutes within 5 errors on a listed program. To produce a two-column open table with title and subtitle from model copy.*

DIRECTIONS *Spacing 1. Line 50. Tab 34 spaces in.*

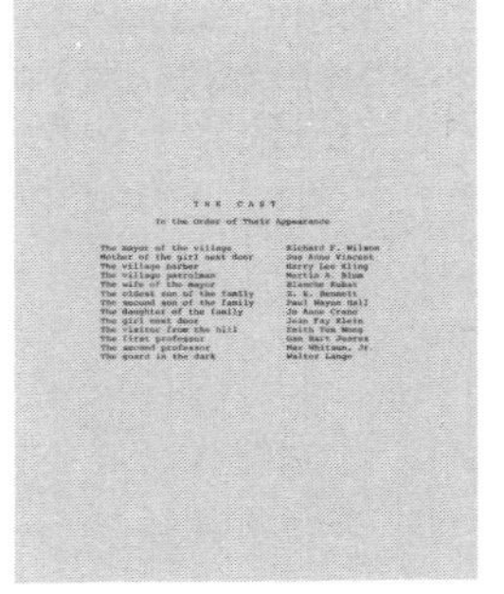

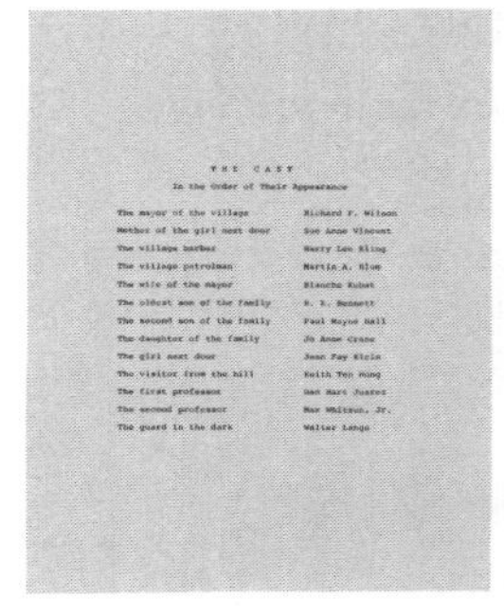

WARMUP PREVIEW

2 copies

1	mayor guard first dark door wife next son the old	10
2	patrolman professor daughter visitor barber Keith	10
3	The wires were quickly fixed by five army majors.	10
4	Get 10 each of items 28, 39, 47, and 56 tomorrow.	10
	1 2 3 4 5 6 7 8 9 10	

4-MINUTE TW

Lines 7 Through 19 Spacing 1

JOB 90·1

OPEN TABLE Full page Spacing 1

OPTIONAL JOB 90·2

OPEN TABLE Full page Spacing 2

5	T H E C A S T			9
6	In the Order of Their Appearance			31
				33
7	The mayor of the village	Richard F. Wilson	10	42
8	Mother of the girl next door	Sue Anne Vincent	20	52
9	The village barber	Harry Lee Kling	28	60
10	The village patrolman	Martin A. Blum	36	68
11	The wife of the mayor	Blanche Kubat	44	76
12	The oldest son of the family	R. K. Bennett	54	86
13	The second son of the family	Paul Wayne Hall	64	96
14	The daughter of the family	Jo Anne Crane	73	105
15	The girl next door	Jean Fay Klein	81	113
16	The visitor from the hill	Keith Ten Wong	90	122
17	The first professor	Dan Hart Juarez	99	131
18	The second professor	Max Whitsun, Jr.	107	139
19	The guard in the dark	Walter Lange	115	147

SI 1.36N

a·i·m 91

GOALS *To practice responding to the bell. To build a speed reserve (140 or more words in 4 minutes within 5 errors) on very easy material.*

DIRECTIONS *Spacing 1 for drills, 2 for TW. Line 50. Tab 5 only.*

AVOIDING KEY JAMS

- Wrists together, for straighter strokes.
- Wrists low, for bounce-off hard strokes.
- Body centered opposite the J key.
- Spell long words silently to yourself.
- Press for smoothness, never for speed.

WARMUP PREVIEW

2 copies

1	how are has two can pin six who say age try had a	10
2	show near rule book just tape make fine much more	10
3	merit badge ought teach spell mixup words learn a	10
4	They quickly fixed five wires he had jeopardized.	10
	1 2 3 4 5 6 7 8 9 10	

a·i·m 177

WARMUP PREVIEW
2 copies
(A–C)

A then same line more page sure much does ten the use one any 12
B article columns trouble length number nearly advice extras! 12
C Junior executives request broad help from weekly magazines. 12
D Repeat the page 185 TW if you have not yet reached the 185/4 goal.

JOB 177·1

PAGE 2 OF 2-PAGE MAGAZINE ARTICLE

Special Notes:
1. When counting the lines, do not count the page-number lines or the (END) line. Do count as 1 line the blank space left after paragraph No. 6 below.
2. Use of all caps in last paragraph is a "style" touch, as referred to in paragraph No. 6.

Elliott / Page 2 ↓3 (Line 7) 10

12

Here, then, is my advice to the typist: 21
1. Type the article with the same length of 31
line that is used in the columns of the magazine. 42
To determine this, type ten lines from the columns 52
of a copy of the magazine; determine the average 62
length and use it. Do not exceed that line length 72
by more than two spaces in any one line. 80
2. Indicate in the heading on the first page 90
the number and length of lines the manuscript will 101
fill. The number of lines is determined by count- 110
ing them after the manuscript has been typed. If 120
extra space must be left before a sideheading, be 130
sure to count that space as a typed line. 139
3. Type the author's name and a diagonal be- 149
fore the page number on all pages after page 1. 159
4. Double-space the manuscript. 166
5. Use standard paper, 8½ by 11 inches. 175
6. Study the "style" of the magazine and use 186
the kinds of display that the magazine features. ↓4 196

197

MY, WHAT A LOT of trouble! Yes, but not nearly as 207
much trouble as it is to write and type an article 217
that is rejected because it does not look profes- 227
sional--does not look as though it "belonged." 236
(END) 241

SI 1.38N

Page 2 of a Magazine Article

a·i·m 178

WARMUP REVIEW
Use A-D in a·i·m 177.

JOB 178·1

MAGAZINE ARTICLE
Retype Page 1 of this article for a different magazine—one that uses a 36-space line.

SPEED DRIVE 4·2·2·4 TW

See page 80.

While we are still in grade school, we ought to be taught how to 14
teach, so that we could learn how to learn. Just like a scout has to 28
show that he can do a thing or two just right before he can pin on a 42
merit badge, so should your sixth grader have to show that he knows 56
how to teach something to a child who is near his age, like how to 69
spell words with an I and E mixup in them or how to say the Greek 82
alphabet, before he leaves sixth grade. 90

If we had a rule like that, each of us would find that the hard 104
thing when you try to teach is to get your student to listen. If he 118
will not or cannot listen to you, he might learn from a book, tape, 131
or show, but he will not get much from you. 140

Now, if all the sixth graders knew that they would learn more if 154
they would listen more, maybe they would listen more when they reached 168
the high school grades and so would learn more. Then they would make 182
fine marks and win the chance to go to college and learn still more. 196
What a great idea! 200

|1 |2 |3 |4 |5 |6 |7 |8 |9 |10 |11 |12 |13 |14 SI 1.08VE

92

GOALS To type at least 116 words in 4 minutes within 5 errors on an alphabetic paragraph. To display column headings by blocking them. To produce tables involving subtitles and column headings.

DIRECTIONS *Spacing 1 for drills, 2 for TW and Jobs. Line 50. Tab 5 at start, changed for Jobs.*

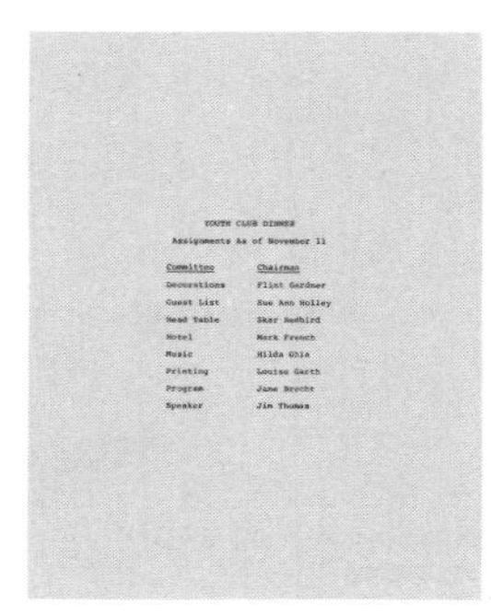

YOUTH CLUB DINNER

Assignments As of November 11

Committee	Chairman
Decorations	Flint Gardner
Guest List	Sue Ann Holley
Head Table	Skar Redbird
Hotel	Mark French
Music	Hilda Ghia
Printing	Louise Garth
Program	Jane Brecht
Speaker	Jim Thomas

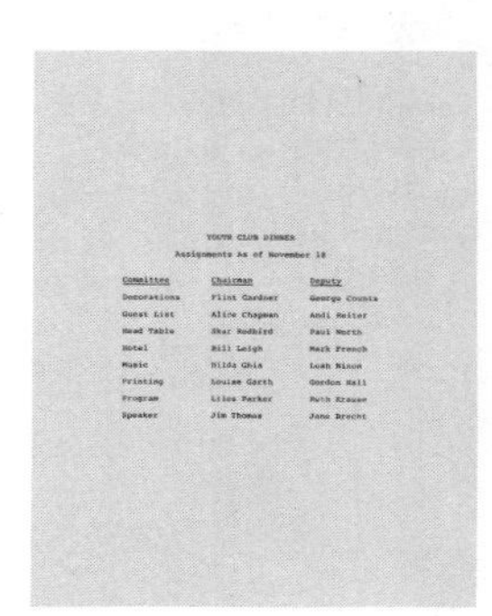

YOUTH CLUB DINNER

Assignments As of November 18

Committee	Chairman	Deputy
Decorations	Flint Gardner	George Counts
Guest List	Alice Chapman	Andi Reiter
Head Table	Skar Redbird	Paul North
Hotel	Bill Leigh	Mark French
Music	Hilda Ghia	Leah Nixon
Printing	Louise Garth	Gordon Hall
Program	Lilia Parker	Ruth Krause
Speaker	Jim Thomas	Jane Brecht

WARMUP PREVIEW

2 copies

draft block judge head over time care one can but 10
expensive adequate instance heading hazard column 10
Why did the team fix the five hazards so quickly? 10
I was for motions 10, 28, 39, and 47, but not 56. 10

|1 |2 |3 |4 |5 |6 |7 |8 |9 |10

4-MINUTE TW

2 copies in 4 minutes
Spacing 2

One can always center a column head over its 10 | 68
column; doing so is safe but is very expensive in 20 | 78
terms of time, care, and hazard of error. A good 30 | 88
typist can judge when it is adequate to block the 40 | 98
heading with the start of the column, as when the 50 | 108
table is in draft form, for instance. 58 | 116

|1 |2 |3 |4 |5 |6 |7 |8 |9 |10 SI 1.32FE

PREPARE a·i·m WB 163–164

a·i·m 176–178

GOALS *To arrange manuscripts in "magazine" style. To type 185 or more words on fairly easy alphabetic, repetitive copy within 5 minutes and 4 errors.*

DIRECTIONS *Spacing 1 for drills, 2 for jobs. Line 60. Tabs 5, center.*

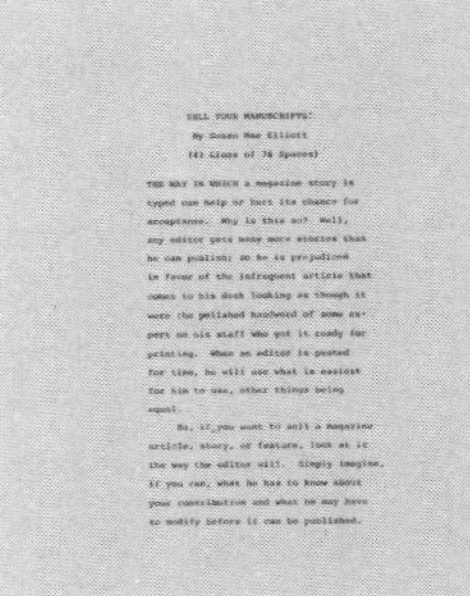

MAGAZINE ARTICLE
1. Spacing double
2. Line length that matches that of the magazine
3. Margins top and bottom as in other manuscripts
4. Style touches and display like that of the magazine

WARMUP PREVIEW

2 copies

A	help hurt gets more want know your many can the has try his	12
B	infrequent prejudiced magazine polished typed equal fill so	12
C	Bored junior executives request help from weekly magazines.	12
D	Five-minute writing on first paragraph in manuscript below.	

5-MINUTE TW

GOAL WRITING
Line 50
Spacing 1
2 copies of paragraph 1 in 5 minutes
SI 1.34FE

JOB 176·1

PAGE 1 OF 2-PAGE MAGAZINE ARTICLE
Read article before typing.
Line 50
Spacing 2
Tabs 5, center

		1	2	
Line 13	SELL YOUR MANUSCRIPTS! (End of 50 spaces)			13
Line 15	By Susan Mae Elliott			28
Line 17	(43 Lines of 50 Spaces)↓3			44
				46
	THE WAY IN WHICH a magazine story is typed can help	10	103	56
	or hurt its chance for acceptance. Why is this so?	21	114	67
	Well, any editor gets many more stories than he can	31	124	77
	publish, so he is prejudiced in favor of the in-	41	134	86
	frequent article that comes to his desk looking as	51	144	97
	though it were the polished handwork of some expert	62	155	107
	on his staff who got it ready for printing. When	72	165	117
	an editor is pushed for time, he will use what is	82	175	127
	easiest for him to use, other things being equal.	92	185	137
	So, if you want to sell a magazine article,			147
	story, or feature, look at it the way the editor			157
	will. Simply imagine, if you can, what he has to			167
	know about your contribution and what he may have			177
	to modify before it can be published.			184
	For example, he has to know how many lines of			195
	space your article will fill, what headings it may			205
	require, what style touches must be injected, and			215
	so on. When you type the manuscript, try to solve			225
	as many of these problems for him as you can.			234

SI 1.37N

Page 1 of a Magazine Article

BLOCKED COLUMN HEADINGS

1. Column heads in open tables are capitalized, underscored, preceded by 2 blank lines, and followed by 1 blank line.

2. Headings are usually centered over their columns, but the head may start even with the column if three requirements are met: (a) the table is for temporary or informal use, (b) the heading is not wider than its column, and (c) there is no restriction (by teacher, office, school, employer, etc.) against this quick but untraditional manner of display.

Practice Type Job 92·1 and Optional Job 92·2 on full pages with double-spacing and 6 spaces between the columns.

JOB 92·1

YOUTH CLUB DINNER — 10

Assignments As of November 11 — 30

Committee	Chairman	
Decorations	Flint Gardner	50
Guest List	Sue Ann Holley	56
Head Table	Skar Redbird	62
→ Hotel	Mark French	66
Music	Hilda Ghia	71
Printing	Louise Garth	76
Program	Jane Brecht	81
Speaker	Jim Thomas ⚲	86

(Column heads line: 44)

OPTIONAL JOB 92·2

YOUTH CLUB DINNER — 10

Assignments As of November 18 — 30

Committee	Chairman	Deputy	48
Decorations	Flint Gardner	George Counts	58
Guest List	Alice Chapman	Andi Reiter	68
Head Table	Skar Redbird	Paul North	77
→ Hotel	Bill Leigh	Mark French	85
Music	Hilda Ghia	Leah Nixon	92
Printing	Louise Garth	Gordon Hall	101
Program	Liles Parker	Ruth Krause	110
Speaker	Jim Thomas	Jane Brecht	118

a·i·m 93

GOALS ⚲ *To type at least 117 words in 4 minutes within 5 errors on an alphabetic paragraph.* ⚲ *To display short column headings by centering them.* ⚲ *To produce tables involving subtitles and centered column headings.*

DIRECTIONS *Spacing 1 for drills, 2 for TW and Jobs. Line 50. Tab 5.*

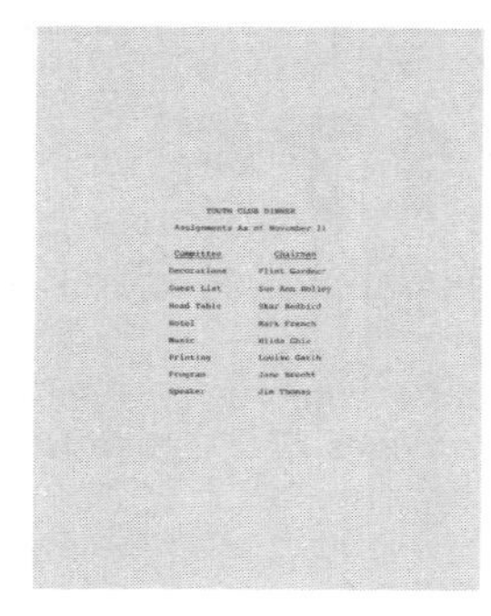

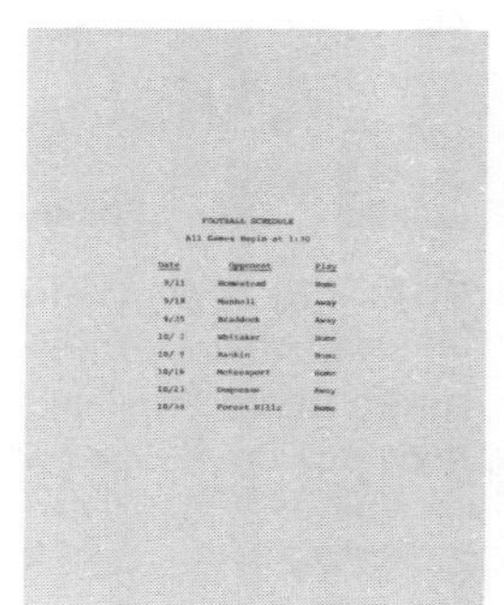

WARMUP PREVIEW

2 copies

```
1  thing split lines take size both drop you any two        10
2  difference pictures exactly between unique boards        10
3  The big man quickly fixed five jeopardized wires.        10
4  We measured 10", 28", 39", 47", and 56" of cloth.        10
   |1   |2   |3   |4   |5   |6   |7   |8   |9   |10
```

JOB 174-2

RULED TABLE
Center on a full page.
Spacing 2

Special Notes:
1. A $ sign is used only at top and bottom, but a % sign is used on every line.
2. An asterisk is typed on the straight side of the column.
3. A short footnote is centered.

ANALYSIS OF LAST YEAR'S SALES 18

By Branch Districts 32

Branch	Budget	Actual	Percent	
				43
				56
				67
Boston	$ 75,000	$ 90,000	120.0%	78
Cincinnati	100,000	122,500	122.5%	89
Los Angeles	250,500	228,300	91.1%	99
Milwaukee	125,800	130,400	103.7%	109
Oklahoma City	205,000	194,000	94.5%	120
*Seattle	150,000	127,500	85.0%	133
Tampa	75,000	67,500	90.0%	140
				153
Totals	$981,300	$960,200	97.6%	163
				174

* Main store closed by fire for six weeks. 203

OPTIONAL JOB 174-3

RULED TABLE
Center on a full page.
Spacing 2

LONGEST AMERICAN VEHICULAR TUNNELS 21

Name	Location	Feet Long	
			32
			41
			52
Bart Tube	San Francisco	19,008	62
Brooklyn Battery	New York City	9,117	71
Straight Creek	Colorado	8,950	79
Holland	New York City	8,557	86
Lincoln	New York City	8,216	93
Harbor	Baltimore	7,650	99
Hampton Roads	Norfolk	7,479	106
Copperfield	Copperfield, Utah	6,989	114
Sidelong Hill	PA Turnpike	6,782	122
Queens Midtown	New York City	6,414	130
			141

a·i·m 175

GOAL *To strengthen skill (185 words or more in 5 minutes within 4 errors) on easy listen-for-the-bell copy.*

DIRECTIONS *Spacing 1 for drills, 2 for TW. Line 60. Tab 5. After warmup, do Accuracy Drive timed writings on lines 18–31, page 181.*

FOR ACCURACY

- Say each letter to yourself silently.
- Stay on the stroke-by-stroke level.
- Type smoothly without spurting.
- Maintain good posture: center body opposite the J key, one handspan from the front of the machine.

WARMUP REVIEW

2 copies, then see page 181.

```
1  Joe did not get to see the box the two men had got for him.      12
2  Jack typed white requisitions for moving large-sized boxes.      12
3  it 85 84 83 or 94 93 92 wo 29 28 27 ri 48 47 46 up 70 69 68     12
   |1   |2   |3   |4   |5   |6   |7   |8   |9   |10   |11   |12
```

4-MINUTE TW

2 copies in 4 minutes
Spacing 1

	1	2
To center one thing over another, whether it	10	69
is two boards or two pictures or two typed lines,	20	79
you take exactly the same steps: you measure the	30	89
size of both things and then split the difference	40	99
between them. The only unique thing in typing is	50	109
just that you have to drop any fraction.	58	117

|1 |2 |3 |4 |5 |6 |7 |8 |9 |10 SI 1.32FE

CENTERED COLUMN HEADINGS (SHORT)

The typist must find how many spaces to indent the column heading to center it: subtract the spaces in the heading from the spaces in the column width, then split the difference (drop any fraction). For example, to center *Opponent* over *Forest Hills:* 12 − 8 = 4 and 4 ÷ 2 = 2 spaces to indent *Opponent.*

Practice Center Job 93·1 and Optional Job 93·2 on full sheets, double-spaced, with each column head centered above its column.

JOB 93·1

YOUTH CLUB DINNER 10
Assignments As of November 11 30

Committee	Chairman	
Decorations	Flint Gardner	57
Guest List	Sue Ann Holley	63
→ Head Table	Skar Redbird	69
Hotel	Mark French	73
Music	Hilda Ghia	78
Printing	Louise Garth	83
Program	Jane Brecht	88
Speaker	Jim Thomas	93

(Column heading line: 50)

OPTIONAL JOB 93·2

FOOTBALL SCHEDULE 10
All Games Begin at 1:30 26

Date	Opponent	Play	
9/11	Homestead	Home	50
9/18	Munhall	Away	56
→ 9/25	Braddock	Away	62
10/ 2	Whitaker	Home	68
10/ 9	Rankin	Home	74
10/16	McKeesport	Home	80
10/23	Duquesne	Away	86
10/30	Forest Hills	Home	93

(Column heading line: 44)

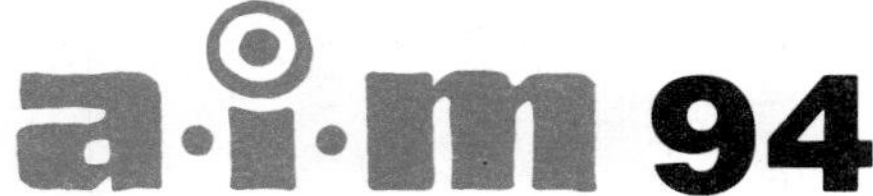 94

GOALS To learn how to center long column headings over their columns. To produce two tables involving long and short column headings.

DIRECTIONS Spacing 1. Line 50.

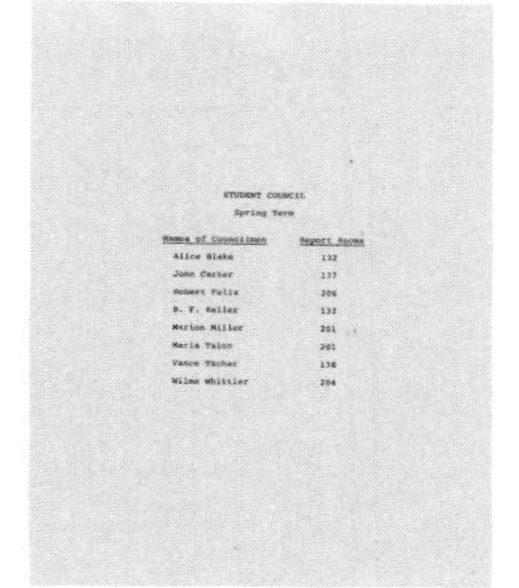

STUDENT COUNCIL
Spring Term

Names of Councilmen	Report Rooms
Alice Blake	132
John Carter	137
Robert Felix	206
B. F. Keller	132
Marion Miller	201
Maria Talon	201
Vance Tachar	138
Wilma Whittier	204

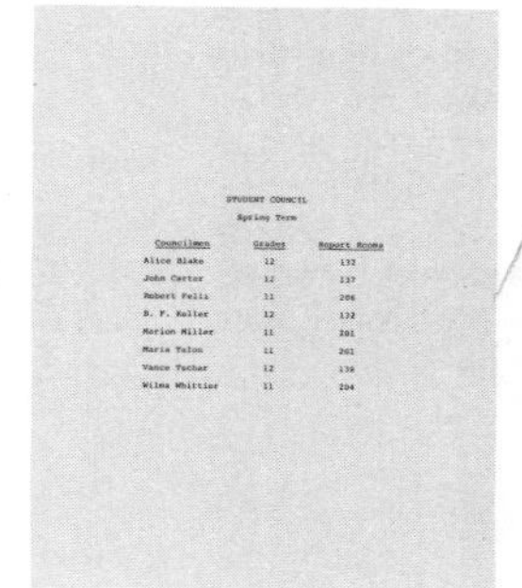

STUDENT COUNCIL
Spring Term

Councilmen	Grades	Report Rooms
Alice Blake	12	132
John Carter	12	137
Robert Felix	11	206
B. F. Keller	12	132
Marion Miller	11	201
Maria Talon	11	201
Vance Tachar	12	138
Wilma Whittier	11	204

WARMUP PREVIEW

3 copies

A Robert Marion Keller Alice Maria Vance Wilma John 10
B Six wires quickly jeopardized those five big men. 10
C Rooms 206 206 204 204 201 201 138 138 186 136 132 10
D Adjust the machine for the table; plan column indention carefully.

|1 |2 |3 |4 |5 |6 |7 |8 |9 |10

a·i·m 173

WARMUP PREVIEW
2 copies (A–C)

A Aaron Crane Ewell Faber Hyatt James Klein Prall Sabin Welsh 12
B Jackson typed requisitions for dozens of wool moving boxes. 12
C 121A 121B 122A 122B 123A 123B 124A 124B 125A 121A 121B 122A 12
D Repeat the 5-minute timing on page 182 if you didn't reach the goal.

JOB 173·1

RULED TABLE
Center on a full page.

ROOM ASSIGNMENTS FOR TENTH GRADERS 21

For the Second Semester 37

Alphabetic Grouping	Room	Teacher	
			50
			59
			72
Aaron through M. Crane	121A	Miss Franks	82
N. Crane through Ewell	121B	Mr. Quinette	92
Faber through Hyatt	122A	Miss Charles	102
Ibbetts through Kwartz	122B	Mr. Klein	113
Lake through J. Morgan	123A	Miss Fleming	123
K. Morgan through Nugent	123B	Mr. Fleischman	134
Oakley through F. Parson	124A	Miss Gates	145
G. Parson through Ryan	124B	Mr. James	155
Sabin through Zinsser	125A	Mrs. Welsh	164
			177

a·i·m 174

WARMUP PREVIEW
2 copies (A–C)

A Economics Athletic Business Science Spanish Hobby Glee Club 12
B Jack typed a dozen requisitions for boxes for moving wools. 12
C $1,825 $925 $900 $350 $240 $200 $175 $150 $125 $100 $50 $10 12
D Repeat the 5-minute timing on page 182 if you didn't reach the goal.

JOB 174·1

RULED TABLE
Center on a full page.

Special Notes:
1. A $-sign at top of a column must line up with a $-sign at the bottom.
2. Totals are set off by ruled lines as shown here.

BUDGETS FOR SCHOOL CLUBS AS APPROVED 22
BY THE STUDENT COUNCIL 37

For the Next School Year 55

Organization	Fall Term	Spring Term	Total Amounts	
				66
				74
				84
				99
Business Club	$100	$150	$ 250	116
Economics Club	100	100	200	127
French Club	100	100	200	135
Girls Athletic Club	200	150	350	146
Glee Club	100	75	175	154
Hobby Club	50	100	150	162
Science Club	100	100	200	171
Spanish Club	50	50	100	179
Talent Club	100	100	200	188
				200
Totals	$900	$925	$1,825	209
				220

CENTERED COLUMN HEADINGS (LONG)

If a column heading is wider than its column, it is the longest entry in the column and is used in the key line for the table. To find out how many spaces to indent the column after the heading has been typed, subtract the spaces in the column width from the spaces in the heading, then split the difference (drop any fraction). For example, in Job 94·1, *Names of Councilmen* is 19 spaces and *Wilma Whittier* is 14 spaces, so 19 − 14 = 5 and 5 ÷ 2 = 2½ (drop fraction) = 2 spaces the column should be moved in after the heading has been typed. ⊙

Practice Center Jobs 94·1 and 94·2, double-spaced, on full sheets of paper.

JOB 94·1

STUDENT COUNCIL 9

Spring Term 18

Names of Councilmen	Report Rooms	
Alice Blake	132	47
John Carter	137	51
→ Robert Feliz	206	56
B. F. Keller	132	60
Marion Miller	201	65
Maria Talon	201	69
Vance Tschar	138	73
Wilma Whittier	204 ⊙	78

(Heading line: 40)

JOB 94·2

STUDENT COUNCIL 9

Spring Term 18

Councilmen	Grades	Report Rooms	
Alice Blake	12	132	48
John Carter	12	137	53
→ Robert Feliz	11	206	59
B. F. Keller	12	132	65
Marion Miller	11	201	72
Maria Talon	11	201	77
Vance Tschar	12	138	83
Wilma Whittier	11	204	90

(Heading line: 40)

a·i·m 95

GOALS ⊙ *To type 119 words or more in 4 minutes within 5 errors on an alphabetic paragraph.* ⊙ *To use extra spaces for line-grouping in a table.* ⊙ *To produce a table involving narrow headings, column headings, and line groupings.*

DIRECTIONS *Spacing 1. Line 50. Tab 5.*

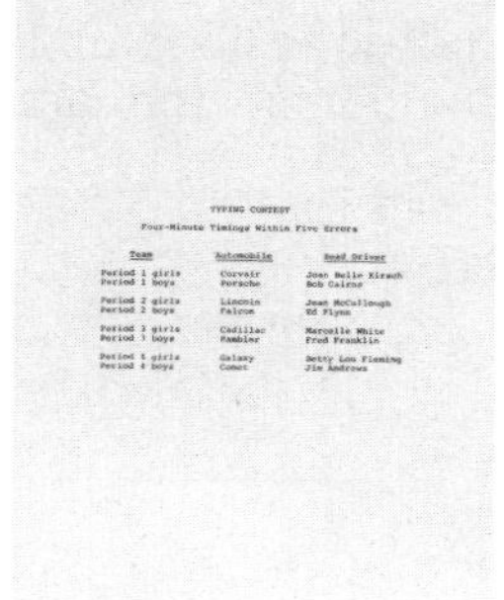

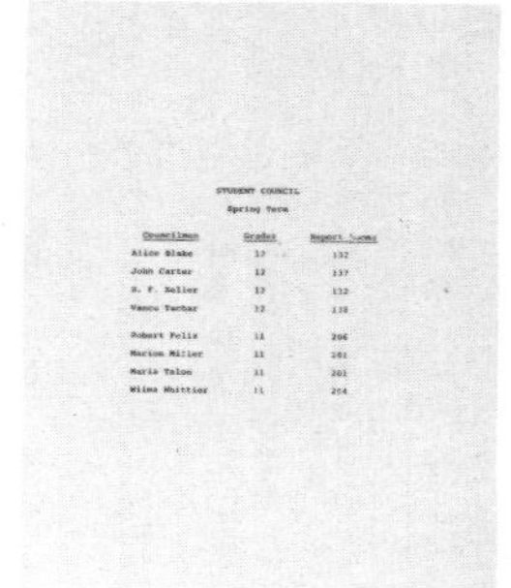

WARMUP PREVIEW

2 copies

1 leave since would left safe rule wide one big six 10

2 question analyzes separate readily answer column. 10

3 The wires quickly jeopardized the five big women. 10

4 Do problems 10 to 28, 39 to 47, and all after 56. 10

|1 |2 |3 |4 |5 |6 |7 |8 |9 |10

a·i·m 172–174

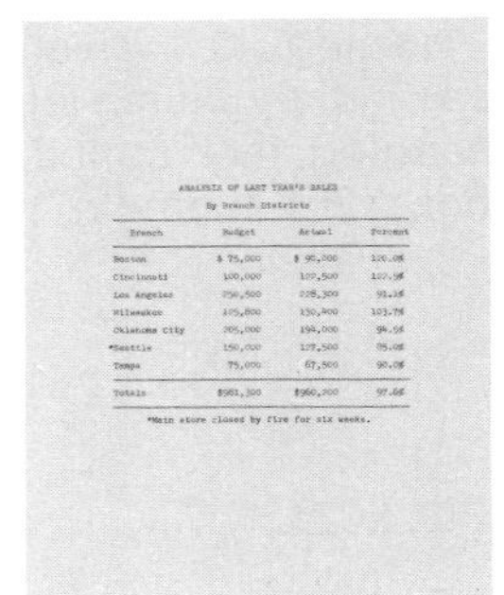

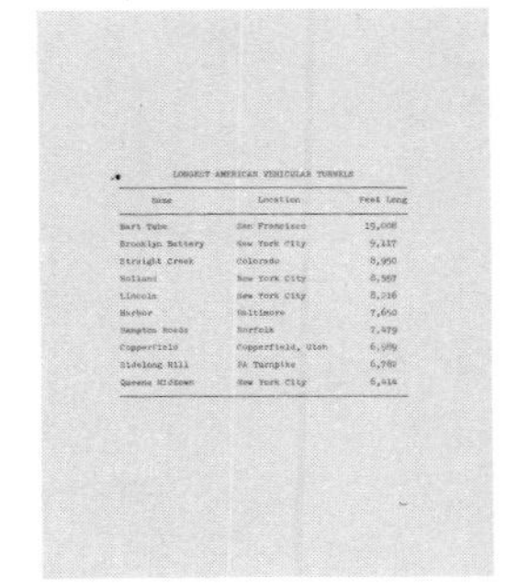

GOALS ⚲ *To arrange tables in "ruled" style.* ⚲ *To type 185 or more words of fairly easy repetitive copy within 5 minutes and 4 errors.*

DIRECTIONS *Spacing 1. Line 60. Tab 5.*

WARMUP REVIEW

2 copies

```
He said that they will rule that page with four long lines.      12
Jack typed requisitions for white moving boxes (long size).      12
we 23 24 25 up 70 71 72 or 94 95 96 it 85 86 87 to 59 60 61      12
|1    |2    |3    |4    |5    |6    |7    |8    |9    |10    |11    |12
```

5-MINUTE TW

GOAL WRITING
Spacing 1
2 copies in 5 minutes

```
                                                                  1 |   2
     A ruled table differs from an open table in three ways      12 | 105
you should know.  First, the parts of the table are set off      24 | 117
by horizontal lines.  Next, headings of the columns are not      36 | 129
underscored.  Third, the right margin stop is set after the      48 | 141
last column, so that the lines will stop where they should.      60 | 153
A ruled table is just like an open table in all other ways.      72 | 165
Both are set up by the same steps; both use the same margin      84 | 177
and tab stops; they are equally easy.          SI 1.26FE         92 | 185 ⚲
```

RULED TABLES

1. Plan top margin as usual.
2. Set tab and margin stops as usual.
3. Set right margin one space after the last column (first space after "e" in "Increase" in Job 172·1) to keep underscores from running into the right margin area.
4. Precede and follow each underscore line by one blank space (single-space *before* and double-space *after* typing it).
5. Don't forget the blank space and line at foot of table; extend the line to the very edge of the table, as shown below.

JOB 172·1

Center on a full page. Spacing 1.

VIDEOX SALES PERSONNEL 13

14

On Permanent Payroll at Year's End 35

District	This Year	Last Year	Increase	
				47
				58
				70
New England	28	41	13	89
East Coast	72	87	15	96
North Central	50	62	12	102
South Central	176	197	21	110
West Coast	54	57	3	116
Southwest	31	43	12	122
⚲				134

4-MINUTE TW

2 copies in 4 minutes

Spacing 1

		1	2
5	One big question that the typist must answer	10	70
6	as he analyzes a table is the number of spaces to	20	80
7	be left between columns. The safe rule to follow	30	90
8	is to leave six spaces, since that is wide enough	40	100
9	to separate the columns but not so wide that eyes	50	110
10	will not jump readily over the blank space.	59	119
	|1 |2 |3 |4 |5 |6 |7 |8 |9 |10	SI 1.34FE	

LINE GROUPING

Tables are often arranged with their lines grouped, for reading clarity, in pairs (as below) or in threes or fours. By leaving an extra space between sections of a table, related materials are tied together. The blank space serves as a "white line" that guides the eye.

JOB 95·1

OPEN TABLE
Spacing 1

11		TYPING CONTEST		10
12		Four-Minute Timings Within Five Errors		37
				39
13	<u>Team</u>	<u>Automobile</u>	<u>Head Driver</u>	67
14	Period 1 girls	Corvair	Joan Belle Kirsch	77
15	Period 1 boys	Porsche	Bob Cairns	86
16	Period 2 girls	Lincoln	Jean McCullough	95
17	Period 2 boys	Falcon	Ed Flynn	104
18	Period 3 girls	Cadillac	Marcelle White	113
19	Period 3 boys	Rambler	Fred Franklin	123
20	Period 4 girls	Galaxy	Betty Lou Fleming	133
21	Period 4 boys	Comet	Jim Andrews	141
	123456	123456		SI 1.42N

OPTIONAL JOB 95·2

Repeat 94·2
Group boys and girls separately.

a·i·m 96

GOALS *To practice listening for the bell. To build a speed reserve (140 or more words in 4 minutes within 5 errors) on very easy material.*

DIRECTIONS *Spacing 1 for drills, 2 for TW. Line 50. Tab 5.*

SPECIAL NOTE

Look at a·i·m 100 Test, pages 106–107. As you do the tables, letters, and skill drills up to that page, ask your teacher whether you may concentrate on the practice you need most instead of typing everything.

WARMUP PREVIEW

2 copies

1 was and the bug bit by, far old who his eye to it 10
2 dawn came long thin gold look room fell pool seen 10
3 through window himself tossed glance working lawn 10
4 The six judges have had a quiet snooze in a cave. 10

|1 |2 |3 |4 |5 |6 |7 |8 |9 |10

a·i·m 171

GOAL *To strengthen skill (185 words or more in 5 minutes within 4 errors on very easy narrative copy, the line endings to be determined by you).*

DIRECTIONS *Spacing 1 for drills, 2 for TW. Line 60. Tab 5.*

FOR ACCURACY

- Concentrate: keep eyes on the copy.
- Concentrate: ignore distractions.
- Concentrate: watch every detail.
- Concentrate: keep the machine going.

WARMUP REVIEW

2 copies

```
The old car was the one you had the day you met the two men.   12
The money for the tax was quickly paid over by a lazy judge.   12
The $56 coat is $47; the $39 coat is $28; the $10 hat is $7.   12
|1  |2  |3  |4  |5  |6  |7  |8  |9  |10  |11  |12
```

ACCURACY DRIVE

See page 162.

Spacing 2

A lot has been said and much has been put in the press about the 14
sad lot of the poor guys who have to ride a train to get to their desks. 29
I am an expert on such matters, and I want you to know that most of 42
the words are not true. As a matter of fact, except for the high cost 57
of the fare, the ride of the man who has to commute on a train is one 71
of the best rides in all the world. True, not all cars are modern and 85
clean and nice like the ones in the trains that I enjoy each day, but 99
the ride is great even when by chance you get the worst cars. 111
What makes a train ride good or bad is not the car you are in but 126
the man in the seat beside you. When you travel on the same trains 139
each day, you become one of a group that takes the same morning 152
train and the same night train. The group sits in a block of seats, 166
the men swap jokes and news bits from the paper, and they form a 179
sort of club or clique of riders. 185

|1 |2 |3 |4 |5 |6 |7 |8 |9 |10 |11 |12 |13 |14 — SI 1.07VE

ACCURACY DRIVE

(For use in a·i·m 175)

The group with whom I share rides is composed of eight men, of 14 | 199
whom you can count on three or four in summer, when others are 25 | 211
away on vacation, and five or six in the winter, when some are absent 40 | 226
on business trips. When anyone who is away comes back, he gets the 54 | 240
treatment you would guess: he is told that his firm has gone out of 68 | 253
business, he is found guilty of neglecting his work, and so on. Since he 82 | 268
expects such talk, he comes back ready. He says that he has bought up 97 | 282
his firm, that his firm has implored him to come back to his desk, etc. 111 | 296
The real sport comes when one of the men finds that he has mis- 125 | 310
placed his ticket. The conductor stands there. The man goes through 139 | 324
his pockets while the rest of us apologize to the trainman. We say 152 | 338
that we do not know why our friend is always trying to get out of 165 | 351
paying his fare, or words to that effect. The trainman just laughs. 180 | 365
He knows all about such talk. 185 | 370

|1 |2 |3 |4 |5 |6 |7 |8 |9 |10 |11 |12 |13 |14 — SI 1.20E

SPEED DRIVE 4·2·2·4 TW

See page 80.

If you respond correctly to the bell, lines will end even.

It was dawn, and the sun came up to thrust a long, thin beam of 14
gold through the window in the corner of the room. The light fell 27
on the floor, so that a pool of bright yellow formed on the rug and 41
grew as the sun rose. The pool flowed across the rug, bit by bit 52
and inch by inch. In a short while the pool had spread as far as 66
the old desk. 69

The man who was working at the desk stirred, looked at the sun 83
streak that had caught his eye, and tossed a glance at the clock. 96
Five, said the hands of the clock, five and dawn. He had worked 109
all through the night, and the four cups told how he had made 122
himself stay with his task. The neat mound of papers was the 134
fruit of the night hours. 140

|1 |2 |3 |4 |5 |6 |7 |8 |9 |10 |11 |12 |13 |14 SI 1.03VE

a·i·m 97

GOALS *To type 120 words or more in 4 minutes and 5 errors on alphabetic paragraph material. To learn about enclosure notations. To produce in correct blocked arrangement a short business letter. To practice responding to the margin bell.*

DIRECTIONS *Spacing 1 for drills, 2 for TW. Line 50. Tab 5. WB 55.*

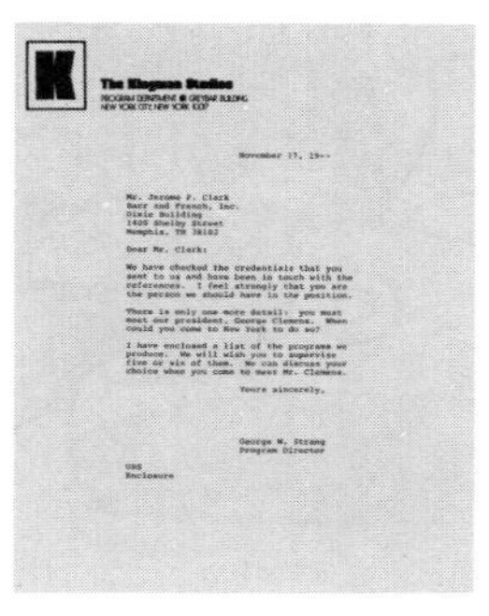

The Kingman Studios
PROGRAM DEPARTMENT ■ GREYBAR BUILDING
NEW YORK CITY, NEW YORK

November 17, 19--

Mr. Jerome F. Clark
Barr and French, Inc.
Dixie Building
Shelby Street
Memphis, TN

Dear Mr. Clark:

We have checked the credentials that you sent to us and have been in touch with the references. I feel strongly that you are the person we should have in the position.

There is only one more detail: you must meet our president, George Clemens. When could you come to New York to do so?

I have enclosed a list of the programs we produce. We will wish you to supervise five or six of them. We can discuss your choice when you come to meet Mr. Clemens.

Yours sincerely,

George W. Strang
Program Director

URS
Enclosure

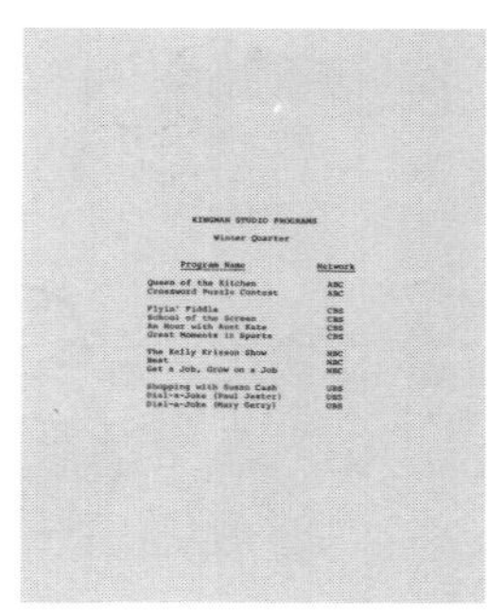

KINGMAN STUDIO PROGRAMS

Winter Quarter

Program Name	Network
Queen of the Kitchen	ABC
Crossword Puzzle Contest	ABC
Flyin' Fiddle	CBS
School of the Screen	CBS
An Hour with Aunt Kate	CBS
Great Moments in Sports	CBS
The Kelly Krisson Show	NBC
Beat	NBC
Get a Job, Grow on a Job	NBC
Shopping with Susan Cash	UBS
Dial-a-Joke (Paul Jester)	UBS
Dial-a-Joke (Mary Gerry)	UBS

WARMUP PREVIEW

2 copies

```
How soon will that fine city firm move its plant?    10
genuinely astounded discovered amazed quiet rival    10
Jack really vexed the farmer by his lazy plowing.    10
Dates to know:  1910, 1928, 1939, 1947, and 1956.    10
|1   |2   |3   |4   |5   |6   |7   |8   |9   |10
```

4-MINUTE TW

When we read in the papers about some of the great things that 14
men have created or discovered, we feel excited; but when we take 27
a quiet look at just a few of the marvels in the world of nature, 40
we feel amazed, astounded, and genuinely humbled. 50

A starfish can grow new limbs; no man can do that. If a billion 64
flakes of snow fall, all will have six sides and yet no two will be 78
the same; a man could not design a thousand such patterns. A man 91
can get lost in a forest, yet a seal can swim three thousand miles 104
and get back home. Will man ever be able to rival the many 117
marvels of nature? 120

|1 |2 |3 |4 |5 |6 |7 |8 |9 |10 |11 |12 |13 |14 SI 1.26FE

Part 8

Overview

Part Eight continues the accuracy drive that began in Part Seven and introduces two new kinds of production experience: new manuscript arrangements and a new way to arrange tables.

Skill You will inch your speed up a little while holding your accuracy constant or improving it as you type material that gradually progresses from very easy at the beginning of Part Eight to normal business vocabulary by the end of the Part. Every fourth a·i·m will be an all-out skill drive.

Manuscripts You will learn how to type magazine articles and news releases so that they have special appeal to the editors who decide whether or not to publish them.

Tables You will learn how to type tables in the "ruled style," which is an arrangement that has horizontal lines of underscores (called "rules") to make them more attractive and easier to read.

Performance Goals

When you finish the 20 a·i·m sessions in Part Eight and take the test on pages 194 and 195, you should be able to demonstrate these abilities:

1. Technicalities You will score 85 or more percent correct on an objective test covering the technical information you have already learned and the additional information you learn in Part Eight.

2. Production You will execute a magazine article in the style of a professional writer from unarranged material of average difficulty; you will produce in ruled style a four-column statistical table, largely from handwritten copy.

3. Skill You will type at least 185 words in 5 minutes (200 words is more likely!) within 4 errors on paragraph material that requires listening for the bell in order to make your own line-ending decisions.

Routines and Procedures

Accuracy Drives You will continue using the accuracy-drive procedure that you began in the preceding Part: a 3-minute writing, then remedial drill from Supplement II (or a 5-minute writing, if you have a high accuracy score on the 3-minute effort), and then a for-the-record good 5-minute writing.

Material for the accuracy drives is provided in a·i·m numbers 171, 175, 179, and 183, with an extra set of drive copy attached to a·i·m 179 and a·i·m 183.

Grouped Jobs Combined a·i·m groupings are used throughout Part Eight for all production work; only the skill-development a·i·m stands alone. The groupings enable you to move more quickly from one production job to the next and to see the relation of one job to the next. In every assignment, however, skill drill and goal timed writings precede the execution of a production assignment.

```
                    Geor
                    Prog
URS
Enclosure
```

```
                    Geor
                    Prog
URS
3 Enclosures
```

ENCLOSURE NOTATIONS

When anything accompanies a business letter in its envelope, the word "Enclosure" (or a number and the word "Enclosures" for more than one) is typed under the initials.

JOB 97·1

BLOCKED LETTER — Body 88 words Line 4 inches Tab center Workbook 55

Today's date ↓5 / Mr. Jerome F. Clark / 12
Barr and French, Inc. / Dixie Building / 19
1400 Shelby Street / Memphis, TN 38102 / 27
Dear Mr. Clark: / We have checked the 36
credentials that you sent to us and have 44
been in touch with the references. I feel 53
strongly that you are the person we should 62
have in the position. 66
There is only one more detail: you must 75
meet our president, George Clemens. When 84
could you come to New York to do so? 91
I have enclosed a list of the programs we 101
produce. We will wish you to supervise five 110
or six of them. We can discuss your choice 119
when you come to meet Mr. Clemens. / 126
Yours sincerely, ↓6 / 131
George W. Strang / Program Director / 145
URS / Enclosure 149

SI 1.33FE

OPTIONAL JOB 97·2

OPEN TABLE — Center on full page. Group as illustrated.

KINGMAN STUDIO PROGRAMS		14
Winter Quarter		26
Program Name	Network	41
Queen of the Kitchen	ABC	48
Crossword Puzzle Contest	ABC	55
Flyin' Fiddle	CBS	61
School of the Screen	CBS	67
An Hour with Aunt Kate	CBS	73
Great Moments in Sports	CBS	80
The Kelly Krisson Show	NBC	87
Beat	NBC	90
Get a Job, Grow on a Job	NBC	97
Shopping with Susan Cash	UBS	105
Dial-a-Joke (Paul Jester)	UBS	112
Dial-a-Joke (Mary Gerry)	UBS	118

123456

a·i·m 98

GOALS *To type 120 words or more in 4 minutes within 5 errors on alphabetic paragraph material. To produce a short business letter with an enclosure notation. To produce a two-column table with centered headings.*

DIRECTIONS *Spacing 1 for drills, 2 for TW. Line 50. Tab 5. WB 57.*

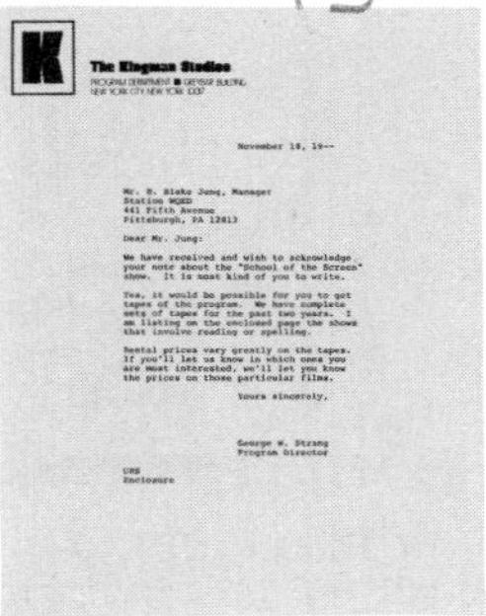

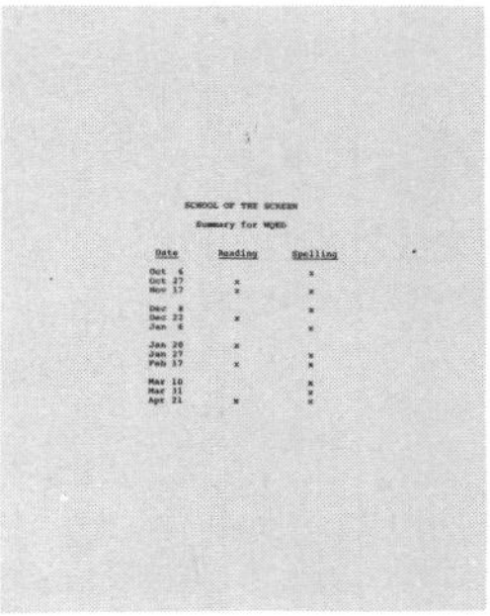

WARMUP PREVIEW

2 copies

```
1  When will that old city firm ever move its plant?   10
2  incredible outwit avoid urchin squid clever brain   10
3  Zebras are housed in quiet cages when they relax.   10
4  I can type tables 10 and 28 but not 39, 47, or 56.  10
   |1    |2    |3    |4    |5    |6    |7    |8    |9    |10
```

TEST 7-D

BLOCKED LETTER
Body 130 words + display
Date at center
Tabs 4, center
Workbook 157

Today's date / Mr. J. Fremont Carter / Executive Secretary / Elec- 17
trical Engineers, Inc. / Rawlings Building / St. Louis, Mo. 63155 / 29
Dear Mr. Carter: Thank you for the prompt reply to my recent 44
letter concerning the hotel reservation for our dinner in March. I have 58
made the reservation for us at the Fort Benjamin, as you suggested. 72
The hotel will send you a confirmation of the reservation at once. 85
The hotel wishes information on these points: 96
1. How many rooms should be reserved for persons coming to the 109
banquet from out of town? 116
2. Does the Association wish the microphone ready for use at 129
the dinner, and will we require any slide projector, screen, or 143
other equipment? 147
3. When will you be able to give the hotel a final, firm count on the 162
number of persons at the dinner? 170
I told the manager, Mr. Thomas Boudeaux, that you would write 184
him directly on these questions./Cordially yours,/Everett T. Thorpe 203
/ Local Chairman / *Initials?* / *Enclosure notation?* 209

|1 |2 |3 |4 |5 |6 |7 |8 |9 |10 |11 |12 |13 |14 SI 1.44N

TEST 7-E

OPEN TABLE
Center on a full page.
Spacing 2

VIDEOX SALES PERSONNEL 13
On Permanent Payroll at Year's End 35

District	This Year	Last Year	Increase	
				58
New England	28	41	13	71
East Coast	72	87	15	77
North Central	50	62	12	84
South Central	176	197	21	91
West Coast	54	57	3	98
Southwest	31	43	12	105

TEST 7-F

MEMORANDUM
Workbook 158

To Thomas P. Morrisey / Executive Vice President / *from* Everett 12
T. Thorpe / Personnel Department / *concerning* Employee Statistics / 24
dated today 29
Mr. Morrisey, this department has made the employee study for 43
which you asked last week. Thanks to the cooperation of the branch 57
managers, we have been able to compile the figures. They are given 70
in the attached table. 75
The gain of 76 persons this year, which amounts to 18.5 percent, 89
is an impressive sign of growth but is much less than the 33 percent 103
to which Mr. Martin referred in the managers' conference in Houston 116
two weeks ago. / E. T. T. / *Initials?* / *Enclosure notation?* 127

|1 |2 |3 |4 |5 |6 |7 |8 |9 |10 |11 |12 |13 |14 SI 1.54FD

4-MINUTE TW

2 copies in 4 minutes

	1	2
The more you see how nature developed living things so that they	13	73
might escape from the jaws of other living things, the more amazed	26	86
you will be. For example, a squid will eject a shower of black ink and	41	101
leave its foe in a dark cloud. An urchin can scissor its way out from	55	115
inside another fish.	60	120

|1 |2 |3 |4 |5 |6 |7 |8 |9 |10 |11 |12 |13 |14 SI 1.30FE

JOB 98·1

BLOCKED LETTER

Body 91 words Line ? inches
Tab center Workbook 57

Today's date ↓? / Mr. B. Blake Jung, Mana- 13
ger / Station WQED / 441 Fifth Avenue / 19
Pittsburgh, PA 15213 / Dear Mr. Jung: / 28

We have received and wish to acknowl- 36
edge your note about the "School of the 44
Screen" show. It is most kind of you to 52
write. 54

Yes, it would be possible for you to get 63
tapes of the program. We have complete 71
sets of tapes for the past two years. I am 80
listing on the enclosed page the shows that 89
involve reading or spelling. 95

Rental prices vary greatly on the tapes. 104
If you'll let us know which ones you are 112
most interested in, we'll let you know the 121
prices on those particular films. 128

Yours sincerely,↓ ? / George W. Strang / 142
Program Director / URS / Enclosure 1.36N 150

OPTIONAL JOB 98·2

OPEN TABLE

Center on full page.
Group body in threes.

SCHOOL OF THE SCREEN 12

Summary for WQED ↓3 22

Date	Reading	Spelling	24 / 42
Oct 6		x	47
Oct 27	x		50
Nov 17	x	x	54
→ Dec 8		x	58
Dec 22	x		61
Jan 6		x	65
Jan 20	x		68
Jan 27		x	72
Feb 17	x	x	75
Mar 10		x	81
Mar 31		x	85
Apr 21	x	x	89

123456 123456

a·i·m 99

GOALS *To type 120 words or more in 4 minutes within 5 errors on alphabetic paragraphs. To preview the a·i·m 100 Test. To produce a letter and a table.*

DIRECTIONS *Spacing 1 for Jobs, 2 for TW. Line 50. Tab 5. WB 59–62. Warmup from a·i·m 98.*

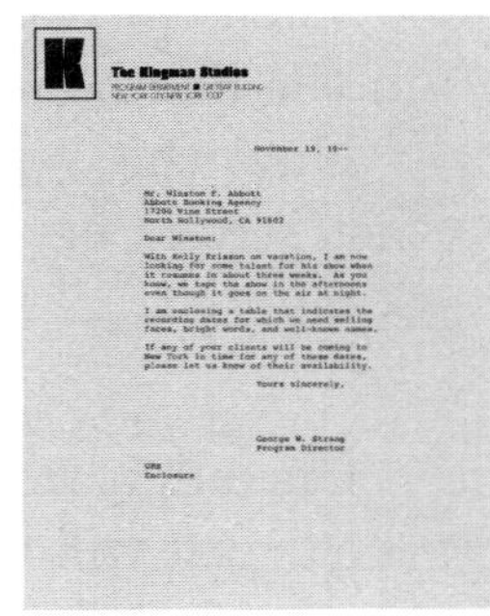

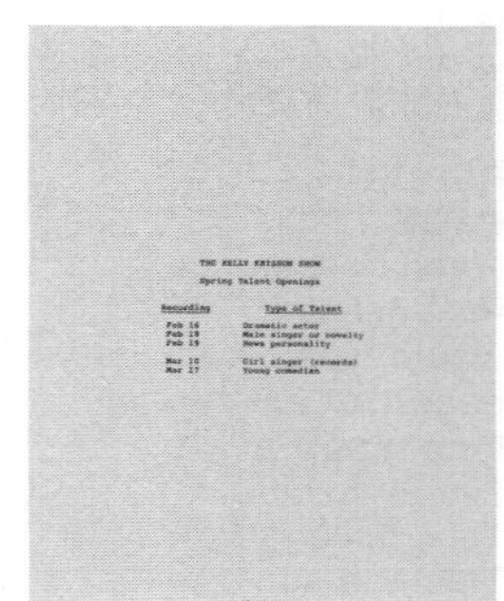

TEST PREP 1 Review the objective-information test on Workbook pages 61–62. Do not mark the test, but look up anything you are not sure of. Be ready to make a high score.

a·i·m 169–170

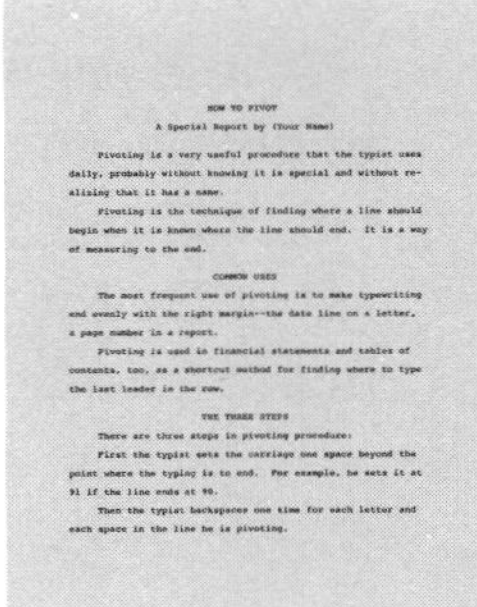

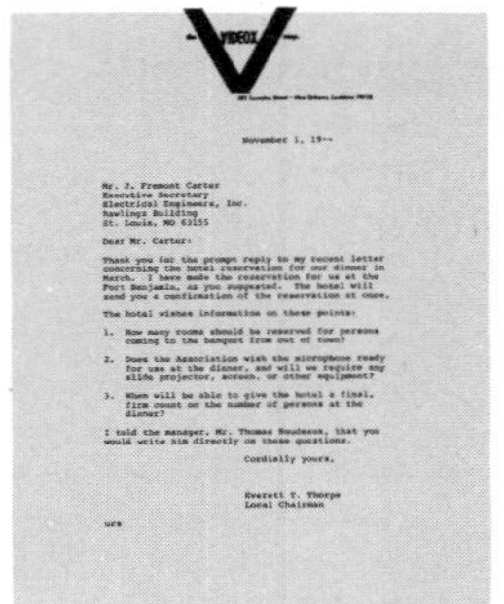

GOALS To type 180 or more words in 5 minutes within 4 errors on average copy requiring bell listening. To produce page 1 of a report. To produce an average length letter. To produce a memorandum. To produce a table. To score 85% or higher on an objective test covering the information reviewed in Part Seven.

DIRECTIONS *Optional warmup from the review on 176. Settings as indicated for each exercise. WB 139, 155–158.*

TEST 7-A

Take a general information test. It may be the one on Workbook pages 155–156 or a similar test that your teacher may give you or may dictate to you.

TEST 7-B

5-MINUTE TW
Line 50
Spacing 2
Tab 5
Omit lines 1, 8, 15, and 24.

TEST 7-C

REPORT PAGE 1
(Type only as much as you would type on page 1 of a long report.)
Line 6 inches
Tabs 5, center
Title and subtitle, line 1
Sideheadings: lines 8, 15, 24

HOW TO PIVOT / A Special Report by [*Your Name*] ..
Pivoting is a very useful procedure that the typist uses daily, 14
probably without knowing it is special and without realizing that 27
it has a name. 30
Pivoting is the technique of finding where a line should begin when 45
it is known where the line should end. It is a way of measuring 58
to the end. 60

COMMON USES ..
The most frequent use of pivoting is to make typewriting end 73
evenly with the right margin—the date line on a letter, a page 86
number in a report. 90
Pivoting is used in financial statements and tables of contents, too, 105
as a shortcut method for finding where to type the last leader in 119
the row. 121

THE THREE STEPS ..
There are three steps in pivoting procedure: 130
First the typist sets the carriage one space beyond the point where 145
the typing is to end. For example, he sets it at 91 if the line ends at 90. 161
Then the typist backspaces one time for each letter and each space 175
in the line he is pivoting. 180
Now the typist is ready to type the material and does so. The 195
last stroke he types will be in the spot where he wants it. The line 209
is pivoted. 211

ONE BIG RISK ..
Once in a while a pivoted line will not work out exactly right, and 226
the typist will be puzzled as to what he did wrong. Almost always any 240
error comes in the first step. The typist is likely to forget to set 254
the carriage one space BEYOND where he wants the line to end. 266

|1 |2 |3 |4 |5 |6 |7 |8 |9 |10 |11 |12 |13 |14 SI 1.40N

TEST PREP 2

4-MINUTE TW
Spacing 2
Line 50
Tab 5

When you hear someone say that it is pouring cats and dogs, you 14
know rain is falling hard. No one knows quite how the expression 27
developed, but it appeared in a book by Jonathan Swift more than 40
two centuries ago. Well, it certainly never does rain felines and 53
canines, but do you realize that it really does rain (of all things) 67
living frogs? 70

A powerful gale can scoop up the live spawn, or eggs, of the 83
frog and carry them way up in the air. The spawn may ride with 96
the wind, traveling many, many miles; some hatch in the air and, 109
taking on weight, "rain" down to the earth below. ⚲120

|1 |2 |3 |4 |5 |6 |7 |8 |9 |10 |11 |12 |13 |14 SI 1.32FE

TEST PREP 3

BLOCKED LETTER

Body 88 words Line ? inches
Tab ? Workbook 59

Today's date ↓? / Mr. Winston F. Abbott / 12
Abbott Booking Agency / 17200 Vine Street 20
/ North Hollywood, CA 91602 / Dear 28
Winston: 30

With Kelly Krisson on vacation, I am 38
now looking for some talent for his show 46
when it resumes in about three weeks. As 55
you know, we tape the show in the after- 62
noons even though it goes on the air at 70
night. 72

I am enclosing a table that indicates the 81
recording dates for which we need smiling 90
faces, bright words, and well-known names. 99

If any of your clients will be coming to 108
New York in time for any of these dates, 116
please let us know of their availability. 125

Yours sincerely, ↓? / George W. Strang / 139
Program Director / URS / *Anything else?* ⚲147

SI 1.36N

TEST PREP 4

OPEN TABLE

Center on full page.
Group body by months.

THE KELLY KRISSON SHOW 13

Spring Talent Openings 30

32

→ *Recording*	*Type of Talent*	49
Feb 16	Dramatic actor	54
Feb 18	Male singer or novelty	61
Feb 19	News personality	67
Mar 10	Girl singer (records)	75
Mar 17	Young comedian ⚲	80

a·i·m 100 TEST

GOALS ⚲ *To type 120 words or more in 4 minutes within 5 errors on alphabetic paragraphs involving listening for the margin bell.* ⚲ *To produce in blocked form a short business letter.* ⚲ *To arrange and center an open table on a full page.* ⚲ *To score 80% or more on an objective test on Part Four technical information.*

DIRECTIONS *Given with each test part.*

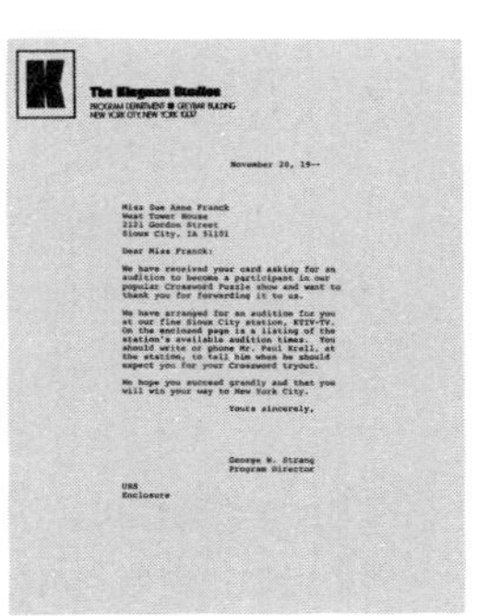

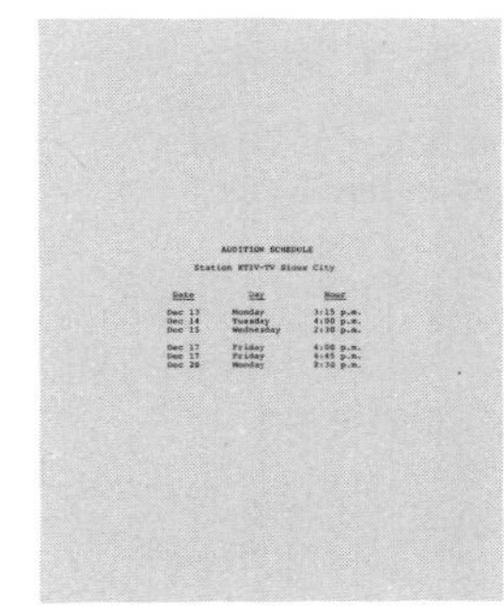

TEST 4-A

Workbook 61–62

Take a general information test. It may be the one on Workbook pages 61–62 or any similar one that your teacher may give or dictate to you.

TEST PREP 4

BLOCKED LETTER
Body 122 words
Line ? inches
Spacing ?
Workbook 153

Today's date / Mr. J. Fremont Carter / Executive Secretary / Elec- 17
trical Engineers, Inc. / Rawlings Building / St. Louis, MO 63155 / 29
Dear Mr. Carter: I have visited the dozen or so hotels in this city 45
and found eight of them that could accommodate the 100 persons 58
that we expect at the quarterly dinner of the EEI on the second 71
Friday in March. 74
As the enclosed list indicates, prices range from $5.00 up to $7.50 89
per plate. To each price a 15% service charge must be added; this 102
includes the gratuity. In all cases there is also a charge of $25.00 for 117
the use of the hotel microphone. 124
Offhand, the Fort Benjamin looks like the best bet. It has a banquet 139
room appropriate to our size, it is newly decorated, it has a fine 152
parking lot, and it offers a rock-bottom price. Shall I reserve it? 166
Cordially yours, ↓4 / Everett T. Thorpe / Local Chairman / urs / 185
Enclosure ⚲ 187

|1 |2 |3 |4 |5 |6 |7 |8 |9 |10 |11 |12 |13 |14 SI 1.43N

TEST PREP 5

OPEN TABLE
Center on a full page.

BANQUET ACCOMMODATIONS			13
Available Second Friday in March			35
	Minimum	Minimum	47
Hotel	Seating	Per Plate	53
Atlantic House	250	$6.00	63
Clairmont Inn	400	5.75	71
Dudley-Plaza	250	7.50	79
Fort Benjamin	125	5.00	87
Merimac Lodge	250	6.00	96
Senate Hotel	300	6.25	104
Shipley-Krown	96	5.00	112
Southern Inn	225	5.50 ⚲	120

TEST PREP 6

MEMORANDUM
Workbook 154

To Harris Wilford / Fiction Editor *from* Doris C. Monsko / Records 13
Department / *concerning* Missing Manuscript Page / *dated today* ↓3 27
A few weeks ago you asked all of us to search for a page missing 43
from a manuscript about the seasons. I went through the active 56
drawers of our files and found nothing. I reported this at that time. 70
Today, however, when I went to one of the inactive files, I found 84
the attached page fastened to the back of one of the file folders. Ap- 98
parently a paper clip had caught it up, so that it was put away with 112
the folder. I do not know whether this is the missing page, but 125
I hope it is. / DCM / urs / Enclosure ⚲ 134

|1 |2 |3 |4 |5 |6 |7 |8 |9 |10 |11 |12 |13 |14 SI 1.38N

TEST 4-B

4-MINUTE TW
Spacing 2
Line 50
Tab 5

One thing that animal life needs is space in which to find food 14
and to grow. Someone once put some rabbits on a tiny tropical 26
island; they grew quickly in size and number, so that they con- 39
sumed the entire food supply in just a few years. That ended the 52
rabbits, precisely as you would expect. 60
The story is also told of an island on which the mice became so 74
numerous that they almost took possession. This island was of 86
unique importance because a rare bush grew there, one whose 98
bark is used in medicine. The hordes of mice jeopardized the 111
medicine and all the people who relied on it.⚲ 120
So the residents brought in some cats to get rid of the mice; they 134
succeeded. But alas, after the mice had disappeared, the hungry 147
cats grew so fierce that they attacked the residents, who then 160
gave up the bush, the bark, the medicine, and the island itself. 174
They abandoned the whole place to the new owners. Today when 186
small vessels circle the place they see packs of cats on the beaches. 200

|1 |2 |3 |4 |5 |6 |7 |8 |9 |10 |11 |12 |13 |14 SI 1.34FE

TEST 4-C

BLOCKED LETTER
Body 97 words
Use WB 63

Today's date/Miss Sue Anne Franck/West Tower House/2121 17
Gordon Street/Sioux City, IA 51101/Dear Miss Franck: 29
We have received your card asking for an audition to become a 42
participant in our popular Crossword Puzzle show and want to 54
thank you for forwarding it to us. 61
We have arranged for an audition for you at our fine Sioux City 75
station, KTIV-TV. On the enclosed page is a listing of the station's 89
available audition times. You should write or phone Mr. Paul Krell, 103
at the station, to tell him when he should expect you for your Cross- 116
word tryout. 119
We hope you succeed grandly and that you will win your way to 132
New York City./Yours sincerely,/ 140
George W. Strang/Program Director/URS/*Enclosure?*⚲ SI 1.40N 158

TEST 4-D

OPEN TABLE
Center wtih 6 spaces between columns.
Center each column head.

AUDITION SCHEDULE 10
Station KTIV-TV Sioux City 28
30

Date	*Day*	*Hour*	41
Dec 13	Monday	3:15 p.m.	47
Dec 14	Tuesday	4:00 p.m.	54
Dec 15	Wednesday	2:30 p.m.	62
Dec 17	Friday	4:00 p.m.	70
Dec 17	Friday	4:45 p.m.	76
Dec 20	Monday	2:30 p.m.⚲	83

a·i·m 167–168

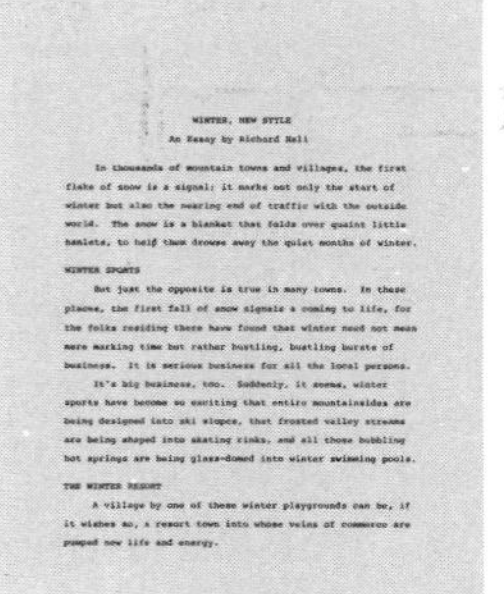

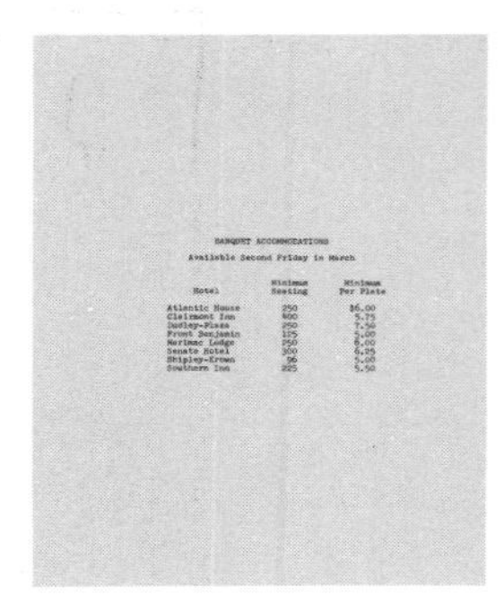

GOALS *To type 180 or more words in 5 minutes within 4 errors on normal listen-for-the-bell narrative copy. To preview the test in a·i·m 169–170. To produce a manuscript, letter, table, and memorandum.*

DIRECTIONS *Warmup spacing 1, line 60. Other settings as directed for each exercise. WB 139, 153–154.*

OPTIONAL WARMUP REVIEW

You may ask the man for the old lid but not for the new one. 12
The lazy judge was very quick to pay tax money for the barn. 12
Please make some price tags for 10¢, 28¢, 39¢, 47¢, and 56¢. 12

|1 |2 |3 |4 |5 |6 |7 |8 |9 |10 |11 |12

TEST PREP 1

Review the objective information test on Workbook pages 155–156. Do not mark the test, but look up any details about which you are not certain; be ready to score high.

TEST PREP 2

5-MINUTE TW
Line 50
Spacing 2
Tab 5
Omit lines 4, 10, 21.

WINTER, NEW STYLE / An Essay by [Your name] ..
In thousands of mountain towns and villages, the first flake of 14
snow is a signal; it marks not only the start of winter but also the 28
nearing end of traffic with the outside world. The snow is a blanket 42
that folds over quaint little hamlets, to help them drowse away the 55
quiet months of winter. 60

WINTER SPORTS ..
But just the opposite is true in many towns. In these places, the 75
first fall of snow signals a coming to life, for the folks residing there 89
have found that winter need not mean mere marking time but rather 103
hustling, bustling bursts of business. It is serious business for all the 118
local persons. 121

TEST PREP 3

REPORT PAGE 1
(Type only as much as you would put on page 1 of a long report.)
Line 6 inches
Spacing 2
Title and subtitle: line 4
Sideheadings: lines 10, 21

It's big business, too. Suddenly, it seems, winter sports have become 136
so exciting that entire mountainsides are being designed into ski 149
slopes, that frosted valley streams are being shaped into skating 162
rinks, and all those bubbling hot springs are being glass-domed into 175
winter swimming pools. 180

THE WINTER RESORT ..
A village by one of these winter playgrounds can be, if it wishes 195
so, a resort town into whose veins of commerce are pumped new life 208
and energy. 211
All through springtime and summer, the local folks prepare for the 225
winter. They construct ski slopes and trails; they fashion new ski 239
jumps, as well, with automatic lifts. 246

|1 |2 |3 |4 |5 |6 |7 |8 |9 |10 |11 |12 |13 |14 SI 1.36N

Overview

In Part Five you will complete the keyboard controls, push ahead in basic skill, and learn several new production arrangements.

1. You will learn the dozen or so symbol keys on the top row of your typewriter. Now that you are moving into practical business production, you need to know these keys.

2. In the preceding Part your skill goal was to type at least 30 words a minute for 4 minutes within 5 errors; in Part Five your skill goal is to sustain (or even increase) the speed level *for 5 minutes* without increasing errors. You will have many skill drives to assist you in achieving this goal.

3. In addition to the letters with which you are familiar, you will produce postal cards, interoffice memos, and invoices.

There are 25 a·i·m experiences in Part Five, each providing about 20 minutes of study or practice. As in preceding Parts, the last a·i·m is a test on the Part and the a·i·m before it is a practice run on the Part Five test.

Performance Goals

When you finish Part Five, you should be able to demonstrate the following skills and abilities when you do the test in a·i·m 125, page 132:

1. Touch Typing You will operate all keys by touch and use the tabulator to tab-indent paragraphs, letter dates and closings, and columns on invoices.

2. Technicalities You will score 80 percent or more on an objective test that reviews the preceding Parts and checks the technical information you will learn in Part Five.

3. Production You will use at least 70 percent of your basic typing skill in the production of a business letter and at least 50 percent in the production of invoices.

4. Skill You will type *at least* 150 words in 5 minutes within 5 errors as you copy alphabetic paragraph material that is not arranged line for line (the 150 is minimal; 175 is more nearly an average expectation).

Routines and Procedures

Speed Drives There are five speed drives in Part Five with extremely easy material to help you achieve speed and accuracy goals. A slightly different routine is used in the 5-minute drives; it is explained on page 109.

Remedial Practice Should you spend extra time on speed? on accuracy? Discuss with your teacher this suggested plan:

If you do not achieve the speed goal or the accuracy goal in a Speed Drive a·i·m, turn to the drills for your level in Supplement II (page 274), spend 20 to 30 minutes on the speed or accuracy drills (whichever you need), then return to and repeat the Speed Drive with which you had had difficulty.

Production Writings Many of the a·i·m sessions will require your taking a timed writing on the letter body or other production task. Doing so will help you apply to production work the typing power you are developing.

Technical Rules The letters, envelopes, and postal cards you type in this Part will be familiar, but the memos and invoices will be different. Type them very carefully, for they are the base of all the forms yet to come.

JOB 165·2

MEMORANDUM
Workbook 149 (or in style shown on page 124)

This memorandum is to John C. Vance / Personnel Department 10
from Orman D. Link, Jr. / Vice President *on the subject of* The 18
Vacancy in Louisville *with* today's date. 28
Thank you for your note about the Louisville vacancy. 41
I am going to Louisville on Thursday of next week to look into 54
some new store locations. I shall probably be tied up all day on 68
Thursday and Friday. I had planned to return on Friday night, 80
but if you think you could arrange appointments for me to meet 93
the two men on Saturday morning, I can and shall plan to stay over. 107
Thank you for your help. / O. D. L. / urs 118

|1 |2 |3 |4 |5 |6 |7 |8 |9 |10 |11 |12 |13 |14 SI 1.38N

a·i·m 166

WARMUP and TW on page 173

JOB 166·1

BILL (invoice)
Workbook 151 (or in style shown on page 127)
Review page 128

- Numbers square on the right
- Words square on the left
- When possible, same tabs used heading/body
- Description and Total line up

the VIDEOX corp.
521 Touraine Street • New Orleans, Louisiana 70118

Invoice

TO Joe Rivers & Sons, Inc. DATE February 11, 19-- 10
211 West Ballard Avenue 15
Birmingham, AL 35201 ↓4 20

23

VIA Our Truck ↓4 No. 37476 25

QUANTITY	DESCRIPTION	UNIT PRICE	AMOUNT	
				28
12	Television Sets, Model SSC 18	100.00	1,200.00	41
12	Television Sets, Model SSC 28	125.00	1,500.00	54
12	Television Sets, Model SSC 88	150.00	1,800.00	67
				68
15	Radio Sets, Model SSC 11	18.00	270.00	80
30	Radio Sets, Model SSC 71	28.25	847.50	91
				92
	Total		5,617.50	99
	Delivery		79.60	107
	Amount Due		5,697.10	115
			Pay Last Amount in This Column	

JOB 166·2

BILL (invoice)
Workbook 151 (or like page 127)

Invoice No. 37477 to J. Paul Thetch, Inc. / 844 South Teague 12
Street / Memphis, TN 38103 / Today's date / Our Truck / 22

10	Television Sets, Model SSC 18	@ 100.00	amount	1,000.00	38
3	Television Sets, Model SSC 28	@ 125.00	amount	375.00	50
3	Radio Sets, Model SSC 91	@ 31.60	amount	94.80	61
500	Booklets, "Your Own Hi-Fi"	@ .03	amount	15.00	73
	Total			1,484.80	79
	Delivery			37.80	87
	Amount Due			1,522.60	95

a·i·m 101

GOALS *To build a speed reserve (175 words or more in 5 minutes within 5 errors) on very easy material.*

DIRECTIONS *Spacing 1 for drills, 2 for TW. Line 60. Tab 5.*

TO BOOST SPEED

- Think **Smooth,** not **Speed.**
- Stress nonstop, nonjam stroking.
- Keep eyes rigidly on the copy.
- Keep fingers curved when stroking.
- Keep wrists, arms motionless.

WARMUP PREVIEW

2 copies

```
The dog did not get the ham she had put out for him to eat.   12
happened printed someone friends dozens talent screen women   12
Jack did such lazy plowing that the farmer was quite vexed.   12
Bob did 10 and 28, Ann did 39 and 47, and Bill finished 56.   12
|1   |2   |3   |4   |5   |6   |7   |8   |9   |10   |11   |12
```

ROUTINE FOR SPEED DRIVE

5 MINUTES

To build a 5-minute speed reserve, take these steps in practice:

1. A 1·1·1·1·1 timings sequence.
2. One 5-minute timed writing.
3. Two minutes of stretch or remedial practice. *Stretch:* Practice repeatedly one more line's worth of copy. *Remedial:* For each word mistyped make (a) three correct copies plus (b) three correct copies with the preceding and following word; for example, if *of* in line 5 is mistyped, you would type *of of of one of the one of the one of the* to remedy that error.
4. Repeat the 5-minute writing.

SPEED DRIVE

```
     News is one of the free things in the world that costs   12
a great deal, as you must know if you ever took a look into   24
the plant where a paper is printed or ever took a second to   36
count how many men or women were on your TV screen when you   48
saw the news at ten last night.  It takes dozens and dozens   60
of folks to get the news or a picture of it, to write it up   72
and edit it, to put it in type or on film, just so that you   84
and your friends can be told what is what and why it is so.   96
     These dozens of folks have to get paid, of course, and  108
you have to pay a good price if you want the best talent to  120
get the news for you--to find it, to screen it for the true  132
facts, to write it up so that the guy who reads it will get  144
the right view of what happened, or of why someone spoke as  156
he did, and so on.  Who pays for this talent?  Who pays for  168
the paper and the print or the film and the screen?  Who is  180
the angel that foots the bills?  He is the man who pays for  192
time or space to tell you what he makes.                     200
|1   |2   |3   |4   |5   |6   |7   |8   |9   |10   |11   |12   SI 1.10VE
```

a·i·m 164

SKILL DRILL ON NUMBERS
Each (a) line once, each (b) line twice.

1a aql ala ala ll axes ll atoms ll apples ll arches ll actions 12

1b DD 111 collided with DE 191 on May 1, 1911, or May 1, 1912. ↓2 12

2a sw2 s2s s2s 22 sips 22 steps 22 syrups 22 sights 22 signals 12

2b Car 222 passed Cars 221 and 223 and caught up with Car 224. 12

3a de3 d3d d3d 33 days 33 dolls 33 doubts 33 dreams 33 dippers 12

3b No. 333 escaped in 1933; and No. 3133 escaped in 1933, too. 12

4a fr4 f4f f4f 44 fobs 44 fires 44 fliers 44 fields 44 figures 12

4b The 444th Regiment included 434 men; the 434th had 444 men. 12

5a f5f f5f f5f 55 fish 55 forms 55 floats 55 forces 55 flashes 12

5b Flight 155 to Portland carried 55 men on February 15, 1955. 12

|1 |2 |3 |4 |5 |6 |7 |8 |9 |10 |11 |12

6a jy6 j6j j6j 66 jars 66 jokes 66 judges 66 juries 66 joiners 12

6b Invoice No. 166,166 was the 166th one she filed on 6/16/66. 12

7a ju7 j7j j7j 77 jets 77 jumps 77 joints 77 jurors 77 jackets 12

7b Train No. 177 left on Track 17 at 7:17 with 177 passengers. 12

8a ki8 k8k k8k 88 keys 88 kings 88 knocks 88 knives 88 knights 12

8b Model 88 has 188 buttons, controlled by 18 men and 88 boys. 12

9a lo9 l9l l9l 99 less 99 lines 99 lights 99 lilacs 99 letters 12

9b The 19 worked here from 1919 to 1929 and from 1949 to 1959. 12

10a ;p0 ;0; ;0; 10 pods 10 pages 10 paints 10 people 10 parties 12

10b Between 10:00 and 11:00, he packed 100 quarts in 10 crates. 12

PREPARE
a·i·m
WB 142

a·i·m 165

WARMUP, TW
on page 173

JOB 165·1

MEMORANDUM
Workbook 149 (or in style shown on page 124)
Review page 125

- Guides/insertions align at bottom
- Left margin 2 spaces inside guide words
- Right margin set to match left
- Writer's initials line up with tab in heading
- Typist's initials as in letters

the VIDEOX corp.

Interoffice Memorandum

TO: Orman D. Link, Jr. FROM: John C. Vance 8
Vice President Personnel Department 17
18
SUBJECT: The Vacancy in Louisville DATE: February 10, 19-- ↓3 29
30
31
As you asked, Mr. Link, we have checked out all the answers 43
to our ad in the Louisville Times. The field has been thinned 62
down to two men who seem to qualify for the position: David 74
Churma and Victor Lewis. Both men live in Louisville. They 87
appear to be well worth the time and cost of an interview. 100
101
If you would like to have a wider field with more applicants, 112
we can repeat the ad or apply to an agency. If you prefer 124
that we interview Mr. Churma and Mr. Lewis before opening the 136
field, I could fly up to Louisville to meet them or invite 148
them both down here to meet you. 156
157
What action do you recommend, Mr. Link? 165
166
J. C. V. 169
urs 170
SI 1.36N

a·i·m 102

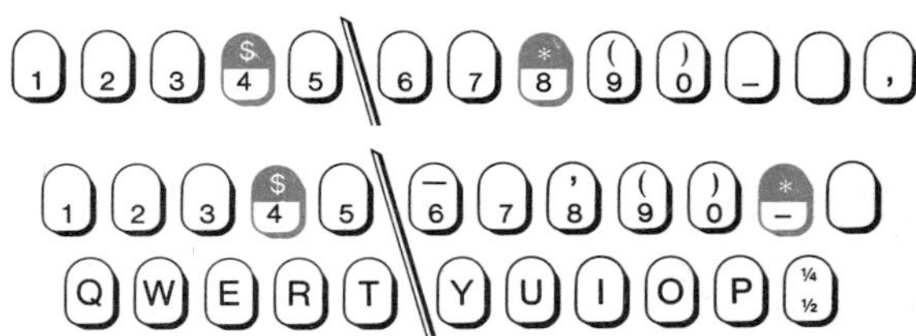

GOALS ◉ *To control $ (shift of 4).* ◉ *To control * (shift of 8 or hyphen).* ◉ *To type 140 words or more in 5 minutes within 5 errors.*

DIRECTIONS *Spacing 1 for drills, 2 for TW. Line 50. Tab 5. K 26.*

WARMUP REVIEW

3 copies

1 Why did the two men get the box from the new car? 10
2 Jack was quiet after he breezily plowed a garden. 10
3 Their voting was 10 to 28, 39 to 47, and 56 to 0.
|1 |2 |3 |4 |5 |6 |7 |8 |9 |10

$ 4 KEY

Shift of 4

4 f4f f$f f4f f$f f4$f Pay $4 or $14 or $41 or $44. 10
5 Buy him the gift for $4 or $5, not for $9 or $10. 10
6 May thought that $14 was about $4 or $5 too much.◉ 10

*** – KEY**

Shift of hyphen (do line 7M) or of 8 (do 7E)

7M ;-; ;*; ;-; ;*; ;-*; Jones* has a ruling on that. 10
7E k8k k*k k8k k*k k8*k Jones* has a ruling on that. 10
8 Jones* used an asterisk (*) in several footnotes. 10
9 * John Jones is an expert on correct punctuation.◉ 10

5-MINUTE GOAL TYPING

2 copies in 5 minutes.

Spacing 2
2 attempts

		1	2
10	Each of the six packages was insured for $10	10	80
11	or $15, which is much less than their value. Joe	20	90
12	said that Mr. Quill* was angry that they were not	30	100
13	insured for $25 or $50, which is just about their	40	110
14	true worth. The firm will have to take a sizable	50	120
15	loss on the order, perhaps as much as $50 or $100	60	130
16	or even $125. The firm can't afford such a loss.	70	140◉

|1 |2 |3 |4 |5 |6 |7 |8 |9 |10 SI 1.31FE

a·i·m 103

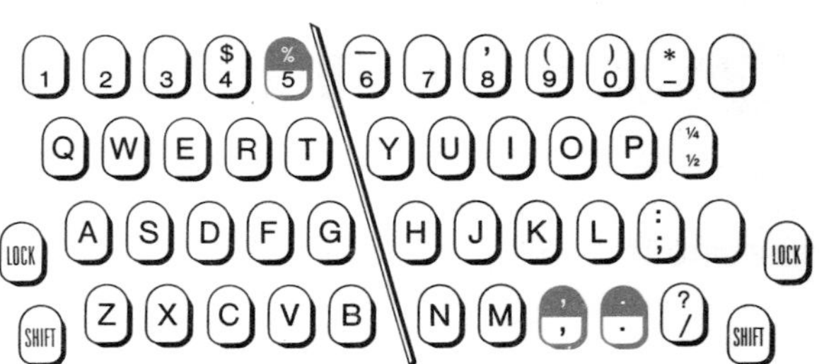

GOALS ◉ *To control the % (shift of 5).* ◉ *To control the "capital" period and comma.* ◉ *To type 141 words or more in 5 minutes within 5 errors.*

DIRECTIONS *Spacing 1. Line 50. Tab 5. K 27.*

WARMUP REVIEW

3 copies

1 The two men did not get the box from the new car. 10
2 Jack was quite breezy after he plowed the garden. 10
3 The two gardens were 10 by 28 and 39 by 47 or 56. 10
|1 |2 |3 |4 |5 |6 |7 |8 |9 |10

a·i·m 163

WHEN DRIVING FOR ACCURACY—

- Type smoothly, as though to music.
- Stay on the stroke-by-stroke level.
- Keep the machine going steadily.
- Silently say each letter to yourself.

GOAL ⚲ *To strengthen skill (180 words or more in 5 minutes within 4 errors) on nearly-normal alphabetic material that requires attention to the line endings.*

DIRECTIONS *Spacing 1 for drills, 2 for TW. Line 60. Tab 5.*

WARMUP REVIEW

2 copies

Why did you ask the man for the new car and not for the old? 12
Maizie quickly paid Jones for the five new taxis she bought. 12
The answers: (10) yes, (28) no, (39) yes, (47) no, (56) no. 12

ACCURACY DRIVE

See page 162.
Spacing 2

When we discuss the names of streets, most of us think of streets 14
and avenues, maybe with a boulevard or drive for good measure. 27
But those four names are just a start. More than thirty names, 40
ranging from lane to plaza, are approved by the post office. You 53
cannot help but wonder how all the names came into being, though 66
some are obvious. Extension, for example, has no mystery nor has 80
square or circle. But take arcade and court; there is mystery to 93
them. Grove may be obvious, as in junction, but where did bypass 106
come from? 108

Without question, some names have snob appeal. Do you prefer a 122
terrace to an alley, a garden to a street, a manor to a mere road? 136
It's hard to explain why, but most persons flinch from rural route 149
but enjoy a vista; we all have some prejudices in such matters. 162
Some words seem to come and go with the times; just now the 174
name plaza is coming back into ⚲ prominence, thanks to the shop- 186
ping plazas we see around us, while trails and crescents are losing 200
out to superhighways. 204

|1 |2 |3 |4 |5 |6 |7 |8 |9 |10 |11 |12 |13 |14 SI 1.34FE

a·i·m 164–166

TO MASTER NUMBERS

- Concentrate on 2 and 6 keys.
- Say each digit silently to yourself.
- Force yourself to type by touch.
- Type confidently—but slowly.

GOALS ⚲ *To develop greater confidence in number typing.* ⚲ *To review procedures for typing on forms.*

DIRECTIONS *Spacing 1. Line 60.*

WARMUP PREVIEW

2 copies in each a·i·m

A The old car was the one you had the day you met the two men. 12
B The money for the tax was quickly paid over by a lazy judge. 12
C We bought 10 shares @ 28, 39 shares @ 47, and 56 shares @ 1. 12
D Repeat 5-minute writing above (omit if you have met the goals).

% 5 KEY

Shift of 5 on all machines
2 copies

4 f5f f%f f5f f%f f5%f We want 5% and 15% and 155%. 10
5 Try to get a 4.5% bond or some 5% stocks for him. 10
6 She wanted 15% interest, but I would pay only 5%. 10

, . KEYS

2 copies

On most typewriters (yours?), the capital of the comma is another comma and the capital of the period is another period. Thus when you type something in all capitals, you don't have to release the shift lock to type them. Practice:

7 Yours truly, J. K. CARTER, INC., Purchasing Agent 10
8 Order from V. R. FRENCH or from K. W. BROWN, INC. 10
9 File J. J. THOMAS, INC. before J. W. THOMAS, INC. 10

5-MINUTE GOAL TYPING

2 copies in 5 minutes
2 attempts

Spacing 1

		1	2
10	The F. Z. DIXON CO., who is the party of the	10	81
11	first part in the contract, has agreed to pay the	20	91
12	sum of $10,000 to J. J. QUILL, INC., the party of	30	101
13	the second part, for the truck if it is delivered	40	111
14	on or before the first of the month. J. J. QUILL	50	121
15	has agreed to a 5% cash discount and a 5% penalty	60	131
16	discount if the truck is more than one week late.	70	141

|1 |2 |3 |4 |5 |6 |7 |8 |9 |10 SI 1.24E

PREPARE a·i·m WB 67–68

a·i·m 104-105

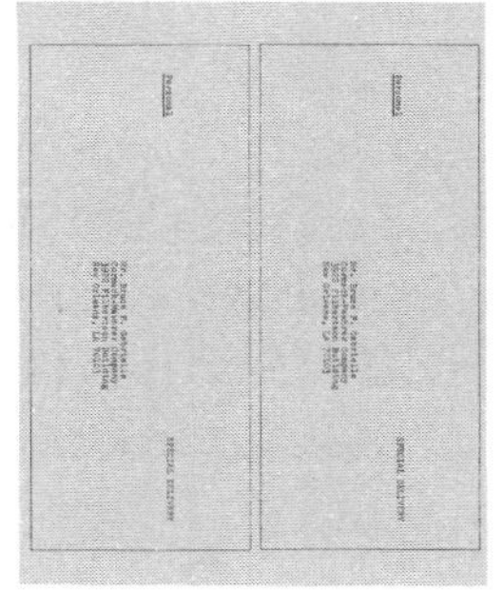

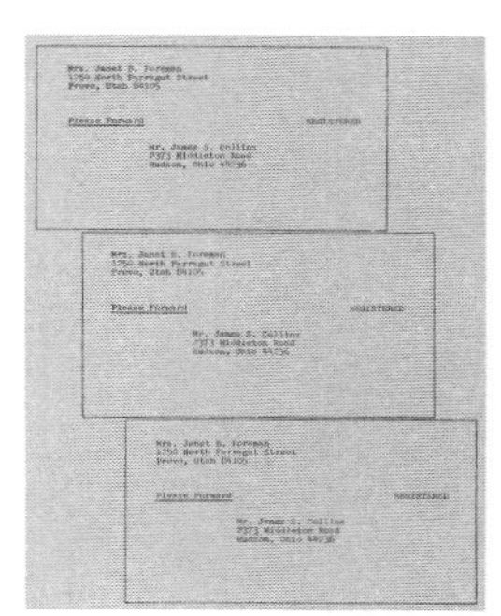

GOALS To type 142 words or more in 5 minutes within 5 errors. To address large and small envelopes. To produce a short business letter. To address an envelope for the letter.

DIRECTIONS *Spacing 1. Line 50. Tabs 5 and center. WB 38.*

WARMUP REVIEW

3 copies

1 Who took the big box that she had put in her car? 10
2 The farmer irked Jan, who had plowed too quickly. 10
3 minimize argument question express subject $4,500 10
4 They give credits of 10%, 28%, 39%, 47%, and 56%. 10

|1 |2 |3 |4 |5 |6 |7 |8 |9 |10

5-MINUTE GOAL WRITING

2 copies in 5 minutes.

Spacing 2

		1	2
5	One subject of endless argument is the ques-	10	81
6	tion of whether the firm should express profit or	20	91
7	loss figures in terms of dollars or percents. If	30	101
8	you want to minimize the change, you will use the	40	111
9	percents; 5% seems less than $4,500. If you want	50	121
10	to make much of the change, you will use dollars;	60	131
11	$4,500 seems like a lot more profit than just 5%.	71	142

SI 1.34N

aim 161

WARMUP
PREVIEW
2 copies (A–C)

A Louisville Times advertised pleased opening receive that we 18
B information application complete writing names file fill in 12
C Jackie quietly gave most of his prize boxers to dog owners. 12
D Repeat the 5-minute timing on page 170.

JOB 161·1

BLOCKED LETTER
Body 71
Line 4 inches
Tab center
Workbook 145

Today's date / Mr. David T. Churma / 427 West First Street / 16
Louisville, KY 40206 / Dear Mr. Churma: / Thank you for writing 31
us about the opening that we advertised in the *Louisville Times.* 50
We are pleased to receive your application. 59

We shall write at once to all the names you listed in your letter. 75
As soon as we have heard from them, we shall write you again. 87

So that we may have complete information about you on file, 100
please fill in and return to us the enclosed application form. 113

Yours sincerely, ↓6 / Orman D. Link, Jr. / Vice President / urs / 134
Enclosure 136

|1 |2 |3 |4 |5 |6 |7 |8 |9 |10 |11 |12 |13 |14 SI 1.41N

aim 162

WARMUP
PREVIEW
2 copies (A–C)

A responsibility supervise reference indicated given name for 12
B responsible accounting confidence appreciate think that you 12
C Dog owners quickly gave most of the boxed prizes to Judith. 12
D Repeat the 5-minute timing on page 170.

JOB 162·1

BLOCKED LETTER
WITH ENUMERATION
Body 147 plus 20
for display of
enumeration
Line 5 inches
Tabs 4, center
Workbook 147

Today's date / Mr. Willard I. Wayne / Wayne & Sons, Inc. / 444 17
Harbor Road / Portland, ME 04105 / Dear Mr. Wayne: / Mr. David 30
T. Churma, a resident of Louisville and an applicant for the posi- 43
tion of manager of our store in that city, has given us your name 56
as reference. He indicated that he worked for you from 1965 until 69
1969. Will you give us some information about him? 80

1. Did Mr. Churma supervise the work of others? If so, did he do 95
this well? 99
2. Was Mr. Churma responsible for the handling and the account 114
of cash funds? If so, how well did he fulfill this responsibility? 129
3. Mr. Churma indicated that he left your firm for a job that 144
would pay more. Was there a reason why you did not pay him 158
more in order to retain him on your staff? 168

We shall, of course, keep in confidence any details that you can 182
give us. We shall appreciate learning whether you would recommend 196
him to us. 198

Yours sincerely, ↓4 / Orman D. Link, Jr. / Vice President / urs 220

|1 |2 |3 |4 |5 |6 |7 |8 |9 |10 |11 |12 |13 |14 SI 1.40N

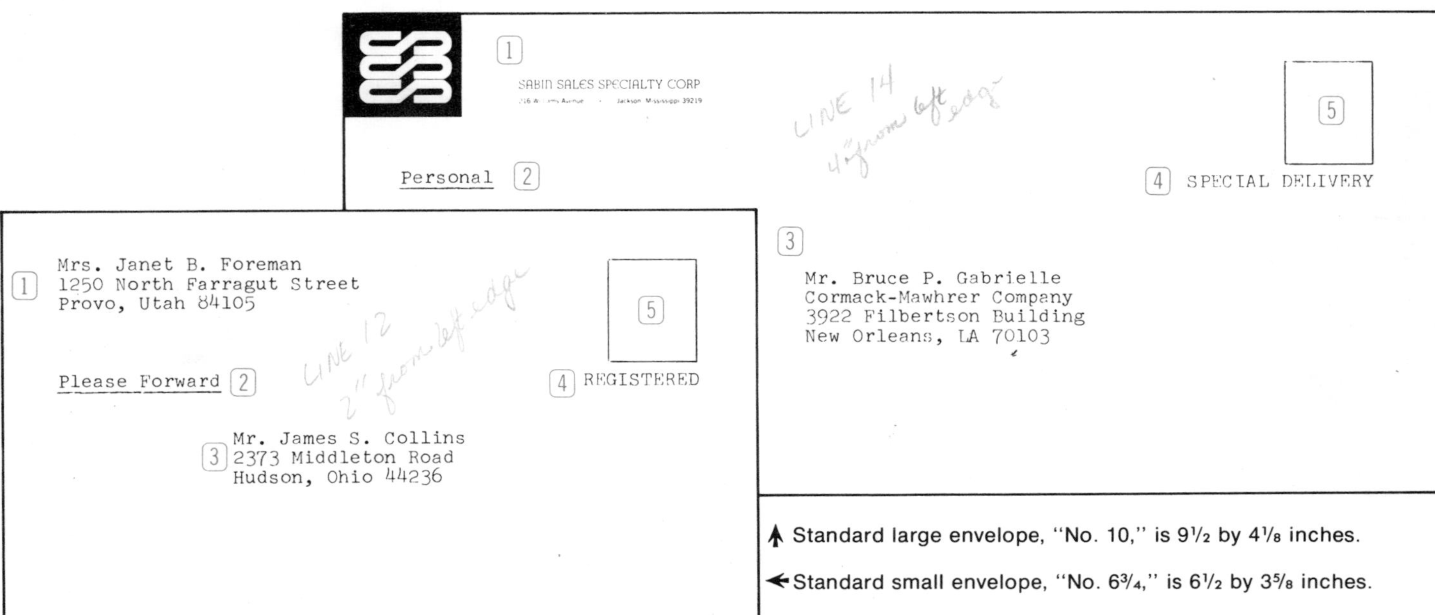

SABIN SALES SPECIALTY CORP
Personal 2
4 SPECIAL DELIVERY
5
3
Mr. Bruce P. Gabrielle
Cormack-Mawhrer Company
3922 Filbertson Building
New Orleans, LA 70103
1 Mrs. Janet B. Foreman
1250 North Farragut Street
Provo, Utah 84105
5
Please Forward 2
4 REGISTERED
3 Mr. James S. Collins
2373 Middleton Road
Hudson, Ohio 44236

Standard large envelope, "No. 10," is $9\frac{1}{2}$ by $4\frac{1}{8}$ inches.

Standard small envelope, "No. $6\frac{3}{4}$," is $6\frac{1}{2}$ by $3\frac{5}{8}$ inches.

ADDRESSING ENVELOPES

Read and remember. Also read and remember Workbook 38.

1. Return address, if not printed, begins on line 3, single-spaced, blocked $\frac{1}{2}$ inch from left edge. The "Mrs." title may be used, but "Miss" and "Mr." are not.

2. On-arrival directions like "Please Forward," "Confidential," "Personal," and "Attention Sales Manager" are typed on line 9 in capital and small letters, underscored, $\frac{1}{2}$ inch from the left edge.

3. Addressee's name and address on a small envelope begin on line 12, 2 inches from left edge; and on a large envelope on line 14, 4 inches from edge. Always use single-spacing and blocked arrangement. City, state, and ZIP must be on same line. State name may be spelled out or abbreviated; post office prefers the new two-letter abbreviations.

In a foreign address, indicate postal zone (if known) after city, and type the country name in all caps on a separate line.

4. Special mail service, if any, is typed on line 9 or 10, positioned to end about 1 or $\frac{1}{2}$ inch from the right edge.

5. Stamp is about $\frac{1}{2}$ inch from top and right edges of the envelope.

Job 104·1. Using slips of paper cut to the sizes indicated in the illustration above, type three copies of the Collins envelope and two of the Gabrielle envelope.

FOLDING LETTERS

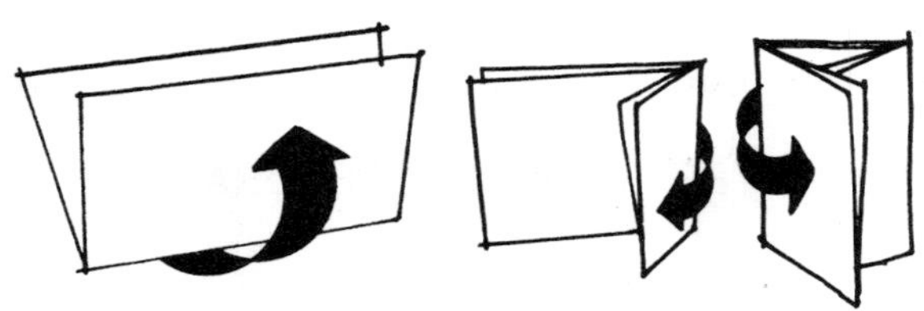

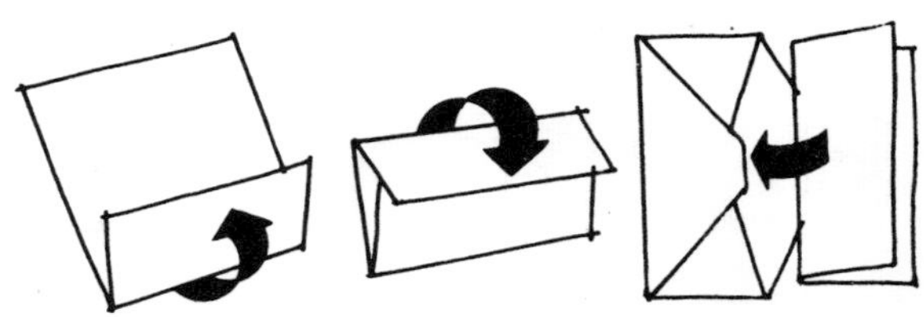

To fold a letter for a small envelope—bring bottom up to ½ inch from the top . . . fold right-hand third toward left . . . fold left-hand third toward right . . . insert into envelope, last crease first.

To fold a letter for a large envelope—fold up the bottom third of the paper . . . fold the top third over the bottom third . . . insert in envelope—the last crease goes into the envelope first.

JOB 160·1

BLOCKED LETTER WITH QUOTATION
Shown in pica
Body 103 + 20 for company signature + 20 for quotation = 143 count
Line 5 inches
Tabs 5, center
Workbook 143

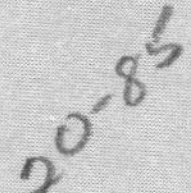

the VIDEOX corp.
521 Touraine Street • New Orleans, Louisiana 70118

Line 15 February 1, 19-- ↓5 4

8

The Louisville Times 12
486 North Rosceil Drive 17
Louisville, KY 40202 21

22

Gentlemen: 24

25

We should like to place the following ad for Help 35
Wanted in your issues for next Saturday and Sunday. 46

47

Indent display 5 spaces on each side.

> We Want a Store Manager! 53
>
> 54
>
> This is a fine chance for a young man of 63
> 25 to 35 who wants a job with a future 72
> and who has had a year or more experience 81
> in managing a retail store. Send full 90
> information and three references to 98
>
> 99
>
> The Videox Corporation 105
> New Orleans, LA 70118 111

112

Please display the heading and our name in a type 122
size that will fill the column width. Payment will 133
be made when proof of publication and your invoice 143
are received. 146

147

Punctuation is standard: colon after greeting, comma after the closing phrase.

Yours truly, 151

152

THE VIDEOX CORPORATION ↓5 159

Orman D. Link, Jr. 163

Orman D. Link, Jr. 168
Vice President ↓2 173

174

Type your initials here.

urs 175

SI 1.41N

Blocked Business Letter with a Quotation Displayed in the Body

a·i·m 105

5-MINUTE GOAL WRITING

Mr. Blaine T. Schroeder / General Manager / Pierce and Orr, 19
Inc. / 1600 Keystone Drive / Tulsa, OK 74111 / *Today's date* 27
Dear Mr. Schroeder: / Thank you very much for sending us your 41
catalog of rings, pins, and emblems for schools, clubs, and other 55
organizations. 58
We have studied the catalog carefully but have not found pre- 71
cisely the design that we are seeking. 79
I am enclosing a rough sketch of the type of emblem in which 92
we would be interested. Please let us know what the charge 104
would be to design a pin similar to the sketch. We would appreciate 118
an early reply. 121
Very sincerely yours, / Mary Ellen Stevens / ⚲ Chairman, 144
Committee / for a New Emblem / URS / Enclosure ⚲ 155

|1 |2 |3 |4 |5 |6 |7 |8 |9 |10 |11 |12 |13 |14 SI 1.44N

JOB 105·1

BLOCKED LETTER
Line 4 inches
Tab center
Body 77 words
Workbook 69

JOB 105·2

ENVELOPE
Workbook 70 or slip of paper

a·i·m 106

GOALS ⚲ *To build speed reserve (175 words or more in 5 minutes within 5 errors) on very easy copy.* ⚲ *To practice responding to margin bell without looking up.*

DIRECTIONS *Spacing 1 for drills, 2 for TW. Line 60. Tab 5.*

BOOSTER DRILLS

- If your speed and accuracy slip below the goals of the a·i·m drives, turn to the motion-control drills in the supplement and work with them for an extra a·i·m session or two.

WARMUP REVIEW

3 copies

```
Why did the man buy the hat and why did the boy ask for it?   12
Were Jack Zimmer's big yellow quilts really that expensive?   12
They owed $10, $28, and $39 to Bill and $47 and $56 to Tom.   12
|1   |2   |3   |4   |5   |6   |7   |8   |9   |10   |11   |12
```

SPEED DRIVE

See page 109.

One of my side aims in life is to meet a man who draws the 13
kind of maps they give you in a gas station or the kind your auto 26
club gives you when you tell them that you wonder how the roads 39
are to your home town. You know what I mean, I am sure. It is 51
a big paper full of lines that zigzag all over the page, dashing 64
from one box to another, or from one shield to another. I am told 78
that each of these shapes has a number on it, but it is too small 91
for me to say it is so. 96
Now, the reason I want to meet a man who can draw such maps 109
is that he needs help and I am willing to give it. He errs on two 122
scores, it seems to me. First, he does not put a date on the map, 136
so that I do not know whether I have one that is just a year old 149
(I never have a new one) or is nine years old. Second, he puts 162
a lot of dash lines to show you where there is going to be a road, ⚲ 175
but he does not tell you when it will be there. 185

|1 |2 |3 |4 |5 |6 |7 |8 |9 |10 |11 |12 |13 |14 SI 1.09VE

PREPARE a·i·m WB 141

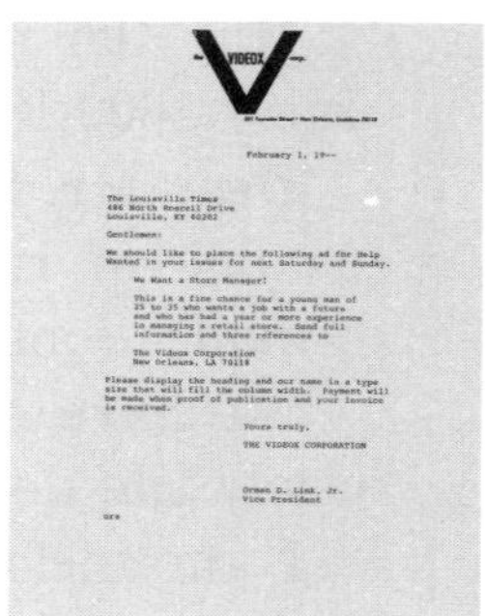

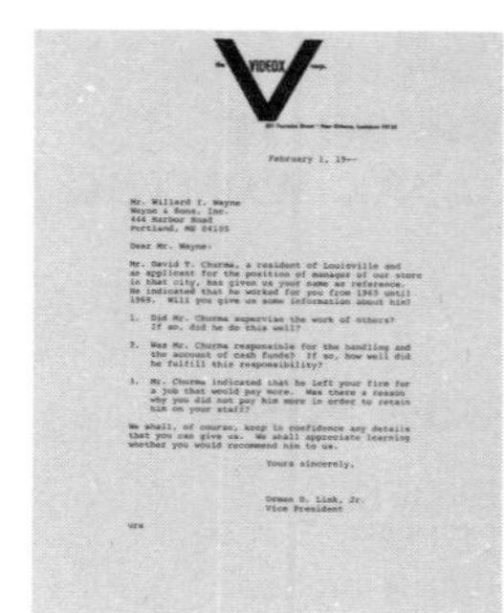

a·i·m 160–162

GOALS *To type 180 words within 5 minutes and 4 errors on normal, alphabetic paragraph material. To review the production of correspondence.*

DIRECTIONS *Spacing 1. Line 60. Tab 5. WB 140, 143–147.*

WARMUP PREVIEW

2 copies in each a·i·m

A proportion formulas sizeable whatever subject equate twenty, 12
B attention signature consider articles company margin framed, 12
C Judge Power quickly gave the six embezzlers stiff sentences. 12
D Take a 5-minute goal-writing timing on the selection below.

5-MINUTE TW

Spacing 2

From the very start of the typewriter, the persons who used it tried 15
to adjust their margins so that whatever they typed would look attrac- 29
tive on the page. Magazine articles said that the typing should be framed 44
by the white space of the margins, and writers offered all kinds of 57
formulas that would equate the margins with the proportions of the 71
paper. But all the time the typists and the writers had trouble in 84
handling the exceptions that did not quite fit the formula. 96

People asked how one could use the same formula when a letter might 111
or might not have a subject line, or attention line, or company signa- 125
ture, or some other display that took a sizeable chunk of space. The 139
answer to the question came when someone found that each display 152
line had the effect of adding an extra twenty words to the letter, which 166
is why we now add that twenty to the body estimate when we are 179
trying to consider whether a letter is short, or average, or long. 192

|1 |2 |3 |4 |5 |6 |7 |8 |9 |10 |11 |12 |13 |14 SI 1.39N

LETTER MARGINS

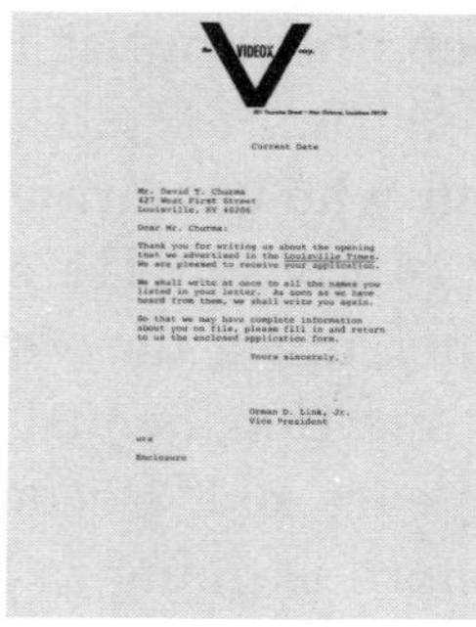

SHORT (4-inch line) has under 100 words.

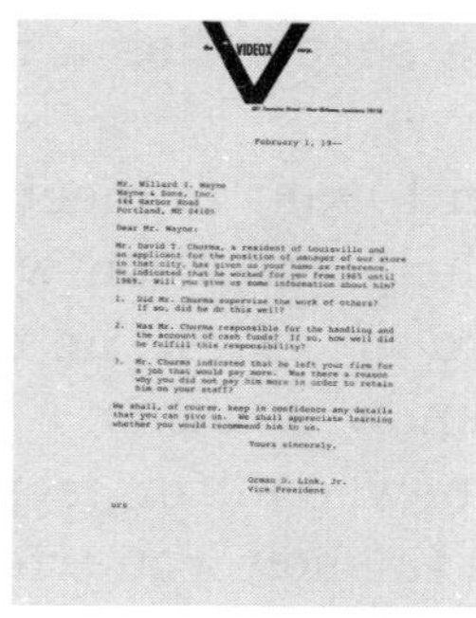

AVERAGE (5-inch line) has 100–200 words.

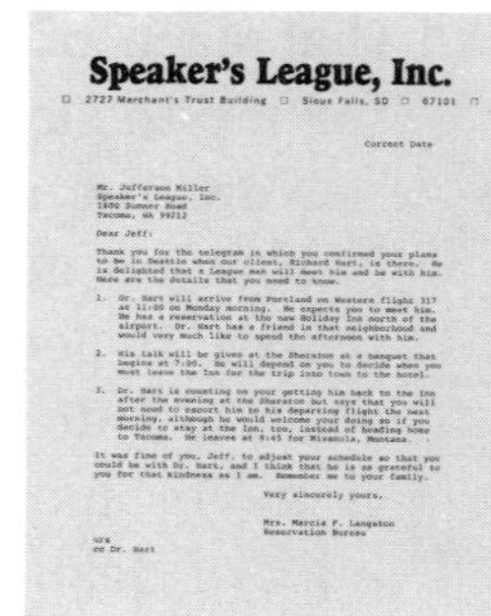

LONG (6-inch line) has over 200 words.

PLACEMENT TABLE
With date on line 15 and center at 50

BODY	PICA	ELITE
To 100 words	40 sp 30–75	50 sp 25–80
100–200 words	50 sp 25–80	60 sp 20–85
200–up words	60 sp 20–85	70 sp 15–90

a·i·m 107

GOALS ◦ *To control # (shift of 3).* ◦ *To control & (shift of 7).* ◦ *To type 143 words or more in 5 minutes within 5 errors.*

DIRECTIONS *Spacing 1. Line 60. Tab 5. K 28.*

WARMUP REVIEW

3 copies

The man did not buy the hat and the boy did not ask for it.	12
Jack Simmer's yellow quilts were not really that expensive.	12
They paid $10, $28, and $39 to Tom and $47 and $56 to Bill.	12

|1 |2 |3 |4 |5 |6 |7 |8 |9 |10 |11 |12

 # 3 KEY

Shift of 3

d3d3d d3d#d d#d#d Order #1131 is for 13# more of #13 nails.	12
John claims Order #31 is for 31#, but Order #32 is for 32#.	12
Who will get the blame if we do not find Order #3311 today? ◦	12

& 7 KEY

Shift of 7

j7j7j j7j&j j&j&j Jones & Sons buy from Wilson & Harris Co.	12
Please write to Dodd & Co., Smith & Sons, and Howe & Blake.	12
It is his duty to lend a hand on the Smith & Blake project. ◦	12

5-MINUTE GOAL TYPING

2 copies in 5 minutes

Spacing 1

	1	2
The & sign is a simple little squiggle that is used as	12	84
the word <u>and</u> in some company names. The & has a fancy name	25	97
that is not used often: ampersand.	33	105
	34	106
The # sign has more than one meaning. When it appears	46	118
before a number, like #33, it means <u>number</u>; when used after	60	132
a number, like 33#, it is meant as <u>pounds</u>.	71	143 ◦

|1 |2 |3 |4 |5 |6 |7 |8 |9 |10 |11 |12 SI 1.29FE

a·i·m 108

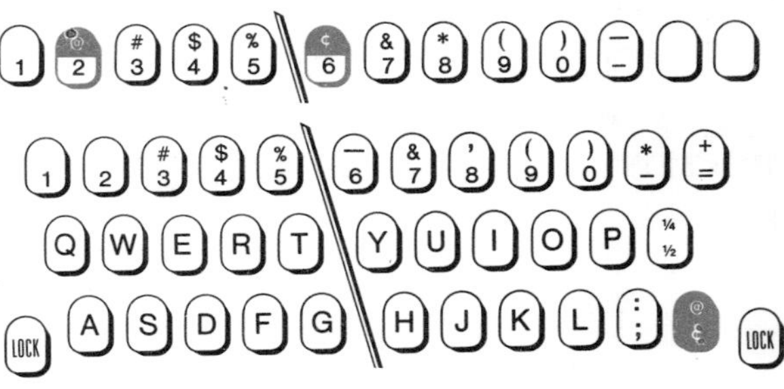

GOALS ◦ *To control ¢ (beside Sem key or shift of 6).* ◦ *To control @ (shift of ¢ or 2).* ◦ *To type 144 words or more in 5 minutes within 5 errors.*

DIRECTIONS *Spacing 1. Line 60. Tab 5. K 29.*

WARMUP REVIEW

3 copies

The man did buy the hat but the boy did not ask him for it.	12
Jeff quietly moved a dozen boxes last night by power truck.	12
Orr & Co. paid $10 on Invoice #28 and $39 on Invoice #4756.	12

|1 |2 |3 |4 |5 |6 |7 |8 |9 |10 |11 |12

a·i·m 158

5-MINUTE TW

3 copies of lines 3–7 in 5 minutes within 4 errors

JOB 158·1

REPORT PAGE 3
Line 6 inches
Tab 5

```
 1                                          Williams / Page 3          7
                                                                       9
 2  SOME OPTIONS                                                      12
 3       It is possible to summarize the broad principles in this  12 24
 4  way:  use double-spacing in formal reports, in reports that    24 36
 5  will be read by a critic, and in those in which space saving   37 48
 6  is not important; but use single-spacing in all reports that,  49 61
 7  for any reason, ought to be kept as short as can be.           ⚲60 72
 8       That statement leaves a great deal of room for options.      85
 9       If the employer says he wants a particular spacing used,     97
10  his saying so is reason enough for doing so.  If the author      109
11  or the typist wants to stretch a report, double-spacing will     121
12  stretch it.  If the wish is to shorten the report, single-       133
13  spacing will shorten it a great deal, naturally.                 143
14       A general guide would be this:  double-space any report     155
15  except when there is some special reason to single-space it.⚲    168
    |1   |2   |3   |4   |5   |6   |7   |8   |9   |10  |11  |12   SI 1.40N
```

a·i·m 159

GOAL ⚲ *To strengthen skill (180 words or more in 5 minutes within 4 errors) on easy material.*

DIRECTIONS *Spacing 1 for drills, 2 for TW. Line 60. Tab 5. For TW, use lines 17–36, page 166.*

WHEN YOU TYPE—

- Sit all the way back in the chair
- Sit erect, leaning forward slightly
- Set feet squarely on the floor
- Place ankles 6 to 8 inches apart
- Hold wrists very close together

WARMUP REVIEW

2 copies

```
1  We might get a bonus if the whole job is done by the fifth.    12
2  Four women quietly gave the sixth prize back to the judges.    12
3  Our discounts of 10%, 28%, 39%, 47%, and 56% vary too much.    12
   |1   |2   |3   |4   |5   |6   |7   |8   |9   |10  |11  |12
```

PREVIEW

2 copies

TW: page 166

```
4  dishwashing retrieve unison driver cannot ahead quite train    12
5  directions shuffled trouble locate family spark hotel after    12
6  hopefully apartment station suburb follow whole while brave    12
7  likely, place, eaten, sleep, that, why, you, all, and, out,    12
```

CHECK YOUR EYE CONTROL

- **New lines** started without looking up
- **Numbers** typed without looking up
- **Symbols** typed without looking up
- **Indenting** tabbed without looking up

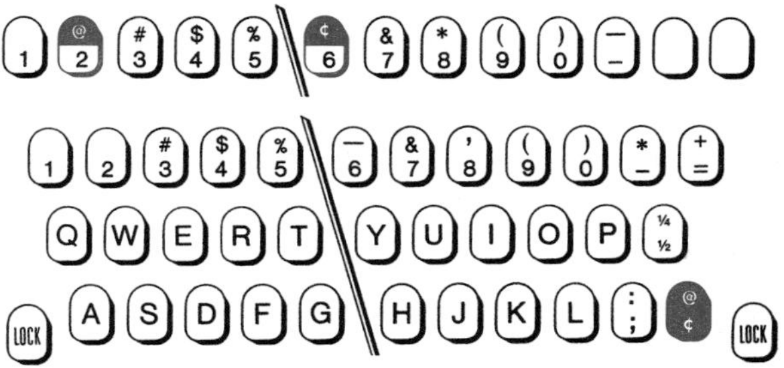

¢ KEY

Beside Sem Key or shift of 6.

2 copies

4M	;¢;¢; ;¢;¢; ;¢;¢; Is it 1¢ to 11¢ each, or 11¢ to 21¢ each?	12
4E	j6j6j j6j¢j j¢j¢j Is it 1¢ to 11¢ each, or 11¢ to 21¢ each?	12
5	I said we have too many 11¢ items and not enough 21¢ items.	12
6	Prices were 10¢, 28¢, 39¢, 47¢, and 56¢ per item, I'm told.	12

@ KEY

Shift of ¢ key or 2 key

7M	;¢;¢; ;¢;@; ;@;@; She asked you for 21 @ 11¢, not 11 @ 21¢.	12
7E	s2s2s s2s@s s@s@s She asked you for 21 @ 11¢, not 11 @ 21¢.	12
8	It ought to be better to buy 20 @ 15¢ than to buy 15 @ 20¢.	12
9	Try to get 10 @ 28¢, 39 @ 47¢, and 56 @ 56¢ sometime today.	12

5-MINUTE GOAL WRITING

2 copies in 5 minutes

Spacing 2

		1	2
10	The first order that Dixon & Zack received was for 100	12	84
11	of the new kits @ 40¢. The second order was for 200 of the	24	96
12	#6 kits @ 57¢. The company did not get any order for 1,000	36	108
13	or more of any one size for nearly a month, which was quite	48	120
14	a surprise. That order was for 1,200 of the #9 kits @ 38¢.	60	132
15	Joe Zack was disappointed. He had expected a better start.	72	144

|1 |2 |3 |4 |5 |6 |7 |8 |9 |10 |11 |12

a·i·m 109

GOALS To learn the arrangement of postal cards. To produce correctly typed postal cards.

DIRECTIONS *Spacing 1. Line 60. Tab none. WB 71–72.*

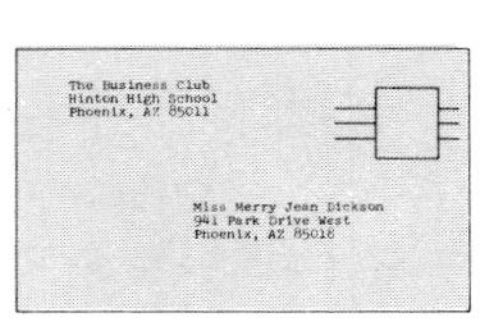

The Business Club
Hinton High School
Phoenix, AZ 85011

Miss Merry Jean Dickson
941 Park Drive West
Phoenix, AZ 85018

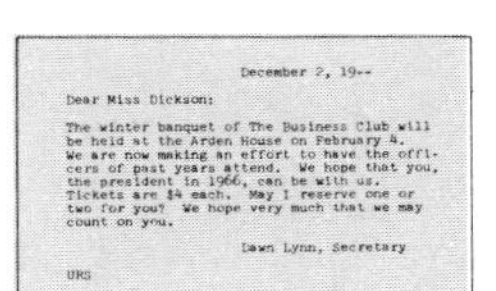

December 2, 19--

Dear Miss Dickson:

The winter banquet of The Business Club will be held at the Arden House on February 4. We are now making an effort to have the officers of past years attend. We hope that you, the president in 1966, can be with us. Tickets are $4 each. May I reserve one or two for you? We hope very much that we may count on you.

Dawn Lynn, Secretary

URS

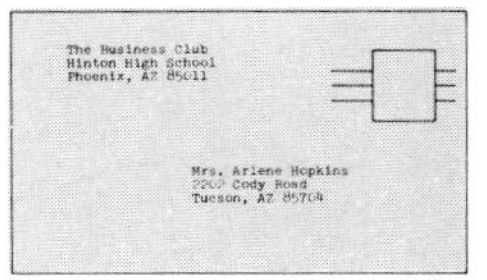

The Business Club
Hinton High School
Phoenix, AZ 85011

Mrs. Arlene Hopkins
2207 Cody Road
Tucson, AZ 85704

December 2, 19--

Dear Mrs. Hopkins:

The winter banquet of The Business Club will be held at the Arden House on February 4. We are now making an effort to have the officers of past years attend. We hope that you, the president of 1964, can be with us. Tickets are $4 each. May I reserve one or two for you? We hope very much that we may count on you.

Dawn Lynn, Secretary

URS

WARMUP REVIEW

1	The boy did ask the man for the hat and the man did get it.	12
2	Did Jeff quickly move away from the blazing box last night?	12
3	The separate items were tagged 10¢, 28¢, 39¢, 47¢, and 56¢.	12

|1 |2 |3 |4 |5 |6 |7 |8 |9 |10 |11 |12

Note that the a·i·m 156–158 report will make three pages, as illustrated here. Page 1 has a deep top margin. Page 2 is a full page. Page 3 is a short page.

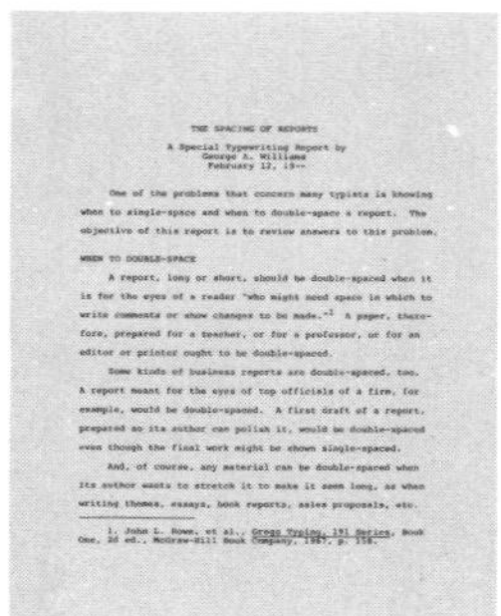

a·i·m 157

5-MINUTE TW

3 copies of lines 7–11 in 5 minutes within 4 errors

JOB 157·1

REPORT
PAGE 2
Line 6 inches
Tabs 5, 10

Williams / Page 2 7
9

WHEN TO SINGLE-SPACE 13

A report is single-spaced when a writer must save space, 26
or money, or time, or all three. Think of space: business 38
reports are kept on file for years, so use of single-spacing 50
to make reports slimmer can be a matter of real importance. 62

If a report is to be duplicated, fewer stencils will be 12 74
required if the report is single-spaced. More than the cost 24 86
of the stencils is involved. If there are fewer stencils, 36 98
less time and paper are needed for printing and collating and 48 110
fewer stamps are needed for copies that are to be mailed. 60 122

One book flatly states that business reports should be 134
presented in single-spacing: 140

> Because reports are ordinarily typed with many 153
> carbons, or duplicated, for wide distribution, they 164
> are usually single-spaced to save supplies, postage, 176
> time, filing space.[2] 183

Even if a report is double-spaced, some parts of it may 196
be shown in single-spacing. A second authority states: 207

> Single-space all special displays, such as 219
> headings that take two lines, quotations that will 230
> fill more than three typed lines, footnotes, list- 241
> ings, and so forth.[3] 248

Single-spacing is also used widely for routine, periodic 261
reports that are prepared more for the record (that is, to be 272
put on file) than for someone to read at once. 283

______________________ 287

2. Ibid., p. 219. 292

3. Alan C. Lloyd et al., <u>Typing 75 Basic</u>, McGraw-Hill 310
Book Company, 1970, p. 113. 317

SI 1.45N

ADDRESSING A POSTAL CARD

Address a postal card the same way you do a small envelope [review page 112]:

1. Single-space and block all lines.
2. Start the return address on line 3, $\frac{1}{2}$ inch from the left edge.
3. Type special directions, underscored, on line 9, $\frac{1}{2}$ inch from left edge.
4. Start addressee's name and address on line 12, 2 inches from the left edge.

Richard F. Carlson
Student Union Building
Reno, NV 89503

Mr. Donald W. Keane, Jr.
Apartment 3-C
1047 East Third Street
Reno, NV 89503

TYPING THE MESSAGE

Message side is typed as pictured here:

1. Use single-spacing.
2. Start date at center of line 3.
3. Align closing with the date.
4. Have side margins of about $\frac{1}{2}$ inch.

If you must save space, you may omit the blank line under the date and may omit unimportant details like the complimentary closing, reference initials, and handwritten signature.

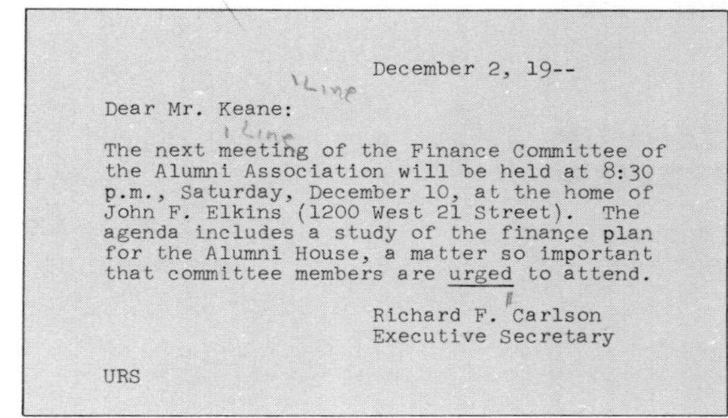

December 2, 19--

Dear Mr. Keane:

The next meeting of the Finance Committee of the Alumni Association will be held at 8:30 p.m., Saturday, December 10, at the home of John F. Elkins (1200 West 21 Street). The agenda includes a study of the finance plan for the Alumni House, a matter so important that committee members are <u>urged</u> to attend.

Richard F. Carlson
Executive Secretary

URS

JOB 109·1

POSTAL CARD
Workbook 71
or slip of paper
$5\frac{1}{2} \times 3\frac{1}{4}$
inches.

From The Business Club / Hinton High School / Phoenix, AZ 85011 / 11
To Miss Merry Jean Dickson / 941 Park Drive West / Phoenix 30
AZ 85018 *Today's date* / Dear Miss Dickson: / The winter banquet 55
of The Business Club will be held at the Arden House on Febru- 67
ary 4. We are now making an effort to have the officers of past 80
years attend. We hope that you, the president in 1966, can be 93
with us. Tickets are $4 each. May I reserve one or two for you? 106
We hope very much that we may count on you. / Dawn Lynn, 120
Secretary / URS 123

|1 |2 |3 |4 |5 |6 |7 |8 |9 |10 |11 |12 |13 |14 SI 1.29FE

JOB 109·2

POSTAL CARD
Workbook 71

Prepare another copy of Job 109·1, addressing it to Mrs. Arlene Hopkins, 2202 Cody Road, Tucson, AZ 85704. *She was the class president in 1964.* Make necessary changes.

a·i·m 110

GOALS *To produce two postal cards. To type 144 or more words in 5 minutes within 5 errors.*

DIRECTIONS *Spacing 1. Line 60. Tabs 5, center. WB 71–72.*

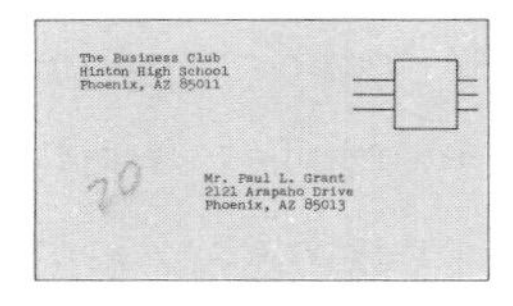

The Business Club
Hinton High School
Phoenix, AZ 85011

Mr. Paul L. Grant
2121 Arapaho Drive
Phoenix, AZ 85013

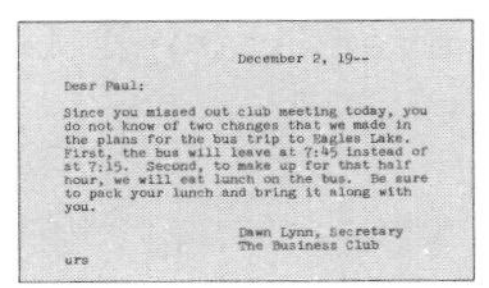

December 2, 19--

Dear Paul:

Since you missed out club meeting today, you do not know of two changes that we made in the plans for the bus trip to Eagles Lake. First, the bus will leave at 7:45 instead of at 7:15. Second, to make up for that half hour, we will eat lunch on the bus. Be sure to pack your lunch and bring it along with you.

Dawn Lynn, Secretary
The Business Club

urs

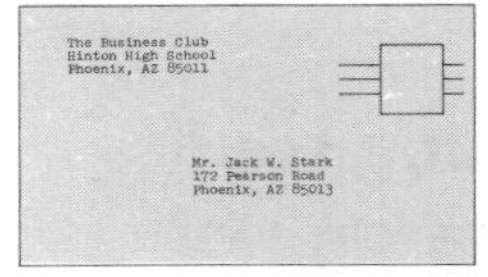

The Business Club
Hinton High School
Phoenix, AZ 85011

Mr. Jack W. Stark
172 Pearson Road
Phoenix, AZ 85013

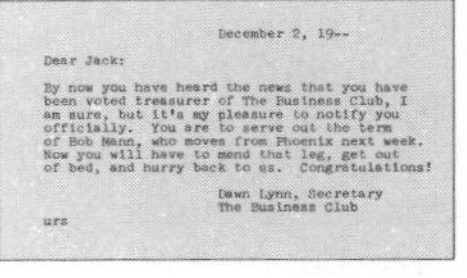

December 2, 19--

Dear Jack:

By now you have heard the news that you have been voted treasurer of The Business Club, I am sure, but it's my pleasure to notify you officially. You are to serve out the term of Bob Mann, who moves from Phoenix next week. Now you will have to mend that leg, get out of bed, and hurry back to us. Congratulations!

Dawn Lynn, Secretary
The Business Club

urs

WARMUP REVIEW

3 copies

```
The hat the man got was not the hat that the boy asked for.   12
Jeff quickly took away five dozen more boxes of light pens.   12
Walsh & Son collected bills of $10, $28, $39, $47, and $56.   12
```

|1 |2 |3 |4 |5 |6 |7 |8 |9 |10 |11 |12

PREPARE a·i·m WB 138

a·i·m 156–158

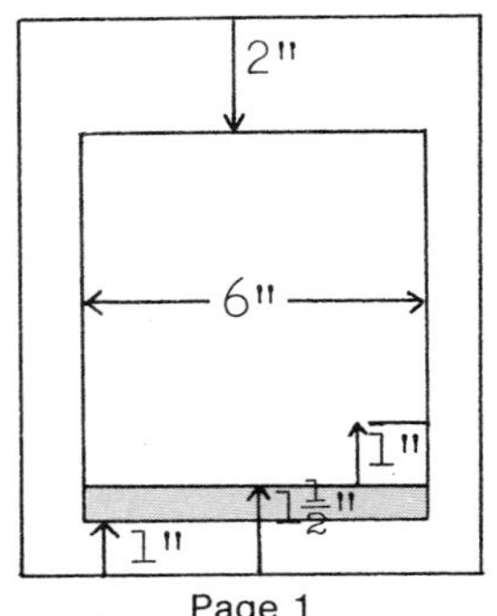

Page 1

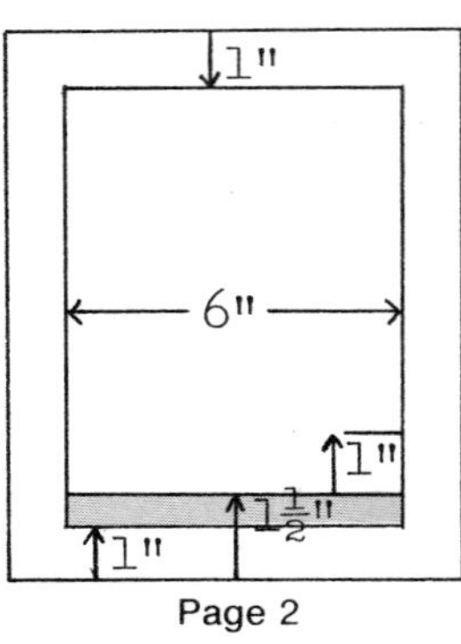

Page 2

GOALS *To type 180 words within 5 minutes and 4 errors on normal, repetitive material. To review the typing of a report with headings and footnotes.*

DIRECTIONS *Spacing 1 for drills, 2 for TW. Line 60. Tab 5. WB 139.*

WARMUP PREVIEW

2 copies in each a·i·m

A collating,[1] listings[2] printing[3] headings[4] spacing[5] needing[6] 12
B double-spacing, single-spacing, double-space, single-space, 12
C Could we six jeopardize their gunboat quickly by two moves? 12
D Take a 5-minute writing on paragraph 2 OR 3 below.

a·i·m 156

5-MINUTE TW
3 copies of lines 9–13 or lines 14–18 in 5 minutes within 4 errors

JOB 156·1

REPORT PAGE 1
Line 6 inches (60 pica or 70 elite)
Start 13 lines from top
Use visual guide Workbook 139
Review pages 141–146

1 THE SPACING OF REPORTS 13
2 A Special Typewriting Report by 34
3 *Use your name* George A. Williams 46
4 *Use today's date* February 12, 19-- 58
60
5 One of the problems that concerns many typists is knowing 72
6 when to single-space and when to double-space a report. The 84
7 objective of this report is to review answers to this problem. 97
99
8 WHEN TO DOUBLE-SPACE 103
9 A report, long or short, should be double-spaced when it 12 116
10 is for the eyes of a reader "who might need space in which to 25 128
11 write comments or show changes to be made."[1] A paper, there- 39 142
12 fore, prepared for a teacher, or for a professor, or for an 51 154
13 editor or printer, ought to be double-spaced. 60 163
14 Some kinds of business reports are double-spaced, too. 12 175
15 A report meant for the eyes of top officials of a firm, for 24 187
16 example, would be double-spaced. A first draft of a report, 36 199
17 prepared so its author can polish it, would be double-spaced, 49 211
18 even though the final work might be shown single-spaced. 60 223
19 And, of course, any material can be double-spaced when 235
20 its author wants to stretch it to make it seem long, as when 247
21 writing themes, essays, book reports, sales proposals, etc. 260
22 ______________ 264
23 1. John L. Rowe et al., Gregg Typing, 191 Series, Book 286
24 One, 2d ed., McGraw-Hill Book Company, 1967, p. 158. 296

SI 1.38N

5-MINUTE GOAL WRITING

Spacing 2

2 copies in 5 minutes

	1	2
If you were asked what you thought was the single most	12	84
frequent use of a postal card, you might say that you judge cards	25	97
are used most for personal notes. You probably don't know that	38	110
a dozen cards are mailed by business firms and by clubs and groups	51	123
for every card mailed by a person. As you might expect, the	64	136
postal card stream is absolutely endless.	72	144

|1 |2 |3 |4 |5 |6 |7 |8 |9 |10 |11 |12 |13 |14 SI 1.28FE

JOB 110·1

POSTAL CARD
WB 71 or slip of paper cut $5\frac{1}{2}$ x $3\frac{1}{4}$ inches

From The Business Club / Hinton High School / Phoenix, AZ 10
85011 *To* Mr. Paul L. Grant / 2121 Arapaho Drive / Phoenix, AZ 28
85013 / *Today's date* 40

Dear Paul: Since you missed our club meeting today, you do 54
not know of two changes that we made in the plans for the bus 66
trip to Eagles Lake. First, the bus will leave at 7:45 instead of 80
at 7:15. Second, to make up for that half hour, we will eat lunch 93
on the bus. Be sure to pack your lunch and bring it along with you. / 107
Dawn Lynn, Secretary / The Business Club / urs 115

SI 1.22E

JOB 110·2

POSTAL CARD
WB 71 or slip of paper cut $5\frac{1}{2}$ x $3\frac{1}{4}$ inches
Don't forget the date!

To Mr. Jack W. Stark / 172 Pearson Road / Phoenix, AZ 85013 13

Dear Jack: By now you have heard the news that you have 37
been voted treasurer of The Business Club, I am sure, but it's my 51
pleasure to notify you officially. You are to serve out the term 64
of Bob Mann, who moves from Phoenix next week. Now you will 77
have to mend that leg, get out of bed, and hurry back to us. 89
Congratulations! 92
Dawn Lynn, Secretary / The Business Club / urs 105

|1 |2 |3 |4 |5 |6 |7 |8 |9 |10 |11 |12 |13 |14 SI 1.28FE

GOAL *To build speed reserve (200 or more words in 5 minutes within 5 errors) on very easy copy.*

DIRECTIONS *Spacing 1 for drills, 2 for TW. Line 60. Tab 5.*

SPEED-MINDEDNESS

- Don't think "Speed!" (you'll jam the keys by trying too hard for speed).
- Do think "Smoo-o-othly" (it calms you, takes off the pressure).
- Do think about "feet on floor!" (keeps you from fretting, worrying).

WARMUP REVIEW

3 copies

```
They look for good jobs when they come here from your city.    12
Did she realize yellow quilts from Jackby's were expensive?    12
They ordered 10# of Hill's #28 and 39# each of #47 and #56.    12
|1   |2   |3   |4   |5   |6   |7   |8   |9   |10   |11   |12
```

ACCURACY DRIVE

See page 162. 180 or more words within 5 minutes and 4 errors.

When I take a business trip, I stay in good hotels. I 12
do not like to stay in private homes. Someone now and then 24
will urge me to stay at his home, but I know that the offer 36
is likely to be just a show of good will and that my friend 48
is holding his breath, not quite sure how he can explain to 60
his wife the importance of having this guest. I always let 72
my host off the hook at once, for I am no more anxious than 84
he to forego my long shower and half hour of reading before 96
I turn out the light and doze off to sleep. No, thank you. 108
When you stay at a hotel, you can do as you wish. You 120
can order up a late snack, take a quick nap if you have the 132
wish to do so, repack the luggage, walk around in your bare 144
feet, write a report, or read all night if the book is that 156
good. You can make a phone call just to see how the family 168
is, relax as long as you like in the tub, or snooze through 180
an hour or two of TV shows. But what is it like in a home? 192

|1 |2 |3 |4 |5 |6 |7 |8 |9 |10 |11 |12

a·i·m 159 ACCURACY DRIVE

(For use in a·i·m 159) See page 162.

In the first place, you have trouble finding the home. 12 | 204
Your host cannot take you, of course, because he has to zip 24 | 216
home ahead of you. If he lives in town, it is in an apart- 36 | 228
ment that your taxi driver cannot locate. If he lives in a 48 | 240
suburb, which is quite likely, the train he suggests is one 60 | 252
that, it turns out, runs just on Sundays. So you catch the 72 | 264
bus, and, of course, the directions he gave you for getting 84 | 276
from the station do not serve to get you from the bus stop. 96 | 288
When you do arrive, the host has hopefully given up on you. 108 | 300
The family has eaten, of course, but it is no trouble, 120 | 312
no trouble at all, to fix up something for you. So you eat 132 | 324
the cold food while the whole family sits there and watches 144 | 336
you, bite by bite. Eyes follow each crumb that falls, each 156 | 348
jiggle of the fork; and heads bend in quiet unison when you 168 | 360
lean over to retrieve a roll from the carpet. Things spark 180 | 372
a bit after you finish. There is a rush of dishwashing and 192 | 384
of packing little ones off to bed; but they do not fall off 204 | 396
to sleep, for they have been shuffled to vacate a bed. But 216 | 408
you are brave and try hard not to think of the lonely hotel 228 | 420
where there would be nothing to do but what you wish to do. 240 | 432

|1 |2 |3 |4 |5 |6 |7 |8 |9 |10 |11 |12

SI 1.17E

SPEED DRIVE

See page 109.

5-minute goal: 200 words within 5 errors

I doubt that there is a sabre that cuts so sharp, or a pain that hurts so much, or a pill so hard to get down deep as the agony of the occasion when a driver finds that he is on the wrong road. He mouths all the regular remarks, like the signs were wrong, were they not, or at least put in the wrong place; and the way that other car cut in front of him kept him from the lane he had to be in when he came off the bridge; and the map was wrong or at least was not readable. But all the while he knows deep inside: he made a mistake.

Some drivers can put up a brave front. They act as if they meant to be on the road where they are. They say that a close buddy from the state highway bureau said this was a fine shortcut; or that they had seen it on a map and always had a yen to try it; or that this area of the country ought to be seen from many views, and this was a new view, right? I admire the man who claims he has been on the road before; watch for a big lake in a mile, he says.

SI 1.13VE

|1 |2 |3 |4 |5 |6 |7 |8 |9 |10 |11 |12

ALTERNATE OR ADDITIONAL SPEED DRIVE

The pain is bad enough when you drive by yourself, but it is a whole lot worse when you have someone with you. He will never, never let you forget that you made the blunder. Ten years from now, even if you do not meet him once in all those years, he will recall what you did and ask if you can recall it, too; and if you see him a lot, it is much worse: you know that he thinks of the event even when he's silent.

If the witness is a member of your family, you will be getting off light if all you get is a jeer or two plus side remarks about who had told you so, or a question about your eyes and your sense of direction, plus a complete review of all those other times when this sort of thing had happened.

Of course there are two sides to each coin. The smart driver tells each rider what he is in charge of, like signs or maps or right turns or bridges or what have you; then if anything goes wrong, he just turns and glares at the person in charge of the thing that went wrong.

SI 1.13VE

a·i·m 154

WARMUP PREVIEW
Line 60
2 copies (A–C)

A Winner Girls Class Fred Anne Ruth Jack Anne Juan Lee Sue di 12
B organization leadership activities principal assembly store 12
C We six could quickly jeopardize their gunboat by two moves. 12
D Repeat the 5-minute timed writing, page 163.

|1 |2 |3 |4 |5 |6 |7 |8 |9 |10 |11 |12

JOB 154·1

OPEN TABLE
Column headings centered
Lines grouped in threes
Spacing 1
Tabs (2)
Review page 101.

WINNERS OF SCHOOL KEYS FOR 16
LEADERSHIP IN SCHOOL ACTIVITIES 37
 38
Awards Assembly, February 11, 19-- 59
 61

Winner	School Year	Principal Organization	
			88
Blaine, Richard	12	Debating Team	103
di Donne, Juan	11	Art League	111
June, Anne	12	Yearbook	118
Mills, Jack	12	French Club	128
North, Ruth Lee	11	Junior Class Play	138
Pream, Stanley	10	Student Council	146
Queens, George	12	Hi-Y	154
Rowe, Sue Anne	10	The Girls Club	163
Trescht, Fred	11	School Book Store⊙	172

CENTER CHECK → (June, Anne)

SI 1.37N

Key Line Blaine, Richard 123456 School Year 123456 Principal Organization

---

a·i·m 155

GOAL⊙ *To strengthen skill (180 or more words in 5 minutes within 4 errors) on easy material.*

DIRECTIONS *Spacing 1 for drills, 2 for TW. Line 60. Tab 5.*

WHEN YOU TYPE—

- Shoulders are level, relaxed, down
- Elbows are loosely close to body
- Wrists are low and close together
- Right thumb over middle of space bar
- Left thumb curled under forefinger

WARMUP REVIEW

2 copies

1 All of us want to get the work done by the sixth or eighth. 12
2 The judge quickly gave back six of the prizes to the women. 12
3 The checks for $10, $28, $39, $47, and $56 seem to be lost. 12

|1 |2 |3 |4 |5 |6 |7 |8 |9 |10 |11 |12

a·i·m 112

GOALS ⚲ *To construct symbols that are not on one's typewriter keyboard.* ⚲ *To know what each symbol means.*

DIRECTIONS *Spacing 2. Line 20.*

CONSTRUCTED SYMBOLS

- Typists do not need special symbols very often, but everyone expects the typist to be able to construct the characters shown below.

JOB 112·1

DISPLAY

Practice constructing each symbol as many times as necessary, using the procedures indicated in Column 3. Then center a double-spaced copy of the 23 display lines. ⚲

1	**Cents**	He charges 2¢	Small letter C, intersected by Diagonal
2	**Star**	☆ ☆ ☆ ☆ ☆	Capital A, typed over small letter V
3	**Caret**	They try/hard (so)	Underscore and Diagonal; center word above Diagonal
4	**Brackets**	He /Johnston/	Diagonals, with Underscores facing inside
5	**Roman numerals**	Chapter XVIII	Capitals of I, V, X, L, C, D, and M
6	**Pounds sterling**	£8 is English	Capital L, typed over small letter F
7	**Degrees**	Freezing--32°	Small letter O, raised slightly (turn cylinder by hand)
8	**Military zero**	Leave at Ø1ØØ	The regular O, intersected by a Diagonal
9	**Times, by**	What is 4 x 5	Expressed by the small letter X
10	**Equals**	11 x 11 = 121	Two Hyphens, one below the other (turn cylinder by hand)
11	**Divided by**	120 ÷ 10 = 12	Colon, intersected by Hyphen
12	**Plus**	87 + 18 = 105	Hyphen, intersected by Diagonal or Apostrophe
13	**Minus**	140 - 56 = 84	Expressed by a single Hyphen, space before and after
14	**Superiors**	$8^2 - 5^2 = 29^2$	Type number or letter above line (turn cylinder by hand)
15	**Inferiors**	H_2O is water.	Type number or letter below line (turn cylinder by hand)
16	**Square root**	$\sqrt{90000}$ is 300	Small V, off-positioned to meet Diagonal, followed by Underscores typed on line above
17	**Divide into**	45)9045 = 201	Right Parenthesis and Underscores
18	**Feet and inches**	Mary is 5' 2"	For feet, Apostrophe; for inches, Quotation Mark
19	**Minutes, seconds**	Time: 3' 15"	For minutes, Apostrophe; for seconds, Quotation Mark
20	**Ellipsis**	He . . . also He I	Three periods, spaced apart (but four periods if there is a sentence ending within the omitted material)
21	**Section**	§20. Symbols	Capital S, intersected by a raised capital S
22	**Paragraph**	¶21. Symbols	Capital P, intersected by the small letter L
23	**Bar graph line**	mmmmmmmmmmmmmmm	Small M, W, O, or X, typed in a solid row ⚲

OPTIONAL JOB 152·2

OPEN TABLE
Lines grouped in sixes
Spacing 1
Tabs (2)

These are the official abbreviations you should memorize and use.

TWO-LETTER STATE ABBREVIATIONS

Including Special Districts

AL Alabama	KY Kentucky	OH Ohio
AK Alaska	LA Louisiana	OK Oklahoma
AZ Arizona	ME Maine	OR Oregon
AR Arkansas	MD Maryland	PA Pennsylvania
CA California	MA Massachusetts	PR Puerto Rico
CO Colorado	MI Michigan	RI Rhode Island
CT Connecticut	MN Minnesota	SC South Carolina
DE Delaware	MS Mississippi	SD South Dakota
DC Dist. of Col.	MO Missouri	TN Tennessee
FL Florida	MT Montana	TX Texas
GA Georgia	NE Nebraska	UT Utah
GU Guam	NV Nevada	VT Vermont
HI Hawaii	NH New Hampshire	VA Virginia
ID Idaho	NJ New Jersey	VI Virgin Islands
IL Illinois	NM New Mexico	WA Washington
IN Indiana	NY New York	WV West Virginia
IA Iowa	NC North Carolina	WI Wisconsin
KS Kansas	ND North Dakota	WY Wyoming

CENTER CHECK → CT Connecticut

a·i·m 153

WARMUP PREVIEW
Line 60
2 copies

A Jeff Stan Jean Carl Jack Bill Herb Dick Phil Curt Mark Fred 12
B Microphones Assemblies Curtains Periods Lights During March 12
C By two quick moves, I could jeopardize six of the gunboats. 12
D Repeat the 5-minute timed writing, page 163.

JOB 153·1

OPEN TABLE
Column headings centered
Spacing 2
Tabs (3)
Review page 100.

STAGE CREWS 7

For Assemblies During the Month of March 33

35

Period	Lights	Microphones	Curtains	
First	Bob Carter	Jack Yahres	Bill Stoner	68
Second	Al Dumont	Herb Lin Kee	Kenny Clark	79
Third	Joe Bentley	Lew Freeman	Mac Thompson	91
Fourth	Sam Winters	Phil Austin	Rick Lloyd	102
Fifth	Tom Wincher	Stan Young	Ed Perkins	113
Sixth	Jeff Staff	Carl Balch	Curt Trane	124
Seventh	Jean de Pax	Mark Doyle	Chuck Reigel	136

(Header line: 57; CENTER CHECK → Third)

SI 1.35N

Key Line: Seventh 123456 Joe Bentley 123456 Herb Lin Kee 123456 Mac Thompson

a·i·m 113

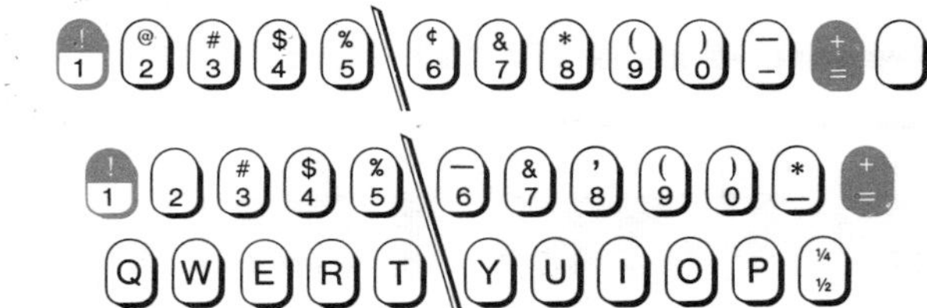

GOALS To control the exclamation mark, equals sign, and plus sign, wherever they are on the machine (or to construct them, if necessary). To type 146 words in 5 minutes within 5 errors on paragraph copy.

DIRECTIONS *Spacing 1. Line 60. Tab 5. K 30.*

WARMUP REVIEW

2 copies

1 Joe and the two men are not sure that you were on the path. 12
2 Jim saw five dozen extra quilts by peeking under the truck. 12
3 Try to speed up on 10 & 28 & 39 & 47 & 56, without looking. 12

|1 |2 |3 |4 |5 |6 |7 |8 |9 |10 |11 |12

NEW KEYS

2 copies of each line

The drills below give practice in controlling the !, =, and + keys. If you don't have these keys, construct them in the manner you practiced in a·i·m 112. If you have the keys, but if they are in a position different from that shown in the keyboard chart, create your own drills for lines 4, 7, and 8.

 **KEY**

Probably is shift of 1.

4 alala ala!a a!a!a Vote for Jones! Vote for Jones! Hurrah! 12
5 He said all he could say! What he said was not said right! 12
6 She counted it down: Five! Four! Three! Two! One! GO! 12

|1 |2 |3 |4 |5 |6 |7 |8 |9 |10 |11 |12

 **KEY**

Probably is beside hyphen.

7 ;=; ;=; ;=; F = 24, A = 29, M = 39, E = 44 (for 5 minutes). 12
8 ;=; ;+; ;+; He said to total a + b, then b + c, then c + d. 12
9 If a + b = 25 and b + c = 45, could a = 10, b = 15, c = 30? 12

|1 |2 |3 |4 |5 |6 |7 |8 |9 |10 |11 |12

SPEED SPRINTS

Each line: 3 copies or a 1-minute TW

10 All of us are glad that the six of you came over to see us! 12
11 Ricky said he must work on his plans for the next big show. 12
12 We know that they can do this work as well as we can do it! 12

5-MINUTE GOAL WRITING

Spacing 1

13 Dear Mrs. Quinn: We want to thank you for the $50 you have 13
14 contributed to the Xavier Fund. Only by the financial help that you 27
15 and people like you give us can the Fund keep on subsidizing the 40
16 vital research projects that we sponsor! 48
49
17 Dear Mr. Jacque: We want to thank you for the $25 you have 62
18 contributed to the Xavier Fund. Only by the financial help that you 76
19 and people like you give us can the Fund keep on subsidizing the 89
20 vital research projects that we sponsor! 97
98
21 Dear Miss Finch: We want to thank you for the $10 you have 111
22 contributed to the Xavier Fund. Only by the financial help that you 125
23 and people like you give us can the Fund keep on subsidizing the 138
24 vital research projects that we sponsor! 146

|1 |2 |3 |4 |5 |6 |7 |8 |9 |10 |11 |12 |13 |14 SI 1.36N

a·i·m 152–154

GOALS *To type 180 words within 5 minutes and 4 errors on easy, repetitive material. To review the typing of "open" tables.*

DIRECTIONS *Spacing 1 for drills, 2 for TW. Line 60. Tab 5.*

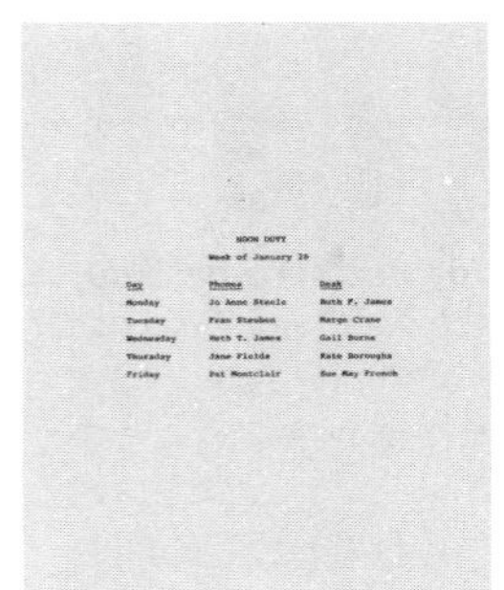

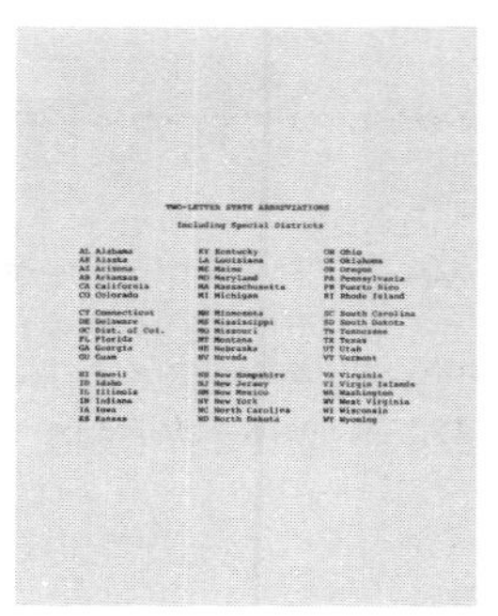

WARMUP REVIEW

2 copies

1 His goal is to get the work done by the sixth of the month. 12
2 Six of the women quietly gave the prizes back to the judge. 12
3 Try to locate reports #10, #28, #39, #47, and #56 for them. 12

|1 |2 |3 |4 |5 |6 |7 |8 |9 |10 |11 |12

5-MINUTE TW

3 copies in 5 minutes
Spacing 2

4 It does not require much time or effort to adjust mar- 12
5 gin and tab stops for tables. Whether you have two columns 24
6 or a dozen, the steps are the same. All you do is pick the 36
7 longest word or item in each column and backspace to center 48
8 the words or items with six blank spaces left between them. 60

|1 |2 |3 |4 |5 |6 |7 |8 |9 |10 |11 |12 SI 1.25E

JOB 152-1

OPEN TABLE
Column headings blocked
Spacing 2
Tabs (2)
Review page 99

Remember: Column heads may be blocked if table is routine and no head is wider than its column.

LINE 25

NOON DUTY 6

Week of January 20 ↓3 19

21

Day	Phones	Desk	
Monday	Jo Anne Steele	Ruth F. James	40
Tuesday	Fran Steuben	Marge Crane	47
Wednesday	Ruth T. James	Gail Burns	56
Thursday	Jane Fields	Kate Boroughs	65
Friday	Pat Montclair	Sue May French	74

(Column headings line: 31; CENTER CHECK → at Monday/Tuesday)

SI 1.31FE

Key Line Wednesday123456Jo Anne Steele123456Sue May French

a·i·m 114

GOALS ⚲ *To type 147 words in 5 minutes within 5 errors.* ⚲ *To align words beside words already printed on the paper.* ⚲ *To learn what fill-in form postal cards are and how to use them.* ⚲ *To fill in two cards.*

DIRECTIONS *Spacing 1. Line 60. Tab 5. WB 73.*

November 17, 19--

Dear Miss Garvey:

We want to thank you for your contribution of

$10

to the Xavier Fund. It is the financial help given us by people like you that enables the Fund to continue to subsidize the many vital research projects that we sponsor.

THE XAVIER FUND, INC.

URS

WARMUP PREVIEW

2 copies

1 Two men said you were on the path, but Joe did not see you. 12
2 variable printed slowly spacer button bottom (knob) you may 12
3 May brought back five or six dozen pieces of queer jewelry. 12
4 The boy was 10 years old. The men were 28, 39, 47, and 56. 12

|1 |2 |3 |4 |5 |6 |7 |8 |9 |10 |11 |12

5-MINUTE GOAL WRITING

Spacing 1

2 copies in 5 minutes

		1	2
5	When you wish to type a word alongside a printed word,	12	86
6	you may need to turn the paper so that the line of printing	24	98
7	will be a little bit higher or lower. To adjust the paper,	36	110
8	press the variable spacer (the button in the left knob) and	48	122
9	turn the left knob slowly, a tiny bit at a time, until your	60	134
10	line of typing is even with the <u>bottom</u> of the printing.	73	147 ⚲

SI 1.35N

USING THE ALIGNING SCALE

Problem: M ss Stil man
Wrong: M^{i}ss Stil^{l}man
Right: Miss Stillman

When you insert paper and must align it with something already printed or typed on the page, you must skillfully use the *aligning scale,* under the line of typing on each side of the printing point. Right now, type the whole alphabet:

1. Note the amount of space between the typing and the top of the scale.

2. Note how closely the vertical lines on the scale point to the center of letters (check with i, capital i, l, v, T, or period).

If, after inserting paper, you find you must raise or lower the paper a bit, press the *variable spacer* (button in left cylinder knob) while you slowly turn the knob.

If you must shift the paper a bit to left or right, depress the paper release, shift paper, restore the release. ⚲

Practice Take out your paper, reinsert it, type over the same alphabet.

FORM CARDS

On a fill-in form card like the one shown above, type the address side and then—

1. Type date (start center of line 3).

2. Type salutation (align it with start of the printing, a double-space above the body of the message (align with the use of the aligning scale).

3. If insertions are to be made in open spaces in the message, center them (by estimate) in the available space.

4. Add reference initials whenever the card has enough room for them. ⚲

Practice Using the top two form cards on Workbook 73, or typing a complete message (like lines 21–24, page 120) on a paper slip cut to card size ($5\frac{1}{2}$ x $3\frac{1}{4}$), acknowledge:

Job 114·1 Miss Jean Finch / 2121 Alamo Drive / Tucson, AZ 85702 / gave $25. ⚲

Job 114·2 Mr. Arthur Gittins / 616 Sixth Avenue / Phoenix, AZ 85025 / $15. ⚲

a·i·m 151

GOAL *To strengthen skill (180 or more words in 5 minutes within 4 errors) on very easy material.*

DIRECTIONS *Spacing 1 for drills, 2 for TW. Line 60. Tab 5. Record best 5-minute score on WB 133.*

WHEN YOU TYPE—

- Feet are apart, flat on the floor
- Back is erect, is leaning forward
- Body is handspan from machine, is centered opposite the J key
- Hands are low, nearly touching

WARMUP REVIEW

2 copies

1 Our goal is to get the job done by the eighth of the month. 12
2 These women quietly gave back the prizes of the six judges. 12
3 Be sure to check pages 10, 28, 39, 47, and 56 of the novel. 12

|1 |2 |3 |4 |5 |6 |7 |8 |9 |10 |11 |12

ROUTINE FOR ACCURACY DRIVE

Step 1. Pretest Copy the first paragraph within 3 minutes, with 2 or fewer errors. If you succeed, omit Step 2 and advance to Step 3.

Step 2. Buildup Turn to the drills for your speed range in Supplement 2 (on page 275 and following) and produce (a) 5 copies each of 3 speed lines if you met the accuracy goal in Step 1, or (b) 5 copies of a set of 3 accuracy lines if you did not achieve the accuracy goal.

Step 3. Sustained Writing Take one or (if you omitted Step 2) two 5-minute writings. Start with line 4. Reach or surpass the goal of this a·i·m (180 words within 5 minutes and 4 errors).

ACCURACY DRIVE FOR 5 MINUTES

4 Of all the kinds of work that a typist may do, what is 12
5 the job that you like best? Do you like to type a table or 24
6 turn out a letter, or what? If you put that question to an 36
7 office typist, you might get more votes for tables than for 48
8 any of the other things that have to be typed. There are a 60
9 number of points for such a choice. Most tables are short, 72
10 with a dozen lines at most. Most tables have just three or 84
11 four columns; it is rare to see six or more. You might say 96
12 that you vote for tables because they are so quick to type. 108
13 It was not always so. There used to be a time when it 120
14 took a lot of thought and effort to plan a table. In those 132
15 days typists thought that the space between the columns had 144
16 to be equal to the space in each margin, and so they had to 156
17 do a lot of math to plan the spacing. Now we realize there 168
18 should not be more than six spaces between the columns, and 180
19 so the math is gone. We treat the job as a task that is to 192
20 be centered, and we get the task done on the backspace key. 204

|1 |2 |3 |4 |5 |6 |7 |8 |9 |10 |11 |12

SI 1.14VE

a·i·m 115

GOALS *To type 148 or more words in 5 minutes within 5 errors, using an alphabetic note. To complete fill-ins on printed form postal cards.*

DIRECTIONS *Spacing 1. Line 60. Tab 0. WB 73.*

HINTON HIGH SCHOOL LIBRARY
Date: November 18, 19--

Charles Aluumbo:

Our records show that the following materials are charged to your name and are now overdue:

TIME magazine, June 14, 1971
Wells' TIME MACHINE

Please return these at once and come prepared to pay the fine of 5 cents a day per item.

Mary Howard, Librarian

URS

WARMUP PREVIEW

2 copies

They will find some more work when they have done your job.	12
subsidizing contributed research projects sponsor vital can	12
James Boxell, the banquet speaker, analyzed a few carvings.	12
The sheets measured 10 x 28, 10 x 39, 10 x 47, and 10 x 56.	12

|1 |2 |3 |4 |5 |6 |7 |8 |9 |10 |11 |12

5-MINUTE GOAL WRITING

Spacing 1
2 copies in
5 minutes

	1	2
Dear Mr. Quinette:	4	78
	5	79
We want to thank you for the $100 that you have contributed	17	91
to the Xavier Fund. Only by the financial help that people	29	103
like you give us can the Fund keep on subsidizing the vital	41	115
research projects that we sponsor. We will enter your name	53	127
in the honor roll of the Golden Club and see that copies of	65	139
our research findings are mailed to you.	73	148

SI 1.32FE

FORM CARDS

For these Jobs, use the printed library overdue cards on WB 73, or type the following message on paper slips cut to card size ($5\frac{1}{2}$ x $3\frac{1}{4}$ inches): Dear . . . Our records show that the following are charged to your name and are now overdue: . . . Please return them at once and come prepared to pay the fine of 5 cents a day per item. Hinton High School Library. School Library.

Job 115·1 Notify Mr. Charles Aluumbo / 164 San Luis Drive / Phoenix, AZ 85024 / that he has two overdues: **TIME** magazine for June 14, 1971 and Wells' **TIME MACHINE**.

Job 115·2 Notify Miss Elizabeth Hetra / 1600 West 18 Street / Phoenix, AZ 85017 / that she has two overdue books: Poe's **SELECTED SHORT STORIES** and Tarkington's **PENROD AND SAM**.

a·i·m 116

GOALS *To build speed reserve (200 or more words in 5 minutes within 5 errors) on very easy copy.*

DIRECTIONS *Spacing 1 for drills, 2 for TW. Line 60. Tab 5.*

FINGERS CURVED

- Curl fingers so you type on the tips, almost on the nails.
- Keep fingers clenched, as though pulling on a heavy bar.
- Keep hands and arms still; do the key stroking with the fingers.

WARMUP REVIEW

3 copies

They look over good jobs with fine pay when they come here.	12
Pete quickly froze the egg mixtures in five old brown jars.	12
I scored cars 10 and 28, then I scored cars 39, 47, and 56.	12

Overview

This point in the first-year typewriting program is normally the start of the second semester.

The new term opens with a review.

A review will help any newcomers (who may have started their typing course elsewhere or with a different book) understand the a·i·m plan of this book, the terminology it uses, and so on.

A review will help everyone if the second semester happens to occur in the fall, after a summer's layoff from the technicalities of typing.

And a review is a good idea anyhow, because it lets everyone concentrate on clearing up any points of confusion that occurred during the first term.

So this is a review. A review with a great many drill sessions for accuracy, because in Part Seven you are to reduce your errors in 5 minutes from 5 to 4. In Part Seven every fourth a·i·m is a drill lesson.

Performance Goals

When you finish the 20 a·i·m sessions in Part Seven and take the test on pages 178 and 179, you should be able to demonstrate as follows:

1. Technicalities You will score 85 or more percent correct (that's 5 percent higher than before) on an objective test covering the technical information you will review in Part Seven.

2. Production You will type in proper form and at a speed not less than 70 percent of your straight-copy speed (a) the first page of a long report, with title, heading, subheading, etc., to be displayed, from complete but unarranged copy; (b) an average-length business letter, from complete but unarranged copy; (c) a memorandum, on a printed business form if you have the Workbook but otherwise on plain paper, from indicative but partly unarranged material; and (d) a table with oversize column headings, from print copy that requires your setting up the problem completely.

3. Skill You will type at least 180 words in 5 minutes (190–200 is more likely) within 4 errors (that's down one error from previously!) on paragraph copy that requires your listening for the bell in order to make line-ending decisions.

Routines and Procedures

Accuracy Drives To help you improve your accuracy, a special routine has been developed for you to use in accuracy drives in a·i·m numbers 151, 155, 159, and 163. The routine, which is explained on the next page (page 162), combines the speed and remedial practice of prior Parts of the book. You take a pretest for 3 minutes, then a remedial-drill buildup for several minutes, and then a 5-minute let's-get-accuracy timed writing. The selections start very easy, and gradually become stiffer until they are normal at last.

Doubles, Triples More combined a·i·m groupings are coming up in order that you may run together quick sequences on tables, letters, etc. The production work will be executed in the same three-step manner that you are familiar with—a warmup preview, a timing (usually on production material), then production of a problem task.

SPEED DRIVE

See page 109.

5-minute goal: 200 words within 5 errors

The six of us found a lane that led to a quiet lake in the woods. The lake was not very big, as far as size goes, but it looked as if it were loaded with fish and just ached for some kind souls like us to help reduce its load. Well, we had come with some such kind thought in mind, and before you could think twice, the fellows were getting the fishing lines dressed. Before the lines got wet, though, a smiling old man came along. I asked him if we were allowed to fish there, and he said that no one would mind at all if we did.

The sun was up just a little, so it must not have been more than eight or nine in the morning when the six sets of lines first hit the water. We laughed when Jim snagged the old bucket and when Bob lost the first hook to a hidden log that, as we told him, must have been waiting for him for at least two or three years. We had no luck at all that morning, though, and when we got a whiff of the bacon that Nick had sizzling, we knocked off for lunch. SI 1.07VE

|1 |2 |3 |4 |5 |6 |7 |8 |9 |10 |11 |12

ALTERNATE OR ADDITIONAL SPEED DRIVE

All during lunch, we joshed each other about the great mess of trout on which we were not dining. We spoke of its fine quality and we agreed that Jim had won first prize for his bucket since it was the only thing caught. We had high spirit when we went back to our rods and reels and the wise old trout to which we would now show no mercy, none at all.

But the old trout stayed wise and out of reach, and by late afternoon most of us were looking a bit anxious. When supper was ready, it was not quite as zestful as lunch was. While we were eating, along came the man who had told us we could fish in the lake. He asked us whether we had had any luck. We said we had had quite a lot of it, all bad. Then he laughed and said he guessed that, by now, we knew why no one would mind if we fished there: There weren't any fish.

You might think that we would be angry, but we were so relieved to find we had not been at fault that we just fell back and laughed until our sides ached. SI 1.07VE

Speaker's League, Inc.

☐ 2727 Merchant's Trust Building ☐ Sioux Falls, SD ☐ 67101 ☐

4

8

TEST 6-D

BLOCKED LETTER
Body 179 words
Line 5 inches
Tabs 5, center
Workbook 124

Mr. Richard L. Hart 12
Central Colorado College 17
2300 Appletree Drive 21
Denver, CO 80211 24

25

Dear Dr. Hart: 29

30

Let me congratulate you on the success of your great tour in 42
the Northwest. We have received great praises for all your 54
presentations, and these praises have come not only from the 65
persons who were your hosts at the colleges you visited but 78
also from the League men. Darrell Da vis, our man in Montana, 89
wrote us that-- 92

93

> Dr. Hart is a dynamo! I wish I knew how he builds up 101
> his stamina. I was with him for about a day, you 112
> know. I pushed some buttons and drove a fewmiles 123
> He talked and performed hours on end. He was still 134
> going strong when he boarded his plane, while I 145
> wearily crept home to a week end of recuparting. He 156
> work me out. 162

163

Tim O'Leary, our man in Utah, has warned be there would be 175
more requests for your services, as a result of the tip you 187
have just taken he is right. Al ready we have have gotten 199
two new requests. One of them is from SantaFe, and one is 210
from Phoenix. 213

214

Would you think of taking a trip to the South west? Say, in 225
6 weeks or so? 228

229

Very sincerely yours, 236

239

Mrs. Marcia F. Langston 246
Reservations Bureau 252

urs 253

SI 1.26FE

 117

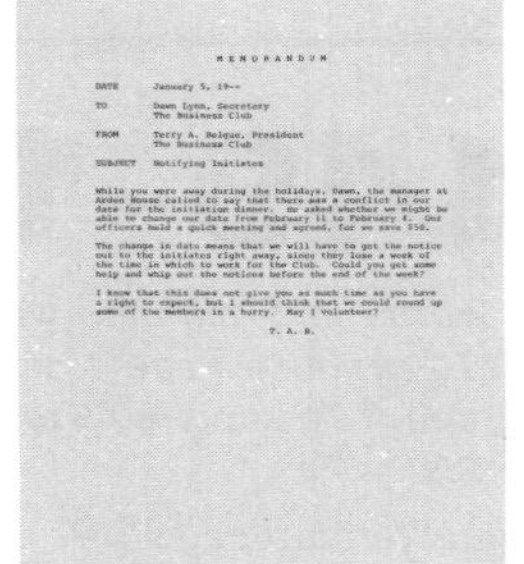

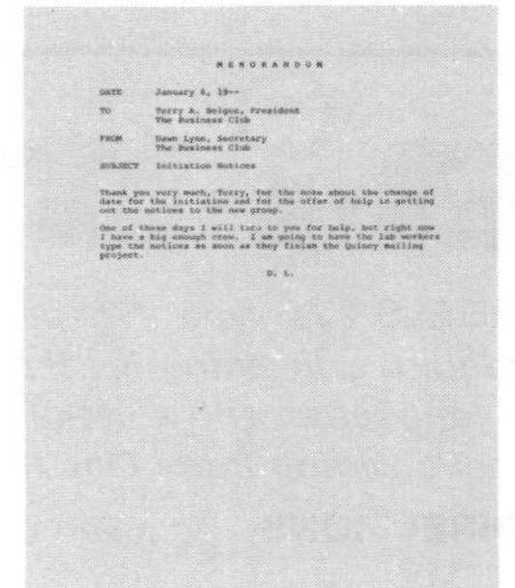

GOALS *To learn how to arrange a fully-typed memorandum. To produce a memorandum. To type 148 or more words of message context in 5 minutes within 5 errors.*

DIRECTIONS *Spacing 1. Line 60. Tabs 10, center.*

WARMUP PREVIEW

3 copies

1	They will look for some good jobs when they come over here.	12
2	initiation volunteer initiates holidays February notice the	12
3	Had Jeff's size helped him to win quickly over Gene Baxter?	12
4	There were 10 to 28 members in 1939 and 47 members in 1956.	12
	1 2 3 4 5 6 7 8 9 10 11 12	

OPTIONAL 5-MINUTE GOAL WRITING

Lines 12–24
Tab center

JOB 117·1

MEMORANDUM
Heading spread center 7 lines from the top
Line 60 spaces
Tabs 10, center
Signature initials start at center

5	M E M O R A N D U M ↓3		12
			14
6	DATE January 5, 19--		19
			20
7	TO Dawn Lynn, Secretary		26
8	The Business Club		31
			32
9	FROM Terry A. Belgue, President		39
10	The Business Club		43
			44
11	SUBJECT Notifying Initiates ↓3		51
			53
12	While you were away during the holidays, Dawn, the manager at	12	65
13	Arden House called to say that there was a conflict in our	24	77
14	date for the initiation dinner. He asked whether we might be	37	89
15	able to change our date from February 11 to February 4. Our	49	102
16	officers held a quick meeting and agreed, for we save $50.	61	114
		62	115
17	The change in date means that we will have to get the notice	74	127
18	out to the initiates right away, since they lose a week of	86	139
19	the time in which to work for the Club. Could you get some	98	151
20	help and whip out the notices before the end of the week?	110	163
		111	164
21	I know that this does not give you as much time as you have	123	176
22	a right to expect, but I should think that we could round up	135	188
23	some of the members in a hurry. May I volunteer?	144	197
		145	198
24	T. A. B.	148	201
	1 2 3 4 5 6 7 8 9 10 11 12		SI 1.36N

Office-Style Memorandum Typed on Plain Paper

a·i·m 149–150

GOALS ⚲ *To type 175 or more words in 5 minutes within 5 errors on copy requiring listening for the bell.* ⚲ *To produce Page 1 of a report.* ⚲ *To produce a long letter with a set-off paragraph.* ⚲ *To score 80% or higher on an objective test covering Parts One through Six.*

DIRECTIONS *As given in margin. Warmup page 157.*

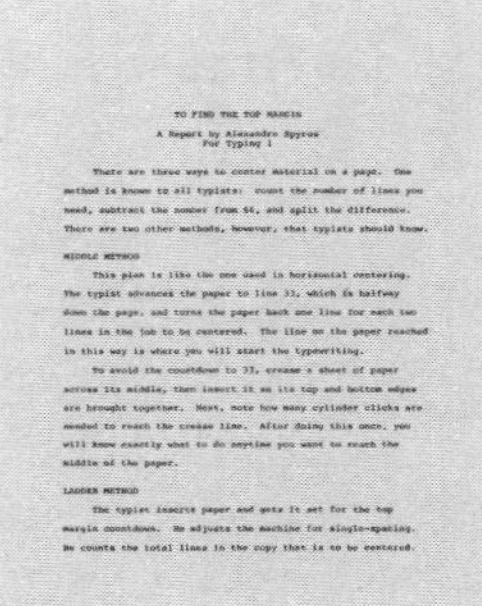

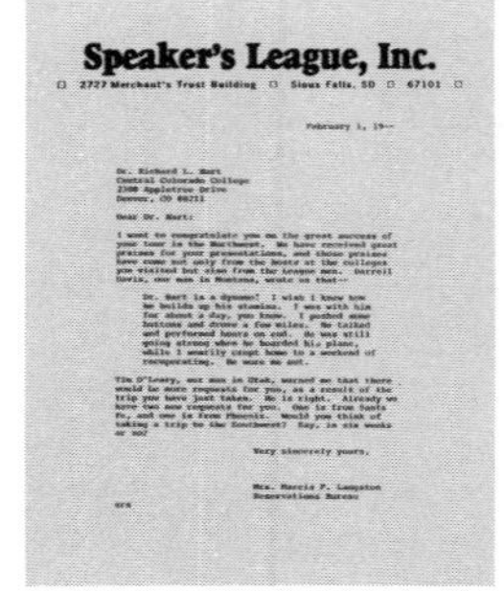

Speaker's League, Inc.

2727 Merchant's Trust Building Sioux Falls, SD 67101

TEST 6-A

Take a general information test. It may be the one on Workbook pages 119–120 or a similar test that your teacher may give you or may dictate to you.

TEST 6-B

5-MINUTE TW
Line 50, Tab 5
Spacing 2
Omit lines 1, 6, and 17
Workbook 121

TO FIND THE TOP MARGIN / A Report by [Your Name] / For Typing I ..
There are three ways to center material on a page. One method 13
is known to all typists: count the number of lines you need, sub- 27
tract the number from 66, and split the difference. There are two 40
methods, however, that typists should know. 50

MIDDLE METHOD ..
This plan is like the one used in horizontal centering. The typist 65
advances the paper to line 33, which is halfway down the page, and 78
turns the paper back one line for each two lines in the job to be 91
centered. The line on the paper reached in this way is where you 105
will start the typewriting. 110
To avoid the countdown to 33, crease a sheet of paper across its 124
middle, then insert it so its top and bottom edges are brought 137
together. Next, note how many cylinder clicks are needed to reach 150
the crease line. After doing this once, you will know exactly what 164
to do anytime you want to reach the middle of the paper. ⚲ 175

LADDER METHOD ...
The typist inserts paper and gets it set for the top margin count- 189
down. He adjusts the machine for single-spacing. He counts the 202
total lines in the copy that is to be centered. If the count is an odd 217
number, such as 41, he increases it to one more, so that it will be 231
an even number, like 42. 236
Next the typist counts by twos, like 44, 46, 48, and so on, all the 250
way to 66. He returns the carriage as he says or thinks each num- 263
ber. As he says 44, for example, he returns the carriage; as he says 277
46, he returns it again. In this way the paper is advanced to where 291
the typing will begin. 295

|1 |2 |3 |4 |5 |6 |7 |8 |9 |10 |11 |12 |13 |14 SI 1.28FE

TEST 6-C

REPORT PAGE 1
(Type only as much as you would put on page 1.)
Line 6 inches
Spacing 2
Tabs 5, center
Heading: line 1
Sideheadings: lines 6, 17
Workbook 123

OPTIONAL JOB 117·2

MEMORANDUM
Plain paper
Line 60 spaces
Tabs 10, center

M E M O R A N D U M ↓3 / DATE January 6, 19-- / TO Terry A. 22
Belgue, President / The Business Club / FROM Dawn Lynn, Sec- 37
retary / The Business Club / SUBJECT Initiation Notices ↓3 51
Thank you very much, Terry, for the note about the change of 64
date for the initiation and for the offer of help in getting out 78
the notices to the new group. 84
One of these days I will turn to you for help, but right now I 98
have a big enough crew. I am going to have the lab workers type 111
the notices as soon as they finish the Quincy mailing project. / D. L. 126

|1 |2 |3 |4 |5 |6 |7 |8 |9 |10 |11 |12 |13 |14 SI 1.47FH

PREPARE a·i·m WB 75–76

a·i·m 118

GOALS *To learn how to arrange memorandums on printed stationery. To produce a correctly typed memo on printed stationery. To type 149 or more words in 5 minutes within 5 errors.*

DIRECTIONS *Spacing 1. Line 60. Tabs as directed. WB 77.*

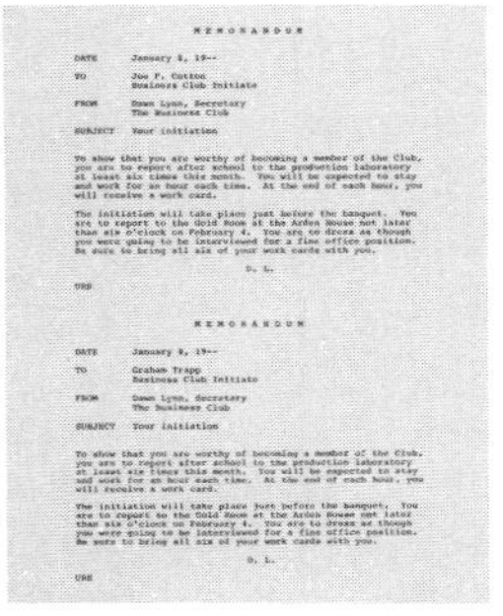

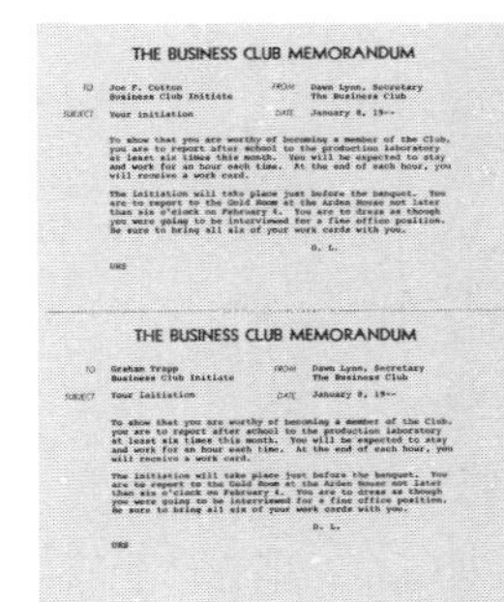

WARMUP REVIEW

3 copies

```
They must and they will come back here with some more cash.   12
Jeff's size had helped him to win quickly over Gene Baxter.   12
Bob had 10 to help his 28, but you had 39 to help 47 to 56.   12
|1  |2  |3  |4  |5  |6  |7  |8  |9  |10  |11  |12
```

PRINTED FORMS

Printed forms are stationery on which words, spaces, and/or lines are positioned to show where to insert information.

Interoffice memos are messages between persons or departments in the same company or organization. They may be typed on plain paper (page 124) or on printed forms (page 126). When a memo form is used:

A. Printed guide words show where to type names, date, and subject in the heading. The insertions should align at the bottom with the printing (use the variable spacer in the left cylinder knob for slight adjustments). Leave 2 or 3 spaces between the printed and the typed words. If one guide appears below another, align their insertions at the same margin stop or tab stop.

B. Separate the heading and body by 2 blank lines (or 3 if the message is very short).

C. Set margins: The left one is determined by the position of the heading guide words. Set the right stop to make the right margin about the same width as the left one.

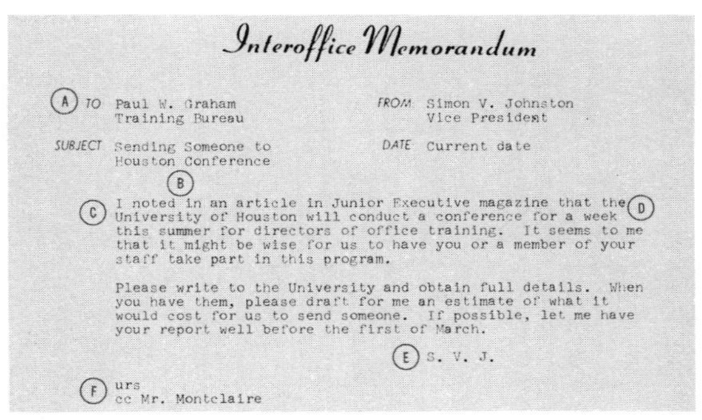

Interoffice Memorandum

(A) TO Paul W. Graham
Training Bureau

FROM Simon V. Johnston
Vice President

SUBJECT Sending Someone to
Houston Conference

DATE Current date

(B)

(C) I noted in an article in Junior Executive magazine that the (D) University of Houston will conduct a conference for a week this summer for directors of office training. It seems to me that it might be wise for us to have you or a member of your staff take part in this program.

Please write to the University and obtain full details. When you have them, please draft for me an estimate of what it would cost for us to send someone. If possible, let me have your report well before the first of March.

(E) S. V. J.

(F) urs
cc Mr. Montclaire

Interoffice Memo

D. Single-space the message body.

E. The closing consists of the writer's title, initials, or name (as he prefers), aligned under the dates 2 lines below the body. If the writer wishes to sign or initial the memo in his own handwriting (not usually the case), type the closing 4 lines below the body.

F. Reference initials, enclosures, etc., are used just as in letters.

The Dommar Company

5650 West Fremont Street • Atlanta, Georgia • 30319

TEST PREP 4

BLOCKED LETTER
Body 176
Line 5 inches
Tabs 5, center
Workbook 117

February 5, 19-- 10

14

Mr. Mowrey Coe, Director 19
Southern Ads, Inc. 23
7333 West 14 ~~Ave.~~ Street 26
Atlanta, GA ~~Georgia~~ 30303 30

31

Dear Mr. ~~Coe~~ Mowrey: 34

35

Ever since the meeting at which ~~all of us~~ we talked about 45
the theme of our spring campaign, I have been thinking 54
about the workding of the first paragraph. It seems to 67
me that it might be better ~~if worded~~ like this: 75

76

> What is space? To a housewife, space is an 86
> empty cupboard. To a scientist, space is the 95
> black void between planets. To us at Dommar, 105
> ~~however~~ though, space is business. 113

114

After reading such a ~~fine~~ paragraph, almost anyone will 127
ask, "How can space be a business"? Thus, a reader is then 138
drawn in to the description of how we help industry to 149
solve spa ce problems of a ~~hundred~~ thousand kinds. 158

159

I am not a copy writer and I know it; yet, I feel there 170
is some worth in this humane approach. May I have ~~the~~ 180
~~benefit of~~ your comments on the whole idea? 187

188

Sincerely yours, 192

195

John Adams, Manager 200
Promotion Department 205

206

urs 207

208

PS: If you think my phrasing is not ~~good~~ an improvement, don't hesitate 222
to ~~speak right up and~~ say so! 224

SI 1.40N

THE BUSINESS CLUB MEMORANDUM

TO:	Joe F. Cotton	FROM:	Dawn Lynn, Secretary	8
	Business Club Initiate		The Business Club	17
				18
SUBJECT:	Your initiation	DATE:	January 8, 19-- ↓3	26

28

To show that you are worthy of becoming a member of the Club, 40
you are to report after school to the production laboratory 52
at least six times this month. You will be expected to stay 65
and work for an hour each time. At the end of each hour, you 77
will receive a work card. 83

84

The initiation will take place just before the banquet. You 96
are to report to the Gold Room at the Arden House not later 108
than six o'clock on February 4. You are to dress as though 120
you were going to be interviewed for a fine office position. 132
Be sure to bring all six of your work cards with you. 143

144

D. L. 147

148

URS 149

|1 |2 |3 |4 |5 |6 |7 |8 |9 |10 |11 |12 SI 1.40N

Interoffice Memo Typed on a Printed Form

MEMORANDUM ON PRINTED FORM Take an optional 5-minute writing on the entire memo. Use plain paper, spacing 1, tab 35 spaces from left margin. Then:

Job 118·1 Type the memo on Workbook 77. If you do not have the Workbook, use plain paper for the memo (see page 124).

Optional Job 118·2 Type another copy, addressing it to initiate Graham Trapp.

 119

GOALS *To learn how to arrange an invoice on plain paper. To produce an invoice.*

DIRECTIONS *Spacing 1. Line 60. Tabs as directed.*

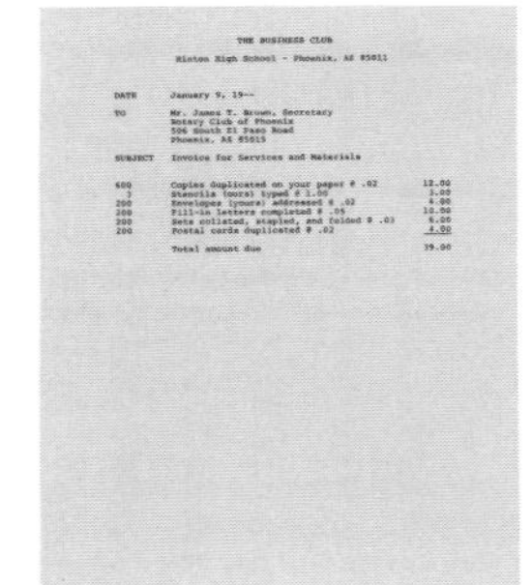

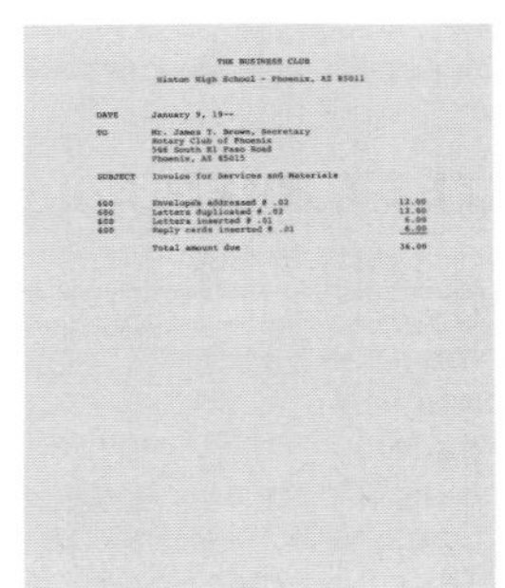

WARMUP REVIEW

3 copies

1 When they get back from town, they will get good jobs here. 12
2 How did Jeff's size help him win quickly over six battlers? 12
3 These five typed 10, 28, 39, 47, and 56 pages respectively. 12

|1 |2 |3 |4 |5 |6 |7 |8 |9 |10 |11 |12

a·i·m 147–148

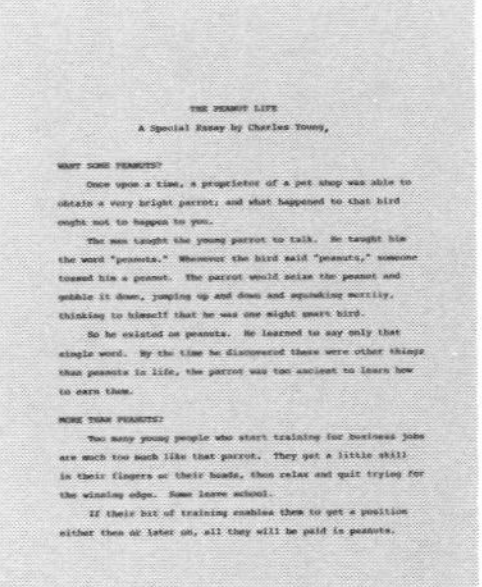

THE PEANUT LIFE

A Special Essay by Charles Young,

WANT SOME PEANUTS?

Once upon a time, a proprietor of a pet shop was able to obtain a very bright parrot; and what happened to that bird ought not to happen to you.

The man taught the young parrot to talk. He taught him the word "peanuts." Whenever the bird said "peanuts," someone tossed him a peanut. The parrot would seize the peanut and gobble it down, jumping up and down and squawking merrily, thinking to himself that he was one might smart bird.

So he existed on peanuts. He learned to say only that single word. By the time he discovered there were other things than peanuts in life, the parrot was too ancient to learn how to earn them.

MORE THAN PEANUTS?

Too many young people who start training for business jobs are much too much like that parrot. They get a little skill in their fingers or their heads, then relax and quit trying for the winning edge. Some leave school.

If their bit of training enables them to get a position either then or later on, all they will be paid is peanuts.

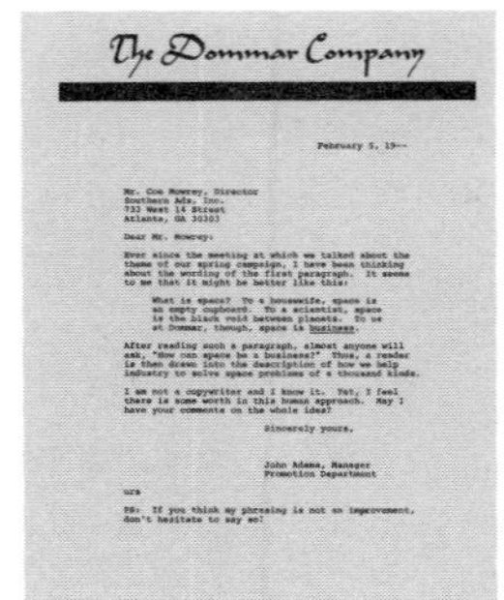

The Dommar Company

February 5, 19--

Mr. Coe Mowrey, Director
Southern Ads, Inc.
733 West 14 Street
Atlanta, GA 30303

Dear Mr. Mowrey:

Ever since the meeting at which we talked about the theme of our spring campaign, I have been thinking about the wording of the first paragraph. It seems to me that it might be better like this:

What is space? To a housewife, space is an empty cupboard. To a scientist, space is the black void between planets. To us at Dommar, though, space is business.

After reading such a paragraph, almost anyone will ask, "How can space be a business?" Thus, a reader is then drawn into the description of how we help industry to solve space problems of a thousand kinds.

I am not a copywriter and I know it. Yet, I feel there is some worth in this human approach. May I have your comments on the whole idea?

Sincerely yours,

John Adams, Manager
Promotion Department

urs

PS: If you think my phrasing is not an improvement, don't hesitate to say so!

GOALS ◉ *To type 175 or more words in 5 minutes within 5 errors on narrative material.* ◉ *To preview the test in a·i·m 149–150.* ◉ *To produce a letter and a manuscript.*

DIRECTIONS *Warmup, Spacing 1, line 60; other settings as directed for each exercise. WB 117–120.*

OPTIONAL REVIEW

1 I do not see how it is that he is to go to the den with us. 12
2 Six big jet planes quickly zoomed over the five old towers. 12
3 We counted 2 or 5 or 8 or 11 or 14 or 17 or 20 or 23 or 26. 12

TEST PREP 1

Review the objective information test on Workbook pages 119–120. Do not mark the test, but look up any details about which you are not certain. Be ready to score high.

TEST PREP 2

5-MINUTE TW
Line 50
Spacing 2
Tab 5
Omit lines 4, 5, and 17

4 THE PEANUT LIFE / A Special Essay by / [Your name] WANT ..
5 SOME PEANUTS? ..
6 Once upon a time, a proprietor of a pet shop was able to obtain a 14
7 very bright parrot; and what happened to that bird ought not to 27
8 happen to you. 30
9 The man taught the young parrot to talk. He taught him the word 44
10 "peanuts." Whenever the bird said "peanuts," someone tossed him a 57
11 peanut. The parrot would seize the peanut and gobble it down, jump- 71
12 ing up and down and squawking merrily, thinking to himself that he 84
13 was one mighty smart bird. 90
14 So he existed on peanuts. He learned to say only that single word. 105
15 By the time he discovered there were other things than peanuts in 118
16 life, the parrot was too ancient to learn how to earn them. 130
17 MORE THAN PEANUTS? ..
18 Too many young people who start training for business jobs are 143
19 much too much like that parrot. They get a little skill in their fingers 158
20 or their heads, then relax and quit trying for the winning edge. 171
21 Some leave school. ◉ 175
22 If their bit of training enables them to get a position either then 190
23 or later on, all they will be paid is peanuts. Like the parrot, they 204
24 simply don't realize that peanuts is all they are worth. 216
25 Maybe it's nice to know that you can rely on having something, 229
26 even though it is only peanuts; but somebody ought to be sure you 242
27 know that there are better things in life, like steaks, that wait for 256
28 you if, by working now, you qualify for them. 265

|1 |2 |3 |4 |5 |6 |7 |8 |9 |10 |11 |12 |13 |14 SI 1.25FE

TEST PREP 3

REPORT PAGE 1
(Type only as much as you would put on page 1.)
Line 6 inches
Spacing 2
Tabs 5, center
Heading: line 4
Sideheadings: lines 5, 17

JOB 119·1

INVOICE
Spacing 1
Line 60
Tabs 10, 55

THE BUSINESS CLUB 10

11

Hinton High School--Phoenix, AZ 85011 ↓4 34

37

DATE January 9, 19-- 42

43

TO Mr. James T. Brown, Secretary 51
Rotary Club of Phoenix 56
506 South El Paso Road 62
Phoenix, AZ 85015 66

67

SUBJECT Invoice for Services and Materials ↓3 77

79

600	Copies duplicated on your paper @ .02	12.00	90
3	Stencils (ours) typed @ 1.00	3.00	99
200	Envelopes (yours) addressed @ .02	4.00	109
200	Fill-in letters completed @ .05	10.00	119
200	Sets collated, stapled, and folded @ .03	6.00	131
200	Postal cards duplicated @ .02	4.00	142
			143
	Total amount due	39.00	149

Ⓜ Ⓣ 10 Ⓣ 55

Invoice Typed as a Memo on Plain Paper

INVOICES

An invoice is a bill listing materials and/or services delivered at one time. It is usually typed on a printed form (page 128) but can be typed in memo form on plain paper as shown above.

Job 119·1 Copy the invoice above. Center the heading on lines 4 and 6.

Job 119·2 Prepare another invoice to Mr. Brown, this one for these items:

600	Envelopes addressed @ .02	12.00
600	Letters duplicated @ .02	12.00
600	Letters inserted @ .01	6.00
600	Reply cards inserted @ .01	6.00
	Total amount due	36.00

120

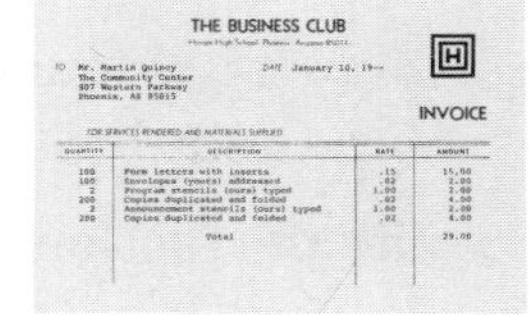

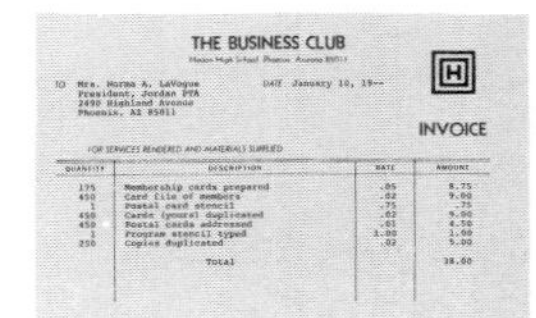

GOALS *To learn how to arrange an invoice on a printed form. To produce an invoice. To type 150 or more words in 5 minutes within 5 errors.*

DIRECTIONS *Spacing 1. Line 60. Tab 5. WB 79.*

WARMUP PREVIEW

3 copies

1 They will soon show them what they won from the other team. 12
2 essential fraction requires exactly sizable equally finding 12
3 Did Jeff's size help him win quickly over Art Goodwin, too? 12
4 We found that Invoice Nos. 1028 and 3947 were both for $56. 12

|1 |2 |3 |4 |5 |6 |7 |8 |9 |10 |11 |12

a·i·m 146

KEEP CALL WHEN—

- Keys jam . . . gently untangle them.
- You lose the place . . . find it.
- You make an error . . . everyone does.
- You're interrupted . . . be polite.
- You do the wrong work . . . we all do.

GOALS *To build a speed reserve (225 or more words in 5 minutes within 5 errors) on easy copy. To learn about carbon paper.*

DIRECTIONS *Spacing 1 for drills, 2 for TW. Line 60. Tab 5.*

WARMUP REVIEW

3 copies

```
If he is to go on with us, he has to be at the lake at six.    12
Five big jet planes zoomed quickly by the six steel towers.    12
They found 1 or 4 or 7 or 10 or 13 or 16 or 19 or 22 or 25.    12
|1  |2  |3  |4  |5  |6  |7  |8  |9  |10  |11  |12
```

CARBON COPIES

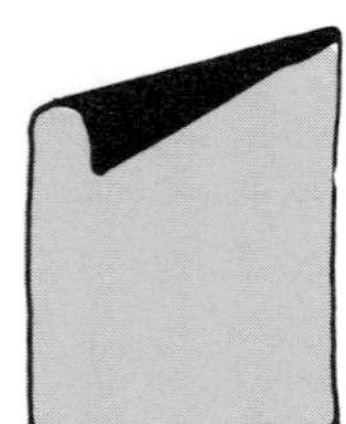

Carbon paper has a dull side and glossy side. The glossy one does all the work.

Put the glossy side against the paper on which you wish to make a carbon copy.

Straighten sides and top of carbon pack before inserting it into your machine.

Hold the pack with your left hand; turn the cylinder smoothly with the right hand.

SPEED DRIVE

See page 109.

Of all the aids that have been dreamed up to help good typists get 14
more work done, the prize goes to carbon paper. It is just about the 28
most useful stuff in the world, and if we did not have such a thing 42
and you thought it up, acclaim and wealth would be yours. Why, it is 56
hard to see how most firms could go on today with no carbon to save 70
typing time. 72

That is, if you use it right. 80

If you do not use it right, carbon paper can drive you wild. Each 94
typist will have to find for himself, once, the fierce madness that can 108
grip him when he finds, after doing a full page of work that shines in 123
its perfection, that all the carbons were in backwards. The rage you 137
feel is enough to make strong men weep and make weaklings into 149
tigers. We say *once,* for after that you will always check your papers. 165

Almost as bad is what happens if you do not jounce the pack of 179
paper so that the carbons are flat and smooth; they crease and 192
wrinkle in a shape like a tree with no leaves on it, and it gives you 206
an odd feeling when you see that shape spread on each one of the 219
carbon copies that you have made. 225

|1 |2 |3 |4 |5 |6 |7 |8 |9 |10 |11 |12 |13 |14 SI 1.11VE

5-MINUTE GOAL WRITING

Spacing 2
2 copies in
5 minutes

	1	2
Printed forms serve a lot of uses. It is obvious that they save	14	89
time; you can fill one in with just a fraction of the work a letter	28	102
requires. It is equally obvious that you are less likely to leave	41	115
out any essential data since forms show you exactly where to type	54	129
what. Ease of mailing them, filing them, finding them, etc., will	67	142
appear on any sizable list of uses.	75	150

|1 |2 |3 |4 |5 |6 |7 |8 |9 |10 |11 |12 |13 |14 SI 1.37N

THE BUSINESS CLUB
Hinton High School, Phoenix, Arizona 85011

H

(A) TO Mr. Martin Quincy DATE: January 10, 19-- 9
The Community Center 13
907 Western Parkway 17
Phoenix, AZ 85015 20

(B) **INVOICE**

FOR SERVICES RENDERED AND MATERIALS SUPPLIED 26

QUANTITY	DESCRIPTION	RATE	AMOUNT	
100	(C) Form letters with inserts	.15	15.00	39
100	Envelopes (yours) addressed	.02	2.00	52
2	Program stencils (ours) typed	1.00	2.00	64
200	Copies duplicated and folded	.02	4.00	75
2	Announcement stencils (ours) typed	1.00	2.00	87
200	(D) Copies duplicated and folded	.02	4.00	99
				100
	(E) Total		29.00	106
Margin ↑	↑ Tab ↑ Tab	(F) ↑ Tab	↑ Tab	

Invoice Typed on a Typical Printed Invoice Form

INVOICES ON PRINTED FORMS

A. Guide words show where to insert address and date. Leave 1 or (preferably) 2 blank spaces between guide and typing.

B. Margin stop is set to line up the quantity items with the address lines.

C. Number columns are straight on the right side, **word columns** on left side.

D. Vertical lines require 1 or (preferably) 2 blank spaces on each side. In last column ("Amount"), typing should end 2 spaces inside the column area.

E. Total line begins approximately under start of word "Description."

F. Tab stops are set at points used most frequently to start items; space in or back for the other column items.

Practice Prepare the following two invoices on the Workbook forms or on plain paper as shown on page 127.

Job 120·1 The invoice above.

Job 120·2 Invoice to Mrs. Norma A. LaVogue / President, Jordan PTA / 2490 Highland Avenue / Phoenix, AZ 85011:

175	Membership cards prepared @	.05	8.75
450	Card file of members	.02	9.00
1	Postal card stencil	.75	.75
450	Cards (yours) duplicated	.02	9.00
450	Postal cards addressed	.01	4.50
1	Program stencil typed	1.00	1.00
250	Copies duplicated	.02	5.00
	Total		38.00

JOB 144·1
Continued

IV. Summary

The guides for the use of headings in reports vary from school 14
to school but are standard in most regards. 23

This report has been typed in a way that illustrates the general 37
agreements: that the headings should show the outline plan, that 50
there should be three ranks of headings (main ones centered, 62
major ones blocked, and minor ones indented), and that pages 74
after the first one should bear a page number. 83

SI 1.32FE

JOB 144·2
BIBLIOGRAPHY
Center
Line 60
Tabs 10, center
Review page 70.

B I B L I O G R A P H Y ↓3

Lloyd, Alan C., and Russell Hosler, Personal Typing, 3d ed., McGraw-Hill Book Company, New York, 1969. TWO AUTHORS

Martin, John, Rules Governing the Typing of Term Papers, 3d ed., Hampton University Press, Chicago, 1970. ONE AUTHOR

Rowe, John L., Alan C. Lloyd, and Fred E. Winger, Gregg Typing, 191 Series, Book One, 2d ed., McGraw-Hill Book Company, New York, 1967. THREE AUTHORS

Wheland, William O., "When You Type Your Term Paper," The Student Activities Monthly, May, 1971, pp. 38-41. ONE AUTHOR

a·i·m 145

JOB 145·1
COVER PAGE

Center lines 1–3 in top half
Center lines 4–6 in bottom half

HEADINGS IN REPORTS

A Report by

Gordie M. Mendez

Typing I

Mrs. Ferguson

January 1, 19--

JOB 145·2
CONTENTS PAGE

Center on full page with
Line 40, Spacing 2

C O N T E N T S

I.	Purpose	1
II.	Research	1
	A. Sources	1
	B. Nature of the Findings	1
III.	Findings	2
	A. Displaying Headings	2
	B. Outlining with Headings	2
	C. Identifying Pages	2
IV.	Summary	3

a·i·m 121

GOAL *To build speed reserve (200 or more words in 5 minutes within 5 errors) on very easy copy that requires listening for the margin bell and making line-end decisions.*

DIRECTIONS *Spacing 1 for drills, 2 for TW. Line 60. Tab 5.*

> **HELP YOUR EYES**
> - Raise the top of the book so there is no shine on the paper.
> - Turn the book so you can read it without bending your neck.
> - Try to keep your eyes relaxed.

WARMUP REVIEW

3 copies

They will find that there are good jobs with good pay here. 12
Jeff's size might help him win quickly over extra battlers. 12
We timed the 10:28, the 3:39, the 4:47, and the 5:56 buses. 12
|1 |2 |3 |4 |5 |6 |7 |8 |9 |10 |11 |12

SPEED DRIVE

See page 109.
Spacing 2

The next time you hear a chairman say that the speaker you have 14
come to hear needs no introduction, shed a tear or two for the speaker 28
and two or three more for the chairman: the speaker will be in a 41
state of fury, and the chairman is certain to learn that he did not 55
do as he should have done. 61
Think of the man who came to make the speech. He must have put 74
in hours and hours on his speech; he took his suit out to be pressed 88
and dug up his best shirt and tie; he had to get there by car or plane 102
or what have you; he had to be away from his home (where there is 116
work to be done, and his wife will have said so more than once); and 129
by and large he has had to go to a lot of trouble to be there on the 143
stage. 145
Now, why does he do it? He has something to sell. It might be 159
himself, and he just might be there to get support from you: your 172
vote, or your hands to haul a sign, or your voice to cheer for him 185
at the right time. What he wants to sell may be a product, the kind 199
that his firm makes; and he knows that you would think well of his 213
firm and his product if you think well of him. The guest has some- 226
thing to sell. 229
So the guest hopes that the chairman will say a lot of nice things, 244
like how much he has done for the party or the city or the Rotary 257
Club, or how often he makes talks or how many books he has written, 270
or that kind of thing. He knows that such things make you think more 284
highly of him and what it is that he wants to sell. He does not want 298
the chairman to go too far or be too lavish, but he does want him to 312
get you ready and eager for what he has come there to tell you. 325
|1 |2 |3 |4 |5 |6 |7 |8 |9 |10 |11 |12 |13 |14 SI 1.10VE

a·i·m 143

5-MINUTE GOAL WRITING
170 words
(Make all indicated revises.)

III. Findings

A. DISPLAYING HEADINGS 4

Headings may be centered, blocked at the margin, or indented the 18
same as a new paragraph. 26

1. Centered. The most important headings are centered, in capital 44
and small letters and underscored, preceded by two blank lines. 62

2. Blocked. The second rank heading is the one blocked at the 79
left margin in all capitals. If it follows a heading, it is preceded 93
by 1 blank line, otherwise it must be preceded by 2 blank lines. 108

Paragraph headings are indented and are underscored. They may 127
be followed by a period or, as in this paragraph, be made the first 141
part of the opening sentence of the paragraph. 147

JOB 143-1
PAGE 2 OF A MANUSCRIPT
Line 6 inches
Spacing 2

B. OUTLINING WITH HEADINGS 154

Most headings of parts of a report are identified by a letter or 168
a number in out line style, so that the organization can be recognized 182
at a glance. The letters or numbers are followed by a period and one 201
blank space. (Only outlines with no narrative have two blank spaces 215
after the period that follows the numbers or letters.) 223

C. IDENTIFYING PAGES 229

Pages other than the first one are numbered on line 7 at the mar- 242
gin, preceded by the word "page." Some typists, including the writer, 256

a·i·m 144
JOB 144-1
PAGE 3 OF A MANUSCRIPT

like to include the name of the writer before the page number to make 14
it easy for anyone to identify to whose report a loose page belongs. 27

The first page of a report or chapter is not numbered (that is, 45
its number is not typed on the page) but the fact that this page has 59
has a 2-inch top margin pages it clear the page is the first one. 68

Page headings, whether they are one line or several are separated 82
from the following text by 2 blank lines. [Continues on page 155.] 91

Revision of Continuation Pages of a Formal Report

a·i·m 122–123

GOALS *To type 150 or more words in 5 minutes within 5 errors while producing a letter. To produce a short business letter on stationery in blocked form. To produce invoices from incompletely arranged copy.*

DIRECTIONS *Spacing 1. Line 60 for drills, 40 pica or 50 elite for TW. Tab center only. WB 81–85.*

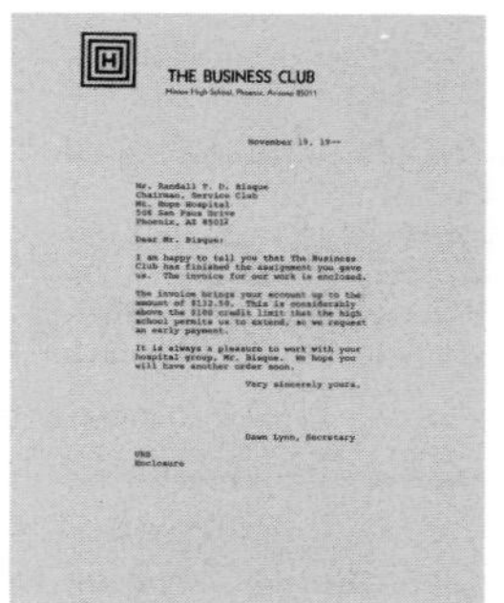

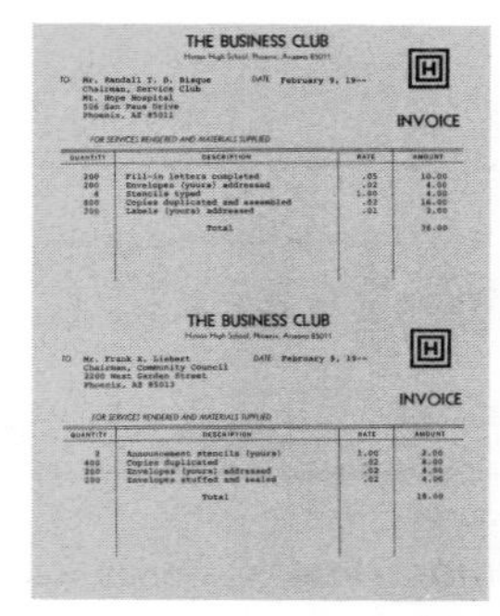

WARMUP PREVIEW

2 copies

The new job has big pay but the six men did not try for it. 12
Six big men quickly won over Jeff despite his greater size. 12
considerably assignment finished $132.50 payment happy $100 12
We sent No. 10 shoes on orders 28 and 39, not on 47 and 56. 12

5-MINUTE GOAL WRITING

Arrange letter as you type it on plain paper.

JOB 122·1

BLOCKED LETTER
Body 78 words
Line 4 inches
Tab center
Workbook 81

Date ↓5 / Mr. Randall T. D. Bisque / Chairman, Service Club / Mt. Hope 19
Hospital / 506 San Paus Drive / Phoenix, AZ 85012 / Dear Mr. Bisque: 33
I am happy to tell you that The Business Club has finished the as- 47
signment you gave us. The invoice for our recent work is enclosed. 61
The invoice brings your account up to the amount of $132.50. This 75
is considerably above the $100 credit limit that the high school per- 89
mits us to extend, so we request an early payment of your account. 103
It is always a pleasure to work with your hospital group, Mr. Bisque. 116
We hope you will have another order soon for us to begin. 130
Very sincerely yours, ↓6 / Dawn Lynn, Secretary / URS / Enclosure 150

1 2 3 4 5 6 7 8 9 10 11 12 13 14 SI 1.39N

a·i·m 123

JOB 123·1

INVOICE
Workbook 83

Date and address as above / 200 Fill-in letters completed @ .05 is 37
10.00 / 200 Envelopes (yours) addressed @ .02 is 4.00 / 4 Stencils 52
typed @ 1.00 is 4.00 / 800 Copies duplicated and assembled @ .02 is 67
16.00 / 200 Labels (yours) addressed @ .01 is 2.00 / Total is 36.00. 87

JOB 123·2

INVOICE
Workbook 83

Date / Mr. Frank X. Liebert / Chairman, Community Council / 2200 15
West Garden Street / Phoenix, AZ 85013 / Invoice for these materials: 22
2 Announcement stencils (yours) @ 1.00 is 2.00 / 400 Copies duplicated 41
@ .02 is 8.00 / 200 Envelopes (yours) addressed @ .02 is 4.00 / 200 57
Envelopes stuffed and sealed @ .02 is 4.00 / Total is 18.00. 76

JOB 123·3

INVOICE
Workbook 85

Date / Mrs. Ruth K. Lemming / Ladies Aid Society / Trinity Cathedral 16
/ 2390 Cathedral Lane / Scottdale, AZ 85001 / Invoice for: 300 Postal 30
cards addressed @ .02 is 6.00 / Total is 6.00. 45

JOB 123·4

INVOICE
Workbook 85

Date / Dr. J. Paul Jorge / 5061 West 14 Street / Phoenix, AZ 85011 / 15
Invoice for: 200 Announcement envelopes addressed @ .02 is 4.00 / 200 31
Announcements inserted @ .01 is 2.00 / Total is 6.00. 48

a·i·m 142-145

GOALS *To type 170 words or more in 5 minutes within 5 errors on report material. To produce a complete formal report as a project in correct report form.*

DIRECTIONS *Spacing 1 on drills, otherwise 2. Line 6 inches. Tabs 5, center. Correct all errors, if any. For daily warmup, use review on page 152.*

FORMAL REPORT PROJECT

- Cover .... JOB 145·1
- Contents page .... JOB 145·2
- Report, page 1 .... JOB 142·1
- Report, page 2 .... JOB 143·1
- Report, page 3 .... JOB 144·1
- Bibliography .... JOB 144·2

a·i·m 142

5-MINUTE GOAL WRITING
170 words
(Omit centered headings in the TW.)

JOB 142·1

PAGE 1 OF A MANUSCRIPT
Shown elite
Line 6 inches
Spacing 2

HEADINGS IN REPORTS Line 13

A Report by Gordie M. Mendez
Typing 1 ↓3

I. Purpose ..

The headings of a report are what distinguish it from an ordinary 14
essay. Headings are important. They are worth study. The purpose of 28
this report is to summarize what most typists do to make the most and 42
best use of heading display. ↓3 47

II. Research ..

A. SOURCES 51

The data in this report come from two sources: 62

1. Interviews. The subject of this report was discussed with six 81
persons: a free-lance typist, two college students, two high school 94
teachers, and a college teacher of English. 103

2. Readings. A number of details were drawn also from a magazine 121
article, from two typing textbooks, and from a new booklet published by 136
the English Department of a college. ↓3 143

B. NATURE OF THE FINDINGS 149

The findings of this report deal with three points: the general 164
arrangement of headings, their use to show the plan or outline of the 177
material, and their use to identify pages. 186

The three points are discussed in detail in the following sections 200
of this report. 203

SI 1.34FE

Page 1 of a Formal Report

a·i·m 124

GOALS *To type 150 or more words in 5 minutes within 5 errors on alphabetic material. To preview the a·i·m 125 Test. To produce a letter and two invoices.*

DIRECTIONS *Warmup from a·i·m 123. Workbook 87–88.*

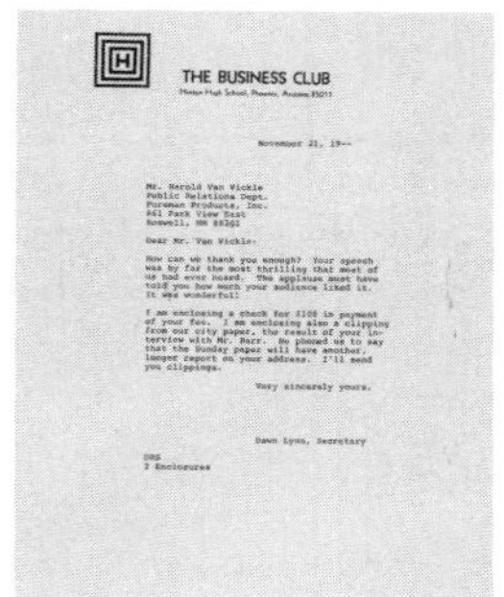
THE BUSINESS CLUB

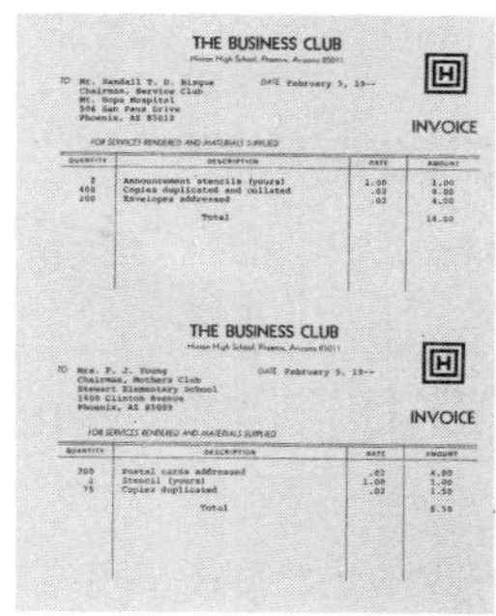
THE BUSINESS CLUB

INVOICE

THE BUSINESS CLUB

INVOICE

OPTIONAL REVIEW

The two men got the big pay for the job but did not use it. 12
Six big men quickly won over Jeff despite his radical size. 12
You will get 180 if you add 10 and 28 and 39 and 47 and 56. 12
|1 |2 |3 |4 |5 |6 |7 |8 |9 |10 |11 |12

TEST PREP 1

Review the objective information test on Workbook pages 89–90. Do not mark the test, but look up any details about which you are not certain. Be ready to score high.

TEST PREP 2

5-MINUTE TW
Line 60
Spacing 2
Tab 5

The postal number that we type so neatly on labels and envelopes 14
emerged from the Zoning Improvement Plan that the Post Office 26
started in the spring of 1963 as a way to speed delivery of the mail. 40
The five figures in the number are a special code that lets mail be 54
sorted much more quickly and accurately. The plan caught on at 67
once, and business firms throughout the nation put the codes on their 81
mailing lists. 84
There are two phases, one concerned with bulk mail and another 98
that has to do with individual cards and envelopes. Although typists 112
are involved only in the second kind, they should know that ZIP 124
numbers do not apply to letters alone. 132
The bulk mail, like magazines and circulars, has to be placed in 145
bags, one for each local postal zone to which the mailing is to go. The 160
mailers like the plan for, once they adjust their mailing lists, it is easy 175
to bag what they are mailing, and the bags start on their way without 189
any delay. You might say they "zip" on their way. 200
|1 |2 |3 |4 |5 |6 |7 |8 |9 |10 |11 |12 |13 |14 SI 1.34FE

TEST PREP 3

BLOCKED LETTER
Body 91 words
Tab center
Workbook 87

Date ↓7 / Mr. Harold Van Vickle / Public Relations Dept. / Foreman Pro- 19
ducts, Inc. / 861 Park View East / Roswell, NM 88201 / Dear Mr. Van 32
Vickle: / How can we thank you enough? Your speech was by far the most 47
thrilling that most of us had ever heard. The applause must have told 61
you how much your audience liked it. It was wonderful! [Turn page and continue] 73

a·i·m 140

5-MINUTE GOAL WRITING
168 words within 5 minutes and 5 errors

JOB 140·1

PAGE 2 OF A 2-PAGE LETTER
Line 6 inches
Tabs 4, center

1 Mr. Darrell E. Davis (Line 7) 4
2 Page 2 (Line 8) 5
3 January 14, 19-- ↓3 (Line 9) 8
10

4 5. Dr. Hart will take part in a conference at the University 22
5 from 9:00 until 12:00 on Wednesday morning. It would be 35
6 a help if you could find out in advance in what building 47
7 and room the meeting will be held so that you can get to 59
8 it without delay. Dr. Hart should be there by 8:30 at 71
9 the latest so that you and he can check the equipment and 83
10 review what you are to do in support of his program. 95
96

11 6. His departing flight will leave Missoula at 1:35, so you 108
12 and he may not have much time to spare when the meeting 120
13 is over. He will have packed his luggage before you pick 132
14 him up in the morning, so you will not have to return to 144
15 the hotel. I imagine that you and he will lunch with some 157
16 of the faculty and then head for the airport. 168
169

17 It will be a busy 24 hours, Mr. Davis, but I am sure that you 179
18 will enjoy them and will make new friends as well. 188
189

19 Very sincerely yours, ↓4 194
197

20 Mrs. Marcia F. Langston 203
21 Reservations Bureau 207
22 urs 208
23 cc Dr. Hart 210

SI 1.26FE

Page 2 of a Two-Page Blocked Letter with an Enumeration

a·i·m 141

GOAL *To build a speed reserve (220 or more words in 5 minutes within 5 errors) on easy copy that requires listening for the bell.*

DIRECTIONS *Spacing 1 for drills, 2 for TW. Line 60. Tab 5. For TW, use Drive 2, page 147.*

WHEN DRIVING FOR SPEED

- Be calm, poised, cool as ice.
- Let nothing upset you.
- Keep your face expressionless.
- Don't speak, sigh, or exclaim.
- Show serene confidence.

WARMUP REVIEW

3 copies

1 See if he is to go with us or to go with one or two others. 12
2 Five or six big jet planes zoomed quickly by the new tower. 12
3 Did he see 1 or 2 or 3 or 4 or 5 or 6 or 7 or 8 or 9 or 10? 12
|1 |2 |3 |4 |5 |6 |7 |8 |9 |10 |11 |12

I am enclosing a check for $100 in payment of your fee. I am enclos- 87
ing also a clipping from our city paper, the result of your interview 101
with Mr. Barr. He phoned us to say that the Sunday paper will have an- 115
other, longer report on your address. I'll send you clippings./Very 131
sincerely yours, ↓6 /Dawn Lynn, Secretary/URS/Enclosures ⚲ 150

|1 |2 |3 |4 |5 |6 |7 |8 |9 |10 |11 |12 |13 |14 SI 1.34FE

TEST PREP 4

INVOICES
Workbook 88 or plain paper

Date/Mr. Randall T. D. Bisque/Chairman, Service Club/Mt. Hope 15
Hospital / 506 San Paus Drive / Phoenix, AZ 85012 / Invoice for: 2 24
Announcement stencils (yours) @ 1.00 is 2.00 / 400 Copies duplicated 44
and collated @ .02 is 8.00 / 200 Envelopes addressed @ .02 is 4.00 / 60
Total is 14.00. ⚲ 68

Date/Mrs. F. J. Young/Chairman, Mothers Club/Stewart Elementary 14
School/1400 Clinton Avenue/Phoenix, AZ 85009/Invoice for: 200 28
Postal cards addressed @ .02 is 4.00 / 1 Stencil (yours) @ 1.00 is 1.00 / 44
75 Copies duplicated @ .02 is 1.50 / Total is 6.50. ⚲ 63

|1 |2 |3 |4 |5 |6 |7 |8 |9 |10 |11 |12 |13 |14

a·i·m 125 TEST

GOALS ⚲ *To type 150 or more words in 5 minutes within 5 errors on alphabetic paragraphs involving listening for the margin bell.* ⚲ *To produce in blocked form a short business letter.* ⚲ *To produce two invoices.* ⚲ *To score 80% or higher on an objective test on Part Five.*

DIRECTIONS *Spacing 1. Line 60. Tab 5. WB 89–92.*

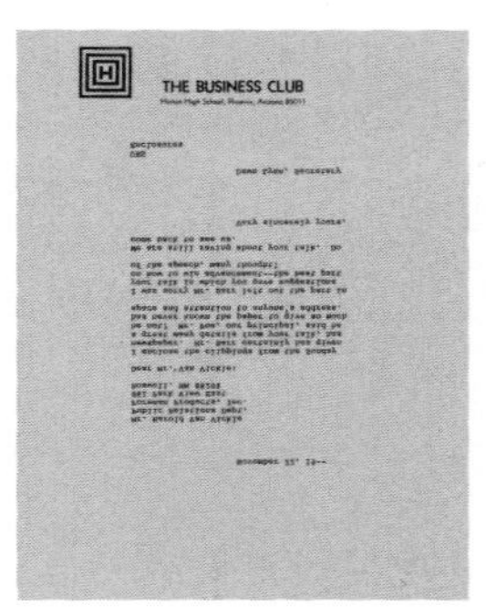
THE BUSINESS CLUB

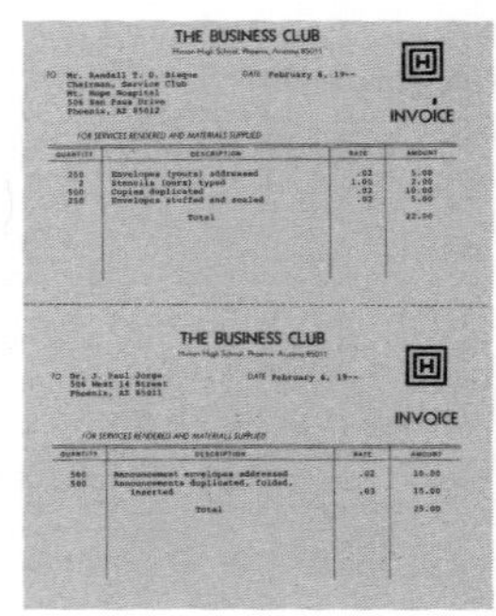
THE BUSINESS CLUB
INVOICE
THE BUSINESS CLUB
INVOICE

OPTIONAL REVIEW

2 copies

```
Why did the men not take the pay they got for that big job?    12
Joe Pott quickly won over six men because of his good size.    12
If he adds 10 and 28 and 39 and 47 and 56, will he get 180?    12
|1  |2  |3  |4  |5  |6  |7  |8  |9  |10  |11  |12
```

TEST 5-A

Take a general information test. It may be the one on Workbook pages 89–90 or a similar test that your teacher may give you or may dictate to you.

a·i·m 139

WARMUP PREVIEW

A Who was the boy and who was the man who got the box for us? 12
B Dave quickly mixed the two freezings in the deep brown jug. 12
C assignment university projector recorders Wednesday o'clock 12
D Where is a 1 or 2 or 3 or 4 or 5 or 6 or 7 or 8 or 9 or 10? 12

|1 |2 |3 |4 |5 |6 |7 |8 |9 |10 |11 |12

5-MINUTE GOAL WRITING

167 words within 5 minutes and 5 errors. Line 60; copy line for line

JOB 139-1

PAGE 1 OF A 2-PAGE LETTER
Blocked style
Line 6 inches
Tab 4
Workbook 115

Line 15 January 14, 19-- ↓5 10

14

Mr. Darrell E. Davis 18
Speaker's League, Inc. 23
2828 Foster Ridge Road 28
Missoula, MT 59801 31

32

Dear Mr. Davis: 35

36

Welcome to your first Speaker's League assignment. You will 49
be working with a very pleasant client, Dr. Richard Hart. I 60
know that you and he will enjoy meeting and working together. 73
Here are the details that you need to know. 81

92

1. Dr. Hart will arrive on Tuesday at 2:30 p.m. on Frontier 95
Flight 474. He will have flown from Seattle to Spokane 109
and changed there for the flight to Missoula. I enclose 121
his photo so that you will be able to recognize him. 134

135

2. We have made a reservation for him at the Hotel Florence. 147
Please take him there from the airport. If someone from 159
the University comes to the airport to meet him, simply 174
trail after them to the hotel. Dr. Hart is counting on 186
your help at the dinner that evening and needs to explain 196
to you what he will want you to do. I know it involves 208
operating the slide projector and the tape recorder about 221
which we wrote you two weeks ago, but I do not know just 234
what you are to do with them. Dr. Hart will tell you. 245

246

3. There is to be a reception for Dr. Hart at six o'clock 258
at the Faculty Club, followed by a dinner and the address 271
by Dr. Hart. Please get Dr. Hart to the Club a little 283
before six so that you and he may check the equipment you 296
are to use in support of his talk. You are to be a guest 308
at the reception and the dinner, of course. At the end 320
of the evening, Dr. Hart will want you to pick up both of 333
the machines and store them for use on Wednesday morning. 345

346

4. Dr. Hart may or may not need a ride back to the hotel; he 358
will let you know at the end of the evening affair. 370

SI 1.27FE

Continues on the next page.

Page 1 of a Two-Page Blocked Letter with an Enumeration

TEST 5-B

5-MINUTE TW
Line 60
Spacing 2
Tab 5

Handling a single card or envelope is different. Such pieces must 14
be sorted in the Post Office. If the cards and envelopes have the full 29
postal zone number in precisely the right place, the sorting can be 42
done ten times as fast by a scanning machine as it ever could be by 56
human eye and hand. 60

What is the proper place? It is after the state name, preceded by 75
some blank space. How much space? The scanner requires but one space– 90
that is, one space bar stroke. The scanner can manage up to a half inch 104
but gets along best if there is just one space between the state name 117
and the ZIP. 120

The use of the new two-letter state abbreviations came after the 135
ZIP got started. Mailers found that there wasn't enough space on their 149
address ⚲ plates for the extra numbers, so the Post Office authorized 162
the new abbreviations to save space. The machines can read state names 177
in full or in new or old abbreviation with equal ease. The Post Office 191
likes and wants us to use the two-letter form. 200

|1 |2 |3 |4 |5 |6 |7 |8 |9 |10 |11 |12 |13 |14 SI 1.30FE

TEST 5-C

BLOCKED LETTER
Workbook 91
Body 87

Date ↓? /Mr. Harold Van Vickle/Public Relations Dept./Foreman Pro- 19
ducts, Inc./861 Park View East/Roswell, NM 88201/Dear Mr. Van 32
Vickle:/I enclose the clippings from the Sunday newspaper. Mr. Barr 47
certainly has given a great many details from your talk, has he not? 61
Mr. Poe, our principal, said he has never known the paper to give so 75
much space and attention to anyone's address. 84

I was sorry Mr. Barr left out the part in your talk in which you gave 99
suggestions on how to win advancement—the best part of the speech, 113
many thought! 116

We are still raving about your talk. Do come back to see us./Very 133
sincerely yours, ↓? /Dawn Lynn, Secretary /URS/Enclosures⚲ 150

|1 |2 |3 |4 |5 |6 |7 |8 |9 |10 |11 |12 |13 |14 SI 1.35N

TEST 5-D

INVOICES
Workbook 92

Date / Dr. J. Paul Jorge / 5061 West 14 Street / Phoenix, AZ 85011 / 15
Invoice for: 500 Announcement envelopes addressed @ .02 is 10.00 / 31
500 Announcements duplicated, folded, inserted @ .03 is 15.00 / Total 52
is 25.00.⚲ 55

Date/Mr. Randall T. D. Bisque/Chairman, Service Club/Mt. Hope 15
Hospital/506 San Paus Drive/Phoenix, AZ 85012/Invoice for: 25
250 Envelopes (yours) addressed @ .02 is 5.00 / 2 Stencils (ours) 43
typed @ 1.00 is 2.00 / 500 Copies duplicated @ .02 is 10.00 / 250 59
Envelopes stuffed and sealed @ .02 is 5.00 / Total is 22.00.⚲ 77

OPTIONAL 5-MINUTE GOAL WRITING

166 words

Today's date/Mr. Jefferson Miller/Speaker's League, Inc./1800 Sum- 18
ner Road/Tacoma, WA 99212/Dear Jeff: Thank you for the telegram in 34
which you confirmed your plans to be in Seattle when our client, Richard 49
Hart, is there. He is delighted that a League man will meet him and be 63
with him. Here are the details that you need to know. 74
1. Dr. Hart will arrive from Portland on Western flight 317 at 11:00 90
on Monday morning. He expects you to meet him. He has a reservation at 105
the new Holiday Inn north of the airport. Dr. Hart has a friend in that 119
neighborhood and would very much like to spend the afternoon with him. 132
2. His talk will be given at the Sheraton at a banquet that begins at 148
7:00. He will depend on you to decide when you must leave the Inn for 162
the trip into town to the hotel. 169
3. Dr. Hart is counting on your getting him back to the Inn after the 185
evening at the Sheraton but says that you will not need to escort him to 199
his departing flight the next morning, although he would welcome your 213
doing so if you decide to stay at the Inn, too, instead of heading home 229
to Tacoma. He leaves at 9:45 for Missoula, Montana. 238
It was fine of you, Jeff, to adjust your schedule so that you could be 254
with Dr. Hart, and I think that he is as grateful to you for that kindness 269
as I am. Remember me to your family./Very sincerely yours, $\downarrow_3$ /Mrs. 289
Marcia F. Langston/Reservations Bureau/urs/cc Dr. Hart 303

|1 |2 |3 |4 |5 |6 |7 |8 |9 |10 |11 |12 |13 |14 SI 1.31FE

OPTIONAL JOB 138-2

BLOCKED LETTER WITH ENUMERATION
Body 240
Line ?
Tabs ?
Workbook 113

a·i·m 139–140

GOALS *To type 167 words or more in 5 minutes within 5 errors on letter material. To produce two-page letters.*

DIRECTIONS *Spacing 1. Line 60. WB 115. Unless teacher states otherwise, erase and correct any errors in letters.*

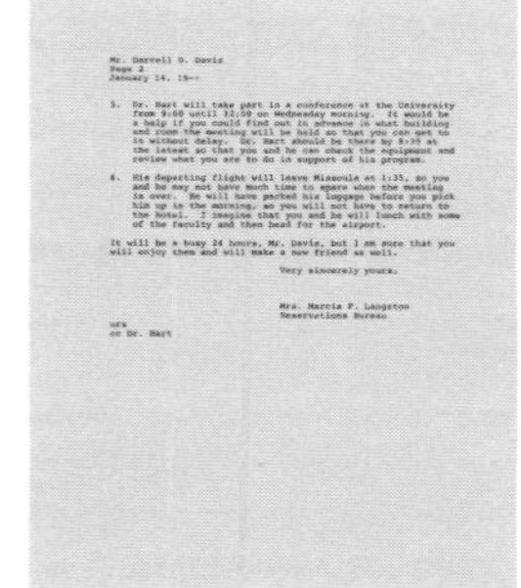

TWO-PAGE LETTERS

When a letter is too long to fit on one page, continue it on another:

Bottom margin on page 1 must be at least 1 inch, can be up to 2 inches.

Page 2 paper should be full sheet of plain paper that matches the quality of the first (letterhead) page.

Line length on page 2 is the same 6 inches used for page 1.

Page 2 heading (note illustration) is typed on lines 7, 8, and 9, leaving a top margin of 6 blank lines (1 inch).

Page 2 body starts on line 12, picking up from where it left off on page 1. At least 3 lines of body must be included on page 2. Bottom margin may be very wide on page 2.

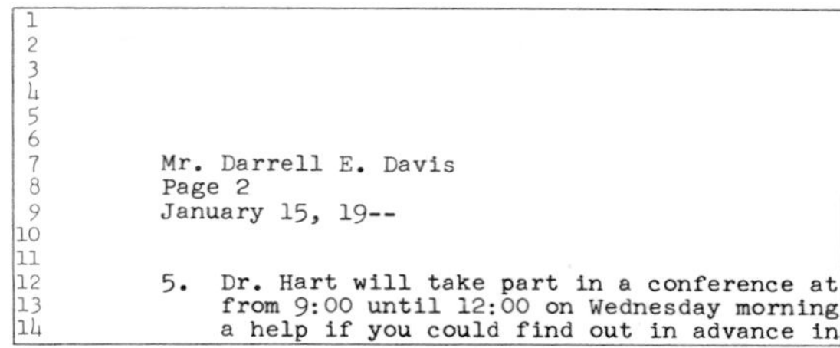

```
1
2
3
4
5
6
7      Mr. Darrell E. Davis
8      Page 2
9      January 15, 19--
10
11
12     5.  Dr. Hart will take part in a conference at
13         from 9:00 until 12:00 on Wednesday morning
14         a help if you could find out in advance in
```

Overview

In Part Six you will get experience in arranging letters and reports with new features and will build added skill in operating the typewriter.

1. Letters Now you will type average, long, and two-page letters. You will type ones with many kinds of display: tables, quotations, enumerations, company signatures, business titles, post scripts, carbon-copy notations, and so on.

2. Reports You will learn to use revision marks of all kinds. You will learn how to display quotations and to acknowledge them in footnotes. You will learn how to use headings, to number pages, to maintain margins, and the like.

3. Skill You will add at least 5 more words a minute speed, with no increase in errors, in sustained typing for 5 minutes.

Performance Goals

When you finish Part Six and type the test on pages 159 and 160, you should be able to demonstrate these skills and abilities:

1. Technicalities You will score 80 or more percent correct on an objective test covering the technical information in preceding Parts (reviewed) and in this new Part Six (emphasized).

2. Production You will type in proper form and at a speed not less than 70 percent of your straight-copy speed (a) the first page of a long report, with title, heading, subheadings, etc., to be displayed, from complete but unarranged copy; and (b) an average-length business letter involving a quotation paragraph, from arranged material in a rough-draft form.

3. Skill You will type at least 175 words in 5 minutes (185–190 are more likely) within 5 errors on paragraph material for whose line endings you will need to respond to the margin bell.

Routines and Procedures

Speed Drives There are five more speed drives (a·i·m 126, 131, 136, 141, 146) to help you develop a speed reserve. Use the same stretch-or-remedy procedure you used in Part Five.

Remedials If you do not achieve the speed or accuracy goal in a drive, and if your teacher approves, (a) turn to the drills for your level in Supplement II (page 275 following), (b) spend 20 to 30 minutes on whichever drills will help you most, and (c) repeat the a·i·m in which you were not able to achieve your speed or accuracy goal.

Production TW Many a·i·m sessions require your taking a timed writing on the letter body or report body of a production task. Welcome such practice, for it will help you apply to production work the power you are developing.

Doubles, Triples As you become able to do production tasks that take several a·i·m sessions to complete, you will find several occasions in which assignments are grouped.

"cc" Notation
If someone is to get a carbon copy of a letter, type "cc" and his name under the reference initials.

I know that you will enjoy the time you spend with Dr. Hart. Already he 247
has told me that he is grateful for your help and is relieved that a 261
League man will be with him./Very sincerely yours, $\downarrow_4$ /Mrs. Marcia F. 282
Langston/Reservations Bureau/urs/cc Dr. Hart ⚲ 294

|1 |2 |3 |4 |5 |6 |7 |8 |9 |10 |11 |12 |13 |14 SI 1.23E

a·i·m 138 WARMUP PREVIEW

A Ask the men how the boy got the box and how he paid for it. 12
B Mixtures prevented the brown jar from freezing too quickly. 12
C arrangements conference engagement available tentative idea 12
D We found a 1 or 2 or 3 or 4 or 5 or 6 or 7 or 8 or 9 or 10? 12

|1 |2 |3 |4 |5 |6 |7 |8 |9 |10 |11 |12

5-MINUTE GOAL WRITING

⚲ 166 words

Today's date/Mr. Mark Jaderstrom/Speaker's League, Inc./1250 17
Bunyan Boulevard/Portland, OR 97209/Dear Mr. Jaderstrom: 30
I have had a visit with Dr. Hart and been able to get answers to 44
your questions about the arrangements for his tour. He is delighted 58
that a League man will meet him and be with him, and he is looking for- 72
ward to seeing you in Portland. Details: 81
1. Dr. Hart will arrive in Portland at 1:00 on Saturday. He will be 96
on Western flight 201. He is arriving this early because he wants to 110
have a conference with Dean Perkins. He has a tentative date to meet 124
him at the University at 4:00 and hopes you can help him keep that en- 138
gagement. 141
2. The dinner at which Dr. Hart is to make his address will be held 156
at the Hilton, so he has a reservation there. ⚲ 166
3. Dr. Hart has no plans for Sunday and expects to fly north to 180
Seattle on Monday, leaving at 9:15 a.m. Dr. Hart is quite a fan of 194
frontier history; if you are available on Sunday, perhaps you could drive 209
him up to Fort Vancouver. This is my idea; he has not mentioned it. 223
Dr. Hart has arranged with the Association for a ticket for you so 237
that you can, if you wish, attend the banquet as his guest and hear his 251
talk. I envy you that!/Very sincerely yours, $\downarrow_4$ /Mrs. Marcia F. 271
Langston/Reservations Bureau/urs/ ⚲ 281

|1 |2 |3 |4 |5 |6 |7 |8 |9 |10 |11 |12 |13 |14 SI 1.32FE

JOB 138-1
BLOCKED LETTER WITH ENUMERATION
Body 2/14
Line ? inches
Tabs 4, center
Workbook 111

OPTIONAL WARMUP PREVIEW

A Ask the boy who the big man was who had bought the old box. 12
B Dave froze the mixtures in the deep brown jugs too quickly. 12
C neighborhood afternoon confirmed departing Missoula airport 12
D We counted 10 or 9 or 8 or 7 or 6 or 5 or 4 or 3 or 2 or 1. 12

|1 |2 |3 |4 |5 |6 |7 |8 |9 |10 |11 |12

 126

GOAL *To build speed reserve (205 or more words in 5 minutes within 5 errors) on easy copy.*

DIRECTIONS *Spacing 2. Line 60. Tab 5.*

CHECK YOUR STROKING

- **Keys** bound back from the paper.
- **Printing** is uniformly dark, clear.
- **Fingers** stay curled when hitting keys.

WARMUP REVIEW

3 copies

I do not see why we could not try the suits before he left. 12
Brown jars would prevent the mixture from freezing quickly. 12
Add up .1 and .2 and .3 and .4 and .5 and .6 and .7 and .8. 12
|1 |2 |3 |4 |5 |6 |7 |8 |9 |10 |11 |12

SPEED DRIVE

Same routine as before— page 109.

We used to raise peppers back on the farm where I grew 12
up as a boy. They were big and green, the kind you like in 24
salads, and we raised them in rows and rows of bushes. One 36
time I asked my dad whether the kind we raised was the same 48
as we shook out of the pepper shaker on the table. He said 60
they were and the shaker stuff was just our kind ground up. 72
Well, I went along with that for years and years until 84
one day a teacher told our class in college that the reason 96
Columbus set out to find a new route to the Indies was that 108
he wanted a lot of pepper. In those days all the travelers 120
were after spice, but what those men called spice is pepper 132
to you and me. All this did nct seem quite right to me, so 144
I read all I could find on pepper. Alas, my dad was wrong. 156
The kind of pepper we use on the table grows on a vine 168
that looks and climbs like ivy. The peppers are berries of 180
the vine that grow in a string or group like currants. The 192
berries may be dried and ground up into the black pepper we 204
like or may be soaked until the black shell falls off, then 216
the white heart is dried and ground into mild white pepper. 228
For hundreds of years the spice ships, including those 240
famous New England clippers, made long trips to get pepper. 252
It was worth so much that the profit on a single trip would 264
pay for the whole ship. Today pepper is still big business 276
all over the world. Why, Americans alone use forty million 288
pounds of pepper a year. This is nothing to be sneezed at! 300
|1 |2 |3 |4 |5 |6 |7 |8 |9 |10 |11 |12 SI 1.19E

Special Note: If your teacher approves, bring a typewriter (ink) eraser to class for use in the next a·i·m.

a·i·m 137–138

GOALS *To type 165 words or more in 5 minutes within 5 errors on letter-body material. To produce long letters with designated variations in display parts.*

DIRECTIONS *Spacing 1. Line 60. WB 109–114. Unless teacher states otherwise, erase and correct any errors in letters.*

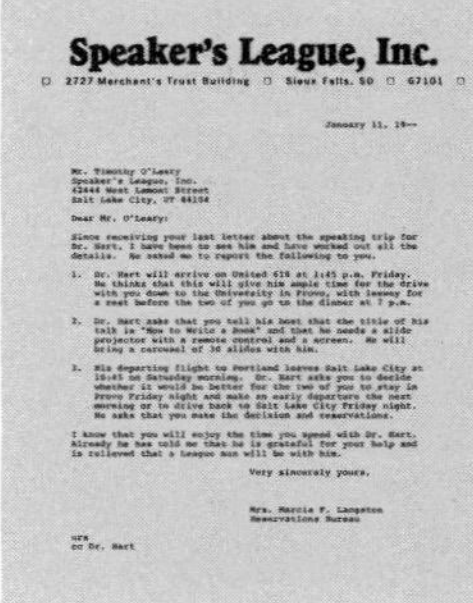
Speaker's League, Inc.
2727 Merchant's Trust Building · Sioux Falls, SD · 67101

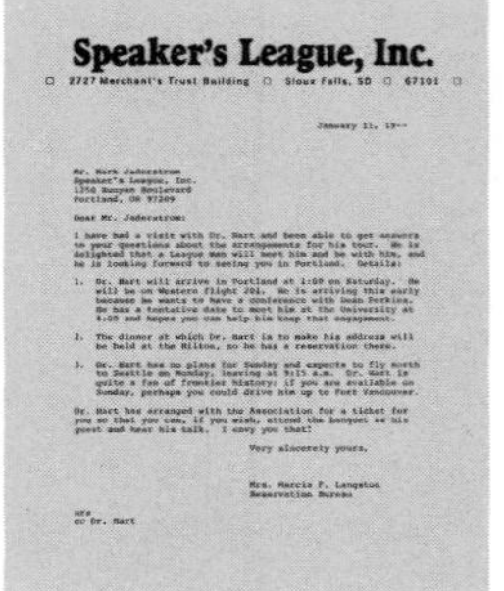
Speaker's League, Inc.
2727 Merchant's Trust Building · Sioux Falls, SD · 67101

LONG LETTERS

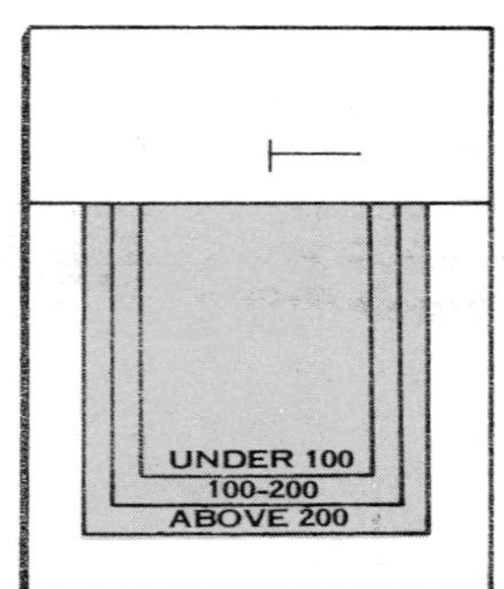

A long letter has more than 200 words in the body or is a 150-word letter with spacetaker display (table, quotation, company signature, etc.). It takes a 6-inch line (pica 60, elite 70). Type date on line 15, at margin.

Use this 20-minute routine for letters 137·1, 138·1, and optional 138·2:

1. Do the warmup lines (2 minutes).
2. Take a 5-minute goal writing as you arrange the letter on a sheet of plain paper; score work (8 minutes).
3. Produce the letter on a Workbook letterhead or on plain paper with a crease $1\frac{1}{2}$ inches from top to represent depth of a letterhead (10 minutes).

a·i·m 137 WARMUP PREVIEW

```
A  Ask him how the men got the box and why the boy may buy it.          12
B  Pat quickly froze the gold mixtures in five old brown jars.          12
C  reservations receiving decision carousel relieved 1:45 p.m.          12
D  Did he get 1 or 2 or 3 or 4 or 5 or 6 or 7 or 8 or 9 or 10?          12
   |1   |2   |3   |4   |5   |6   |7   |8   |9   |10   |11   |12
```

5-MINUTE GOAL WRITING

165 words within 5 minutes and 5 errors. Spacing 1

Today's date / Mr. Timothy O'Leary / Speakers League, Inc. / 42444 West 19
Lamont Street / Salt Lake City, UT 84104 / Dear Mr. O'Leary: 31

Since receiving your last letter about the speaking trip for Dr. Hart, I 47
have been to see him and have worked out all the details. He asked me to 62
report the following to you. 68

1. Dr. Hart will arrive on United 616 at 1:45 p.m. Friday. He thinks 84
that this will give him ample time for the drive with you down to the Uni- 98
versity in Provo, with leeway for a rest before the two of you go to the 113
dinner at 7 p.m. 117

2. Dr. Hart asks that you tell his host that the title of his talk is 133
"How to Write a Book" and that he needs a slide projector with a remote 147
control and screen. He will bring a carousel of 30 slides with him. 161

3. His departing flight to Portland leaves Salt Lake City at 10:45 on 178
Saturday morning. Dr. Hart asks you to decide whether it would be better 192
for the two of you to stay in Provo Friday night and make an early depar- 207
ture the next morning or to drive back to Salt Lake City Friday night. He 222
asks that you make the decision and reservations. *[Continues next page.]* 232

|1 |2 |3 |4 |5 |6 |7 |8 |9 |10 |11 |12 |13 |14

JOB 137·1

BLOCKED LETTER WITH ENUMERATION
Body 228
Line 6 inches
Tab 4, center
Date at right margin
Workbook 109

a·i·m 127

GOAL To learn how to make corrections.

DIRECTIONS *Spacing 1. Line 60.*

```
They can help if you ask.
They will help if we ask.
They can help if you ask.
```

WARMUP REVIEW

3 copies

```
1   I had to leave as soon as the men had tried on their suits.   12
2   Dave quickly froze the two mixtures in the deep brown jugs.   12
3   Ship 1 or 2 or 3 or 4 or 5 or 6 or 7 or 8 or 9 or 10 or 11.   12
    |1  |2  |3  |4  |5  |6  |7  |8  |9  |10  |11  |12
```

CROWDING AN EXTRA LETTER

Problem In making a correction, how can one squeeze in an extra letter?

Advice You must move the new word a half space to the *left* so that only 1/2 space precedes and follows it. To do this, you must keep the carriage from spacing normally. Depending on your make of machine, there are three ways you can control the carriage movement: (1) press your fingertips against the end of the cylinder, (2) depress the halfspace key if your machine has one, or (3) partly depress the backspace key.

Practice Type lines 4 and 5 *exactly* as shown, then insert "said" in each of the two blank areas in line 5.

2 attempts

```
4   They say they will help us.  They say they will be careful.   12
5   They     they will help us.  They     they will be careful.   12
```

SPREADING AN EXTRA SPACE

Problem How do you spread a word so it will occupy an extra space?

Advice You must move the word a half space to the *right* so that $1\frac{1}{2}$ spaces precede and follow it. This requires your controlling the carriage just as you did in the preceding exercise.

Practice Type lines 6 and 7 *exactly* as shown, then insert "say" in each of the two blank areas in lines 7.

2 attempts

```
6   They said you will help us.  They said you will be careful.   12
7   They      you will help us.  They      you will be careful.   12
```

CORRECTIONS

1. Turn the paper so that the error will be at the top of the cylinder.

2. Move carriage far to left or right (use margin release) to make eraser grit fall outside the typewriter.

3. Press the paper tightly against the cylinder with the left fingertips.

4. Using a typewriter (ink) eraser, erase each letter to be deleted. Use quick, light strokes and blow eraser grit away.

5. Turn back to the writing line.

6. Insert the correction.

Other Notes Errors on carbon copies are erased with a soft (pencil) eraser, with a stiff card placed *under* the sheet of paper on which you will erase to keep smudges from showing on copies below.

If you find an error after removing the paper, it and its carbon copies must be erased, reinserted, and corrected one at a time. So: always proofread your work *before* taking it out of the machine.

Practice Type line 8, then correct it so it looks like line 9.

As many attempts as necessary.

```
8   They say they will help us.  They said you will be careful.   12
9   They said they will help us. They say  you will be careful.   12
```

|1 |2 |3 |4 |5 |6 |7 |8 |9 |10 |11 |12 |13 |14

SPEED DRIVE 1

See page 109. ⚲ 215 words within 5 minutes and 5 errors.

Dick Foreman was on the spot. No doubt about it. His great grand- 14
mother had been famous as one of the first women to learn to type by 28
touch, back at the turn of the century; Dick knew all about her, for he 42
had been told often enough. His grandfather had won some kind of typing 57
crown, too; and his mother, well, she was quite nice about it, but she 71
took time now and then to tell Dick just how she had won a state typing 82
contest back in her high school days. All this left Dick out on the 99
limb. He could race along at sixty words a minute, but he seemed to make 114
a dozen errors a minute, too. 120

How could he cut down on the errors? He though about that question 135
night and day; it nagged at him all the time. Then, like a bolt coming 150
out of the blue, he got help. One day the speaker at a school assembly 164
was Nathan Zimmer, the tennis expert. The theme of his talk was prac- 178
tice; he said that anyone could be a champ if he found out what he should 193
practice and then did it. Dick sagged down, his jaw on his hand. This 207
speaker, he told himself, is not a typist! ⚲ 215

|1 |2 |3 |4 |5 |6 |7 |8 |9 |10 |11 |12 |13 |14 SI 1.23E

a·i·m 141

SPEED DRIVE 2

For use in a·i·m 141. ⚲ 220 words within 5 minutes and 5 errors.

A minute later the bolt came out of the blue. As Dick was dozing in 15 231
a dream in which he was smacking a typewriter with a tennis racket that 29 245
had a long handle like an ax, the speaker said that he had had trouble, 44 259
and a lot of it, with errors when he had learned to type. Dick sat up. 58 276
Then the speaker went on to say, quite as though it were nothing the 72 288
least bit odd, that he had found accuracy in typing was the same as ac- 86 302
curacy in tennis or dancing or golf or any skill: accuracy comes from 100 312
good posture and from unhurried rhythm. 108 322

Dick sat back and thought. True, he had been reminded to sit up, to 123 339
keep his feet braced, and so on, a hundred or more times, but he hadn't 138 353
realized that he should do so for the sake of getting rid of errors. 152 367
True, he had been given drills by the dozens to help him to type evenly, 166 382
but he had not really tried hard to conquer rhythm, for he had felt 180 396
it was more exciting to gallop along at top speed than to push for 193 409
smooth typing. And that, ladies and gentlemen, was how a *tennis pro* 211 427
helped me, Dick Foreman, to become a champion. ⚲ 220 436

|1 |2 |3 |4 |5 |6 |7 |8 |9 |10 |11 |12 |13 |14 SI 1.23E

Note that any words shown in italic (slanted) printing, like "tennis pro," should be underscored when typed.

a·i·m 128–130

GOALS ⚲ *To type 155 words or more in 5 minutes within 5 errors, on letter material.* ⚲ *To produce letters with standard variations in date lines, titles, body displays, company identification, initials, postscripts, etc.*

DIRECTIONS *Spacing 1. Line 60. WB 97–102. Unless teacher states otherwise, erase and correct any letter errors.*

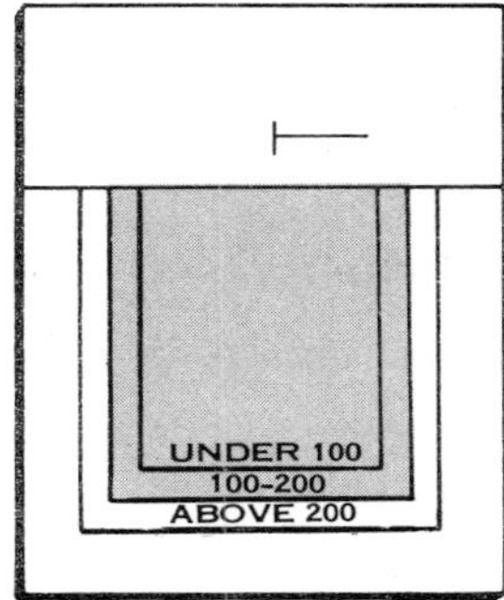

AVERAGE letter has 100–200 words in body or is short letter with body display (table, quotation, etc.) and takes a 5-inch line (pica 50, elite 60). Date on line 15.

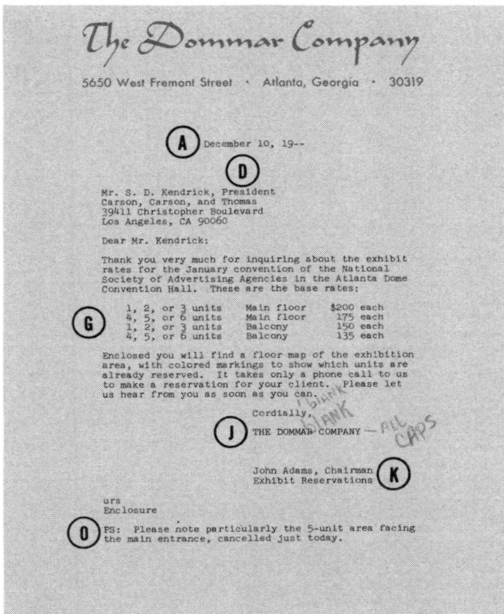

The Dommar Company
5650 West Fremont Street · Atlanta, Georgia · 30319

(A) December 10, 19--

(D)
Mr. S. D. Kendrick, President
Carson, Carson, and Thomas
39411 Christopher Boulevard
Los Angeles, CA 90060

Dear Mr. Kendrick:

Thank you very much for inquiring about the exhibit rates for the January convention of the National Society of Advertising Agencies in the Atlanta Dome Convention Hall. These are the base rates:

(G)

1, 2, or 3 units	Main floor	$200 each
4, 5, or 6 units	Main floor	175 each
1, 2, or 3 units	Balcony	150 each
4, 5, or 6 units	Balcony	135 each

Enclosed you will find a floor map of the exhibition area, with colored markings to show which units are already reserved. It takes only a phone call to us to make a reservation for your client. Please let us hear from you as soon as you can.

Cordially,

(J) THE DOMMAR COMPANY

John Adams, Chairman
Exhibit Reservations (K)

urs
Enclosure

(O) PS: Please note particularly the 5-unit area facing the main entrance, cancelled just today.

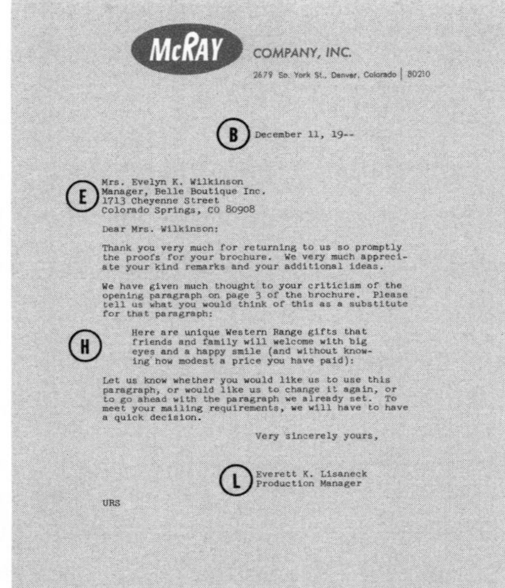

McRAY COMPANY, INC.
2679 So. York St., Denver, Colorado | 80210

(B) December 11, 19--

(E)
Mrs. Evelyn K. Wilkinson
Manager, Belle Boutique Inc.
1713 Cheyenne Street
Colorado Springs, CO 80908

Dear Mrs. Wilkinson:

Thank you very much for returning to us so promptly the proofs for your brochure. We very much appreciate your kind remarks and your additional ideas.

We have given much thought to your criticism of the opening paragraph on page 3 of the brochure. Please tell us what you would think of this as a substitute for that paragraph:

(H)
> Here are unique Western Range gifts that friends and family will welcome with big eyes and a happy smile (and without knowing how modest a price you have paid):

Let us know whether you would like us to use this paragraph, or would like us to change it again, or to go ahead with the paragraph we already set. To meet your mailing requirements, we will have to have a quick decision.

Very sincerely yours,

(L) Everett K. Lisaneck
Production Manager

URS

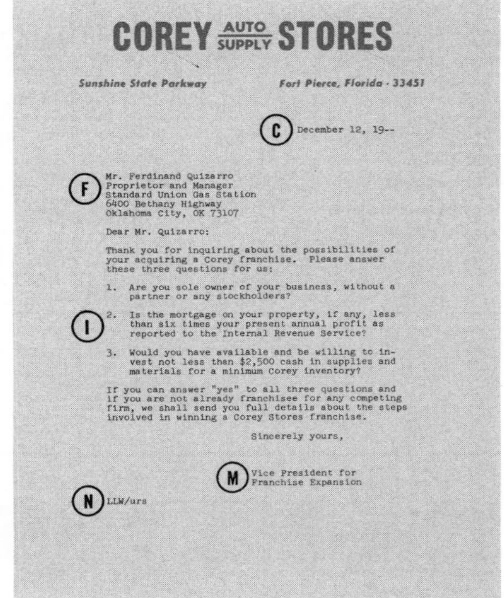

COREY AUTO SUPPLY STORES
Sunshine State Parkway   Fort Pierce, Florida · 33451

(C) December 12, 19--

(F)
Mr. Ferdinand Quizarro
Proprietor and Manager
Standard Union Gas Station
6400 Bethany Highway
Oklahoma City, OK 73107

Dear Mr. Quizarro:

Thank you for inquiring about the possibilities of your acquiring a Corey franchise. Please answer these three questions for us:

(I)
1. Are you sole owner of your business, without a partner or any stockholders?
2. Is the mortgage on your property, if any, less than six times your present annual profit as reported to the Internal Revenue Service?
3. Would you have available and be willing to invest not less than $2,500 cash in supplies and materials for a minimum Corey inventory?

If you can answer "yes" to all three questions and if you are not already franchisee for any competing firm, we shall send you full details about the steps involved in winning a Corey Stores franchise.

Sincerely yours,

(M) Vice President for
Franchise Expansion

(N) LLW/urs

STANDARD LETTER VARIATIONS

Read and remember

Date may be Ⓐ centered, Ⓑ begun at center as you have been doing, or Ⓒ aligned at right margin by backspacing from the margin (slow) or estimating the starting point (fast). Choice depends on employer's or typist's preference.

Business title may be Ⓓ at end of line, Ⓔ at start of line, or Ⓕ on its own line, whichever makes the lines in the address block most nearly even.

Body may include Ⓖ a table. Allow 4 or 6 spaces between the columns.

Body may include Ⓗ a display paragraph. Indent it 5 spaces on each side.

Body may include Ⓘ an enumeration. Indent run-over lines 4 spaces.

Company name Ⓙ in all caps a double space below closing, is used if employer wants it or if letter is a contract.

Signer's title may be Ⓚ after name or Ⓛ under it or Ⓜ instead of it.

Dictator's initials Ⓝ are included, ahead of typist's initials, whenever his name is not typed under his signature. Many styles are acceptable, like

HIS/urs   HIS:URS   HIS urs

Postscript Ⓞ is added as a final paragraph. Type PS: at its start.

20-MINUTE ROUTINE FOR EACH LETTER

1. Do warmup lines (2 minutes)
2. Take 5-minute goal writing as you arrange the letter on sheet of plain paper; score (8 minutes).
3. Produce the letter (correct any errors) on Workbook letterhead or on plain paper with crease $1\frac{1}{2}$ inches from top to represent letterhead depth (10 minutes).

JOB 135·1
Continued

If the last page of a formal report is short, any foot- 119
note on that page goes at the bottom of the page. Remember 131
that the footnote should end on lines 57–60, so you can 142
count the lines you used for typing and top margin, and then 154
estimate how many to drop down before starting the line. 168

D. SUMMARY 172

If a person displays quotes as they should be and if he gives 183
credit in footnotes, as he should, not only can he borrow from 193
the writings and thoughts of other persons but also can be 201
seem to be scholarly just by doing so! 209

__________________ 217

3. Alan C. Lloyd and Russell J. Hosler, Personal Typing, 227
3d ed., McGraw-Hill Book Company, N.Y., 1969, p. 115. 238

4. Rowe, op. cit., p. 136 245

|1 |2 |3 |4 |5 |6 |7 |8 |9 |10 |11 |12 SI 1.23E

Op. cit. should not be underscored. It means "in the work cited."

a·i·m 136

GOAL *To build a speed reserve (215 or more words in 5 minutes within 5 errors) on easy copy that requires listening for the margin bell.*

DIRECTIONS *Spacing 1 for drills, 2 for TW. Line 60. Tab 5.*

CHECK YOUR WORK FOR ABSENCE OF—

- Overlapping characters.
- Very light or dark letters.
- Omitted or extra spaces.
- Omitted or repeated words.
- Raised capital letters.

WARMUP REVIEW
3 copies

The tall man who set the pace for him did not win the race. 12
Jars prevented the brown mixture from freezing too quickly. 12
Try to get 1 or 2 or 3 or 4 or 5 or 6 or 7 or 8 or 9 or 10. 12

|1 |2 |3 |4 |5 |6 |7 |8 |9 |10 |11 |12

RHYTHM DRILL
3 copies

first women learn touch often quite sixty dozen night theme 12
back spot turn knew been told some kind took time just nice 12
his had one all won too now and her cut day got out jaw lot 12

PREVIEW WORDS
3 copies

grandmother champion practice posture century gallop nagged 12
grandfather accuracy exciting dancing speaker errors dozens 12
typewriter unhurried assembly conquer hundred rhythm sagged 12

a·i·m 128

WARMUP PREVIEW

For our to our to see if you in our it is to us or if do so 12
Director Southern Newsweek Atlanta Georgia Score Inc. Ads I 12
Dave quickly spotted the four women dozing in the jury box. 12
Adjust machine for Job 128·1; practice typing the table.

5-MINUTE GOAL WRITING

155 words

Today's date $\downarrow_5$ / Mr. Coe Mowrey, Director / Southern Ads, Inc. / 733 West 19
14 Street / Atlanta, GA 30303 / Dear Mr. Mowrey: 29
Thank you for reminding us that it is time to take steps to hold space 44
in the April issues of the big journals. I may now authorize you to obtain 59
space in our name for these four inserts for April: 70

Life	Half page	Black only	79
Newsweek	Full page	Two colors	88
Score	Full page	Black only	96
Sunset	Full page	Full color	105

If you follow your normal schedule, and I assume you will do so, you 120
should have the ads ready for us to review in two or three weeks. I shall 135
look forward to our meeting then, for I am eager to see how you come along 150
with the plans for our spring campaign. 158
Sincerely yours, $\downarrow_2$ / THE DOMMAR COMPANY $\downarrow_4$ / John Adams, Manager / 177
Promotion Department $\downarrow_2$ / urs / PS: I shall be away for a few days. To 192
set up the date of our meeting, please write to Mr. McHugh. 204

|1 |2 |3 |4 |5 |6 |7 |8 |9 |10 |11 |12 |13 |14 SI 1.31FE

JOB 128·1

BLOCKED LETTER WITH TABLE
Body 109
Line 5 inches
Date centered
Workbook 97

a·i·m 129

WARMUP PREVIEW

we should to place he wrote at once am much be very we feel 12
convenient colleagues campaign statement magazines requests 12
The four women quickly spotted Dave dozing in the jury box. 12
Adjust machine for Job 129·1; practice the set-in quotation.

5-MINUTE GOAL WRITING

156 words

Today's date $\downarrow_?$ / Mr. Dennis G. McHugh / Assistant Sales Manager / The 18
Dommar Company / 5650 West Fremont Street / Atlanta, GA 30319 / Dear 31
Mr. McHugh: 34
In his last letter, Mr. Adams asked us to reserve space in the first April 50
issue of four magazines. We shall write at once to place the space requests. 66
I note that Book is not included in the list. When he wrote us on No- 82
vember 13 about the success of the winter campaign, Mr. Alison said: 96
I am much impressed by the results of our fall ads in Book. 113
Let us be very sure to include Book in our next spring campaign. 128
In view of the firmness of that statement, we feel that we should raise 144
the question: Should Book have been included in the list? 157
Would it be convenient for you and your colleagues to review the spring 173
campaign plans during the last week in January? If so, what date would 187
be best? / Sincerely yours $\downarrow_4$ / Coe Mowrey, Director / initials? 205

|1 |2 |3 |4 |5 |6 |7 |8 |9 |10 |11 |12 |13 |14 SI 1.32FE

JOB 129·1

BLOCKED LETTER WITH QUOTATION
Body 138
Line 5 inches
Date at center
Workbook 99

JOB 134·1

REPORT, PAGE 1
Line 6 inches
Spacing 2 but 1 in heading
Start line 13
Tabs 5, center

QUOTES AND FOOTNOTES

A Report for Typing 1

Change to your name — By T. T. Jehler

Use today's date — March 1, 19-- ↓3

A. INTRODUCTION 3

The purpose of this report is to summarize the general 15
rules about ^the typing ^of quotes and foot‿notes in a report, as given 28
in ~~contemporary~~ current and recent typing textbooks. ↓3 36

B. QUOTATIONS 41

One text~~book~~ says, "A quote that ~~will~~ would fill three or fewer 56
lines when it is typed is shown in quotation marks"[1] (just as 67
shown in this sentence). ¶ The same ~~textbook~~ goes on to say, 79
". . . a longer quote must be given special display: It is 91
single-spaced and ^is indented (5) spaces on each side margin"[2] (as 106
shown on page 2). 109

The quotations in a report are numbered in sequence, the 121
number shown as a ~~superior~~ raised figure after the ~~final~~ last word (or 132
after the punctuation mark, if there is one, after ~~it~~ the last word). 145

Each quote has to be ~~referenced~~ explained in a foot‿note, given ^the 157
same number, which is typed at the bottom of the same page. ↓1 168

____________________ 174

1. John L. Rowe, et al., Gregg Typing, 191 Series, Book 189
One, 2d ed., McGraw-Hill Book Company, New York, 1967, p. 136. 201

2. Ibid. 204

For raised number, turn roll slightly and hold it there as you type the number.

Three-period ellipsis shows that something is left out.

Line is 2 inches of underscores. Don't underscore "et al." or "Ibid."

"Et al." means "and others."
"Ibid." means "in the same place."

|1 |2 |3 |4 |5 |6 |7 |8 |9 |10 |11 |12 SI 1.27FE

Page 2 ↓3 1

JOB 135·1

REPORT, PAGE 2
Start line 7

C. FOOTNOTES 5

Each footnote ~~should be~~ is arranged as ". . . a separate 14
paragraph. It is numbered. # It is single-spaced. It is ~~also~~ 27
indented."[3] The footnote must be kept apart from the body ^of the report: 43

Separate a footnote from the text above it by 57
a 2-inch line of under‿scores--that would be 20 pica 68
spaces long ^or 24 elite spaces long. Be sure, also, 78
to double-space after typing the ~~underscore~~ line, 86
so that one blank space will be left between ^the typed 96
line and the first footnote below the line.[4] 109

Long quote is displayed. No quote marks.

a·i·m 130

WARMUP PREVIEW

```
April issue asks that will note for the and let us be so it      12
reservation surcharge assurance section confirm color where      12
The four women in the jury box quickly spotted Dave dozing.      12
```

Adjust machine for Job 130·1; practice the inside address.

5-MINUTE GOAL WRITING

157 words

Today's date ↓?/Miss Claire A. Parnell/Sales Manager, <u>Sunset</u>/72 20
North Lei Nilla Drive/Los Angeles, CA 90017/Dear Miss Parnell: 33
I enclose a reservation for a full page, four colors, for the April 4 48
issue of <u>Sunset</u>. Please note that— 58
1. Our client would like the page to appear in the LOOK TO THE 73
FUTURE section of the issue. 79
2. Our client asks that his page be placed where it will not face 95
color on the adjacent page. 101
3. If a surcharge must be paid to obtain these two requests, our client 116
will pay it. 119
4. The insert is for your Western issue and is not to appear in your 135
other editions. 138
Please confirm the space and let us have assurance that you will note 153
and observe the two requests we make in regard to the location of the 167
ad./Sincerely yours,/SOUTHERN ADS, INC.↓4 /J. Edward Viska/As- 192
sistant Manager/Initials?/other notations? 199

1 2 3 4 5 6 7 8 9 10 11 12 13 14 SI 1.36N

JOB 130·1

BLOCKED LETTER WITH ENUMERATION
Body 120
Line ? inches
Tabs 4, center
Date at right
Workbook 101

OPTIONAL 5-MINUTE GOAL WRITING

158 words

Today's date/Mr. Arnold F. Rogoff/Sales Manager, <u>Score</u>/972 Tran- 20
sit Avenue/Flint, MI 48502/Dear Mr. Rogoff: 30
I enclose a reservation for a full page, black only, for the April 4 45
issue of <u>Score</u>. Please note that— 56
1. Our client would like the page to appear as near as possible to <u>The</u> 71
<u>Score on Business</u> section. 84
2. Our client asks that his page be placed where it will not face 99
color on the adjacent page. 105
3. If there is an extra charge to be paid to obtain these two requests, 121
our client will pay it. 126
4. No copy will need to be set. Our 7 x 10 plate will reach you at 142
least two days before your closing date. 150
Please confirm the space and let us have assurance that you will note 165
and observe the two requests we make in regard to the location of the ad. 180
Sincerely yours,/SOUTHERN ADS, INC.↓? /J. Edward Viska/As- 204
sistant Manager/initials?/other notations? 213

1 2 3 4 5 6 7 8 9 10 11 12 13 14 SI 1.25FE

OPTIONAL JOB 130·2

BLOCKED LETTER WITH ENUMERATION
Body 131
Tabs 4, center
Date at right
Workbook 102

Page 2 1

JOB 133·2

REPORT, PAGE 2
Line 6 inches
Spacing 2
Tab 5
Start line 7
Workbook 108

D. BOTTOM MARGINS 6

The bottom margin should be *at least* 1 ~~full~~ inch (preferably 1½ inches) 20

wide to make the page look *well* balanced. 28

Suggestion: to keep from running ~~right~~ into the bottom margin, 40

draw a light *pencil* mark in the margin, about 2½ inches from the bottom, ~~edge~~ 55

to serve as a warning singal. ~~You can~~ erase it later. 64

E. SUMMARY 68

Most of a report is double-spaced, with single-spacing ~~reserved~~ *used* 76

for lists, tables, foot notes, and quotations ~~that are~~ longer than 91

3 lines. When protected by margins of at least 1 inch on all 4 sides, 106

the report will then be attractive to theeye and create a favorable 120

impression on the reader. 123

a·i·m 134–135

GOALS *To type 162 or more words in 5 minutes within 5 errors from easy revised copy. To produce a 2-page report involving footnotes, from a working draft.*

DIRECTIONS *Spacing 1 for drills, 2 for TW. Line 60. Tab 5.*

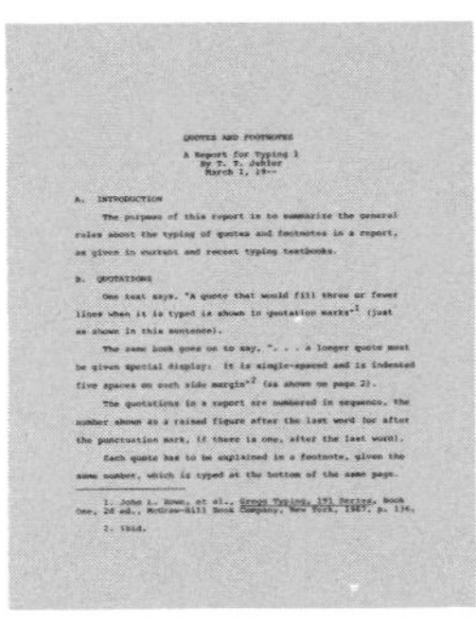

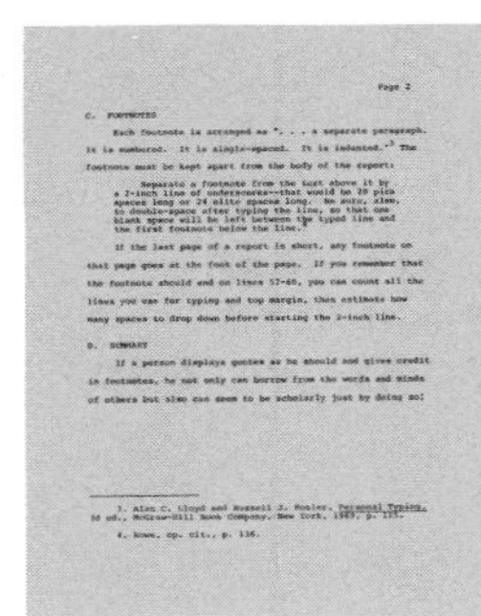

WARMUP PREVIEW

3 copies

1 The one who can try but did not try for the job may get it. 12
2 The faker who got the money prizes was vexed by Jacqueline. 12
3 underscore footnote superior figure bottom margin 2-inch 20 12
4 She got us 1 or 2 or 3 or 4 or 5 or 6 or 7 or 8 or 9 or 10. 12

|1 |2 |3 |4 |5 |6 |7 |8 |9 |10 |11 |12

UNARRANGED REPORT

When a person prepares a report, he will usually organize his material, write a quick draft, edit the draft for correctness and completeness, and then retype it. As he retypes, he pays attention to arrangement, margins, display, etc.

The material that follows is ready for retyping. It will make a page and a fraction. You must watch for the point at which to end page 1. After reading the essay and taking the 5-minute goal writing, type the report in correct form.

a·i·m 131

GOAL *To build a speed reserve (210 or more words in 5 minutes within 5 errors) on easy copy.*

DIRECTIONS *Spacing 1 for drills, 2 for TW. Line 60. Tab 5.*

CHECK YOUR POSTURE

- **Feet** apart, braced on the floor
- **Back** erect, leaning forward from the waist
- **Body** centered opposite the J key
- **Hands** low, close together, fingers curled

WARMUP REVIEW

3 copies

As soon as we had tried on the blue suits, we had to leave. 12
Brown jars prevented the mixture from freezing too quickly. 12
Just order 1 or 2 or 3 or 4 or 5 or 6 or 7 or 8 or 9 or 10. 12

SPEED DRIVE

See page 109.

There is no air on the moon, none at all, a fact which 12
lies at the root of many of the problems that must be faced 24
by the brave men we place up there. Since there is no air, 36
there is none for them to breathe; but that is just a part, 48
and a small part, of the risks they take because of no air. 60

In the first place, with no air there can be no sound; 72
so, the moon is a place of hush, of silence. A boulder may 84
fall from a high cliff to the ground and bound toward a man 96
with no crash, no noise, no warning at all. A crater could 108
cave in, a hill could collapse, all with no sound to signal 120
a man and put the man on his guard. No air means no sound. 132

In the second place, with no air there can be no water 144
or snow or ice; so, there is not a tree, not a plant, not a 156
blade of grass to be seen nor a sign of life as we know it. 168

In the third place, with no air there is no way to mix 180
up the hots and colds. With no air to act as a filter, the 192
sun makes boiling hot what it falls upon. With no air mass 204
to spread the warmth, where the sun does not hit there is a 216
freezing chill. To go from sun to shadow would be just the 228
same as to jump out of a furnace into an ice cream freezer. 240

So the man who roams the moon must be on guard against 252
the strange risks of that world. He must wear a space suit 264
that protects him from heat and cold and feeds him his air. 276
It gives him radar for ears and radio for voice. What else 288
a man needs—heart, brain, soul—he must build for himself. 300

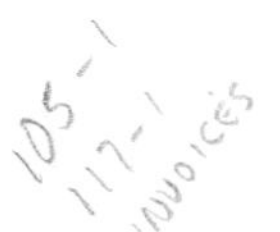

|1 |2 |3 |4 |5 |6 |7 |8 |9 |10 |11 |12 SI 1.07VE

JOB 133·1

UNBOUND REPORT
Line 6 inches
(70 elite)
Spacing 2
Tabs 5, center
Start line 13
Workbook 108

PWC

THE MARGINS ON A TERM PAPER 16

A Report by Verne J. Harris ↓3 34

36

Sideheading in all caps.

A. INTRODUCTION 39

Many persons learn to typewrite so that they ~~can~~ may use the skill in 53
typing term papers and other formal reports that are assigned to them 67
in high school ~~or~~ and college. The purpose of this report is to review the 82
rules about margin requirements specified in (2) college handbooks and (3) 97
typing textbooks. ↓3 101

103

B. TOP MARGINS 106

Paragraph heading underscored.

On page 1 of a report or ~~each~~ of a chapter of a report, the top margin 124
should be 2 inches (12 blank lines). The title of the report or chapter 138
is, therefore, centered on line 13. 146

On other pages, the top margin should be 1 inch (~~5~~ 6 blank lines), 165
so the page number is on line 7 at the right margin. ↓3 176

178

C. SIDES MARGINS 181

It is standard practice to use a 6-inch line, which is 60 pica or 201
70 elite spaces. Centered on the paper, a 6-inch line gives margins of 215
1¼ inches on each side of the paper. 223

If the paper is to be bound (that is, put in a ~~stiff~~ binder), move both 247
the paper guide and the paper ¼ inch to the left. Doing ~~so~~ this will reduce 262
the right margin to 1 inch but expand the left margin to 1½ inches, 275
with extra room for binding. 281

Page 1 of a Two-Page Unbound Report (Elite). Page 142 for same page in pica.

PREPARE a·i·m WB 105–106

a·i·m 132–133

GOALS ⚲ *To learn to read revision marks.* ⚲ *To type 160 or more words in 5 minutes within 5 errors from easy revised copy.* ⚲ *To produce a 2-page report.*

DIRECTIONS *Spacing 1 for drills, 2 for TW. Line 60. Tab 5. Read report to determine margins and spacing.*

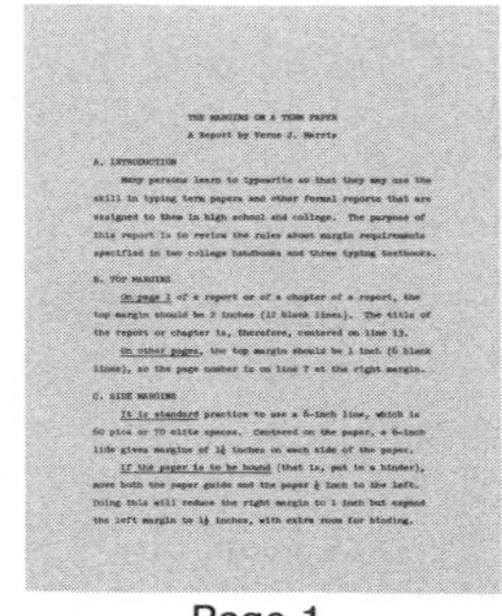
Page 1

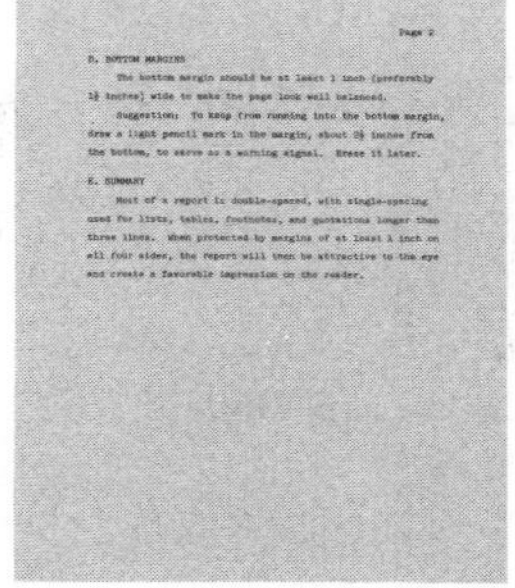
Page 2

WARMUP PREVIEW

3 copies

1	They that seek good work will find good pay with this firm.	12
2	Jacqueline was vexed by the folks who got the money prizes.	12
3	(binder), 70 elite, 60 pica, margins, spaces, $1\frac{1}{2}$, $1\frac{1}{4}$, and $\frac{1}{4}$	12
4	Ask us for 1 or 2 or 3 or 4 or 5 or 6 or 7 or 8 or 9 or 10.	12

|1 |2 |3 |4 |5 |6 |7 |8 |9 |10 |11 |12

REVISION MARKS

Study and remember.

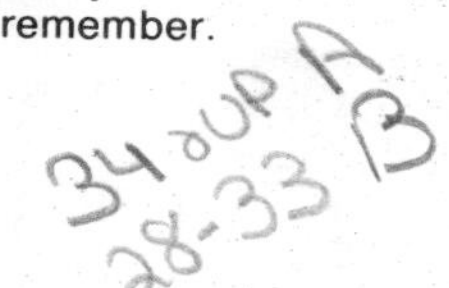

	Mark	Example
5	∧ Insert word	and ∧so it
6	Omit word	and ~~so~~ it
7	.... No, don't omit	and ~~so~~ it
8	\ Omit stroke	and so\ it
9	/ Make letter small	/And so it
10	≡ Make a capital	if he is
11	Make all capitals	I hope so
12	—] Move as indicated	and so—]
13	= Line up, even up	TO: John
14	‖ Line up, even up	‖ If he is
15	ss[Use single-spacing	and so it
16	∽ Turn around	had it so
17	ds[Use double-spacing	and so it
18	= Insert a hyphen	white=hot
19	5] Indent — spaces	5] If he is
20	# Insert a space	and∧so it
21	Insert a space	and so it
22	⁀ Omit the space	10 a m.
23	__ Underscore this	It <u>may</u> be
24	Move as shown	it is (not)
25	Join to word	the re port
26	word Change word	and ~~if~~ so he
27	∘ Make into period	to him;
28	⬭ Don't abbreviate	(Dr.) Judd
29	⬭ Spell it out	(1) or (2) if
30	¶ New paragraph	¶ If he is
31	✓ Raise above line	Halel says
32	+#→ More space here	+#→ It may be
33	−#→ Less space here	−#→ If she is
34	2# 2 linespaces here	It 2# may be ⚲

5-MINUTE GOAL WRITING

⚲ 160 or more words on page 142. Start line 3.

FORMAL REPORTS

1. Paper. Type reports on plain sheets of $8\frac{1}{2} \times 11$ inch paper.

2. Margins. Read pages 142–144.

3. Spacing. Use double-spacing for the body of the report, with one extra blank line (a) before each sideheading and (b) between the heading and body of each page. Use single-spacing for lists, long tables, quotations longer than three typed lines, footnotes, and other displays.

4. Page Numbers. Type "Page" and the number on line 7, positioned to end even with the right margin (see page 144) but omit the number from the first page.

Practice. After reading pages 142–144, type a correct copy of the whole report.

JOB 133·1

UNBOUND REPORT
Line 6 inches
(60 pica)
Spacing 2
Start line 13
Workbook 108

(MAT 13–78)

LINE 13

THE MARGINS ON A TERM PAPER

A Report by Verne J. Harris ↓3

TW

Sideheading in all caps.

A. (2 SPACES) INTRODUCTION 3

Many persons learn to typewrite so that they ~~can~~ may use the 16
skill in typing term papers and other formal reports that are 28
‖assigned to them in high # school ~~or~~ and college. The purpose of 40
this report is to review the rules about margin requirements 52
specified in ② college handbooks and ③ typing textbooks. ↓3 65

67

B. TOP MARGINS 70

Paragraph heading underscored.

<u>On page 1</u> of a report or ~~each~~ of a chapter of a report, the 86
top margin should be 2 inches (12 blank lines). The title of 98
the report ^or chapter is, therefore, centered on line 13. 110

<u>On other pages</u>, the top margin should be 1 inch (~~5~~ 6 blank 128
lines), so the page number is on Line 7 at the right margin. ↓3 139

141

C. SIDE~~S~~ MARGINS 144

<u>It is standard</u> practice to use a 6-inch line, ¶ which is 161
60 pica or 70 elite spaces. # Centered on the paper, a 6-inch 174
line gives margins of 1¼ inches on each side of the paper. 185

<u>If the paper is ^to be bound</u> (that is, put in a ~~stiff~~ binder), 209
move both the paper guide and the paper ¼ inch to the left. 221
Doing ~~so~~ this will reduce the right margin to 1 inch but expand 233
the left margin to 1½ inches, with extra room for binding. ¶ 245

Page 1 of a Two-Page Unbound Report (Pica). Page 143 for same page in elite.